Gene

Merry Christmas
2008

Love,
June

# *Tales from Great-Grandpa's Trunk*

## A Lighthearted Look at Rural Life

**Second Edition**

## About the Cover

**G**reat-grandpa relaxes in Grandma's rocking chair, his red handkerchief on his lap as he points to each dot and counts it. I leave my little rocker to stand beside him and watch. I'll soon be able to count, too. His trunk from Germany sits in the background, showing off one of Grandma's quilts, and on the shelf above it stands Grandpa's clock, the one that traveled to Wisconsin in a covered wagon when he was two. When Great-grandpa needed a spittoon, Grandma found a flower pot that was just the right shape. She protects the rag rug she had made by placing the spittoon on a newspaper. Little does she know the problem that will create. Using pictures of the actual family items, Pat Wietholter of New Knoxville painted the cover.

# *Tales from Great-Grandpa's Trunk*

**A Lighthearted Look at Rural Life**

**Second Edition**

**by**

**Glenna Meckstroth**

The Wooster Book Company
Wooster • Ohio
2004

The Wooster Book Company
*where minds and imaginations meet*
205 West Liberty Street
Wooster, Ohio • 44691
*www.woosterbook.com*



Printed in the United States of America.

ISBN: 1-59098-410-2

To order additional copies of

***TALES FROM GREAT-GRANDPA'S TRUNK:***
***A Lighthearted Look at Rural Life***

| | | | |
|---|---|---|---|
| _____ Copies | @ | $25.95 each | $_______ |
| Sales Tax | @ | $ 1.95 each | $_______ |
| Postage and handling | @ | $ 5.50 each | $_______ |
| Total amount | @ | $33.40 each | $_______ |

(Author's second book)

***SURVIVING WORLD WAR II:***
***Tales of Ordinary People in Extraordinary Times***

(See page 373)

| | | | |
|---|---|---|---|
| _____ Copies | @ | $29.95 each | $_______ |
| Sales Tax | @ | $ 2.25 each | $_______ |
| Postage and handling | @ | $ 5.50 each | $_______ |
| Total amount | @ | $37.70 each | $_______ |

Send checks to: Glenna Meckstroth
P.O. Box 502
New Knoxville, Ohio 45871

# *Back by Popular Request!*

*Tales from Great-Grandpa's Trunk: A Lighthearted Look at Rural Life* is now presented in a new and improved format. Thanks to all the faithful readers, it was necessary to produce more books. Two thousand six hundred twenty-five were not enough! Several additions suggested by readers are included in this second edition. An every-name index was frequently requested, as well as a 5-generation chart making it easier to identify various family members. [It's amazing how many people are related to me!] Additional pictures have been included, and there is further identification of some of the earlier ones. Also included are elevation maps of the Miami-Erie Canal locks and the path the canal takes as it meanders across western Ohio.

At the suggestion of David Wiesenberg of the Wooster Book Company, *Tales from Great Grandpa's Trunk* has been reprinted as a companion book to the author's second book, *Surviving World War II: Tales of Ordinary People in Extraordinary Times.* The hardcover makes the book a little more classy and much more durable as it is passed to other family members and friends or is set back for the enjoyment of future generations.

# *What Others Have Said:*

Humorous, poignant, very personal–these vignettes are an intimate portrayal of family history and tenacity set against the backdrop of rural Auglaize County history.

Writing with vivid imagery, Glenna has the ability to make the reader feel, hear, smell, taste, and see as she relates stories down to the most minute detail.

As I read Glenna's memories I not only lived her story with her, I also relived many of my own childhood, teenage, and family experiences–some of which I had almost forgotten. A great reading experience!

Annett Kuck,
Retired Teacher/Principal
New Knoxville, Ohio

The author has a wonderful power of colorful expression in her writing which captivates the reader as she shares the most interesting highlights of her early childhood and adolescence, leading ultimately to her marriage.

The book is very informational giving detailed, interesting historical events that happened during that specific time in her life. It is also a very entertaining book as she relates many comical happenings which the reader will definitely enjoy. One gets a cozy feeling reading the book and experiences nostalgia.

Her writing will provide fascinating reading for every member of the family.

Mary Boertje Smith,
Retired Teacher/Pastor's Wife
Lima, Ohio

## Dedication

To our three gifts of love
Michael Allen, Steven Lynn, and Nancy Kay;
to their earthly father, William Arthur Meckstroth,
whose love and encouragement
have helped make this book possible;
to our son-in-law, David Humphreys;
and our grandchildren, Brian and Heather
and to our Heavenly Father who was in charge of it all.


## Acknowledgments

With sincere thanks and deepest appreciation to my family, to my brother Don for his input on childhood events, and to Annett Kuck for the long hours she spent evaluating and correcting my manuscript in its earlier stages. Also, my deepest love and appreciation to my son, Michael, for the insight he gave me into the world of computers, which was, until now, a foreign language. To him, I also owe my gratitude for his untiring efforts in encouraging me through the aches and pains of publishing.

Special thanks to canal expert Ray Zunk, to friends at church, Genealogy Society, and the community for their encouragement.

To those newspaper, book, periodical publishers and others who granted permission to use the many excerpts which further explain and enhance the stories, my sincere thanks.

My gratitude and respect go to those busy persons who took time to read my manuscript and were willing to say a few kind words of endorsement. This was a new venture in my life, and their encouragement was greatly appreciated.

# *How in the World?*

"How in the world did you decide to write a book," I've often been asked. It started years ago when a cousin in Florida asked for family information from Ohio. I searched courthouse and library records, and the information I found was quite enlightening. As I became more interested, I began talking to those older relatives who were still living. My family enjoyed the stories so much that Michael suggested I try to preserve them by writing down some facts about butchering, threshing, childhood Christmases and so on. I was convinced, and jumped into the writing pool feet first with my eyes wide open.

Soon the few essays somehow blossomed into a gigantic effort more familiarly known as *Mom's Book.* As suggestions turned into stories, other thoughts came to mind. At no time did "writers' block" become bothersome. Erma Bombeck once described writer's block as that time when your fingers showed up for work, but your mind was out to lunch. I like that, don't you?

"Hello, Glenna. This is Cathy. How are you?" the voice at the other end of the line inquired. When the conversation turned to my book, Cathy expressed delight that I was preserving the events that so vividly portrayed my early days.

My cousin, Tom Huenefeld, married Cathy, a Southern girl. Like many from that area, her Uncle Ed had written a family history. Cathy sent information about the family even mentioning Lizzie, the family dog. When a couple of family members pointed out small errors in Uncle Ed's book, Cathy decided to have some fun. Uncle Ed had described Lizzie as a "winsome little gray dog." Lizzie felt this was a bit ho-hum and didn't fully describe her best attributes. With a touch of loving indignation, Lizzie, the dog, "wrote" this to Uncle Ed: "Winsome--Dad says it means winning and cute, which is okay. You didn't mean anything pathetic, did you?" Lizzie suggested that instead of calling her a little gray dog, he could have used more descriptive words: gorgeous, amazing, magnificent, adorable . . . . Would Ed be most impressed by her "sports ability, singing talent, tricks and cute dog stunts, or other?" To everyone's delight, Uncle Ed fired a letter back to Lizzie. Again, Lizzie "answered." Uncle Ed from the South can't believe that for ten years he has corresponded with Lizzie, the dog from Cincinnati.

Lizzie is honored to be in print, but Cathy and Tom are concerned that she may become quite vain with all the notoriety. I'll tell you, that Lizzie has a real way with words. Soon we will be seeing whole books in print that have been written by this precocious "winsome little gray dog" named Lizzie. I recognize talent when I see it!

Since this book is based mainly on my memories and is not a date-and-place, accuracy-inclined family record, I feel the necessity of making a comment right at the beginning. I have talked to numerous older folks and discovered that even their memories don't always agree. I've done my best to check and double check for accuracy and have even included old newspaper items for the enlightenment of the readers.

My purpose for writing was not just to entertain (although any enjoyment gained from it would be quite acceptable). It was also my desire to teach—no, that word might be offensive to some. Perhaps a more satisfactory word might be to *share* the events of my early life. But I must issue the following warning! The older generation may find that this book has retrieved memories which may have escaped decades ago. Please remember that since this book is about MY memories, prompted in part by items from Great-grandpa's trunk, they may not be quite the same as YOUR memories. If that is the case, then I must lovingly ask that instead of messing with my memories, please, just *go write your own book!* Thank you!

# TABLE OF CONTENTS

# Chapter 1.
## Great-grandpa's Trunk

It's just a plain wooden trunk, a rectangular box with dovetailed corners and a lid that's rounded end-to-end. It has no drawers or shelves, just an inside covering of faded wallpaper that's seen better days. Handmade handles and latches are attached to the trunk's rough outside. A segment of shipping tag at the end of the trunk spells out "*BRE,*" probably for Bremerhaven, the port where many German immigrants boarded ships for the New World. No, the trunk isn't much to look at, but what a story Great-grandpa's trunk could tell if it could talk.

When I was little, the family spoke of Great-grandpa Henry Schwartz's "Wander-Book," but no one really knew what it contained or why it was valuable. Mrs. Charlotte Callahan, a German immigrant and employee of The Ohio State University library, agreed to translate this book, which a cousin had inherited. After seeing her translation, we finally gained a better understanding of the true significance of Henry's special little book.

Heinrich Schwarz left home to become an apprentice miller when he was but seventeen years old. The year was 1858. He became a part of one of the old German guilds that adhered to a system of strictly enforced *laws* which regulated the training and practice of skilled craftsmen. Emil W. Deeg of Lemoyne, Pennsylvania, provided this explanation, "There were three levels of accomplishment: *Lehrling* (apprentice), *Geselle* (craftsman), *Meister* (master of the trade). Accuracy of records contained in the Wanderbook was necessary to show that the master-candidate had expanded his professional knowledge, applied it successfully under a wide variety of circumstances and demonstrated the human qualities expected from a master of the trade."

Henry carried his "Wander-Buch" with him as he moved about in his work. Leaving his home and family, he was no doubt lonely as he traveled from job to job, mostly by foot, knowing that strict rules were enforced in each area with a threat of punishment or jail for violating them. As she read the account of Henry's travels and work, Charlotte felt quite sorry for him. Some of the writing was very hard to read, especially the names. Charlotte said much of it had been written by crude, uneducated men who were often harsh in dealing with the young apprentices.

Upon entry into each town, the book was to be stamped and employers' comments were to be written concerning the quality of his work and behavior: "he worked hard and was well-behaved," "he is a good worker," "behaved well during his stay."

The first page of the little book contains a description of the apprentice Schwarz with his signature at the bottom. Unlike many of the uneducated Germans who signed Auglaize County Courthouse records with an "X," Henry's signature is quite easy to read and it is obvious that he was educated.

The "laws" listed on the front page were established by the guilds, not by the many little dukedoms and kingdoms of 19th Century Germany. Be thankful you're an American!

INSTRUCTION and WARNING

1. The apprentice shall keep his Wanderbook clean, undamaged and must not lose it. He or any other person are not permitted to add, erase or otherwise alter the document. This is dangerous and could result in arrest and fines.
2. Should the apprentice lose this Wanderbook, he must at once report this to the nearest local authority and state his loss. He must be able to prove his loss and must ask to have his book replaced at the last place which had documented his stay. Should he not be able to get such a document, he must ask for a pass from town to town until he reaches his hometown or the place where his book was issued.
3. The apprentice must show his book at each place of employment and have it properly signed, stamped and dated by the local authorities. It will then be noted in his book, if he acted noble, worked hard and behaved well.
4. After leaving each place of employment, he must look for work as soon as possible; should he not find employment he must still have his Wanderbook stamped, dated and signed by the local authorities.
5. Since the Wanderbook must contain the holder's whereabouts at all times, it must be shown to local authorities at each new place of employment. He must state where he plans to travel and by what mode and route. This is to be obeyed. Should he change his mind and take a different route or go to a different place, he must tell the local authorities the reason for this change.
6. Should he not be able to work due to illness, he must note this in his book.
7. The apprentice who travels around aimless, begs or becomes a public burden must expect the punishment according to the laws of the land for vagrants or beggars. He also will be deported over the border and must return to his hometown.
8. The apprentice who doesn't comply with articles #3, 4, 5 and 6 will have to be punished.
9. The apprentice must obey the following rules made by the Federal Work Congress on December 3, 1840: All governments of the United German countries have made rules which all apprentices must obey. They may not belong to outlawed parties or organizations, participate in apprentice courts or strikes.
    a. Apprentices having broken the laws of the state which is not their homestate will be punished according to the laws of such. All Wanderbooks, passports, etc. will be taken from the holder after incarceration and returned to the home authorities.
    b. After release such persons must be returned to their home by designated route and watched by local authorities and not permitted to leave their homestate to work elsewhere.
    c. The government of the homestate will note all fines or jail sentences of the holder and will mark this in his Wanderbook or passport.
    d. Every apprentice must make himself familiar with all the rules and regulations of each state he works in or passes thru during his travel.
    e. All rules shall be posted with local authorities within two months.
10. Breach of any of the above rules will be punished with jail sentences according to act #182 and #183.
11. The Wanderbook is only valid till April 1, 1861, starting today. Should this be extended it will be noted in this book.

Because of the military conditions in Germany, Wander-Buchs were also used in part to help pinpoint the whereabouts of young men of military age. Thousands left Germany to avoid the military lottery—some walking across borders to freedom, some escaping by night, some hiding in hay wagons as they crossed to farms in neighboring countries. Most were poor working men who had no desire to fight someone else's battles. On the first day of April 1861, Henry drew his freedom from military service through the yearly lottery. He was twenty-one years old and continued learning his trade until 1864 when he was logged lottery number 144. The Wander-Buch says he was granted an extension until 6 February 1864, but he was now twenty-four years old and apparently decided to take no more chances with the military lottery system. He packed his trunk and within a few weeks, he left Germany to join the rest of his family near Hamilton, Ohio. With all his earthy possessions carefully tucked inside, Great-grandpa's trunk was placed aboard a sailing ship and accompanied him to America where he hoped to make his fortune.

What would Henry have carried in his trunk? No one knows exactly, but most men from Germany brought extra clothing that would have been quite simple and probably consisted of an extra pair or two of pants and shirts, underwear, stockings, handkerchiefs, gloves, a heavy wool coat and a hat. He would have needed a drinking cup and container for water, plate, silverware, a cook pot or kettle, candles, towel and soap, and a pillow and blankets. He no doubt brought a few tools–a mallet or hammer, knife, pliers, nails or tacks, string or twine, and the tools he used as a miller. On some ships the food was provided in the cost of the journey; on others, each person was responsible for his own food. In either case, extra food would have been packed for any emergency that might arise. Dried foods such as beans, rice, dried apples and dry bread would have traveled well, along with the German staples of potatoes and sauerkraut, some lard for frying and salt for flavoring. Many of the immigrant farmers had packed various grains and seeds from fruit trees which they lovingly planted and cared for on their new farms. There were numerous other items which Grandpa may have brought, but of one thing we are quite sure, the Wander-Buch he had been required to carry for the last seven years was now tucked into a corner of the trunk for the trip to America.

With his arrival in Hamilton, Ohio, the remaining family members were once again united, his widowed mother Maria, sisters Mary and Helena and brothers Conrad and John. An unknown child was said to have remained in the Old Country.

By the time Henry reached his new home in Ohio, the trunk had no doubt spent several weeks in the hold of the ship, had bounced across miles of land in the bottom of a horse drawn wagon or coach, and rested on a boat as it floated down the Ohio River to Cincinnati, then up the Miami-Erie Canal to Hamilton. Henry eventually followed the canal to Auglaize County where he built a log house, married the next door neighbor's daughter and raised a family of eight children. Although one died as a child, and another at the age of 54, he and the remaining six children all lived to the *ripe old ages* of from 81 to 98 years.

Great-grandpa and his trunk came to live at my house when I was just a toddler. He died when I was three years old and the trunk remained in the spare room which he had occupied. After his estate was settled, Grandma stored some clothing and other special items in it.

For the next forty years the old trunk sat along the east wall of that room. When I was twelve, the room was cleaned out and it became my very own bedroom. Grandpa built a little closet behind the door, and I helped Grandma select yellow striped fabric for curtains. Since I thought the old trunk was so ugly, she also made a covering for it. It had been emptied and now became the treasure chest for my little-girl things: the pressed flower from a party, pretty shells from along the lake, Bible School ribbons and those special school papers.

As I reached maturity, the old trunk took on new meaning. As some of the childhood treasures were eliminated, I began filling the expanse with items for my hope chest. At first, there were only little things: the relish dish I had won by throwing balls at the county fair, the dish towel Grandma had gotten in a box of soap, the pot holder and towels I had made in 4-H. When a real boy friend became a reality, the pursuit of items for the hope chest began in earnest. My long Saturday afternoons in college were spent embroidering pillow cases. While other girls dated college guys, I remained true to Bill, my fellow back home, and hand stitched guest towels and cotton aprons. Numerous flowered feed sacks were turned into useful items for my future home.

When that home became a reality, the trunk was emptied. Its treasures became a part of my household. But the trunk didn't remain empty for long. After three years the Lord blessed us with a son, and his outgrown baby clothes went into the trunk for any future baby we might have. Sure enough, two years later, out came the tiny outfits for our new baby boy to enjoy. By the time he had outgrown them, another two years had passed and we had added a baby daughter. Now the trunk was emptied and we made a trade. As our boys outgrew them, the little shirts and suits were handed on to my brother's sons, Richard and Roger Davenport. The dresses that his daughters, Linda and Marilyn, had outgrown were sent back to us. They were packed in the trunk until Nancy grew into them. How she loved spending rainy afternoons looking through the trunk with me. Each piece of clothing was held up and analyzed. If it looked about the right size, she tried it on. Then we discussed how we could freshen its look by tearing off a limp ruffle and adding a new one, replacing a faded ribbon or adding a vest or flower. I enjoyed those cozy afternoons. Nancy knew I would sew plenty of new dresses for church and school, but she looked forward to the dresses from her favorite cousins. After all, they were "big girls."

After the girls no longer outgrew their dresses, the trunk became Nancy's treasure chest just as it had been mine, storing the keepsakes that she had acquired. When our family moved to the New Knoxville area, the trunk was finally removed from the east wall of the little, low-ceilinged bedroom. Our sons were now strong, sturdy teenagers and they loaded the trunk in preparation for the ride to its new home where a special spot awaited its arrival.

With a gradually increasing thirst for more information about my family, the old wooden trunk took on new significance. It now became the focal point of my family history. Bill made a little shelf which slid into the bottom to hold an assortment of pictures and notebooks, one for each of our family surnames. Where could I have found a more appropriate place to store family information than in the trunk that Great-grandpa brought from the Old Country well over a hundred years ago?

As I lay in bed one night, thinking about all the memories the old trunk had held through the decades, the stories seemed to come to life. Suddenly we realized we had found the title for this book . . . *"Tales from Great-grandpa's Trunk."*

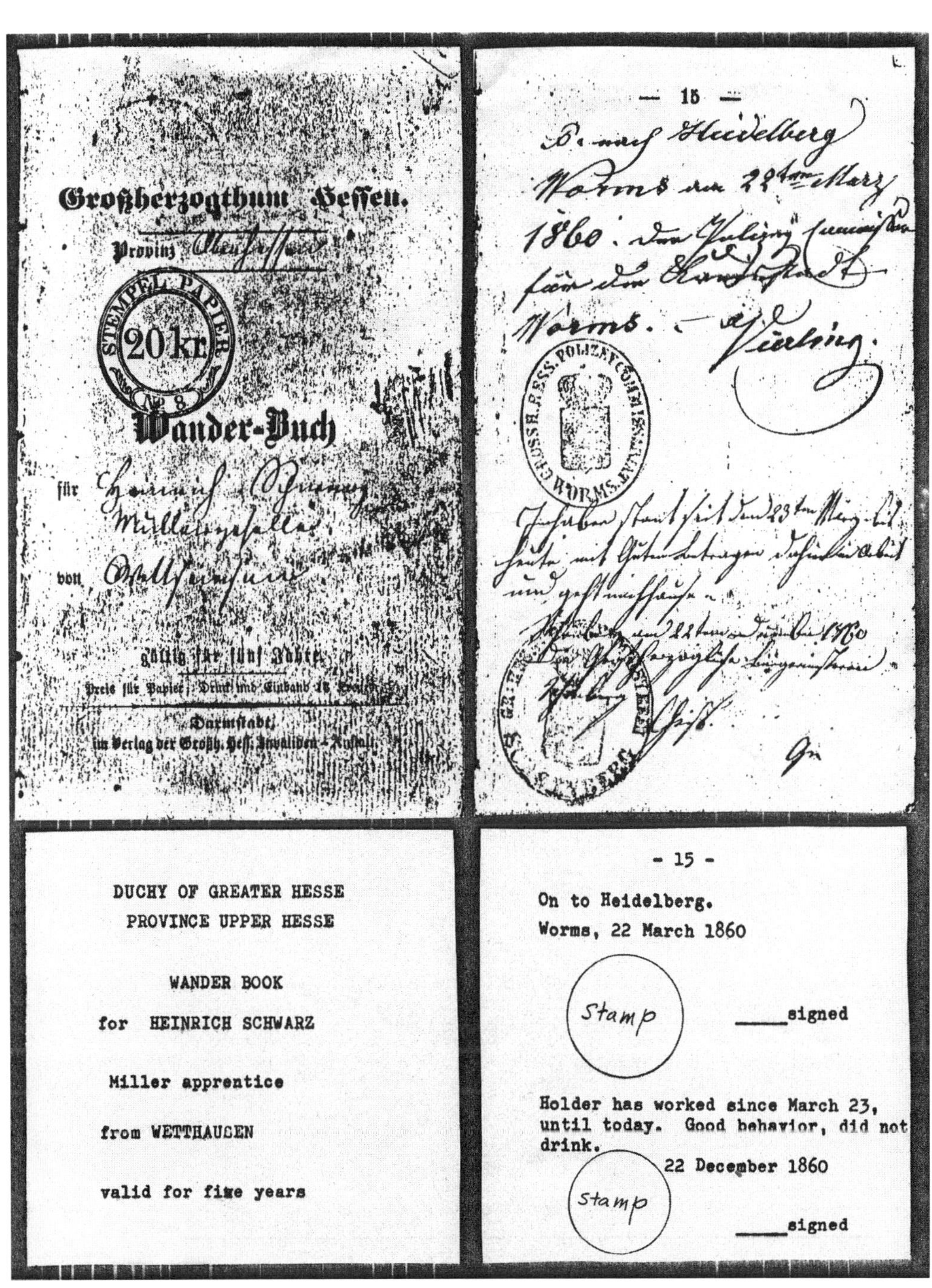
Großherzogthum Hessen.

Provinz

STEMPEL PAPIER 20 kr. № 8

Wander-Buch

für

von

gültig für fünf Jahre

Darmstadt,
im Verlag der Großh. Hess. Invaliden-Anstalt.

— 15 —

DUCHY OF GREATER HESSE
PROVINCE UPPER HESSE

WANDER BOOK

for HEINRICH SCHWARZ

Miller apprentice

from WETTHAUSEN

valid for fime years

- 15 -

On to Heidelberg.
Worms, 22 March 1860

Stamp ____signed

Holder has worked since March 23, until today. Good behavior, did not drink.

22 December 1860

Stamp ____signed

Cover and sample page from Great-grandpa's Wander-Buch.
The fact that Henry had the book and was entered as *Müllergesell* shows that he was already beyond the second level and was getting ready to go for the master miller.

Glenna Mae Davenport
b. 22 Apr. 1930
m. 24 Jun. 1951

Omen Bernard Davenport
b. 7 Oct. 1899
m. 8 Apr. 1926
d. 27 Oct. 1984

Henry Franklin Davenport
b. 14 Sep. 1877
m. 24 Jul. 1898
d. 30 Jul. 1971

John Wesley Davenport
b. 19 Nov. 1845
m. 3 May 1869
d. 13 Mar. 1923

Nathan Davenport

Elizabeth Foster

Laura Francis Daniels
b. 5 Jun. 1850
d. 13 Jun. 1888

Abner Daniels

Rebecca Eggleston

Nora Leona Schwartz
b. 29 Jan. 1880
d. 11 Jul. 1961

Heinrich Schwartz
b. 13 Nov. 1840
m. 25 Apr. 1871
d. 17 Dec. 1933

Maximilian Schwartz

Maria Elizabeth Cyliax

Catherine Elizabeth Aufderhaar
b. 24 Nov. 1855
d. 24 Feb. 1927

Heinrich Adolph Aufderhaar

Christine Catherine Elisabeth Hünefeld

Lena Edith Sophia Briggs
b. 5 Apr. 1905
d. 23 Nov. 1930

William Roscoe Briggs
b. 29 Apr. 1870
m. 23 Sep. 1891
d. 16 Nov. 1954

Charles Marion Briggs
b. 25 Jul. 1842
m. 9 Jul. 1869
d. 18 Jun. 1925

John Marion Briggs Jr.

Susanna (Carr) Harter

Amanda Edith Vest
b. 18 Jul. 1848
d. 4 Jul. 1904

Roland Vest

Edith (Edwards) Hawkins

Charlotta Adelheid Dorothea Frech
b. 17 Apr. 1870
d. 3 Sep. 1949

Johann Heinrich Frech
b.
m. 27 Aug. 1854
d. 1874

Louise Sophie Dorothea Nietert
b. 16 May 1830
d. 22 May 1901

Friedrich Nietert

Maria Elisabeth Speckmann

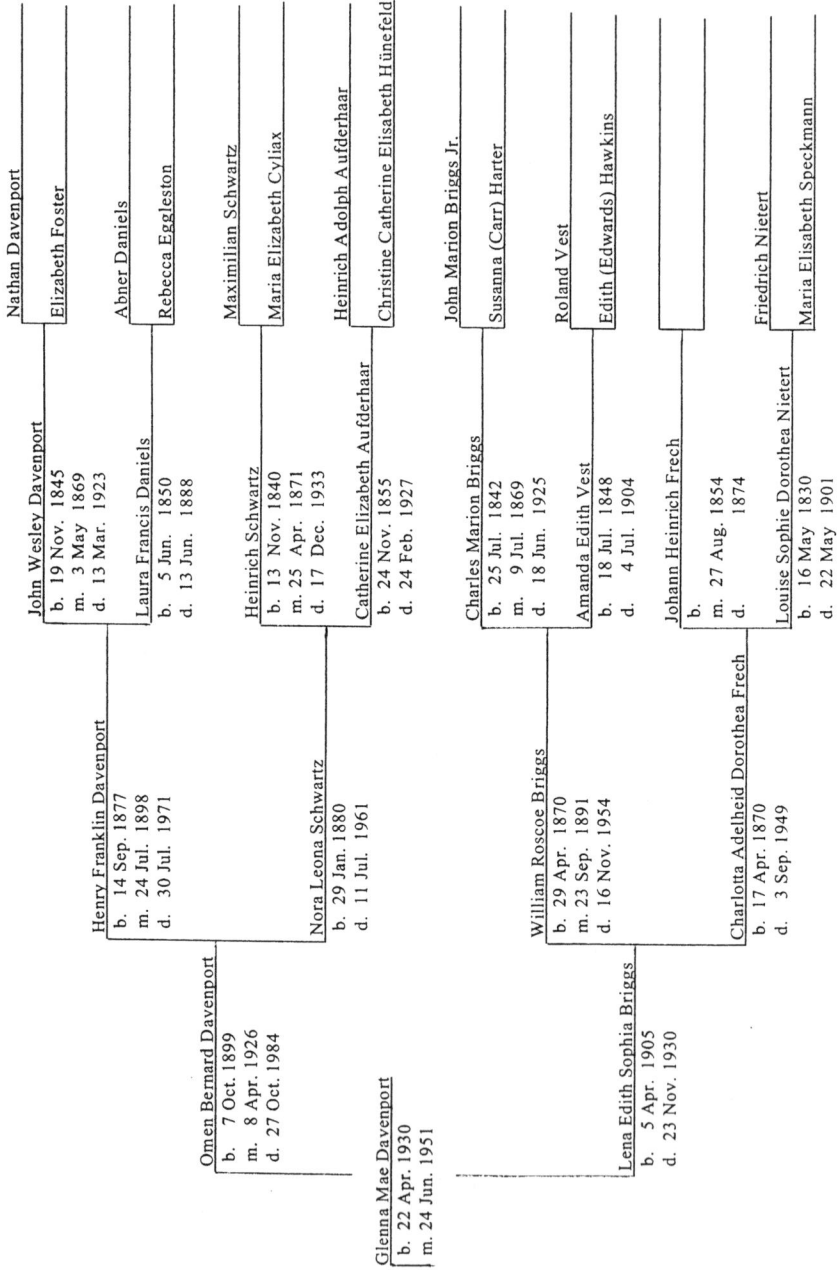

Five Generation Chart

## Chapter 2.

# The Bearded Immigrant

Who was this immigrant and what was his story? "In the year of our Lord eighteen hundred and forty, on November 13 in the afternoon at three o'clock was born to the citizen Maximilian Schwarz and his wife Elisabeth nee Ciliax (Cyliax), their sixth child Heinrich which was the 3rd. son." The above was translated from church records in "Wettsaasen, a tiny village in Oberhessen near Giessen," and was sent upon request from the Archives in Darmstadt, Germany. Since my other great-grandparents died before I was born, Henry Schwartz was the only one I knew.

When he came to the United States in 1864, he "Americanized" his name as many others had done, and Heinrich Schwarz became Henry Schwartz. His Certificate of Citizenship, dated March 21, 1881, Auglaize County, says that Henry Schwartz of Germany declared his desire to become a Citizen of the United States of America on the 30th of March 1878. William Pfeifer and Ernest Afderhar (Aufderhaar) gave their oaths that he had resided in the United States for five years and was of good moral character.

In its original German, "schwarz" is translated as the color, "black." As his daughter, Eva, entered Ada Normal School (now Ohio Northern University) in the 1890s, they called her Miss Black, but she explained that her family had retained the German and that she was to be called Miss Schwartz.

When Henry came to America, he worked for a while in Hamilton at a water-powered grist mill, where employees worked around the clock by lantern light. One night he was hurt rather badly. As he tried to put a metal piece on top of a barrel of flour, it flipped off. On the second try, it flipped over and fell to the floor. When he reached down to pick it up, he got his fingers caught in the nearby machinery and lost all but his index finger. The accident changed Henry's activities, but life went on. After the accident he always wrote with a short stub of a pencil while moving his whole hand.

The first four children born to Henry were girls, my grandma being one of them. Being females didn't spare them from the hard work usually done by males. Even as children, the girls worked beside their dad as he tilled and harvested the fields. Like most old German men, Henry was occasionally quite harsh with his family. Grandma spoke many times of "getting a licking" from her dad for some transgression she had committed. When he got excited, he often reverted back to his native tongue. When he yelled at the children in German and they did not understand, his wife, Kate (who also understood German) patiently explained to the children just what their father wanted.

Are you on speaking terms with a skunk? One day Great-grandma heard a commotion coming from her henhouse. The chickens were frightened and were running for their lives, creating quite a noisy disturbance. Henry went to investigate, and there, amidst the frightened chickens, stood a fully grown skunk. Since Henry had no sense of smell, he grabbed the nearest thing (probably a shovel or broom) and started beating the skunk, either to kill it or to scare it out of the building. The smell didn't bother Henry, but when he went into the house, Kate turned up her nose in a violent reaction to his horrendous odor. In his broken English, Henry asked, "Does she shmell, Kate, does she shmell?"

I also heard a similar story about a skunk that somehow found its way into their basement. I don't know if there were two separate skunk episodes or just confusion over the one. In either case, neither the skunk nor his bad "shmell" seemed to bother Henry Schwartz.

My dad remembered frequent visits to the home of his grandpa and grandma Schwartz when he was just a little child. At Christmas, a big dinner was held for all their children and grandchildren. Henry was usually quite tight with his money, even though he owned several farms and was known to be one of the more well-to-do men in Salem Township. Grandma had no income, except perhaps for the butter and egg money that most farm wives were allowed to keep, yet she always managed a gift for each one at Christmas. I remember my grandma showing me a pretty postcard which she said had been her only gift from her mother one year. It eventually ended up in Grandpa's trunk with my postcard collection. Grandma Schwartz gave a book to each grandchild one Christmas, and Dad's had been a copy of the children's book, *Black Beauty*.

On one of his visits to his grandparents' house, my dad was running and fell, striking his head against something sharp. When it began to bleed profusely, his grandma quickly got down her Bible, then put her hand on his head as she read several verses. The bleeding stopped at once. We asked Dad what she had read but he didn't remember. He was young and although she explained what she had done and said, he couldn't remember the words. Great-grandma Schwartz also used Bible verses when taking the *fire* out of a burn. She had done that on a burn Dad had received one time.

The Schwartz family was very strong in urging their children to get an education. Back in Germany, the schools had no blackboards, books, or papers, so students were taught to do a lot of the math and other subjects in their heads. Henry was very smart and was quick at figuring in his head. I think that is one reason he really liked my grandpa Frank, because he was also very quick at figuring things in his head. Education was important, and Henry's brother, John Schwartz, encouraged his son, John, to go to college and become a teacher. He eventually became a very highly recognized history professor at Bowling Green State University during the 1940s. Our family visited him many times.

Henry and Kate Schwartz's daughter, Elva, shared a story with me in 1983. She and Floyd Wilkins selected Christmas Eve, December 24, 1911, for their marriage date. After the wedding, they went to the Christmas Eve service at the Kossuth Church. Since they were still dressed in their wedding finery, they were very much admired and were the focus of attention. They felt quite special. The next day, the Schwartz family celebrated Christmas with a large dinner at their big house north of Kossuth. The family kept track of the newlyweds for a while, but when some of them went home briefly to do chores, the couple sneaked up to the attic where they hid for a couple of hours. After the family had all returned, they hunted all over the house for Elva and Floyd, looking under beds, in closets, outside in the barn and sheds and, as the newlyweds watched from the attic windows, the family even looked around the corn shocks in the fields surrounding the house. Finally the young couple got tired of hiding and missing all the fun. They quietly returned to the kitchen with the rest of the crowd. The others couldn't figure out where they had been hiding. The whole family had a good laugh about the newlyweds' caper.

Henry Schwartz Jr. said his mother, Catherine, had gone to school only two weeks in her life and that was when she lived at New Knoxville. She was sick a lot as a child and when they moved to the Kossuth area, she no longer went to school. "Mother started working out as a hired girl when she was eight years old," Aunt Elva told me. "Young girls often helped in homes when a new baby was born, and she had even baked bread."

Henry Schwartz was a shrewd businessman, and after the girls were grown, he usually had several men working for him. Many times they would be a little short of money and would ask him for an advance on their salary. Henry Jr. said several times he had seen his dad pick up a smooth chip of wood and write a "check" out on it. The men took those wood chips to the bank and I.B. Post gave them their money. Henry went in later and picked up his "chips." One snowy day when Henry Jr. was a young teen, he went with his dad to Spencerville to borrow $200 to pay off a note. Because the Spencerville bank didn't have large amounts of money to lend, Henry bought farms using notes from Wapakoneta banks. He had sold some grain, animals, etc. to pay his note but lacked $200. I.B. Post had only $200 in the bank that day and agreed to lend it to Henry Sr. if no one came into the bank needing money before closing time. No one came, and Henry got the money, leaving only a few cents in the Spencerville bank. Mr. Post said he would have to round up some money from local merchants before the bank could be opened the next morning.

When they arrived home, Henry told his teenage son to carry the bag with the 200 silver dollars into the house. Henry Jr. told me, "It was all I could do to carry it!" His dad had also bought a sack of nails while he was in town. As the boy got out of the sleigh, one of the men working for his dad told him to bring that sack over right away, since he needed some nails. But Henry Sr. said, "That sack doesn't hold any nails. They are still in the sleigh. Come over here and look in this sack." When his dad told him to set the heavy sack down, young Henry gladly obliged, since it was a struggle carrying it through the snow. His dad opened the sack so the man could look inside. When he saw that sack of silver dollars, he could only gasp, "My God, where did you get all that money?"

After my mother's death in November of 1930, my grandparents welcomed Dad, Don and me into their home. Two years later, they again opened their arms, this time to Grandma's father, Henry Schwartz. Again the wooden sea trunk traveled with him as he settled into our spare bedroom for the remaining months of his life.

At ninety-three years of age, Great-grandpa was no longer active, and spent long hours sitting in his chair where he enjoyed his cigars. The problem was finding a place to put the ashes. A brass spittoon was expensive in those depression days, so Grandma solved the problem with a green spittoon-shaped flower pot which she placed on a newspaper on the floor beside his chair. He could easily drop the ashes into this makeshift spittoon.

One spring day, as Grandma was outside working, she left me in the house to "keep an eye on Great-grandpa," (or, more probably, he was supposed to keep an eye on me). He dropped some ashes that day, but they missed his spittoon and fell on the paper. As it began to smolder, I became really frightened and ran to the garden as fast as my little legs would go, screaming at the top of my lungs, "Grandma! Grandma! Come quick! Great-grandpa set the house on fire!" I was still only two years old when this happened, but I've never forgotten my exact words. No, the house didn't burn down. Grandma rushed in and quickly stomped the smoldering paper, putting the fire out before it could do any real damage. But that vivid memory of Great-grandpa setting the house on fire has never faded from my mind.

A big red *work* handkerchief was often spread out on Great-grandpa's lap as he sat in his chair. Unlike the white ones used for Sunday, his everyday handkerchief was covered with rows of white quarter-inch dots with a border on a red background. Henry spent many hours counting those dots, touching each one with his finger as he said the numbers. This not only helped him pass the time, but it also helped me to learn my numbers by hearing them over and over. My brother was in school by then, and Great-grandpa kept me amused while Grandma did her gardening, fed the chickens, baked, and so on. His dot-counting procedure was repeated so often that those white dots finally wore through. In my mind I can still see that strange-looking dotted handkerchief–but there were no dots, just holes!

Another unforgettable picture was of Great-grandpa's long white beard. He didn't always have that beard, and according to family stories, it was a good thing. He once got his face singed in a rather unconventional way. He had built a new home, the big cement block house located one fourth mile north of Kossuth on Schwartz Road. (Yes, it was named after him.) Since electricity had not yet come to the farms in this area, he installed carbide lights. A storage tank for the carbide was placed in the basement. One evening the lights began to dim and Kate suggested Henry might check to see if the storage tank might need some attention. Henry lit a match and bent over the fuel tank to see what the problem might be. A sudden flash of fire burned the hair right off his face! Fortunately he was not badly burned, but Henry Schwartz quickly learned a few dangers of *modern* conveniences that evening.

Life in the new house was definitely made easier by those "modern conveniences." The Schwartz household no longer made regular trips to the outhouse. They now had an "indoor" bathroom. The windmill near the back door provided the power to force water from the well to a tank in the attic. Pipes from the tank extended down to the bathroom where the pull of gravity allowed the stool to be flushed and hands to be washed. Quite modern for that day!

Although Henry and Catherine's family were basically dirt farmers, there were a few hints of money among the relatives. Catherine had a very wealthy uncle, Ernst Huenefeld, who lived in Cincinnati. He came to visit the Schwartz family in the early 1900s, having been driven up by his chauffeur who stayed at the hotel in Spencerville. Before he left, he gave Catherine a gift of money, possibly $100. She had told her children she was going to save that money to pay for her burial. She died February 24, 1927, and Henry died six years later on December 17, 1933. They are buried side by side in the Kossuth Cemetery. Henry worked hard and saved his money. Like most Germans, he pinched each penny tightly and when his will was read after his death, each of their seven surviving children (Eva, Tilla, Nora, Bertha, Henry Jr., Elva, and Lehr) inherited a farm in the Kossuth area. The bearded immigrant prospered when he sought a land of freedom.

This portrait of the immigrant Henry Schwartz and his family was taken about 1906.
Back: Elva, Henry Jr., Eva and Tilla. Middle: Bertha, Henry (father), Catherine (mother) and Lehr standing.
My grandma, Nora, sits center front.

Four generations posed in 1930: Great-grandpa Henry Schwartz sits beside my brother Don. Grandma Nora and Dad stand behind. All lived within a mile of the Miami-Erie Canal.

Four generations enjoyed the 60th anniversary of Frank and Nora (Schwartz) Davenport on July 24, 1958. Glenna Meckstroth stands beside her dad, Bernard, with her children in front of his parents. They are Steven, age two; Michael, age four; and Nancy, age two months.

## Chapter 3.

# Digging the "Big Ditch"

When the first two Meckstroth brothers arrived in America in 1834, they traveled 106 miles 's "through" mud roads from Cincinnati to their destination near what is now New Knoxville. The situation had not improved when their parents, brothers and sisters arrived a year later. But when the last son and his wife arrived in 1842, they found a much more pleasant means of travel. The first eighty-three miles north of Cincinnati were mud-free as they traveled by canal boat to Piqua, leaving only thirty miles of mud road to traverse to the New Knoxville area.

Travel was exceedingly slow and difficult in the 1820s. There were few roads. Much of this area, at the edge of the Great Black Swamp, was marshy and wet most of the year. Many felt that canals, which were being built in eastern states, were the answer to transportation problems in Ohio. Cincinnati was easily accessible by the Ohio River, and Toledo could be reached via the Great Lakes, so a canal was proposed between these two industrial cities. In 1825, the Ohio legislature provided funding for a system of canals in the state.

Congress granted 500,000 acres of northwest Ohio land to be sold, much of it for $1 to as low as 10¢ an acre, and thus the Miami-Erie Canal was begun. At the time the first shovelful of dirt was turned on July 21, 1825, Lima was just a small town, and the entire population of Allen County was less than 100 households. This included our home areas of Kossuth and New Knoxville, since Auglaize County was not formed until 1848, mainly from parts of Allen and Mercer counties. By 1828, the first section of the Miami Canal was finished from Cincinnati's Ohio River to Dayton. [1]

The second section, called the Miami Extension, reached from Dayton to the Defiance area where it joined the Wabash and Erie Canal. This canal was built from Lake Erie to Ft. Wayne, Indiana.

Due to famine in Europe, many Germans and Irishmen had come to this part of Ohio where workers were needed to build the canal. According to a paper, *German Communities in Northwestern Ohio: Canal Fever and Prosperity*, written by Wolfgang Fleischhauer at The Ohio State University, "The construction of the canal meant hard money in the pockets of the pioneer settler . . . . Groups of German pioneer settlers from New Bremen and Minster, for instance, worked on the Wabash and Erie Canal in Indiana before the Miami and Erie Canal passed through their settlements." [2]

Ray Zunk explained that the heavy physical labor of digging the canal was done mostly by Irishmen, many of whom had been bog workers. As he put it, "They were the poorest of the poor." Many local Germans, especially from northwest Germany, had helped build the canals in neighboring Holland. Many of these men were experienced in canal building and became the engineers and foremen of the crews of workers on the Miami-Erie Canal.

Since most of them owned or were buying farms in the area, they went home when the weather was not suitable for canal work. Many of them used their canal earnings to pay for farms in the area of New Knoxville and the canal towns of New Bremen and Minster. Money was also saved to pay the travel expenses of other family members who were eventually brought to America.

Although the canal brought with it the promise of an improved transportation system, it also had an impact on the local price of land. As the canal (or "Big Ditch") was being dug, the price of land increased. A March 31, 1836, letter from Griffith John, of Allen County to his father (possibly still in Germany) reads, "Improved land is raising in value very fast. I have been offered ten dollars an acre for part of mine. Corn is worth 37 cents per bushel, wheat is $1.25 and bacon 10 cents per pound. I have sold about 700 bushels of corn since last fall at from 25 to 37 cents per bushel. The demand is chiefly by emigrants to this country. There can yet be some good entries made here in land . . . We had a long and hard winter here.

"The seasons here are more mild and variable (than in my former Pennsylvania home). Summer heat nor winter's cold are not so intensive as it is there . . ." [3] The increased prices only made it that much more difficult for those doing the more menial jobs to save enough money to buy property. Some who owned property sold it for a healthy profit, then moved their families farther west, where they bought cheaper ground.

When the canal camps closed for the winter, most of the Irish had no place to go. Many died of disease or exposure. Some helped the Germans clear their land in exchange for food and shelter. When the Irish canal workers died, there was no Irish Catholic burial place for them. My friend, Rita Hoying, archivist for St. Augustine Catholic Church in the canal town of Minster, explained that the bodies of many Irish workers were buried in that parish's cemetery. Other workers, some of whom were prisoners, found their final resting place in the actual canal banks. It took several years before the first Irish settlement and parish were established near Glynwood.

Bill's great-grandfather Herman William Meckstroth came from Germany about this time and worked on the canal as a water boy for 17¢ a day. As part of each man's pay, a jigger of whiskey was also included. It was thought to be of medicinal value, a form of protection against malaria and "canal fever." Many of them died anyway. Another of Bill's great-grandpas, William Feldwisch, arrived from Germany during the final years of canal construction and worked on a crew until the project was completed.

Henry Herman Fledderjohann, Bill's great-great-grandfather, came to America in 1835 and settled in Washington Township. He started to work as a common laborer on the canal, but because of his experience as a carpenter, he was soon raised to the position of foreman. He learned the carpentry trade from his father in Germany and was given the job of constructing several of the locks near the "divide" section of the canal. The continental divide ran through this section between Piqua and St. Marys. It was the highest point of the canal and contained the largest concentration of locks in the entire length of the canal. Grandpa Fledderjohann had plenty of work to do, but he was up to the task. He later built a sawmill which he operated for forty years on the banks of the canal at Lock Six.

A historical marker erected beside the lock in New Bremen reads:

Loramie Summit–The Miami and Erie Canal built 1825-1845. 244.5 miles long. Was a transporter of passengers and freight between Lake Erie and the Ohio River. This section is Loramie Summit, a 21 mile long plateau of water, retained by lock 1-N (This marker) and lock 1-S at Lockington. Water supplied by Summit feeders from reservoirs Loramie and Lewiston (Indian Lake). Lock 1-N was one of 105 locks which lifted boats 513' from Cincinnati to the Summit, lowered 395' to Toledo. Lock chambers of wood and stone were 90' by 15'. Canal here was 50' top 26' bottom and 5' deep. The half-way marker, lake to river, is 1.5 miles north this site. Fare passengers 3¢-2¢ ton mile - 1.5¢ over 100 miles. Boat tow was 4-5 miles per hour. [4]

Unlike most canal systems, the Miami-Erie numbered the locks going outward from the Loramie Summit; thus there was a lock two "north" and a lock two "south," and so on.

Much of the area through which the canal was to be built was swampy. In order to drain the swamps and provide the water needed to feed the canal, three reservoirs were built: the Lewistown Reservoir (we now know it as Indian Lake), Lake Loramie, and the Mercer County Reservoir.

The Mercer County Reservoir was started in 1841 and was the largest manmade artificial lake in the world until the building of Hoover Dam. (St. Marys folks called it "Lake St. Marys," Celina people used the name "Grand Lake," but my family just called it "The Reservoir.") Dirt embankments were built at each end of a ten-mile long natural basin which was spring fed. Since a large part of this area was forest, the trees were either cut down or were girdled so they would die before the water came in.

St. Marys residents were afraid the water would cause the trees to rot and that diseases such as malaria would sicken or kill those living near the lake. (The water actually preserved the downed trees, and the stumps measuring four feet across are still being pulled out in such perfect condition that the ax marks are clearly visible.) Canal officials said the water would cause no problems, and allowed it to cover the basin. Many people had not yet received proper payment for their flooded land and were quite angry, since funds for the construction of the lake, part of which was to pay them, had been appropriated. When the lake continued to fill with water in 1843 and they had still not been paid, 150 to 200 residents from the Celina area gathered together, and with picks and shovels, cut a channel through the West Bank. "They were arrested for their deed and it was the first time in the country's history that all of a city's (Celina) and county's (Mercer County) officials were arrested and charged with a crime." No grand jury would convict them, and they were released, but it cost the state $17,000 to repair the damage. [5]

Facts about this reservoir are stated on a stone marker near the East Bank shelter house:

Grand Lake Saint Marys. Originally Mercer County Reservoir was world's largest man made lake when constructed 1837-1841. Water supply for Miami-Erie Canal from here to the Maumee River at Defiance - 17,603 acres. In 1856 lake level lowered 5.4 feet to prevent flooding -15,748 acres - cost 528,222.07.

World's first offshore oil well drilling occurred here 1891- Piles were driven to support a platform for derrick and drilling rig - Oil well derricks were as numerous in the lake as the surrounding land area. [6]

Several interesting events were recorded during a couple of the very dry years. "In October 1872, the water in the lake was so low that there was practically no water on the east end of the lake. Dead timber on the east side of the lake bed dried up. Luxuriant weeds and vegetation grew where a short time before there had been water several feet deep. It was in that month that the weeds and timber caught fire. Sparks were blown in over St. Marys, and local citizens were alarmed about their properties."[7] Although it was a smoky autumn in the area, no great damage was recorded. Unfortunately, it didn't burn off many stumps in the lake.

The lake's water level has often dropped during dry years, but as we look at the expanse of blue water today, it is hard to believe that it was so dry one year that most of the fish died, and the lake bottom dried up enough for farmers living nearby to plow several acres and plant a crop of corn. An area near the north shore was plowed up and a good crop of celery was harvested by local farmers.[8]

Axes and saws had worked well for cutting down the huge trees to form the lake, but even in dry years, there was no way to tear out the stumps that lurked just below the surface.

"The Reservoir, as it was known in those early days, wasn't a lake at all, just a water-filled pasture full of trees. It took four men with long pike poles, two on each side, to pole a boat loaded with merchandise over and back." During the heyday of lake travel, a steamboat ride to Celina and Montezuma cost 30¢ to 50¢ round trip from St. Marys. At one time seven steamboats worked on the lake. Some of those operating there were *The Niagara* in 1849, and in later years, *Steamboat Clipper, Pilgrim*, and *J.M. Davidson.*[9]

Larger boats were quite popular during the 1890s. St. Marys historian Clara Kellermeyer mentioned a problem which one of the larger boats encountered. A 45-foot wood-burning double-deck stern wheeler, called *City of Celina* occasionally got stuck on some of the stumps below the water's surface. The captain would blow his whistle, then a second boat, the smaller 30-foot long *Bo Peep* would come to its rescue, seesawing the bigger boat back and forth until it was dislodged from the stump.[10]

According to New Bremen Historical Society papers, William Combs Jr., a former canal boat captain, recalled the trips across the reservoir to Celina. "A man named William Barnbook operated a steamboat on the reservoir. There was a deep channel from the bulkhead all the way across to Celina. Barnbook would wait until five boats were lined up ready to cross. He would tie two boats to each side of the steamboat and then trail the fifth one."[11] Wouldn't that have been a sight to see?

As equipment has progressed, additional stumps have been removed when the lake's water level has been low. Over the years, many boats have been damaged because of the stumps. (When our kids were teens, the motor on our pontoon raft broke several shear pins on stumps just below the water's surface. When it was built one hundred fifty years ago, who could imagine all the speed boats zipping around the lake?)

According to local historians, oil was first discovered in Auglaize County on July 24, 1886, in St. Marys. In his book, *The St. Marys Story*, local author, Frank Shuffleton described that exciting scene. A group of traveling actors had been presenting *The Mikado* for the "local gentry" who were gathered at the town hall. When the cry, "They struck oil!" was shouted through the streets and into the hall, everyone including the actors rushed to "David Armstrong's cow pasture" to see the excitement.[12] It was a glorious day.

The *St. Marys Argus* of January 24, 1891, states: "It is said that an oil well derrick has this week been put up on the reservoir, three or four hundred feet from the shore at the northeast corner. Verily, the days of the reservoir are numbered." Although it sounded like the demise of the lake, it was not. Old photos show numerous oil derricks (nearly 150) scattered throughout the lake. St. Marys canal historian, Jim Kite explained that eight to ten of these derricks were connected with pipes, giving them a spider-like appearance. A central steam engine then pumped out the oil. The derricks and pipes were so numerous that Kite said it was possible to walk most of the way from the north shore to the south shore without touching water. Only one channel was left open for the canal boats to travel through on their way to Celina."[13]

Lew Hines, husband of Grandpa's sister, Effie, was one of the last pumpers of those wells. In 1936, ice harvesters on the lake were cutting chunks of ice frozen twenty-two inches thick, the thickest in years. They predicted it would get even thicker if the cold spell continued. Lew died as a result of working those oil wells one bitter cold February day. The Wapakoneta *Daily News* obituary on February 24 says he became so cold that he died after being a patient in St. Rita's hospital for "three weeks, suffering from infection of brain caused by being severely frozen."

Maybe the greatest challenge of the Miami and Erie Canal system was what is known today as Deep Cut. It was a huge engineering feat that took place north of Kossuth where the canal was cut through a deep hill and is now designated as a Registered National Historic Landmark. On a pretty autumn day, I sat on a cold concrete bench in the park directly above the *deep cut* and recorded the following:

> You are on that section of the Miami and Erie Canal where the greatest excavation was made–a section that has been known over the years as "Deep Cut." The huge ditch, 6,600 feet long and 5 to 52 feet deep was dug and blasted through the tough blue-clay ridge which separates the St. Marys watershed from that of the Auglaize.
> Strong muscled farm boys, brawny Irishmen, and sometimes convicts sentenced to hard labor, toiled here with picks, shovels, and barrows, from sun-up to sun-down for 30¢ a day. They lived in shabby unsanitary camps and were often ravaged by malaria and other diseases. Bad blood among the construction gangs and whisky, which "flowed like water," led to frequent brawls. Spencer Township, Allen County, where this marker is located, and Spencerville, just to the north, are both named in honor of Colonel William Spencer, member of the State Board of Public Works which had charge of Ohio's canal system. [14]

In many areas, the canal needed only to be dug out of the flat ground, but as it was built across lower, more level areas such as that found in much of Auglaize County, the soil was piled in levees to form the canal banks eight to ten feet above the surrounding farmland. Much of the dirt removed from the deep cut was used to fill in these low areas. Ray Zunk said the excess dirt was moved to the south by a horse-drawn tramway. Regardless, the canal system, having been built without the benefit of today's massive earth moving tools is a tribute to the energies of those who built it.

When the entire canal was finished, the total cost was 8.026 million dollars for the three reservoirs, 103 lift locks, three guard locks, and nineteen aqueducts. It generally took four days to travel the full length. When the canal was at its peak in the 1850s and 1860s, records listed four hundred boats on the canal at one time. (That would have been two boats in almost every mile of canal!) Additionally, passenger traffic was at its highest with as many as 200,000 persons per year.[15]

The canal system is noteworthy for a number of reasons. Apart from Lake St. Marys having been the largest inland manmade lake and the location of some of the very first off-shore oil platforms, the fact that the Continental Divide runs through it also contributes to its uniqueness. Excess water from the west (Celina) side drains into rivers flowing into the Gulf of Mexico, while water from the east (St. Marys) side goes north into the St. Lawrence River! It was quite a "ditch" those determined men dug!

---

[1] Ray Zunk, private conversations and canal presentations, Auglaize County Genealogical and Historical Society meetings, 1980-1997.

[2] Wolfgang Fleischhauer, *German Communities in Northwestern Ohio: Canal Fever and Prosperity*, from The Report: 34, A Journal of German-American History, published by The Society for the History of the Germans in Maryland, 1970, used with permission.

[3] Griffith John, personal letter written 31 March 1836, Allen County Museum Library, Lima, Ohio.

[4] Historical Marker placed at New Bremen lock by Auglaize County Historical Society 1968.

[5] Pam Crabtree, "Grand Lake St. Marys; From Canal Feeder to Recreation Hotspot," Back to Future Progress special 1992 edition, *Evening Leader*, St. Marys, Ohio, used with permission.

[6] Historical Marker placed by Auglaize County (Ohio) Historical Society, 1978.

[7] Hal Miller, "As I See It," *Evening Leader*, St. Marys, Ohio, July 15, 1988, used with permission.

[8] Cathy Schreima, "Controversial History Attached to Grand Lake St. Marys," St. Marys *Evening Leader*, February 28, 1997, used with permission.

[9] Hal Miller, "As I See It," *Evening Leader*, St. Marys, Ohio, October 12, 1990, used with permission.

[10] Cathy Schreima, "Controversial History Attached to Grand Lake St. Marys," *Evening Leader*, St. Marys, Ohio, February 28, 1997, used with permission.

[11] Janet Fledderjohann interview of Forest Combs in *Evening Leader*, St. Marys, Ohio, 1974, used with permission.

[12] Janie Southard, "Early Ohio Oil Boom has Roots in St. Marys," *Evening Leader*, St. Marys, Ohio, October 16, 1991, used with permission.

[13] Jim Kite, Canal Historian, private conversation, February 3, 1998.

[14] Historical Marker placed by Allen County Historical Society, 1961.

[15] Wayne Wenning, "Lock One Sets Astride a Key Portion of Miami-Erie Canal," *Evening Leader*, St. Marys, Ohio, March 25, 1996, used with permission.

[16] *Travel Back in Time,* Ohio Department of Natural Resources and MECCA, p. 21, 2003, used with permission.

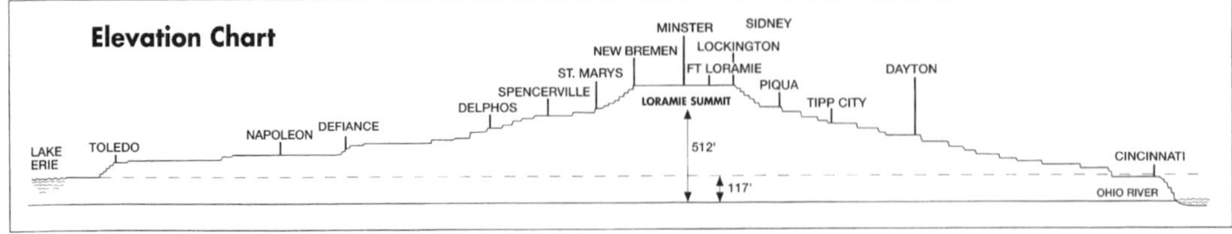


Elevation chart of Miami-Erie Canal locks from Lake Erie to the Ohio River.
From *Travel Back in Time,* Ohio Department of Natural Resources and MECCA.[16]

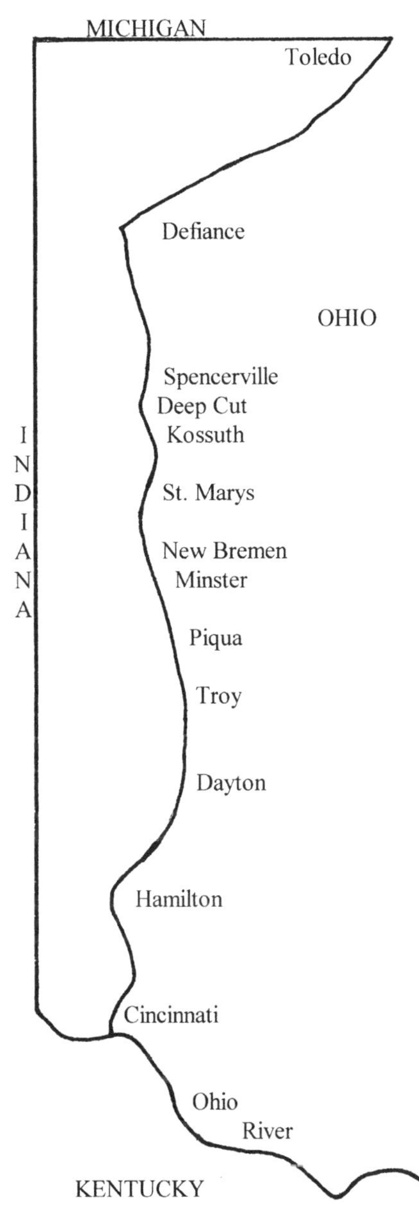


The path of the Miami-Erie Canal as it extends south from Lake Erie to the Ohio River.

The world's first off-shore oil wells were at the Reservoir, now Grand Lake St. Marys. (*Photo courtesy of George Neargarder*)

The Bulkhead lock as seen from the Reservoir. The lake's water level appears to be low. (*Photo courtesy of Tom Hevlin*)

The east side of the Bulkhead lock in 1895. It was here canal boats entered the Reservoir. (*Photo courtesy of Tom Hevlin*)

## Chapter 4.

# *Life Along the Towpath*

> This was a gala day for Spencerville, people coming for miles to witness the triumphant entry, towed by a beautiful team of horses decorated with plumes and highly decorated blankets. The boat was in charge of Captain George Cook and entered the settlement amid ringing of bells and the cheer of the passengers aboard the boat . . . From this time for nearly half a century the Miami and Erie Canal was the principal means of mercantile transportation for the territory it served as well as considerable passenger service. [1]

It was July 4, 1845. Great-great-grandpa John Briggs had taken his children to see the first canal boat as it passed through Acadia (changed to Spencerville in 1867). W.W. Rider, the son of a canal boat captain, gave the above description of the momentous day. It may seem like a big deal about nothing, but for many, the canal was their first means of public transportation, and was instrumental in "opening up the area."

Although the first canal boat may have received a warm reception as it opened the new and primary means of transportation, not all of the boats that followed were so well received. One of the oft repeated stories in our area concerns the 383 freed slaves of John Randolph of Virginia who came up the canal to New Bremen in 1846. Land had been purchased for them in Mercer County, but disgruntled citizens met the boat and refused them permission to disembark. The freed slaves were returned to the Piqua area where they were allowed to remain.

The canal brought a variety of boats to the wilderness area of that time. In a 1982 *Country Living* article, Karin Deneke indicated that "passenger packets, grocery boats, freighters, pleasure crafts, and log rafts made up a colorful array of canal traffic." Ray Zunk even described a special canal boat, one that was highly decorated in circus wagon style and housed a circus troupe which entertained along the canal. Sounds like fun!

As might be expected, local farmers took advantage of the canal as a means of transporting their goods to market. Part of New Bremen's and Minster's original wealth was attributed to the raising of hogs. During the peak of canal traffic in the 1860s "an estimated 10,000 hogs were slaughtered and shipped from five plants in the village of New Bremen and a sixth in nearby Lock Two."[2]

Surprisingly, there was an even larger "crop" that went to market—ice. "Reports show that for decades, more tons of ice went down the canal than any other cargo combined. Some of it continued to be shipped as far as South America."[3] Boatloads of ice were harvested from ponds near the canal. Imagine that, shipping ice that far away! Wow!

The common method of keeping ice in those days was to pack it in sawdust in a barn-like building called an ice house. New Bremen, like many small towns, had a pond where ice was harvested each year, and the blocks of ice were closely packed into the nearby ice house. Harvesting ice was very familiar to Forest Combs, the son of a canal boat captain. In a 1974 interview, he said that after a week of cold, zero temperatures, the crop would be ripe. He gave the following account:

> You could hear the ice cracking or thumping on the quiet of the night as it froze. Ice was tested for thickness by using a six-foot drill, like an auger and was measured each day until ready. Dad never put it up until it was seven to 9 inches thick; sometimes it was thicker. At times it was necessary to remove snow from the pond by hand or by using a light horse pulling a big scraper. Harvesting the ice crop required at least 25 people and one or two horses during the three-day process. Often, the night before the harvest, a post and flag would be erected, marking the center of the far south end of the pond and the center of the west side. Rather often, the first and most important score was made by lantern light. Similar to the farmer directing his horse to plow a straight row, one man would lead the horse over the ice while the other guided the marker. The plowing phase was similar to marking, only it made a deeper cut. Ice harvesters worked from the center of the pond outward–north and south,–then east and west the same way, marking the 22-inch squares. A saw was the tool for the actual harvest. The product was stored in an ice house year round.[4]

So what was life really like along the towpath? My grandparents, parents, brother and I spent our childhoods living within a mile or two of the canal and there have been some interesting happenings. Grandpa told us of frequent trips to Lock 14 north of St. Marys. He was only eleven years old when his mother, grandma and baby brother all died in 1888. As the oldest son, he had to take on additional responsibilities to help out, including getting the family's corn ground at the nearest mill. His pa would place a sack of hand shelled corn onto the back of the family horse and then give him a boost up behind the sack. He then followed either the towpath or the dirt road to Bloody Bridge where he no doubt crossed the canal on his way to the village of Lock 14.

Take a moment and imagine the anticipation this young farm boy must have felt as his horse trotted down the dirt path into the village. The promise of excitement would have been great as he watched the turning of the mill's water wheel (much as I did years later when I went with him to the mill in Spencerville). While he waited for the corn to be ground, I'm sure he would have watched with great anticipation as the lock tender did his job, opening up the south gate and allowing a canal boat being pulled by a team of mules to enter the lock. The gate behind it was then closed and the wicket gate (a roughly two and a half foot square sliding door built into the north gate) was opened.

When enough water had escaped through the wicket gate so that the water level in the lock matched that on the "down" side of the lock, the north gate was opened and the boat exited. Maybe a south bound boat was waiting, and immediately entered the lock. The north gate (and its wicket gate) would then be closed, raising the boat up to the level of the canal south of the lock. Sometimes boats, especially the bigger ones, would scrape against the side of the lock while going up or down, causing them to rock from side to side.

While he was waiting, Grandpa occasionally bought needed items from the grocery store run by a gentleman named Fred Hauss. After the cornmeal had been ground, the sack was loaded on the horse. When it was tied down, Grandpa would start the ride back home. Much of the narrow dirt road went through deep woods that were no doubt becoming quite dark as the evening approached. And of course, there was the hollow clip-clop of the horse's hoofs as they traveled across that wooden structure known as Bloody Bridge where, just three decades before, a notorious murder was committed. On short winter days, the ride home may have been concluded in the darkness of night. Quite a day for a youngster!

More work was waiting at home. After returning with the coarsely ground corn, it would be sifted through a sieve to separate the corn meal from the coarse outer cracked corn. Then it would be fine enough for making bread or cooked as cornmeal mush.

All that remains of Lock 14 today are remnants of the concrete lock and a couple of nearby houses. Recently, I climbed the canal bank and stood mesmerized as I stared at the swiftly flowing water in the lock below me, then read from the county's historical marker:

> Lock 14–This concrete lock built in 1907 replaced original white oak wooden structure. In this area was a church, locktender's house, sawmill, blacksmith shop, general store, ice house, and homes. Boats were drawn by mules - horses using the towpath.[5]

Bloody Bridge, just north of Lock 14, was well known in canal days. First of all, it was used in winter as a docking place for some of the boats. The owners tied their boats on the heel path side of the canal and lived on them all winter or until the ice had thawed. Neighbors in that area kept the teams of mules in their barns throughout the winter.

The Sullivan family owned at least two canal boats, the *Nautilus* and the *Sing Shelley,* and lived on one of them.[6] There may have been a family connection. Grandpa had mentioned that when his pa remarried, his stepmother, Nellie Sullivan, had come from "over west." (He nodded toward Bloody Bridge.) His pa, John Wesley Davenport, had worked on a canal boat. Could it have been one of the Sullivan boats? Since Nellie's parents had both died, would she have lived with or visited on a Sullivan boat? Would that be where John met Nellie? Hmm! Guess we'll never know.

Bloody Bridge was best known as the location of the dastardly deed that took place there one night in 1854. The story was known to canal men from Cincinnati to Toledo, and I suppose passengers on each boat passing the area no doubt heard the details of the terrible event. The nearby historical marker gives this brief account:

> Bloody Bridge–During the canal years of the 1850's a rivalry grew between Bill Jones and Jack Billings for the love of Minnie Warren. This became hatred by Bill because Minnie chose Jack. On a fall night in 1854, returning from a party, Minnie and Jack were surprised on the bridge by Bill armed with an ax. With one swing, Bill severed Jack's head. Seeing this, Minnie screamed and fell from the bridge into a watery grave. Bill disappeared, and when a skeleton was found years later in a nearby well, people asked was it suicide or justice. [7]

Although there was not a lot of *scheduled* boat travel on the Miami-Erie canal in Grandpa's teen years, it still got a lot of use. He especially enjoyed skating on the canal in the wintertime. I was surprised when he showed me his skates one winter day. I had just received a pair of shoe skates for Christmas, but his didn't look at all like mine. They were heavy steel clamp-on skates that needed a key to tighten the clamps around the soles of a good solid pair of work shoes. A strap from the back of the skate came to the front where it was fastened across the ankles. When I attached them to my shoes and stood up, I soon discovered it would have been rather difficult to skate on them, but it was the best they had at the time and they enjoyed the winter activity. I have seen an early picture of kids skating on the canal near the Pratt Bridge a mile south of Kossuth and wondered if Grandpa was in the crowd.

The canal provided a lot of enjoyment in summer as well as winter. Grandpa was a strong swimmer and had much of his fun in the area of the aqueduct south of Kossuth. It was at this spot that, as a young lad, he had held his breath and walked across the bottom on the wood plank floor of that aqueduct, scaring the boys who were swimming with him.

Perhaps I should explain the purpose of an aqueduct. Aqueducts were used to carry the canal water over the streams and rivers along the way. They were from 500 to 700 feet long and some were as high as thirty-five feet above the streams.

In Mary McClintock's 1966 interview of Grandpa, she quoted his words: "There is a spot two miles south of Kossuth where the canal crosses over Six-mile Creek, Frank told us. This was an exciting place when he was a youngster. He liked to watch the boats pass through a great big wooden box which had been built into the canal. There was water in the center of the box for the boats, a walkway on one side for the mules and plank on the other for pedestrians."[8]

Well, folks are still fascinated by that picturesque aqueduct beside Route 66. It is frequently visited by tourists, as well as photographers hoping to capture the beauty of its blooming buds in early spring, its cool green foliage in summer, its vibrant colored leaves in fall and the splendor of the frozen ice cascade in winter. At any time of the year, the aqueduct is beautiful!

The canal has never lost its appeal. I had been raised listening to my grandparent's stories. When I was a child, I loved to spend lazy afternoons there, too, many with my best friend, Rosemary Rothe, whose house was right beside the canal. A little diving board was still fastened to the old canal bridge near her house, and we occasionally splashed around in the water. By then the dirt and silt had washed into that area, making the mud nearly as deep as the water. When a pipeline was put through from Texas to Lima, a round metal pipe was placed across the canal where Grandpa and his friends had skated. As kids, we dared each other to walk across it.

Grandpa used to catch fish by the hundreds in the canal, but we weren't that successful. Rosemary and I used to sit on the canal bank, lean against a tree and fish—sometimes with a proper pole and line, but sometimes by just taking off our shoes and tying a string to our big toe with a hook and bobber on the other end. We sat and talked and giggled and fished. Did we catch many? No, but we most certainly had fun!

The Kossuth church sits beside the canal, and children for many decades have been intrigued by the nearby water. In summer, the boys were especially eager to go out the church door and directly to the canal bank, where each tried to outdo the other by getting the most *skips* when skipping stones across the water. It seemed that some kids tried to see how close they could get to the water without falling in, and there were several boys (and a few girls) who went home with a wet foot. One of the most frequent Sunday admonitions was the adult's cry of, "Get away from that canal!" In winter, the first question the kid's asked was, "Is the ice thick enough for skating?"

In the 1940s, ice skating was quite popular. The bigger boys often skated south on the canal to the Forty Acre Pond or north to Spencerville. A few girls enjoyed skating, especially Rosemary and me. We were exceptionally brave one winter day and joined the boys as they skated to Spencerville. They had made the trip many times and had spent hours playing rough games of hockey on the ice, but the trip was a real struggle for Rosie and me. We couldn't keep up with those strong skaters, so we stayed closer to home after that. Winters must have been colder then because there were many weeks when Rosie's brother, Donald Rothe, skated to school and back on the Miami-Erie Canal.

If the canal's ice was not quite thick enough to be safe, we usually tried the shallow pond in Kossuth. There was little danger of falling through the ice and getting wet, as some had done on the canal. Many nights the boys built a bonfire on the ice, and we skated long after dark, often by the glow of a luminous full moon. I remember one of those nights when the canal ice was not safe, and we moved to the pond. It had warmed up, and the pond ice was rubbery. It was really funny to watch as the thin ice sank beneath the skater's weight, then came back up behind him. What a strange feeling to be gliding over ice that felt like a sheet of rubber as it rolled with each movement.

Ice skating was a favorite winter sport then, but the cold, fresh air sometimes made us thirsty. While sitting on the ice, we whacked it with the pointed back side of our skates to chop a hole. When the cold water flowed in, we quenched our thirst by prostrating ourselves on the ice beside the hole, then drinking the cold water. I guess we knew it wasn't pure. After all, when we fished in the summer, we saw soap bubbles flowing into the canal from nearby kitchen drains. We also saw a few animals that had drowned, but now it was winter and we were thirsty. No one became ill!

Grandpa occasionally talked about sleigh rides, but as teenagers, our church youth group held a hayride one night. Some brave person thought it would be fun to drive the tractor and wagon loaded with kids along that canal bank. The state had kept the bank clean near the bridge, but our adventure suddenly came to an abrupt halt in a growth of thick underbrush. Now what? There wasn't room to turn the tractor around, so the only way out was to back up—not an easy job with a load of excited teens yelling conflicting instructions. The driver finally backed far enough to turn around in Earl Hoverman's back lot. That was the last time we tried that!

When Grandpa was a youngster, Kossuth was much larger than it is today. The village had been born with the advent of the Miami-Erie Canal which cut a swath across the countryside and through the middle of town.

The 1880 Auglaize County Atlas shows a drawing of the American House Hotel, J.H. Wipfler, proprietor, Kossuth, Ohio. It also shows a map of the village. Included are east and west streets of Wayne, Main (old Route 66 and still the main street), and Walnut. The streets to the north and south included Ash (present State Route 197), Elm, Vine (old Route 66 beside the Methodist Church), Race, and Pike.

Grandpa said Kossuth had been well known along the canal for being a rough town. Offenders were even put in the local jail which was located in a building later owned by Great-uncle Bert and Aunt Eva DeLong. When I was a little girl I couldn't imagine a real jail in little old Kossuth, and I was really quite curious. Uncle Bert showed it to me.

A June 19, 1890, newspaper account in the *Auglaize County Republican* reports on this event that they felt was newsworthy. It took place in the Kossuth area.

> In a vote on drink or no drink, the 'wets' won by 33 votes. Kossuth had been 'dry' for two years but voted a change. John Schaibley who will start a saloon at Kossuth celebrated the

wet victory last Saturday night by letting the inebriating ale flow freely to all. Men and boys could be seen imitating the swine by weltering in the street gutters, the only visible point of difference being the absence of the bristles. When will men cease to be porkers? We are in favor of increasing the Dow tax to $500. We believe the majority of the saloon-keepers could not afford to pay that sum, at least not in unincorporated villages like Kossuth where law and order are unknown.[9]

In contrast to this account from the *Republican*, the *Democrat* paints a different picture just two years later. An 1892 newspaper describes Kossuth in more glowing tones:

For the benefit of those readers of the *Democrat* who may never have the privilege of visiting Kossuth, we will give a graphic description of the town and its various industries and institutions. The founding of the town dates back some forty-five or fifty years or about time the Miami and Erie canal was built. Since then it has been the center of an active trade in hoop-poles, cord wood, tobacco and beer. At present it is in a very prosperous condition. It has two saloons which are doing a thriving business, two stores, two saw mills, two blacksmith shops, an excellent hotel, a carriage shop, a shoemaker, three doctors, a good school house and a church. Its people are of a literary inclination of the art of public and dramatic speaking. It also numbers among its citizens a divine [preacher] and a lawyer. In point of morality it will favorably compare with any town within a radius of two miles. To our knowledge there has been no arrest made for ill behavior within the last two years and there are no reasons to believe that any will be made for some time to come. In conclusion we will say that if any one doubt the veracity of this description he need only come and see for himself to be convinced of its truth.[10]

Grandpa's family, the Davenports, lived approximately three miles southeast of Kossuth, but Grandma's Schwartz family grew up north of town, between Kossuth and Deep Cut. After Grandma's father, Heinrich Schwartz, lost most of the fingers from one hand in the mill accident, he could no longer work there. He applied for a job at a place that sold firewood. The owner hired Henry to supervise the cutting of lumber up in Auglaize County.

Other men were hired to do the actual sawing and labor. The man knew of about 120 acres of land for sale north of Kossuth. Henry was to see that the land was cleared and the wood split and piled on the canal bank, ready to be loaded onto boats. The boatloads of wood would then travel to Hamilton and Cincinnati to be sold for firewood. When enough lumber had been cut, the farmland would be his.

Leaving his mother, brothers and sisters in the Hamilton area, Henry boarded a canal boat and rode to Auglaize County, to the land he was promised near the big curve north of Kossuth. He eventually settled there and married Catherine, the daughter of his neighbor, Heinrich Adolph Aufderhaar. Canal travel was still going strong at that time.

Since Henry's land was near the canal, his children used the towpath when walking to the one-room school at Deep Cut. It was much closer than walking on the mud roads which were sometimes impassable after heavy rains or snow. It was also quicker than going through the fields, where they would have to climb rail fences.

Grandma told of watching with interest when two canal boats met and passed. Boats traveling upstream had the right of way and the downstream boats had to unhitch their team, allow their boat to hug the side of the canal bank, then drop their towline rope into the canal where it sank to the bottom, permitting the other boat to pass over the top. As the mules of the oncoming boat walked over the line on the ground, they pulled their boat past the other one and went on. The remaining team was then hitched up and walked on in the opposite direction, taking up the slack in the boat's towline as they proceeded down the towpath.

One of Grandma's favorite memories was of the day she was heading to school and met a white haired man on the towpath. She said he was dressed in "fancy" clothes and was riding a beautiful horse. He had nodded and said, "Good morning," to the little girl who later found out more about this elegant gentleman. He was part of a show performing in Spencerville and had been an Indian fighter, a buffalo hunter and owner of his own Wild West show— none other than William Cody, better known as "Buffalo Bill."

Grandma's youngest sister, Aunt Elva Wilkins, told me of an event that happened when she was a small child. One cold winter day she and her brother, Henry Jr., rushed out of school to the canal bridge. They planned to cross the "swing" bridge and walk home on the tow path. The bridge swung around parallel with the banks, allowing the canal boats to pass through. Some swing bridges had to be opened and closed by manpower. Others opened when a boat bumped them and then closed automatically after it had passed. This bridge had not closed completely after the last boat had gone through and when the children got to it, Henry realized his little sister, a first grader, would not be able to jump over the gap between the road and the partially closed bridge. Since he was bigger and stronger, he decided he would jump the gap and close the bridge so Elva could walk across. But when he jumped, he didn't quite make it all the way. The little girl watched in horror as her big brother fell through the gap and into the icy water below.

Not knowing what to do, Elva started to cry, but Henry pulled himself out of the water and up the bank, reassuring her he was all right. Without the bridge, they knew the only way to get home was to walk south to the next bridge. They began to walk as fast as they could toward Kossuth two miles away. The going was slow because Elva's little legs couldn't go very fast, and Henry's clothes were starting to freeze to his body.

The children finally reached the Lew Reed home, about halfway to Kossuth. Mrs. Reed was a kindly lady and told the children to warm up for a while. Henry had to go behind the cookstove and remove his clothing. She threw a warm blanket over him and then dried the clothes by the stove. When they were warm and dry, she told them to hurry on home. When they finally reached Kossuth, they crossed the canal bridge and headed back north to the Schwartz farm. A worried mother was happy to see them when they finally reached home. The tired children walked more than four miles in freezing weather. Aunt Elva never forgot that day, even though it was ninety years later when she told me.[11]

Actually, Henry was very lucky! Frank Sunderman of New Bremen told of crossing a swing bridge as he walked to school at Lock Two where the Miami-Erie canal "cut across their trail like a giant furrow." They felt they were quite fortunate if they got there as a boat arrived. They would "jump the swing bridge and get a free ride as it swerved open to let the boats through." This was great fun that sometimes ended in tragedy. One youngster "tried to leap off the bridge before it completely closed. He jumped and missed and before he could pull himself up, the bridge swung shut and smashed his legs."[12]

Ralph May, New Bremen historian, described a swing bridge: "There was a circular track on which castor-like wheels moved in turning the bridge from one side to the other. The track was located to the one side and that end of the bridge was weighted down with heavy limestones to give it the proper pitch in swinging around." It was quite a thrill for the children in those days who were brave enough to "get the bump of the bridge when the bow of the slow-moving boat hit the heavy timber on the outer side of the Bridge."

The October 7, 1887, Spencerville *Journal-News* said: "The swing-bridge across the canal at Fourth Street, was damaged yesterday, by a boat bumping it; it being in bad repair and the stay-rod broken, previously. It should be repaired at once." W.W. Rider wrote in the *Journal-News* that when the canal was first built, "all bridges were of the high type, permitting boats to pass underneath." Later these were removed and swing bridges installed. Swing bridges were on a level with the roadways which eliminated the steep climb for horses to pull a wagon over the high bridges. Some of the canal bridges were lighted. A Salem Township Treasurer's Record shows a sum of $6 being paid on October 5, 1901 to Grover Rapp for lighting the lamps on the Kossuth bridge. He received another $2 on December 7. On January 6, 1902, Elza Shafer was given $19.85 for lighting the Pratt bridge and on December 1 another $15.15 was given to Wm. Shively for lighting the bridge during that time.

I spent a delightful afternoon reminiscing about the "old days" with Grandma's brother, Henry, when he was in his 90s. As a little boy, he had seen fires burning in all directions as he looked out across the woods and fields. People clearing "new ground" hauled large tree limbs to the homesteads for firewood. Medium-sized trees were used for log houses, barns and sheds. He said the really huge logs were too hard to split and were so plentiful that the neighbors would get together for a log roll. Helping each other on their farms, the neighbors used their teams of horses to roll these large logs into huge piles which were burned. Some of the more manageable logs were loaded on canal boats or tied into rafts and shipped to Cincinnati and Hamilton to be sold as firewood or where they were sawed into lumber for constructing large buildings in those growing cities. He said a stack of those huge logs had for some reason never been shipped. For many years they lay along the canal bank where they eventually rotted down.

Henry remembered seeing the canal boats, many of them lit up with torches and lanterns, as they traveled by night. As a small boy, he sat on the porch of their log house and watched those boats a half mile or so away. One night he saw seven boats, all lighted and moving around the big curve near the Schwartz farm. He sometimes heard music from fiddles, mouth harps or concertinas. He had also seen folks dancing on the tops of some boats. That would be no problem in the open country, but sometimes people on the top deck were forced to prostrate themselves when going under low bridges. As a little boy, Henry was intrigued by the sights and sounds of those canal boats, whether they carried produce, lumber, animals or humans. In those days of mud roads, it was the best way to travel and it made a fascinating and unforgettable picture in young Henry's mind.[13]

Boats presented an enchanting view to the boy, but actual travel wasn't always exciting to passengers. Much of our Auglaize County area was swampy and mosquito infested. To the north lay the Great Black Swamp. Ronald E. Shaw's book, *Canals for a Nation,* paints a verbal picture of canal travel of that day: "Yet boats passed through the wilderness areas, where the yellow light of the canal boat lantern and the almost silent rippling of the boat as it glided over the water added to an overpowering sense of loneliness. This was especially true . . . on the canals of Western Ohio and Indiana. After a trip in northwestern Ohio in 1851, Moritz Busch left an account of his journey through the Black Swamp on the Miami and Erie Canal. His readers can feel his deep sense of isolation."

> We were still in the Black Swamp, but we were approaching its border. The boat glided slowly in a straight line along its waveless watery path through the moonless forest landscape. The dark woods rose without interruption on both sides. . . . Everything was quiet in the cabin. Not a breath of wind, only the soft lapping of the water on the keel disturbed the deep calm all around. The beam of the hanging lantern below flitted about on the water and ran like an uncertain, nimble will-o'-the wisp through the mists and shadows on the shore . . . . A bell began to tinkle and was answered by ours. Then another canal boat floated past us, with red-curtained, faintly illuminated cabin windows. Then silence and solitude again. [14]

The boat on which he traveled was "overfilled with travelers of all sorts." A dozen others "had to spend the cold, damp night upon the roof of the cabin."

Shaw's book gives numerous personal comments made by famous people as they traveled various canals. Nathaniel Hawthorne expressed enjoyment at seeing "a vessel that seemed full of mirth and sunshine. It contained a little colony of Swiss, on their way to Michigan, clad in garments of strange fashion and gay colors, scarlet, yellow and bright blue, singing, laughing, and making merry, in odd tones and a babble of outlandish words."

Charles Dickens describes the dinner fare which included "tea, coffee, bread, butter, salmon, shad, liver, potatoes, pickles, ham, chops, black puddings, and sausages." Ray Zunk mentioned that many canal boats had a shelf above the heads of the mules or horses in the stable area. Crates of chickens, rabbits or other small animals were stored up there to help provide food for passengers and crew.

John Quincy Adams told of the divisions within the larger canal boats such as those found on New York's Erie Canal. At the bow or front of the boat were "two settee beds, for the ladies, separated by a curtain from a parlor bed-chamber, with an iron stove in the centre, and side settees, on which four of us slept, feet to feet." Next came a stable for the mules or horses, then "a dining-hall and dormitory for thirty persons; and lastly a kitchen and cooking apparatus."

British traveler-critic, Harriet Martineau described daytime travel on the top as being pleasant "(except for having to duck under the bridges every quarter of an hour, under penalty of having one's head crushed to atoms)." She described the horrors of night with its "heat and noise, the known vicinity of a compressed crowd, lying packed like herrings in a barrel, the bumping against the sides of the locks, and the hissing of water therein like an inundation, starting one from sleep; these things are disagreeable."

Harriet Beecher Stowe wrote in *Godey's Lady's Book* about moments of "a most refreshing slumber" and the pleasant sound of the "rippling of the rope in the water." She didn't care for the jar of boats going through locks or for the noise of children on board.

Actress Fanny Kemble wrote, "I like travelling by the canal boats very much," but she didn't care for the "horrible hen-coop allotted to the female passengers," and Frances Trollope stated that women getting ready for a canal boat journey looked like "hedgehogs, with every quill raised." Philip Hone, president of the Delaware and Hudson Canal Company described sleeping travelers as "packed away on narrow shelves, fastened to the sides of the boat, like dead pigs in a Cincinnati pork warehouse."[15]

How about a few facts about these canal boats? Costing about $2,000 each, canal boats were of three types. The "state" boats were used when doing repairs. It was the duty of the repair crews to check for washouts or leaks in the canal banks caused by muskrats and groundhogs or by heavy rains, to see that bridges and locks were kept up and to do any necessary repairs to keep the canal safe for boat travel. The second type of boat was the "packet." Used to haul passengers, the packets were usually 78 feet long, 14 feet 10 inches wide, and completely decked over with cabin compartments containing separate sleeping areas for men and ladies. A larger cabin was used for the men's sleeping bunks and for dining and lounge facilities. Beds were made of 3-foot "shelves" with straw mattresses and pillows. The crew, which had separate quarters, consisted of a captain, two mule or horse drivers, a cook, and two steersmen. Those boats not carrying extra mules on board got them at the mule yards located along the canal. The third type of canal boat was the "line-boat" which was used for hauling freight. These freight hauling boats were usually eighty feet long with cabins on one or both ends for the crew's sleeping and cooking area. The remainder was left open for hauling freight.

When Spencerville held its centennial celebration on August 12-13, 1942, an 1870 picture of the canal boat, the *A. Millett*, was made into a zinc etching. This picture was used to publicize the event as follows:

> The "A. Millett" was 70 feet long, 14 feet wide. . . . She carried the following crew: Captain, 2 Steersmen, 2 Bowmen, 2 Drivers, and a cook. Her cargo consisted of coal, flour, lumber, stone, gravel, ice, etc. Power for the "A. Millett" was 6 mules. Three of the mules pulled while 3 mules ate and rested. The stable for the mules was in the center of the boat. With good luck, and not too many locks and fights, the "A. Millett" could average close to 3 miles an hour.[16]

What was it like to work on the canal? Great-grandfather John Wesley Davenport worked on the Miami-Erie canal for a period of time, but unfortunately, little information was passed down concerning his experiences. Grandpa said his dad had driven mules pulling the boats. The animals were stabled on the boat, working six hours and resting six hours. When the six hours were up, the captain stopped the boat and a change of mules and drivers was made. Grandpa said the towpath was kept as smooth as a road.

St. Marys druggist, John J. Hauss, who had at one time worked on the canal in his younger days, provided an excellent description in a newspaper account. In the spring of 1870, at the age of 14, he began working for $20 a month as a mule driver on the canal boat, *Thomas Tilton*. "Getting up at sunrise and working until the next sunrise was not so unusual in the good old canal days," explained Hauss, who said his possessions then consisted of the clothes on his back, a pair of canvas baseball shoes, a 10-cent Barlow knife and two red bandana handkerchiefs.

In a newspaper column John Hauss described his first 120-mile trip to Cincinnati:

> All I had to do that trip, and on later trips, was to help load and unload freight, drive the mules, feed and curry the mules and then, after we had laid up for the night, saw the wood, carry water and scrub the boat.
>
> I slept on the locker in the kitchen cabin with my legs and feet hanging to the floor, so when my feet got wet, I knew it was time to get up and pump water out of the boat. Boats always leaked, more or less, so I could pump any time. Sometimes I pumped until it was time to start the fire for breakfast. I had to peel potatoes and help the cook prepare breakfast and afterward I had to wash the dishes. Then after breakfast I had to clean the

> big bow lamps and the cabin lamps and the lantern, trim the wicks and fill them with oil. I did not have to drive all the time. I could steer part of the time. And then too, if I had all my work done I could pump awhile for a change.[17]

Canal men were mostly a rough bunch with brawls and fights being quite common. Many a race took place, with the winning captain traveling the length of the canal in less than three days. Although competition was keen, these races were discouraged because of the damage caused by the boats' wakes to the dirt banks of the canal. Ultimately, officials had to set a 4-mile an hour limit.

W.W. Rider said the traffic would average a boat each way, each hour of the day, as most boats ran day and night. Although it was discouraged, races between boats were fairly common as each tried to be first in reaching their destination in order to unload their cargoes or load the most favorable merchandise, (barrels of flour that could be rolled on instead of heavy sacks of grain or smelly live animals, especially hogs.) Stories of encountering bears, wild cats and other animals were common as the boats passed through some wild and rugged countryside.[18]

We can't imagine this area having wild animals, but one of Hal Miller's columns provided proof: "On January 22, 1881, a 400-pound black bear was killed between Kossuth and Deep Cut and it was the first one shot in the area since 1857."[19] Grandma was a one-year-old living in that area. Do you suppose her dad saw the bear? Spencerville, the next town north of Deep Cut, held one of the favorite spots of my childhood, Kolter's Mill. Don and Mary (my brother and sister-in-law) sat at our kitchen table one night as we discussed the "good old days," especially our childhood visits to Kolter's Mill. Mary grew up in Spencerville and Charlie Kolter, who ran the mill, lived next door. She and a neighbor boy, Joe Sutton, played together most of the time and loved visiting the mill.

One day Charlie took them to the very top where Mary found all the noise and long flopping belts to be quite scary! She and Joe used to play in the rocky area under the mill run where it was cool in the summer. They weren't supposed to play under there because, although Mary didn't know it, her Uncle Ira had been killed there. Someone was shooting rats there when a bullet had ricocheted off a rock and hit him. She and Joe loved to sit among the rocks and play with the lead toy soldiers which Joe brought along. The youngsters' mothers didn't know they played there and wouldn't have approved.

Kolter's Mill could be described as a complete flour mill. They ground the wheat and ran it through the rolling mills that mashed the bran out, leaving the remaining flour almost pure white. The mill race above the canal lock was long, extending over to the mill on the east side of the canal near the present VFW hall. The mill had an overshot wheel with the water coming off the sluice at the top and pouring down over the wheel. It had wooden gears with a peg and box drive. The wheel had pegs and the drive shaft had dowel-like protrusions in the holes. When the pegs on the wheel engaged those, it turned the mill and the grain was ground.

The waste water flowed into a pond area and then once again flowed into the canal below the lock. Mary said the pond was very pretty in winter when hoarfrost coated everything around it. The kids weren't allowed to ice skate near it because the moving water kept it from freezing over easily. The same was true of the area just above and below the canal lock west of the mill. Don skated too close to it one winter day and fell in. It was a mighty cold bath!

I loved going to that mill with Grandpa and watching the water splash and tumble over that huge wheel into a frothy cascade below. I was sad when the mill finally closed and was torn down. Don was told that when everything was cleaned up, that big mill wheel was buried under the VFW building, and that because of some settling of the dirt covering it, the floor of the new building had some problems. It seems ironic! The original mill wheel was buried, then a few years later a new bank building was built not far from there. Remembering the historical aspect of the area, they used the old mill as the theme for the new building, complete with a fancy new water wheel. The cost of that wheel alone was probably more than the total cost of the original mill!

I've often regretted that the canal boat era ended long before my time. On June 5, 1854, the first passenger train steamed into Allen County, and transportation began to change. Canal boat travel started a steady decline. By 1885 there was only one *scheduled* boat a day, although many others used it. An article in the *Lima Gazette* stated, "The railroads have done it to the canal." Indeed they had! By 1890, the canal was rapidly losing its fight to stay alive as more and more trains traveled through the area. An 1890 Kossuth news item says, "We noticed a boat on the canal one day last week. The canal has had its most useful days and might as well be abandoned."[20]

A November 23, 1892, article in the *Sidney Daily News* stated that "Unless considerable money is spent in dredging the canal it is but a question of time until boats cannot find passage. A boat with half a load sometimes spends a day getting through town, if it is going upstream, the numerous sand bars holding it. The water is low for this time of year, it being less than three feet deep in some places, but dredging has not kept pace with the gradual filling from hillsides, and the stream, never ornamental, is becoming useless." Canal boom towns were fading and preservation methods tried and failed. Ralph May of New Bremen explained, "At one time the boats were to be propelled by a trolley line along the towpath. It was used for a time between Dayton and Cincinnati but did not prove successful."

Ray Zunk said the last working canal boat traveled this area in 1913 when Captain Billy Combs' freighter carried a load of stone from Newport. Grandpa's friend, Spencerville historian Ernie Robison, said James Norbeck captained the last canal boat to travel to Spencerville from Delphos in 1905. The records differ from area to area due to the availability of locally owned boats traveling only short distances locally. Eventually some areas of the canal were closed because of weather and animal damage to the banks.

The final blow ending canal travel was the Great Flood of 1913. It completely washed out the banks in many areas and the canal was abandoned. Many of its towns became what Ray Zunk calls "ghost towns." In some areas, sections of the canal remain, mainly as sources of water for fighting fires.

Although the 1880 atlas shows a post office, stores, and several homes in Deep Cut, this tiny village that was once larger than Spencerville has disappeared. All that remains today of Deep Cut is a lonely roadside park with a pump, a shelter house, a view of the "deep cut" in the canal. The few tourists who stop cannot imagine the determination and intestinal fortitude involved in making the deep cut that was so necessary for building the canal. It was indeed a remarkable era!

---

[1] W.W. Rider, "Time Marches On," *Journal-News*, Spencerville, Ohio, August 13, 1942, used with permission.

[2] Wayne Wenning, "Lock One Sets Astride a Key Portion of Miami-Erie Canal," *Evening Leader*, St. Marys, Ohio, March 26, 1996, used with permission.

[3] Karin Deneke, "Miami Erie Canal: An 18th Century Engineering Marvel," *Country Living*, July 1982, used with permission.

[4] Janet Fledderjohann interview of Forest Combs in *Evening Leader*, St. Marys, Ohio, 1974, used with permission.

[5] Historical Marker placed at Lock 14 by Auglaize County Historical Society.

[6] Harriet Ann Hill, personal letter, September 3, 1988.

[7] Historical Marker placed at Bloody Bridge by Auglaize County Historical Society 1976.

[8] Mary McClintock, "Mary-Go-Round" from Recollections of Miami Canal, *Wapakoneta Daily News*, Wapakoneta, Ohio, December 1, 1966, used with permission.

[9] *Auglaize County Republican*, "Logan Township," June 19, 1890.

[10] *Auglaize County Democrat*, "Kossuth," February 18, 1892.

[11] Elva Wilkins, personal interview by author, 1990.

[12] Naomi Sunderman, *Historical and Genealogical Record of the Sunderman Family*, "Sketches of Life and Times on the Original Sunderman Homestead (1887-1900)," used with permission.

[13] Henry Schwartz Jr., personal interview by author, 1983.

[14] Ronald E. Shaw from *Canals for a Nation: The Canal Era in the United States, 1790-1860,* pp. 180-197. 1990, The University Press of Kentucky, reprinted with permission.

[15] Ronald E. Shaw, *Canals*, 1990, reprinted with permission.

[16] W.W. Rider, "Time Marches On," *Journal-News*, Spencerville, Ohio, August 6, 1942, used with permission.

[17] W.W. Rider, "Time Marches On," *Journal-News*, Spencerville, Ohio, August 6, 1942, used with permission.

[18] W.W. Rider, "Time Marches On," *Journal-News*, Spencerville, Ohio, August 13, 1942, used with permission.

[19] Hal Miller, "As I See It," *Evening Leader*, St. Marys, Ohio, used with permission.

[20] Kossuth item, *Auglaize County Republican*, Wapakoneta, Ohio, June 19, 1890.

## Chapter 5.

# Hiding from the Natives

"Run and hide when the Indians come!" John Briggs Jr. had warned his children Nancy Jane and Charles Marion. John was a woodsman and spent many hours working in the dense forests of Allen County. He had married Nancy Hempleman on September 2, 1819, and they moved to Allen County in 1836. When she died that November, John eventually courted Charles Harter's widow, Susanna, and married her three years later. After only six years, she also died, and John was left to rear their children. Until his third marriage a year later, five-year-old Nancy and three-year-old Charles, my great-grandfather, were left alone for several hours at a time while their father worked in the woods. Indians in the area were friendly and occasionally visited the pioneer homes. According to the Spencerville *Journal-News*:

> Nancy Briggs was a lovely child with black hair and dark eyes. It seems the Indians were partial to that coloring and was [sic] known at times to kidnap children. Nancy was warned by her father to run and hide whenever the Indians came. Just a short ways from the house, the Briggs family had an enclosure made of rails where they stored corn husks to be used for mattresses. Whenever the Indians would come, as they approached the house, they would let out a whooping sound announcing their arrival. Nancy and Charles would run and jump in these corn husks and cover themselves. The Indians were friendly and never harmed the family, but would take any food in sight.[1]

John Briggs Jr. had met Indians before coming to Allen County. He was the son of John Briggs Sr. and a grandson of Joseph Briggs, my great-great-great-great-grandfather, who had entered Virginia in the 1780s. The land there was very pretty with green trees, rocky hills and winding creeks. A few hearty pioneer families lived in an area populated by "many wild and savage Indians" as described in the book, *The Joseph Briggs Family of Hardy and Pendelton County, Virginia.*

Many of their friends and neighbors had been captured by Indians during a fierce battle just a few miles from the Briggs home. Some were killed, others escaped, but many were taken captive and brought north "through the beautiful Valley of the Ohio with its lush grasslands and on up to the Great Lakes country with its great forests," possibly on their way to Canada. A few of these settlers managed to escape, and when they arrived back in Virginia, they painted a glowing picture of the rich soil and lush grasslands of the Ohio country. After years of farming the steep hills and rocky soil in that part of Virginia, the Briggs brothers and their neighbors were anxious to travel to this wonderful new area.

In 1803, the Briggs' sons decided to move to Ohio, although their father, Joseph, preferred to stay in his log cabin home in Virginia. His faithful slave stayed with him until his death, then buried him in the meadow behind the barn. The compilers of the book visited the Briggs' homestead many years later, and as they walked into that meadow, the family dog chased a deer from a nearby corn field. The unmarked grave of Joseph Briggs was a mound of dirt covered with "blooms of scarlet fire weeds."

When John Briggs Sr. arrived in Ohio in 1804, he eventually settled in Clark County. The area was wild and primitive, and Indians were camped near his log home. The Ohio natives seemed a bit more friendly than those of Virginia, and the Briggs boys frequently played or wrestled with the little Indian boys. The Briggs' cabin was one of only three in the county at that time and church services were held there until a log school house was built. As another Virginian, George Hempleman, and his family traveled through the area, they noticed the Briggs' cabin. Turning to his wife who was riding a pack horse, he said, "I wonder what fool ever got out to this God-forsaken country." After a venison supper and a night of rest, the family decided to stay in the area. They traveled about four miles, then selected land and built their own cabin. A Hempleman daughter eventually married a Briggs son.

As some of the Briggs family traveled to other areas, one of them joined the Gold Rush to Pike's Peak. When he returned, he bought his father's Indiana farm. Included in the land was the site of the Indian village which was the capital and residence of Little Turtle, chief of the Miami tribe. Mr. Briggs and his wife preserved the site.

Some of the Briggs descendants in Whitley County, Indiana, had an interesting encounter with Indians. Old Settlers Day was held in Columbia City, and the Indians watched from the nearby woods as the citizens enjoyed a huge picnic. After the group had finished eating, there was still an abundance of food left over. The pioneers invited the Indians to eat, and the food tasted delicious to these natives. They ate so much they soon became ill, but they didn't blame their suffering on the array of rich foods so foreign to their bodies. No, they were convinced the settlers had poisoned them. [2]

---

[1] Wanda Leis, "More History of Canal and the Village of Spencerville," *Journal-News*, Spencerville, Ohio, September 11, 1958, used with permission.

[2] Kenneth B. Briggs, Mrs. Gaylord Younghein, and Mrs. Arthur Campbell, *The Joseph Briggs Family of Hardy and Pendelton County, Virginia*, used with permission.

The Briggs family on Lena's wedding day, April 18, 1926. Front: her sister Dorothea beside Lena. Back: parents William and Lottie Briggs, and sons Roy, Marion, and twin sons Leo and Leon.

## Chapter 6.

# "Grandpa's Little Girl"

"Grandpa, tell me about when you were a little boy. Please, Grandpa, please," I had often pleaded. With childish curiosity, I wanted to hear about the activities and way of life of my grandparents.

When my mother died, Daddy moved us home to Grandpa's house. I was told they had problems finding a milk that "agreed" with me, so I must have been a difficult infant. I suspect Grandpa spent many hours rocking me while Grandma tried to keep up with all the household duties for a family of five or six people. Grandpa always seemed to have patience with me and I adored him.

By the time I was two, Great-grandpa Schwartz had come to live with us for the final few months of his life, Dad was ditching away from home, and Don was in school. The responsibility for keeping me out of mischief often seemed to rest on Grandpa and I soon became *his* little girl. If he washed his hands, I always had to join him in washing mine.

I thought Grandpa's life was one of the most exciting of anyone around. He was born and lived during one of the most progressive centuries in history, stretching from a cross-country ride in a covered wagon to a TV view of native Neil Armstrong's space flight from Cape Canaveral to the moon and back. He had stories and tunes to keep me occupied and quiet for many hours.

My favorite story, and one which Grandpa enjoyed telling, took place when he was a two-year-old, bumping and bouncing his way to Wisconsin in a covered wagon. His memories of the trip, which were "few and far between," consisted mostly of pointing to the mantel clock that had made the trip with them, and telling of his encounter with a big "dog." (I wish I would have asked him for more details when I got older.) I've found records showing his parents, John Wesley and Laura Frances (Daniels) Davenport, apparently traveled with John's sister and her family, Elsie and Bill Bradford to Barron County, Wisconsin. They joined Laura's sister, Cynthia Jane and Henry Beltz and their children who had traveled there from Minnesota. The 1880 Wisconsin census shows the three families living next door to each other.

After the birth of a new baby to each of the two Ohio families and a bitter cold Wisconsin winter with little to eat, the families returned by train to Auglaize County. But the experience had been quite exciting and at an early age Grandpa had been thoroughly bitten by the "adventure" bug.

After I got old enough to walk, I was beside him as he worked in the shop or barn or fields. I learned to do some mighty dirty jobs, just because I wanted to be with him–things such as loading smelly hogs, then shoveling their smellier manure, working with the animals in muddy barnyards, or making hay that was itchy on hot summer days. If Grandpa was using his big scoop shovel to sack dusty grain or to shovel snow on cold winter days, I used my smaller one to help. He taught me to whistle and sing those early "fiddlin'" songs.

As we "worked" side-by-side, he often told me stories of his birth (September 14, 1877) in a log house three miles southeast of Kossuth. He had pointed out the house as we drove past it while taking a trailer load of homegrown sugar cane to New Knoxebille (as I called it) to Lasses Kuck's. Grandpa usually grew a patch of cane, then when it was ripe, he sliced it off just above the ground with his sharp corn cutter. I loved sucking the sweet juice out of the stalks as Grandpa loaded them into his trailer before the trip. At Kuck's, the juice was squeezed out of the cane, then boiled down to the tasty molasses Grandpa loved. He had smiled, "I've got to have something to spread on my bread!"

As I helped him stack wood by the woodpile, Grandpa explained about names. My name was special because I was named after friends of my mother. His name, Henry Franklin Davenport, was also special because his mother had named him after her brothers, Henry Daniels, a newspaper man "out west" and Franklin Daniels, a farmer living nearby. He seldom, if ever, saw his Uncle Henry, but Uncle Frank was one of his fiddle playing group who got together almost weekly when he was a young man.

Grandpa shared his love and sympathy with me because my mother had died when I was a baby. He tried his best to answer my questions about that. He had also lost his mother when he was just a boy. At the age of eleven, he had lost his grandma, mother, and baby brother, Archie, all within a few short months. His grandma had lived with his family until her death. (With some searching, I found that his grandma, Elizabeth Foster, had married Nathan Davenport in 1836 in a part of Allen County which is now Auglaize County. Nathan had apparently died before Elizabeth traveled with the Davenports to Wisconsin and back.)

On the days when Grandpa and Grandma (and I, of course) worked in the fields, he often talked of life when he was younger. As a teenager, Grandpa recalled walking a mile through the nearby woods to a "play party." On the way, he encountered a rattlesnake lying in his path. After he killed it, he cut off the rattles, stuck them in his pocket and went on to the party. One of the games played was "Heavy, Heavy, Hang Over Thy Head." He held the rattles over the head of a blindfolded girl, and when she couldn't guess what it was, he shook the rattles. Those country kids were all too familiar with the dreaded sound of a rattlesnake. Grandpa said, "The party almost ended right there!" Afterward, he gave the rattles to one of the girls to wear in her hair because it was thought this would prevent headaches.

What do you suppose I found in the old trunk when I was just a child? A clown suit, of all things! Now that needed an explanation, and Grandpa told us of an exciting time in his life. When he was in his late teen years, he spent a summer traveling in this area of Ohio and Indiana with the C.G. Phillips Co. and their road show, *Uncle Tom's Cabin*. As the show approached a town, its wagons lined up for a parade to promote the event. Grandpa showed Don and I how he had woven the reins through his fingers as he drove a circus-type six-horse-hitch team pulling the bandwagon. He said, "My fingers were really kept busy, especially when we had to turn a corner." Once he got the first team going around it, the second and third teams usually followed.

A large tent was erected in the town and benches were placed in neat rows. When show time began, Grandpa donned his fancy suit and, along with a very stubborn donkey, he performed as a clown to keep the crowd happy between scenes.

Grandpa sat me on his lap and told me about the play. The slave girl, Eliza, was being hunted by her mean master, Simon Legree. His bloodhounds (played by the troupe's watchdogs) were hot on her trail as she hurried to safety across the ice on the Ohio River.

Occasionally a problem occurred after the show was over. If locals picked a fight or tried to steal something, the cry "Hey, Rube!" rang out, and the tough roustabouts took care of the problem. The roustabouts were the brawny fellows who helped put up the tent, unload the benches, and do the heavy work involved in presenting the show. Grandpa said that at night, all the men slept under the wagons. He laughed as he said, "On chilly nights, we snuggled up to those bloodhounds just to help keep us warm." With the coming of cold winter weather, Grandpa finally decided he had experienced enough show business and he returned home to a warm log cabin. Grandpa's clown suit came home with him and was packed away in the old wooden trunk. As a little girl, I played "dress up" with it until it was tattered and torn. Grandma finally had to throw it away. What a shame! At least I have a picture of my grandpa in his clown suit.

As a young man, Grandpa was a farmer, but he also worked as a teamster (a man who used his team of horses and wagon for commercial hauling). Grandpa had some really nice horses, and a December 1, 1910 *Auglaize County Democrat* said, "Sodom--Frank Davenport lost [to death] a valuable horse Wednesday of last week." I'm sure that was very hard for Grandpa to accept. Don remembered hearing Grandpa tell how he needed his team of horses to haul white oak bolts and butts to the St. Marys Spoke Works. The two-foot long bolts were used to make wagon wheel spokes and the butts were one foot long bottom or "stump cuts" and were made into the tough wagon wheel hubs. Grandpa also hauled straw to the St. Marys paper mill and moved oil well machinery–steam boilers, engines and "draw works," to new oil well locations in the area, especially around St. Marys. Oil wells were definitely the topic of conversation in the late 1880s and 1890s. Local papers included the names of farms on which new oil wells had been drilled. In the 1890s the Spencerville *Journal-News* even carried a weekly column just about oil drilling and production.

I had a nice dinner pail to take my lunch to school, but Grandpa explained that when he was working as a teamster, he ate his lunch from a small lard bucket as he sat under a tree. The lard bucket worked well in keeping the ants out of his food. He and a friend teamed together and talked as they ate. His friend usually had a piece of pie that was placed on top of the sandwiches where it wouldn't get smashed. Most people would have set the pie aside until the sandwiches were eaten, but not Grandpa's friend. He took it off and ate the pie first. Then if he got full, the sandwiches could wait until later, but he surely didn't want to eat them and not have room for the best part, that piece of pie! I think Grandpa agreed with that philosophy. His sweet tooth was very active. (When Bill and I drove Grandma and him to Florida in 1954, we had to stop in the middle of the afternoon so he could have a piece of raisin pie and a cup of coffee. Grandpa really loved his pie!)

Nora Leona Schwartz was the nice young lady from north of Kossuth who attracted Grandpa's attention. She was a hard worker and enjoyed music. She knew how to chord on a piano, and at the turn of the century, she occasionally joined Grandpa, his cousin and two uncles as they provided "fiddle" music for parties and "barn raisings" in this area. Grandpa and Grandma lived for a short time at the edge of Glynwood, and though none of the family was Irish or Catholic, the fiddlers played for several years at the "Glynwood picnic," an event held each year at that Irish Catholic settlement north of St. Marys. Grandpa used to put me on his lap and sing some of their favorite songs—"Turkey in the Straw," "Red River Valley," "Oh, Susanna" and others.

The August 6, 1914, *Democrat* says: "Last Friday night there was a good old-fashioned ice cream supper served at the country home of Mr. and Mrs. Frank Ward, with all the ice cream and cake you could eat, and all you had to do was just to hop to it till you had your fill. Besides there was plenty of music, consisting of two pianos and violins. They all departed early in the morning, thanking Mr. and Mrs. Ward for their splendid entertainment but not wishing for any more ice cream for twenty-four hours. My, how the crowd got away with five and a half gallons of ice cream and two large cakes."

Another event was reported two weeks later: "Quite a few friends gathered at the home of Mr. and Mrs. Bert Montague Tuesday evening to enjoy themselves with some good music consisting of piano and several violins. At ten o'clock ice cream and cake were served and at 12 o'clock they all departed for their homes, thanking Mr. and Mrs. Montague for their splendid entertainment." Dad was fifteen as he accompanied his parents to the party. Fifteen to twenty friends and neighbors met nearly every week just to play, eat, and enjoy those wonderful evenings of good, clean fun and fellowship, all done to the accompaniment of this fiddle playing family.

Grandpa and I made many trips on State Route 66 following the canal from Kossuth, past Deep Cut, and on to Spencerville. Grandpa loved to "show me off" to his friends by asking me to hold out my hands. I was just a little girl, but Grandpa would say, "Look at those nice, long fingers. She's going to be a piano player some day." He helped to make that a reality when he usually took me for my Saturday morning accordion lessons. I was only eight then but later on, he was proud when I learned to play piano and organ. Grandpa encouraged us to do our best in everything we tried.

Grandpa felt it was his patriotic duty to vote each year and to salute our beautiful American flag. He taught us to respect the dead as we attended the Decoration Day (Memorial Day) services at the Spencerville Cemetery each year. Grandpa helped me hold my ears shut, then wiped my frightened tears when the guns fired their salute. I tried very hard to show my respect by not stepping on any of the graves. Grandma made fresh bouquets from her peonies and iris which we placed on the graves of each of our ancestors in the Kossuth Cemetery. Grandpa always pointed out each grave and I helped put the flowers in place. The prettiest flowers always went on Mama's grave.

When he worked in the woods, Grandpa taught me to recognize trees by their leaves or bark and to keep up my end of a crosscut saw. (Too bad they didn't have "Jack and Jill" sawing contests back when Grandpa and I were at our peak!)

Sometimes when we drove to Wapak, he stopped at the old "powder house" north of Wapakoneta where he bought the dynamite that he used to blast huge stones out of the middle of a field or to reduce to slivers an immense tree stump in a fence row. Grandpa had used enough dynamite when building roads to know how much to use for each job. I was curious about things and loved looking at the many tools and other items of interest in Grandpa's shop. One day he took Don and me inside and showed us a glass jar full of a liquid. He explained that it was nitroglycerine, a clear explosive liquid used to detonate dynamite. He explained that we were never, ever to touch it. If we were to pick it up and drop it, it might explode, and we would be badly hurt or killed. Believe me, I never went near it, but I remember the palm-sweating experience of watching as he dug a trench beside a huge tree that stood in the corner of a field several hundred feet from the house, then placed a stick of dynamite beside it. I peeked around the corner of the house and watched as the charge was set. The explosion blew large chunks of roots and dirt high into the air. The large tree quivered from the blast, then slowly fell to the ground.

Our farm was almost self-sufficient when I was a child. Although the trees in our orchard were usually rather scraggly, Grandpa often found enough apples to make some cider in the fall. We also got some apples from a tree on the John Wesley Davenport farm that my dad had bought after his grandpa's death. There was also a pear tree in that front yard. Grandpa always said, "A few pears will give the cider a sweeter taste." Grandpa was right. We loved his fresh cider. Another of Grandpa's favorite treats was parched corn. I don't know how he made it, but the taste was delicious.

When nights were freezing and days were warm, the sap began to flow in the maple trees in the woods and yard. This was Grandpa's signal to start tapping the trees for sugar water. I watched as he took his auger and drilled a hole into the side of the maple trees. He sliced a round piece of wood in half, then hollowed out the center and inserted this spout into the hole where it allowed the sap to flow down it into one-gallon buckets hanging underneath. Each day, someone (usually my brother) emptied the small buckets of sap into a large bucket. This sweet sugar water was brought to the house and strained, then boiled down in the cookstove oven until it was a thick maple syrup. I've heard the proportion of water to syrup was 50 to 1. That means fifty gallons of sugar water boiled down to make one gallon of syrup. There was no better taste! (Today's syrups are sanitized and homogenized and sterilized and who knows what other kind of "ized" before they are allowed to be sold. Somehow today's maple syrup and cider just don't have the good fresh taste like that which Grandpa made!

While working in the woods one day, Grandpa noticed a "bee tree," a hollow tree where a swarm of honey bees had set up housekeeping. That night he and Dad showed us how to get the honey out of it. (Bill remembers his Grandpa Fred Wierwille quoting a poem about swarms of wild bees.)

A swarm of bees in May is worth a load of hay.
A swarm of bees in June is worth a silver spoon.
A swarm of bees in July isn't worth a fly.

"Uncle Sam Needs You!" the sign proclaimed. This bigger-than-life portrait of Uncle Sam appeared on the side of a shed at the south edge of Spencerville. He was pointing his big, long finger at us as we drove into town. I always wondered why he needed me. I was only a child! Grandpa explained to me about the war (World War II) as we made our weekly trip to buy groceries at the Kroger Store, gasoline for the car, cookies from Wright's Bakery and hopefully an ice cream cone from the Creamery. After "Granny" Gochenour stopped coming around to our home to pick up the cream from our cows' milk, we took it to the creamery in Spencerville. This always meant an ice cream cone–a real treat in the days before home freezers. My favorite flavor was orange-pineapple. When I finally learned to eat cones from the top instead of biting off the pointy bottom first, Grandpa spoiled me by buying a larger cone with an extension on each side, one designed for three dips–one on each side and one on the very top. Now I had a super-duper cone that lasted a long time, especially when I savored it one lick at a time.

Grandpa was always interested in new developments. Many inventions came during his lifetime–the telephone, radio, television, automobile, airplane, and even space ships. He never rode in an airplane, but in his later years he longed to travel the Alcan Highway that was being built in Alaska. I wish he could have seen it. The old road builder would have marveled at their huge machinery and modern methods.

Grandpa always had a keen interest in cars, especially the Nash. In 1937 he drove a new one to Oklahoma. The next summer, Grandma's cousin from Indiana, George Nicholson, drove his new Hudson to a reunion at our house. As the men gathered around to admire it, they noticed the floor boards were much lower than the running board. Grandpa finally said, "Well, I guess it's a nice car, but I sure wouldn't want one. Trying to get in that thing would be like stepping into a bathtub." Grandpa's next car—yes, it was another Nash.

It was Grandpa who taught me responsibility and work. He gave me a runt pig to raise. The money from it bought my first sewing machine which I still use. He also taught me to milk a cow, then gave me her calf. I sold it and bought the fur coat I wore during my college days.

One year Bill and I raised a few sheep. The ewes had trouble delivering the large lambs, and after helping deliver one, Bill thought everything was all right. He went on to work. I checked every hour or so, and soon realized other ewes were also having trouble. With no one there to help, I spent most of that day in the barn pulling those baby lambs.

Grandpa lived just down the road, and after Grandma died, he didn't have much to do. He was lonely and loved being with me and my family. He often walked down to our house and just "puttered around" in our barn, tossing hay in for the sheep or fixing a broken board. On this particular afternoon, he came into the barn and found me helping those ewes. Grandpa was raised in a day when young ladies did not deliver lambs. That was man's work. He insisted he would do the job. But by now Grandpa was close to ninety years old and he didn't have the strength he'd had as a young man. He had pulled many a calf when he was younger, but now, he just wasn't strong enough to get those huge lambs out. I knew what I had to do, but I had a hard time saying it. "Grandpa," I finally said in my most loving tones, "I'm sorry, but you're going to have to step aside and let me do that. You're working too hard. I don't want you to have a heart attack." I realized it was one of the hardest things either of us had ever done, but we both knew it had to be that way. I delivered the last lambs, and we saved every one of them, but it was the end of an era for Grandpa.

Grandpa had always been a hearty man, and although he couldn't be of much help to me that day, he wasn't about to give up. At the age of ninety-two, he decided to paint his house. When we urged him not to climb so high, his comment was, "I would rather wear out than rust out!" He painted his house. Grandpa finally wore out at ninety-four. He just never stood still long enough to rust out—not my grandpa!

Now that Grandpa is gone, I appreciate even more the kind of life he lived. I miss his hugs and words of encouragement. He had more than his share of excitement, yet Grandpa remained firm in his active spiritual life. Grandpa, a deeply religious man, lived his faith daily in all that he did. Everyone knew that his handshake was a binding contract! It somehow seemed appropriate that "Grandpa's little girl" sat beside him, holding his hand as he peacefully entered the gates of heaven!

Grandpa Davenport's family portrait was taken about 1898.
Standing: Grandpa's sisters Elizabeth "Lizzie," Ella, Effie and Addie
Seated: the father, John Wesley (my great-grandpa) and Grandpa Frank

Grandpa's 1914 political campaign card for Auglaize County Recorder

My Grandpa Frank's dad, aunts and uncle: his "Uncle Nate" Nathaniel Davenport; his Aunt Ellen (Davenport) Bradford; his father, John Wesley Davenport; and his Aunt Susan(Davenport) Folk. This photo was taken in 1916.

All dressed up are these cousins, all nieces of Frank Davenport: Inez, daughter of Effie (Davenport) Montague; Nina, daughter of Elizabeth (Davenport) Doute; and Muriel daughter of Ella (Davenport) Craft.

Chapter 7.

# A Little Girl's Grandma

Delicate little balls of yellow fuzz that go "peep, peep." Those were the baby chicks that Grandma got every spring. When I was just a very little girl, Grandpa and Grandma hatched their own chicks using the big red incubator that sat in our basement. I was too young to understand how it worked, but I remember Grandma turning the eggs each day as they lay on a pullout tray at the front. The incubator was heated by a kerosene heater. Eventually, I could look in the narrow glass window in the front, and there would be little chicks looking out at me! That was exciting, and I knew I would get to play with the fuzzy little chicks as soon as they were moved to the brooder house. Eventually Grandma bought her chicks from a mail order catalog, and they were delivered by the mailman. He placed the boxes of chicks on the back seat of his car, and as he pulled into our driveway, he honked his horn. On many spring days, his car was filled with the sounds of those "peep, peeps." Maybe he enjoyed the company. When we see how letters today are sometimes folded, spindled and otherwise mutilated, we are amazed that the chicks survived, but he took good care of them.

Sometimes the chicks were purchased from local hatcheries in Wapak or Celina. Boxes were stacked high on the counter as the supply of chicks was made ready for the area farmers. I couldn't wait to get the cuddly little balls of fluff home. Grandma had scrubbed the small brooder house in the orchard, and I helped spread clean yellow straw over the floor. The brooder stove stood in the middle of the room with the chimney going out through the top of the roof. The stove had a tin hood called a "hover" that extended in a circle around it. Grandma had started a fire in the stove the day before, and now the room was warm and cozy, even on a chilly spring day.

The chicks arrived in cardboard boxes with little round air holes punched in each side so they could breathe. There were often a few of these cardboard circles that hadn't fallen out. I usually pulled the remainder of them out to be used later for play money.

After the boxes were brought into the warm building, the chicks were removed and set near the hover so they could warm up again. While I played with the chicks, Grandma filled the stone crocks with sour milk. These round-top crocks were turned upside down while the milk was poured in, then a pie-pan-shaped saucer was placed on top. As Grandma quickly turned the crock over and set it on the floor, the milk slowly seeped into the saucer as the chicks drank from it. Although I eagerly tried to fill these crocks, I usually flipped them over too slowly or wasn't careful enough and often spilled some of the smelly sour milk down my front or onto the floor.

The little stove was the important item when raising baby chicks because they had to be kept warm. Grandma went out several times a day and into the night to check that little stove. The temperature had to be kept constant so the chicks would not get too cold and die. The baby chicks were Grandma's responsibility.

Grandma also had to give her attention to baby pigs. Occasionally a sow gave birth on the coldest night, and the newborn pigs would nearly freeze in the barn. There were many days when a bushel basket of pigs was brought into Grandma's kitchen and set on the cookstove's open oven door where the heat would quickly revive them. Sometimes the basket was then placed on a hot air register until the pigs were strong enough to go back to the barn and the waiting mama sow.

Grandma and Grandpa were married on July 24, 1898, by the Justice of the Peace at Kossuth. They worked hard to turn an old log house into a home, and about fifteen months later they became the parents of a baby boy who became my father. Grandma told me it had been a hard delivery and she made up her mind that very night that she was not going to have any more children. The doctor smiled and said, "I'll be back next year!" But he didn't have to return. Dad remained an only child.

When it came to field work, Grandma could hold her own. Many times I saw her working beside Grandpa as they shocked wheat and husked corn. She helped haul manure, especially when the hen house and brooder house had to be cleaned out each spring. Another job that she didn't care for was chasing the hogs back into the lot after they had rooted under the fence and escaped. I didn't like that either.

One of her most fascinating stories took place shortly after she and Grandpa were married. They were making hay at the back of the farm, and while Grandpa forked the hay up to her, she used a hayfork to distribute it evenly over the wagon. Suddenly she heard a noise that was very familiar in those days—one which usually brought fear to the hearer. A rattlesnake was shaking its tail in unmistakable anger. Grandpa had pitched the snake onto the wagon along with a forkful of hay. Grandma quickly jumped down from the load, then steadied the frightened horses who had also heard the rattler. Grandpa slowly pulled the hay back onto the ground until he spotted the snake. After he had killed it, they both heaved a sigh of relief. You just didn't mess with a rattler!

Every family seemed to have a rattlesnake story. Grandma told of a friend who had placed her baby in the shade of a tree in the front yard. The child was a year or so old and was contentedly playing when a rattlesnake crawled through the grass toward it. (Remember, there were no lawnmowers back then.) When the mother looked out to check on the baby, she was horrified to see the snake crawling toward it. She knew that if she ran to grab the baby, the snake would surely bite it. Not daring to move, she stood and watched as the snake crawled across the child's arms and legs, then she heaved a sigh of relief as it disappeared in the grass on the other side. Thank goodness rattlesnakes eventually disappeared from this area.

Grandma liked animals and usually made sure our dog, Curly, got the table scraps. After Curly died, a new puppy was given to us by neighbor, Farrell Bruner. As he drove past our house one day, the puppy darted into the road where Mr. Bruner accidentally ran over it. He really felt bad about that, but my brother and I learned about life and death that day. It was also a good lesson in road safety. The next puppy was Don's Mickey. Mickey was tiny when Don got him, and being a hound, his ears stuck out. Those big ears reminded Don of Mickey Mouse, and Mickey became his name. Mickey really enjoyed Grandma's attention, especially in the morning. She usually made two bowls of Post

Toasties, complete with milk and sugar—one was for her, one was for our dog, Mickey!

Mickey was an excellent hunting dog. When he went hunting with Don, Mickey knew the difference between the animals. When he gave a quiet little "oof, oof," Don said he knew it was a hen pheasant which they weren't allowed to shoot. But, if it was a louder "woof, woof, woof," it would be a rooster pheasant, and Don would get a shot as Mickey flushed him out. Don laughed as he told me that if Mickey got really excited with a fast, continuous "WOOF, WOOF, WOOF, WOOF," the critter was a rabbit, and Mickey knew he was in for an exciting chase. After our marriage, Bill and I lived with my family for a couple of months while their new home was being built. Nearly every morning, Bill saw Mickey race around the orchard and farm buildings, chasing a rabbit. Bill thought it was the same rabbit every day, but he couldn't decide who enjoyed the chase the most—the dog, the rabbit, or was it Bill himself as he grinned from ear to ear and watched the merry chase?

The Ladies Aid at the Kossuth Church was one of Grandma's favorite organizations. She spent many hours helping serve meals at the Auglaize County Fair dining hall. The proceeds were used to help pay for the new church. This Ladies Aid also served dinners for most of the farm auctions and other special meetings held in the area. I especially loved their wonderful homemade pies and their delicious made-from-scratch chicken noodle soup. Um-ummmm!

Other activities which Grandma especially enjoyed were her flowers and the Kossuth Garden Club. The club was organized about the time I was out of college and I drove us to the meetings.

When folks in the Southwest referred to the "range," they were speaking of the pasture land on which their cattle grazed. In other areas, "range" referred to a local string of mountains. But out here in the middle of northwestern Ohio's flatland, when our grandma said the word "range," she meant the faithful "Home Comfort Range" cookstove that stood in the corner of her kitchen. It was her steady companion as she fired it up each morning and kept it going all day. Grandma was so familiar with her stove that she knew just what kind of wood Grandpa needed to bring in to provide a more steady heat when baking a cake or pies. When she baked a cake, we children had to tiptoe through the kitchen so it wouldn't fall. I loved Grandma's pies, especially the butterscotch. As she browned the butter and brown sugar, she usually made a little extra for a hard, candy-like brittle for us to eat. Was that ever good!

When power lines came through our area, Grandma got her first electric stove. That helped keep the kitchen cooler in the summer, but it didn't make any warmth for the winter; thus, the old wood stove still stood in the kitchen, providing the extra heat needed for the colder months. After Don and Mary were married and the rest of the family moved into the house next door, the old stove was taken out to the yard for disposal, making room for my refrigerator to sit in the kitchen, instead of in the dining room as Grandma's always had. One day someone saw the old stove in the yard and asked if he could have it. I was glad someone could use it and gave it to him.

Grandpa, Grandma, and Dad joined the Grange after returning from North Carolina in the 1920s. Since Dad often ditched away from home during the week, Don and I went to meetings with our grandparents. Eventually Nellie Wright organized a Juvenile Grange for the children and when we were fourteen years old, we graduated to the *big* Grange.

One year the ladies of Kossuth were asked to present the State Grange Rose Drill at

Memorial Hall in Lima. I was quite excited that Grandma and I were both asked to take part. It would be our first opportunity to wear fancy formals. We had several practices to learn the complicated drills. (A drill consisted of marching in time to music in various formations. We might form a single line and march down the center of the room, then divide at the end with one person going to the right and the next to the left. They might go to opposite corners and file past each other in the center, forming a moving X.) It was a very pretty sight with lots of lovely flowers, and all the ladies dressed in formals of varying colors.

Grandma took care of those school activities requiring help from a mother— making valentine boxes, special treats for birthdays, attending band mothers' meetings, and calling to see if friends could stay overnight. I especially remember my junior prom. The class mothers were responsible for preparing the food for the special prom night banquet. Grandma worked all day alongside my classmates' younger mothers, doing everything she possibly could to make it a special evening for all of us.

Grandma was always faithful in getting everyone ready for church and we never missed unless we were sick. Sunday mornings were very busy for her. She had to check on her baby chicks or pigs, have something planned for Sunday dinner, get us ready and then get herself ready. I remember one Sunday morning when she was so busy getting everything done that she forgot to take off her house slippers and didn't notice until she was sitting in church. She just laughed about it.

It was from Grandma that I acquired my love of sewing. When I was little, Grandma made all my dresses. They were very simple, but they served the purpose. You couldn't buy the fancy braids and decorations available today, and sewing machines made no fancy stitches back then. They didn't even sew backwards. Any lace or trim she might put on a Sunday dress was usually something she had crocheted or tatted. One time she decided to teach Don and me how to do tatting. (Webster describes tatting as "a kind of knotted lace made from cotton or linen thread wound on a shuttle." Since the thread is finer than that used for crocheting, it makes a rather delicate looking lace and consists of a lot of tiny loops joined together.) Don was old enough to understand her instructions and he learned to do some of the simple things. I was too young and never got the hang of it. It didn't interest me as much as sewing, and I never learned to tat, knit or crochet. Grandma spent many evenings tatting a large table cover that I used on the cake table at my wedding. Later she made some tatted lace to trim a baby dress for my daughter, Nancy.

My friends' dresses, like mine, were usually cotton and rather plain. They were wrinkled by the time I got to school, although Grandma stood over the ironing board for several hours, pressing out the wrinkles with the heavy "sad irons."

After making our dresses and aprons from pretty cotton fabrics, Grandma saved the remnants. I was allowed to use some for doll dresses. Grandma taught me that working with fabrics could be fun. When I was about six, she showed me how to use her treadle sewing machine. My legs were almost too short to reach the treadle that moved up and down, making the machine sew. If I forgot to move my foot, the machine forgot to sew.

Grandma never used a "store bought" pattern when making her dresses. Using old newspapers, she showed me the basic designs for cutting out a sleeve, a blouse, and a skirt. It worked well for those first crude doll clothes I made for my Betsy-Wetsy doll. My big baby doll only opened and shut her eyes, but Betsy did real things. If I gave her a bottle, she drank, and then, guess what? That's right, I had to change her diaper. When I was a little girl, that was real progress in the world of dolls! I still have her complete wardrobe, although my poor rubber Betsy must have had too many bottles and far too many wet diapers. She didn't survive the hot, humid days in the attic while I was in college.

Grandma had other uses for leftover fabric scraps. She carefully cut them into various shapes for quilt patches. My great aunts often came over several days during the winter to help Grandma with the quilting. There were many days when I sat under the quilt frame and played while they sewed and talked. If I could turn back the clock, I might hear some family gossip that would make interesting reading, but alas, I was just a child who was not fascinated by adult conversations.

When those cotton dresses, aprons and shirts finally wore out, Grandma found another good use for them. Many winter evenings were spent tearing them into rags that she later crocheted into rugs. While we did homework or sat and listened to the radio, Grandma sat in her rocker with her feet, clad in felt house slippers, resting on the warm furnace register as her wooden crochet hook wove those rag strips into a useful rug.

Like most housewives of that day, Grandma crocheted "antimacassars." Now I can hear you saying, "What in the world is an antimacassar?" It is the pretty little covering that was often placed on the arms and backs of chairs and sofas to help keep them clean. Some folks called it a "tidy." As the man of the house relaxed in the easy chair, he laid his elbows on the arms or his head against the back where the dust and oil from his hair soaked into the antimacassar which could easily be removed for laundering. The only problem was that the rest of the chair eventually became soiled around it, making it necessary to return the antimacassars to the chair as soon as possible after they were washed, starched, and ironed. Wash day was not a good time to have company. The overstuffed furniture looked bare.

Very little was wasted in those days. Sweaters were usually made of wool since the soft nylons and orlons were not yet manufactured. One of my wool sweaters had been worn until a few areas were beginning to fray. Grandma unraveled the remainder of the sweater and rolled the good yarn into a ball, then used it to crochet a "fascinator" for me. Have you heard that word? My *Webster's Collegiate Dictionary* of 1948 describes a fascinator as a crocheted head covering for women. Grandma's version was a long strip about ten inches wide that covered the head and then crossed over beneath the chin, with tails that were either left to hang loosely or were tucked into the front of the coat. That wool fascinator was quite warm, and I loved to wear it while skating with its tails flying out behind as I raced across the ice.

Housework was a bit different when I was a child. Before the electric lines were put in, Grandma swept the *entire* house with a broom. Imagine! When she purchased a new broom, she soaked it in hot salt water. This was supposed to make it last longer. The rugs at that time were mostly of wool. As she swept, she dampened the broom occasionally to help keep the dust down. Our roads were mostly stone and every car that passed left a little more dust on the furniture.

Grandpa helped provide another source of daily dust as he shook the grates in the furnace down in the cellar. Each shake brought a thin cloud of soot and dust up through the floor. On Grandma's official "spring cleaning day," the living room rug was rolled up and taken outside to be hung across the clothesline. Don and I liked to pretend it was a tent or Indian tepee, but there wasn't much time for play. We had to take the carpet beater and bang away at that rug until no more dust came out. Grandma usually placed a layer of newspapers on the floor under the rug to keep the furnace dust from coming up from the basement. Since we had no rug pads, it also helped protect the back of the rug. After the carpet was placed on the clean papers, the old ones were burned.

I remember the day Grandpa took Grandma to Lima to the Montgomery Ward store to look at a new electric vacuum cleaner. To demonstrate it, the man dumped a sack of lint and dirt onto the store carpet, then turned on the vacuum cleaner and sucked it all back into the sweeper bag. We watched in awe. Grandpa was impressed enough to buy this new gadget, and Grandma's housework became much easier after that.

Grandma always had a good garden. She consulted the Old Farmer's Almanac about planting things in the proper sign of the moon. (I am not sure that helped. I never paid any attention to the signs, yet we also had good gardens. I guess Grandma gave me her "green thumb.") She spent many long hours canning all the vegetables needed to last us through the winter. Canning had to be done in a huge kettle on the cookstove. The water bath method never seemed to work for peas and many of them spoiled, so Grandma had to buy cans from the store. Even now, I don't enjoy canned peas. Some of her canning jars used a rubber ring which tightly sealed the glass lid on top to the jar beneath. A wire bail crossed the top of the glass lid and secured it. She also had a different style canning jar that used a zinc lid which screwed down onto a rubber ring. I was thrilled when the metal rings with replaceable center lids came on the market. Now I listen for those little lids to "ping" and I know my cans are sealed. Grandma seldom purchased tin cans of "store bought" vegetables because they just didn't taste as good, and the whole family was grateful when rented frozen food lockers became available.

Werner's Market in Wapakoneta was one of the first to install a "locker plant." We were thrilled to be able to have the more appealing frozen foods. The weekly trip to the locker was quite an event. Werner's always had several big coats hanging outside the heavy metal locker door. In summer, it was a pleasure to leave the hot outdoors and walk into that huge cool room lined wall-to-wall with storage boxes of various sizes. We had a key which fit only our locker, and believe me, once we were inside that room—"Brrr!" We hurried to unlock our door and fill our basket quickly with the frozen food. By now we had a refrigerator at home, and the frozen foods were placed into its small freezer compartment. We no longer had to can vast amounts of our fresh meat, but put them in the freezer instead. Eventually refrigerators had larger freezer compartments. Finally home freezers came on the market and the locker plants in town were closed. One of our early purchases as newlyweds was a large chest-type freezer.

Grandma always grew and canned a lot of pickles. Using a nail, she made holes in the bottoms of large tin cans such as those used for juice; then she set the cans among the pickles. Every few days someone carried a bucket of water to the pickle patch to fill the tin cans. This allowed the water to soak down into the ground slowly. She always grew more than enough pickles and cucumbers.

Sauerkraut was made in a large crock each fall. Grandma trimmed the coarse, outer leaves off the cabbage, leaving just the plump white heads. These were cut into quarters and pushed back and forth across the sharp kraut cutter, shredding the cabbage as it moved. This was not a job for a child because the knives in the cutter were very sharp, and it was too easy to take a slice off the fingers or heel of the hand. After putting a layer of cabbage in the crock, she added a handful of salt. I was then allowed to use the potato masher to stomp that cabbage down until a juice was formed. More cabbage and salt were added and pressed down. This continued until the crock was almost full. There had to be a little space left at the top because the kraut expanded as it fermented. Grandma usually washed some of the largest leaves from the grape vine and placed them across the top of the kraut. Then she covered the crock with a large plate on which she placed a clean stone, one heavy enough to keep the cabbage under the salty brine. In a few weeks, we had sauerkraut, sausage and potatoes—a popular dish in keeping with her German heritage.

Grandma didn't have much time for gossip, but she did enjoy talking on the phone with her friend, Doris Romshe, who lived a mile to the north; or with our neighbor, Helen Mack, who kept her informed about the activities of her dad, Joe Frank, who had just moved to Texas. He had been Grandpa's hunting partner and one of his best friends. These occasional talks were a welcome break in Grandma's weekly routine.

It's hard for me to think of Grandma as being a little girl at one time. After all, she was always a grandma when I knew her. Retha Rohrbach, a former neighbor of Grandpa Briggs, told me that her aunts, Dora and Elizabeth States, had been Grandma's best friends when they were little girls. She said her aunts had told her how they usually played with Grandma and had even stayed at each other's houses occasionally. Grandma occasionally mentioned their names.

Back in their younger days, Grandma and Grandpa were often involved with entertaining and being entertained by a group of friends who seemed to get together almost every week for fun and fiddlin' parties. Grandma's garden helped provide the refreshments for some of these gatherings. A 1914 party was described as having twenty friends and neighbors who gathered to enjoy "drinking cider and eating musk and water melons, and playing the violins and organ, and listening to it."

There were also little get-togethers of the ladies only. Those gals didn't spend all their time bending over scrub boards or hot stoves! As an example, on August 13, 1914, The *Democrat* "Out West" column stated that Mrs. Frank Davenport and three friends had spent Friday with Mrs. Frank Ward. Several weeks later we read: "The ladies who took dinner with Mrs. J.L. Bitters Tuesday were:" and the names of nine ladies were mentioned. It concluded by saying, "First a full house and then a full table and then . . . ." and the rest of the story was left to our imagination. Yes, those country gals found time for some fellowship, too!

Some of the things I remember most about Grandma were her many aprons. They were usually made from feed sacks or from a pretty cotton that was on sale in the fabric department of the J.C. Penney or Uhlman's stores in Wapakoneta. Those aprons were used for many things on the farm. Mental pictures come into my mind of Grandma gathering eggs into that apron, carrying a cold newborn pig to warm up in the house, bringing in produce from the garden and fruit from the orchard, and of her flapping a corner to shoo hens into the henhouse when a storm was approaching. If it began to rain, she threw the apron over her head and hurried to the house. If it was chilly, she threw it over her arms and shoulders or over us children to keep us warm.

Grandma's apron was used to wipe our tears or even our runny noses, and if a spot of dust had been missed, a corner of the apron quickly erased it. Kindling to start the morning fire was gathered in it the night before, and after such exertion, a corner was lifted to wipe the sweat or to use as a fan to cool her tired body. When unexpected company drove in, hands were quickly washed and wiped on a corner of the apron that was then tossed down the cellar steps in readiness for next wash day. With all the uses Grandma found for her apron, I wonder how I have managed all of these years without one.

Grandma taught me a very important lesson. Never complain about your husband. She mentioned several times that my other grandmother always seemed to have some kind of complaint about what her husband did or did not do. Although Will was a school teacher and a well-educated man, she always seemed to find fault. Grandma always told me that she would never complain about Grandpa. She was very proud of him and his lifestyle. He was an honest, hard working man who was in church teaching his class every Sunday. One day as we shopped in Wapak, Grandpa walked down the street ahead of us. "Look at him!" Grandma proclaimed. "He's standing so straight and tall!" Grandpa was in his seventies by then but he was still straight as a stick, and Grandma was obviously quite pleased and very proud of him.

I didn't give Grandma enough praise and thanks for all the lessons she taught me about homemaking and living. The values she instilled in me have helped make me a better person. With Grandma's death, the family circle as I had always known it was broken. Grandma died at home, and Grandpa immediately stopped the old mantel clock. In accordance with family tradition, the clock was stopped at the death of a loved one and started again after returning from the funeral. I was an adult with children of my own, and it was difficult for all of us; but the one who felt it the deepest, of course, was Grandpa—her marriage partner of almost sixty-four years!

Grandma and Grandpa Davenport are ready to leave for a
road building job in North Carolina in 1923.

## Chapter 8.

# *Did Your Daddy Wear a Dress?*

Did your daddy wear a dress until he was two? Did he have a bow in his hair? If so, he was probably born around the turn of the century when "baby raising" was done a bit differently. I have seen numerous pictures of little boys dressed in this manner. Born in 1899, Dad's earliest pictures show him in a dress, quite the "proper" attire for little boys! When he was two, his hair hung in long curls as he gazed at the camera. Bill's Aunt Alwina said she thought little boys usually stayed in dresses until they were toilet trained and, as she put it, "knew what pants were all about."

By about four years of age, Dad appeared in his Little Lord Fauntleroy suit of maroon velvet, complete with brass buttons, wide ruffled collar and a big bow at the neckline. His dark eyes sparkled, and a small bow held his dark curls in place. This outfit, quite elegant for little country boys at the turn of the century, was stored for many years in Great-grandpa's trunk.

Before I was born, many country homes didn't have lawn mowers. Chickens, ducks and guinea hens usually roamed inside a fenced yard, keeping the grass down. Babies were often placed under a shade tree where they played contentedly in the dirt (and other assorted items found in the yards of farmers who had chickens, ducks and guinea hens. Yuck!). When Mother husked corn or worked in the garden, baby played in the dirt beside her. One lady remembered seeing a toddler wearing black diapers. Sounds quite practical, don't you think?

Raising a baby in those days was a bit different from today's methods with our rows and rows of prepared baby food. Many mothers gave their babies dry bread or zwieback to chew. Its hard surface felt good against tiny teeth that were trying to come through the gums. Since there were no prepared baby formulas then, it was essential that mothers nurse their babies. When a mother started her baby on more solid food, it was usually the same thing she served the rest of the family. She just mashed it up with a fork. Potatoes and gravy were popular, and homemade applesauce was a favorite.

Preparing meat for children was a bit more difficult. I have heard of mothers who chewed the meat first, then gave it to their little one. (Somehow that idea doesn't sound too appetizing, yet they did what was necessary to keep the children healthy.) Even so, many nineteenth-century babies died before the age of two. Cemetery and church records show the terrible death rate for children.

Bill's Aunt Alwina said she didn't have many toys as a child. Her older sisters had cloth dolls with tin heads. She finally got just one small doll to call her own. Some children had porcelain dolls which were delicate and easily broken.

By what names were early babies known? Lulu, Effie, Fanny, Frettie, Hattie, Beulah, Madie, Bessie, Hester, Mattie, Bertha, Tillie, Maggie, Zeke, Wilbur, Darius, Clem, Lemuel, Frederick, Ephriam, Isaac, Cloide, Rufus, Lafe, Casper, Harvey, Enoch, Elmer, Jeb–all common and proper names, but birth announcements today seldom list them. (If so, the baby was probably named after grandparents.)

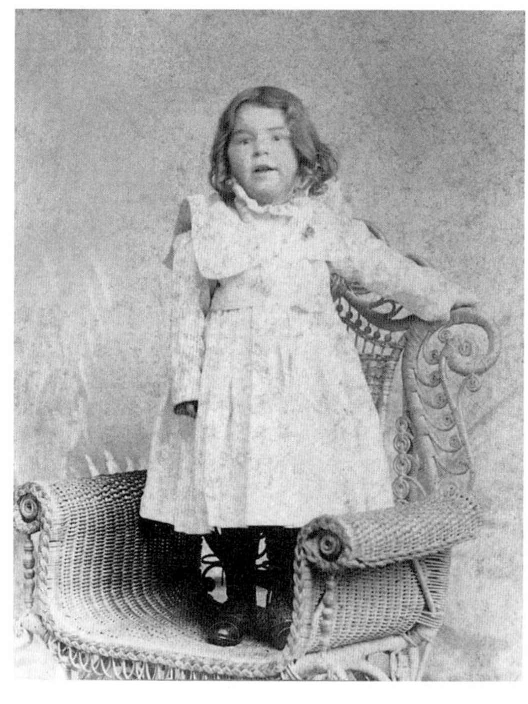

My daddy, Bernard Davenport, wore a dress and curls for this 1901 baby picture.

Dad posed in 1903 in his maroon velvet "Little Lord Fauntleroy" suit, complete with brass buttons and a lace edged shirt.

## Chapter 9.

# The Good Old Days

With childish curiosity, I wanted to hear more about the activities and way of life of my ancestors. To what did they refer when they spoke of the "good old days?" Grandpa Frank's families had come to Ohio in the 1830s, so they no doubt saw Indians and plenty of wild animals. Some may have lived in the log Indian huts left after the natives were moved west to reservations, log huts described by one old lady as having "puncheon floors and greased paper windows." Life was simple. They made their own candles and spun their own fibers into crude cloth. A fireplace in one end provided the only heat in their log cabins and the schools which were eventually built. One early settler explained how they captured wolves by building pens with frail coverings. As a wolf jumped on top, he fell in and could not get out. His pelt could then be sold or made into warm winter clothing.

What were early Auglaize County homes like? Of course, the pioneer settlers of the area built log houses. Even after the early frame and brick homes were built, there was not a great abundance of elegant furniture, especially in the farm homes. Most homes seemed to have one or two pieces of furniture that were of great importance to the family, usually because Grandpa had brought them all the way from Germany or England or wherever.

Although my childhood home had more than enough furniture, there were a few pieces that seemed especially important—Great-grandpa's trunk, the library table and the dining room sideboard. As a child, I also remember a "fainting couch" sitting along the west wall of the living room. This was a bed-like couch with one rounded end elevated above the other. It was just the right angle for someone who had to rest because they were feeling "fainty." When Bill and I were married, a fainting couch also sat in the bedroom of his grandparents.

Until the mid-1930s, Grandma's kitchen held the old cookstove, a small granite-topped work table, a plain wooden rocker, and a wooden table and chairs. She kept an oilcloth covering on the table, and if the electricity was off for any reason, a coal oil lamp was placed in the middle to provide light. In a family postcard, Tillie Fledderjohann described the care of coal oil lamps. "Once a week we would bring all the lamps on the kitchen table and refill them with oil. Then, too, the next big job was to wash all those lamp chimneys. I just hated to do that but it had to be done. We used to have a hanging lamp above our long kitchen table and we could pull that up and down to get better lighting."

Like most farm kitchens, ours also had a cupboard with two double glass doors where Grandma's dishes, glasses and food items were stored. Wooden drawers just below held the silverware and kitchen tools. Pots and pans, sacks of sugar and flour were stored in the bottom half of the cupboard behind wooden doors. The cupboard served well until the luxury of built-in cupboards came about in the mid-1930s, then it went to the basement where it stored Grandma's delicious home-canned foods. There were no non-stick frying pans, no electric mixers or microwave ovens back then!

But what was my grandparents' social life like before my time? After listening to their comments years ago, I've tried to recall a few of the activities filling their lives from the 1880s to the 1920s.

Of course school took up much of their early lives, but as newlyweds in 1898, they spent a lot of time working together. (Because farm couples needed each other to survive, divorce was virtually nonexistent then!)

Many farm activities of that day became fun because friends helped each other by working together. Barn raisings were one of those events. Grandpa was a young man when many of the large old barns of our present day were being built in Auglaize County. On the day the barn was to be started, family members, friends and neighbors gathered together for an enjoyable day, but one that was very tiring. Working together, they soon had the frame up, and the barn began to take shape. Depending on the number of people, a barn could be erected in a relatively short time and at little expense above the cost of materials, most of which came from the farm. The trees had been cut down earlier and were sawed into the lumber needed for the barn. Things went fast when everyone worked together. While hammers rang throughout the morning, the ladies prepared a huge dinner for the hungry men. By "chore time," everyone was ready to go home and relax by the side of old Bossy as the evening milking was done and the animals fed. Our Amish friends still build their barns in this manner. A day of hard work becomes a "labor of love," as well as a time of good fellowship among neighbors.

"Swing your partners and do-si-do," was the tune of the caller as neighboring families joined the fun at a barn dance in many of those brand new farm buildings. Grandpa, his cousin Freed Daniels, and Uncles Lew and Frank Daniels, all played fiddles for many of those early barn parties. The June 28, 1917, *Auglaize County Republican* contained an item in the Sodom news stating: "Frank Davenport had his new barn raised Monday. Look out for a big dance when completed."

The most active form of entertainment for my grandparents was visiting family and friends. How those folks loved to visit! A high priority was placed on visits and they were often reported to the local newspapers. This became very obvious while looking through some of the old Auglaize County newspapers. An example from the *Republican*, August 18, 1904, Sodom area states: "Frank Davenport and family spent Sunday as the guests of Ed Thiesing and wife near Kossuth." Items such as this appeared each week. There were also elaborate descriptions of surprise birthday parties with fifty or more family members and friends attending, each mentioned by name in the paper. Another social event was the family reunion where relatives met for a huge dinner and day of fun. These were usually reported in the paper, often listing by name everyone who attended. My, how those folks loved to see their names in print!

Getting mail was somewhat different in Grandpa's day. People faithfully watched the county newspaper under the column, "List of Letters." Names of those receiving letters were published here with the admonition that they were to pick up their mail in two or three weeks or it would go to the dead letter office. An 1898 notice said, "Persons calling for letters in this list will say 'Advertised' and pay one-cent postage for advertising." Would they have gotten their letter if they had not said 'Advertised' or would it have cost more? Farmers who belonged to the Grange felt a need for some form of delivery of letters. They worked toward getting "Rural Free Delivery," established in 1896. Men such as Dusty Miller drove their buggies or sleighs or rode horses to deliver mail to the country areas. Eventually cars and mail trucks did the job, bringing a touch of the outside world to the farmer's door. Would there be a letter from a distant friend or relative? My family sent a lot of post cards back then, many with family pictures on the front. Since there were no telephones, a penny postcard was the cheapest way to send a message. For instance, Grandma received a picture postcard from her friend, Grace Daniels, with a 1911 Lima postmark. The picture on the front was of the Billy Sunday Tabernacle and the message read, "Will look for you Saturday or Saturday aweek sure. We got home all OK. Heard Billie Saturday night. Am feeling fine. G.D." (Grace refers to Billy Sunday who was in Lima for a huge revival at the "Billy Sunday Tabernacle" built in his honor.)

Church activities then, like now, often included "potluck" dinners. Some folks called them "covered dish dinners." (That term created a real problem many years later when a cousin, Bob Warnock, returned from World War II, accompanied by a sweet young Irish "war bride" named Hazel. Although she spoke English with an Irish brogue, our customs were new to Hazel and she didn't understand some of our common expressions. One day she was invited to a "covered dish" dinner. She said she looked through every dish in her cupboard and couldn't find a single one with a cover. She was afraid she wouldn't get to go since she had no "covered" dish. A friend gently explained. You were to bring some food in whatever dish you might have. If it didn't have a cover, you used a towel or wax paper to cover it. Then Hazel understood!)

These dinners were known by several names—potluck, covered dish, community feed. In the southern part of the United States the noon meals at the churches were often referred to as "dinner on the grounds." Since many country churches had no basements, these dinners were often held outside underneath the trees in the church yard, probably upwind from the hitching rail where the horses were tied and where the gentle breezes would be less fragrant!

An occasional form of entertainment in rural areas was traveling stage shows. Grandpa had worked for a time in Uncle Tom's Cabin. I saw this show when I was a very little girl. A large tent with a stage and a lot of benches was set up on a vacant lot in Spencerville. Smaller tents were placed outside the main entrance where roasted peanuts and popcorn were sold. I believe there were also a couple of wild animals, much like those found in a small circus.

Family portraits were quite popular at the turn of the century. It was considered quite a privilege to receive a portrait from relatives who lived at a great distance. Even those living nearby often gave each member of the family a recent portrait for a Christmas gift.

Cameras were sophisticated contraptions that were anything but convenient, so these old photos are now priceless reminders of past ancestors. What great pleasure it is to look at the facial expressions, the styles of clothing, the intricately painted backgrounds and the wicker furniture that seemed to be such vital accessories in many early pictures.

A June 20, 1896, story in the *St. Marys Argus* told of a really big event of the good old days. A crowd of 10,000 visited Spencerville the previous 4th of July, and an attempt was to be made in 1896 to eclipse that figure. "The program will include a gorgeous industrial and circus parade in the morning, horse races, bicycle races, tub races on the canal, football, baseball, rope and slack-wire walking, Sun Bros' Circus, menagerie and hippodrome, both afternoon and evening; closing with a magnificent display of fireworks. All to take place in the beautiful Keeth Driving Park Grounds. An effort will be made to arrange for the 'shooting' of an oil well near the park grounds sometime during the morning; also, several pumping oil wells will be in operation, nearby. Admission is free to the grounds." How's that for excitement? (No fire trucks with sirens screaming, no politicians riding in sleek convertibles, and no prancing girls twirling batons!) Grandma would have been sixteen. I wonder, did the Schwartz family attend the big celebration or did she have to stay home to work in the fields as usual?

An occasional medicine man show was eagerly anticipated as it arrived in the villages and towns. Trotting his horse-drawn wagon into town, the "doctor" loudly proclaimed that he had an amazing medicine that was sure to make everyone feel better. In minutes, word had spread that a medicine man was visiting Kossuth (or wherever), and a crowd would gather. He and his associates, (often his wife and kids), would then present some form of free entertainment, usually dressed in fancy costumes designed to attract attention. At the conclusion of the show, he extolled the virtues of his amazing medicines which could cure almost any ailment known to man. (I have heard the medicine consisted of about 95% alcohol. No wonder it made people feel better, at least for a while!) His associates moved through the crowd with bottles of the wonder-medicine in their hands and were happy to accept the money thrust at them by customers eager for a cure. Grandpa's family always enjoyed the free show, but he said they never purchased the cure-all medications.

Organizations such as the Grange had large picnics each year at a grove or backyard in the neighborhood. One paper reported such a picnic being held in the grove of trees at the home of Great-grandpa Henry Schwartz, north of Kossuth. Another favorite spot was in the woods beside the Prairie Creek south of Kossuth.

Community Farmers' Institutes were held each winter in many farming areas, including Kossuth, Buckland and New Knoxville. We recently saw a program from the Seventh Annual Farmers' Institute held on January 31 and February 1, 1913, in New Knoxville. One of the members of the executive committee was Bill's grandpa, Fred Wierwille. These institutes were exciting times for the whole community. Although the main idea was to provide interesting and informative speakers for the farming community, there were also fun-type contests between the speeches. A favorite was to bring four or five people to the front of the room, then give each one a balloon to blow up. The winner was the first person to burst the balloon. Another was to pass out a handful of soda crackers, and the winner was the first one to finish his crackers, then whistle loud enough to be heard. Children were included in these contests, as well as the older people. The person in charge knew the personalities of the audience and knew that certain people would be wet-blankets and you didn't ask them to come forward to participate in the fun. Others could always be depended upon "to put on a good show." The Institute's closing event was always a home talent play, a hilarious comedy, of course. (Kossuth's Community Institute continued until after we were married. Bill and I were participants in the last of those rib-tickling comedies.)

The Auglaize County fair had already existed for many years when my grandparents were young. A day spent at the fair was a special treat for them. It was geared mainly to the farmer's interest. There were also numerous band concerts around the area. Even small communities such as New Knoxville, Buckland and Spencerville showed off their bands made up of a dozen or more local men. Parks or the town square often had a band shell for such concerts. Sporting events were also quite popular, especially baseball.

A baseball excursion advertised in an 1898 *Auglaize County Democrat* was to be held on Sunday, August 21, to League Park in Cincinnati for a game of ball featuring Wapak versus the Shamrocks. The round trip train ticket cost $1.50 and included free admittance to the ball park and grandstand. The excursion train was to leave Wapak at 6:11 a.m. and arrive in Cincinnati at 9:30 a.m. It would leave there at 9:00 p.m. in the evening, allowing ample time for a visit to Coney Island, the Zoo, Lagoon and Chester Park. Other special excursion trains took large groups to Cedar Point Amusement Park, to State Fair and so on. Folks from New Knoxville traveled by train to the 1893 Columbian Exposition in Chicago, where the main attraction was the world's largest Ferris wheel. Bill's Grandpa Wierwille joined others from the county aboard one of the many trains carrying eager visitors to the 1904 fair in St. Louis, where he bought a beautiful cup from the Jerusalem Exhibit. Bill's family lived only two miles from Moulton, where they could "catch" the interurban line to Wapak or Lima, then board a train.

Train travel was a common mode of *long*-distance transportation, making it possible to visit relatives in distant states. I recently found a copy of a 1966 *Wapakoneta Daily News* interview with Grandpa Frank. He mentioned traveling to Wisconsin in a covered wagon in 1879, then returning a year later by train. He told me of a visit by his Uncle Lew Daniels who homesteaded in Idaho and then returned by train to visit relatives back in Ohio. While in Spencerville, he purchased a rifle from Pohlman's Hardware, one which he took back with him. A family portrait taken in the 1880s at a studio in this area of Ohio showed Grandma's aunt, Caroline (Aufderhaar) Wiethoff, along with her husband and ten children, including twins Mary and Martha. Since they lived in Minnesota, we must assume they made the trip via a train. What an exciting event that must have been for those ten children.

Another form of transportation that sounds exciting was the use of a horse and sleigh in the winter. The *Republican,* on February 4, 1915, had the following: "Joe Frank and family, Frank Davenport, wife and son Bernard, Freedus Daniels and wife, Frank Ward, wife and daughter Esta, formed a sleighing party and were conveyed to the home of Mr. and Mrs. Bert Montague, Saturday evening, where they had a good social time." After having talked to some of the old folks who had to use sleighs, I don't think we missed too much. Bill's Aunt Alwina explained that her dad didn't own a real sleigh, but had lifted a wagon box off its wheels and sat it on wood runners for traveling in snow. The family sat on straw in the bottom of the wagon bed with heavy wool lap robes and bricks warmed in the oven of the wood stove. Even so, the ride was extremely cold. Eunice Miller related that her uncle, Dr. Foreman, often made winter calls in a sleigh, covered by a heavy buffalo hide lap robe. Sleighs were about the only means of transportation in the winter when buggy wheels didn't function well on the snow covered ground.

Buying a sleigh was no real problem in the Kossuth area. "A 100-Year Chronology of Spencerville" was compiled by *Journal-News* editor, Paul W. Cochran, and published August 6, 1942, in the column, "Time Marches On." It states: "1871–F.B. Miller sleigh factory at Kossuth turned out 100 cutters." A cutter was a one-horse sleigh. (The same article mentions that in "1892– Of the choir made up of 15 convicts at the Ohio State Penitentiary, 5 were from Spencerville.")

Even a buggy ride to town for a day of shopping was exciting. Grandpa and Grandma were married on July 24, 1898. City streets were still dirt then and that day's *Democrat* records a huge sale at the store of Timmermeister and Rogers in Wapakoneta. (Do you suppose they drove over for a special honeymoon day of shopping to supply their home?) Table oilcloth was 10¢ a yard, 5¢ cotton flannel was reduced to 3¢, men's plow shoes, regular $1.25 were now only 89¢, ladies' oxfords and slippers were 49¢ and linen hats for men and boys were 25¢. The best buy seemed to be men's shirts "well made" for only 25¢ each. Not to be outdone, Werst and Collins, also of Wapakoneta, listed their specials: 25 boys waists (shirts), clearance sale price 19¢, 4¢ gingham aprons clearance sale price of only 2½¢ each. Their best buy was 25¢ all-wool dress goods clearance sale price only 16⅔¢ each. You wonder how they paid two-thirds of a cent? At that time fabrics were seldom more than a yard wide and it would have taken about six yards for a simple long dress. That adds up to an even amount of money.

"Grab your gun! I just saw a pheasant out behind the hen house!" This excited call came frequently in winter when the men looked forward to days of hunting the rabbits and pheasants that were quite plentiful. The sound of guns was quite familiar. Since there were no freezers, the women depended on the fresh meat brought home by the family men.

"Ker-boom!" The louder sound of a dynamite explosion was also common in the late 1890s and early 1900s, especially in the oil fields in this area. Dynamite was also used when clearing the "new ground" of the huge tree stumps from the woods that nearly covered this area of the county. After reading a story in an 1894 county newspaper, I found there were some adults who didn't seem to know much about using dynamite correctly. A man foolishly stored half a box of dynamite in the oven of the kitchen stove. Later, when the fire was started, it exploded, killing five of the eight people in the room. Three others were not expected to live. He wiped out his entire family in that one act of carelessness. A few years ago, the television show, *Little House on the Prairie*, featured a story about Pa and his neighbor taking a job hauling dynamite in order to earn money to save the farm. I watched that show with sweating hands. It brought back memories of a story Grandpa had told us of a man he knew with a similar job. The unstable material had suddenly blown up. They were unable to identify *anything*, not the man, nor his horses or the wagon.

When men weren't working, many enjoyed a rather passive pastime—whittling. A sharp pocketknife and a piece of wood were all that were required for hours of enjoyment. Grandma's uncle, Herman Metz, from St. Joseph, Missouri, was extremely talented with a knife. He was a fireman, and with a lot of time between fires, he carved out many toys for the local children. He was also well-known for the household items he made that featured his carvings. I have seen at least four of them: a chair, a marble cane, a candy dish and a hat rack with a mirror. Several stockyards and packinghouses were located in St. Joseph. Herman used cow horns to form the rounded arms on the chair and to hold hats on the hat rack. Some horns were split and soaked in water, then opened out to dry. He used these to make the candy dish.

Each item included one or more hands made from black balls used on pool tables. The carving on these tiny hands was beautifully done with fingernails an eighth of an inch long and the wrinkles delicately carved at the knuckles of each finger. Three of these hands helped form a pedestal for the candy dish, several decorated the chair and the hat rack, and the cane was topped with hands. Herman also made a room full of very unique furniture which was on display at the 1904 St. Louis World's Fair.

I found it interesting that the St. Joseph fire department was organized in 1865 and their first steam engine was horse drawn, cost $5,000, and was named the "Blacksnake." Some of the equipment was pulled by volunteer firemen and other citizens–there being ropes to accommodate all who desired to "run wid de masheen." (How's that for a good German expression?) As Herman drove to a fire in 1918, his horses stumbled, throwing him against the front of the fire wagon. He died that night from a punctured lung. Grandma received pictures of the funeral procession.

When I wrote to the St. Joseph library, they sent a copy of Uncle Herman's obituary. The funeral was described in part as follows: "The procession then will start for Mt. Mora cemetery, headed by Chief Pat Kane. Then will come Maupin's Band, followed by thirty firemen on foot. The wagon which Metz was driving at the time of the accident, draped in mourning, will convey the coffin. On the seat beside the driver will be the hat and coat the dead man wore. There will be a group of firemen to greet the procession at the beginning of Frederick Avenue and another at the cemetery. The pallbearers are firemen."

After the tragedy, his unusual pieces of furniture were disposed of. Although distant relatives have tried to locate them, they have been unsuccessful. If you see an item with cow horns and tiny black hands, Uncle Herman may have made it. They were his trademarks.

A popular saying was that "Women's work is never done." The ladies were kept quite busy with the usual household chores, but they also looked forward to winter when they could put up the quilting frame and enjoy long hours of chitchat and stitching together. This pastime continued into my childhood when Grandpa's sister, Ella, often visited for a week or more. (I rather reluctantly gave up my bed and slept downstairs on the couch.) Aunt Tillie was always dependable as a good quilter. She was also a great conversationalist. (I remember hearing a few moments of discussion about other family members who were not usually included on quilting day. No, it was really nothing personal. These gals simply made their stitches too large and uneven. Ladies took pride in their handiwork.)

In looking through several 1914 Auglaize County newspapers recently, I was interested in the style of writing, especially the *flowery* obituaries. The headlines were also very descriptive: "Angel of Death Takes Aged Lady"; "Two Oil Well Shooters Killed"; "Editor-Aeronaut Falls to his Death" (fell from a balloon); "Man Died Instantly in Fall From Derrick Today" (oil well); "Horse Run Down by Locomotive"; "Bull Attacks Horse and Injures Man"; "One Cent Postage Must Come" (It had been raised to two cents but people thought that was too high and they could easily get by on one cent.); "Horse Thieves Are Finally Caught"; and "Suffragettes Busy as Buzzing Bees."

The important thing that for generations has made a house into a home has not been the size of the building nor its elegant furniture. It has not been the activities available for the family to enjoy nor the places they could go. The important thing has been the love and respect that has been shared by family members within the four walls of that home. It was true in the *good old days*. It's still true now!

The log cabin of my grandparents, Frank and Nora Davenport, in the autumn of 1900. Their baby son, Bernard, stands in his buggy. The horses and cow were their most valuable possessions. Grandpa made the picket fence and shingles for the cabin.

## Chapter 10.

# The D & D Construction Company

Aren't brothers wonderful? Don gave me the answers to many of my questions about "The Company." Not only is he older, but by working with Dad and Grandpa for many years, he heard quite a few of the stories from their lives in the past. The importance of the Davis & Davenport Construction Company became clearer as the childhood stories began to come to life.

Grandpa was a teamster, "one who drives a team of horses or is in the business of hauling with a team."[1] That describes the early work of Frank Davenport. Although his dad didn't have much of the world's goods, he had a team of horses. The horses provided a means of making a living as they did their share of work on the farm and then helped him haul for others. Horses were the semi-tractors of that day, hauling anything that needed to be moved.

The country was developing, and with the exception of a few main roads that had been "piked," everything else was mud roads. Piking was the forming of "proper" roads by digging drainage ditches and covering the road's surface with gravel. Davis and Davenport formed a partnership when Grandpa received the contract to pike the Townline Road, the road that ran past his dad's house. Grandpa was responsible for hauling the gravel, while Charlie Davis was responsible for obtaining it. Of course, they also hired family members and neighbors to help them. The gravel was dug out of the Peterson gravel pit located along the Prairie Creek near the present Hugh Core home. Davis set up a Sauerman drag line, a machine which helped dig the stone out of this gravel pit. It was then loaded on wagons whose bottoms were made of 2x4's or 2x6's that stood on edge. Handles on the ends allowed the operator to lift the boards up so the gravel could run out below. This eliminated shoveling the heavy stone.

After they had piked many of the roads in the area, the natural progression led from building stone roads to more sophisticated concrete roads. They bought machinery and officially went into the road building business. A road leading into Mercer, a little town in Mercer County, was their first job. Other jobs were bid in Troy, Reynoldsburg, and in the Amish area near Berlin, Navarre, and Millersburg. Dad had his ditching machine on that job, putting in the side road drainage. They also built roads at Marietta and were getting jobs all over Ohio, enough that they were rapidly becoming one of the largest concrete road builders in the country. Grandpa became friends with the Miami Portland Cement Company salesman, Herb Roller. If Mr. Roller heard of a job being "let," he informed Grandpa so the company could put in a bid. Grandpa may have sold his half to W.W. Wilcox, because the name was eventually changed to the Davis-Wilcox Company.

Although Herb Roller had proven to be an honest man in his dealings with Grandpa, not all salesmen could be trusted. Some were less than honorable in their dealings with potential customers. For them, the idea of "salesmanship" was to "wine and dine" the company officers while discussing business. When they were sufficiently drunk, the salesmen could cut a better deal with more profits for themselves! It didn't work with Grandpa! Grandpa didn't drink alcoholic beverages, which is one of the reasons he had been elected as the company's treasurer. When it came time to "sign on the dotted line," they were sure Grandpa would be sober!

Grandpa often talked about attending the Chicago Road Show, a trade show in which the suppliers presented their latest road building equipment and accessories. A less-than-honorable salesman tried to work his magic, but it backfired. Ikey Davis was enjoying the road show to the fullest, and this salesman convinced him the company needed a new roller, which was used to prepare the road bed before pouring the concrete. Ikey had enjoyed a little too much strong drink by this time, and a new roller certainly sounded like a great idea. He willingly signed his name to the purchase agreement. The next morning, the salesman came to Grandpa and told him he had sold a new roller to Ikey the night before. He would like to have a check for the payment now. When he showed Grandpa the paper with Ikey's signature, Grandpa just laughed and said, "No, you didn't sell a new roller to anyone. Ikey's name on that paper isn't worth a dime. I'm the company treasurer. It's my signature that counts, and you're not getting it." Grandpa saved them several thousand dollars.

As the company grew larger and branched out, someone, possibly Herb Roller, told them of a little town down in North Carolina that wanted to have their city streets paved for the first time. A postcard dated 18 November 1921 was sent from Grandpa in North Carolina back to Grandma in Ohio and mentions, "The letting is at 12 a.m." The successful bid was his and Grandpa boarded a train for Washington, D.C., then back home to Ohio.

The next eight weeks were spent in preparation for the trip to Bessemer City, North Carolina. Early in January, with Grandma beside him, Grandpa pulled his automobile into a convoy of cars, four trucks and machinery headed for the South. My dad drove a 5-T Clydesdale truck, one of four making the trip, and he occasionally recorded their progress with photographs. The best route available at the time was the National Trail that wound through the Allegheny Mountains. On the 12th of January, 1922, the entourage crossed the Ohio River at Wheeling, West Virginia, and headed east. Two days later, everything came to an abrupt halt in four-foot-deep snow on a flat stretch of road near Keysers Ridge in the Allegheny Mountains of Maryland. It was Saturday, and area farmers brought horses and a Fordson tractor to try to pull the snowbound vehicles out of the four-to seven-foot drifts. Although they worked the remainder of that day and all of Sunday, they made little progress in what the local folks called "the hold-up." Dad snapped several pictures as the Maryland road maintenance crew eventually came in with several men and shovels and helped dig them out. By the 18th of January the caravan had traveled through the narrows near Cumberland, Maryland, and were on their way south to Bessemer City, North Carolina. As they reached their destination at 4 p.m. on January 26th, the trucks were lined up for one last photo.

Grandpa and Grandma occasionally talked about that exciting trip. Seven young men accompanied them, taking turns driving the trucks on the long trip. Grandma delighted in telling about the day she and Grandpa took those sturdy young truck drivers into a restaurant. Someone turned to Grandma and asked, "Are all those big boys yours?"

Travel between Ohio and North Carolina was usually done by train. Grandpa had a problem though. If the train berth was made up the normal way, he got deathly sick as he rode. He had a hard time convincing the porter to make that bed up backwards and put the pillow on the other end, so he could sleep on the trip.

Working on the southern side of the Mason-Dixon line meant that things were going to be different and that he had some lessons to learn, especially since he was from the North. When Grandpa expressed a need for local laborers, it was suggested that he contact Ed McNell, a highly respected man from the nearby town for "colored folks only." When Grandpa contacted him, "Big Ed," as he was called, accepted the position and offered to help Grandpa with the hiring. He helped educate Grandpa about Southern ways and the reality of 1920s segregation. He told Grandpa (and I quote the words of this black man), "Mr. Davenport, you got's to hire singin' n....s. If dey don't sing, dey don't work." Big Ed knew his people well and the pickaxes swung in tempo with the singing. Breaking up the rocks was extremely hard work, but Big Ed's men sang and beat those rocks until they were broken up and the road was built. Ed took a liking to Grandpa, and did everything possible to help and protect him. One late afternoon after work, Grandpa had driven a truckload of Ed's men back to their homes. It was beginning to get dark, and some of the company men didn't think Grandpa should go, but Big Ed vowed he would see that Grandpa was safe, and he was.

The company's employees noticed and appreciated that fact that Grandpa treated all of them with fairness and dignity. One day he was sick and unable to come to work. When he hadn't returned after another day or two, Big Ed went to Grandpa's house to see how he was doing. He soon found that Grandpa and Grandma were both quite ill with the flu. When he realized Grandpa was too sick to bring in coal for the stove, he made it his business to not only bring in several day's supply of coal, but he also cleaned out the ashes and hauled them outside, then did all he could to make things easier for Grandpa and Grandma. After he had finished, Grandpa offered him money for the work he had done, but he refused. He hadn't done the work for money, but as a favor for a man he loved and respected. Grandpa finally asked, "Ed, isn't there something we can do for you to repay you for your kindness?" Big Ed finally told Grandpa that he had always admired the buckle that he wore on his belt. If it wouldn't be asking too much, he would sure be proud to have that buckle. Grandpa took off his belt and was happy to give it to him. The day was made brighter for both men.

Grandma also made some discoveries about "Southern" ways, and those women learned a thing or two about ideas from the North. While they were in North Carolina, Grandpa and Grandma rented a house where Grandpa's first job was to put up a clothesline. That doesn't sound like anything to get too excited about, does it? But you see, the ladies of Bessemer City had never seen a clothesline! They always spread their laundry out on the grass, bushes and wire fences. Grandma said that many of the towels and clothing had stains from those rusty fences, and a strong wind usually sent the clothes all over the neighborhood. As soon as her line was up, her laundry was waving gaily in the breeze. The neighbors all began to notice what the "damyankees" (pronounced as one word) from up north had done. Soon clotheslines were popping up all over Bessemer City. By the time they left, Grandma said nearly every housewife in town had a clothesline!

The fine print in a contract was not always visible back then and the company really got themselves into some difficulties. The bid called for six inches of concrete, meaning they had to dig down below the grade six inches, take out the dirt and put the concrete up to grade. Now that sounds rather simple, and it would have been relatively easy to do back home, but this was Bessemer City. As the roadbed was being prepared in the downtown area, it was discovered that there weren't six inches of dirt to remove. Granite rock reached almost to the surface. No one had mentioned that possibility, and to fulfill the terms of the contract, that rock had to be blasted down to the six-inch level and the concrete poured on top of it. This cost them a mint. The company had to hire experts from near Knoxville, Tennessee, who knew how to work in bedrock. They drilled holes in the rock and put checkerboard set shots on the granite, then covered it with cocoa mat and set it off. Those people really knew how to do the blasting, and although this was in the downtown area with storefronts all around, they cracked only one window in the whole town of Bessemer City.

Dad developed a unique operating system for the beds of the company trucks. The paver could only operate in batches. Dad developed "batch gates" in the truck bed. He hung hinged gates in the dump box, dividing it into four sections. When the truck bed was raised, he tripped a lever which opened the gate, allowing only enough cement for that batch to pour out into the "skip." The paver skip was rather like a bucket with a winch line to pull it up. When you dumped the cement in, the skip would pick it up and dump it in the mixer bowl. Then you left it down and dumped in the correct amount of sand. A third dumping added the gravel. Dad developed that Ezy-Dump Batch Box Endgate but never patented it. He should have!

Besides the four Clydesdales that were driven south, they also bought five Republic trucks and several Relay trucks. The Republics were fairly lightweight with no cabs or roofs over them. The Relays may have had only a roof over them but no windows.

A description under one of Dad's photographs says, "Home of the Davenports while in Bessemer City, N.C. Jan. 30th. to Aug. 1st. 1922." I don't know when Dad and Grandma returned to Ohio, but a postcard dated May 3, 1923, is addressed to him at Wapakoneta from his parents as they arrived in Cincinnati. Dad had purchased a fancy car in North Carolina and may have driven it back at that time. Grandpa returned to Bessemer City to finish the job, and many postcards traveled between the two states. In a postcard he sent to Grandma on September 14th, his birthday, he mentions that Mrs. Johnson had one boarder besides him. During a period of three years, Grandpa spent much of his time in Bessemer City. He often mentioned the occasional train rides back to Ohio to spend some time with his family. Grandma also told of spending several months in North Carolina when she and Grandpa rented a room with various local people with whom they became lifetime friends. They corresponded until their deaths.

We don't know when the entire company moved back to Ohio, but the last card we found from North Carolina was one Grandpa sent to Grandma on March 15, 1926. Within three weeks, Grandpa was back in Ohio to attend Dad's wedding.

Some of the men who worked for the company were Charlie Davis's sons—Homer, who was called "Ikey," and Russell, who went by the name "Red." An older man from Spencerville named John Klink, whom they called "Jake," was the licensed engineer in charge of the Huber steam engine that ran the paver. George Hydaker, secretary of the company, his wife and young daughter, Gay, lived in North Carolina, as did Orvie Cooper, his wife and little son, Ted. All of these people returned to Ohio upon completion of the road. Another familiar name was John F. Carey, a civil engineer from Georgia. (When we drove Grandpa and Grandma to Florida in 1954, we stopped for a visit at the home of John and his wife, a sweet lady whom he lovingly called Miss Lena. John had a powerful sense of humor and used to send letters to “Dem ditch diggin’ Davenports of Wapakoneta, Ohio” or just to “Dem ditch diggers on Route Three, Wapakoneta, Ohio,” no name or specific address was given. We were always amazed when those letters from Georgia actually arrived at the home of Dad and Grandpa in Ohio.)

Another person who appears quite often in the North Carolina pictures was W.W. Wilcox, along with his wife and their little daughter, Joy. Coxie, as he was called, usually appeared in the photos dressed in a fine suit and tie with a hat on his head. His wife’s attire was quite elegant with huge feathered hats and elaborately decorated dresses and coats. While doing some research about the company, Don talked to George Hydaker’s daughter, Gay Edwards. She was just a little girl when they went to North Carolina where her daddy was the company bookkeeper. Gay explained to Don why the “Davis-Wilcox” Company went South, but the “Davis-Davenport” Company returned to Ohio. Not only did the company encounter some expensive problems with all those rocks in North Carolina, they also had another financial problem. It seems Mr. Wilcox had walked away with the company’s money and was never heard from again. Gay remembered it quite well because as a little girl, she had placed her precious savings with the company’s money. When he took off with it, she lost every penny of her savings. No, she never forgot Mr. Wilcox.

When Grandpa and the company went south, the trucks they took were relatively new, and they ended up purchasing more new equipment when they got there. They even had to set up their own stone quarry and crushing plant. When they got done with that difficult job, they had a bunch of old worn-out trucks and machinery. They drove some of the trucks back here and sent some of the machinery back by rail. Don and I remembered seeing one of the old trucks out behind the garage when we were kids.

The stone crusher was shipped to a plot of land that had been purchased near Red Key, Indiana, with the idea of starting their own stone company. When they started to prospect the area, however, they found out the limestone was too soft to use. They abandoned the aging crusher and pulled out, leaving the property go until the taxes ate it up. We drove over there in the 1940s, and everything was still there—the crusher, the screens, everything. We don’t know why they didn’t start it right here in their own backyard.

Upon their return, the Company officers went back to the bank in Spencerville and said “Well, we’re twenty-two thousand dollars in debt. How about it, Posty? (Referring to Ira Post, head of the bank.) Will you loan us $12,000 to buy machinery?” He said, “We can’t do that until we have a bank meeting. I don’t know. This is bad! If you don’t repay the $22,000 debt, it’s going to close the bank. (This was an enormous amount of money then, especially for a small-town bank like Spencerville’s.) We’ll have to have a bank meeting and let you know.” The bank officials met and finally told them, “Well, it’s going to put the bank under if we don’t do it, so we decided we’re going to scrape $12,000 together, and we’re going to trust that you’ll go back and get the thing done.” So they started building roads again in Ohio, and began making money. Grandpa mailed a 1929 postcard from McConnellsville, Ohio, to Grandma at home. The company name was now the D&D (Davis and Davenport) Construction Company, and things were looking good. With

George Hydaker as the bookkeeper and Grandad as the treasurer, the two kept abreast of any developments. They didn't allow anyone to plunge them into further debt with new machinery.

Evalyn Sandkuhl's family and mine had been very good friends. One day in 1927 her dad, Clarence Leffel, decided to drive down to Troy, Ohio, to see Grandpa and Grandma and some of the equipment that the company was using while they completed a job in that area. The Leffels had asked Dad and Mother to go along so our grandparents could see the new baby boy, my brother Don, born the 26th of August. With the ladies in the back seat and the men up front, Clarence headed for Troy.

Evalyn said she remembers the day quite well because she was just nine years old, and, like most little girls, she was interested in the baby that Dad was holding on his lap. She especially remembered Dad giving the tiny boy his bottle as they drove down the highway.

Don reminisced about a later trip, "I remember going down to Troy to visit a work site. This was after our mother died. We ate at a restaurant there, then spent the afternoon at the job site. They set me up on the seat of the new roller they had purchased and said, 'Here's our new roller operator.' I would have been three and a half to four years old," Don said. "And that's one of the few things I remember at that early age."

Grandpa mortgaged his farm in order to finish the Bessemer City job. When the company made enough money to pay off its debts, he finally got his farm paid off. Then he said, "I've had enough of this poker game! I'm getting out!" And Grandpa sold out his half of the company to Herb Roller, the friendly salesman from the Miami Portland Cement Company.

Clarence and Florence Whetstone had done the farming and lived in Grandpa's house while they were in North Carolina. When Grandma and Dad returned, the Whetstones found another place to live, but they continued to farm until Grandpa sold the company. By then my mother had died and Dad, Don and I were living with Grandma and Grandpa. They were happy to be out of the business, and after several years of being separated for months at a time, they were even more happy to be back together in their own home. Grandpa and Dad returned to farming in the mid-1930s.

What happened to the company? After Franklin Roosevelt was elected as President of the United States, he developed the Rural Electrification Act (REA), which helped finance the construction of electric lines in rural areas. By now the company was called the Davis-Hydaker Company, and they saw the potential in building REA power lines, erecting some of the first ones in this area. Bill remembers the day his family got power lines installed in June of 1937. One of the young men who had worked for Grandpa and had made the trip to North Carolina and back, Floyd Crow, was now married and working on the REA installations. His fellow workers were teasing him because he had just become a new father—of a set of TRIPLETS! When I was nine or ten years old, our family went to Spencerville to visit the Crows. The triplets, Dana Lee, Dianna Bee, and Darling C., were a couple years old and into everything. I wasn't used to being around little children, and my goodness, there seemed to be babies everywhere I looked.

When the power lines were about all installed in Ohio, the Davis-Hydaker Company moved to Michigan where they were quite successful and became big-time operators. Davis eventually sold out to George Hydaker and he took a new partner by the name of Wheatlake. The Hydakers owned a big home on Birt Lake near Camp Modock where my brother's in-laws, Corinne and Rob Mitchell, went for an occasional fishing vacation. Mr.

Wheatlake finally purchased the Hydakers' home on the lake and the company which continues to build power lines in the Michigan area. This 1990s company got its humble beginnings before the 1920s with Grandpa and Charlie Davis "piking" the mud roads back in the Kossuth area. Quite a story!

---

[1] *Webster's Collegiate Dictionary,* G.C. Merriam Co., 1948, p.1023

Top: Pouring concrete for a road in Marietta, Ohio, June 25, 1927
Bottom: Finishing a 42-foot wide continuous poured concrete street in Bessemer City, North Carolina, in 1922

More pictures from the Davis & Davenport road building company

## Chapter 11.
# Davenport the Ditcher

"Davenport the Ditcher." That was the name printed on the front of the ditching machine Dad used when putting drainage tile into the farmers' fields and that's the name by which many people knew him. But Dad was also a great music lover. Fritz Kreisler, Jascha Heifetz, Yehudi Menuhin–all well-known violinists of which Dad often spoke. These were his idols in the music field. Dad gave his children an inheritance that money can't buy–the love of classical music. Grandpa had been a "fiddler" and loved down-home country music, but Dad was a "classical" violinist, having taken lessons from Ted Eisenbach, an excellent teacher from Spencerville. He was active in several ensembles, starting with the Blume High School orchestra in Wapakoneta. According to Henry Moser, a fellow violinist who sat beside Dad, he was very good, far better than any of the other players. When I met Mr. Moser at a genealogy meeting, he was thrilled to know I was Bernard's daughter. For several minutes he told me how, seventy years earlier, he had enjoyed playing violin beside Dad in the Blume orchestra. "But I wasn't nearly as good as your dad," he said. "None of us were. Bernard was a professional."

Dad eventually took lessons from Mathilda Helmstetter from St. Marys. After his lesson, one of the Helmstetter girls, all maiden ladies, would say, "We've got a new piece here. We want you to try it." The other sisters joined in, and they all played together, Mathilda and Dad on the violin, Agnes on the viola, and Maya on piano. Those gals loved to play, and so did Dad. They would make music together all afternoon. When Dad and Mother were married a short time later, Agnes played the violin at their wedding. Maya eventually became my piano teacher.

The Helmstetter sisters entertained troops overseas during World War I. After the Great Depression, President Roosevelt started the Works Progress Administration (WPA) program to give people jobs. This program sponsored musical groups, including a Kossuth orchestra with the Helmstetter girls in charge. Some of Dad's music had WPA printed on it. He no doubt participated in the program reported in a 1936 *Wapakoneta Daily News*:

> Postponed Minstrel Will be Presented at Kossuth Friday. The Kossuth WPA Emergency Singing Group, under direction of Maya Helmstetter of St. Marys is to present the Witmark Minstrel in the Kossuth Grange Hall Friday evening. The minstrel was postponed due to severe weather, several weeks ago. Forty persons make up the Kossuth WPA singing group. No admission charge is to be made, H.H. McPheron, county WPA emergency school supervisor said, but a collection will be taken.[1]

A log house on the Shaeffer farm two miles from Kossuth was the birthplace of Bernard Davenport. The log house was deserted after the Shaeffers built a new house. Grandpa lived a half mile south and was hunting a place to live so he could marry Nora Schwartz from north of Kossuth. He went to Mr. Shaeffer and told him he wanted to get married and needed a house. Could he rent the old log house? The roof was falling in, and the house needed a lot of work, but Grandpa said he would put on a new roof and fix up the house to make it livable. Mr. Shaeffer agreed to let him have it rent free if he wanted to do that. As a result, Grandpa split the shakes for the new roof, repaired any other bad areas, and hand-hewed a picket fence for around the yard.

The earliest memento of Dad is a picture of the log house with him standing in a baby buggy in the front yard. He told us of waking up many times as a child with a light misting of snow on his blankets. It had sifted through under the eaves and around the chinks in the logs of that old house.

The family later moved from the little log house to a larger home on the west edge of Glynwood. Eventually, with some help from his father-in-law, Henry Schwartz, Grandpa bought the farm next to their first log house. They lived for a while in what was called a "pump shack," a small house used by a man who stopped regularly to pump the oil wells in the area. When the new modern house was built about 1918, the pump shack became a part of Grandpa's chicken house.

What did Dad do as a child? He accompanied his parents to many of the parties held by their friends every week or so. Bernard's name, along with a few cousins and neighbor kids, was usually in the newspaper lists of those attending. Like most children, he visited his grandparents. A March 30, 1911, *Auglaize County Republican,* Sodom item says: "Bernard Davenport spent Sunday with his grandparents, Mr. and Mrs. Henry Swartz." Dad was eleven.

Like his father before him, Dad walked a little over a mile to Sodom School east of their home. Although they were no longer called "Sodom Indians," there was still mischief going on, and Dad did his share. I remember hearing something about an outhouse being tipped over with the teacher still inside.

There were also other accounts of the family's activities. On September 3, 1914, the *Auglaize County Democrat* says, "Mr. and Mrs. Frank Davenport and son, Bernard, visited Sam Longworth at St. Marys Sunday," and in the same issue, "Bernard Davenport returned home last Wednesday after a few days' visit with relatives in Lima." (His Aunt Tillie and Uncle Ed Thiesing and their children, Homer, Edna and Doris. He was fourteen years old.)

A large stone monument at Ft. Amanda Park was to be dedicated July 5, 1915. At the age of fifteen, Dad was chosen to represent all the Auglaize County school children by reciting the Gettysburg Address. To prepare for the occasion, he took elocution lessons from his violin teacher's sister, Miss Ella Eisenbach. Grandpa and Grandma often spoke of the good job he had done, and after having heard the story so many times, I recently checked several local newspapers for a full account of the festivities. The official program with its list of distinguished speakers had been published in area papers. Mention was made of the 1,000 or so people who attended and of the hundreds of cars and buggies that filled the surrounding fields; but not one single word was said about Daddy and his eloquent recital of the Gettysburg Address.

Bernard was four years old when the Wright Brothers flew their first airplane at Kittyhawk. As a teenager he built a model plane that attracted a lot of attention at the

Auglaize County Fair. Later, he had his first ride in a Jenny, a plane that helped win the first World War. When he was more than eighty years old, his last plane ride was to Florida and back in a jet liner.

After Dad finished the eighth grade at Sodom School, he spent the next three years at Spencerville High School. He probably chose this school because he could stay in town for his violin lessons.

Since this was during World War I, the school playground was used for activities other than just playing. Dad told of sitting in class and hearing the commands of the young men as they practiced military drills on the playground outside. Dad was actively practicing, too, but he practiced for sports. He was one of the biggest guys on the Spencerville football team. In about 1917, one particular scrimmage game remained special in his mind, and we loved to hear him tell about it. Spencerville was quite small compared to the big Lima city school. Spencerville's team was composed primarily of hardworking country boys who enjoyed the fun of football. Their uniforms were plain and quite old, but Lima had fancy new uniforms. It had rained hard before the game, and the field soon became a muddy mess. That didn't bother the Spencerville guys. They tackled and slipped and slid through that mud without a thought of their appearance. But those poor Lima guys didn't want to get those fancy new uniforms dirty. They got skunked by Dad's small-town football team.

Dad transferred to Wapakoneta Blume High School for his fourth year and graduated in 1919. He may have chosen Blume School because of its fine orchestra. Dad drove his Ford to school each day, picking up three young ladies along the way: Sodom School classmates Vida Richardson and Riva Bowersock and Buckland resident, Llewena Marsh. All four young people entered Blume for their senior year. Since Buckland had no four-year high school at the time, the girls chose to attend Wapak for the additional year of education because all three wanted to be school teachers.

Dad's yearbook, *The Retrospect*, shows the following quote under his picture: "Bernard Davenport, 'The power that rises higher than our heads.' Orchestra. This fellow sought Blume High last fall in a Ford. He has been a splendid pupil and has always remained firm to his ideas. He had portrayed his likes and dislikes to a great extent on the question of labor strikes." Like Spencerville, Blume also had boys learning military drills. With Sinon McCarty, a senior, in charge, they met for one hour every other evening. The local newspaper stated, "There came that memorable eleventh of November. The commander of the Blume High School army came to the parade ground in the evening of that day and found it entirely destitute of soldiers. The so-called soldiers were marching down Blackhoof street, yelling and howling at the top of their voices, 'The war is over! We don't want any more training!' The commander reluctantly turned away, utterly at a loss what to do at this wholesale and flagrant desertion." [2]

After graduating, Dad went to work at the Lima Locomotive Works, living for a time with his Aunt Tillie and Uncle Ed. His first job was running a radial drill most of the time, then he later moved to the assembly line. The locomotives were put together on the assembly floor in the main erecting shop. He worked in that area for three or four winters when he couldn't do farm work. Years later, his son worked in the same area of the Lima Locomotive works.

A flu epidemic closed the schools when Dad was sixteen years old, so he helped a man operate a ditching machine. He enjoyed the work and purchased the machine. He ran it long enough to finish a job on the farm that eventually became the old Wapak Airport where Astronaut Neil Armstrong, first man on the moon, learned to fly. Dad had to rebuild the ditcher's single-cylinder engine before he could work again. He put in ditches along the sides of some of the roads built by the Davis-Davenport Construction Company which was co-owned by his dad. When they were awarded the bid in 1922 to build the first concrete streets in Bessemer City, North Carolina, Dad drove a truck down and worked with them.

Dad's days were spent on the job, but many of his evenings were occupied in the local motion picture theater where he played classical violin music as a background for changing silent movie film rolls. Not only did he earn a little extra cash, he saw all the films free of charge and became quite a popular gentleman with the young ladies of the town. One, Eugenia Gerth, stayed in touch and years later accompanied friends whom my family knew in North Carolina as they drove to Ohio for a visit. Even then, when both had lost their mates and were senior citizens, she said she would have married Dad if he'd asked.

While Dad was in North Carolina, a circus came to town and some of the people did some car trading in Bessemer City. One car was a twelve-cylinder Premier which Dad bought and drove back to Ohio. It had a big engine and was so long he could get only the front end into the garage. It ran like crazy, going eighty or ninety miles an hour–*really fast* for that time. Dad laughed as he said it would pass everything on the road but a gasoline station! It was a "gas hog" and he didn't keep it long. He eventually traded it off and bought a new Model T Ford.

When Dad and Grandma returned to Ohio, Dad called Minnie Graessle, a young lady he had known before they left, and asked her for a date. Minnie's shocked reply had been, "Oh, Bernard, I can't! I'm getting married tomorrow!" She said she hadn't heard from him while he was in North Carolina and assumed the flames of romance had died, so she married someone else. (Minnie told me this fifty years later when both spouses had died, and she and Dad had married each other.)

When I was a child, Dad practiced his violin in the evenings, especially for special events when he played solos at church programs, Farmer's Institutes, Grange and community meetings. He was also a member of the Kossuth area trio: Dad on violin, Danny Graessle on flute and Iva Grassley on piano. I had accepted Dad's music as just a part of my life when I was a child, but after seeing the difficulty of those classical violin solos he played, I appreciate even more the talent he had.

When his grandpa John Wesley Davenport died, Dad purchased his farm. The October 7, 1926, *Wapakoneta Daily News* told of two Kossuth boys, ages 18 and 16, who had stolen eight sacks full of chickens from Arthur Craft. He reported it and officers found the chickens hidden in an old shed on the untenanted Davenport farm. Officers stationed themselves nearby and waited for the thieves to come for their loot. Then they were arrested. Seventy years later, as I sat in my brother's living room and read this to him, he burst out laughing and said, "Oh, yes, I remember Dad talking about that." He then told me this story.

At one time there had been eight oil wells in the immediate area of John Wesley's farm. A man came out, usually from the Buckland area, and pumped those wells. Since this required quite a bit of time, the pumper often stayed overnight in a nearby pump shack. When Dad bought the farm, he moved this shack to the barnyard, and it became his shop. (As a child I had often wondered why large strips of wallpaper were still visible on the walls and ceiling of Dad's shop. It had been the pumper's occasional overnight home.)

Chickens had been stolen, not only from Dad's first cousin, Arthur Craft, but also from others in the neighborhood. One day Dad discovered the chickens in his building and reported it. Since he was an ambitious young man, he decided to try to catch the thieves himself. Dad carried a gun with him one night to a hiding place near the pump shack. As he waited for the thieves to show up, he heard a noise nearby. With gun drawn, he emerged from his hiding place and yelled for the thieves to stop where they were because he had a gun. To his surprise, it was not the chicken thieves at all. It was the county sheriff's men who also had guns drawn. They told Dad it was a good thing he made himself known immediately. When they heard him moving in the shadows, they assumed it was the thieves. But the story ended well. As we read in the paper, the neighborhood chicken thieves were eventually caught, and Dad gave up playing Sherlock Holmes.

Since there was only the old log house on Dad's newly purchased farm, he and Mother lived with his parents, Frank and Nora Davenport for the first year or so of their marriage. It was in Grandpa and Grandma's house that my brother, Donald Eugene, was born.

Dad purchased a house in Buckland that had quite a story behind it. Either Buckland was going to have to expand their two-year high school to four years, or their students would have to attend schools in Wapakoneta or St. Marys. The issue was put on the ballot in the fall of 1926 and approved. A house, standing on the site, had to be moved before the school building could be constructed. Dad purchased this house, and after digging the cellar drain, he hitched the house to the back of his ditching machine and pulled it home. I have simplified the event considerably, but he actually used a very ingenious method of moving it. The house was placed on telephone poles which rolled on the road under it. As Dad pulled it with the ditcher, the poles moved it slowly down the road. When the back pole rolled free, it was brought to the front each time and the strange procession rolled its way out of Buckland and west on Route 197 to a spot near the Lewis Bowersock farm. There it bridged a creek and proceeded across the fields to Dad's farm. It must have been quite a sight! Folks probably stood in yards along the six-mile route and watched the house roll slowly by.

By the time I came along three years later, this house had been fixed up and it was there that I made my first appearance. The Great Depression was in full swing and everything seemed to fall apart for Dad. Mother never regained her strength and Dad was eventually left with two little children and lots of bills—bills from the hospital and doctors, bills from Hoge Lumber in New Knoxville and Plikerd's Hardware in Spencerville for materials used to fix up the house, and bills from Collins Furniture Store in Spencerville for the furniture. Mr. Collins was very sympathetic and took back the furniture that was still new. In an ordinary year, Dad's ditching jobs would have paid these bills, but with the depression, farmers didn't have money to pay for ditching, so Dad's income nearly ended for a few years. He went back to his parent's home where three-year-old Don and the seven-month-old baby, (me), grew up.

When I was about two years old, I had a rather strange idea. Dad was ditching quite a distance from home and was not going to get back for several weeks. Since I was quite small, they didn't want me to forget my daddy. Dad's nearly life-sized graduation picture in a large oval frame hung on the wall. My grandparents often lifted me up and showed me the picture and said, "That is your daddy!" They had me so convinced that weeks later when Dad finally got home, I wouldn't have anything to do with him. They held me up to him and said, "This is your daddy!" But no one was going to fool me! Shaking my head, I pointed to the picture on the wall and said, "No! That's MY daddy!"

Dad was a hardworking man, and even in the toughest of times, he always managed to find a job. During the depression he worked for the Launders Construction Company as foreman for the hand-ditching crew as they worked on Lima's West Street Road job.

As my brother grew older, he worked with Dad in his farm drainage business. It was then he got to hear the rest of the story. All of Dad's creditors agreed to settle for a certain amount. Dad paid that as soon as he got a Federal Land Bank loan on his forty-acre farm. In order to complete this payment, he needed a few more dollars. Don offered his daddy what little money he had saved in his bank account. Those few dollars were enough to complete the payment to Dad's creditors. That made a deep impression on Don, and he says it may explain why he has been very frugal all of his life.

When Dad negotiated the settlement with his creditors, he promised that when he was able, he would pay each one of them the remaining amount with interest. That is exactly what he did! Several years later, Don was working with Dad as he did some ditching for Wes Plikerd. When the job was finished, Wes asked how much he owed Dad for his work. Dad said, "You don't owe me anything!" and he handed Wes an itemized bill that included all the interest Dad owed. He marked it paid and handed it to Wes. Mr. Plikerd was overwhelmed. He said he hadn't expected to get his money, but Dad kept his word.

Although hard times took their toll on many men, my dad did not crumble in defeat. He had always gone to church, and he continued to put his faith in the Lord. He was still a young man and he didn't dwell on the hardships that had come his way, but with the Lord's help and my grandparents' support, he just kept plugging away until he had triumphed over the adversities.

In October 1933, the First National Bank of St. Marys, Ohio, was robbed by members of the notorious John Dillinger Gang. One of his men was caught two years later and put in the Allen County jail in Lima. The gang planned his escape, and in the process, Jess Sarber, Allen County sheriff, was shot and killed by the daring gang. Everyone in the area was quite nervous for several weeks since one of the gang, a man named Makley, was from St. Marys. Was the gang hiding out in this area? One night Grandma woke up and noticed a light in our garage. She woke Dad and Grandpa. They quickly slipped into their clothes, grabbed their shotguns, and walked through the back yard to investigate. Were the Dillingers about to use one of *our* cars as the getaway car for their next crime spree? No, not quite! A faulty switch had turned on the car's lights. Thank goodness, it was not the Dillingers because I was four years old and had followed Dad and Grandpa outside. As they investigated, I stood shivering, brave but scared silly, in the middle of our dark back yard.

Dad was usually in good health, but I vividly recall one time in the mid 1930s when everyone was quite concerned about him. He was ditching for a family near Waynesfield. Since it was a long way to travel back and forth from home each day, he usually stayed with the family during the week. One night our phone rang in the wee hours, an unusual occurrence that usually meant something was wrong. The family in Waynesfield called to inform us Dad was deathly sick. Grandma told them she and Grandpa would come as quickly as they could. Just then our good neighbor, Helen Mack, broke into the phone conversation, "Nora, bring the children down here. I'll take care of them while you're gone." Bless her heart, Helen knew that two longs and a short ring on the party line in the wee hours meant the Davenports had a serious problem. She was eager to help if she could. How grateful Grandma was!

We later heard the rest of Dad's story. The housewife had served sauerkraut and wieners for dinner. Since they had no refrigerator, the leftovers were set in the cupboard, still in the aluminum pan. The food was warmed over for supper, and Dad had gotten ptomaine poisoning from it. Although others had also eaten it, only Dad became ill. After supper, he went out and sat down under a tree. When it got dark, and he hadn't come in, they went to hunt him. Finding him in that condition, they called the doctor at once. He was much too sick to move, even to a hospital and for several days they took care of Dad in their home. When he was finally able to return home, he was blind, crippled and walked with a cane. It was a scary time for us children. We had to be as quiet as possible so Daddy could rest. He eventually recovered fully, but he never cared much for sauerkraut and wieners after that. I understand why!

Dad enjoyed singing. He and Grandpa joined several other Kossuth men to sing in the Spencerville Men's Chorus sponsored by the Methodist Church. This group sang for many church and social functions in the Spencerville area. Although I was still quite small, I really enjoyed hearing men sing. (I never lost that enthusiasm. During my college days, I enjoyed the men's Fraternity Sing a lot more than the girls' Sorority Sing.)

Another of Dad's musical groups was the Kossuth Men's Quartette. This group was made up of Fred Graessle (high tenor), Carl Seewer (lead tenor), Dad (baritone), and Bob Henne (bass). They sounded quite good for amateurs and everyone loved hearing them at church and community events. I especially enjoyed hearing Bob with his really low bass voice. Little did I know then that someday I would marry a low bass.

It was almost Christmas of 1936. Don and I were to be in the school program, but I had pneumonia. In late afternoon of program day, Dad was rushing to the doctor's office in Spencerville to get medicine for me. At the north edge of Kossuth, his car hit a patch of ice and slid onto the canal bank beside the road. As the car teetered precariously on the edge, Dad carefully climbed out, trying not to tip it on over into the water. He walked back into Kossuth to call Grandpa who picked him up and drove to Spencerville for the medicine. We were sure Don would miss the program, but they got back just in time for Dad to drive Grandpa's car to the school. Dad's car was rescued with little damage, but I always gazed in awe at that spot where Dad almost dumped his car into the canal.

Dad wanted his children to enjoy music as much as he did. When Don was six years old, Dad bought him a junior size violin and gave him lessons. Don later studied with Miss Vivian Arnold in Wapakoneta. At the age of eight, I began accordion lessons at the new Wurlitzer studio in St. Marys.

As we improved on our instruments, Dad purchased trio music and we joined him in a group he named the *Davenettes,* little Davenports. We could tell by the way Dad introduced us to people that he was really pleased with our accomplishments, especially our music. Don went on to play the flute in the Buckland High School Band, while I was the pianist for many school activities. Dad also encouraged both of us to learn how to type. He always used the "hunt-and-peck" system. I'm glad I can type the right way.

One of our favorite childhood radio programs was *Jack Armstrong, The All American Boy*. It came on soon after we got off the school bus. For some reason, perhaps as punishment, I was not allowed to listen to that program one week. It was always very exciting, but we had to listen every day to keep up with the story. I figured out a way to circumvent the problem. I sneaked out to the garage, and since Dad's Plymouth had a radio, (Grandpa's Nash didn't), I turned the key and played the radio long enough to hear my program. After a couple of days of this, Dad had to go to a meeting, and for some unknown reason, his car wouldn't start. The battery seemed to be dead! How could such a thing have happened? Did I ever confess, you may ask? Yep, I told my brother last week! (A little bit late, huh?)

When World War II began, Dad was asked to do his patriotic duty as a member of the Auglaize County rationing board. Rationing was used to save needed items for the military. This involved regular trips to ration board meetings in Wapak when they looked over requests from folks needing new tires, more sugar for canning, additional gasoline for trips to the doctor, or whatever their needs might be. Since supplies of these items were very limited, the board looked at each request and supplied the needs of as many as possible. Dad was selected for the tire board, along with Colby Pepple, a man who became his good friend. There were many nights when people actually came to our house to see Dad and to plead with him for help in getting new tires so they could drive to the doctor or to visit distant relatives. He was only one of the committee, and although he tried to be as impartial as he could, he always felt bad when he had to tell them he could do nothing to help them. All they could do was add more patches to the inner tubes or put a "boot" in the tire. A boot was a piece of old inner tube or tire that was placed inside the tire casing to prevent the inner tube from sticking out through the hole or slit in the tire. It was not too reliable but it usually kept them going for a few more miles.

In the 1940s, the government came up with a plan that farmers thought was crazy. Under this new plan, farmers were told to kill their little pigs, and they were not allowed to raise wheat. Now, being told what to raise and when to kill their animals was not very popular with the farmers. As a result, a group was formed to protest the government rules. They said, "We're not paying attention to Roosevelt's plan," and they raised wheat anyway. The government wouldn't let them market their wheat, so they organized a group they called the Ohio Marketing Quota Protest Association. Dad was an active member, and along with a man from near Hume, one from Attica, and others, they went to Washington, D.C., to protest the Roosevelt plan. I thought that was really something—MY dad going to Washington to tell them how to run the government! Wow!

One winter in the 1960s after Grandma had died, Dad and Grandpa decided to take a vacation. They went to North Carolina where they walked on some of the same Bessemer City streets they had built in the 1920s. They were very pleased to see that the streets had remained in excellent condition. They also visited a few people they knew when they lived there so many years before.

Florida was their next stop. After a good time visiting friends and tourist spots there, they started west for Texas and a brief stop at Longview. There they met R.G. LeTourneau, the well-known Christian man who invented the electric wheel, the huge earth movers, and many other large pieces of equipment that are used extensively today in road building, construction, and manufacturing. Because of his expertise in seeing a need and building something to fill it, Mr. LeTourneau was encouraged to share his knowledge. He started an engineering school in Longview, Texas, then informed others of his work and need for support for the task with his little magazine called *Now*. As a little boy, our son Steven heard his grandpa talk about Mr. LeTourneau. He occasionally read some of the magazine stories and was impressed with the pictures. Years later, when Steve decided to attend college, he chose LeTourneau. His first Texas Thanksgiving dinner was spent as a guest of "Mom" LeTourneau and her family. R.G. "Pop" had already gone home to be with the Lord. Eventually Steve graduated from the university with two engineering degrees. Grandpa would be proud!

As Dad grew older, he had more time to relax. He joined Don and a few Schwartz cousins for deer hunting in Pennsylvania. I wasn't sure how Dad would manage all the mountainous walking and living in a primitive hunting shack. He did quite well, and was very proud of his first deer. He had the head mounted for his office wall.

Dad's favorite hobby was working with cameras. As a young man, he had taken a picture which puzzled me. It was snapped during a solar eclipse on September 10, 1923. Fastening the camera on a tripod, Dad snapped a picture at regular intervals, thus exposing the film many times. As a result, one picture showed the process of the eclipse from a full sun to nearly complete coverage and back to full sun. In later years, he bought a movie camera, then updated it with sound. He could now take the picture and tell about the action at the same time. After he married Minnie and retired from ditching, he spent many days looking at catalogs of the latest camera equipment, updating information, editing and splicing film.

Dad never stopped being his children's number one fan. He was extremely proud of our talents, especially in music, and we were grateful for his Christian faith and for the musical inheritance he left his family. Many of the older folks still remember him as "Davenport the Ditcher."

---

[1] *Wapakoneta Daily News*, Wapakoneta, Ohio, February 26, 1936, used with permission.
[2] *The Retrospect,* Wapakoneta High School Yearbook, Wapakoneta, Ohio, 1919, used with permission.

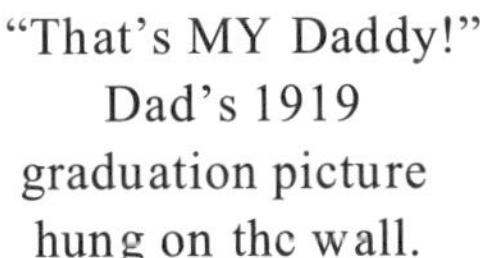
"That's MY Daddy!"
Dad's 1919
graduation picture
hung on thc wall.

Sodom School, April 20, 1906 with Dad age 6, last on right of middle row

# DAVENPORT GRANTED PATENT ON DRAIN-TILE LAYING DEVICE

Bernard Davenport of the Kossuth community informs us that he has received official notice from the United States Patent Office, Washington D. C., that on December 10, 1957 he was granted Letters Patent covering an "O. B. DAVENPORT-DRAIN TILE LAYING DEVICE."

This is a machine for installing and properly spacing drain tile in a newly excavated trench directly behind a trenching machine, thus eliminating the back-breaking task of a man having to grasp the tile off the trench bank, and bending down to a point where he can deposit it at his feet, repeating this cycle each foot the trenching machine travels.

The Pilot model of this machine which has undergone three years of testing has already saved more than one-half million such back-bending cycles, which is quite a saving of back-ache.

Mr. Davenport has also been informed by his Ottawa, Ontario representative that on December 3, 1957 his Canadian application for Patent was allowed.

Mr. Davenport who began his drainage career forty years ago this month, eventually becoming widely known as "Davenport the Ditcher", has recently joined in partnership with his son Donald under the new name of "DAVENPORT DRAINAGE SERVICE".

BERNARD DAVENPORT

When Dad's drainage tile laying invention was patented in 1958, the Spencerville (Ohio) *Journal News* made the announcement. (*Used with permission*)

## Chapter 12.

# *Until Death Do Us Part*

A New Year's Eve party with a surprise twist took place at Grandpa's house in 1925. The society column of the *Wapakoneta Daily News* gave the following account of the big event.

> Members of the Ladies Aid Society of the Kossuth M.E. Church entertained their husbands and families at a watch party Thursday evening, December 31, at the country home of Mr. and Mrs. Frank Davenport, west of town.
>
> The following program was rendered: music by trio, Miss Iva DeLong, D.B. Graessle and Bernard Davenport; reading, Mrs. D.B. Graessle; piano solo, Mrs. Sam Graessle; vocal solo, Dorothy Briggs; reading, Mrs. Sam Graessle; music by trio; address by W.R. Briggs. A number of stunts caused merriment.
>
> At 10:30 o'clock Miss Iva DeLong took her place at the piano, while Lois DeLong sang softly, *I Love You Truly*. At the strains of a wedding march, little Miss Dorothy Briggs acting as bride and Frederick Bowers as groom took their places at an altar, where the following announcement was made. "On the 8th. day of April 1926, Miss Lena Briggs will become the lawful wedded wife of Mr. Bernard Davenport." The announcement came as a surprise to their many friends.
>
> Miss Briggs is a graduate of Fort Wayne Business College and at present is employed at the McCook aviation field at Dayton, while the groom is a prosperous contractor in the western part of Auglaize County.
>
> At 11 o'clock a three-course lunch was enjoyed. At the midnight hour, as the "Old Year" passed out with his big scythe, the New Year came in with cards of greetings.[1]

Forty-seven guests were in attendance for this unusual "Wedding Announcement and New Year's Eve Party."

How did all of this start? Don worked with Dad for many years and one day he asked, "Dad, how did you meet Mother?" Did you know that doing a good deed can change your life? Mother officially met Dad when he was the Good Samaritan who stopped to rescue the lady in distress with a flat tire. As Dad drove winding old State Route 66 toward Spencerville, he noticed a car pulled off to the side of the road near Deep Cut. It obviously had a flat tire and the driver was the pretty young lady who lived a mile west on Briggs Road. Dad stopped and changed the tire for her.

Although my dad was not a knight in shining armor riding in on a white horse, he was a gentleman who had rescued the fair maiden. From this act of kindness the two became better acquainted. Their paths met more frequently after that, and eventually merged.

Thus began the romance that brought about one of the prettiest weddings the Kossuth church had seen. The Wapakoneta Daily News society column described the day.

> One of the most beautiful events of the spring season was the marriage of Miss Lena Briggs, daughter of Mr. and Mrs. Wm. R. Briggs, to Mr. Omen Bernard Davenport, son of Mr. and Mrs. Frank Davenport, west of town, which took place at the Kossuth M.E. Church on April the eighth, nineteen hundred twenty-six, at high noon, in the presence of a large assemblage of relatives and friends to witness the ceremony. Miss Lucille Bowers sang softly *Beloved*, followed by a violin solo by Miss Agnes Helmstetter accompanied by Mrs. Bernice Skinner Baxter at the piano, after which Miss Bowers sang, *I Love You Truly*. As the hands of the clock approached the appointed hour, at the strains of Mendelssohn's Wedding March, Master Lester Schwartz proceeded up the aisle and opened the locked gate to admit the bridal party. Miss Iva DeLong and Mr. Homer Grassley, attendants, were the first to approach the altar, followed by little Misses Evelyn Leffel and Dorothy Briggs strewing flowers along the way, after which came little Miss Genevieve Rothe and Master Leonard Rothe, each bearing a ring in a white lily. Next came the bride on the arm of her father, who was met at the gate by the groom and conducted to the altar, where Rev. Metz of Spencerville proceeded, using the double ring ceremony, during which time Miss Helmstetter, Mrs. Skinner Baxter played softly a beautiful selection.
>
> The bride was prettily attired in a blue and white printed georgette over blue satin with white bandeau of orange blossoms, slippers and hose of gray, and carried a bouquet of brides roses and fernery, while the bride's attendant was attired in rose georgette over rose satin, carrying a bouquet of pink roses. The groom wore a becoming suit of gray with a white carnation in the lapel of his coat.
>
> Immediately after the ceremony a three course luncheon was served to the immediate families at the home of the bride's parents. Miss Helmstetter and Mrs. Baxter rendered several beautiful selections, during the lunch hour. Mr. and Mrs. Davenport left on their honeymoon trip by motor to Washington D.C., Gettysburg and other places of interest in the east. The bride's traveling suit was of gray poiret twill. The bride is a graduate of the Ft. Wayne Business College of Fort Wayne, Ind. and has recently been employed at the McCook aviation field at Dayton, while the groom is a graduate of Blume High, and a prosperous contractor in the northwest part of Auglaize County. Mr. and Mrs. Davenport will reside on the groom's farm in Logan Township. [2]

This wedding was the biggest social event around Kossuth and was indeed "the talk of the town," said Retha Rohrbach, a Briggs neighbor. Grandma explained that several ideas had come from an elegant wedding they had attended while in North Carolina: opening a gate at the front of the church as the bride approached, carrying the rings in lilies, and including several children.

At the conclusion of the festivities, Dad and Mother climbed into Dad's Model T Ford coupe and departed for Washington, D.C. Honeymoon pictures included the Gettysburg battlegrounds in Pennsylvania. Lena's grandfather had been a member of the cavalry during the Civil War, so she would have been interested in the Civil War battlefield. There were also pictures of the Capitol Building taken from atop Washington's Monument, a nice one of the White House, and several of Mt. Vernon.

I'm sure it must have been fun for my grandparents as they helped Dad and Mother with their wedding plans. The event was such a contrast to Grandpa and Grandma's wedding day. Grandpa hitched up the horse and buggy, and they drove into Wapakoneta where they got their license at the Courthouse. After waiting the three days required by law, they again hitched up the buggy and stopped to pick up two friends on their way to Kossuth to see Thomas J. Barnett, Justice of the Peace. He read the vows, they drove home, and that was it! They were married! But the simple ceremony "took." A July 30, 1914, *Auglaize County Democrat* mentioned a party at Grandpa and Grandma's house as thirty-one friends and relatives helped celebrate their sixteenth anniversary with a musical program and a three-course lunch.

A Troy, Ohio, picture was taken on their thirtieth anniversary—July 24, 1928. Grandpa was working on a road job and Grandma said she was surprised the picture turned out at all, since she said, "I had a really bad sick-headache that day."

On July 24, 1948, Frank and Nora celebrated their fiftieth wedding anniversary with an open house at their home near Kossuth. Seven years later the family gathered for their 57th anniversary at Lyman's Restaurant in Wapakoneta. Also celebrating his first birthday was our Michael Allen, their first great-grandson. It was quite a day, and that little boy knew how to dive into a birthday cake. The waitresses stood by and smiled, while other patrons stopped eating to watch the fun. He definitely became the focal point.

My grandparents' longtime marriage ended July 11, 1961, when Grandma died thirteen days before their sixty-fourth anniversary. Dad and Mother never had the chance to enjoy many years of life together. After only four years, the following appeared in the *Wapakoneta Daily News*: November 23, 1930, Spencerville item:

> Mrs. Lena Davenport, 25, wife of Bernard Davenport, died in Lima City Hospital at 6:30 a.m. Sunday. Surviving are the husband; two small children, Donald Eugene and Glenna May; her parents, Mr. and Mrs. William Briggs, of near Spencerville; four brothers, Leon, of Denison; Leo, of Van Wert; Marion of New Bremen; Ray [should have been Roy] of Toledo; and one sister, Dorothea Briggs, of near Spencerville. Services will be held at 2 p.m. Tuesday in the Kossuth Zion M.E. Church. The Rev. Robert Herrier will be in charge. Burial will be made in the Kossuth cemetery.[3]

As a child I had dug into the old wooden trunk in my room and found a blue and white georgette flower. I had never seen a fabric rose, and when I showed it to Grandma, she explained that it had adorned Mother's wedding dress. Also in the trunk was the picture taken on that special day with Mother and Dad in their wedding finery. Dad was sitting proudly as Mother stood beside him, holding her arm bouquet and smiling sweetly. I treasure that picture. It is still carefully packed away in Grandpa's trunk.

---

[1] "Society Column," *Wapakoneta Daily News*, Wapakoneta, Ohio, January 2, 1925, used with permission.
[2] "Society Column," *Wapakoneta Daily News,* Wapakoneta, Ohio, April 10, 1926, used with permission.
[3] "Obituary," *Wapakoneta Daily News*, Wapakoneta, Ohio, November 23, 1930, used with permission.

Dad and Mother's wedding day, April 8, 1926

The Briggs-Davenport Wedding Party

First row: flower girls Evalyn Leffel and Dorothea Briggs. Second row: violinist Agnes Helmstetter, pianist Bernice Skinner Baxter, receptionist Lucille Bowers, bride Lena Briggs, groom Bernard Davenport, maid of honor Iva DeLong, best man Homer Grassley. Third row: Pastor Rev. and Mrs. H.S. Metz. Fourth row: receptionist Lois DeLong, and W.R. Briggs, father of the bride.

## Chapter 13.

# *"My Mama is an Angel"*

Everyone who knew my mother loved her—family, friends, neighbors, school chums, teachers, and most of all, my dad and grandparents. Lena Edith Sophia Briggs was born to a farmer/schoolteacher, William Roscoe Briggs, and his German-born wife, Charlotta, whom he called Lottie.

Iva DeLong, one of Mother's best friends, lived a mile or so east of the Miami-Erie Canal and Lena's home was about a mile west of it. The girls were the same age, both had a parent who was a schoolteacher, and both were in the same class at the Deep Cut one-room school taught by Iva's mother, Eva (my grandma's sister). Lena's father, Will Briggs, graduated from Defiance College, then taught in one-room schools. He also taught at the two-room school in Kossuth and at Spencerville junior high school for three years.

What kind of person was my mother? I never had the joy of knowing her, since she died when I was only seven months old. From what I have been told, I know I would have loved her dearly. She was vibrant, alive, full of fun and well-liked by everyone.

What were my feelings about not having a mother? When I was quite young, I didn't realize our family was different from others. When Dad and my grandparents attended our special programs at school, the other little boys and girls began to notice that we didn't have a mother and if anyone mentioned it to me, I always replied, "My mama is an angel." I knew she had died and was with Jesus. Since I had heard of angels being with Him, I assumed she was now an angel. Sometimes I felt cheated because I didn't have a mother like the other kids, but my caring family was so closely knit that I always felt quite secure and loved. In fact, my childhood seemed to be just one step away from perfection.

During the days of World War I, three of Mother's four brothers were stationed in the same army camp and fought in the same battles in France. I'm sure she must have written numerous letters to those big brothers. One of the special treasures carefully tucked away in a box in the old trunk was the beautiful, sheer pink apron which those soldier brothers brought back from the war as a gift for their young sister, Lena.

Mother had pasted numerous unmarked clippings from the Spencerville *Journal-News* into her scrapbook. They told of various parties, school functions, community and church activities in which she was a participant. She and Iva, both now sixteen years old, provided music between the acts of a 1921 school play and also participated in other productions.

Lena and Bernard were both in attendance at the Salem-Logan Township Sunday School Convention on May 27, 1923. A Convention program found in Lena's scrapbook showed that Dad had played his violin in a solo, in a duet, and in the Salem orchestra.

"Stereoptic" pictures of the Philippines were shown by Bert DeLong who been a soldier in the Spanish American War. He was Aunt Eva's husband and the father of Lena's best friend, Iva.

In relating the history of Mother's 1923 Spencerville High School senior class, the local paper gave numerous details. Mother was one of those reported: "Lena Edith Sophia Briggs was born in Auglaize County, April 5, 1905. She is five feet and six inches tall, and weighs 134 pounds. Lena is the jolliest of all our girls, always furnishing some little remark for us to laugh about. Lena is known as the belle of Kossuth and judging from the many changes made in her escorts she keeps the boys constantly asking the question 'Whose turn next?'"[1] I was rather surprised when I saw the class descriptions with their weights printed for all to see. How embarrassing that must have been for one of Lena's friends, who was always "pleasingly plump." The class proverbs said–Lena Briggs, "Smile and the world smiles with you." A few of her friends who are elderly now said that was indeed true. She was a happy person and smiled a lot.

After graduation, Lena attended Business School in Ft. Wayne, Indiana, then got a job as a clerk typist in the Engineering Division of the War Department at McCook Aviation Field in Dayton, Ohio. Her salary was $1140 per annum.

According to official government papers, Mother's resignation to the Secretary of War in Washington, D.C., was submitted on March 17, 1926. After three days, she hurried home to prepare for her wedding two and a half weeks later. Within a year, everything from McCook Field was transferred to a larger area which became quite well known. I'm sure you've heard of it—Wright Patterson Air Force Base, Dayton, Ohio.

Lena's dad asked her to wait with marriage until she was twenty-one years old. She was obedient and on her birthday, she and Dad drove to the county seat to apply for a marriage license. After the three-day waiting period, they were married on April 8, 1926. (Her little sister ignored their dad's rule and got married as a teenager.)

Dad and Mother lived a year or more with his parents, Frank and Nora Davenport. They both told me they had dearly loved my mother. She was such a very sweet person and so easy to love. The next spring after they were married, Grandma noticed that as they prepared the meals together, Mother frequently made a sudden dash outside for a few minutes. Dad and Mother finally told Grandpa and Grandma that a baby was on the way. Years later, as Grandma told me the story, she smiled and said, "I knew that was the problem, but I certainly wasn't going to say anything to spoil their surprise."

That baby was my brother, Don, who was born on August 26, 1927, at Grandpa's house. In a 1997 conversation with Evalyn (Leffel) Sandkuhl, she remembered a car had stalled that day on the big curve on Route 66 north of Kossuth. She was about nine years old and noticed the car as she was looking out the window. While she continued to watch, a Ford car had raced past their house, stopped at the stranded car, picked up a lady, then turned around and came back. My dad was the driver. The stranded car, driven by Grandpa's young half-brother, Homer, was bringing his mother, Nellie Davenport, out to assist in the birth. By the next day the news was spreading that the Davenports had a new baby boy, Donald Eugene.

A few years later, Mother was shopping in Spencerville when she met an old friend, Fern Miller, who had just had a new baby boy. As the two young mothers admired the new baby, Mother asked what they had named their son. Fern said, "We chose a name that we have never heard used before. We call him Donald Eugene." Mother burst out laughing and said, "You're looking at one. That's what we named our boy." The two friends enjoyed a laugh over that. Strange as it may seem, Donald Eugene Davenport married Donald Eugene Miller's first cousin, Mary Mitchell.

Sometime after Don's birth, Dad and Mother moved into the home Dad had purchased in Buckland and moved to the land he had bought from the estate of his grandpa, John Wesley Davenport. It was that house in which I was born. It eventually passed to John's great-grandson Don, and is now occupied by his great-great-grandson, Roger Davenport and his family.

After my birth, a young lady from Kossuth, Luella Mees, came to help Mother for the first few weeks. I spent a delightful afternoon with 84-year-old Luella (Mees) Lenhart in 1996. Her mind was really sharp. She was happy to see me and as I left, she said, "Now you come back. We could talk all night!"

Luella and her sister, Janie (Mees) Leffel, had both worked "baby cases." Babies were born at home then, and most families had a hired girl during that time. Luella said they would stay two or three weeks at a time. (At one time a doctor in Spencerville had kept Janie so busy that during the summer, her own son, Bob, often stayed with his Aunt Luella and Uncle Bob Lenhart.) My family had known the Mees family for many years. Fred Mees had at one time worked for my great-grandpa Schwartz, and my family knew the girls were hard workers. Luella was eighteen years old, out of high school and not yet married, when she came to work for a month after my birth. She helped to take care of the three-year-old big brother and the new baby whom they had named Glenna Mae. That's me! I was named Glenna after Mother's friend from the airfield. Mother's aunt and a Kossuth friend were named Mae.

While she worked at Dad's, Luella cooked the meals, did the laundry, kept the house clean and took care of us children. As Luella and I talked, she said, "Oh, I gave you a bottle and changed your diapers many times." That thought brought a hearty laugh from both of us mature ladies as we talked and shared stories together.

During her time with Mother, Luella and Lena had gotten along really well. "Oh," she said, "your Mother was a really wonderful person! We just got along great!" One day when Mother was feeling really good, she said, "Let's have a picnic!" Luella fixed a lunch and brought down a blanket, then they walked over to the woods across the road from Dad's house. While Don played, they placed the blanket on the ground and placed me on it. Then Mother, Luella and Don sat down and ate dinner amid the sounds of birds and the sweet springtime aroma of the woods. She said they had enjoyed it immensely.

One day they had gone to a circus near Celina. Luella didn't remember much about it except that they had elephants and other animals. They were surprised to see a neighbor, Martin Hager, with his sons, Norman and Maurice. Years later, these boys and Don and I were in the same Sunday school class and other community activities.

Luella said Mother was very good at playing the piano. I have numerous pieces of sheet music which had belonged to her. I practiced until I was finally able to play them.

After Mother began to get her strength back, Luella was no longer needed and returned home. Later that summer, though, Mother's condition worsened and she wasn't able to care for a baby and three-year-old. She had to have help again. Luella was not available at that time, and an older lady was hired. She was "set in her ways" and was not handling an active little boy and baby as my family wished. As soon as Luella was available, she returned, and the older lady was asked to leave. Everyone was glad to have Luella back, and she was pleased to come because she and Lena had gotten along so well.

In spite of the love and good care Mother received from family and friends, her health continued to deteriorate. When nothing seemed to be helping, the doctor ordered surgery at the Lima City Hospital. The family was apparently given the idea that it was some sort of "female problem," the term used in those days when referring to anything personal. Further information was usually not given.

Grandma Davenport told me a story that I have never forgotten. She had gone to Lima to the hospital to see Mother after the surgery. Mother was quite ill that morning. As she lay quietly in the hospital bed, she listened for a while, then said to Grandma, "What a beautiful morning! Listen to the birds singing outside my window. Aren't they beautiful?" Grandma said she looked out the window and listened carefully, but there were no birds. It was six-thirty in the morning on Sunday, November 22, 1930, and Mother had just died! With tears in her eyes, Grandma shook her head sadly as she quietly said, "Why couldn't it have been me? I've lived my life. She was just starting hers!"

As news commentator Paul Harvey would say, "And now, the rest of the story." In the spring of 1949, as I was a student at Wittenberg College in Springfield, Ohio, I was not feeling well and went to the college infirmary where I received a shot of a highly acclaimed new miracle drug, penicillin. It was no miracle for me! I had an immediate allergic reaction to the "wonder drug" and spent the next two days in an infirmary bed. I was the only student there, so the nurse spent some time talking to me. When she heard my name was Davenport, she mentioned that she had taken care of a lady named Davenport when she was in nurses' training. I asked her where that had been and when she answered, "Lima, Ohio," I immediately asked what year it had been. She answered, "I was in training there in 1930." "That was my mother!" I explained, telling her what I had been told concerning Mother's death. She quickly returned to her work and we said no more about it.

The next day the nurse entered my room and gently explained, "I think there is something you should know. Someday you will get married and have children and you will worry about something happening to you." I admitted that I had indeed thought about that. She then told me the devastatingly true story that none of my family or friends had ever heard.

I was born at home with a doctor from Spencerville attending. My mother had apparently had some hemorrhaging during my birth. The doctor used a gauze packing to stop the bleeding. But when he removed it later, he didn't get all of it. After several months, gangrene had developed. By the time the surgery was performed, it was already much too late to save Mother's life. That was why the doctor had been very vague in explaining the cause of her death. He did not want the real reason known. Those in the operating room were not allowed to tell. As often happens, the doctor would bury his mistake!

But time had passed, the doctor was now dead and the hospital was no longer used. The nurse felt she had an obligation for my sake to tell me the real reason that had been kept a secret all those years.

So now you know why my knowledge of my mother is very limited. I have been told over the years that I look a lot like her and that I am very much like her in personality and talents. I've never heard an unkind word about her. I'm sure I would have loved her very much if I had only had the opportunity to know her. She influenced my life greatly. I always felt she was looking down at me from Heaven, and I didn't want to do anything that would disappoint her. Just think! Someday we shall sit in our heavenly homes and get acquainted for the very first time!

---

[1] *Journal-News*, Spencerville, Ohio, June 14, 1923, used with permission.

My dad, Bernard Davenport, proudly shows off his brand new Ford.

My mother, Lena, stands beside the car as they honeymoon in Washington, D.C.

## Chapter 14.

# *Making Do: the Depression*

I was a depression baby. Born in 1930, the year of the Great Depression, I never quite knew *why* we did what we did. Was it because of the German half of my heritage, because of the English half, or because of the depression? Many people were extremely poor during depression days and were sometimes said to be "down on their luck." In the days before government welfare, the ordinary citizens often had to "foot the bill" for surgeries or funerals of poor folks. The township trustees often used tax money to pay their bills. I remember some adults talking about a person who was in and out of the hospital with one surgery after the other. Each time the township had to pay the bill. Folks were getting a little tired of it, especially since the "patient" seemed to be in better health than some of them. Some wondered if all the hospital stays weren't just a ploy to get some sympathy and rest away from the children and responsibilities at home. President Roosevelt eventually initiated a new form of federal government assistance which folks sometimes called being "on the dole" or "on relief." We didn't hear the word "welfare" then.

Nearly all the folks in our neighborhood were farmers. Unlike their city relatives who received a weekly paycheck from their factory jobs, farmers never received paychecks. They learned to make do between the sale of the hogs and the harvesting of the crops in the fall. The only regular checks came from the sale of milk and eggs, and that wasn't much on those small family farms. Everyone did things in about the same way, so I had no idea who was poor and who wasn't.

Living on Grandpa's farm probably had the greatest influence on my family's success in making it through the depression. We always raised the garden produce and animals needed to keep us fed. As for the other things, we just made do with what we had. It was too difficult to get to town to buy something we thought we needed, but found we didn't have the money for and could get by without because we just made do! There, is that a good enough explanation?

Some people were adventurous and sought a better life elsewhere. One of Grandpa's friends went "out west." My grandparents received a post card dated July 1, 1929, from Dodge City, Kansas. "Roads sand and mostly mud," he wrote, "Working in harvest fields, move on in two weeks." It was difficult work, but at least he had food and shelter.

Nearly every farm had a large garden. Farm wives spent long hours planting and harvesting food. Most farms had a good supply of manure from barns, hog houses and chicken coops which was spread liberally on fields and gardens in the fall, so fertilizer wasn't needed. The big ears of corn and the plentiful supply of fresh vegetables grown the next year were the welcome payment. Most farmers also raised several animals to provide meat for the year. We usually killed a beef, most of which had to be canned until frozen food lockers were made available for rent in town. We also killed two hogs each year, providing some ham, bacon, and sausage.

Grandma always had a good-sized flock of chickens that supplied all the eggs we needed, as well as additional meat. After the young pullets began laying, some of the old hens whose egg production had slowed down became Grandma's source for chicken and noodles or sandwiches. The young chickens made the best fried chicken and were usually saved for Sunday dinners. We also had a variety of other meats. I remember a few times when my brother headed out to the woods and, like Daniel Boone, returned with a couple of squirrels which Grandma fried for dinner. He was a good shot. At least one time he shot some pigeons in the barn. Grandma made pigeon potpie. Grandpa and Dad did some shooting during hunting season, and the pheasants and rabbits provided a variety of fresh meat during the winter months before butchering day.

A lot of folks were poor in the depression days. What could they do when the food ran out? Why, they went to visit their relatives, that's what! Times were hard, but families were helpful! Grandpa told about his aunt who came to visit and returned to Buckland with one or two of his runt pigs which she carried home in a bucket. The pigs ate table scraps and whatever they could root for in the neighborhood until they were big enough to butcher and provide her with some meat.

Grandma found several uses for the milk from our cows. After it had gone through the cream separator, the skim milk was often given to the chickens or pigs. She sold the extra cream but saved back enough to be churned into butter and a little extra to be made into whipped cream for a special dessert. Yummy! She also made her own cottage cheese, a delicacy for which I had no appetite. Ugh!

We usually made our own butter. I spent many hours turning the crank on our glass butter churn. Eventually Grandma gave up making the butter and bought the newfangled oleomargarine. Although the first "oleo" that was sold was supposed to be better for you, it came in a pale white color. People who were used to rich, yellow butter found this pale new product very unappetizing. The dairy farmers put up a fuss when the officials decided to color it yellow to make it more appealing. It was a threat to their butter sales. So, either a little packet or tablet of yellow food coloring was then placed in each box of oleo. After she had purchased it, the housewife colored her own. Several farmers became rather irate when they came into the house after doing the evening milking and realized their wives had placed oleomargarine, the forbidden food, on the supper table directly in front of them. Talk about an insult!

Like most kids, we loved ice cream, but we seldom used our hand crank ice cream freezer. The only available ice was sold at least five miles away in Spencerville. We usually didn't spend money for luxuries such as that during the Great Depression days. We got our nickel cone when we went to town during the hottest summer days, but in winter we loved to make "snow ice cream" from new-fallen heavy, wet snow. After we packed the largest drinking glass we could find with clean, white snow, Grandma poured a little milk over it. Then we stirred in a spoonful of sugar, a little vanilla and it was ready to eat. What a treat that was! It was even better because we had made it ourselves. We no longer make snow ice cream. Pollution, you know!

Grandma looked forward to spring and the appearance of the first tender, green dandelions. She always made a "mess of dandelion greens" for what she called our "spring tonic." There were no fresh salad makings in the stores then, so those wilted greens tasted quite good when she cut a hard-boiled egg into them, added crispy crumbled bacon, then a homemade sweet and sour type of dressing. When the dandelions were full grown and tough, they were no longer used for salads.

There was no cafeteria when I first started to school, so we took metal dinner buckets with cold meat or peanut butter sandwiches. Bill even mentioned having a lot of cold fried egg sandwiches. It certainly didn't sound exciting, but that's about what everyone had.

When my shoes got holes in the bottom, Grandpa cut out a piece of cardboard to slip into them, and they were good for another few weeks. If the heel came off, a smelly cement was smeared on, they were placed on the floor to dry overnight with a chair leg sitting on the heel, and in the morning they were as good as new. Occasionally new half-soles were purchased at the five-and-ten-cent store and glued in place. Sometimes these came loose at the front. They became a real nuisance then, as they flapped up and down when you walked. This year's Sunday shoes became next year's everyday shoes. If they got too short, Grandpa got out his trusty pocket knife, cut off the toes and they fit for the rest of the summer.

If a dress got too short, the hem was let down, and the resulting hemline was covered with rickrack or a piece of lace. If there was no hem to let down, a contrasting ruffle might be added. Slips were often made from white flour sacks and could easily be lengthened with an added ruffle. Since we didn't wear everything "skin tight," this added a year of wear to children's clothes. When the clothing was no longer wearable, it was taken apart, then torn into rags for Grandma's crocheted rag rugs. She saved all the buttons, snaps and zippers for use on next year's new dresses. Coats of that day were always wool. Many of the adult coats were later torn apart, brushed and washed, and reused to make children's coats, sometimes using the inside of the old coat as the outside of the new. I've made several of my own children's little coats using these old techniques. As much thread as possible was saved from these recycled garments and used later as basting thread when sewing new clothing.

The good parts of a sheet were cut down to make pillow cases, and the less-worn ends of towels were later turned into washcloths. Many items were patched to make them last a bit longer. A rip in a man's shirt might end up with a flowered patch on it, but it could be worn that way for many more months. Grandma never allowed any of us to wear patched clothing to school or town, though. Any clothing that was patched was considered "everyday" and we wore it only around home.

When I was just a child, I had seen an establishment in Lima which intrigued me. As we walked by the big window, we saw the owner working nearby, steam cleaning and brushing men's felt hats. Haven't seen that done in years! Grandma seldom took anything to a dry cleaner, but any article she did take came back with a brown paper sack covering it. She usually "spot cleaned" things at home. When the collar on Grandpa's suit coat began to look soiled, Grandma moistened a rag with naphtha or gasoline and rubbed the spot until the dirt came out. Then she took the coat outside and hung it on the clothesline to air out until the smell had gone. Grandpa wore his good suit only on Sunday, and since he had taken his Saturday night bath, the collar stayed clean for a long time. He removed it as soon as he got home from church. Suit coats usually lasted longer than the pants, which eventually became shiny and threadbare and were no longer fit to wear. Grandpa usually paired the coat up with new "work" pants or with overalls and continued to use it for weekday trips to town, visiting relatives and other less dressy events. I don't remember him ever owning a windbreaker or casual jacket. Winter overcoats reached below the knees and were made of wool–heavy and cumbersome–but very warm.

Hand-me-down clothing was also used extensively. In some families, that practice continues today, but usually within the immediate family. Garage sales didn't exist back then. I was thrilled when an older cousin gave me a pretty dress she had outgrown. When a sweater began to show signs of age around the elbows, patches (dignified-looking leather ones for the men) were used to cover the worn spots. A worn sweater was often cut apart and unraveled, wrapped into a ball and reused later to patch a pair of mittens, darn holes in socks and gloves, or knit a muffler. A muffler is what the older folks called a scarf that was tied around the neck, keeping it warmer in the winter. Grandma didn't knit, but some ladies used that ball of yarn for knitting mittens or baby soakers. The soft scraps were often used as the stuffing for a little cloth ball for baby. Very little was wasted during those depression years!

Old bed sheets found many uses. They were thrown over strawberry beds and garden plants on cold nights to keep them from getting bit by "Jack Frost." Strips were torn from the sturdier areas and used as bandages for wrapping sprained ankles and such. Grandma wrapped hams in sheet strips for curing. The most worn parts were saved for shop rags, folded bandages and other necessities used by the ladies. The softer pieces were cut into squares and hemmed for everyday handkerchiefs, especially for Grandma and me. I used many of them when I was a runny-nosed kid! How I detested sticking those wet, yucky hankies into my dress pockets. Tissues had not come on the market yet, so it was either use a cloth handkerchief or let the old nose drip. Both Bill's family and mine used those cost-free homemade items for everyday blowing. Pretty handkerchiefs of cotton or linen were saved for Sunday. Since they were rather inexpensive but thoughtful gifts, most ladies had a dozen or more. I still have some that have never been used, but when I have a cold, I don't dig them out. Instead, I thank God for soft, throw-away Kleenex!

Home remedies were used extensively to save on the expense of a trip to the doctor. If we didn't have regular toothpaste, we used baking soda and salt. Cornstarch from the kitchen was always sprinkled on a baby's little bottom. I really had to laugh a few years back when the makers of baby powder started including cornstarch in their products and praising its benefits. Mothers had been using cornstarch for years and knew it was not only cheaper, but was the best thing available for keeping a baby dry and comfortable. My box of cornstarch and I raised three children successfully.

The medicine cabinet included a large jar of Mentholatum for colds or stuffed up noses. Iodine or Mercurochrome was used for cuts. Scraped knees on the school playground were an ample excuse for running to the teacher for a generous dab of this medication. It left a bright red knee as a sort of status symbol for all one's friends to view with appropriate gasps of "Oooh" and "Does it hurt?" Castor oil was a common laxative, but thank goodness Grandma didn't go overboard in its use! Epsom salts were also in the medicine chest for use on sprains or to soak the "bad stuff" out of a foot that had accidentally stepped on a nail. Grandpa always kept a bottle of Carter's Little Liver Pills there, also. A paste made of baking soda helped take the pain out of a bee or wasp sting and a spoonful of soda in a glass of water helped to settle a "bilious stomach" or to "sweeten a sour stomach." Wool socks were tied around sore throats, and a wool scrap that Grandma called my "pneumonia jacket" was placed over my chest each day to keep me from getting pneumonia again. Most of the school year seemed to be filled with days of itchy long underwear with lumpy long socks pulled up over them. Ghastly attire for a little girl!

The school provided library paste for projects made there, but if we wanted to make something at home, our paste was water mixed into plain flour from Grandma's flour bin. I still have a mental picture of an old zinc mason canning jar lid sitting on the corner of my dresser while I pasted a picture together. The paste dried before I was finished and once that flour and water had hardened, I don't think a sledge hammer could have pounded it out of that lid. The papers that had just been glued always seemed to remain a little lumpy and wrinkled, too. A tiny scrap of brittle paper recently fell from Grandma's old cookbook. On it was this recipe: "A Good Library Paste–Into a cup of flour stir enough cold water to make it like thick cream. Then pour over this 4 cupfuls of boiling water, stirring all the time. Cook this five minutes. Then to this paste add 1 teaspoonful of powdered alum, pour into a bowl and beat until cold. Then add 1 teaspoonful carbolic acid, the same amount of oil of cloves or wintergreen. Stir well and pour into jars. When cold pour paraffin over top of jars that are put away for future use. Keep in a cool place." Sounds interesting, but we never made the fancy recipe. Plain flour and water for us!

Grandma used homemade lye soap for doing the laundry for many years, but she didn't make much of it after we came to live with them. The lye was powerful stuff and dangerous to have around children. Maybe she just didn't have time to make it. Her recipe for lye soap was: Dissolve 2 boxes Red Seal lye and 1/4 pound Borax in 2 quarts rain water. Stir once in a while until dissolved. Put 10 pounds clean grease (she often used old meat fryings and leftover lard that had gotten rancid) in granite pan and pour lye water into it. Add 5 cents worth sassafras extract and stir ten minutes. Grease pan and pour soap into pan. Set in cool place.

Cakes of Fels Naphtha soap finally became available at grocery stores and were popular and affordable. The problem was that Grandma had to shave little slices off the cake of soap into the wash water to dissolve it. Eventually boxes of soap powder came into the stores. Although she thought they were really too expensive, they were much easier to use. To encourage the thrifty housewife to buy its product, one company included a hand towel inside each box of soap. It knew those thrifty ladies would purchase its brand just to get the "free" gift inside.

Other money-saving recipes in Grandma's collection included one for making your own rose cream face lotion from quince seeds, bay rum, glycerine, rose water and 5-cents worth oil of geranium. Wallpaper cleaner was made from flour, salt, ammonia, carbon oil and vinegar. Bleach for clothes was made from chlorinated lime, sal soda and soft water. The recipe for furniture polish called for vinegar, motor oil and turpentine.

Grandpa and Grandma were faithful readers of *Successful Farming* magazine, and many of the helpful hints found between its covers were published in a booklet, *How to Save Time, Save Money and Make Profits in Farming and Homemaking.* The copyright date was not listed, but this booklet seemed to have the answer for almost everything, from how to regulate a windmill so the cattle tank doesn't overflow to how to keep horses from chewing the boards of their feed trough. (Nail old buggy tires to the top board.) It solved the problem of keeping a dog from sucking eggs, something which could not be tolerated on a farm. (Punch a tiny hole in each end of an egg and blow the contents out, then fill the empty shell with red pepper and place it back in the hen's nest. One bite of that, and the dog will never look at another egg.) The booklet also suggested using rubber bands cut from an inner tube to keep the horses' tails from trailing in the mud during rainy weather. That doesn't sound like much, but one swat in the face by a horse's muddy tail would tell you why this was an excellent idea–that is, if it worked.

In the days before plastic, ladies used wax paper and tinfoil to cover the leftovers after a meal. If they were lucky enough to have an ice box, it was no problem, but we had none. Grandma covered our dishes and set them in the cupboard until the next meal or took them to the cool basement. After using the wax paper or foil, it was usually washed and reused until it was too limp and ragged to use again. Grandma crumpled the wax paper and brushed it over the top of the wood stove. The wax gave the stove a bit of a luster or shine. Having served well, it was then pitched into the fire.

Wooden boxes that had contained fruit, nuts, or other products were also used again for children's toys, storage, chicken nests, book shelves, or for holding small items. Bill's Grandpa Wierwille provided his whole shop with lots of little compartments for storing bolts, nuts, screws, and small parts–all made from wooden cigar boxes. He liked to work with wood and added drawers to an old radio, turning it into a beautiful sewing cabinet. A square metal cigar box made a handy holder for Grandma Davenport's buttons. Children with nothing to play with could sit for hours sorting and stringing that colorful assortment of buttons. After at least three generations of children had played with that button box, I took it to the county fair where the judge of antiques suggested I remove the buttons and preserve the box. "That old thing," Grandma would have laughed!

Storage space was at a premium in our house because there wasn't much built-in closet space. For many years, Great-grandpa's old trunk from Germany was used to store seldom-used items that Grandma wanted to keep.

Our daily newspapers were saved for various uses. They were ideal for starting the fire in the wood cookstove each morning. Layers of newspapers helped extend the life of a carpet by providing the only padding under the large rugs covering the dining room, living room and our grandparents' bedroom floors. They provided extra warmth and kept the furnace dust from coming up into the rooms above. Since I was the one who usually had to dust the furniture, I appreciated that. However, with all these old papers being used around the house, it was hard to keep one's mind on housecleaning each spring. As soon as the rugs were taken outside to have the dust beaten out of them, Don and I were down on the floor. We just had to reread those year-old funnies that we had long ago forgotten!

Newspapers had other practical uses. They were used to line dresser drawers and kitchen shelves. Clothing was often wrapped in paper to keep it clean and insect free. In winter, when someone killed a rabbit or pheasant during hunting season, it was taken to the basement to be cleaned. I helped quite often. It was much more comfortable to do the job inside, rather than outdoors in the cold. We always put several layers of paper on the basement floor first, then the bunny fur or pheasant feathers fell on the paper. I usually held the rabbit while Grandpa skinned it. Then, as he gutted it, the blood and intestines fell on the paper underneath. When the job was complete, the papers were folded up and burned in the nearby furnace.

Letters and bills were received in envelopes that were also reused. While the bills went into the record files, the envelopes became scraps of paper for writing notes, grocery lists, garden maps, "scratch paper" and drawing paper for restless children during church. A scrap of paper and a stub of a pencil kept me occupied for many a long sermon.

The life of a household broom was said to be prolonged by soaking it in salt water before using it. A broom was the only thing Grandma had for sweeping her house for many, many years. Aging brooms often went to the barn or hen house. When it was no longer usable there, the handle was cut off and kept for future use. I remember a window or two being propped up with a piece of broom handle until the broken rope was replaced with a new one. Handles were used to stir buckets of hog slop and to prop gates open while animals were moved from one field to another. Grandpa often kept one handy in the barn when he was working with the animals. A tap on the nose pointed hogs in the right direction. It was also a means of self-defense, should one of those porkers get unruly or mean.

When one of the car's inner tubes no longer held air and had been patched more times than he could count, Grandpa cut it into strips looking much like large rubber bands. These were used to hold many things together. One day Grandma said a kitchen chair leg had come loose. After cleaning it and putting on new glue, Grandpa used one of those giant rubber bands to hold the chair together until the glue dried.

Little girls in our area didn't have "proper"playhouses when I was a child. But we certainly made our own versions of a playhouse. I used the smokehouse and hung a few pictures on the wall and added an orange crate set of shelves for my dishes. I didn't take my nice set of toy dishes out there, but dug in the trash pile behind the shop for the cracked dishes that Grandma had discarded—cracked plates, cups with no handles, clean Karo bottles that became flower vases for my many bouquets of dandelions, wild mustard, chicory and other blooming weeds growing around the farm. I usually didn't cut Grandma's special flowers.

One day my family visited friends near Kemp. I went with their girls to search through the junk pile for pretty dishes and vases. We found a nice variety and spent a pleasant afternoon playing house. Little girls who were determined to play house could find a variety of spots to use—a corner of a barn, an empty corncrib, the basement, the unused silo. The most unusual one? I remember going to Mary Ramga's house to play. We turned an unused pigpen into a playhouse for the day. It was a little *fragrant* and dusty, but it worked. One thing I will not forget about that day was that, like most farms, there was an abundance of flies that seemed to be especially attracted to our "playhouse." I swallowed one! "You swallowed a fly?" Yep! Sure did!

On the farm, baling wire and twine string were often used to hold things together, at least temporarily until they could be fixed properly. This included wire fences through which a wayward hog had broken or that had been snagged by a piece of machinery. Most repairs were made at home, or at least were cobbled up to last a bit longer. If something had to be replaced, it was first torn apart and any usable parts were salvaged to keep something else going a bit longer in the future. "Save everything!" was the farmer's motto. I've seen quite a few electrical cords taped together with black tape, and there are bins and bins of little bolts and screws which both our grandpas had salvaged for possible future use.

Almost every home that had children also had an old tire hanging by a long rope in a tree near the house. This was the kid's swing. When Don and I asked for a swing, Daddy and Grandpa rigged up some heavy old pipes with rods to brace them. Two sets of chains were connected to wooden board seats, forming an ideal swing.

Anyone who was working or playing outside was encouraged to use the old wood outhouse instead of "traipsing through the house" to use the fancy indoor plumbing upstairs. Using it was more expensive because flushing meant running the water pump, and the toilet paper cost more than the free paper provided by the old Sears Roebuck catalog in the outhouse. (Grandpa always called it the privy.) There, it became the farmer's version of toilet paper. For modesty's sake, Grandma always tore out the ladies underwear pages. It would not be proper to display such suggestive material before the men! Ed Johnson, a popular radio and TV farm editor, spoke at a local meeting on the topic of life on the farm back in the "good old days." His grandma used the old Sears Roebuck in her outhouse, too. I told him afterward that my grandma had done the same thing, but that it didn't go to the outhouse until the ladies section was torn out. He laughed and said, "I'll have to add that to my speech." (I wonder if he did.)

A couple of inches of water in the tub was plenty for our once-a-week baths. We had to be careful we didn't use too much cistern water. If it was a dry year, the cistern would run dry for sure. Water was never left running while we rinsed dishes. That was wasteful!

I guess the most thrifty person I knew was an old gentleman who lived near us. When winter came, he put his car up on jacks to save the tires. He even picked out any stones that may have gotten stuck in the tread. With the advent of World War II a few years later, he was pleased that he had saved his precious tires.

Even our electricity was "home grown" and used sparingly. Both Bill's family and mine had small power plants that worked similarly to the portable engine/generator combination sets having 110/220 volts used today for temporary service in case of power outages. Bill's family had a Marco mounted in an outside shed. Ours was a Delco located in our basement. They were connected to a series of two-volt batteries totaling a charge of thirty-two volts. The batteries were glass jars containing acid. Round balls located inside these jars floated at the top when the batteries were fully charged. As the energy was used, the balls gradually dropped to the bottom. The engine then had to be run several hours to recharge them. It was often a quick trip for Don and me to run down and check those balls to see if they would need to run the Delco the next day. Sleeping was difficult if it was operated at night. Too noisy!

Don received his train while we still had the Delco, and he remembers Dad hooking it up to two of those batteries. When they ran down, he hooked it up to the next two. What fun it was to run the train in the middle of the living room floor. Mickey, our dog, would bark at it, then jump aside as it headed down the track directly toward him, then rounded a curve and took off in the opposite direction. It looked like such fun for barking at and chasing, but he was never quite sure where it was going next.

People without a generator did not have electricity. They depended on kerosene lamps, scrub boards and wood stoves. Gallons of water for the animals had to be pumped into buckets and carried to the barns every day. The Delco was a real advancement for farm families. Most of our neighbors had one and it was a very common to walk outside and hear the engine putt-putting at a neighbor's house in the area. The Delco provided sufficient electricity for operating light bulbs, radios, and small motors for the water pump, the cream separator and washing machine. With no refrigerator or ice box, many food items were placed in the basement to keep them cool. The depression was over by the time the REA began erecting power lines in our area. Nearly everyone hooked up, but some thrifty families like mine waited until the old Delco wore out. Mustn't waste anything!

When changing to REA, everything had to be changed over to 110 volts, even light bulbs. A new transformer was needed for Don's train. Since electricity was now cheap and abundant, we used more of it. We no longer had to make do with Delco batteries that ran down! Grandpa bought electric motors to run the cream separator and the water pump. He eventually added a stoker to the furnace, so he no longer had to bank the fires at night and get up early in the morning to get them going again. Grandma purchased her first electric stove and an Admiral refrigerator. (After almost fifty years of use by at least four generations of the Davenport family, the Admiral still runs.)

"*Making do*" in those depression days seemed to be popular in almost every house in our part of the country. As a result, I often think back to those days as I tear open an envelope and throw it into the wastebasket, or relax in a tub with *three* inches of water, or run the drinking water down the drain until it gets nice and cool. Such wastefulness almost makes me feel sinful. I guess I've lived this way for so many years that "making do" is simply a way of life.

Members of the Ladies Aid Society of the New Knoxville Evangelical and Reformed Church gathered in the fall of 1923 to make apple butter for the children's home at Fort Wayne. An early newspaper reported them as: L to R. (standing) Callie Eversman, Mrs. Herman Holtkamp, Mrs. Henry Oelrich, Mrs. Mary Kuck, Mrs. John Engle, Mrs. Ben Cook, Mrs. F. Schneider, Mrs. Christina Eschmeyer, Mrs. Henry Lutterbeck, Mrs. Sophia Peters, Mrs. Hartung Kuhlman, (sitting) Mrs. William Hoelscher, Mrs. Elizabeth Maher, Mrs. A. Meckstroth, and (kneeling) Mrs. John Henkener. This picture was taken by Bill's dad and made from his original glass negative.

## Chapter 15.

# A Day at the Davenports

I loved summer mornings when sleeping a bit later was a real luxury, although the most peaceful moments of the day were those of early morning: the sounds of a killdeer calling through the distant haze and the subtle answer of its mate from the pasture beyond the barn, the red-combed rooster stretching his neck to the morning sun as he vocally welcomed the new day, frisky little half-grown kittens who tumbled and twirled as they chased each other's tails in a frenzy of excitement. Wake up, world, the day has begun!

It was Grandma who usually came downstairs first each morning, dressed in one of her simple cotton everyday dresses and wearing cotton stockings with sturdy shoes. Since she usually made her own everyday dress patterns from newspapers, most dresses looked quite similar. Some had a front bow added or a different type collar, but basically they were the same, each made from a different colored print. Grandma's Sunday dresses were usually "store-bought" or "ready-made."

Grandma's first task of the new day was to shake the grates to remove the cold ashes from the firebox of the cookstove. Then, taking her little shovel that just fit through the door, she shoveled the ashes into the bucket sitting behind the stove. She was now ready to start the fire for another day. Crumbling an old newspaper, she placed it on the bottom of the wood compartment of the stove, then covered it with small twigs and chips of wood. With the touch of a match, the paper began to burn.

While the wood was getting a good start, she went around the corner into the washroom and washed her face and hands, then combed her hair. For many years Grandma had allowed her hair to grow and then braided it, fastening it into a bun on the back of her head. When this was finished, she put on a clean apron, then added some sticks of wood to the fire and got out the coffee pot and frying pan.

By now, Grandpa was dressed and downstairs. In winter he went to the basement to attend to the furnace. The process was much like that used by Grandma with the cookstove. He soon had the ashes removed and the fire stoked for the day. Since Grandpa had banked the fire the night before, it had lasted through the night, and he needed only to add a few chips until it was blazing, then throw on a couple of good-sized pieces of wood or the large chunks of coal which lasted for a few hours. Several years after the Great Depression, he purchased a stoker which made it much easier to take care of the furnace. He needed only to keep the hopper filled with stoker coal, then remove the clinkers left in the bottom of the furnace. With the furnace taken care of, Grandpa climbed the steps to the washroom and was soon ready for his breakfast.

If Dad was digging ditches in farm fields at distant places such as Waynesfield or New

Hampshire, the thirty-mile trip was much too far to return home after each long day's work, so he occasionally made it home only on weekends. During the winter snows when Dad was home, he might put on his heavy Mackinaw coat, and after pulling the tabs of his cap down over his ears, he shoveled a path to the barn before breakfast. Then he would spend the rest of the day in his workshop, repairing and updating his ditching equipment.

If school was in session, Grandma called Don and me to wake up and get dressed. Breakfast was ready by the time we got downstairs. If it was foggy or snowy, we kept one ear tuned to the telephone. Would school be closed? Since many people didn't have radios, the best way to spread the news was by telephone. Central rang one very long ring and everyone listened in as she announced the closing of school for the day.

I didn't get too excited about breakfast, especially when it consisted of oatmeal or corn meal mush. Eggs weren't too exciting unless they were served with our home-cured ham or bacon. If we had toast, it was usually a piece of day-old (or older) bread into which Grandma stuck a fork, then removing one lid from above the firebox of the stove, she held the bread over the coals until it was brown on one side. Pulling the fork out, she stuck it in the other side, and soon we had our toast. Although I don't remember it, Don said there had been a four-sided wire toaster in the shape of a pyramid. A slice of bread could be laid on each side of this wire rack, then Grandma removed the lid from the smallest hole in the top of the cookstove and placed this "toaster" over it. When the hot coals had browned one side, she turned the slices and toasted the other sides. Then the stove lid was replaced and the toaster set aside to cool. Four slices of toast at one time. Real progress, huh?

When we had finished breakfast, Grandpa prepared to shave. He had a well-rehearsed routine that I loved to watch. First, he had to make sure his straightedge razor was sharp. This was done by securing his razor in one hand. The top of the leather razor strop was securely fastened to the back of the wash room door. Grasping the bottom of the strop and pulling it taut, he moved the razor back and forth until it was sharp. Then, dropping his suspenders and removing his shirt, he stood in his short-sleeved underwear top and work pants with legs spread apart and hunkered down so he could see in the mirror. He used that straightedge like an expert. When the task was finished, he washed his face, put a little powder in his hands and patted his cheeks, then put on his shirt, pulled up his suspenders, and he was ready for the day!

While Grandma did the dishes, Grandpa fed the animals. Then they did the morning milking. Sometimes Don and I had to help with the milking, but in winter we were usually on the bus shortly after breakfast.

After the breakfast dishes were washed, the daily routine of work commenced. In winter, the ashes that had cooled sufficiently were carried outside and scattered across the garden or thrown on the driveway near a shed. The chickens had to be fed and the eggs gathered. Grandma had the washing and ironing to do, usually early in the week. There were hogs to be moved from one lot to another, calves to be separated from their mothers at weaning time, baby chicks to be cared for, and always there was the large garden to be tended from spring to late fall. I spent many a hot summer day sitting on the back steps shelling peas or in the porch swing snapping beans. The two jobs I most detested were picking the slimy slugs out of the strawberry patch and knocking potato bugs off the plants into a tin can. I often wondered what God had in mind when he made them. But I guess I had it rather easy with our one or two rows of potatoes. Bill said his family raised a large patch of them and he used to get terrible headaches from bending over those buggy potatoes. As he and Aunt Alwina remembered those backbreaking days, they also mentioned the large field of flax that his grandpa grew one year. When the plants bloomed, the blue flowers covering the entire field made it look like a lake of blue water. As the wind blew gently, it formed waves.

Grandpa and Grandma worked together on jobs such as husking corn and shocking wheat. They also made hay for the cows and loaded it on the trailer hooked to the back of the "Old Hoopie." This was a 1927 Pontiac Coupe that Grandpa kept for field work where it felt more at home than on the road. I loved that old car. It had a rather wide "shelf" up behind the seat. I remember laying up there many days, taking a nap while Grandma and Grandpa worked in the fields or woods. Don was in school and I had no one with whom to play. A nap in that cozy little area helped fill the afternoon. The Hoopie was the first car I ever "drove," sitting on Grandpa's lap and steering while he ran the pedals and shifted gears.

When the sun was high in the sky, Grandpa and Grandma knew it was time to get dinner. They went by the sun and moon for a lot of things. They didn't plant the garden without first consulting *The Old Farmers Almanac* to see if the "sign" was right. The almanac listed days that were good for planting root crops such as potatoes and carrots. Other days were best for planting crops such as lettuce, spinach and garden flowers. Still other days worked best for planting above-ground crops such as peas and beans and tomatoes. How was this determined? By the position of the moon! The *Almanac* still lists the best days for planting these various crops.

While Grandma started dinner, Grandpa got the mail and read the paper. We often had fried potatoes for dinner, and Don said Grandma usually used a skillet with a steel bottom that she placed directly over the fire after removing the stove lid. It got hot very quickly. Because of that, she occasionally burned the "spuds." Usually she browned them on one side, then turned them with a spatula, added a little water, and steamed them until they were done.

Don especially remembers the lid Grandma used on her skillet. Its original handle had been a round ring in the center of the lid, but the ring had come loose, so she used the tines of a fork to lift that lid on and off. Why put out good money for a new lid when this one still worked? I don't remember the steel-bottom skillet, but I do remember her lifting the lid with a fork as she fried potatoes in the old cast iron skillet! There was nothing better for making good fried potatoes. Bill's mom often boiled potatoes in good sized chunks, then sliced and fried them. Grandma didn't fry cooked potatoes unless they were leftovers from a previous meal. If we had baked potatoes or boiled potato chunks for supper, those that were left over would probably be sliced and fried for dinner the next day. Since they wouldn't have that freshly sliced taste, she often fried onions or home cured bacon along with them to improve the flavor. How we enjoyed those delicious potatoes!

One of Grandma's favorite company-style dinners was fried chicken, fresh from the henhouse. Oh, how I long for some old time country-fried chicken. No layers of fat were hidden beneath the skin of those active gals. They spent their days in the fresh air and sunshine where they kept their girlish figures by actively pursuing the barnyard bugs and the orchard grass seeds. Grandma plucked the feathers herself, and after removing the large stove lid, she singed off the fragile pin feathers by slowly turning the chicken over the flames beneath. When we ate Grandma's crispy fried chicken, we knew we were eating only good homegrown fowl. There was no fat and definitely no feathers.

Grandma seldom used a recipe, but when she did, her cookbook words seemed funny to me, things like "Brine strong enough to float an egg" and "Smoke hard with sassafras wood." I smile now as I look at some of those old recipes. They usually specified as to whether sour milk or sweet milk was to be used. Measurements seemed anything but accurate: "tin cup full cream, lard the size of an egg, two handsful of flour, scant cup sugar, 4 tins of water, butter size of a walnut, pinch of salt." Temperature for wood cookstove ovens also seemed quite indefinite: "hot oven, slow oven, fast oven."

Grandma often sang as she worked in the kitchen. One of her favorites was the cheerful hymn, "Brighten the Corner Where You Are." Grandpa used to sing to us occasionally, but when he was at work, we were more apt to hear him whistling "Oh, Susanna" or "My Old Kentucky Home" or one of his favorite hymns. I especially remember him standing in church with his head back as he heartily sang, "Let the Lower Lights Be Burning."

When we had finished eating our meal, Grandma "redded up the table" and got out the granite dishpan, which she filled with hot water from the tank on the side of the cookstove. She swished her bar of homemade lye soap through the water to make some suds, and the dinner dishes were soon sparkling clean. Grandma had acquired a habit from earlier days when her only storage space had been one small kitchen cabinet. It was easier to "store" the dishes by leaving them out from one meal to the next. Many of the older ladies did this, some placing them back on the table, upside down. Grandma set her dishes right side up, each place sitting ready for the next meal. She then covered the table with a large white table cloth. When supper was ready, she removed the cover and the table was already set for the meal.

While Grandma did the dinner dishes, Grandpa usually read the newspaper, often falling asleep! After his nap, the afternoon's routine was carried on much the same as in the morning. The day's work continued with such activities as picking apples, berries or cherries in the summer or chopping and sawing wood in the winter. The kitchen stove was kept burning all day, sometimes because sugar water was being boiled down into maple syrup in the early spring, sometimes to help provide extra hot water for washing down walls or ceilings, or for any job that might need warm water. It also provided heat for the kitchen on cold days. When the electric power lines went through and we finally hooked up, Grandpa purchased a hot water heater that now guaranteed plenty of warm bath water. Operating the electric hot water heater, however, was a luxury that was not to be overdone! Grandma still liked to heat water for kitchen chores with the old wood stove. (Even after we were married, Bill's mom heated their dishwater on the wood cookstove.) After all, if it was heated in the tank on the side of the cookstove, it was "free."

Well, little in life is actually "free." Keeping that "range" supplied with wood was a day-in-day-out task requiring someone (usually Don or me) to go out to the woodpile and bring in several loads of wood to fill the wood box (one of the ways I "contributed" to the family). That sometimes seemed like a lot of work, especially if it was cold and snowy and Grandma was doing some extra baking, but it was nothing compared to Grandpa's "contribution."

Each fall Grandpa hitched his trailer to the Old Hoopie and we drove to the woods to cut our winter's supply of firewood for the cookstove. When working in the woods, Grandpa didn't cut any more trees than absolutely necessary. He looked for trees that might have blown down or were dead, but not yet rotten. Rotten trees did not burn well in the stove. Any large branches that may have blown off were also put in the trailer. It took several loads to supply sufficient wood for the kitchen cookstove and the furnace in the basement.

Fall's woodland aroma was powerful as the colorful leaves fluttered silently down, forming a thick, colorful blanket over the ground. While the adults loaded the trailer, we kids usually looked under the trees, amidst the fallen leaves, for walnuts or hickory nuts that had fallen. These would be brought to the house where the outer shell would be removed. Some cold winter day, Grandpa would take them to the shop and crack them. That evening we'd sit and pick out the good tasting meat inside. Sometimes Grandma baked a hickory nut cake or added the nuts to a batch of divinity candy she usually made at Christmas. Yummy!

Grandpa owned his own sawing equipment. A buzz saw (a circular saw with sharp teeth on the outer edge) was set into a wood frame which Grandpa called a sawbuck. After a trailer load of wood was brought to the house and unloaded, a long belt was connected from a pulley on the side of the sawbuck to another pulley attached to the side of the tractor. Smaller logs or tree branches were laid across the shelf or saw table behind the buzz saw. This table was then pushed forward, causing the log to be cut on the revolving saw blade. When the wood was all sawed into pieces about a foot and a half in length, it was stacked on a pile nearby. The pieces that were more than seven or eight inches thick had to be split into smaller pieces. An iron wedge was pounded into the large chunks of wood with a sledge hammer, splitting them into two pieces. Using an ax, Grandpa or Dad then split these chunks into smaller pieces that were piled on the stack of wood. It was from this wood pile that Don or I carried in the fire wood for the stove. That wood created a lot of heat: as Grandpa and Dad worked to cut it up and prepare it, as Don and I brought it in, as it burned in the stove, and as Grandma worked over it while preparing meals. Makes you tired just thinking about all that work!

When the sun began to sink lower in the west, Grandpa and Grandma came in from the field or barn and started the milking and evening chores. We usually got home from school about four o'clock, and after changing clothes, we had to help with the chores. One of my jobs was to dust the living room furniture. In those days of the 1930s, states such as Kansas and Oklahoma were experiencing terrible dust storms caused by little or no rain for many months. The soil and crops dried up, and the strong winds that were so prevalent blew the powdery earth about into giant drifts much like our winter snows. Although we were hundreds of miles east of the Dust Bowl area, our skies were affected by those powdery fine dust particles blown into Ohio by the strong westerly winds. Occasionally the sky had an ominous pinkish/gray cast which dimmed the afternoon sun, then a fine sifting of dust penetrated the tiniest cracks around the windows of the house, leaving a layer of fine dust over everything.

We really didn't need any additional dust since we already had a local creator of excess dirt. Like nearly every other road in the area, State Route 197, which ran in front of our house, was a stone road. It had a lot of traffic, and that meant lots of dust. Usually once or twice in the summer, the State Highway Department sent a truck to spray oil on the stone in front of the houses. The farm wives welcomed this with great relief. Although it brought a pungent oily smell with it, it did indeed help to settle the dust for a while. That was really an improvement. The roads to the north and south were mud roads. They had no stone and after a day or two of rain—my goodness! What a slimy, muddy mess!

Keeping the furniture dusted was probably a whole lot easier than dealing with the window curtains. Actually, washing the curtains was not really hard. Grandma soaked them in cold water to loosen the dirt, then wrung them out gently and washed them again in rather hot water. The big pain came when I helped put the lace curtains on curtain stretchers. Little pin points stuck up from a wood frame that was adjusted to form a rectangle the same size as the curtains. The clean, wet curtain was attached to the pins on one side of the frame, then pulled and stretched until the other edges could be placed over the remaining pins. If the curtains were getting older, this was when the lace tore and Grandma had to mend them later with a needle and thread. The stretched curtains were placed in the sun to bleach and dry. When done properly, the dry curtains were smooth and ready to hang. With nine windows and a door in our living and dining rooms, our fingers were nearly raw by the time all those curtains had been pinned and unpinned.

One day, Grandma decided to get rid of lace curtains and try the popular new Venetian blinds. They sounded as if they would make life a lot easier for our hands, but we hadn't been introduced to the woes of Venetian blinds. The downstairs window blinds were sharp metal blinds. By the time Grandma made the decision to try them on the upstairs windows, World War II had claimed the metal. Only wooden blinds were available. These flat wood slats and the curved metal ones were about two inches wide and lay on two cloth tapes which had a rope in the center for raising and lowering. The slats were tilted by gently pulling a rope on the side, allowing more or less light to enter the room. These slats had to be dusted weekly and washed once or twice a year. Because my hands were smaller and would fit between the slats, guess who got the cleaning job? Dirt and dust really clung to the slats, making them hard to wash. All that grime left the hands extremely dry and occasionally cut and bleeding from the sharp edges of the metal blinds or splinters from the wooden ones. I vowed I would never have lace curtains *or* Venetian blinds in my house! I don't have!

Besides the dusting, I usually had to peel the potatoes. While Grandma cooked the meal, I did my school homework. In those days, we didn't have a pencil sharpener, so Grandpa got out his jackknife and whittled away at the end of my pencil until the point was nice and sharp.

After supper, Grandma usually gave me a choice as to whether I wanted to wash dishes or practice my accordion lesson. Guess what I did! I practiced! That's why I learned to play musical instruments.

I often helped with the evening milking, especially when I had my own cow. I had raised Flo from a calf. We had several cows, but I especially remember a big, broad cow named Star who gave a large bucket of milk each morning and evening. I was glad I didn't have to milk her.

After the outside chores were done, Grandpa usually sat in the kitchen and cleaned the eggs. I sometimes helped with that job, but was glad when it was finished so we could all sit down in the living room and listen to the radio. Grandpa always liked to hear Gabriel Heatter—"Ah, there's good news tonight." Don and I were more eager to hear *Henry Aldrich* and *Lum and Abner*. Grandpa always joined in the excitement of the *Old Ranger*, while Grandma usually kept busy with her Bible reading, tatting or rug making. Many nights she sat with her feet on the warm air register and tore our old clothing into strips that she then crocheted into rag rugs. For a time I had a hobby of collecting picture post cards. I loved to get them out of Grandpa's trunk, then sit in the old wicker rocking chair in the living room as I listened to the radio and admired the pictures over and over, sorting them according to states. Occasionally Don and I played checkers or *Terry and the Pirates* and ate popcorn popped in a skillet, briskly shaken over the wood cookstove. Each fall Grandpa bought a bushel of apples that we happily munched on cold winter evenings.

It was Grandpa's pocket knife that often cut up those apples. That was one of his most useful possessions–it was used to cut up and peel apples and pears, to open his mail at noon, to cut the twine around sacks of grain or the string tied and knotted around a package. Outside on the farm he used it to stick the side of a bloated cow, allowing the gas to escape, or to castrate the male hogs or dig the warbles out of a cow's hide. (What is a warble? Webster says, "Warble—a swelling caused by the maggot of a botfly or warble fly under the hide, especially the back of cattle.")

Grandpa's knife was a necessary tool for personal hygiene—cleaning barnyard dirt out from under fingernails, or cutting those nails when they became too long. As a small child, I watched in awed silence as he scraped the excess growth off the big toe he had permanently damaged in his younger days. I was certain it had to hurt, but he assured me it really didn't. Grandpa often wiped the knife on the side of his work pants, but did that wipe dirt off or just add more? I do remember seeing him light a match, then holding it under the blade of the knife to sterilize it before digging a splinter out of his finger or out of mine. Oh! Ouch! *That* hurt! There was no end to the uses Grandpa had for that pocket knife. He tested it for sharpness by stroking it across his thumb. In the evening, he often used a little stone to whet the knife to make it sharp. Whether it was sanitary or not, it didn't seem to make much difference because we were usually healthy, and Grandpa's knife certainly stayed active doing a variety of assorted jobs around our farm.

If it was Saturday night, Grandma made sure that Don and I had our baths while Grandpa took down his Bible and spent extra time preparing for his Sunday school lesson.

By nine o'clock, it was bedtime. While we got ready, Grandpa broke up the clinkers in the furnace and banked the fire for the night. He also checked the hot air registers to make sure nothing was lying on them. Our little neighbor, Roberta Mack, had fallen onto a register when she was just a toddler. She was not able to get up quickly and the hot little squares in the register's pattern seared into her tiny leg, leaving nasty scars that grew in size as she grew. We had also heard of fires starting because of something left carelessly lying on a hot register overnight.

When everything was finished for the day, Grandpa locked the door, turned off the lights downstairs, then came upstairs and got ready for bed. Since he slept in his longjohns, it didn't take long! Our busy day concluded with the saying of our prayers. Then Grandpa always kissed me goodnight before climbing into bed. That bedtime kiss routine continued until I started dating.

*The Waltons*, a popular TV show when our kids were young, always closed with a call of "good night" from every room. That is exactly how our day ended. After a big yawn and sigh, another day at the Davenports was brought to a finish! The final sound of the day was often someone calling, "Goodnight! Sleep tight! Don't let the bedbugs bite!"

## Chapter 16.
# Let's Go Visiting

Organ music provided a beautiful background for birds as they sand and chirped, filling the room with vibrant sound from the radio. These were the main attractions of the Sunday dinners at Grandpa's sister, Aunt Lizzie and Uncle Bert Doute in St. Marys. Because they lived in town, they already had their funny papers. Ours didn't arrive on the country rural routes until Monday. What an exciting privilege to view them a day early, especially when their paper also had a children's page with puzzles, poems, and such. Aunt Lizzie let us take them home. When I finished looking at them, I carefully folded them and put them with my treasures in Grandpa's trunk.

Visiting was a part of country living, especially after folks had begun to recover from the depression. From then until the start of World War II, family visits were one of the main forms of staying in touch.

I am told we took a short one-day trip to Troy in 1934 to see the area where Grandpa's road building company was currently paving new roads and to see the house in which Grandpa and Grandma had lived for a short time a decade earlier. Don told me about that trip, but since I was quite small, I have no memory of it. What can I say? I went, I saw, I quickly forgot!

We also enjoyed our Sunday dinners with Grandpa's sister, Aunt Effie. One time, I was allowed to spend a week at her house. Although she'd had some sad events in her life, I loved her sunny outlook. You see, her first husband had worked in the oil fields around St. Marys and had died in 1929. Five years later she married Lew Hines who was also an oil man, having worked for the Ohio Oil Company for thirty-three years. Lew died as a result of pumping the wells in the bitter cold winter of 1936.

I was six years old when we went to Aunt Effie's home for her husband's viewing. She cried so hard as she hugged and kissed Grandpa and Grandma, but I was too young to comprehend death. I was quite puzzled by all those tears from my usually happy great-aunt Effie. Although I grew up with the knowledge of my own mother's early death, I had no idea how devastating it was for her to lose two husbands in such a short time.

Mag Catterlin was a tiny little lady not much taller than I was as a child. How we kids enjoyed going to her home! Her spinster sister, Alta Folk, lived with her. They were Grandpa's cousins. Mag's grandson was about my age. He was often there when we visited. Then Don and I enjoyed playing with him, and we especially enjoyed riding the large spring-type rocking horse that Mag kept for the children. How I loved rocking and bouncing on that horse! I was so sad when I finally got too big for it.

Other Sunday dinners were enjoyed at the home of Grandma's brother, Uncle Henry and Aunt Ida Schwartz north of Spencerville. A pretty ornamental iron fence enclosed their yard to keep out the guinea hens which usually pecked at bugs in the barnyard and driveway. In order to avoid hitting them, Grandpa had to slow down as we drove in. The older Schwartz sons were married by then and the younger sons and daughter, Mary Alice, usually had something else to do that day. I guess playing with a couple of little kids wasn't too much fun for them. I didn't mind, though, because Aunt Ida usually brought down a beautiful big doll which kept me quite happy the rest of the day.

Betty Eileen Lowman was Don's age. We children always had a good time playing together when our family visited. Russell and Opal Lowman, Grandma's niece, were young and full of fun. They usually had plenty of ideas for things to keep us busy. Betty and I had a great time during one summer's week-long visit.

Aunt Tillie's little canary usually greeted us with a welcome song when we visited her and Uncle Ed Thiesing in Lima. It made a pleasant background for the dinner conversation. Aunt Tillie always took time to listen to our childish prattle and usually had something creative to entertain us. Aunt Tillie was a lover of flowers. While she and Grandma looked over her many flower beds, Don and I enjoyed watching the goldfish in the pool Uncle Ed had built. She had surrounded it with flowers, making it quite pretty. After his death, she had to leave her beloved flowers and goldfish and move into an upstairs apartment. With no place to grow real flowers, Tillie turned to making her own bouquets from crepe paper. (There were no lovely silk flowers then.) She enjoyed working with crafts and was on the lookout for old picture frames. We saw many of the artistic sprays of paper flowers that she arranged on painted chicken wire and placed in elegant old frames. Especially pretty were those with large paper roses which she hung on her wall.

I didn't know much about weddings when I was a child, but I thought receptions were fine. We were invited to the Glynwood area home of Grandpa's nephew, Arthur Craft and his wife, Sylvia, after the marriages of their daughters, Dorothy and Lowella. Even before that, I was quite small when we attended a party at Doc and Ocey Ward's old log house–the one in which Grandpa Frank was born. It had no electricity, and I remember the coal oil lamp burning in the middle of the oilcloth-covered kitchen table.

Another one-day visit was to North Baltimore to see Grandpa's niece, Inez, and her husband, Merlin Luedeke. It was 1938, and I was eight years old. We drove on Route 25 north of Lima where, for several miles, a train track ran parallel to the road. I was fascinated by the closeness of a passing train and waved at the engineer and the people in the cars, some of whom were eating in the dining car. I wished I could be there with them. It looked like such fun. When we got to the Luedeke home, we had more things to enjoy including a little baby boy. I had hoped to get to hold him, but unfortunately for me, he slept most of the day. I'm sure his mama was most grateful though. His daddy showed us pictures of the baby lying on a bearskin rug. Frankly, I was quite shocked! He wasn't wearing a stitch of clothes, something we were taught was just not proper. I had even heard that one could be arrested if one took off one's clothes. "How had the photographer dared to develop a picture of someone who was naked?" I had innocently wondered.

Who would get excited about ice cubes? I would! I'd never *seen* an ice cube. We didn't own an ice box or refrigerator. Ice cubes were new to us country kids. When Inez gave us some of the frozen little cubes, we spent the afternoon sucking on those fascinating objects. They were wonderful on a hot summer day. (I still love crunching on ice cubes.)

With the price of gasoline so cheap, it was not unusual for our family to take an afternoon drive to see how area crops were doing, to visit historical sites, or to check out the fall leaves. Another sign of fall was the annual afternoon drive to the orchard near Lima where Grandpa bought at least two bushels of apples for the winter, one for cooking and baking and another for eating raw. On cold winter nights, as Grandpa got out his pocket knife to cut up an apple for us, we often heard Grandma in the kitchen, and soon the smell of popcorn filled the house. The warm coals left from cooking supper were just right for heating the cast iron skillet that Grandma shook back and forth until the corn popped. We don't use a wood cookstove and cast iron skillet anymore, but we still enjoy home-grown popcorn on cold winter evenings.

So, who would get excited about a whole piece of chalk? Me! Several times we traveled up to visit Grandma's cousin, John Schwarz who was a history professor at Bowling Green State University. I remember two things from the visit we made the summer after I was in first grade. Although it was closed on Sunday, he pointed out the *Falcon's Nest*, a student union for the kids at BGSU. Then he took us to his classroom where he picked up two pieces of chalk and gave them to Don and me. I had never had a *full* piece of chalk before. Our school teachers had always broken the chalk in half, and we had to write with the shorter pieces. I never understood why, but I know that day Professor Schwarz delighted one shy little country girl with a *whole* piece of chalk. I think that was the moment I decided to some day get a college education. (I eventually went to Wittenberg because of their good music department, but they also allowed me to use whole pieces of chalk. Yeah!)

Although other meats may have also been prepared for the dinners between visiting families, fried chicken was the most commonly used. After all, a skillet of fried chicken was no farther away than a farmer's back door. A dinner for seventeen friends and family members was glowingly described in the *Auglaize County Democrat* of October 8, 1914. My grandparents were in the group who met on Sunday at the home of Mr. and Mrs. Bert Montague for what one guest described as a "good old-fashioned chicken dinner, with all the trimmings that can be found on a farm. And, I tell you, some of the old boys liked chicken all right. They made you think that they were preachers the way the chicken disappeared." Don't you love the descriptions in those old newspaper stories?

It was a nice fall day in 1938 when my family decided to go for a ride to Geneva, Indiana, to visit the fourteen-room Limberlost cabin, home of author Jean Stratton Porter who had died fourteen years earlier. Geneva is located in the Limberlost country of Adams County and was made famous by her novels: *A Girl of the Limberlost, Freckles* and *The Harvester.* After our visit, I was eager to read and enjoy all of her books.

Families worked harder at remaining connected when I was a child. There were at least two or three family reunions each year. The Aufderhaar Reunion was occasionally held in Bluffton or Muncie, Indiana. It made for a long day, and by the time we started back to Ohio, we were a tired but happy family. After such a strenuous day, I often enjoyed a nap that kept me busy on the long trip home.

World War II brought about many changes, and the number of visits and distance driven were limited, since gas rationing was instituted to conserve petroleum products. Grandpa always had enough gas to get us to church and to Spencerville for our Saturday grocery trip. He often bought his hog supplement and a few gallons of gasoline at the elevator. Sometimes he left me off at the nearby Erie Railroad Station where my "pinching uncle," Frank Swaney, was the station master. It was exciting to stand on the platform beside the tracks and watch as trains went through, especially when they had to pick up or deliver train orders or mail bags on the arm sticking out to catch them. Uncle Frank had no children and his idea of fun was to pinch me. I didn't like that one bit, but put up with it in order to see the trains and to occasionally play with the "Key" where messages were sent in Morse Code. Did he send out a message that a little girl was going to "play" with it? I never knew. Our afternoon usually ended with him giving me a nickel, another incentive to put up with the pinching. I was not the only one he pinched. My sister-in-law, who was from Spencerville, told me he playfully pinched all the kids.

When we had finished, we occasionally visited Grandpa's half-sisters, Marie Croft and Hilda Young and their families. Sometimes we stopped at historic Deep Cut which overlooked the Miami-Erie Canal. At that time the park consisted of just a pump and a path down to the water, but it was so far down that *deep cut* that we had to be impressed. Occasionally we stopped to see mother's brother, Leo Briggs and his family who lived just south of the park. With so little gasoline to use, we had to cover as much as possible on that weekly trip.

Dad usually drove to Columbus to Farmers' Week, a time of classes and activities geared to informing farmers of the latest in agriculture. Since he was doing a lot of custom farm ditching, he wanted to keep up with the new ideas. He often spoke of his friend, Virgil Overholzer from The Ohio State University. Farm groups were usually provided entertainment for the event. The Granges of Auglaize county were asked to perform, and plans were made to travel in a local school bus. They accepted the invitation. Then gas rationing started in November and by performance time in late January, travel such as this was discouraged. Since they had promised to perform, those in charge felt they should go ahead as planned. The road to Columbus, U.S. Route 33, was a two-lane road then. The hill at Bellefontaine always presented a challenge, especially since there were no passing lanes. That hill was known throughout the state as a tough one, especially for trucks. They just kept going slower and slower as they tried to climb that steep incline. Sometimes traffic backed up for several miles. We had just descended this hill when someone yelled, "There is a highway patrolman, scoot down in your seats and look like a bus load of kids going to school. Maybe he'll leave us alone." I don't know if that helped or if he had more important things to do, but we drove on toward Columbus. Our group did a good job of singing. I was especially impressed with a young lady from the east end of the county who sang "Indian Love Call" so beautifully that it brought tears to my eyes. Oh, the love of music!

While the rest of our group returned home on the bus, Don and I stayed overnight with Dad at the elegant Deshler Wallick Hotel in downtown Columbus. I was impressed by a room that had mirrors along the walls. What fun to see ourselves from several angles in several mirrors at the same time!

Dad took us on a grand tour of the Columbus area. I was never fond of high places, and the AIU Tower was the city's tallest building. It was definitely higher than any place I'd ever been before. A 1939 picture post card proclaims: "The American Insurance Union Citadel is one of America's most beautiful buildings. It is a 45-story skyscraper, 555.5 feet high, erected by an Insurance Company founded in the City of Columbus. It is one of the world's tallest buildings. Powerful searchlights on the tower guide the way of night flyers over the city." That magnificent tall building was definitely impressive in those days.

My heart pounded as we rode the elevator to the top, and I wondered when it would stop. It was a much longer ride than the two- or three-story elevators back at J.C. Penney, The Leader or Greggs department stores in Lima. I remember the important things–stepping gingerly out of that elevator and seeing the words “Kilroy was here!” scribbled on the side of the wall! The highest part of the tower was an open area with a walkway around it. As I tiptoed over to the surrounding wall, my hands were sweating, and I trembled as I leaned over, straining to peer at the street far below. So breathtaking, but oh, so scary!

The beautiful paintings in the rotunda of Ohio’s State House were magnificent. We gazed up at them until our necks ached. We also visited the offices of our governor and other state officials and walked into the “almost sacred” area where our state senators and representatives conducted their business.

The old State Penitentiary was located near the downtown area, and Dad thought we should see it, too. We parked outside the gray walls surrounding the prison, high and forbidding with armed guards at each corner, then visited the gift shop where items made by prisoners were sold. Daddy bought me a little pin that was made from a flattened penny with the Lord’s Prayer imprinted on one side. (When I wore it to school a few days later, it came unpinned. Another girl found it. After a few days, she wore it to school, insisting it was hers. I knew better. Her daddy hadn’t taken her to the prison. Mine had!)

Dad finished the tour with a drive among the many buildings at The Ohio State University. (I certainly would not have believed my own son would some day be working, studying and teaching classes in some of those same buildings.) Of course, no campus visit would have been complete without a look at the huge *Ohio Stadium*. I was overwhelmed by its size as we walked up and down through the rows and rows of seats. We had sat in our living room and rooted for the OSU team as we ate popcorn and listened to the football games on Grandpa’s big console radio. Now, as I stood gazing at the playing field below, I could almost hear the radio commentator saying, “And it’s another win for Ohio State!” Go Bucks!

Dad’s interest in college encouraged me at Wittenberg. The college music honorary sorority, Sigma Alpha Iota, members, patronesses and alumni enjoyed the Christmas party in December of 1949. I’m wearing a velvet and lace formal, third from the left in the front row.

## Chapter 17.

# Planes, Trains and Things That Move

What is your very first memory? One of my earliest recollections involved a car. I was not quite three when Grandpa and I were driving to Spencerville. We were moving slowly, (well, didn't all cars move slowly in those days?). Suddenly I was quite surprised to see one of our wheels rolling and bouncing out through the field. When I turned to Grandpa, his look was as startled as mine. I don't remember any problem with the car, so it was probably the spare tire which seemed to have a mind of its own. The spare tire on those 1930s cars was often stored beside the hood in front of the right passenger door. Anyway, that runaway wheel was certainly having a jolly good time bouncing and jolting across that field in a scene I've never forgotten.

School buses have changed over the years. Until Salem Township bought their first bus, Mother, like the other students, had to find her own transportation. A friend of hers told me recently that a barn was located near the school. The kids' horses were stabled there during the day. One girl was quite proud of her horse because it was white. Most of the others were dark colors. The new bus was purchased in the early 1920s and was a great improvement over the horse and buggy days. Basically, it was a square box mounted on narrow wheels with four windows on each side. The top half of each window folded up and was fastened near the roof, while the bottom half folded down. Edgar DeLong, Dad's cousin, once told me he had driven that first bus from the Kossuth area to Spencerville School. He showed me a wooden model he had made.

My first school bus was an old Reo which had already seen better days. It was similar to the one Mother rode in. There were no seats, just benches down the center, along each side and across the back. It got very cold in the winter and I'm not sure it even had a heater. We were about the last ones to get on the bus and usually the only empty spaces were at the very back, meaning we had to climb over everyone's feet to get there. On my first day of school, I got on the bus and was trying to squeeze through all those knees to get to the back when I accidentally stepped on the toes of one of the "big" girls. When she yelled at me I don't remember if I cried, but I probably did! I remember trying to keep my distance after that. (Her name sounded like Walk-*off*, but I really upset her when I accidentally walked *on* her!) It strikes me as funny now, but it certainly didn't then! I was so little, and the world was so big!

I loved the first bus driver, Lester Bowersock. Since we were the last ones on the bus, we were also the last ones to get off. When the bus was almost empty, he allowed me to slide to the front and talk to him. He had a little girl in my class and he teased and talked to me. In the winter, as we drove down the Townline Road, I used my wool mittens to clear the ice from the left window, making a little hole just large enough for him to see if anyone was coming as we approached the stop sign. I was sure I was being very helpful by clearing that tiny spot in the glass.

Interest in traveling in the early 1900s blossomed with the advent of the exciting interurban. What an improvement over the horse and buggy! The interurban cars ran on tracks much like a railroad, but were fed by electricity through heavy overhead cables. Since the cars could not run backwards, a turntable was needed at the end of each line. The first cars to travel from St. Marys to Lima arrived on March 10, 1902. Other tracks crisscrossed Ohio, making it easy to travel to other parts of the nation. The first paved road in the area was built from New Bremen to St. Marys in 1917 and thus began the downfall of the interurban. The last car ran January 16, 1932.[1]

Many of the local older folks still talk about going north to catch the interurban at Moulton or Stop 30. When I talked to Aunt Alwina, she said she had boarded it there many times. As she remembered, if you wanted to get on, you stood on the track and waved as it approached. When the conductor saw you, he rang his bell, you got off the track, then waited for him to stop. Her dad had been on the board of the Equity Creamery in Lima and had traveled on the interurban many times. When Bill was five or six years old he rode the interurban to Lima with his grandpa.

Steam engines still chugged through Buckland when I was in grade school. As I sat at my desk in the top floor classroom on cold winter days, I watched in fascination as those "puffer bellies" huffed and puffed through town, billowing immense fluffy white clouds into the clear blue sky above. How I loved the unmistakable sound of those steam engines as they whistled for the Main Street crossing!

I finally got to ride on steam-powered trains to Cincinnati and back on two 4-H excursions. These trips included not only my first train ride, but my first ride on a ship, the *Island Queen*, a beautiful paddle wheel ship that left from downtown Cincinnati and traveled east to Coney Island Amusement Park and back. Some of the horses used today on a Kings Island merry-go-round are the same ones used at the old Coney Island park, but they had quite a trip before arriving there. During a flood which inundated Coney Island in 1937, the horses broke loose from the ride and many of them traveled down the Ohio River, some for many miles. One "swam" all the way to Memphis, Tennessee. Eventually they were recovered, and although some were badly damaged, they were restored and used again until Coney Island closed. When Kings Island was built in 1972, the merry-go-round was moved there. What a fascinating story some of those beautiful handmade horses could tell![2]

Trains seemed to fill the rails during World War II, not necessarily carrying the general public, but transporting military personnel, vehicles and equipment across the United States. Trains were quite long, many with more than one hundred cars. It seemed to be a universal pastime to count the cars as we waited patiently at railroad crossings. Some of the cars were covered with huge tarpaulins and we often speculated as to what might be under those strange looking bulges . . . huge tanks, cars with camouflage paint, giant cannons? War was serious business, even on the home front.

A lively topic of interest in the 1920s was that of airplanes. An early historical moment was recently written about by Kim Kincaid for the Jan. 22, 1997, issue of the Lima News.

> Lima has the distinction of being one of the first places in the United States where mail was delivered by Airplane. This occurred at the spring meeting of the Lima Driving Park Association, held at the fairgrounds in June 1912. A temporary post office was erected on the grounds, and mail from there was flown to the public square and deposited. However, the event drew such a crowd that one of the flights had to return to the fairgrounds with its original contents because there were too many people downtown for the plane to land.[3]

Traveling by airplane was just becoming the talk-of-the-town when my brother was born in 1927. World War I pilots had flown in daring dogfights over the battlefields of Europe and proven the reliability of aviation. The public was starting to accept the airplane, although the "If God wanted man to fly, He would have given him wings" skeptics still existed! Others sought to silence the skeptics, however. Richard E. Byrd and Floyd Bennett became the first people to fly over the North Pole on May 9, 1926. The next year, Charles Lindbergh was the first to fly alone nonstop across the Atlantic Ocean in his *Spirit of St. Louis*. The date was May 20-21, 1927. Lindbergh's flight soon spurred the adventurers to new heights and the newspapers were filled with stories of airplanes, pilots and their daring adventures as they tried to set new records for speed or distance. I was surprised at the number of stories about women learning to pilot planes. They were becoming more daring now that they were allowed to vote. Especially amazing was a front-page picture of a ten-year-old girl seated in the plane she was learning to fly.

In their frenzy for fame, several pilots lost their lives or were turned back in defeat. Such was the case in a flight by the German plane, the *Bremen,* described in the August 16, 1927, *Wapakoneta Daily News*. The headlines proclaimed "Attempt To Cross Atlantic by Gedman Airplanes Fails. The Junkers monoplane *Bremen*, one of two which left here [Dublin, Ireland] yesterday morning for the U.S. returned this afternoon, the plane and pilots baffled by their task." The pilot of the *Bremen* was August Loose who told of encountering heavy fog and high winds, forcing their return. However, on April 12-13 of 1928, the *Bremen* made the east to west flight with a new crew aboard. Their names were Herman Koehl, Capt. James Fitzmaurice, and Baron Guenther von Huenefeld. This trio was the first to fly from Europe to North America. The pilots were welcomed with a ticker-tape parade. Their plane rests in the huge Henry Ford Museum in Detroit, Michigan. Were we related to the Baron? Some of my Huenefeld relatives would like to claim him as an ancestor, but the Baron, a bachelor, seemed more interested in flying than marriage!

I was a bit puzzled when I read the August 9, 1927, headlines:

> First 'Air Truck' Goes Into Service. Will Perform Delivery Service to 500 Cities–Can Land Cargo by Parachute. The world's first 'air truck', an all-metal tri-motor, the newest development in the conquest of the air, and particularly in the advancement of commercial aviation, has been delivered to the Royal Typewriter Company . . . The new air delivery truck is a Ford-Stout tri-motor, all metal plane, with a cruising radius of 500 miles . . . powered by three Wright Whirlwind motors of the type used by Col. Lindbergh, Commander Byrd and Chamberlin on their trans-Atlantic flights. [4]

We have indeed come a long way since those first *air trucks* flew a whopping 500 miles to deliver typewriters. I saw the following in a *Wapakoneta Daily News*, Nov. 8, 1927–Delphos, Headline–"Delphos Inventor Has Patent Rights on Landing Field. An airplane landing field with many runways and a system of block signal lights, arranged so it might be operated in either good or inclement weather is one of the many inventions of Peter J. Backus of Delphos." Ever hear of Peter? He also had several other patents.

By the early 1940s, Earl Hoverman's 21 year-old-son, Austin, had developed an interest in flying and purchased a plane. We occasionally saw it fly overhead. One day he and a friend, Earl Wheeler, wrecked it in a field on the Wheeler farm. Earl was hurt, but recovered. A few days later Austin's dad drove past our house with the plane's wings removed and the sad remains resting on the back of his truck.

Airplanes became so numerous during World War II that, instead of occasionally running out to see one plane, we saw many planes almost daily. Great clusters of planes were flown across the United States. Some flew under the low hanging clouds so that we could actually see the pilot sitting in the cockpit. We occasionally heard the very distinctive sound of B36 planes as they flew over. These big six-engine pusher-type planes made a very low, prolonged rumbling sound that was especially noticeable at night.

Bill said Grand Lake St. Marys seemed to be used as a test area during the war. (Such things were never made public at the time.) Since their house was due east of the lake, they often saw fighter and escort planes flying over, then swooping low over the water. He speculated that they might be pilots from Wright-Patterson Air Force Base in Dayton flying practice runs over the lake. There would be less chance of someone getting hurt than on low runs over inhabited areas.

Identifying airplanes became a favorite school-boy hobby. One day a plane flying over Bill's house as his family was eating dinner made a much different sound than any of the planes they had heard. Bill ran out to see what kind it was, but even though he hurried, it was out of sight before he got there. Very unusual! It was later that they learned the plane which had made the sound was a recently developed flying machine called a "jet" plane.

Can interest in aviation be inherited? Before her marriage, Mother had worked at McCook Aviation Field in Dayton, Ohio, shortly before the field was closed and everything moved to Wright and Patterson fields. (I was even able to obtain records about her employment stint from the government!) Don eagerly took flying lessons and enjoyed flying. One nice clear day he took me for a ride and I was quite nervous about the whole thing. I didn't share his great enthusiasm for flying. I did all right as we flew over the countryside, but when we got to Spencerville, Don noticed a huge circus tent erected just east of town. Elephants were staked near the tent, and Don said, "Oh, let's go down for a closer look." As he tipped the plane and zoomed downward, my innards stayed up in the sky. I was sure I would tumble out through the side of the cabin and plummet to the ground below. It was during those moments my flying pattern was firmly established. I'm a white-knuckle flier! So much for those genes!

As little children, Don and I were fascinated by high-water buggies and a wood-paneled school bus, by puffer-belly steam engines that chugged down the tracks and by low-flying little planes that occasionally flew over our house, tipping their wings as we waved. Today's cars and buses are modern and streamlined. Only a few trains still run through our area. Huge airplanes fly so fast and so high that we see only vapor trails drifting lazily into the sunset. My, how times have changed!

---

[1] Supplement to *Combined Atlases of Auglaize County*, p. 71, 1994, used with permission.
[2] *Ohio Magazine*, June 1990, used with permission.
[3] Kim Kincaid, "Command Central," *Lima News*, Lima, Ohio, January 22, 1997, used with permission.
[4] *Wapakoneta Daily News*, Wapakoneta, Ohio, August 9, 1927, used with permission.

Grandpa and Grandma are ready to travel in their new car.

My mother, Lena Briggs, rode this old-time Salem Township school bus to Spencerville High School. My first bus was a newer model of a similar style.

## Chapter 18.
# *Strictly Personal and Oh, So Delicate*

**R**ight now, before we start, I want you to know that I was raised in a very modest home, Never did anyone run around the house without wearing clothes! Well, I can't honestly say that, either, can I? Since I was the youngest member in the family of five (Grandpa, Grandma, Dad, my brother Don, and me), I really don't know how I may have appeared when I was less than three years of age. That's the time when little "streakers" delight in their naughtiness, isn't it!

The strictly personal items often referred to as "unmentionables" are the current topic of discussion. If the delicate nature of the subject offends you, please turn the page and do not under any circumstance read even one more sentence. If you believe yourself to be capable of holding up under the strain, then read on!

The words "longjohns," "drawers," and "union suits" seem to have changed meaning over the years. Drawers were the knit underpants worn by some men. When I was a child, Grandpa's summer attire was usually lightweight "cotton" longjohns–a one-piece ankle length knit outfit with short sleeves and buttons down the front. In winter he switched to long-sleeved longjohns made of "wool." (Pardon me, but even as I write, the very thought of it makes me feel like scratching.) The only way to shed these garments was to unbutton all those front buttons, pull them off the shoulders, and step out. This would be an impossible task in a cold privy on a windy winter day. Thus, a narrow slit was located in the front and a two-button "trap door" was conveniently located in the back, of course. This took care of any emergency which a refined gentleman of that day might encounter. I never knew of my grandpa wearing anything but these two types of "unmentionables."

Now Dad, on the other hand, had a different type of summer attire. I think Grandma called them union suits. They were made of a lighter weight cotton than those worn by Grandpa and were low-necked, sleeveless, with short legs and the front slit. Instead of a two-button drop seat, they had a long one-button slit which parted sufficiently to provide ample space for sitting, once the trousers were dropped. The look somewhat resembled men's 1920s style swimsuits.

When it came to shopping, the men of the family didn't go with Grandma and me when we *girls* went to D. Armstrong Co. in St. Marys. They would have been too embarrassed! This was the store where Grandma purchased her unmentionables—girdles, corsets, "all-in-ones" and slips (which she called petticoats). Since these outdated words may be confusing to the younger generation, I feel it is my duty to issue an explanation for their benefit. Webster's Collegiate Dictionary, published 1948 was brand new when I entered college. It conservatively describes a girdle as "a light corset supporting the body below the waistline." A girdle was a smaller, less complicated article of clothing than a corset. Some girdles were made of heavy cloth with boning (a strip of whalebone or steel, used for stiffening), while others were made only of rubber. A college friend wore one of the rubber variety, and I could always tell if she was in the ladies' room. Not only was it a real struggle to step into and pull up to one's waistline, it also made a funny, rubbery slapping noise. (I was thankful I was skinny at that time. I didn't have to worry about such a nuisance.)

This was before the days of Spandex and nylon, so these garments were a major purchase and deserved the proper attention for correct fit. In days of such extreme modesty, I was always amazed that those dignified ladies who entered the Armstrong store would shed their outer clothing so that a clerk could come into the dressing room to fit them with a girdle or corset, poking and punching until everything was squeezed in just right.

I will try to explain those "all-in-ones" before dealing with the corset. The only way I can describe this garment is with a question mark. I really don't know what it was! I heard Grandma speak of it, but I have no remembrance of exactly what in the world it looked like. I guess the name explains it.

So, with that behind us, we shall go on to the corset. Webster describes it as "a close-fitting, boned undergarment reaching from the bust to below the hips, worn by women to support the body, or to mold the figure." Now that was a piece of equipment! My grandma wore one of those outlandish contraptions. Her corset was a marvelous outfit made of heavy pink cotton with strips of boning running the full length of the back, top to bottom. Actually it could have been called an "over-garment" since it was worn *over* one's undergarments. Heavy hooks joined the two sides together with a series of lacings that had to be drawn up as tightly as possible. If I remember correctly, straps crisscrossed in various places to help keep one's body in the best possible shape.

The corset was not worn for everyday. No, no! You put it on for church, ladies' meetings and especially for picture taking when one wanted to appear as trim as possible.

I remember the day I first came face to face with one of those monsters. As a child, my bed was in the corner of Grandpa and Grandma's bedroom. As I played with my dolls one day, I needed a blanket to cover them. Grandma was downstairs, so I opened her dresser drawer to see if there might be something there I might use. I'd never searched through Grandma's drawer before and I shouldn't have on that day! I was really puzzled when I unearthed that unusual conglomeration of straps and stays and strings. After a confused analysis, I quickly replaced it. But when Sunday came, I was a bit more attentive as to what certain people were putting on when getting ready for church. It was then I finally discovered the real purpose of that strange-looking item!

My conclusion today is that these garments may have improved the appearance, but they did nothing for the disposition. They had to have been vastly uncomfortable! That is why, if you look very carefully at early photographs, you will notice that the ladies are never smiling. Their faces show a very sober, almost pained expression. I am convinced it is because they laced those corsets entirely too tight!

## Chapter 19.

# "Shave and a Hair Cut, Two Bits"

Um, um! How good that smelled! But what was it? Grandpa went to the barbershop regularly, even though he had very little hair left to cut. Since I usually went along to town until I was old enough to go to school, I accompanied him into the barbershop and sat while he got "the works"!

I could always tell the barbershop from the other stores, even before I could read. It was the one with the big stick of red and white peppermint candy outside the door. (At least, I liked to think it was a giant stick of peppermint candy!) I especially remember the barber shop in the basement beneath one of the banks on the north side of Wapakoneta's Auglaize Street. The traditional red and white barber pole stood beside the steps leading down to the shop. Nearby stood a post that was topped by the big round clock advertising Hartman's Jewelry Store. That clock kept the shoppers on schedule and many checked their watches as they passed by.

Once inside the barbershop, Grandpa took a seat, and I squeezed as close to him as I could. Since he usually went to Wapak during the week, the kids were in school and the younger men were at work, leaving only the old men, Grandpa, and me as we sat along the wall and waited patiently.

Everyone seemed to know when it was his turn, and as the barber said, "Next," Grandpa put down the magazine he was reading and took his place in the chair. The barber pushed down repeatedly on the handle at the side of the chair. As if by magic, the chair rose higher into the air. Grandpa was soon "pumped up" to a suitable height. Covering him with a large white cloth, the barber grasped his pointed shears in one hand and a comb in the other and started snip, snip, snipping. It didn't take long to finish trimming the small amount of hair that Grandpa had. I loved the sweet smelling liquid he now rubbed into the hair. I didn't know until recently what that fragrance was called. As Bill and I visited the old-time barber shop in the Sauder Village Museum near Archbold, Ohio, the village barber did a quickie haircut to show us the routine. When he got down his bottle of Lucky Tiger Hair Tonic and started rubbing it into the man's hair, memories flooded back. *That* was the smell I remembered from Grandpa's trips to the barber long ago. Lucky Tiger not only smelled good, but the barber said it also helped control dandruff.

After the tonic was thoroughly massaged into the scalp, the barber combed the hair and flipped a soft brush back and forth on Grandpa's neck to eliminate any loose hair. For those not wanting a shave, the barber finished the job by carefully removing the white cloth with a flourish. And the next man stepped up to get "the works."

You have no doubt heard the old expression, "Shave and a hair cut, two bits." The two bits equaled twenty-five cents, a reasonable price in early days for both a haircut and a shave. By the time I was old enough to go with Grandpa, the price had gone up. The most exciting part of the event was watching as Grandpa got shaved. A hot, steamy white towel was wrapped around his face. While it softened the skin and whiskers, the barber grabbed his leather razor strop in one hand and, opening the blade of the straight-edged razor in the other, he stroked it back and forth, making a very satisfying slap, slap, slap sound. The barber then brought down a shaving mug with soap in the bottom. Wetting a soft bristled shaving brush, he moved it quickly back and forth with a slop, slop sound as he worked up a lather in the bottom of the mug. Removing the towel that had now cooled, he "painted" Grandpa's face with thick, white foam. I loved that part.

There was a knack to shaving with a straight razor. The barber didn't open the razor all the way. It had to be bent at an angle with the fingers holding the blade and cover at the hinge, in a manner that allowed the sharp edge to be drawn toward you, cutting the whiskers as it moved. He gently pushed the sides of Grandpa's face this way and that so that he could shave off every whisker. A good barber could cover a balloon with foam, then shave it with a straight-edged razor without bursting it. When the shaving was finished, the barber wiped Grandpa's face with the damp towel, removing all traces of lather. Pouring a sweet-smelling aftershave into the palms of his hands, the barber patted it on Grandpa's face. I always thought his *pat* was more like a *slap*, but Grandpa said that was just to stimulate the skin and it really hadn't hurt.

When I was small, Shirley Temple was the most popular little girl in the world. She was two years older than I, and her birthday was only a day or two away from mine, so I felt a real kinship. But when it came to looks, I felt I was a born loser. I wanted, oh, so badly, to have bouncy curls like Shirley had, but alas, I was destined for a lifetime of straight hair. I sat for hours, twisting my hair around and around my finger, hoping somehow it would end up in one of those plump little curls for which Shirley was so famous. But it never happened! One day Uncle Henry and Aunt Ida Schwartz were visiting, and after watching me twist my hair for a while, she turned to Grandma and said, "Whatever is wrong with that child? What's she trying to do with her hair?" I don't remember what Grandma said, but it wasn't too long before we went to Spencerville for my first chance at curls.

A beauty parlor was located on the lower level of the old Conservatory Hotel. An elderly lady, Bertha Gesellchen, owned the establishment. Her claim to fame at that time was a new permanent wave machine. Had I not been so terribly anxious for curls, I think I would have taken one look at that contraption and headed for home at once. Resembling something from outer space, the machine had lots of wires coming down to clamps that were fastened on my hair. I'd never seen an electric chair, but this surely had to come close! With the dastardly deed done, I peeked into the mirror and decided this lady had never seen Shirley Temple. Instead of soft, plump curls, I saw stiff little kinky curls that smelled faintly of burned hair! Oh, dear!

I learned a valuable lesson from that experience. If the Lord had wanted me to have curls, He would have given them to me. That was my first and last experience with that monstrous machine. When new and improved methods of curling hair were devised, I finally got my curls.

We have some memories of our own children's haircuts. We didn't cut Steven's hair until he was two years old. By then, he had curls reaching to his shoulders and had been mistaken more than once for a girl. His hair was so pretty, we hated to have it cut, but a visitor at church one Sunday wondered why I had taken such a pretty little girl to church wearing pants. That did it! That boy's hair had to be cut! As the barber set Steven on a special board across the arms of the chair and pumped it up as high as it would go, four-year-old Michael stood by and watched. When the barber said something to him about his brother, he proclaimed, "Steven is a girl." He had said that before and when we said, "No, Steven is a boy," he had responded by shaking his head and matter-of-factly stating, "No, Steven's a girl." After the barber had cut off the curls around the front of Steven's head, Michael had a puzzled look on his face. Finally he said, "Well! . . . Steven *IS* a boy!!!"

Spencerville, Ohio's oil boom prompted the building of this beautiful 65-room Keeth Hotel in 1882. It boasted running water from a storage tank in the attic. Parked on the left are the guests' buggies and the sign above the canopy says "Oil Well Supplies." Johnzy Keeth brought big-city elegance to this small town. (Later generations spelled the name Keith.) When the hotel was sold in 1910, it became the home of the Ohio Conservatory of Music and Art. It was here Dad took violin lessons as a young man. When this enterprise failed, it became the Conservatory Hotel. I received that dreaded first permanent in the basement, formerly the ballroom, of this building.

(*Photo from the Zeitha Wierwille collection, courtesy of Lee Schnelle*)

## Chapter 20.
# *Goliath of the Barnyard*

Regardless of whether you spell it threshing or thrashing, it meant the same thing–a lot of hot very dirty, very dusty work. I was still rather small when the last Goliath of the Barnyard, the threshing machine, came down the road to our house for the final time. I have joined my memories with those of a few friends and relatives to paint this picture of threshing day when the huge machines, the Goliaths of the Barnyard, were in charge.

"Rain, rain, won't this rain ever stop? How in the world will we ever get our wheat threshed?" Dry weather was needed for threshing, but folks back in 1896 were getting concerned. Great-grandpa Schwartz lived in Salem Township where a July 30 item in the *Auglaize County Republican* explained: "Owing to the frequent rains of the past week much damage is done to wheat and oats. Some of the wheat shocks are perfectly green from growing wheat."

In earlier years, the grain had been cut with a hand sickle, then tied into bundles or sheaves. With the invention of a horse drawn grain binder, farming methods changed. It cut and bundled the wheat or oats, ready to be placed in shocks. The bundles were stacked in a way that allowed the water to run off the shock without damaging the grain. During that wet summer of 1896, the farmers may have been able to save some of the inner bundles, but those that were growing on the outer edges of the shock would have spoiled.

The more progressive farmers in the area purchased huge steam engines and threshing machines to thresh the grain out of the bundles. In the *Republican* of July 10, 1890, Logan Township, home of the Davenport family, boasted of "six or seven threshing machines within a radius of five miles."

Threshing was a big job and several men were needed to take care of all the various activities. Neighborhood "threshing rings" were formed with several men working together to harvest crops. The man responsible for starting a fire in the steam engine boiler had to be up by three or four o'clock in the morning. He had to have a good head of steam going by the time neighbors arrived to start the day's work with their teams of horses and wagons.

Keeping the proper pressure in a boiler was an item of concern. An interesting incident was recorded in the September 13, 1900, *Republican:* "New Knoxville: Messrs. Kruse and Schroerluke, the threshers, came near having a catastrophe last week with their recently purchased boiler. That the boiler did not imitate a balloon and make an ascension is due to the timely discovery that the water in the boiler was dangerously low. The water was found to be below the second row of flues. The crown sheet and upper row of flues were so badly burned that some time was consumed in making the necessary repairs." Someone was a bit over-zealous in reporting the incident and by October 25, the following appeared: "Some time ago we stated through these columns that Benjamin Schroerluke, engineer of Kruse and Schroerluke's thrashing rig had a narrow escape from having their boiler take an ascension and parachute descent. Since then we have conversed with parties who were present at the time in question and they tell us that it was misrepresented. This led us to making inquiry and we now take pleasure in stating that the circumstances were altogether different from the statement made in our former article. The engineer may have been negligent in some degree but not to the extent of endangering the loss of life or property."

The job of water tender was to see that an ample supply of water was available for maintaining a good head of steam in the engine's boiler. A team of horses pulled a water wagon that held a large water tank, usually made of wood. As the tank was emptied, the team pulled the wagon to the nearest source of water. In the area around Kossuth, that was usually the Miami-Erie Canal or the St. Marys River.

Another job was the blower tender whose assignment was to build the straw stack. Some knowledge of this job was necessary to guarantee a stack that would stay put during storms and provide a form of shelter for the cows as they huddled against it, trying to avoid the wind. Some farmers used a wooden frame when building the straw stack. As the blower blew the straw around and onto this framework, it formed a nice, enclosed room where the cows could get inside in bad winter weather. Again, there was a knack in knowing how to build this stack, since new straw was extremely slippery and hard to manage.

The barn at Bill's childhood home had a second floor straw mow. Here, the tender had to see that the straw was distributed evenly, especially into all the corners.

Another important job was filled by the man who took care of the threshing machine. Before the threshing began each morning, he greased and oiled the machines, making sure everything moved freely. He also made sure the belts stayed in place.

Another man took care of the steam engine itself, adding wood to the firebox as needed. The farmer usually had an ample supply of wood piled up in the yard near the steam engine. The steamer's location was very important. It had to be downwind from the thresher so that sparks from the firebox wouldn't ignite the chaff or straw near the machine. The thresher was located at least fifty feet away from the steamer with a long belt connecting the two.

When threshing day finally arrived, I could hear the procession, with its squeaks and clangs of pulleys and metal parts bumping together, and the sheer excitement of the occasion brought a generous supply of goose bumps. The parade of huge threshing equipment coming down the road was indeed a sight to behold! In the 1920s, much of the threshing in our Kossuth area was done by Jacob Leffel with his huge Baker steam engine and Baker threshing machine, sometimes referred to as the separator since it separated the grain from the straw. By the time I was born, the steam engine had been replaced by a huge gasoline tractor.

Some of the men used teams of horses and wagons with hayracks to carry the bundles of wheat from the shocks in the field to the barn. Wheat straw was very slippery, so the heads of grain were laid end to end, meshing them together for more stability. The butt ends of the sheaves of grain were carefully placed around the outside of the wagon to form a solid foundation, then the rest of the sheaves were packed down in the center. If done properly, the load would not shift or slide off as it swayed and bumped through rough fields on its way to the barn. There was an occasional friendly rivalry as each farmer tried to outdo his neighbors. The Kossuth area winner was usually Jake Scholl. He had a lively team of horses and was very particular in loading his wagon. Jake was always delighted when he (with help from his team of hard working horses) was declared Kossuth's winner each year.

In Bill's Grandpa Wierwille's family, just as in the Schwartz family, the daughters were all unfortunate enough to have been born first, so they had to work like men to help on the farm. One year Aunt Alwina and Aunt Caroline helped haul the sheaves of wheat out of the field across the road. Caroline later told Alwina they had hauled forty-five wagon loads of sheaves to the barn to be threshed. Folks, that is an awful lot of work, especially for a couple of girls!

Meanwhile, the rest of the men set up the machinery in the barnyard. After the separator was in place and the tractor was placed so its pulley was lined up with the one on the threshing machine, the long, long belt was put on and tested for accurate placement. When all was in readiness, the signal was given to commence threshing. I was engulfed by the sound of wheels turning, gears meshing and belts slapping as wagon after wagon load of sheaves were pulled alongside the thresher. Men using pitchforks threw the bundles of wheat into the separator. The endless itch of wind-blown chaff soon descended on everything in the area, including me. Even with that little irritation, threshing was almost more excitement than a four-year-old could handle! I loved it!

On the Wierwille farm, the thresher was placed near the barn with the straw being blown into the strawmow. When that was full, the rest of the straw was blown onto a straw stack beside the barn. Having straw in a mow above the animal stables was quite handy. When bedding down the animals, the straw was pushed through a hole in the floor to the stable directly below. This eliminated a lot of heavy work, making it a good chore for the children.

Bill's cousin, Ralph Hoelscher, was a young boy when he and neighbor boy, Casper Hoelscher, went to the barn to play in the fresh straw, something they really were not supposed to do. As Ralph looked over at his friend, Casper suddenly disappeared, right before his eyes. While walking through the fresh straw, it had started to slide, allowing Casper to slip right down through that hole to the cow stable below. Ralph was really scared because he was sure Casper would be badly hurt. Fortunately, the fall didn't break any bones, and by the time Ralph had climbed down out of the mow, Casper was walking away as though nothing had happened.

But back to threshing. No one seemed to remember the cost of threshing, but the price had been set according to the number of bushels each farm produced. This seemed an equitable way to do it, since the man with a bumper crop that required extra time and energy would pay more than the farmer with the same number of acres but whose crop might not have been quite as good.

A counter on the thresher kept track of the number of bushels of grain. Using a bagger, the grain was placed in sacks and loaded onto the narrow grain wagons that were so popular at that time. These wagons were then pulled into the granary and unloaded.

Each ring had a few rules of their own making. For instance, Bill's grandpa had gone to each of the other men in his ring and paid them a little extra money because he had the largest acreage and had required more of their help than he had furnished them in return. The money evened things out a little. In another neighboring threshing ring, the farmer who had grown the best wheat provided a real treat for the rest of the group—ice cream.

Huge dinners were the highlights of threshing day. What a job it must have been to cook for a threshing crew, using only a wood cookstove on hot summer days. Lola Lammers' mother baked fruit pies and crusts for filled pies on the day before threshing, since the oven would be filled with the meat and other items on threshing day. Chickens were killed and cleaned the day before, then left to soak overnight in salt water to keep them from spoiling. Since they had no refrigeration, the filling for cream pies had to be cooked on threshing day in large pans on top of the wood stove. Vegetables were also cooked there, and chickens were fried in huge cast iron skillets on the stove's top. Lola's dad left the threshing crew for a short time and went to the Kettlersville meat market, bringing back a huge roast that covered most of the big pan used to bake it in the oven. Margaret Henschen's family always had huge amounts of steak which her mother had baked in the oven. Cookstoves, like farmers' wives, worked long hours of overtime on threshing days.

Occasionally city relatives came to spend threshing day on the farm. Extra ladies could be very helpful in the kitchen. The July 23, 1914, *Auglaize County Democrat* told of a threshing dinner at my grandparents' home. "William Bradford and wife (Grandpa's aunt) and Mrs. George Hoopingarner from Wapakoneta motored out to Frank Davenports to spend the day Friday and to eat a good old threshing dinner. Bill said: 'My, those ladies are surely some cooks, and if I don't stop eating chicken pretty soon I will never get home.'" Although the men's names were not included, at least eight ladies were mentioned, all relatives and friends who may also have come to help celebrate the Davenports' fifteenth wedding anniversary the next day.

Of the older folks who remember threshing days, most remember the disappointment of seeing all that wonderful food on the table. Children were not allowed to eat until the men had eaten their fill and gone back to work. Only then would the women and children finish the leftovers.

One of the foods served quite often at threshing dinners was a newly developed product, Jell-O. It was cool, tasty and very refreshing in the dusty, dry throats of the men. Lola Lammers recalled hearing a story about her grandfather's first experience with Jell-O. He was one of those old-fashioned, no foolishness, very strict German men. When the housewives of America were first introduced to Jell-O in 1897, it was considered a luxury item on the farm; however, Lola's grandma had tasted Jell-O at the home of a friend and she loved it. Determined to have some for her family, she secretly bought it and hid it away until she could prepare it without her husband's knowledge, since she was sure he would complain about such an extravagant waste of money for such a foolish thing as Jell-O. One day she prepared it, placing it to set up on the coolest spot on the farm, the basement floor. When her husband had gone back to his farming after dinner, she brought the dish up to the kitchen where she and the children ate all of it. They enjoyed it so much she occasionally made up other flavors, but it was never mentioned to her thrifty-minded husband.

As the family ate dinner at a neighbor's house one day, the lady placed a special bowl of dessert on the table. Lola's grandpa helped himself and enjoyed it so much that he turned to his wife and said, "You ought to get some of this, too." She was very happy to oblige and from then on, the *entire* family enjoyed that delicious new dessert, Jell-O!

When the threshing was finished, the equipment moved slowly onto the road and proceeded to the next job. I was told there were often two whistles on a steam engine. Their signals varied, but in one area, the whistle was blown three times to signal that the threshing was done and the machine would be moving to the next farm. If that farmer was not ready, the engine would go on down the road, blowing the other, more shrill whistle to tell the next farmer it was on its way and to get ready for the thresher. Those old steam engines had a whistle that could be heard for quite a distance. Charles Sandkuhl often heard the Leffels blowing their steam whistle just for fun as they drove through Kossuth.

Because of the weight and length of a steam engine and the long separator which followed it, the operator had to be careful when crossing bridges. In those days there were no bridge inspectors or load limits, so every man took his chances. My grandpa told of a threshing machine that had started across the canal bridge at Kossuth in 1917, and the bridge had collapsed under the extreme weight. When he had to cross bridges that didn't look too sturdy, Evalyn Sandkuhl's dad, Clarence Leffel, always started the steam engine slowly across the bridge, then jumped down and let it cross by itself, in case it fell through. He walked over the bridge after the last piece of equipment was safely across, then ran to catch up with the slow-moving engine and jumped on board, proceeding down the road .

As a little girl, Evalyn ran down the side of the road to meet her daddy as he brought the threshing outfit home after the completion of a job. They could always hear him coming, and as she ran toward the big engine, he stopped, picked her up, and let her enjoy the rest of the trip with him. When the threshing equipment needed repairs, she also enjoyed the ride up to Swanton for parts.

One such trip was quite memorable for her. When *faster* became *better*, the Leffel family decided to modernize. They would trade the steamer for a gasoline tractor. But the new tractor just didn't have enough power to operate the huge separator and the decision was made to drive it back to Swanton and trade it on an even larger model. Since Evalyn was an only child, a cousin was allowed to ride along. The procession started out with them sitting in their Cadillac as it was pulled behind the slow-moving tractor. When night approached, the tractor was parked in a farmer's barnyard, they got into the Cadillac and drove home. The next morning the two men drove the car back to the barnyard and finished the slow trip to Swanton. By now the Leffel family had seen enough slow trips with cumbersome tractors. The larger tractor was shipped on a railroad flat car to Spencerville, and the Leffels made the return trip in the comfort of their automobile.

What did the owners of steam engines do the rest of the year? The next crop to be harvested was the oats, which were so necessary for feeding horses. Farmers also had to harvest clover seed. Much like making hay, the mature clover was mowed and left to dry. Then it was brought to the barn and run through a cleaner that was powered by a steam engine. This separated the seed from the dried plants, cleaning the weed seed out and preparing the clover for next year's hay planting. The steam engines also provided the power to operate the corn shredders, and occasionally it provided power for drilling water wells. Some owners used one to saw the large piles of wood needed for the winter's fuel supply. On cold winter days, the owners stayed inside and did the repairs needed to keep things running smoothly. In the days before electricity, the steam engine was the real "work horse" when it came to the big jobs on the farm.

I was a bit envious of my "water boy" brother when they did the threshing on our farm. I had been cautioned to stay far away from the huge machines and all the activity, but Don got to walk right up to the sweaty men and give them a drink from the water jug.

Have you noticed how water containers have changed over the years? Don carried water to the thirsty men in a wooden keg with a wire bail or handle on top and two holes just below it. The larger hole was wide enough to allow an ample flow of water to quench the thirst. Grandpa had whittled a tapered wooden plug until it was smooth and round. That was used to close the drinking hole. The smaller hole allowed air to enter the jug so the water could pour out in a stream.

Grandpa's water jug was used year-round. During spring planting it sat in the tall grassy fence-row, ready for a drink at the end of the newly planted row. A shady spot under a tree kept it cool in summer as the men plowed the weeds out of the cornfield. In the fall it sat on the ground beside the corn shocks as Grandpa and Grandma used their husking pegs to get the bright yellow ears of corn out of the dry husks. When the men brought in the year's supply of firewood in the winter, the water jug nestled in the thick carpet of leaves beside the huge oak tree. Water kegs went by the wayside after the introduction of thermos jugs, but when I was a child, the water boy's wooden keg was always a welcome sight to thirsty threshers.

As I said, my brother was the water boy. After one particularly long, hot day, I awoke to hear him mumbling something as he walked down the stairs. He was half-way down before Dad reached him. "What are you doing?" Dad asked. "I've got to get some water out to those men," an extremely tired little boy replied. Don was exhausted, yet he was so concerned about keeping water for those thirsty men that he felt he had to go back out. The problem was–it was the middle of the night–Don was still sound asleep!

Threshing machines were indeed the Goliaths—the giants of the barnyard—but like Goliath, they were eventually brought down by the little Davids, the small combines that area farmers eventually purchased. Steam equipment still fascinates farmers. Shows are held throughout the United States featuring these monstrous machines that were once the workhorses of the mechanical world. Threshing days have disappeared from the farm scene in Auglaize County, along with steam engines, separators, straw stacks and shocks of wheat, but my, weren't those the days! [1]

---

[1] Information compiled from Don Davenport, Alwina (Wierwille) Niemeyer, Charles & Evalyn (Leffel) Sandkuhl, Silas & Lola Lammers, Ralph Hoelscher, Adrian & Martha Settlage, Margaret Henschen, Elmer and Reuben Henschen, and others attending the October, 1996 Historical Society Platt Deutsch meeting.

Threshing day at the home of Bill's grandparents in the 1920's
This picture was taken by Bill's dad and was made from the original glass negative.
It shows the complete process, from the wheelbarrow of wood on the right to the straw stack on the left.

## Chapter 21.
# *The Burying of the Dead*

**F**razier's Bottom, West Virginia, is where we saw it. The owner pointed to a bench-like piece of wood and asked if we knew what it was. We certainly didn't. It looked like a two-foot wide slab of tree cut about six feet long with four tree-branch legs holding it up. It seemed too wide to use as a seat. He explained that it was "a cooling bench," a bench upon which a body was placed after death to "cool" in the proper position for burial. Several decades earlier it had been passed around in the neighborhood, and when a family member was near death, someone searched the area to locate the bench. I had never heard of a cooling bench, and if one was used locally, it was definitely before my time.

At one time, Bill's mother mentioned that the dinner bell was sometimes rung when there was a death in the family. Neighbors usually came as soon as they heard the sad news. While family members often tenderly washed their loved ones and dressed them for burial, neighbors helped clean the house in preparation for the viewing. Furniture was moved aside, making room for the casket to be displayed, usually in the living room.

One of my first memories with death was of sitting on Grandma's lap in a kitchen filled with women, while the men stood in clusters on the front porch and in the yard. Family and friends brought food and gathered to support the bereaved. The viewing of the deceased was held in the person's home. In fact, this was such an important event that one of Bill's relatives in Iowa said the only reason they had put a front door in the house was to get the family caskets in and out. (Friends and relatives always entered through the back door.) Either a large wreath of flowers was fastened at the front door or a floral arrangement stood beside it to let folks know that a family member had died. For friends and relatives who may have arrived by train or driven in by buggy or car, it was an easy method of identifying the correct home. Also, door-to-door salesmen knew they shouldn't bother these sad homes as they drove through the countryside. In fact, Gloria Eddingfield said the old custom of door wreaths signifying a death was so ingrained in the local people that when she first placed an attractive wreath on her home's front door as a decoration, her mother just didn't think it was quite proper!

Someone always offered to stay overnight in the home, especially if the lady of the house would now be alone. While the funeral service was being held at the church, two or three neighbors stayed at the house and returned the furniture to its original place. When the family and closest friends returned from the cemetery, the house looked normal again, food was laid out, and a time of fellowship brought a form of comfort to the home. During this time someone might mentioned how "old John sure had been a good neighbor. Remember the time he . . . " and the mood eventually changed from one of sadness to a time of laughter, recalling some of the tricks old John had played. "Do you remember how he was so used to driving his team of horses that when he drove his first car, he kept talking to it, but it wouldn't listen!" It was a time of healing and as the group departed, old John's widow felt she would not be forsaken by these good friends and neighbors.

Great changes have been made in coffins. A late 1800s coffin for a child was recently displayed at the New Knoxville Historical Museum. Made from simple wooden boards, the coffin narrowed above the head. The sides flared out toward the shoulders, then narrowed toward the feet. The simple box was often lined with a favorite blanket or quilt. More elegant models eventually became available and were rectangular with a fancy satin or velvet lining, much like those of today. While the early coffins were placed directly into the ground or into a rough box, one must now buy a concrete vault. Coffins are designed with elegant carvings and handles, with rubber seals, with indestructible vaults, with everything imaginable to *preserve* the body! Does no one remember the Biblical admonition, "Ashes to ashes and dust to dust?" And by the way, they are no longer "coffins." Now they are "caskets" or "burial containers."

Speaking of "preservation," there have been many other changes since "cooling boards." Embalming in its more modern form came about during the Civil War. Due to the number of soldiers dying on battlefields far from their homes, a form of embalming was used to preserve the bodies until a decent burial could take place. For many, this meant they could be returned to their homes. The methods of embalming were rather crude, and up until the 1930s, the undertaker did the embalming in the family home. Because many homes did not have window or door screens, flies from the barns were quite prevalent. Thus, a sheer, light-colored veil was placed across the coffin. It was through this veil that the body was viewed. I don't know when the veil was discontinued but probably about the time the viewing changed from the home to the funeral parlor. I don't remember exactly when that happened, but I do remember that when some of the first families started showing their loved ones at funeral homes, some neighborhood gossips figured it was probably because their home wasn't good enough for the viewing or that it was just too much trouble to clean it. That may not have been a very gracious attitude, but it was one that I had heard expressed more than once.

Are you old enough to remember when the local furniture dealer was usually the undertaker? Since the man who made much of the furniture had the tools and expertise to work with wood, he also made the caskets used to bury the dead. As the process of embalming became more sophisticated, the furniture man not only made the furniture and the caskets, he or one of his employees, often his son, acquired the knowledge to embalm the body. C.B. Miller (better known as Patsy Miller) at one time had a furniture store and undertaking business in Kossuth. Don married his granddaughter, Mary Mitchell. When our daughter married David Humphreys, we discovered that his grandfather had owned the same type of business in Columbus Grove many years ago. The two grandpas apparently knew each other!

Over the years, even the names used by the professionals have changed. As a child, I heard the men referred to as undertakers or morticians. Their place of business was called the funeral parlor or mortuary. Later they were called funeral directors and funeral homes.

As a child, I do not remember funerals ever being held any place other than a church. Even the scalawags who had flaunted their sinfulness were properly "preached and prayed over" in the sanctuary of the local church. Since there were no air conditioners in those days, the Miller Funeral Home, as did many others, kept a supply of advertising fans available at the church. They were not only good for fanning during warm funeral services, but also were nice to have on hot and humid Sunday mornings. The earliest models were woven of straw with the funeral home name and logo printed on the side. Later fans were of cardboard with pretty pictures on the sides, the advertising imprinted below, and a wooden handle to hold. Another model was made in three sections fastened together at the bottom.

Another custom that has changed deals with when the body is viewed and the casket closed. In our present day, the body is usually taken to the church an hour or so before the funeral. Guests may view it there if they wish. Sometimes the casket is closed at the beginning of the funeral before the family is ushered into their seats at the front of the church. At other times, the casket is closed at the conclusion of the service and the family is escorted out first with the other guests following. Others skip the church entirely and have "grave side" services at the cemetery. When I was a child, the casket remained open at the front of the church and at the end of the funeral service, the friends and relatives in attendance were asked to walk past the casket in single file for one last look at the deceased. Then they left the church and stood respectfully in the church yard as the immediate family spent a few moments alone with their loved one. As the family left the church, the casket was closed and brought to the hearse while the assembled crowd dispersed or entered their cars for the procession to the nearby cemetery.

Even the names associated with the burial have changed! During my grandparents' generation, loved ones were "laid to rest" in the burial grounds or the graveyard, sometimes jokingly called the "bone yard." And some were even buried beneath a favorite tree near the family home. Today our "deceased" loved ones experience "interment" in a "memorial garden" and sometimes inside a "mausoleum."

When someone is hurt or becomes ill today, a square-boxed emergency squad vehicle answers a 911 call and rushes that person to the hospital. As ironic as it may seem, when I was a little girl, the hearse that carried the corpse to the cemetery was the same vehicle that answered the call when someone had to be rushed to the hospital. At that time, the funeral home was the only business having a vehicle long enough to transport a person while lying down. A three-inch high advertisement in the September 27, 1927, *Wapakoneta Daily News* read as follows: "Ambulance Service–Home Furnishers and Undertakers. Phone Main 1859. Heinl and Swonger, Wapakoneta." Some undertakers eventually purchased a separate vehicle which was kept for ambulance use only, but of course it was an expensive vehicle. As medical knowledge progressed, specially-trained people became Emergency Medical Technicians (EMTs) who made use of many items not available in the old ambulances. Thus, today's emergency vehicles are designed with lifesaving features built into them. Can you imagine what would happen today if a seriously ill person called for an ambulance in order to be transported to the hospital and a funeral car or hearse pulled up to do the job? Oops! The words "funeral car" and "hearse" are no longer viable. My friend Ron McClaren, who works for a funeral home, informs me they are now called "funeral coaches."

At the same time, the improvements in medicine have had a significant impact on the circumstances surrounding death and dying. It is rare to experience "epidemics" such as our ancestors did. During the cholera epidemic of 1848 to 1850, the local carpenters could scarcely keep up with the desperate need for coffins, and one winter the wooden boxes were stacked in a corner of the grave yard until the ground had thawed enough to dig graves in the spring.

We often forget the risks associated with bringing new life into a world without delivery rooms and incubators for premature infants. My grandpa's Grandma Rebecca Daniels went to her eternal rest in the late 1860s with her newborn twin babies, one on each side, lying on a blanket inside a hollowed-out log casket. They were buried on the family farm with a simple wooden cross stuck in the mound of dirt above the grave. Shortly after, her husband and the younger children left for a new life in Minnesota. Yes, living and dying were both difficult for those early pioneers.

Bill's father took this picture of a horse-drawn funeral hearse from the Arcade in New Bremen, Ohio. It was used at the death of a relative in the early 1900s. This copy was made from his original glass negative.

## Chapter 22.
# *The "Old" Folks*

Why are some people *old* at fifty while others are still *young* at seventy? When I think back to the "old" people of my childhood, I am amazed to find that many of them were much younger at that time than I am today. Many things seemed to make those folks appear older.

People usually didn't live as long back then, so relatively speaking, they *were* old. But age is a state of mind, and folks seemed to *think* and *act* old then. Like many others, Bill's home and mine had three or more generations living in the house. There was always someone to take care of the "old folks." Grandmas then were content to sit and peel potatoes, do the mending and rock the baby. Today's Grandmas have to squeeze baby-sitting in somewhere between aerobics and tennis class. Back then, ladies did not have hobbies to occupy their minds. They got their exercise doing the daily chores–washing clothes and hanging them outside (summer and winter), carrying wood for the stove, milking the cows, hauling feed to the henhouse and baskets of eggs back to the house, weeding gardens and flower beds, chasing escaping pigs back into the hog lot–all things a farm wife had to do. And anyway, to have wasted precious time for something frivolous like a hobby would have seemed almost sinful!

When looking at old pictures, people appeared to be older because of what they wore. Dresses worn by the ladies were quite long, almost to the ground, with long sleeves and high necklines. They were rather bulky and loose fitting. (I remember Grandma being upset when, as a teenager, I wanted my clothes to fit tighter. To show the outline of one's figure seemed quite inappropriate.) A 1996 *Lima News* article, "Clothes for Fashion and Function," caught my eye. The Ohio Legislature had an interesting bill submitted in the 1920s to prevent selling "any garment which unduly displays or accentuates the lines of the female figure." It would also forbid the wearing of a "shirtwaist [blouse] or evening gown which displays more than three inches of her throat." Lastly, it would not allow a female "more than fourteen years of age from wearing a skirt which does not reach to that part of the foot known as the instep."[1] No one seemed interested, and the bill failed.

Although the pictures I have seen from the 1920s and 30s were not in color, it is easy to see that the clothing worn by the older people was dark, even in summer when the younger women were in white and pastels. I don't think I ever saw Bill's grandmother, who lived to be ninety-eight, appear in public in dresses of any color other than black, brown, navy or possibly gray (but only if it was *dark* gray). She had a good sense of humor and always said she didn't care what color a dress was, just so it was *black*!

Besides the dark clothing, the eye glasses made people look older. Frames were little round metal-rimmed styles. Because of their one-size-fits-all design, they often slid down on the nose.

Older ladies often wore their hair in tight little buns or other styles that were easy to care for. Ladies did not wash their hair every day or two. How about every month or two? (In the pioneer days, many of the women washed their hair two or three times a year, *whether it needed it or not.* The rain water needed for washing hair was usually used for more important things like washing dishes, faces and babies.) Grandma's older relatives came to reunions with their hair braided and wrapped around their head in tight little buns. This style worked well with hats, and of course hats were the thing to wear–to town, definitely to church, and even to family reunions held out of doors in parks and backyards. Yes, getting dressed up was certainly proper back in those days.

Although there were some quite stylish hats with elegant feathers and fancy flowers, usually the older the lady, the plainer the hat. In keeping with their dresses, the hats also had to be a very dark color. Bill's grandma preferred black hats. A recent display at the New Knoxville museum suggests that a lot of other ladies felt the same way. The hats were all black. I was told that the more well-to-do and influential ladies in town usually wore the large, wide-brimmed hats with lots of long feathers, huge flowers, and a magnificent long hat pin to keep everything in place on their heads. An elegant display indeed, but woe unto the unlucky person who was seated behind them in church. About the time they got situated where they could see around the hat, the lady shifted positions and they had to start over. I am told these ladies of importance did a lot of nodding and moving from side to side because they delighted in seeing the long feathers flutter about the face.

One of the special items I enjoyed when I played dress-up as a child was the long purple feather from one of the elegant old hats which Grandma had saved and stored away in Grandpa's trunk. On rainy days, I loved to put on her long dresses (well, they were long on me), plop an old hat on my head with a feather sticking straight up, then clomp around the room in a pair of her old shoes. My roles varied: the Queen of England, a silent movie heroine, a missionary among the heathen, or one of the sisters from my book of *Little Women*.

Ladies' hosiery consisted of heavy cotton or woolen stockings that were either fastened to a corset, a girdle or had a band of elastic placed at the top of the stocking, then rolled down two or three turns to make it stay up. (During World War II when elastic was not available, Grandma figured out a way of twisting the top of the hose, then tucking it in and rolling it down. It stayed fairly well.)

Gloves were usually worn when outside the home and were an absolute *must* when going to church. Grandma once made the remark that she was glad they wore gloves to church. After a particularly hard week of outdoor chores, the gloves were a good cover for her rough, red hands. You must remember that a farm wife's hands spent a lot of time in a pan of dishwater three times a day, as well as in the huge tub of hot wash water each week. Then they worked in the fields beside their husbands, pitching hay, shocking wheat and husking corn. Even with heavy cotton work gloves, these activities created rough, red hands.

Some of the methods of conveying food to the mouth were a bit different for those older folks. Both Bill and I remember seeing people pour their hot coffee into a saucer, then hold it up to their mouth to blow on it until it was cool enough to drink. Some poured it back into the cup and drank, others drank it directly from the saucer. Most of that generation also loved to dunk–donuts, toast, cookies, stale cake. Grandpa dunked his sugar cookies in his cup of coffee, so I followed his example and dunked mine in my glass of water! We've also seen older people eat peas with a knife, pushing them on with the back side of a fork held in the other hand, then balancing them carefully as the knife was raised to the mouth. Eating peas required steady nerves.

Shoes were another item that seemed to add years to a person's looks. The older ladies wore plain, dark colored shoes that were sturdily built with low, flat heels and strings that tied in the front. When I see that particular style shoe today, a little inner voice whispers, "old lady shoes!" Guess what? Those *old lady shoes* are the type I now wear around home. They certainly are comfortable, thank you!

When was the last time you heard someone say, "I'd better put on my galoshes."? Grandpa always slipped his rubber galoshes over his shoes if it was raining or snowing. How about gum boots? They were knee high and went straight up the leg with no fasteners. They were a necessity on the farm where a man waded in mud, manure or snow up to his knees. I still have a vivid mental picture of my great-uncle Lehr Schwartz wearing his gum boots, standing on the back of his mud boat, smiling and waving as his team of horses pulled a load of wood to the house in preparation for winter. When Dad went ditching in snowy weather, he put on what he called his "artics" (arctics), boots reaching almost to his knees with pleats at the front for ease in putting on and off. The pleats then folded in and the boots were kept on by fastening four or five buckles down the front. Although I never saw any in our house, some men owned hip boots, high rubber boots that went up to the hip. Any serious fishermen in the area usually had a pair of waders which were the overalls of the rubber footwear industry. Our Baptist preacher still uses a pair during baptismal services.

Many of the older ladies never learned to drive. That was a job for the men of the family. As a result, the ladies could not attend any activity unless their "men" took them and returned for them later. Many men did not have time for this if they were busy on the farm, so the ladies had to be content to stay at home. Favorite activities of these ladies seemed to be knitting (Grandma didn't learn this), crocheting (she usually made rag rugs), and tatting (she made laces, doilies, and a huge table cover.) For several years she usually made or helped someone else make a quilt. They spent hours sitting around the quilt frame in the dining room, talking and sewing those tiny little stitches required for a nice quilt. Since much of the older ladies' time was spent sitting for these activities, many of them lost their girlish figures very early and looked more *frumpy* than elegant.

Like the ladies, the older men also dressed in dark colors and plain suits. There were no light-blue or tan suits for men and no sport coats. They would be shocked to see some of the plaids and bright colors used in sport coats today. Grandpa once had a suit with tiny pinstripes, but the only plaids he ever owned were his blue everyday flannel shirts. Grandpa never owned a sport coat. When his Sunday suit pants wore thin and became shiny, he wore the coat over his blue work shirts and dark pants when he went to town. For church and other dress-up occasions, he sometimes wore spats over his shoes and elastic bands on his arms. The men at my genealogy meeting said those were called "sleeve garters." Shirts used to come in one sleeve size, so these were used to keep the sleeves at a comfortable length, rather than drooping down over the hands. I suppose matching suspenders and sleeve garters were considered the sexy attire of their day, especially if the young man also wore spats on his shoes and a sailor or boater straw hat.

Most older men wore suspenders. Some called them by their British name, "braces." Grandpa often referred to them as "galluses." He wore only blue chambray shirts and a pair of heavy dark pants for working on the farm. Sometimes in the winter he stayed warmer by wearing bib overalls over the pants, but he never owned a pair of denim blue jeans.

Grandpa didn't have a lot of hair, so he needed a warm winter hat. He usually wore a wool or corduroy cap with a bill in the front and ear tabs that could be folded down to keep the ears warm. Farmers wore loosely woven straw hats in the summer, which allowed the air to flow through, but protected them from the sun. Grandpa wore a hat nearly all the time except in the house. He had a black derby or bowler hat that he called a "Stiff Katy." I loved to see him wear it, but I don't remember him doing that very often. I guess the wearing of such a fancy attire on one's head was out of style by the time I came along.

If Grandpa entered a home or church, he took off his hat. In large buildings such as department stores, Grandpa always removed his hat as he entered the elevator. As he walked down the street, he nodded or gave a greeting such as "Good morning" or a quick "Howdy-do" to all the people he met, and he always tipped his hat if it was a lady. That showed respect and was just considered good manners. Grandpa was always a real gentleman!

I nearly forgot one of the more prevalent things that made older people seem old–that was the lack of teeth. Many of them never made it into a dentist's office in their entire life. If a tooth hurt, it was often the doctor who pulled it. If they lost a tooth, it was just gone. If they lost all their teeth, they just "gummed" their food. Many could not have afforded a new set of teeth and for those who could, a dentist was often not close enough to bother. At the turn of the 20th century, most small towns had a doctor, even tiny Kossuth, but there weren't many dentists in the county.

When I was a little girl, many of the doctors felt that if an older person was not feeling well, it just might be his teeth. The doctor often recommended pulling all of them. At that time the dentists pulled just one or two teeth at each visit, so it took a long time to get a full set of teeth pulled. Then they usually suggested waiting several months or longer for the mouth to be completely healed. Thus, many of the older folks went for long periods of time without teeth. This definitely made them look older.

I remember one story of a doctor suggesting that the teeth were the cause of an illness, but it didn't quite turn out as the doctor expected. Uncle Ed Thiesing hadn't been feeling well and went to the doctor. After examining him, the doctor said, "Ed, I believe you would feel a lot better if you had those teeth out." Now, Uncle Ed had an ornery streak, and when the doctor suggested having his teeth pulled, Ed reached into his mouth and pulled them out, handing them to the doctor. He had gotten false teeth several years before, but the doctor didn't know it. As he looked at that handful of teeth, the poor doctor was speechless! That was the last time he suggested Ed get his teeth pulled.

It wasn't just clothing and appearance that made people seem *old*. The demands of day-to-day living for the early settlers were much more physical in nature than most of today's lifestyles. They had to work extremely hard their entire lives—cutting down trees and hauling away the logs, dynamiting stumps and plowing new ground, doing everything the hard way because there was no easy way, accepting sickness and aches and pains because there were no miracle drugs to help them. These were all things that tended to make people old. Yes, old before their time!

---

[1] "Clothes for Fashion and Function," *Lima News*, Lima, Ohio, December 4, 1996, used with permission.

These daughters of Heinrich Adolph Aufderhaar enjoyed a 1920 family reunion. Standing: Sarah Peters, Elizabeth "Lizzie" Suhr, Emma Suhr. Seated: my great-grandma Catherine Schwartz and Anna Nicholson. Second wife Elizabeth (Huenefeld) Aufderhaar was the mother of Sarah, Catherine and Anna. Third wife Rebecca (Kurtz) Aufderhaar was the mother of Lizzie and Emma.

All dressed up! My grandparents stand to the left of Grandpa's fiddlin' cousin, Freedus Daniels and his wife, Grace. Standing behind is their Uncle Lew Daniels who homesteaded in Idaho.

## Chapter 23.
# *Two Longs and a Short*

If the phone rang, we listened. If it sounded like two long rings and a short ring, we answered it. Telephones were the farmer's communication with the outside world, especially if he needed help. When Grandpa got sick in the middle of the night, as he occasionally did when I was a child, Grandma went to the phone and cranked the handle once. The night operator at Buckland came on and asked whom she was calling. After a few minutes, Doc Doughty answered at his home in Spencerville, and within a half hour, he would be at our door. We knew Grandpa would be all right.

Our first telephone was a wooden rectangular box that hung on the wall behind the kitchen door. Two circular bells were at the top with the clapper between. Directly below was the mouthpiece that could be tilted up or down. Since Grandma was short and she did most of the phoning, it was usually tilted down. The pear-shaped hearing device called the receiver hung on a U-shaped prong on the left side of the box. When the receiver was lifted, the phone was activated and you could place your call. Our phone book listed the people on our line and their rings, one short and one long, a long and two shorts, and so on. When placing a call on your own line, you didn't call the operator but just turned the crank on the right side of the box the appropriate number of times. Three times around, a pause, and one turn of the crank would have been one long and one short. Farm wives listened for their ring as they went about their daily routine.

When calling someone on a different line, the routine was to lift the receiver, crank the handle, and when central (the operator), said, "Number, please?" you gave her the number. She then rang the party with whom you wished to speak. She stayed on the line until your party answered and sometimes carried on a conversation with you, perhaps ending with, "Well, it doesn't sound like they are going to answer. You'll have to try later," or "I think they are visiting her mother in Texas." How long has it been since you have had a friendly conversation with your telephone operator while waiting for someone to answer?

I got one of the biggest scares of my life from a telephone when I was just a little girl. A very big thunderstorm had come up, and I was standing in the middle of the kitchen, about three feet from the telephone box on the wall. Suddenly, lightning hit, and a ball of fire jumped out of that telephone right in front of me! It must have stunned me for an instant. When I finally got up off the floor, I was tingling all over. After a good cry, I felt much better. (But I still don't go near a phone when a thunderstorm is in full swing!)

If an emergency arose, you grabbed that crank and just kept turning it around for a dozen or more times. Everyone on your line could hear that long ring, and every housewife would grab the receiver and listen to see what was wrong. If you had a fire, within minutes all the neighbors would be there to help carry things out of the house and pass buckets of water until the fire department could arrive. This long ring could also be rung from the telephone office in Buckland and was frequently used in winter to tell us that school was canceled due to snow. Hurrah! Community announcements were sometimes made over the phone: "The Farmer's Institute Play will be presented Saturday night in the school auditorium. Everyone is welcome!"

When our country party line phones were removed, they were sadly missed by the gossips of the community. Many of the older ladies had very little to do, especially in winter when the gardening was all finished. Every time the phone rang, they knew by the number of rings just which neighbor was being called. Down came the receiver with the hopes of hearing what was going on in the neighborhood. One lady was so quiet she was sure no one knew she was listening. She forgot about the kitchen clock ticking away beside the phone. When a young man called his girl on Friday night, the heavy breathing was usually not from his girl. It came from the lady down the road who was listening in! One high school senior called his girlfriend, and in the course of the conversation, he said something that upset her and she hung up the phone. Knowing the nosy neighbor always listened in, he said, "Well, Flossie, (not her real name), she hung up on me, so I guess you and I will have to talk." Bang! Down went Flossie's receiver.

Flossie and the other eavesdroppers got frustrated trying to listen in when Bill had a conversation with his New Knoxville family and friends after we were married. Why? Those conversations were in German!

How many families were on a party line? The most we ever had was thirteen, and that sometimes made it difficult to get the phone when you needed it. When Grandma died, Grandpa had asked Rev. Gerald Erter, our fine young preacher who had just been moved to a different church, to come back and preach the funeral. With only an hour until time for the funeral, he still had not arrived at our house where we hoped to have a few minutes together before going to the church service. Finally, we decided to call his home and see if there was a problem, but someone was using the party line. I waited, then lifted the receiver again in a few minutes, but they were still talking. I waited a little longer, and as the clock was moving as fast as that woman's mouth, I was getting desperate. Finally I picked up the receiver and said, "I'm sorry, but we really need this line. It's a life or death situation." "Well!" she said and hung up.

When Michael first went to college in Missouri, he usually called on Saturday night at about eleven o'clock. We thought this was an hour when everyone else would be in bed asleep. Not so! Nearly every time he called, an elderly lady came on the line after we were talking and asked, "Linebiz?" I couldn't figure out who was talking or what she was saying and ignored it, but in a few minutes she said the same thing. This time Bill listened and said, "She is asking, 'Is the line busy?'" If people are talking, the line is definitely busy. That was her way of letting us know that *she* wanted that phone, and she wanted it right now. One time I wondered whom she was calling that was more important than our talking to our son way out in Missouri, so I hung up and waited for her to make her call, then *I* listened in. Her *important* call was to a friend down the road for the purpose of discussing what to wear to church the next morning!

Thank goodness, it wasn't long before the phone company broke up the party lines. We were placed on a semi-private line with only Bill's mother. Yippee! She was in bed asleep by ten o'clock, long before Michael called, so we had the line to ourselves.

Other small problems with party lines were the children who loved to play with the phones. When they heard the phone ring, many were not old enough to tell if it was their family's ring. If Mom was outside or in another room, they just picked up the phone and began to talk, perhaps in the middle of your conversation. I came up with a solution to that problem, though. When a child picked up the phone and began to talk, I talked to them briefly in a nice, friendly manner. When I had their full attention, I asked them if Mommy was there. She always was, so I just asked them to go tell Mommy someone wanted her on the telephone. In a few minutes they came back with Mommy, who usually caught on as to what had happened and the receiver went down immediately. If not, a quick, "Hi! Did you know your child was playing with the phone?" usually did the trick. She apologized and hung up. Problem solved!

The party line had some good benefits. We often had traveling salesmen driving through the countryside, going door to door selling books, salves, magazines and household gadgets. If a stranger selling something stopped next door at Helen Mack's, she usually called to let us know that someone was coming. After I was married, Grandma lived in a new house next door, and she would call me. Lester Skinner lived in the next house to the east, and his wife was in poor health, so I called her right away. This went on for several years. One time a salesman said to me, "What's going on here? Every time I knock on a door, the lady tells me she isn't interested. She already knows just what I'm selling, even before I get a chance to show it." I said, "I'm sorry, but in this neighborhood we just take care of each other." He walked away, shaking his head and grumbling to himself.

Long distance calls were very unusual when I was a child. First of all, after the Big Depression, it was considered too expensive to make a long distance call unless it was an *emergency*. To make a long distance call, you cranked out one ring for the operator. When she came on the line, you told her the name of the person you were calling and the city in which they lived. Sometimes it took several minutes before the call finally got through. If the operator had difficulty getting the call made, she occasionally told you to hang up and she would call you back when she had reached the person you wanted. This might take quite a few minutes.

I was about twelve years old when I made my first long distance call. It was such a traumatic experience that I wondered if I might not pass out before it was completed. My heart pounded so hard I could barely talk when I was finally connected. In those early calls it was not always easy to understand what each of us was saying. We had to almost shout to be heard above the static. But then what could we expect? After all, we were hundreds of miles apart! When the newer phones were installed and more long distance calls were being made, there were many comments about how it was now so clear that, "Why, it's like talking to someone right in the very *next room*!" Imagine that!

By the time we got married, the wall phone had been replaced with a newer desk model. It had a separate wooden box for the ringer that was placed on a nearby bookshelf. The phone was a round cylinder with a wider base on the bottom. The mouthpiece was at the top, and the hook for hanging the receiver was on the side. We no longer had to crank a handle to get the operator. We just lifted the receiver, the operator said, "Number, please," and we gave her the number we wanted. Then she placed the call.

For a while it seemed that our phone stopped working every time we had a thunderstorm. This meant a call to the phone company. The line repairman, Jim Kurtz, would have to come out to fix it. Usually the problem was that lightning had struck close enough to blow the fuse in the box outside the back door. We got tired of losing our phone after every storm and Jim eventually gave us a generous supply of fuses to keep on hand. After that, storms weren't such a bother. We just put the fuses in the box ourselves.

One time we had a phone problem, and when Jim opened up the wooden box beside Bill's desk, he found that the entire inside was charred. At sometime, lightning had struck nearby and come in on those telephone lines, starting a fire inside the box. It had smoldered long enough to blacken the whole inside, but because the lid was closed, it didn't get sufficient oxygen. The fire had gone out. How thankful we were that it had! It could have burned down our house!

Bill remembered a man named A.H. Stienecker who was the first manager of the New Knoxville telephone company. An article found in the November 20, 1926, *Wapakoneta Daily News* listed the following under New Knoxville news: "A.H. Stienecker, manager of the New Knoxville Telephone Company motored to Lima Thursday accompanied by several of his Hello Girls to attend a district telephone convention which convened there." I had forgotten that girls we called *Central* were sometimes called *Hello Girls.*

One of the best known telephone stories around New Knoxville concerned "Old Doc Fledderjohann." Since he lived with his daughter and son-in-law, Zella and Ferd Eversman, he was there when Bill took his late Saturday night voice lessons. Doc often wiggled his finger at Bill as he motioned for him to come into his room where they could talk. One evening he told Bill about the dastardly deed that was done one late night years before. A young wife was in labor north of town and when they tried to call the doctor on the phone, they couldn't get through. Finally, a neighbor drove his horse into town and got Doc out of bed. He dressed, hooked up his buggy and hurried out to deliver the baby. It was a long, difficult delivery, and when he got back into town the next *afternoon*, the place was buzzing with excitement. Someone had thrown a brick through the window of the telephone office, frightening the daylights out of the poor operator. Mr. Stienecker said if he found out who had done that awful thing, he was going to prosecute him to the fullest degree. "Then start prosecuting, because I'm the man who threw the brick," Doc said. Everyone who heard this comment was aghast! Why would the town doctor break a window in the telephone office?

As Doc told the story to Bill, he said he minced no words in explaining things to Mr. Stienecker. The farmer had tried to telephone the doctor when his wife needed help, but the operator never came on. Doc said he guessed that since it was the middle of the night, the operator had shut off the ringer so she could take a nap on the office couch without being disturbed. "I reached down and grabbed a brick as I climbed into my buggy, and when my horse rounded the corner by the telephone office, I gave that brick a mighty heave. It sailed through that second-story window and right into the telephone office." Night operators were supposed to keep that ringer on all night for just such emergencies. The lives of a mother and baby were at stake. Doc never got arrested for his late night brick throwing episode, but that night is still a frequent item of conversation around New Knoxville.

The new direct-dial phones brought misgivings for our family doctor, Dr. Herbert Wolfe, of New Knoxville. If he would be out of the office, he had always called the operator to let her know of his plans. If someone needed him, she told them where he could be reached and when he would be back. With the new direct-dialing phones, he worried that someone might need him and there would be no operator to let them know where he had gone or when he would return.

Direct-dialing capability eliminated the need of operators to make routine phone calls, and soon many of the smaller phone companies were bought up and consolidated into bigger ones. Since Buckland and New Knoxville remained small, independent phone companies and we made few long distance calls, our bills were only two or three dollars a month, much smaller than our city friends. Life was simpler back then, and a whole lot cheaper! Those were what my generation refers to when we think of the “good old days.”

## Chapter 24.

# Family Fun on the Farm

"What can I do? There's nothing to do!" Mothers, do you ever hear that from your children today? We didn't get much of a chance to worry about what to do when I was a child. There was always wood to haul to the cookstove, and we often helped with the milking, especially in the evening. In the summer there were weeds in the garden that had to be pulled. I remember a time or two when we hoed weeds out of the big fields of soybeans. There were peas to shell, beans to snap, and spinach to be looked over, one leaf at a time, in case a bug decided to play hide-and-seek in a crinkly leaf. Many of our jobs were once-in-a-while jobs. For example, I remember pushing the rotary blade lawn mower over the huge yard, digging potatoes, gathering eggs, putting feed in for the pigs, throwing hay down from the haymow and putting it in the cow mangers, helping husk corn, pumping water for the livestock, shoveling coal back into the pile away from the hot furnace, helping milk the three or four cows we usually had, hauling water to the tin cans Grandma usually placed between the pickle and melon vines, working in the garden and helping can the produce from it, hauling a bucket of water or sour milk to the baby chicks in the brooder house and filling the stone crocks, breaking the ice on the cattle tank in winter, and lots and lots of peeling potatoes for supper. There were so many things to do on the farm that with such a wide variety, we didn't get extremely bored. Well, maybe just a little bored with all that potato peeling.

As we waited for the school bus on winter mornings, Don and I often played "fox and geese." By sliding our feet through the snow, we made a big circle covering most of the side yard. Of course, we had on our rubber boots. Mine were an ugly brown and were difficult to get on and off, but Don could easily get into his black high tops that buckled in the front. After scooting through the snow to form the outside circle, we made a + through the entire circle, stamping down a small area in the very center. It now looked like a giant wheel with four spokes and a hub. "It" (the fox) had to chase the others (the geese) along the paths while trying to catch them. If a goose ran into the center hub area, he was safe and the fox had to chase someone else. Although it was a lot more fun to play with a group of kids during recess, Don and I managed to make it fun while occupying our time and keeping us warmer until the bus came.

Girls enjoyed making snow angels, although teachers didn't encourage this if the snow was quite wet. We carefully lay down in the snow, then spreading our arms and legs, we moved them back and forth. The resulting impression in the snow looked like angels with long skirts and wings (and our snow-covered back sides made us resemble snowmen).

Sledding was always exciting on snowy winter days. Occasionally we took our sled to the canal near Herman Rothe's and slid down the canal bank into their pasture. As I got older, I received a pair of shoe-type ice skates for Christmas. If the ice was solid, we could also skate on the canal between sled rides.

At home, Don and I usually pulled each other on the sled. He was older and stronger, so he probably pulled more than I did. Once in a while, Grandpa or Grandma took a turn pulling us, but it was usually toward the barn when it was time to feed the animals and milk the cows. I remember one special time when I pulled a sled to the house with a bushel basket of baby pigs on it. They were born during a bitter cold winter night, and were nearly frozen by morning. Grandpa loaded them into the basket, and I pulled the sled to the house where Grandma took the basket of pigs into the kitchen and set it on the open oven door of the wood range. After several hours, the baby pigs had warmed up and were getting hungry. Then it was time to sled them back to their mamma.

I loved playing with the baby pigs. They were so cute! When Grandpa put them back with their mother she was very protective of them. He warned us not to get too close when a sow had baby pigs. Even a gentle sow would become dangerously aggressive and rush at us with a loud "bush, bush, bush!" as she snapped her teeth.

By the way, this was about the time I learned the facts of life. I asked Grandpa where the baby pigs had come from and he told me the mother sow had rooted in the straw and found them under there. (Now that really puzzled me. I had helped put that same fresh straw in the pen a day before the pigs were born and I surely didn't see any pigs under that straw then! Hmmm!)

One thing that always provided fun for farm kids was feeding the cats at milking time. Our cats were well-trained in this procedure. They stood near the cow as we milked by hand. Occasionally we turned one of the cow's teats toward our kitties and squirted the milk in their faces. Standing on their hind legs, they begged for more, then wiped their mouths with their paws, licking them carefully to save every drop.

We had more time to play in the house on winter evenings, and that was when the train was set up in the middle of the living room floor. Occasionally a picture puzzle was put together on a long winter night, and games such as bingo, checkers, and dominoes were played. A game of Monopoly was sure to keep us occupied for several hours, especially if we happened to be snowed in. One of the family's favorite pastimes was reading: books, magazines, and newspapers. We also loved to listen to the radio. The first model I remember was an Atwater-Kent which sat on top of a small cabinet. Grandpa's favorite show was the *WLS Barn Dance* on Saturday night. It featured Lulubelle and Scotty who became the special act at the county fair one year. Of their many songs, my favorite was a humorous one called "Does Your Chewing Gum Lose Its Flavor on the Bed Post Overnight?"

Other family favorites were *The Old Ranger*, sponsored by Twenty Mule Team Borax, *Lum and Abner*, *Fibber McGee and Molly*, *Henry Aldrich, Amos and Andy*, and a little girl called *Betty Lou*. I sent in a box top or two from something and received an authentic Betty Lou spoon. Standing shyly at the top of the spoon, she wore a cute polka-dot dress and curls that I so envied. Her name was spelled out down the handle. We loved the antics of Edgar Bergan and his dummies, Charlie McCarthy and Mortimer Snerd. The *Fred Allen, Baby Snooks*, and *Eddie Cantor* shows were also fun. Don liked shows such as *Gangbusters*, *The Shadow*, and *Inner Sanctum* with its squeaky door, but these scared me too much! I preferred music, singers such as Bing Crosby, Morton Downey, and Kate

Smith who made "God Bless America" famous. The big band sound was popular, and Glenn Miller was the best. In my younger days, Grandma didn't listen to the radio during the day, but when I was a teen, she occasionally tuned to *Don McNeil's Breakfast Club* or *Queen for a Day*.

Little girls loved playing jacks, whether it was winter or summer. In cold weather, we played on the floor of our school classroom. In warm weather, we used the sidewalk or the cistern behind the school. We each had a little sack of jacks and a ball. The idea was to throw the jacks down on the floor, then toss the ball into the air, pick up one jack and catch the ball on the first bounce. After you had picked up each jack, you started on your "twosies." Now you threw the ball and picked up two jacks each time. If you got through that, you went to three, then four and so on until you had to throw your ball quite high and pick up the whole bunch at one time. If you missed the ball or didn't pick up the correct number of jacks, the next girl had a turn. We spent hours playing jacks while the boys played softball or marbles. Our hands developed some real calluses from scraping them on the concrete each time we grabbed the jacks. Ooh! Ouch!

Girls also liked to swing, teeter-totter, and ride the Giant Strides until we got blisters on our hands. And of course, there was skipping rope. I don't remember any of the singsong verses we said as two people turned the rope and one or two girls jumped. I was good at jumping with my own rope, but when two people turned a long rope and I had to run in and start jumping, I was not too successful. Since I was the tallest girl in my class and the others were all much shorter, it didn't seem as if they got that rope up high enough. Was I too tall or too clumsy or both?

When I was little, Dad had welded some pipe together and made a large swing for us. It was much taller than the little swing sets sold today. There were two seats, so Don and I could both swing at the same time, sometimes racing to see who could go the highest. He was much braver than I was and often sailed high into the tree branches before I had gotten a good start.

When I was about five, the Big Ringling Brothers, Barnum and Bailey circus came to town. We had never been to a circus and Daddy decided Don and I were both old enough to enjoy it. My goodness, where was a little girl to look? There were so many things going on at the same time in those three rings that I hardly knew which way to turn. I didn't want to miss any of it. Huge elephants walked on their hind feet with their front legs on the back of the elephant in front of them. I had never seen an elephant, and to watch them walk in this manner was quite exciting! There were trapeze artists, a man shot out of a cannon into a net and clowns galore. What was my most vivid memory of that day? Promise you won't laugh? My brother lost his little red baseball cap. (You said you wouldn't laugh. I remember the really important things, don't I?)

I was also five years old when our neighbor, Joe Frank, was honored by having a new grandson, Joe Mack, named after him. With two people named Joe living in the house next door, we devised a way to tell them apart. Grandpa was called Big Joe and the baby became Little Joe.

Occasionally, after Joe was three or four years old, Grandma would ring his mother's number on the telephone party line and asked if I could come over to play with him. Grandma watched from our dining room window as I walked down the side of the road to their home. Following my progress from their living room window were Helen and Little Joe. After playing a game or two with the little boy, I usually headed for their old garage where my feet and fingers flew on the ancient pump organ stored there. Although I hadn't yet learned to read notes, I *played* great oratorios with expertise, covering every note on the organ. Since Joe was five years younger, his interest in my concert soon faded, and I played on in happy abandon. Eventually I grew tired (probably from the ill sounding music), and Joe and I returned to hide-and-seek or some other game. Helen occasionally treated us to a tea party on the front porch and gave me my first taste of a new candy called Tootsie Rolls. When Joe was tuckered out, Helen bedded him down for his nap, and it was time for me to go home. Helen rang two longs and a short on the telephone and told Grandma I was on my way. Again my steps were followed by a pair of eyes from each house until I was safely back home.

Sometimes I was called the "doll baby" little girl. I could never get enough dolls, and I nearly cried the Christmas I asked for a doll with a suitcase full of clothes, but the suitcase under the tree was actually a typewriter for Don. I held back the tears, but it wasn't easy. I started making clothes for my little doll family when I was about six or seven years old. It was a little difficult to make the tiny clothes on Grandma's big treadle sewing machine, so Santa brought me a little chain stitch toy machine. It was fun to turn the handle on the side and watch it run, but it never did sew correctly. I usually got frustrated and returned to the big machine. Making the crude doll clothes developed a love of sewing that was strong enough to last a lifetime. It was great fun playing "pretend" with my dolls, doll bed and wicker baby buggy. I was Mommy, and I dressed the dolls and pushed them around the yard in the buggy. Occasionally, when one of our barn cats would cooperate, I would dress it in doll clothes, too. Now this was fun for me—having a real live *baby*, but my kitty eventually got tired of it, especially when I tried laying it in the doll buggy—on its back. Away my kitty would run, doll dress and all. I nearly lost some of my very best doll clothes that way!

Before I went to school, I was not allowed to use sharp scissors, but I had a little blunt-edged pair for cutting my paper dolls. No, they were not the fancy books of dolls with pretty clothes designed just for them. My earliest paper dolls were people I carefully cut out of the Sears Roebuck or J.C. Penney catalogs. Dresses didn't always fit quite right, and the dolls were not very sturdy, but they were all I had, since we were still in the depression years. Sometimes I made a dollhouse by cutting windows and doors in a shoe box. Pictures of beds, tables and couches were cut out of the catalog and pasted on the inside walls of the box, using homemade flour-and-water paste. Happily, when I was old enough to take care of them, I was given *real* paper dolls. Although they are well-worn, I still have them, dolls such as Shirley Temple, Princess Margaret and Princess Elizabeth (now Queen Elizabeth of England), Kewpie, Mortimer Snerd and Charlie McCarthy. I also have my coloring books of Shirley Temple, the British princesses, Jeanette McDonald, Nelson Eddy and several others.

One Christmas, I received a real dollhouse. No, not the sturdy wood or plastic houses of today, but a two-story cardboard house with cutout windows and a door that folded open and shut. It wasn't strong, but it was the best they made. I loved rearranging the furniture and taking my little doll family through their paces. While Mother leaned stiffly against a corner of the room, holding the baby awkwardly in her movable arms, the maid dusted the cardboard furniture, and Father sat in his flimsy chair, looking sternly upon the scene. The young son and daughter slept peacefully in the cardboard beds upstairs. When the cardboard house had seen better days and had to be discarded, the little family was gently returned to their silver box, and placed in the corner of Grandpa's trunk.

When I was a child, there was something I didn't like about warm weather. It was warm! Air-conditioning hadn't been invented, and we had no electric fans. Our only fans were cardboard funeral home advertising fans. How I loved those breezy summer days when we could open the windows and play beneath the curtains that blew gently to and fro.

During several summers, we attended Saturday night movies in Buckland. No, they didn't have a theater. Someone came to town with a big cloth screen that was fastened up in the vacant lot beside the fire station. Since folding lawn chairs were not yet available, everyone brought blankets and sat on the grass to watch the movies. I don't remember the names of any movies or actors, but they were all good, clean, family-style shows. We were a very disappointed bunch of kids, though, if the movie was canceled because of rain.

One night a man presented a magic show. Daddy knew him from Spencerville School many years before, and he told Dad some of the secrets of his magic but made him promise not to give away the details.

We went swimming at least once or twice each summer. It was a special treat to go to the *real* pools in Spencerville or Wapakoneta. Family reunions occasionally provided a few hours of swimming fun. The Aufderhaar Reunion was sometimes held near a pool in Indiana. What fun those reunions were. After a bountiful dinner spread across tables in a back yard, the children looked forward to playing with distant cousins they hadn't seen for a year. A program was usually held after dinner. We were anxious to run and play, but we couldn't go until after the program. This was the time when each child was encouraged to say a piece or sing a song, possibly something learned in Sunday school. My accordion was always put in the trunk of the car. I knew I would have to perform before we could play or head for the near-by swimming pool.

A favorite pre-war activity was a trip to Lima to visit the Eldora Dairy and the nearby airport. Gasoline was cheap and folks were recovering from the depression, so an afternoon jaunt to Lima was exciting for the whole family. Eldora was known, not only for its wonderful ice cream, but also for the huge windows which separated the store from the dairy, making it possible to watch the cows being milked while licking an ice cream cone. Everyone was fascinated and it was a learning experience for the city kids. Since we knew more than enough about milking cows, we were anxious to get on with the day and a stop at the airport just west of Lima on Baty Road. A parking area at the end of the runway allowed cars to pull off the road to watch the fun. Planes took off and landed while we finished our ice cream cones. At one time, there was even passenger service via North Central Airlines. For country kids, watching airplanes was real excitement and cheap entertainment.

Sunday school class parties and Ladies' Aid outings held at Villa Nova Park offered us an afternoon of swimming in the lake. The Davenport family held a birthday get-together there one year. We got to swim that afternoon, but not until I had played my accordion.

Our family enjoyed the relaxed atmosphere near the lake. Don and Grandma were the fishermen of the family and they enjoyed fishing there. Eventually, Grandpa built a cottage at Villa Nova near St. Marys. Grandma and Don could fish as much as they wanted now, and we could swim more often. The 1948 political conventions were being held as we worked on the house. I remember scooting around on the floor as we varnished woodwork with the little radio tuned to the conventions. After all, I was voting that year for the first time. We enjoyed that cottage, but as college took me away and Don got more involved in a job, Grandpa finally sold it. Neighbors Oliver and Minerva Fritz loved flowers and fishing as much as my grandparents, and the two couples stayed good friends for the rest of their lives.

Popcorn was always a part of our lives on the farm. Grandma often popped corn in the evening, especially in winter. (Bill and I still enjoy that custom in our home. Our family loved popcorn, and we spent many Saturday evenings with our children gathered around the television as we watched Lawrence Welk and munched on the warm corn.)

As teens, Don and I often borrowed Dad's car and met the neighborhood kids at the parking area in front of the church at Kossuth. Summer fun often included an afternoon swim at Stoner's gravel pit a couple miles south of town. Mr. Stoner allowed the kids to swim there, and he kept an eye on things. We had to be very careful since some parts of the gravel pit were quite deep.

Occasionally we went to a theater in one of the nearby towns where we saw exciting movies starring Gene Autrey and Smiley Burnette or Roy Rogers. Most of these theaters have now closed. Some had real "class" with very ornate ceilings and elegant red velvet curtains that parted as the show began. Many had been used years before as opera houses and vaudeville theaters. Going to a movie was exciting fun for the entire family. We purchased our tickets at the booth on the sidewalk, then admired the huge pictures displayed in glass cases, each depicting scenes from the movie. As we entered the lobby, we saw walls covered with more pictures of movie stars being featured in the coming attractions. We didn't get to attend movies very often, but those huge posters certainly made us *want* to.

Theater lobbies were carpeted, and near the magnificent popcorn machine were glass counters displaying candy bars and gum. The aroma of the warm corn with its generous twirl of butter on top tempted us. If we were lucky enough to have money for such delicacies, we clutched the warm boxes in our hands and walked through the double doors where an usher greeted us. Using a flashlight, he guided us down the dark aisle to empty seats. If we were early, we had time to stare at the elegant surroundings and experience the dramatic dimming of the lights, the parting of the curtains, and the beginning of the newsreel. Since there were no televisions with evening news, the movie newsreel was the nearest thing to reliving the events that were making history then. During the war, there were a lot of action films from the European front or the Pacific. Because we had never seen live action such as that in our little corner of the world, most of us watched with real interest. Some kids had daddies, brothers or uncles who were fighting in those battles.

The cartoons were everyone's favorites–Woody Woodpecker, Mickey Mouse, or Donald Duck. To encourage regular attendance, an exciting adventure film was presented in serial form. For those who went every week, the show was a continuous story. Since we seldom attended and the plot was vague, we didn't know the good guy from the bad unless he was wearing his white hat.

Next were the coming attractions–a short segment, (usually very exciting) taken from the feature films which would soon be shown. Sometimes prizes were given to those attending the movie. We received a dinner plate one night. The idea was, if you didn't miss a single new feature, you would eventually have a complete set of dishes.

Something new came to the area when I was a teenager—a drive-in movie theater. Now it was easy for a family to attend a movie together. Cars parked in a semicircle around a large screen. Since the front of each parking space was elevated, even those in the back seat could see the screen. The projection and sound equipment were placed in a centrally located building that also had restrooms and a snack bar where hot dogs, candy, popcorn and paper cups full of pop were served. The first drive-ins had large, outdoor speakers which could be heard when the car windows were lowered. When cool nights created a problem, individual sound systems were developed with a pole located between two cars. Small metal speaker boxes were then brought into the car. The window could be closed, allowing only enough room for the small attached wire. Later yet, the system was improved and the sound came through the car's radio. What luxury!

Often a set fee was charged for each car, making it cheap enough for even large families to see *Oklahoma,* the Marx Brothers, or some other favorite movie, especially if they brought snacks from home. Some drive-ins introduced playgrounds below the screen at the front of the lot. While the children played, parents relaxed, enjoyed a snooze, or visited with friends in neighboring cars. As the sun began to sink in the west, the lights went on at the sides of the screen and the children headed for Dad's car. A few minutes later, the lights dimmed and the movie began.

The routine was much the same as in the theaters–a newsreel, cartoon, coming events, and a feature film. No one really dressed up, so when a child in pajamas had to visit the little girl's room, mom grabbed her hand and away they ran. Not wanting to miss anything, most families tried to put such trips off until intermission, if possible. When the lights came back on, some folks went for refreshments while others leaned out their car windows to yoo-hoo at friends near-by. It was a friendly, relaxing evening.

Occasionally someone got impatient for the show to resume, and headlights flashed at the screen. Then a horn or two blared their encouragement for everyone to hurry. Soon other viewers joined in and the variety of car horns was a veritable symphony of sound.

Like many other young people of that era, we enjoyed many dates at drive-in theaters where we saw good musicals—*State Fair, Show Boat*, the Nelson Eddy/Jeanette McDonald and Gordon McCrea films and many more. Morals were important then and an adult helped keep things under control with a flashlight and a walk among the cars. Teens had a form of privacy but were still accountable for their actions.

Drive-ins were a delightful addition to life in the boondocks. (I remember quite well the night we put our firstborn into the little car bed on the back seat and we went to the Midway Drive-In near Moulton to see the movie, *The Ten Commandments*. I could never have taken a newborn to a regular theater.)

Having fun in those days didn't require a lot of complicated equipment or expensive paraphernalia. We enjoyed afternoons with our family or with friends whom we knew from Sunday school and youth fellowship meetings. Don and I played in the snow and on ice in the winter and swam and rode bicycles in the summer. I wistfully remember those good times. How I wish today's young folks could grow up in the safe, happy environment we enjoyed! We just lived our lives and tried to enjoy each day as we came to it. Farm folks were quite good at that!

These kids attended a 1932 Davenport family reunion.
I'm the little tyke at the right. Don is standing behind me.

An Aufderhaar family reunion was held at Grandpa Davenport's house in June of 1940.
I'm sitting in the front row with the white hair band. Don is the third to my left wearing a hat.

## Chapter 25.
# *Fortress of the Farm*

It is a cold snowy night with the wind howling and darkness fast shrouding the earth in its wintery clutches. A touch of the finger and the pole light glows dimly through the fast falling flakes which seem immense in size. Wrapping ourselves in cocoons of winter garments and leaving the warmth and friendly light behind us, we set forth for the barn. As we trudge through the white wilderness to the barn door, we grasp its cold handle and step inside, shutting it quickly against the raging storm. The quiet barn-world is hushed, and its occupants rest peacefully in silence. Grunting softly, the pigs express to each other the feelings of mutual satisfaction over their last grains of corn. In the calf pen, the new little white-face butts its mother and shows its desire for just a little more milk, please. The milk cows wait patiently in their stanchions, anxious for the evening's milking to be over. Some stand in drowsy contemplation, and others relax peacefully in the warm clean straw, contentedly chewing their cuds and resting their heads. As we enter the stable, they glance at us with timid, long-lashed eyes and with a soft 'moo' inquire if it is really necessary for them to rise. A little fresh hay and a few nubbins of corn help them make their decision. With painstaking effort they yawn and stretch their way to a standing position, and with a look of self-satisfied boredom, they munch the hay and stand quietly while the milking is finished. As we switch off the barn light and open the door to leave, we hear the heavy breathing of the sleeping pigs and the long sighs of the cows as they settle back into the straw for the night of rest. We reluctantly close the door against the warmth and contentment within, and clutching the bucket of warm, steaming milk in a wooly mittened hand, we return through the glistening fairyland to the welcoming light inside the kitchen door.

Did you enjoy my winter barn description? I wrote that forty years ago for my friend, Eugenia Gerth. Gene was a "Southern" city woman who knew very little about barns, and being from Bessemer City, North Carolina, she had very little knowledge of snowy winter weather. Gene was an artist and loved my "painting" with words.

Most farms had a variety of buildings, and the big barn was indeed the fortress of the farm. It was the castle of the cows and a porker's paradise for piggies, especially on those blustery winter evenings. Although the house was the most important building for the comfort of the family, life on the farm really revolved around the barn. The farmer was very careful in planning the location of those early barns. They needed to be on higher ground for good drainage, but they must also be near a good water supply for the animals. They were usually located downwind from the house for obvious reasons. Grandpa's barn, however, was west of the house where it provided a lot of protection against the strong westerly winds, but did little to protect us from the occasional whiff of "Eau de *Manure*!"

Other buildings on his farm included a hog house, a chicken coop (also called a hen house), a brooder house (for the baby chicks), a double corn crib with a driveway between, and an oil house where the oil and gasoline were stored. Some farms also had a well house or pump shed, a machine shed (where farm equipment was stored), and a straw shed which formed the base for the straw stack. Of course, every farm had that little house behind the big house which was called the "outhouse" or the "backhouse."

Whoever heard of a telephone in a barn? No one had when I was a little girl, although it is quite common now, especially in dairy barns. Don and I just may have been the very first to have a barn phone! Nearly all the older barns had haylofts upstairs, and those sweet smelling areas made wonderful places to play. The loose hay was piled into the north loft of our barn. Grains such as beans, wheat and oats were stored in the south loft, some in bins and some in sacks. Occasionally Don and I used a long string pulled tightly across the driveway to connect our telephones. Then we carried on a conversation between his tin can in the north mow and mine in the south. It didn't work exceedingly well, but it surely kept us out of mischief for a while.

Ours was a hip roof barn. The roof went out at an angle, then made a turn and extended down from there, much as a human hip extends out from the waist and down, thus the name "hip roof barn." A grain bin was built high above those two haymows, almost against the roof. A small sliding door in the bottom could be opened, allowing the grain to run out into a truck in the driveway below. Grandpa's pigs and an occasional calf claimed the pens under the north mow.

Grandpa had built a feed storage bin under the south mow where he usually kept some ears of corn. He stacked sacks of ground feed on a wooden platform on one side of the bin, keeping them off the dirt floor where they could easily mold. This feed was mixed with water in five gallon buckets, then taken out to "slop the hogs." A small hog house in the lot south of the barn sheltered the pigs in the summer, but cold weather signaled the time for Grandpa to move them into the warmer pens inside the barn.

Grandpa's corn sheller was located beside the feed storage area. Don and I often shelled the corn for the animals to eat. It was really rather fun—but only for a short time. Our arms soon got tired from turning the handle and pushing the corn into the hole at the top. The grains were stripped off the ear and fell into the bucket below.

The cow stanchions occupied much of the south end of the barn. This was where the real action took place! Every morning and every evening of every day, the cows had to be milked. We usually milked only three or four, and that was done the old-fashioned way— by hand. Sanitation rules were unheard of then and we usually just brushed the loose dirt off the cows' udders (milk bags). If it had rained and they were muddy or coated with manure, we washed them off.

To milk a cow, we approached from her right side, quietly called her name, patted her on the side, then brushed against her hind leg and said, "Heist." She then knew we wanted her to move that leg back so we could get to the teats (milk spigots). Setting our bucket under her udder, we sat down on our little milk stool and got to work, alternately squeezing our left hand, then right, then left, and so on. The first squirts of milk ping, ping, pinged into the empty bucket. When it was obvious that there were only a few squirts left, we "stripped" the cow. No, that doesn't mean we took her clothes off. To strip meant to put our fingers together and gently pull down on each teat to get out the last drop of milk.

Although cows usually stood still while they were being milked, there was more than one time that a cow got tired or scared by a sudden movement or noise and took a step forward. When that happened, she occasionally put her foot in the bucket, or upset the bucket with the milk running down our leg and through the straw into the gutter. As the old saying goes, "It's no use crying over spilled milk." When this happened, we tried to calm the frightened cow by talking nicely (well, as nicely as possible under such circumstances), then picked up our bucket and tried to finish the job. By this time, the entire cat population had heard the good news–"Spilled milk!" All were present and accounted for, waiting for us to finish so they could lap up their share of the spilled milk.

My favorite spot in the barn was definitely the north haymow. New hay smelled absolutely wonderful. Mama cats loved to hide their newborn kittens in nests they made in the hay. It was a special place to sit quietly and watch them play while tiny dust particles danced through the bright beams of brilliant sun peeping through little knotholes or shining in full force through the window high up in the hayloft. Sometimes we climbed to the very top on the ladder fastened to the north wall, then looked out of the top window to the barnyard far below. Clinging to the ladder for safety, we pretended to be firefighters making a rescue at the top of an apartment house or park rangers looking for smoke in a nearby woods.

Before the days when hay was baled (and stacked in the mow) or chopped (and blown into the mow), the usual method of moving hay from the wagons to the mow involved a "hayfork." Just under the center of the roof was a track that ran the entire length of the barn (and on some, the roof and track extended past the side of the barn). Suspended from that hay track was a carrier or trolley, which could be moved along the track. The track was set up so that the carrier could be locked at a specific position. A big rope was attached to the carrier, and then looped down, passing through a pulley (or sometimes a set of pulleys) from which was suspended a hay fork with two sets of opposing prongs that looked something like fingers. That big rope then returned to the carrier, where it passed through another pulley or two or three in order to reach a source of power (such as a horse or tractor) located outside the barn. In our case it was tied to the bumper of the Hoopie, that wonderful old car that thought it was a tractor.

Loaded hay wagons were backed into the barn and the hay fork was dropped onto the hay. There were several kinds of hay forks with different methods of operation, but basically, the forks came together under a load of hay and were locked in place. When a load was secured, the signal was given to tighten the rope and draw the hay fork up to the carrier and track in the top of the barn. When it reached the carrier, a mechanism automatically locked the hay fork to the carrier so it could not fall. The same mechanism that secured the fork to the carrier also released the carrier to move freely on the track. The rope that had lifted the hay from the wagon now pulled that fork to the place where the hay was to be released and dropped to the mow floor. At the desired release point, a second, smaller trip rope attached to the hay fork was pulled, allowing the hay to drop.

The man with the most unpleasant job was the one who had to stand at the edge of that mow where the temperature often reached more than one hundred degrees. He had to pull that trip rope, and wait for the hay to drop, knowing that as it came, so did a great amount of dust and dried up leaves that stuck to sweaty arms and faces, making them itch like crazy. Using a pitch fork, he then had to distribute the hay evenly over the mow floor. No one seemed anxious for that job.

After the hay had dropped, the person operating the Hoopie was told to back up (releasing the tension on the big rope). Then someone inside the barn pulled the smaller trip rope to return the carrier and hay fork back over the hay wagon. When it reached the loading position, the carrier was automatically locked in place and the hay fork was released to pick up another load of hay.

Those hay ropes also made a wonderful indoor swing for farm kids. With the carrier locked in place and the hay fork removed, we tied the rope securely to a big support post that was a part of the barn structure, allowing us to swing on the end. This swing had no seat, just a big knot that we held on to for dear life! Don swung out far enough to drop off into the south mow. I was not that brave, but it was certainly fun swinging out over that vast expanse of driveway below. We could swing a lot higher than on our regular swings out in the yard. I'm sure we must have really overworked our guardian angels though!

In order to get into the mow, we had to place a ladder against the mow floor and climb it. When the ladder was being used somewhere else, it was easy for us kids to just climb the rope. We wrapped our legs around it, and going hand over hand, we soon reached the mow. Coming down was much more fun. We just slid down that rope in the same way a fireman slides down his pole. The only difference was that a rope quickly gives burns! Little girls did not wear jeans as they do today. In the winter I had long underwear with long stockings over them and everything went well. But in summer, that rope really scratched the bare legs and arms when I slid down. It's a wonder I didn't set my britches on fire! But the momentary pain seemed to be worth it though, considering the fun we had.

At one time our family had a dog who loved to climb up the ladder into the haymow, especially if someone happened to be up there. The problem was that, although he had no problem climbing up, he absolutely could not climb back down! Someone always had to pick up that awkward pooch and literally carry him down the ladder. If he didn't show up for a couple of hours, we usually looked in the haymow where he often sat, patiently waiting for someone to find and rescue him.

I did a crazy thing once when I *walked* hand over hand from one end of the mow to the other, hanging by my hands underneath that track at the top of the barn. I was so proud of myself for having done it, but too afraid to tell anyone. It makes my head swim now, just thinking about those daredevil things we did in that barn. The Lord must give farm kids just an extra bit of divine protection!

When hay balers first made their appearance, Grandpa hired the Wagners from Buckland to come out and bale our hay. Now our playground area changed. We could climb up and down those giant bale steps, move the bales around to form tunnels, make fortresses and playhouses. One year we got a real surprise though. When some bales were moved, the men noticed an area where the hay had gotten too hot and a black, burned out section appeared in the center of a large group of bales. In other words, we had come very close to having a fire that would have surely burned down our barn. Farmers always had to be very careful when making hay. A barn might burn due to spontaneous combustion if hay was too damp when it was packed tightly into a hayloft. Wet hay often got hot, which seemed to attract lightning during bad summer storms. It was rather common to have a barn or two burn each summer in rural Auglaize County with its vast number of farmers who made hay for dairy cattle and steers.

A concrete silo, ten feet in diameter and approximately thirty-five feet high, stood just outside the small barn door on the east side of our barn. At one time a beanie-type roof had covered the silo, but high winds had hit several years before I was born and the roof was blown away, leaving it open to the sky. No longer used to hold silage for the animals, it made a great "jungle gym" for hours of play for a couple of eager farm kids. We loved climbing up those concrete doors with their metal bars for opening and closing. Grandpa often told us of the time lightning had struck the silo and pointed out the spot where it had hit, knocking out a chunk of concrete. I wasn't brave enough to climb to the very top of the silo, but I went high enough to scare myself. There was also one thing that gave us a very funny feeling. When we were standing in the middle of the empty silo floor looking straight up, the clouds drifted slowly overhead, giving us the feeling was that the silo was moving, not the sky.

Most farmers had a few barn owls and an occasional screech owl near their barns, but an owl and I had quite a night after Bill and I were married. I awoke after hearing a very loud, low rumbling noise. Not being able to figure out what the sound might be, I woke Bill up. We listened as that noise penetrated the quiet night. After staring out the window for several minutes and listening to that chilling sound, I finally made out the figure of a gigantic great horned owl sitting on the roof of our barn. That was my only encounter with one. I still get goose bumps thinking of that eerie rumbling hoot in the middle of the night!

Many of the big old barns, such as the one we loved so much as children, are no longer being used and are falling into disrepair. Working barns display such quiet dignity and delight the senses with such a variety of elegant smells and sounds. What a pity to see the demise of these wonderful old fortresses of the farm!

## Chapter 26.
# *One-Room Schools*

"What was school like when you were little, Grandpa?" As children, Dad, Mother, Grandpa, and Grandma had all attended small one-room schools. Mother and Grandma had walked to the Deep Cut School, while Dad and Grandpa attended Sodom School. In these small schools everyone sat in the same room, regardless of age or grade. Imagine being the only child in the fourth grade. If you were a good reader, you might study with the fifth grade. If you got behind in your arithmetic (or do you call it mathematics?) you might study it with the third graders. Grandpa didn't use either of these words. He called it "ciphering," and he was good at it. Although his schooling stopped at eighth grade, he was able, even as an old man, to figure in his head faster than I could with a pencil and paper. Grandpa was amazing!

In this area, after 1825, townships were given the authority to establish schools and eventually most of these, which largely were one-room schools, were located about two miles from each other. Usually no child had to walk more than one or two miles to school. (No five-mile trudges through waist-high snow while carrying an armload of books and a lunch bucket!) This system worked quite well in Ohio's flatlands. Many of the early one-room schools were 20 X 24 feet with one door and three or four windows on each side of the building. They were furnished with a potbellied stove, benches or desks, chalkboard, portraits of Lincoln or Washington, and a drinking pail.[1]

Grandma attended "Deep Cut School" north of Kossuth. Dad and Grandpa went to "Sodom School" southeast of Kossuth. New Knoxville used one-room schools late enough that my husband, Bill, attended the "Chapel School" for his first few years of education. One of this area's last one-room schools in use was at Egypt, west of Minster, which closed in the 1960s. Many one-room school buildings remain in the area, although most are used as sheds for animals or farm equipment. A few have been remodeled and made into unique homes.

The very early school teachers were usually males. After the men marched off to fight during the Civil War, more women filled the gap and became teachers. There were very strict rules for these lady school teachers. Since female teachers were required to be single, they often got their room and board with a local family. If a lady teacher got married, she no longer taught.

A one-room school teacher was in charge of everything. She had to arrive at the school early enough to pump a fresh bucket of drinking water to bring into the building and to build a fire in the wood stove so that the school would be relatively warm by the time the students arrived. Grandpa and Grandma both agreed that even on good days, they were apt to be red-cheeked from the heat on the side nearest the potbellied stove, while the other side would still be cold.

Teacher's rules were passed in early 1900. Ivan Knapp listed these 1915 rules:

1. You will not marry during the term of your contract.
2. You are not to keep company with men.
3. You must be home between the hours of 8 p.m. and 6 a.m. unless attending school functions.
4. You may not loiter downtown in ice cream stores.
5. You may not ride in a carriage or automobile with any man unless he is your father or brother.
6. You may not travel beyond the city limits unless you have permission of the chairman of the board.
7. You may not smoke cigarettes.
8. You may not dress in bright colors.
9. You may under no circumstances dye your hair.
10. You must wear at least two petticoats.
11. Your dresses must not be any shorter than two inches above the ankle.
12. To keep the school room neat and clean, you must sweep the floor at least once daily; scrub the floor at least once a week with hot, soapy water; clean the blackboards at least once a day; and start the fire at 7 a.m. so the room will be warm by 8 a.m.[2]

Now that you've read the rules, how would you like to be a teacher?

One-half hour before school started, the teacher gave several tugs on the school bell rope. This was a warning to the children that it was time to leave home, allowing sufficient time to walk the mile or two to school. A half-hour later, the bell rang a second time to signal the start of classes. Woe to the slowpoke who scooted into his seat after the bell had stopped ringing. My grandparents spoke of occasionally having to run the last half-mile so they wouldn't be late and have to stand in the corner. The teacher then opened classes, usually starting the day with a prayer and the Pledge of Allegiance to the flag of our United States.

The teacher was in charge of the discipline. There was no office where a wayward child could be sent. The teacher was the law, and no one dared disobey! To do so would probably mean two spankings, one from the teacher and one from your pa when you got home. Since other brothers and sisters sat in the same classroom, someone was sure to let it slip that you had received a spanking.

Students in one-room schools ranged in age from approximately six years old to the ages of eighteen or nineteen. Since the children attending my grandparents' schools were all farm children, many of the older boys were often kept home for spring planting or harvesting in the fall. As a result, they continued going to school when it was convenient until they reached adulthood. Sometimes the school year was broken into segments of three or four months. A "teacher" who was not doing well might leave at the end of this short time.

One of Grandpa's favorite stories was about the big boys and the teacher. When a new teacher came to the Sodom School, it was usually a man. No woman could handle those "Sodom Indians." Usually the first day or two decided whether the new teacher would stay or leave. The biggest boy in the school would challenge (or provoke) the teacher to a fight. Now you must remember these were husky farm boys who were used to doing hard manual labor. Learning was not necessarily their first choice of activities, since many didn't think they needed to know a whole lot of "book learnin'" to run a farm. The unwritten rule was that if the biggest boy could whip the teacher, the teacher left, and a new one had to be hired. Some of the teachers were rather frail young men who were not physically strong enough for the rigors of farming. This challenge of the new teacher usually took place soon after the school year started. If the teacher was the winner, he stayed for the rest of the school year and was usually respected by all the students.

But just because the teacher had earned the respect of the school by passing "his" first big test didn't mean that it was smooth sailing for the rest of the year. One of these mischievous boys' favorite tricks was to place a board over the top of the school's chimney, making the smoke back up into the school building. The classes couldn't carry on in that thick black smoke, and the teacher had to send the students home for the day. Another favorite trick was to upset the outhouse. Occasionally a snake was brought to school and *accidentally* let loose in the classroom. Those things didn't prompt a day off from school, but they did keep things exciting for a little while until the teacher could deal with the situation. Grandpa never told us if *he* had been involved in any of those pranks. One time something happened that had not been caused by the big boys. A skunk got under the school building one day and ended classes before they began. No one wanted to mess with that unwelcome visitor. He left quietly during the night without leaving a trace of his bad odor, and the next morning classes resumed as usual.

Most one-room schools regularly held spelling bees for their pupils. Grandma always enjoyed the "spell down," and both she and Grandpa were quite good at spelling. After a student had won the champion speller title, he or she might be asked to compete in a spelling bee with another area school. Grandpa told of one occasion when a visiting school came for a spelling bee. Some of their older boys criticized the Sodom teacher and Grandpa said everyone piled on those boys and *cleaned up on them*. "Sodom Indians" became their nickname because of incidents like this. Every teacher in the county knew about them and their fearsome nickname!

The following paragraphs were copied from a 1942 Spencerville *Journal-News* article, "Echoes of Days Past and Gone," written by Dr. J.R. Welch. The doctor died unexpectedly at the age of 83 before the series could be completed. (During his 60 years as a practicing physician in Spencerville, he delivered 4,212 babies, of which I was one.) He wrote of attending an old log school house.

> The only books that I can remember of having was a McGuffey spelling book and reader. Those of you who have studied that spelling book will remember that there were long columns of words to be pronounced and spelled. We were drilled on this work until we were able to pronounce and spell the entire column after the teacher had pronounced the first word of the column. Another plan was to have the class line up on the floor and the teacher would pronounce the first word of the column, then each scholar was expected to know his word and spell it. If he did not know his word, or misspelled it, he had to sit down. The result of all this drilling was that our school just about won the pennant in every spelling contest. In those days spelling schools were about all the excitement that the youngsters had to look forward to. As I now remember, we nearly always went in sleds with large wagon boxes full of straw. [3]

Dr. Welch remembered that his first trip to Spencerville had been to participate in a spelling school. When their school was the winner, the children were taken to the Roeckner Hotel which stood west of the old Kolter mill. There they ate an oyster supper.

Grandpa said teachers occasionally played games with the children during recess or the noon hour. While the older children played ball, some of the smaller ones played “drop the handkerchief” or "fox and geese." If it was winter and there was a pond or stream nearby, ice skates were clamped onto shoes and skating continued until the teacher rang the bell for classes to resume. These activities often proved to be enjoyable for the teachers as well as the students, since many of them had been students themselves just a year or so before.

Teachers were also the school nurses, taking care of any emergencies that might arise. I’ve never forgotten the warning my grandma gave me one cold winter day. She said, “Don’t ever stick your tongue against any kind of metal when it is cold outside.” When she was in Deep Cut School, someone dared one of the “smarter” girls to lick the metal pump handle on a bitter cold winter day. She foolishly licked it, and her tongue froze to the handle. Someone hurried to tell the teacher. I don’t remember hearing how she got the girl’s tongue loose, but Grandma decided right then and there that a girl who was dumb enough to lick a pump handle when it was freezing just wasn’t as smart as she thought she was! I never forgot her warning.

Occasionally the students presented an evening program for their parents. This was a very special time! Grandma said it seemed really strange to come back to the school at night, dressed in their Sunday best, with Mom and Dad driving them in the buggy or wagon instead of walking as they did each day. In a card from Tillie Fledderjohann to Bill’s mother, she said, “Do you remember the coal oil lights we used to have in our country school? We had a small lamp at each window and it had a shiny reflector on it to give better light. We used them whenever we had Spelling School or Box Socials.” The families arrived carrying lanterns in their buggies or wagons. Upon arrival, these were often hung up for additional light. Benches were placed along the sides and at the back wall, just inside the cloakroom. Moms and dads were seated there with squirming little brothers and sisters on their laps as they listened to the pupils say their “pieces” and sing songs. A makeshift stage was made from curtains hung on a rope tied to nails on each side at the front of the room. Grandma thought these programs were definitely the highlights of the year in a one-room schoolhouse.

Occasionally teachers also had monthly “literaries”at their schools. While talking to Lola Lammers, I asked what she knew about literaries. She laughed and said she once heard a story about a group of rather uppity ladies who were quite pleased with themselves as they attended the local literary meetings where they studied some of the great works of literature. Their husbands, who were all doctors and other educated professional men, had to laugh at their wives and the pride they took in attending these literaries. In reality, the literature was far above their heads and they understood very little of what they were reading, but these hoity-toity ladies thought it seemed to be an appropriate activity for the wives of such intellectual gentlemen.

“Who will buy my box?” the girls wondered. Grandma gave us an account of another school event, the box supper. The excitement mounted as the time for the auction approached. Box socials ranked high on the list of enjoyable activities. Each young lady brought a box she had prepared and wrapped as pretty as possible. Inside was placed a supper that she hoped would be fit for a king. Grandma said many of those boxes contained home-fried chicken. (Sorry, Colonel Sanders. Your Kentucky Fried Chicken was not the first to be sold in a box!) A local man acted as auctioneer while each box was displayed and sold to the highest bidder. There were many anxious moments as each girl waited hopefully for the right young man to buy her box. The successful bidder then had the privilege of eating supper with the young lady whose box he had purchased. The money was used to help buy a new dictionary, new reading books, or whatever the teacher and school board deemed most needed at that time.

If students wanted to attend high school, they were required to pass the Boxwell-Patterson Exam. After exam day, the questions were often printed in local papers. I have seen some of those questions, and believe me, they were difficult. Not every teacher had college training. Some received approval after passing an exam, and by the next year they were teaching. My grandpa Briggs, who was in Spencerville's first high school graduation class, taught at several schools, including the two-room school in Kossuth. One of his fellow teachers was Meta Meckstroth, a distant cousin of Bill's who later became Mrs. Art Hoge. Bill's dad taught at a one-room school south of New Knoxville, and many of his aunts, uncles and cousins were teachers. My grandma's first cousin, Professor John Schwarz, even worked his way up the education ladder from a one-room school teacher to a college professor.

Bill remembers quite well a lesson he learned in the one-room Chapel School. The teacher had finished the lessons with Bill and the other younger students seated on the left side of the room. She turned her attention to the older ones on the right. They were studying about the western United States. She shared events from her summer trip "out west." Bill listened in and has never forgotten one statement she made, "When you are that far away and meet someone from Ohio, it is like meeting your next door neighbor back home."

Those one-room schools may have been small and archaic by today's standards, but their graduates are testimony to their effectiveness.

---

[1] Ann Bowers, Bowling Green State University Archivist, Mercer County Historical Society meeting, April 1996, used with permission.

[2] Ivan Knapp, *Evening Leader*, St. Marys, Ohio, March 17, 1987, used with permission.

[3] Dr. J.R. Welch, "Echoes of Days Past and Gone," 1942, reprinted January1 and 8, 1976, *Journal-News*, Spencerville, Ohio, used with permission.

Chapel one-room school southwest of Moulton in 1932

First row left to right: Roger Howe, Carl Kogge, Paul Kogge, Cletus Ballweg, Emerson Howe, William Meckstroth, Wilson Kruse

Second row: Elmer Schultz, Donald Sudman, Willis Schultz, Frederick Arnett, Ralph Schultz, Adrian Kruse

Between second and third row: Ruth Wibbeler (with bangs) and Gladys Schneider (blond)

Third row: Melba Ballweg, Marie Clausing, Treva Ballweg, Esther Wibbeler, Alice Katterheinrich, Beulah Aufderhaar, Forest Stolte, Lillian Schneider, Vernita Schwaberow

Fourth row: Vernon Meckstroth, Mary Arnett, Henrietta Schneider, Rachael Katterheinrich, LaHoma Ballweg, Walter Wibbeler, Vernon Kogge

Teacher Roger Smith stands in the center of the back row.

(Identified by former students Vernita Fark, Bill Meckstroth, Mary Rohrbaugh, and Ralph Schultz)

Chapter 27.

# Country Living Makes a Lot of "Scents"

The nose was kept at peak performance from the wide assortment of smells on those old-time farms. The olfactory nerve is one of the more important parts of the body, and those country farms produced some smells that still bring back great memories. For instance, the smell of coffee reminds me of Grandma's old coffee pot sitting on the back of the wood cookstove. How I loved the smell of coffee as it brewed and as she poured the steaming liquid into the cups on the dinner table. Since I thought it had such a fabulous aroma, I decided as a tiny girl that I wanted a taste. After begging Grandpa to give me a sip, I was certainly disappointed. It didn't taste at all like it smelled, really very nasty tasting stuff! As a result of that experience, I never took up coffee drinking. How could something that smelled so good, taste so bad?

There were a lot of other smells that I associate with Grandma's kitchen—the warm sugar water as it boiled down into delicious maple syrup each spring, the sweet aroma of fresh-baked pies cooling on the shelf at the top of the cookstove, and homemade jellies and jams which she stirred until they were just the right consistency. Taking a large spoon, Grandma skimmed the foam from the top of the pan so that the jelly would remain clear and sparkling. I usually ran for a spoon to enjoy this delicious *residue*. Grandpa loved the sweet jam or jelly spread on his bread. He always said he just couldn't eat bread without something on it!

Breakfasts were made special by the smell of freshly cut slabs of bacon, brought in from the smoke house and fried as an accompaniment for the fresh eggs gathered the day before in the henhouse. That smell, wafting up the stairway, was sure to get even the sleepiest heads out of bed and ready to greet the day. The smell of hot chocolate or a pot of homemade vegetable soup simmering on the back of Grandma's cookstove was always welcomed on cold winter days.

Fresh baked goods were also a most welcome smell. When I was just a little girl, Jesse Bourne, the county agent, taught Grandma's homemaker class how to make an apple coffee cake. That wonderful coffee cake was the only yeast product Grandma ever made. How I loved that warm yeasty smell as the apple cake baked in the oven of the wood cookstove!

Fresh, sweet apple cider not only had an inviting aroma, it also had a wonderful taste in the fall. Mixed with the smell of freshly popped corn, the two became symbols of a relaxing evening at home when everything seemed to be right with the world.

Then there was the questionable smell of newly made sauerkraut. The fresh cabbage had a delicate odor, but we knew it would change drastically in a few short weeks. Once the cabbage had fermented, the smell of the kraut reminded us of something much more disagreeable. Oh, my goodness! Was there a dead mouse in the house? Oooeee!

We always looked forward to the smell of grapes and sweet, red ripe strawberries direct from the patch. There was a delicate aroma from the muskmelons and the ripe watermelon as it was sliced, breaking open with a crack. Then we had the pleasure of enjoying the wonderful taste as well as the aroma.

When we came home from school on cold days and opened the door to the smell of fresh straw in the kitchen, we knew a basket of shivering newborn baby pigs would probably be sitting on the oven door of the cookstove. Now we could hold, pet and play with them without worrying about the mother sow being there to hurt us.

Outside the house most smells were seasonal. In spring there was nothing sweeter than the honeysuckle flowers as the vine meandered up the lightning rod at the corner of the house. Another early spring smell was the backyard lilac bush in full bloom. It usually bloomed about the time we were planting the garden and we had to pass near it when we walked through the garden gate. Ummm! How sweet it smelled. Grandma loved the smell of the hyacinths and planted several in her teardrop flower bed in the center of the driveway. A sure sign of spring was the sweet aroma of the blossoms from the various fruit trees blooming in the orchard. We were always fearful of a frost during the time they were blooming. If the blooms were frozen, there would be no fruit that summer. Although the tree blooms smelled delightful, we had to look out for the bees they attracted!

When our city friends visited the farm, they occasionally watched as we milked, a job they found quite interesting. After the cows had been turned out on pasture in early spring, they ate the *green* grass and often belched loudly, then hunched their back, raised their tail and let it fly! This resulted in a hurried movement by the person milking as they tried to escape the inevitable "splat" that was sure to follow. If you weren't quick enough, you spent the remainder of chore time with the strong odor of those smelly brown spots decorating your legs and shoes.

Even our yard had the fresh smell of spring as the reel-type lawn mower was taken from the shed and pushed through the lush green growth. The style of mower has changed, but the aroma of freshly cut grass hasn't.

The earthy aroma of freshly turned brown dirt in the spring was tantalizing with the promise of another growing season just ahead. Setting out the onion plants with their distinctive odor was just another sign of the harvest to come, complete with its many tears as we cut the juicy onions into soups and casseroles. Onions gave the meat roasts a most delicious aroma and we enjoyed the taste, forgetting the tears. I think that is rather akin to life and its problems. Once we have enjoyed the sweet aroma of success, we soon forget the tears of failure.

Summer on the farm brought many distinctive smells. We always enjoyed the scent of the many flowers that Grandma grew. I especially liked the smell of the roses. A climber spread its flowers over the back fence, and a pale pink moss rose stood in the corner of the yard. An old-fashioned single yellow rambler bloomed near the water pump. Grandma always had lots of old-fashioned zinnias with their stiff heads standing erect at the front of the garden. She also grew marigolds, the pretty orange and yellow flowers with the strong smell that was supposed to chase bugs out of the garden.

A wagon loaded with wheat had a very identifiable smell. Grandpa showed us how to chew on the fresh grains to tell if it was ripe. It was rather like a farmer's form of chewing gum. Haying season on the farm promised a variety of smells, since the sweet clover hay had a fragrance different from alfalfa. When that fresh new hay was put in the barn's hayloft, the whole building smelled wonderful! Even today, as we drive through the countryside, we enjoy the familiar fragrance of the newly mown hay. Although not as strong a smell, the new straw had a subtle, clean scent of its own as it was scattered in the calf pens and the chicken house. The animals loved to lay in the clean, fresh straw.

A tramp through the woods each fall offered a delightful array of smells. The dried leaves that formed a carpet of gold under the huge trees offered an unforgettable "woodsy" smell. As Grandpa took the Hoopie to the woods for a jag of logs and branches, he often built a fire to burn some of the smaller twigs and branches, and to provide some warmth for cold hands and toes. It gave off the distinctive smell of burning wood and leaves. In years past, leaves were raked into the gutters along city streets in our area, then burned. I loved that aromatic smell. It was one of the most obvious signs that fall had arrived.

A familiar odor found only in winter was that made by wet wool socks and gloves as they dried near the open oven doors and on the hot air registers. Wool was the fabric most used for outer clothing when I was a kid, and we all had at least one pair of wool mittens. The men's work socks were also wool.

Some smells, however, never changed. Who can forget the smells associated with the freshly ground feed in Grandpa's feed room in the barn and the chicken house? Neither will one forget the smell associated with the other end of the animals!

City folks usually turned up their noses at the odor of the pig pens, the cow lot, and the chicken coop, all perfectly normal on a farm and something that farmers jokingly described as "the smell of money." I didn't mind most of the smells, but I didn't like the smell of the chicken coop. If bad weather prevented it from being cleaned out, the smell of ammonia was very strong and we were happy when the weather cleared and the job was finally finished. Just driving by a field with a new coating of fresh manure was more than some city noses could handle, but the potent fragrance of the road-kill skunk was almost more than even the farmers could take.

When we were working outside, we often used the conveniently located outhouse. Now that had some real fragrances that our city friends didn't like! Even the damp Sears Roebuck catalog had a subtle aroma of its own.

The smell most familiar to every farm family was the smell of honest sweat after a day of hard work. Perspiration may be the fancy word for it, but when a farmer did it, it was just plain old-fashioned, hard earned sweat!

Even Grandpa's old trunk had a smell of its own. When my grandparents moved from North Carolina they brought back a small cedar tree and planted it in the front yard. When it had grown to be a good sized tree, a winter storm broke off a branch. A piece of its fragrant wood was smoothed and placed in the old trunk. The cedar smell helped repel any moths who might have gotten the idea of taking up housekeeping there.

There were smells galore on our childhood farm, both in the house and out. Some were not too sweet, but there was no better smell than the wonderful aroma of freshly washed clothes that had dried on an outside line in the sunshine and fresh air. When rainy weather demands it, I am thankful for my wonderful clothes dryer, but if the weather permits, I still enjoy hanging my clothes out in the fresh air and sunshine. No smell is quite as nice as those clean, sweet smelling bed sheets perfumed by God's special outdoor fragrances! Ah, what a good night's sleep they provide at the end of a busy day!

## Chapter 28.

# The Sounds of Silence

The farm was such a quiet place that when a farmer went to the big city, he could scarcely sleep. It was just *too doggone noisy* with all the sirens from police cars and fire engines, loud whistles from factories, and quieter ones from the policeman on the corner, the chiming of city hall clocks and church towers, and trains whistling and rumbling through town. But when the city man came to the country, he had the same problem. He could scarcely sleep. It was just *too doggone quiet!*

As any farmer would tell you, farms had lots of sounds, some very obvious and some as soft as a whisper. Sunrise brought the obvious with the crowing of the neighborhood roosters as they welcomed the dawn. In the early morning stillness, that first rooster's greeting could be heard for a mile or more. As his fowl friends down the road joined in, the whole neighborhood quickly knew it was morning. No alarm clocks needed here!

If you stood still and listened, you could hear many sounds—the quiet clucking of the chickens as they scratched the ground, pecking for bugs; their excited cackle when they found some; a cow lowing softly to her newborn calf; then weeks later the bawl of the calf that had just been weaned from its anxious mother; the lambs baaing in the pasture as they frisked and frolicked, jumping straight up into the air in sheer exuberance; a Delco power plant putt-putting away during the day; the tree frogs and crickets chirping at night. A very reassuring sound on winter nights was the sound of the snowplow as it cleared the drifts from the country roads. An exciting sound for Don and me was the steady drone of an airplane passing overhead. We rushed out the door and gave a friendly wave to the smaller, low-flying planes, hoping the pilot would see us and tip his wings in response. Airplanes were scarce in those days and this simple recognition added an extra dimension of delight for farm kids like us.

Farm skies were alive with an abundance of birds. Where there was feed for the animals, the birds instinctively knew there would be some for them. We most often heard the tweet, tweets of hundreds of ordinary sparrows. Occasionally a redheaded woodpecker bombarded our ears with the steady rat-a-tat-tat of his sharp little beak as he searched for a fresh bug dinner, drilling deeply into the bark of our huge maple tree beside the kitchen window. All too often we heard the raucous squawks of a flock of blackbirds as they swooped low over the farm fields, their beady little eyes searching for any exposed grains of corn or wheat. Blackbirds, like crows, often played havoc with a farmer's garden and crops. Although hawks and owls thrived on mice and rats, they were not welcome around Grandma's brooder house. We occasionally saw these large birds zero in on a flock of baby chicks and help themselves to the poor little unsuspecting victims.

Some birds, however, were the farmer's helpers. They ate the moths, beetles, caterpillars, and other insects that devoured the tender plants in the garden! The bobwhite with his two-word vocabulary, "Bob White, Bob White," is capable of eating up to 15,000 weed seeds in one day! My favorites in the bird kingdom are the songbirds such as the little wren, the bright red cardinal which is also the state bird of Ohio, and the robin who is so eager to bring spring that he usually makes his first appearance weeks before the last snow of the season. As children we often caught a glimpse of a blue jay standing defiantly in the back yard maple tree, scolding other birds who ventured near. The big crane who balanced on one spindly leg as he stood at attention in the nearby Prairie Creek was always a source of wonder to me. These awkward birds resembled the pictures I had seen of storks, and I often wondered if they might bring a new baby to the neighborhood, perhaps even to our house! A special treat was to watch the tiny hummingbirds, flitting from flower to flower in search of the sweet nectar. For some reason, I especially remember the sound of the morning dove with its gentle "coooo, coooo." Grandpa always said that sound was "a sure sign of rain."

Although bird sounds were more prevalent, we occasionally heard the whinny of horses. By the 1940s, however, horse sounds were being replaced by tractor sounds. Most farmers could tell by the sounds the tractors made just which neighbor was working his field that day. When I was in high school, we often heard a voice singing and finally located its source. Our neighbor, Mac Lishness, sang as he drove his tractor through the fields, plowing and planting and harvesting. I'm sure we could hear him much clearer than he heard himself as the sound carried above the noisy tractor.

Another sound that was all too common was the buzzing of flies, especially the big horseflies that were so prevalent then. They delighted in biting the cows' legs and backs, sometimes forming big welts. When a cow who was relaxing under a favorite tree suddenly took off running, tail flying high in the air, old Mr. Horsefly was usually circling for a landing. Bad smelling fly spray was often applied to keep the cows calm during milking, but open pasture fields offered them no help. All the poor cows could do was try to outrun their enemy. Many farmers placed leather fly nets over the backs of their horses. Constant movement kept each narrow strip of leather twisting and turning, thus providing an unstable landing field for the horseflies. Any farm that had animals had a lot of flies. Bill and I both remember hot summer days when the screen doors would be nearly black with flies, each one waiting patiently to get inside the house. Our kitchen light usually had a sticky fly paper hanging beneath it, ready to catch and hold any passing insects. Of course, we had to be careful that, as we passed by, we didn't get our hair caught in the sticky mess. Although we never tried it, some people cut newspapers in narrow strips and tacked them to the top of the screen door. As the door was opened, the strips fluttered in the breeze and chased away the flies, allowing time for you to enter . . . hopefully without the flies.

The quietest creatures on the farm were the oats bugs. These were tiny little black bugs about an eighth of an inch long that seemed to be in great abundance everywhere. Do you have any very old pictures in your attic? If you look carefully, you may still locate a few carcasses in the corners beneath the glass. There were a lot of oats grown to feed the horses back then and those pesky little bugs seemed to appear at harvest time, walking through screens and up and down any human flesh they could find inside the house or out. They came during the hottest time of the year and the more you perspired, the more they crawled around your face and arms. We don't have any of these silent little oats bugs bothering us today, perhaps because with fewer horses, oats is seldom grown. I haven't seen any of the little bug varmints in many a year. They seem to have disappeared and believe me, that's good! No farmer would want them back! No siree!

Now don't laugh, but even the sounds from a country bathroom were different from their city cousins. The city people had indoor plumbing, so their bathroom noises ended with a swish and the sound of bubbling water as the tank filled, but many farms did not have indoor plumbing and the only sound in the outhouse was a trickle, trickle, plop, plop! I remember some of the church ladies saying they enjoyed coming to Ladies Aid meetings at our house because Grandma had *indoor* plumbing.

Occasionally there were sounds we did not wish to hear. Sudden squawks from the chickens were usually a sign that some animal had gotten into the chicken yard or hen house and they were frightened. Feathers usually flew in all directions and someone ran to the rescue. Another sound that we did not like was the steady bawl of a lonesome cow whose calf had just been sold. Her fretting call might continue for several days.

One summer a young city friend, David Jodry, was going on a two-week mission trip with our church youth group and because it would interrupt a summer job, he was unable to find an employer who would allow that. Since our son was also going, we understood David's plight and Bill found some work for him at our store. One day David kept hearing high-pitched squeals coming from the barn across the road. "What is wrong with those pigs?" he finally asked. Our other employees were a bit more farm-oriented and they had to smile as David discovered the cause. The neighbor was castrating his pigs! David eventually married a farmer's daughter, became a preacher, and now has a family of his own. But, he has never forgotten that summer day. When we last saw Dave, he grinned as he recalled its events.

Night sounds on the farm were usually quite pleasant. One of the first sounds of a warm spring night was that of the tree frogs calling from the nearest woods. There was also the steady chirping of crickets that blended with the sound of the cicada. (The farmers usually called them locusts.) There was also the katydid that, like the locust, resembled a grasshopper but was wider and greener.

A very undesirable sound that we heard at night was the high-pitched whine of the mosquito. These usually prompted a battle between humans armed with a fly swatter and the tiny rascals armed with wings that moved at incredible speeds. Just when a tired farmer had settled down for a pleasant night of rest, "Bzzzz Bzzzz" sounded a mosquito as he checked his victim for a suitable landing site. Recognizing the imminent danger of attack, the farmer jumped to his feet and grabbed the nearest object, often a shoe. After several unsuccessful trips around the room with arms flailing and swatter swatting, tripping over shoes and upsetting chairs, traipsing across beds and muttering under one's breath, the human might be fortunate enough to disable the critter, thus guaranteeing undisturbed sleep for what little amount of the night that might remain.

Our dog occasionally barked at night and we often heard an answering bark from his lady friend a mile away. When I was a child, our neighbor's dog once howled forlornly all night long. The next day we found out his master had died during the night. Had he understood what had happened?

One of the most welcome sounds for a hungry farmer was the ringing of the dinner bell. Although we had a bell, I don't remember Grandma ever using it to call Grandpa for our dinner. We did occasionally hear others in the neighborhood. Bill said they rang their bell for dinner when the men were working out in the woods. It had been used in earlier days to let neighbors know there was an emergency, especially a fire. In our area, the dinner bell got its biggest workout on *belling* nights. When a young couple got married, their friends usually surprised them with a very noisy belling party.

What was the most joyous sound on the farm? It was the laughter of children at play. With a whole farm as a playground, there was excitement from morning to evening—from swinging on the haymow rope to running through the open fields, from concentrating on the tiniest bugs on the ground to exploring the giant trees in the woods, from reading a good book in the big easy chair to teaching the new puppy how to shake hands, from whistling triumphantly during the walk to the mailbox to yelling for the sheer joy of yelling while running through the pasture to bring the milk cows to the barn, from greeting the morning with a welcoming whoop while diving into a pile of rustling fall leaves to the quiet whispers of a child's prayer at bedtime. Farm children were involved in a lot of work, but they also had a way of turning much of that work into fun and that fun had a way of bringing lots of laughter. Yes, farms had a variety of sounds, but the laughter of children was the happiest!

Smiles were plentiful on a 1937 western vacation. Standing in front of an Oklahoma oil well are Don and I beside cousin Betty Lowman. Behind us are Grandpa, Aunt Eva DeLong, Grandma, Aunt Bertha and Uncle Carl Crawford and their son, Otho.

## Chapter 29.

# Tourist Cabins and Travel Tales

They weren't much more than chicken coops, those overnight accommodations in 1937. Long-distance travel was quite a contrast to the ease and comfort of traveling today. Main roads were paved and were two lanes wide, but with few of the safety features we expect today. White lines along the sides and reflectors in the center had not yet been developed.

The longest trip of my childhood was taken in the summer of 1937 as we drove to Missouri and Oklahoma to visit some of Grandma's relatives. Grandpa and Grandma, Aunt Eva DeLong and Don and I motored west in the new Nash automobile Grandpa had just purchased. As Grandma described it in an August 23 post card mailed from St. Louis, "Have driven over 1000 miles. Nash is acting fine." The roads were narrow but fairly good by then and we had no problems with the car. (There were no huge semi trucks beating down the roads in the 1930s. Everything was shipped by train, then loaded into *small* trucks to be taken to its destination at stores and businesses.)

While driving in a big Missouri city, Grandpa approached a yellow traffic light. He stopped and waited until it had turned red and then to green. After driving another block, he again had a yellow light and again stopped and waited. Suddenly a car pulled up beside him and a red faced man yelled over, "You don't have to *stop* for yellow lights. They are just a *warning* light." And then he added, "*Keep On Driving*!" Now we country hicks from Ohio had never seen any of those big city yellow warning lights, so Grandpa thanked him and the man took off in a *big* hurry . . . right smack through a *red* light! How we laughed. Even *country hicks like us* knew you didn't run red lights!

Spending that first night in a "tourist cabin" was a new experience for everyone in our family. The idea of locating drive-in motor hotels (later called "motels"), conveniently along the side of the highways was something new. Prior to that time, folks needing a place to spend the night usually had to drive to a hotel in the center of town, find a parking place, and then drag everything up several floors to a hotel room. This was not easy for five people, especially when two were older ladies and two were children. Besides that, hotels took more time and cost more. Did you tip the bellhop?

As evening approached, we looked anxiously for "Tourist Cabins Ahead" signs. It was always a relief to locate one, even though the cabins were not much more than chicken coops with a potbellied stove in the center and metal beds around the walls. Some form of modesty was attained by undressing behind the stove. The bathrooms, located fifty or a hundred feet away, were merely glorified outhouses. No, glorified is not the best word. The word "odoriferous" comes to mind as a more suitable description. Showers consisted of a square wooden box-like area with a bucket of water, usually cold, which hung above the head and was activated by pulling a string that tipped the bucket of water over on you. To this day, I hate showers and love tub baths. I blame it all on those ridiculous cold showers near the 1937 tourist cabins.

Don and I were amazed when we got ready for bed that first night. Opening her mouth, Aunt Eva reached in and pulled out a complete set of teeth, then placed them in a glass by her bed. I was aghast! I'd never seen anyone do that. I was horrified as I looked down at those teeth grinning up at me. Who ever heard of such a thing? As I stared with wide eyes at Aunt Eva, her toothless grin did nothing to reassure me. "How did she do that?" I wondered, "My teeth don't come out like that."

Our first visit was at Macks Creek, Missouri, at the home of Aunt Bertha. She and Uncle Carl ran a tourist/souvenir/filling station not far from Bagnell Dam near the Lake of the Ozarks. At night, we could hear coyotes howl in the woods behind the house. I determined I was never going to the bathroom, the little house out back with a half moon in the door. I was afraid I might meet up with a coyote, or worse yet, a rattlesnake. I had heard about those things. The adults and I slept in one of the tourist rooms, while Don slept in front of the fireplace in the store's main room. While there, we watched a neighbor as he made clay pottery. Grandma bought one of his planters to bring home. I was intrigued by a life-sized wax lady that sat along the road in front of his pottery shop. When it started to rain one day, we ran down to help carry her inside.

While driving toward Bagnell Dam, we stopped for supper at a nearby restaurant. It was there that Don and I got our first taste of iced tea. Don told me later that he really liked it and said, "Boy, that was good!" I must not have been very impressed with it because I don't even remember drinking it. But then, I still don't really care for iced tea!

When you purchased an item in Missouri and paid a tax, you received a little round cardboard token. We'd never seen those because Ohio gave paper tax stamps. We also saw our first slot machine. Uncle Carl had one in the front of his little store. People would play a nickel or two as they stopped for gas. Sometimes that "one armed bandit" would so captivate a persistent customer that he would stand in front of it, putting in nickel after nickel after nickel. Finally he would give up and drive on. Carl sometimes put in only a couple of nickels and would hit the jackpot. We didn't put any money in it, though. Our Sunday School teacher had told us we weren't supposed to gamble.

After a couple of days, we drove on to visit relatives in St. Louis, a small oil town in Oklahoma. A roller skating rink was located just behind our cousin's house. I listened to the music as I lay in bed. By propping myself up on one elbow, I could watch the skaters as they seemed to fly around and around. (Little did I know I would eventually meet my future husband while roller skating back in Ohio.) Oil wells dotted the landscape, and even in this small town the sound of the pumping engines was heard day and night.

The dirt in that Oklahoma town didn't look like our dirt back home. It was red! What fun it was to walk down town after a rainstorm and watch the red mud squish up between our toes. Although there were sidewalks made of boards like those in the old wild west movies, it was much more fun for us children to slosh barefoot through the red mud.

One afternoon we drove to the site of an oil well where our relatives were working. That was quite an adventure for us children and was of great interest to Grandpa. As a young man, he had hauled timber and helped build oil well rigging during Ohio's oil boom at the turn of the century. Aunt Eva's camera recorded us standing by the oil well.

By the time we left, a nice layer of red dust and mud covered our car. Don remembers stopping at a very modern filling station, one of those with the 1930s-type roof extending out over the gas pumps. The attendant talked with a real drawl. When he saw all the mud on our car, he asked, "Where'd ya'll git all that raid" (that's how he pronounced red) "that raid mud on your car?" Don and I giggled at his "foreign accent."

From there, we drove to St. Joseph, Missouri, to the home of Grandma's Aunt Sarah Peters. Sarah was a widow who shared her home with two daughters. Hazel was severely disabled, but Bernice was young and a lot of fun. There were no children to play with, and in an August 23, 1937, postcard to Daddy back home in Ohio, Grandma wrote, "G.M. (that's me) is homesick for you."

Bernice and I got along well and she shared her bed with me. As I woke up that first morning, I heard my name being called, but where was I? They continued to call, but couldn't find me. Sometime during the night I had apparently fallen out of bed, rolled underneath and now I was completely out of sight!

Grandpa drove through St. Joseph while Sarah told us about the sights. We went to the top of a "mountain" in the middle of town. Coming from flat northwestern Ohio, it seemed awfully high to me. (As an adult, I looked for that *mountain* as we drove through there. I saw only a rather small *hill*!)

Aunt Sarah asked Grandpa to drive to the drugstore where her son, Alvah, worked as a pharmacist. He greeted us warmly and gave Don and me coloring books and colors, as well as our first "Fudgsicls." We loved those cool treats instantly. The coloring books helped entertain us during the long drive ahead. (Believe it or not, fifty years later when Bill and I visited Alvah, I showed him that coloring book which I had kept all those years.) Those books helped pass the time for us, since boredom was the worst enemy for us children. I don't remember much of the travel between towns. I suspect I took an awfully lot of long naps.

Some of our most exciting moments always came as the car approached the next state. Don and I would lean forward as far as we could into the front seat and yell, "I beat you into Missouri," or Illinois or whatever the state might be. Since Grandpa did all the driving, I'm sure he must have braced himself for our shouts every time we approached a new state. We must not have behaved too badly, though. I don't remember any severe scoldings or spankings on the trip.

We really had some funny moments with Aunt Eva. Cameras were new to her and it took her a while to line things up the way she wanted them for her first photographs. Someone stopped her before she actually snapped one of them and reminded her to turn the camera around. She had it pointed directly at herself! Thank goodness it was early in the trip and she didn't lose any of her pictures. (Wouldn't that have been terrible if she had gone all the way to Oklahoma and back, only to find out that all the pictures she had taken were of herself?)

On our first day out, Aunt Eva had ordered hot tea in a restaurant. When the waitress set a steaming cup and saucer in front of her, she took a sip and said, "This tea is certainly weak." No one drank tea at our house and as Grandpa glanced at her saucer, he saw something laying on the back side and said, "What is that, Eva?" She turned the saucer around and picked up the little paper bag and read it. It said to place the bag into the cup of hot water. Aunt Eva had just met her first tea bag! She enjoyed the laugh along with us. Travel in the 1930s was a whole lot different from today–slower, less sophisticated, but what a good time we had. It took so little in those days to make a young child happy!

Later trips included our honeymoon, of course, and then a trip to Florida with my grandparents after we were married. By that time, Grandpa no longer felt comfortable driving such a long distance. Instead, he and Grandma asked if Bill and I would do the driving and they would pay most of the expenses. It sounded good, but I was in a rather "delicate" condition at the time. But after checking with the doctor, we packed our bags and headed south in Grandpa's Nash.

While we were there, we visited the usual Florida attractions at that time. Disney World wasn't there yet, so Florida was a lot less populated and life was a great deal more simple. One night we stayed in tourist rooms located in a private home. As we prepared to leave the next morning, Bill backed the car out of the parking space and wham—right into a tall palm tree that stood smack dab in the center of the driveway. We hadn't seen it in the darkness the night before, but we certainly felt it when we came to an instant stop that morning. Thank goodness, there was no damage to the tree, the car, or its occupants.

Grandma was now in her seventies and having some difficulty in getting around quickly. While walking through the lovely gardens surrounding one of the attractions, Grandma was enjoying the beauty of the flowers, but was not able to keep up with the guide's fast pace. He talked rather unkindly to her and grumbled about people who wouldn't walk fast enough. Grandma was really hurt by his remarks, and I finally told him to just go on with his tour and we would come when we could. I'm sure if we were to visit there today, there would be provisions for sweet little grandmas who just can't keep up. (That guide would be in his seventies today. Wonder how he's doing?)

The attraction Grandpa and Grandma enjoyed most was the boat trip around the Miami area. They had never been on a good-sized boat and were a bit skeptical. We really had to talk them into it. As we cruised near the shore and saw the beautiful skyline with its elegant hotels and homes of rich people, they relaxed and enjoyed it immensely.

For Bill and me, this was almost like a second honeymoon (except you normally don't take your grandparents on your honeymoon, do you?) Though I had a few uncomfortable moments with "morning sickness," I handled the trip quite well. At the first smell of hot grease each morning, I had a few dry heaves, but then recovered rather quickly. I've never forgotten the comment Bill made after that trip, "I wouldn't mind driving to Florida if I didn't have to go through Georgia." There were no interstate highways and Georgia's roads were so rough that he worried about my delicate condition on all those bumps.

Bill and I eventually earned many enjoyable business trips to various parts of the world, but the little girl still within me has never quite forgotten the excitement and childish thrill of that first *big* trip, the one to Oklahoma. (Maybe it's because the other trips didn't include Aunt Eva with her camera, tea bags and a glass full of grinning teeth!)

## Chapter 30.

# Corn, a Harvest of Gold

It was fall and the corn stalks swayed with each gentle breeze, their brittle leaves rustling in a discordant rhythm. The dog and I played together, running in and out of the standing corn or hiding behind the newly made shocks yelling, "Find me, Grandpa." Poor Don. He had to spend his days in school, but I was still too young. In my mind, I can still see Grandpa and Grandma toiling in a patch of ground south of the henhouse as they cut down the corn with its ears of golden grain hanging full and ready for the harvest. Working side by side, Grandpa swung the sharp corn knife, slicing the stalks off near the ground and Grandma carried them to the shock.

Shocks were the original "grain driers." Grandpa's method was to leave four stalks of corn standing in the form of a square and then wrap another stalk around them, giving it a final twist to secure it. Other stalks were then placed evenly around this square. When a shock had been formed, he finished off the job by twisting two stalks together to form a "rope." String was not wasted for such things during the depression. Although the stalks of corn appeared to be dry, fall weather was needed to dry the kernels sufficiently. Finished shocks stood in rows throughout the field like brown sentinels waiting patiently. Although wind and rain would buffet the shocks, any farmer worth his salt knew how to fasten them so they would stand up to the storms until husking or shredding time.

Corn shocks also served another purpose. When working in the field, farm folks found them to be ideal for squatting behind when "Mother Nature" called. The leaves and husks made awfully scratchy toilet paper though! But then, when you were out in the fields or woods, you made do. That's how farmers handled such matters.

After the corn had dried sufficiently, it was time to return to the field, this time with Grandpa at the wheel of the Old Hoopie with the little two-wheeled trailer fastened behind. The shocks were then slowly taken apart as Grandpa and Grandma husked out the dry ears of golden corn and threw them into the trailer. A special tool, a husking peg, fit over the glove on one hand and made it easier to grasp and pull off the husks surrounding each ear. I tried to be a big girl and "help," but my feeble attempts at husking corn didn't amount to much. "Maybe when I get bigger," I thought. As before, my activities were to run and play hide-and-seek behind the shocks. When weariness finally overtook me, I climbed into the Hoopie and took a long nap.

Sometimes, if the weather was extremely wet and it was feared that the corn might mold if left in the field, the shocks were disassembled and stalks (with ears still attached) were taken into the barn. When the ears had dried, they were then removed from the stalk and husked. This job was usually done on a cold or rainy winter day. Although some of the ear corn was shelled in a "hand" powered corn sheller, most of the ear corn was fed to the animals without further processing. The remaining fodder was still useful. Cattle were sometimes fed the husks and dried leaves, while the stalks could be used for bedding.

I'm sure a corn binder was used on our farm, but I just don't remember it. I do remember some of the corn being harvested "by hand" by my family. Many farmers got together and helped their neighbors, depending on how much corn had been planted and the availability of machines, like corn binders and shredders in a given neighborhood. Binders and shredders were less expensive to buy than threshing machines, so more farmers owned their own or worked out arrangements with close neighbors. Sometimes several men in an area went together to purchase the equipment. The *Auglaize County Democrat* of Thursday, October 29, 1914 listed the following under the New Knoxville heading: "A company of farmers, including Messrs. W.D. Arnett, C.A. Meckstroth (Charles was a cousin to Bill's dad), H.A. Holtkamp, and Wm. Haberkamp last week purchased a complete corn shredding outfit, consisting of a Deering six-roll shredder and a fifteen horsepower Fairbanks oil engine. The sale was made through the agency of The Detjen Grain Company at this place." In Grandpa Wierwille's case, he owned his own shredder, one made by the Appleton Co. of Appleton, Wisconsin. It was kept inside the barn and out of the weather. The source of power was a twelve-horse, one-cylinder engine made by the Olds Co.

Since my knowledge of corn shredding was quite limited, Bill described the operation as it was done on their farm. The cutting of the corn stalks by hand was replaced with a sled that was pulled between the rows. It had winged-extensions containing knives that cut the stalks, which then fell to the ground. These sleds were later replaced with corn binders which were pulled by a team of two or three horses into the field where they cut just one row of corn at a time. Early binders cut off the stalks about six to ten inches above the ground, making bundles of a dozen or so stalks which were bound with string. Later binders had "bundle carriers" which allowed the bundles of stalks to accumulate and be discharged together, eliminating the need to pick up many individual bundles strung across the field. Every method required quite a bit of time. An *Auglaize County Republican* item of October 4, 1917, pointed out that in Grandpa's area near Sodom, "The corn binders can be heard at this place at eleven o'clock at night." That would be quite late for folks who were used to going to bed shortly after sundown. Was the moon shining? Remember, those horses didn't have headlights out in front to guide them.

On Bill's grandpa's farm, a wooden triangular apparatus was set on the ground and used as a base to build the shock of corn. When that shock was completed, the base was moved on until the field was finished. The shocks were always set up in rows, but the ground continued to be worked right around the corn shocks. The little sled affair (used prior to the introduction of the binders) was taken through the corn rows. It cut off the remaining stubble closer to the ground. After that, a disc or harrow was brought in to loosen the ground around and between the shocks. Wheat was then planted.

A second important machine was a corn shredder. It performed several tasks. The stalk and ear were fed into the machine between two snapping rolls which removed the ear from the stalk. The ear fell down into the husking bed: several rollers that pulled the husks off the ears of corn. The ears were then discharged into a wagon and placed in corn cribs. The fodder, which had continued past the snap rolls, entered either a "cutter" head or a "shredder" head. The cutter head cut up the stalk, husks, and leaves into small pieces. It was often fed to the cows. The shredder head just mangled the fodder, with the stalk generally remaining in one piece. It was then used as bedding.

Corn shredding day was very much like threshing day. As colder weather approached and it became each farmer's turn to harvest the corn, the steam engine that had done the threshing came down the road again, this time to be used on the corn shredder. While some of the men got the steamer and shredder in place with the long belts between them, others drove teams of horses into the field, loading the bundles that formed the shocks and bringing them to the barn for processing. As usual, the women also had their work to do. The *Republican* newspaper of January 7, 1915, mentioned: "Mrs. Frank Davenport and Mrs. John Bowersock assisted Mrs. Fredus Daniels in cooking for the corn shredders Monday." They no doubt returned the favor for Grandma.

When the entire operation was completed, most farmers went back to the fields and planted wheat in the strips where the corn shocks had previously stood. If it had been an excessively wet fall and they were not able to get back into the fields, oats were often planted in the spring, instead.

There were also other "labor saving devices" that were used on many farms. Bill's grandpa had a Hexel bank which chopped up oats (stalk with head and grain) into a mixture that was fed to the horses. The stalks had to be fed into the machine by hand, where two rollers directed them into a cutter head. The small pieces were then blown into a storage bin close to the horses. One man told me that when making feed for their horses, the farmers used only the best oats grown on the farm.

Other machines were used to cut wood. Bill remembered a little hill back in their woods which was used for their huge wood pile. Sawing the wood was dangerous, and he was not allowed in the woods while the machinery was in operation. Later, he often pulled a small wagon there and loaded it with wood, then brought it back to fill the wood shed.

Farm machinery did not have the safety features required today and was dangerous to be around. Steam engines could explode. There were always a lot of dust and chaff which made the leather machinery belts quite slippery, posing a danger if a belt slid off a pulley. (Bill's Grandpa coated the belts with castor oil to keep them soft and make them sticky so they wouldn't slip) Shields were not generally installed because of the need for constant maintenance. The "hand fed" nature of the machines also meant that some workers got a little too close and ended up feeding *their* hands to the machine. Bill's Uncle Harry lost two fingers on his right hand when, as a young man, he tried to unplug the corn shredder. Bill remembers that it was a terrible shock to the whole family. They didn't think such a thing would happen in their family. One man in the community had bragged that he was too fast for a piece of machinery to catch him, but he eventually lost a whole hand. I knew two men from the Kossuth area who lost arms in shredders.

Local New Knoxville physician, Dr. Henry Fledderjohann, a distant relative of Bill's, told in a 1949 *Evening Leader* interview about a case he had.

> I remember when Mr._had his arm crushed in a corn shredder. They called me and I came on the run. His arm was a mangled bloody mess, almost made me sick to look at. All that I could do there was stop the bleeding. We bundled him in my buggy and set out for St. Marys, over exerting my good horse in the process. We went to a doctor's office there, gave him chloroform, trimmed the stub of his arm, and he got along fine. . . We used chloroform because ether was explosive and we sometimes operated by kerosene lamp. [1]

When the first mechanical corn pickers came on the market, they were pulled by a tractor. Thus, it was necessary to "open up the fields." Several rows of corn were husked out by hand to keep the tractor from knocking down the stalks and destroying the corn as it made its first trip around the field. With self-propelled harvesters, even that has become a thing of the past. Now, it is primarily the Amish who continue the old traditions while harvesting the gold.

---

[1] Andrew K. interview with Dr. Henry Fledderjohann, *Evening Leader*, St. Marys, Ohio, October 22, 1949, used with permission..

This machine shredded corn at the Ernst Meckstroth farm near New Knoxville. The picture, taken by Bill's father, was made from his original glass negative. It was at this bank barn that he later fell off a hay wagon and died.

## Chapter 31.
# Butchering Day on the Farm

What was one of the most exciting days on the farm? Butchering day! The day was usually cold and crisp with an occasional cover of an inch or two of snow on the ground. Heavy snow made it fun for kids, but a bit difficult for the adults. Bill's Aunt Alwina said her dad often butchered a beef on election day, then took the hide to market before going to vote. The women didn't go along, of course. They were not yet allowed to vote!

Perhaps you might not wish to read this chapter if you have a squeamish stomach, but for the younger generation who have no idea of how we survived on the farm, these are the routines of butchering day. Along with helping with the birthing of baby animals, hauling sloppy manure and other unpleasant tasks, the events of butchering day were just another part of life on the farm.

When I awoke on butchering morning, a fire would already be burning in the back yard with the butchering kettle hanging on a metal pipe suspended between two barrels. The water in the kettle was being heated in readiness for scalding the hogs. As I opened my eyes and saw the reflection of the fire dancing across my bedroom ceiling, I knew this was a special day. It didn't take long to get up because there was a lot of activity and I didn't want to miss any of it, (except, of course, the part I most disliked.) I usually stayed in the house and held my ears shut so I wouldn't hear the crack of the rifle that killed the animal. Both Grandpa and Dad were good shots with a rifle and that was necessary so the animal would not suffer. Usually only one bullet was needed to drop the hog. Someone with a really sharp knife then stuck the jugular vein so it would "bleed out," quickly and completely, thus making a better tasting and healthier meat. Bill's family, as well as my Schwartz family, saved the blood for blood pudding, but we didn't make blood pudding at our house.

My memories of butchering hogs are the most vivid, since that was usually done on Saturday when we kids would be home to help. We usually butchered three hogs at a time, but Bill said his family always did six. They had a lot more adults at home to eat it and to help with the butchering and the preserving. In their neighborhood, they actually had a butchering ring, neighbors who exchanged help with them. This ring included the Schroeders, Reinhart Rain, George Katterheinrich, the Aufderhaars and the Henkeners. Some of these same people were also in the threshing ring. In our area, our good neighbor, Joe Frank, often helped.

At Bill's house, after the hogs were killed, they were dragged to a scalding trough. This was a tapered rectangular wooden box large enough to hold a hog. The rest of the year it was used to mix corn, oats and supplement for feeding the calves, but on butchering day it was partially filled with very hot water and was used for scalding. Ropes were draped under the hog in such a way that after it was scalded on one side, it was just rolled over to do the other side. At our house, we used a wooden barrel that was set up at an angle on a platform beside the garage. Hot water from the butchering kettle was carried to the barrel and it was filled about half full. With Grandpa on one side and Dad on the other, they slid the carcass into the barrel head first, left it for only a few seconds and then pulled it back out. It was turned around and the back half was immersed in the hot water. A person had to be experienced to know just how long to leave it and that depended on how hot the water was. The purpose of scalding was mainly to loosen the hair so it could be scraped off. It also washed off any dirt that might be left on the hide. If the animal was left too long in really hot water, the skin tended to come off while scraping off the hair.

The men used a round cup-shaped scraper to remove the hair from the hog's hide. When this was completed, they tied the animal to a three-cornered tripod that kept it hanging up off the ground. The tripod was made from three wooden rails (like those used in making a rail fence). A large bolt was put through the top of the rails and they were raised upright, looking much like a tepee. After the animal carcass was tied to this tripod, a sharp knife was used to slit the belly. A tub was placed underneath to catch the intestines as they fell out. Usually the pigs were not fed the evening before so the intestines would not be so full. One of the men cut the small intestines out and drained them before taking them to the house for cleaning in preparation for stuffing the sausage. Bill's family saved some of the larger intestines to be filled with summer sausage and blood pudding. The blood pudding was mixed and placed in the casing, then cooked in the outside kettle of water to make it firm. The rest of the intestines were given to the chickens or hogs. When cutting out the liver, the men were careful not to cut into the gall bladder. If this was accidentally cut, the bitter gall left a very nasty taste on any meat it touched.

The carcass needed to be washed before the meat was cut up. Grandpa dipped a bucket into cold water, then literally slung it as hard as he could onto the back of the hog and into the stomach cavity to clean out the debris and blood. Because the air was so much colder than the warm carcass, it usually steamed for a bit. If any spots of hair had been missed, hot water was poured on that spot and the hair was scraped off. With the pig now washed clean inside and out, the men usually took it into the garage where they could work out of the wind and cold. Saw horses with boards laid across them formed the table on which the carcass was placed for the cutting-up process. The entire procedure was repeated for each of the other hogs.

By this time Grandma had brought out the largest pans and crocks she could find. The water had been emptied from the butchering kettle and it was now ready to hold the pieces of fat which would be made into lard. As they cut up the hog, the fat was cut away from the lean meat and tossed into pans. The pans containing the fat were then emptied into the kettle for "cooking down" into lard. Some knowledge of this job was needed since it took more than just heating the fat to make the lard. Good lard would be almost pure white with a pleasant aroma. A "slow" fire was kept burning under the kettle so the fat would melt. If the fire got too hot, the fat would burn, making the lard dark in color with a poor taste and smell. It needed to be stirred frequently to keep it from burning. As the fat melted, any hair or other foreign matter came to the top where it could easily be skimmed off. Carrying wood to keep the fire burning and running errands for the grown-ups were things we children could do while the adults were busy cutting up the meat.

The heart, tongue, and liver were usually put in a dish pan and taken to the house where Grandma washed them thoroughly, then cut them up. Some folks made a liver pudding, but there was no method of keeping the liver fresh, and since we couldn't eat all of it before it spoiled, the excess was given away. That meant our mailman, Dusty Miller, would find a "mess of liver" in the mailbox the next day. Other neighbors did the same thing and I often wondered if Mrs. Miller didn't sometimes get tired of eating all the fresh liver Dusty found in mail boxes along his route on those winter butchering days.

If no one wanted the liver, it made a sweet delicacy for the farmer's dog. Every farmer had at least one dog and the saying was that raw liver gave the dog a little extra "sass," something that was very desirable on a farm when animals got out or when unwelcome visitors started "nosing around" the area. In those days there were still some gypsies that drove by with their horses and wagons. One of their favorite schemes was for one man to engage the family in conversation at the front door while others climbed out of their covered wagons and stole some chickens out of the henhouse, a pig from the hog pens, apples from the orchard, or produce from the garden. When we saw a gypsy wagon coming down the road, we children ran to hide in the house and the adults remained on guard until the wagon had lumbered on down the road. I remember one day when we were in the back yard picking up wood for the cookstove. A gypsy stopped and came back to talk to Grandma. He got a little smart with her, and she told him he'd better get back to his wagon or she would call her husband. The man hesitated and Grandma turned around toward the henhouse and at the top of her lungs yelled, "Frank, will you come here? Right now!" The man quickly walked to his wagon and left. Grandma heaved a real sigh of relief, because Grandpa had gone to town that day and she was really alone with us kids. She had just pulled a good bluff and praise God, it had worked!

But back to butchering. The meat was cut up with huge butcher knives that Grandpa had sharpened the day before. They always said it was more dangerous to use a dull knife than a really sharp one when cutting the large slabs of meat, although I didn't understand the reasoning back then.

The pig's feet were sawed off to be cooked later. Although we never pickled the feet, some families did. Bill's family used an ax to cut off the toes, but our family boiled them until the toe nails came off, then added the tail and made soup from them. Bill's Aunt Alwina said the tail meat of a cow was the sweetest meat in the whole animal. It made wonderful "ox tail soup!" The tongue was another delicacy that was boiled, then peeled and eaten or sliced to be fried later. Both our families sometimes saved the brains and these were rolled in flour and fried. I'm not sure I would want to eat them now, but at that time, *any* fresh meat on the table in winter was welcome. Even the pig's snout was used. Another expression was that we used everything but the squeal! By the way, do you know why farmers put rings in the pig's nose? When a pig was in a dirt pen, he used his snout like a small bulldozer. Pushing it into the ground, he shoved the dirt aside until he had made a "wallow hole." He often made a hole deep enough under a fence that he could escape from the pen. If one hog found a means of escape, the others usually followed. By putting a ring in his snout, the pressure of pushing would hurt his tender nose, thus discouraging the animal from rooting.

Some farmers had a real talent for cutting up the hog carcasses. Bill's Grandpa Wierwille was *very* particular about the looks of the finished hams and shoulders, and he trimmed his to a beautiful shape. Mrs. Aufderhaar, a neighbor from the butchering ring, always insisted no one but Fred should trim their hams and shoulders. After the hams, shoulders, pork chops and side meat were cut out, there weren't a whole lot of other large pieces of meat left. Smaller scraps were thrown into a large tub to be ground into sausage. Those who did not like heart and tongue usually put them into the sausage. But I don't know of anyone who put in the liver. Its strong flavor would have spoiled the sausage.

Making sausage was the part of the day I liked best. When I was quite young, the sausage grinder handle was turned by hand. One person turned the crank while someone else fed the grinder. As children, we were allowed to turn the handle and occasionally drop the pieces of meat into the top of the grinder, but we had to be *very careful.* If a piece of meat didn't fall all the way in, we didn't dare try to "help it in" for fear we might get our fingers into that sharp grinder.

After the meat was all ground into a large tub, it was time to season the sausage. Grandma, who was in charge of this, came out with her sack of Morton's salt, pepper, allspice, and the other spices used to make good sausage. After putting in what she thought was about the right amount of salt and spices, she dived into that tub with both hands and pushed and pulled and squeezed and turned the meat over and over until the spices were spread throughout. When it appeared to be well mixed, she pulled off a little piece of meat and formed a patty that was fried on top of the little round coal oil (now called kerosene) stove used to heat the garage on butchering day.

I was always eager for that first taste of the fresh sausage. After everyone had a tiny bite, a brief discussion was held as to what was needed to make it just right. More spices were added and everyone tasted again. When it was agreed that the flavor was perfect, the meat was ready for the sausage stuffer.

While the men had been cutting up the hogs, Grandma had been busy scraping out the intestines and washing them over and over for use as the casings for the sausage. As I got older, Grandma asked, "Would you like to learn how to clean the casings?" She taught me to run the intestines between my finger and thumb, pushing the contents out one end. Then we ran water through them, turned them wrong-side-out and washed them again. Holding a sharp knife very carefully, she showed me how to scrape them clean. That was the most difficult part. Even the tiniest nick meant a "blow out" of the sausage when it reached that spot. The casing then had to be washed again and cut into shorter sections. We tied a knot into one end of each section to keep the meat in place. Farmers usually wormed their hogs before butchering time. Worms tended to weaken the casings, causing them to break easily. I finally got the knack of cleaning casings about the time we stopped butchering!

"It's time to stuff the sausage," Grandpa would call through the kitchen door. This was Grandma's signal to bring out the little water-filled granite pan which held the clean casings. She pushed these gently over the spout of the sausage stuffer. The seasoned meat was then packed into the stuffer and pressed down to fill the entire area. When it was full, the lid was closed, locked in place and the handle turned until it forced the meat out through the spout at the bottom. As the sausage came out of the spout, it filled the casings which curled gently in a slow circle into a pan below. (The last few years we butchered, Dad got the bright idea of connecting the handle of the sausage grinder to the back wheel of a car that had been put up on a jack. The car was then run slowly and the handle moved along at a good speed, much easier than cranking it all by hand. Very ingenious!)

By the time the sausage was finished, the fat in the butchering kettle had been cooked and the fire was allowed to die down. The sausage stuffer was washed and scalded to remove any remains of the meat. It was then wiped dry and a special liner covered with small holes was placed inside the stuffer so it could be used as a lard press. The pieces of fat meat were removed from the kettle and ladled into the sausage stuffer. The lid was replaced by a smaller one that fit down into the inner lining. It was again cranked down so the fat meat was compressed and the lard drained through the small holes, running out of the spout at the bottom. This lard was poured through a white sugar sack to strain out the "settlings," then put into metal lard cans where it was allowed to cool.

When all the lard had drained out of the spout, the handle was turned in reverse until the lid could be opened up and the solid cake of remains in the bottom (the cracklings), could be removed. "Anyone want some 'cracklins'?" someone would call and we broke off crisp little chunks to nibble on while it was still warm.

By the time the lard was finished, night was approaching and it was time to clean up the mess. Everything had to be thoroughly washed and scrubbed. Knives were usually washed and put away at once, lest someone, especially children, might get hurt on them. The meat was placed in the smoke house or basement until the next day. The men had to put away the saw horses and boards, the kerosene stove, the barrel—everything that had been used. When the evening milking was done, a quick supper was eaten, and a tired butchering crew was ready for bed.

The next day was another big day in the farmhouse. Since this was before freezers, electric stoves, and pressure canners, there were not too many ways to preserve fresh meat. Butchering was always done in the winter so some of the meat could be hung up in the smoke house to cure where it would stay cold for many weeks. When meat was needed for a meal, a sharp knife was taken to the smoke house, a slab or slice of cured meat was cut off and brought back to the kitchen. Some of the side meat was cured for bacon and the rest was always sliced thin, then "fried down" in several large skillets on Grandma's old Home Comfort wood cookstove. The fat that fried out was poured over the meat after it was placed in a large crock. This kept it fresh for several months and it needed only to be warmed up and served, a real convenience.

A favorite winter treat for Bill's family was "head puddin'." Water was put on to boil in a large kettle on the cookstove. In it were placed the jowls (the pig's chubby cheeks), the snout, tongue, heart, ears, skin from the bacon slabs, some scraps of meat, and any other meat from the pig's head, thus the name "head" pudding. After being thoroughly cooked and taken off the bone, the meat was ground up and mixed with oatmeal (older New Knoxville folks said they sometimes used "pin oats," a name that is unfamiliar to me.) It was then made into loaf-shaped cakes that were placed in large flat pans in the oven and cooked until the remaining fat was fried out. The loaves were packed in crocks and covered with lard. These were later cut into half-inch or thicker slices, fried, and served with eggs for breakfast. I remember Bill's mother making this when our children were small and all of us enjoyed eating it. I wish we could have a taste of it again. By the way, no one I knew ever called it "pudding." It was just "puddin'!"

At our house a side of pork meat would usually be "cured" by salting it down and wrapping it in cloth. It became the bacon that would taste so good for breakfast. The hams were cut out in one large piece and were rubbed with Morton's Sugar Cure, then wrapped in clean white strips from old sheets and hung up to cure and drain. Sometimes Grandma unwrapped them and added more curing mixture. Bill's family sometimes smoked some of the meat in the smokehouse. A small, slow fire was kept burning on the dirt floor for several days to cure the hams and sausage. Since we had a wooden floor in our smokehouse, Grandpa usually smoked our meat by partially filling a five-gallon bucket with corn cobs which were lighted, then hickory chips were placed on top to give the meat a nice hickory flavor. The slow burning cobs and chips gave off a smoke which permeated the meat in the small smokehouse. The hams, shoulders, sides, and pork chops were placed on tables along the sides of the building. The coils of sausage were hung over the end of a rail that was fastened from the ceiling. Grandma usually fried down some of our sausage until it was done, coiling it inside a large crock, and covering it with lard or putting it in large-mouthed jars, covering it with hot lard, and then sealing it. This sausage needed only to be warmed up before eating. It tasted really good for those cold winter night suppers. If I were asked which meat I liked best, it would be hard to decide between those wonderful home-cured hams or the fresh sausage. I still love both.

Frying down, salting and wrapping all the meat took most of the day. Since these methods worked well for preserving pork, Grandma seldom canned any of it. By the time all the crocks were scrubbed, the meat fried and packed into them, the skillets, knives, forks and ladles used to cut and turn the fried meat were washed and put away, it was time to make supper and do the milking.

Although we butchered our own hogs, we didn't do the butchering of our own beef. Instead, Abe Holtzapple and his son, Frank, usually came to our house and butchered the beef while we were in school. Although the process has some similarities, I know there was one big difference. When butchering a hog, the hair was scraped off the hide, and the hide and fat meat beneath it were cut up and thrown into the kettle and made into lard. Beef hides were not scalded nor the hair removed. Instead, the hides were given to the Holtzapples as payment for their work. Wintzers in Wapakoneta bought hides which were tanned and could be used for something large, such as a leather coat. When skinning the carcass, they were very careful that the knife did not cut through the skin. Damaged skins did not bring a premium price and could be used only for small leather items such as shoes, belts or purses.

Beef was butchered during the coldest part of the winter. Large slabs or quarters of beef were hung in the smokehouse where they froze or stayed cool until they were eaten. Grandpa often used a butcher knife to cut slices of steak or roasts which he brought into the house to be cooked. The smaller chunks of meat were often canned using the "cold pack" method. Until pressure canners were developed, cold packing beef was the accepted method, since one didn't preserve beef in the same way in which one preserved pork (salting, sausage, etc.). Even then, Grandma sometimes had cans of meat that spoiled.

We eagerly awaited butchering day each year. It was a very busy and tiring time on the farm, but it was a day when the whole family worked side-by-side to preserve the meat needed for another year. I wouldn't have missed it for anything!

## Chapter 32.
# *Chicken Little and Summer Storms*

The lightning cuts a gash into the sky
And frightened clouds above me rush along,
I hear the sound of thunder roar nearby.
Seeking shelter, birds have hushed their song
And flutter quickly through the deepening blue.
Each bush and tree waves wildly in the breeze
And groans amid the rush of air, and through
The clouds that hover near the dancing trees,
The rain, in torrents, pelters to the ground.
As suddenly as it has come, it leaves
And silence reigns where storms had touched. No sound
Disturbs the charming pattern sunshine weaves
Upon the earth, for after storms, we seem
To know that all was made by God supreme.
Author's school poem (age 13), received an "A."

Squeak, squawk, squeak, squawk. The soft rhythmical sound was comforting as Grandpa and I relaxed on the porch swing, swaying gently back and forth in a slow rhythm. The night was dark, and the crickets had stopped their chirping. The cows had seemed restless at milking time and now the dog lay beside the door, glancing nervously at the darkening sky. The only sound was the soft squeak of the old wooden porch swing and the faraway murmurings of the distant thunder. The day had been hot and dry. The animals seemed to know a thunderstorm was imminent. As the volume of the thunder increased, the dog walked to the swing and nervously nudged Grandpa's legs, as if to say, "Don't forget me. I need comforting too."

Thunderstorms and I were never very compatible. Like Chicken Little, I was always afraid the sky would fall. As a little girl I had been quite frightened of storms and had found a perfect refuge. I hid behind the couch in the living room, shutting my eyes tightly with my hands pressed against my ears. That's where I stayed until I was quite sure the storm had passed. If we happened to be in bed when a storm broke, I drew the covers over my head and didn't come up for air until it had rumbled off into the distant darkness.

Grandpa encouraged me to get over my fear of storms as we sat quietly in the old porch swing, listening to the approaching thunder. We watched the heat lightning as it playfully flickered across the sky harmlessly, but now the storm was developing into a full-fledged thunderboomer. Lightning slashed through the western sky, lighting up the barnyard. As the force of the winds increased, the nearby tree limbs danced and twirled in the flashing light. The cows gathered together, pressing closely to the south side of the barn, out of the worst of the wind and rain that now began to pelt the countryside. First came a few large drops, then as the intensity of the wind increased, the number of drops grew to a noisy downpour. One large clap of thunder crashed nearby. I had heard enough! Raising my hands to cover my ears, I rushed into the house.

Daddy and Don often stood on the front porch and watched the summer storms. Unlike his little sister, Don was not afraid of them and enjoyed watching the streaks of lightning as they played tag across the dark sky, often resembling a giant version of the fireworks we had seen each summer at the county fair. During one storm, Grandpa sat on the glider on the front porch with Don straddling the porch railing and Dad leaning against the wooden support post in the corner. As that storm approached, I became quite concerned for the safety of the men of my family. I ran to the open door where I childishly called through the screen, "You guys better come in here quick before that lightning gits you!" I, like Chicken Little, was a bit of a worrywart.

Storms such as this are a part of life on a farm. They are God's way of providing the necessary moisture to keep the hay green and growing. The thirsty fields of corn, whose leaves have curled up and stretched toward the sky, hoping for a good drink of water, now soak up every drop as it slides down their pointed leaves, refreshing the soil around the roots below. Even the lightning is beneficial as it releases nitrogen from the air to help keep the soybeans and other crops growing. The rain seems to wash the atmosphere and leaves the dry, parched earth smelling fresh and clean. Now, for several days, Grandma won't have to worry about watering the pickles and melons in her garden. The cistern is filled, assuring her of a plentiful supply of water for doing the family laundry for several more weeks.

There is no sound quite like the silence on a farm after a big thunderstorm has passed. But as the sun returns to brighten the scene, the once quiet barnyard is soon teeming with the happy sounds of insects and birds who have left their shelters to emerge into the warm sunshine and a fresh new earth. Birds dip down to the big water puddles in the driveway and drink deeply, then splash and preen in their temporary giant-sized birdbath. Soon they chirp and flutter from tree to tree and the world returns to normal.

Occasionally storms produced unusual sights. One day after such a shower, Bill's Grandpa was amazed to find two small fish lying on the sidewalk by the barn. Both were still alive. You've heard of it raining cats and dogs. How about raining fish?

Not all storms are beneficial for a farm. I recall many days when the rain continued in a never-ending flow. As we watched day after day, the little green weeds emerged in the fields and began to choke out the corn and bean plants. By the time the soil was dry enough to cultivate, the weeds had taken over and were difficult to kill.

Occasionally hail accompanied a sudden rain, and within minutes, acres of good crops could be ruined by the pounding of the little balls of ice. After a half-hour of crushing hail stones, a field of tall, beautiful corn can be reduced to an inch of muddy flat rubble that no animal would find appetizing.

There were dry years when the corn leaves curled up and turned yellow. Soybean plants sat in pathetic little clusters, refusing to grow until they got that much needed drink of water. Fields of hay were so dry that the leaves shattered and fell off and the animals were destined to eat the unappetizing stems. Many times the rains eventually came, but were too late to help the crops. The farmers had to tighten their belts and try to survive for another year.

When I think of summer storms, I think of one particularly dry summer day during hay-making season. It was obvious that a large storm was approaching from the southwest. The men had worked as quickly as possible to get the last load of hay into the barn before the storm broke.

As I looked out of the dining room window, I could see the loaded hay wagon rolling into the barn just as the first big drops of water spattered onto the dusty driveway. As the men stood just inside the big double doors on the east side of the barn, they brushed the dusty remnants of the hay off their clothes and grinned into the sky as the rain we so desperately needed for our thirsty cornfields had at last come. Our prayer was answered.

The wind increased and the rain dashed against the double dining room windows in front of me. I could no longer see through the downpour to the men standing inside the barn doors. Suddenly I let out a horrified shout, "Grandma, there's water running down the wall." As she wiped her hands on the corner of her apron, Grandma hurried in to look where I was pointing. One quick glance was all she needed and she rushed back to the kitchen to grab a handful of dish towels. As an afterthought, she reached down and pulled the old rag rug from beneath her rocking chair, then hurried to the west windows. Little ripples of water were now running down the wall, rapidly seeping into the cold air register just below. Throwing the rug on the floor, she took a towel in each hand and began to sop up the water that now covered the window sill and continued to run down the wall below the glass. It seemed like an eternity before the booming thunder ceased, and the rain ended in an uncertain trickle. We were finally able to stop the mopping process, but the ugly brown stains from the intruding water were left on Grandma's pretty new wallpaper where they would stay until the paper would be replaced a few years later.

The men left the shelter of the barn and walked through the last remaining drops of rain toward the house. While they washed for supper, they expressed their gratitude that the load of hay was safely in the barn and discussed the real "goose drowner" we had just had. In our neck-of-the-woods that was farm language for a really big storm. "Oh, look!" Don called out, and we rushed to peer out the washroom's little diagonal window. There, with its colors showing vividly against the darkness of the receding storm, was God's gift at the end of the day—a perfect rainbow!

## Chapter 33.

# "Old Eddard's Sayings"

Where did the name come from and to whom did it refer? Neither Don nor I have any idea, but we often heard Grandpa use what he called "Old Eddard's Sayings." Was it really "Edward's" sayings? Where did he get the expression and how is it spelled? These were just his by-words, but each one had a subtle meaning in the pattern of life as he thought it should be lived–expressions such as: "Every dog has its day," "You never miss the water until the well runs dry ," "Don't put off until tomorrow what you can do today," and "One rotten apple will spoil the whole barrel."

Grandpa worked in the woods a lot and often watched the hogs as they rooted for fresh acorns in the grass under the huge oak trees. His expression, "Even a blind hog will find an acorn once in a while" encouraged us to try things, even though we might be hindered or have less natural ability than others. If we kept trying, we might be fortunate enough to *find an acorn*.

"Every hog has to carry his own hide to market" was often used by both grandparents and we knew they meant for us to be responsible citizens. If we did something wrong, we would be the ones to carry the responsibility for our actions.

As a child, I remember hearing one of Grandpa's expressions when I told him about someone who had done something wrong and seemed to be getting away with it. "Now don't you worry," he responded. "Give a calf enough rope and it will hang itself."

Grandma often said "You can catch more flies with honey than with vinegar." In other words, you are more apt to get what you want if you treat people nicely with kind words and a smile (honey) than if you treat them badly with nasty words and a frown (vinegar).

Grandma tried to mend our clothing as soon as it developed a problem. She always said, "A stitch in time saves nine." She knew that a little rip could be sewed shut right away with just a stitch or two, but if we wore the clothing again without being mended, the small rip would get bigger and require nine or more stitches. Other favorites were: "Don't let the cat out of the bag" (Don't tell anyone), "It's no use crying over spilled milk." (I had done enough milking to know that if the cow kicked over the bucket, the milk was gone and no amount of tears could bring it back. If something happens and we can do nothing about it, our lives must go on), "You can't make a silk purse out of a sow's ear" (Grandma often said this when we were shopping for dress fabric. You just can't make a really nice dress out of really cheap fabric.)

"What a tangled web we weave, when first we practice to deceive." Now, there is one from which we should all learn. If we tell one little white lie, we soon have to tell another to hide that one, and then we must tell a bigger one to cover both of them. Soon our web of deceit is not only overwhelming us, but now there seems to be no way out of the mess.

There were numerous other little expressions we often heard. I include my definitions of each: “white as snow”–The color of the sheets on the Monday morning clothesline; “black as the ace of spades”–A cloudy night with no moon or stars shining as we walked to the barn; “red as a beet”–My complexion after a day in the hot sun; “good as gold”–What we children were just before Christmas; “scared as a jack rabbit”–What I was just before I got a spanking; “gentle as a lamb”–What my cow, Flo, was when I milked her; “cute as a button”–Something I never was; “strong as an ox”–Anyone who could carry a 5-gallon bucket full of hog slop in each hand; “smart as a whip”–What I hoped to be in school; “sharp as a tack”–Someone with great intelligence; “poor as a church mouse”–What a lot of folks were during the depression; “higher than a kite”–What the local drunk was on Saturday night; “big as a barn”–What the old sow was before delivering thirteen pigs; “slower than molasses”–Now that was slow; “slower than the 7-year itch”–Even slower than molasses; “dead as a doornail”–What a mouse was when the cat finished with him; “naked as a jay bird”–What a two-year-old was when he escaped from the bathroom after his Saturday night bath; “a straight shooter”–An honest and upright man such as my grandpa and dad; “a snake in the grass”–Just the opposite of a straight shooter; “crooked as a dog’s hind leg”–Occasionally used to describe politicians; “birds of a feather flock together”–Pick your friends carefully. Would you rather swim with the swans or eat “road kill” with the turkey buzzards?

Grandpa had several expressions that pertained to the weather. “Don’t plant corn until an oak leaf is as big as a squirrel’s ear” was a good one for farmers. A squirrel’s ear is quite small, but if an oak leaf had started to grow that much, the farmer knew the ground was warm enough to start planting his corn crop. Another was “Mackerel skies and mares’ tails, stormy weather prevails.” If the clouds looked somewhat like fish scales with long stringy *tails* between, it was usually a sign of an approaching storm. The final expression came in several forms. Although Don remembers hearing “rainbows at night” and others used “red skies at night,” I remember it as: “Red sails at night, sailors delight. Red sails in the morning, sailors take warning.” Grandpa had told us of one of his ancestors who had been an English sea captain. He would have had plenty of time to study those red sails and the changing weather patterns. Was the expression handed down from this unknown ancestor who *sailed the seven seas* of the past? We will never know, but we do know that whoever Old Eddard was, he had some very wise sayings.

# Chapter 34.
# The Men in my Life—Before Marriage

These pages are a tribute to the men who were a part of my life when I was growing up on an Auglaize County farm. Some played a very prominent part in my childhood and remembering them brought back many happy memories. I saw others only occasionally and few memories remain. In the 1930 to 1950-era, most of these men visited our neighborhood on a regular basis, some weekly, others less often and some only once a year. Family and friends came and went, but these men played a vital part in keeping things running on the farm. Written in alphabetical order are the stories of these "men in my life—before marriage."

## *The AUCTIONEER*

Who could stand up all day, yell loud enough to be heard for a country mile, keep a restless crowd alert and listening, and do it in summer or winter, even with an icicle hanging from his nose? Why, it was our friendly auctioneer, Ross Downing. He must have had vocal chords of steel, because everyone could hear every word as they parked along the roads and walked to the farm having the auction. This was long before the days of loud speakers and relief help. It was Ross you heard from the start of the sale until the finish, sometimes even after dark.

Since Ross "cried" sales in a half-dozen counties, everyone seemed to know him. He was a large-boned man with a big booming voice that was distinctive. When you heard his auctioneer's cry or patter, there was no mistaking Ross. He was much sought after because he knew about how much things were worth and how to get a good price for the seller. He was very adept at inserting a joke just when things were beginning to lag. If a box of ladies' hats was being sold, he might pull out the most outlandish looking one and plop it on his head at a rakish angle. Even the men would giggle at Ross's antics, and the bidders would perk up.

Bill was at a farm sale where Ross used his creativity to sell a scoop shovel. Holding the shovel up, he called for a bid, but none came. He kept trying, but to no avail. Finally he took a nickel out of his pocket, placed the coin on the outstretched shovel, smiled and said, "Now, will somebody give me a nickel for this scoop shovel?" Everyone laughed, but Ross had no trouble selling his scoop shovel!

My first remembrance of Ross Downing was at a farm sale on the Lew Reed farm north of Kossuth. As Grandpa and I looked over the sale items, I spotted a little corner whatnot shelf that I liked. I had never bought anything before, but I asked Grandpa if I could try to buy it. He gave his permission, and when Ross held that little shelf high above his head and asked, "Who will bid a dime for this shelf?" My hand flew into the air and I shouted, "I will!" Everyone saw that I really wanted that shelf. Although Ross asked if there were any other bids, no one wanted to spoil it for a child. He called out, "Sold to the little girl for a dime." I was so pleased that I carried it around all afternoon, wearing a smile that had to have been at least a half-mile wide. I still have that little corner shelf.

When my daughter, Nancy, was little, she went with me to an auction in the area. She told me recently that she had gotten rather upset with a few people that day. As the crowd followed down the line of items being sold, they paid no attention to where they were walking. They were trampling down all the flowers that had been carefully planted in the yard. Someone had worked hard to plant those flowers there. As the crowd trampled them, Nancy thought, "Have you no decency?"

When she got tired, Nancy sat down on a swing to rest. As Ross worked down the line of household items, he came to the one on which she was sitting. Before she realized what was happening, Ross had the swing almost sold. To clinch the sale, he announced, "And the little girl goes with it." About that time, she realized what he had just said. Up she popped with eyes as big as saucers! Everyone smiled at her, including the kindly auctioneer.

Long before I became interested in horses, races were held at the Big Auglaize County Fair. Most were run with a horse pulling a sulky and driver, but the kind that finally interested me were the running races where the jockey actually sat on the horse and raced, much like the present-day Kentucky Derby. Before they had microphones to call these races, they used those iron vocal chords of Ross Downing. He stood on the top level of the little octagonal gazebo-type building that stood opposite the grandstand. From there he could see the horses as they ran the complete distance around the race track. Using a megaphone he described the race as it progressed. No one missed a word, and he made it an exciting experience for everyone.

Ross was active on the fair board for several years, and for thirty years was superintendent of the New Hampshire Methodist Church's Sunday School. As Ross got older, he brought a young man, Eugene Meyers, into his auctioneering business. Now Ross is gone, Eugene has retired, and the next generation carries on the business. Many of today's auctioneers have fancy boxes to stand on, matching tables to hold the dishes and pans, and sound systems that magnify the patter so everyone can hear. Ross had none of those fancy things to help him sell, only an iron clad voice and a personality that made everyone his friend. And that includes at least four generations of my family!

## *The BREAD MAN*

"Omar Man" he called out as he knocked on the door. After the last visit from the huckster wagon, Grandpa usually bought the family's groceries in town. There was a time after World War II, however, when bread was delivered through the countryside by the Omar Man. "OMAR" was painted on the side of a small red and white panel truck which pulled into the driveway. A man in a snappy-looking Omar Bakery uniform jumped out and loped up the sidewalk to the back door. He always seemed to be friendly, full of energy and in a hurry. After a quick knock on the door, he would call out "Omar Man!" In the wintertime, Grandma invited him into the back porch. He usually held a couple of loaves of bread in his hand. He knew she would probably want them, but he also carried one or two nice looking sweet rolls that he also hoped to sell to her. In the summer, we often walked to the back of his panel truck and looked over his display of sweet items. If Don or I happened to be there, he made sure we saw those yummy looking rolls because he knew we would say, "Oh, Grandma, won't you buy a roll? They look so good! Please? Please? Pretty please?" And she usually did! If Grandpa was working near the house, he was sure to pick up a roll or two. He was the adult with the biggest sweet tooth and couldn't resist those tasty items! All his life, he loved pies and cakes and rolls—anything sweet. I could never figure it out. How did Grandpa stay so skinny when the Omar Man was there with all those sweet rolls?

## *The CARPENTERS*

I can almost hear the zwizz, zwizz of the hand saw as it cut through the boards. Just smell the delightful aroma of that freshly sawed lumber! No other smell is quite like it. I loved playing in sawdust and watching as Grandpa did repair work in his shop. It was great fun to fasten a board in the vise, then saw it in half as Grandpa had taught me. He also taught me to cut out simple designs with a key hole saw, to keep a slow but steady pace on one end of a two-man cross cut saw, and—the most fun of all—how to use a plane to shave off curls from a smooth board. Several of these curly shavings attached to my straight hair with bobby pins made reasonably satisfactory substitutes to fulfill my childish desire–lots of plump, gorgeous curls like Shirley Temple's.

There were two teams of carpenters that I remember as a child. Lew Biederman and his son, Merle, had built Grandpa's house before I was born. A few years later, they added the front and back porches. They eventually purchased a lumber company in Spencerville where we stopped on many occasions as Grandpa bought a few boards or nails or doors. There always seemed to be time to stand and briefly "pass the time of day." Saul Bowsher and his son, Pearl, who lived in our neighborhood, were also carpenters. Grandpa occasionally asked them to do some repair work on the farm buildings when a storm's strong winds had blown through, causing loose boards or other damage. It was the Bowshers who had constructed the first built-in cupboards in Grandma's kitchen when I was quite small. The cabinet in the basement that held her canning jars had been used before that. I don't remember ever hearing that she had a pitcher pump, but I was in several homes as a child where such a small pump sat in a crude cupboard in the kitchen and was the source of water in the house.

Driving nails was an interesting pastime for me. Grandpa showed me how to hold a nail and use a hammer. He gave me a board of rather soft wood and a handful of nails. I spent most of an afternoon banging away with the hammer. I smile as I think back to how that poor board looked when I was finished. Nails stuck out like porcupine quills, some straight and some bent over at odd angles. It was lots of fun, but I knew I wasn't destined to be a lady carpenter.

As a child, I often heard the names of Bowsher and Biederman, but there was one carpenter who was even better known in our house. That was Jesus, the young man from

Nazareth who worked in His father's carpenter shop until He was thirty. Not known for great buildings or fine furniture, He is remembered for the families He built and the lives He changed!

## *The COAL MEN*

The Gaberdiel Brothers Coal Yard wasn't far from the Miller Funeral Home in Spencerville. Dan and Albert worked together, and like most business men in those days, they enjoyed a friendly chat with their customers. They brought in large truck or train loads of coal directly from the mines in Southern Ohio and West Virginia. The coal was stored in huge piles on the back of their lot. I remember seeing some of their employees as they shoveled coal from those large piles into the delivery trucks. They were so black from the oily coal dust that it was hard to believe they were really white men.

In the next few days after our visit, the Gaberdiel coal truck would pull into our yard. Delivering coal was a dirty and unpleasant job, and Grandma's landscaping didn't make the job any easier. When delivering coal, the truck needed to back in from the road, turn at a right angle to avoid driving over Grandma's teardrop flower bed, then back over the sidewalk while keeping a safe distance from her "pergola." If all went well, he had about another five feet to go to reach the basement window. The driver then set up a long metal trough-like chute that reached from the back of the truck through the open window to the bin in a corner of the basement. Bill's family actually had an enclosed room for their coal.

When everything was in place, the driver raised the bed of the truck slightly, then, using a shovel, he guided the coal into the chute. As the load emptied, he raised the bed of the truck a little higher. When those hard chunks of coal bounced and slid down that metal chute, they made an awful clatterty-bang racket that could be heard all over the house. There is no other sound quite like it, but in the middle of the winter when it was bitter cold and the coal supply was about depleted, this was a very comforting sound!

One fall, a young, very inexperienced driver had a little problem. As he backed the truck toward the basement window, he avoided running over the flower bed, and everything looked good. But he hadn't noticed the overhanging *arms* at the top of the fancy pergola, an arbor with a trelliswork roof that Grandma saw in her garden magazine. (Grandpa had built one over the water pump.) As the truck bed was raised, a corner of it was also lifting up several of the pergola's arms. Before the driver could get the truck bed stopped, it had raised one whole section several inches off the ground. Oh, my! Grandma was not happy! The driver really felt bad about it and apologized several times. After he left, Grandpa was able to repair the damage, but from then on, when the coal truck made a delivery, Grandma was looking out of the dining room window to make sure the driver missed the flower bed *and* the pergola! She never had the problem again!

We didn't see the Gaberdiel Brothers much after we were married. Bill often sent one of our big trucks to the mines in Southern Ohio to bring back our own stoker coal.

More than fifty years after the pergola episode, Bill and I visited our son, Steve, in Roseau, Minnesota. As we concluded a tour of the Polaris factory where he was an engineer, we got into our car to leave. But a pickup truck pulled up behind us, blocking our way. A man climbed out and walked over to our car. "I see you're from Auglaize County, Ohio," he said. "I was born near there. Where are you from?" We answered,

"From New Knoxville." Now he really grinned as he said, "I was born in Spencerville!" "Well, I was born near Kossuth," I replied. We finally found out he was a Gaberdiel grandson, now selling Polaris products at his store in Michigan. While I knew some of his family, he also knew some of mine. It's a small world!

## *The CREAM MAN*

"Granny Gochenour," they called him. (Yes, "Granny" was a man!) Ralph Gochenour, his real name, lived west of Deep Cut and was our cream man. I have no idea where he got the name Granny, but that's what everyone called him.

When our evening milking was finished, Grandpa poured the bucket of milk into the large round bowl at the top of the cream separator. As Don or I turned the separator handle, the lighter weight cream came to the top where it ran out of one spout. The watery skim milk ran out of the other into the bucket below. My grandparents often referred to skim milk as "blue milk" because it lacked the yellow color from the rich cream. Skim milk was usually poured into the troughs for the pigs or chickens. After each morning's and evening's milking, the milk was run through the separator. Grandma then took it apart, washed each piece very carefully and rinsed it with a teakettle of boiling water. Then it was ready for the next day.

Since we had no ice box or refrigerator, the cream was kept in the cool basement. It was often divided, with most going into a five-gallon can that Grandma kept shiny clean. The remainder stayed in a brown crock that she covered with a clean white cloth to keep the flies away. That was for use in the house. When that was used up, Don was sometimes sent down to scoop a cupful of cream out of the can. It was brought to the kitchen so Grandma could whip it and put it on top of cool Jell-O. Yummy! How good that whipped cream tasted. Each day, the new cream was added to the can. On his weekly trips, Granny collected the cream and took it to Spencerville where it was eventually made into ice cream, cheese, cottage cheese or butter.

I remember those weekly visits of Granny Gochenour, especially the ones when I was not old enough to go to school. Whenever I saw him drive in, I had just enough time to run to the kitchen. Then, opening the inside cellar door, I would dash to the bottom of the basement steps and hide around the corner before he could enter the outside cellar door. As he walked down the steps, I would jump out and yell "Boo!" Granny always pretended to be really quite surprised, and that delighted me. We would laugh and talk as he collected Grandma's cream. Sometimes I "helped" him carry it back up the steps, then we would say "Goodby." I always knew that a week later, he would return for more cream and another "boo."

## *The EGG MAN*

Once a week a big truck from the egg auction drove in and the driver would get out, carrying an empty egg crate in each hand. He went around to the back of the house and down to the cellar where he brought up the filled crates of eggs from the week. Crates were about fifteen inches wide, thirty inches long and eighteen inches high with cardboard sections that held about two dozen eggs. A flat divider went between each section, and each case held twenty-four dozen eggs. That would make quite an omelet, wouldn't it?

I remember a few times when Grandma had some "setting hens." These were often White Rocks or Hampshire Reds whose eggs were brown. We always had a few roosters around, so the eggs were fertile and could develop into baby chicks. After laying several eggs, the hen then sat on them until they hatched. Grandpa usually had a couple hundred White Leghorn chickens whose eggs were white and were sold to the egg auction. Grandpa always laughed at the difference between the size of the eggs, depending on whether you were buying or selling. It seemed that if we were *selling* "large" eggs, they might be classified as "mediums" which would bring us less money, but if we were *buying* the same eggs, they might now be listed as "large" or "jumbo," and we would have to pay a premium price. Hmmm!

Every day, morning and evening, someone had to go to the henhouse and gather the eggs in large wire baskets. Not in the largest stretch of the imagination could I enjoy the job of gathering eggs. There were usually a few hens sitting on the nests. Grandpa would gently slide his hand under them and bring out the eggs. Why was it that when I did it, the hens had a way of cocking their heads to one side and staring at me with their beady little eyes and a look that said "How dare you take those eggs! They're mine, mine, mine!"? Then, with a sharp peck on the back of my hand, (Ouch, that hurt.), a drop of blood reminded me not to try again. I figured out a way to outsmart them, though. I knew I shouldn't, but I often scared the hen until she flapped her wings and flew off the nest. Then I could gather the eggs in peace. The only problem was, as the frightened hen flew, she usually broke an egg or two.

Another interesting experience was gathering the little eggs the pullets laid. Pullets were young hens who were laying eggs for the first time. They weren't too well informed yet as to what those wooden boxes containing straw were to be used for, so they just laid their eggs wherever they happened to be when the urge came. Many of them were laid in the straw and manure on the floor. When gathering eggs, one had to watch where one walked until those dumb little pullets got the hang of it and put their eggs in the nests.

I detested cleaning the eggs each night. They often had dried manure that had to be washed off with a wet cloth. Wet eggs have a funny smell! So does wet manure! Put the manure on the egg, and you have a nasty cleaning job. I was always glad when I didn't have to clean eggs. After they were clean and dry, they were weighed to determine their proper size. If the eggs were sorted and packed according to size, the farmer received a small premium in the next check. The eggs were taken to the basement where they were packed into the big egg crates and stayed relatively cool.

Driving through the countryside picking up heavy egg crates was not an ideal job, so we never had the same egg man long enough to remember his name. Most were young men who took any job until they could find a better one. Their work was very necessary and much appreciated, especially after the auction when Grandpa received his check!

## *The FAIR SECRETARY*

It was the summer of 1898. An advertisement in the *Auglaize County Democrat* featured a sale by Kahn Brothers and Co. in Wapakoneta. There were bargains in shoes and fabrics, but the main idea of the advertisement seemed to be the promotion of the "Greatest and largest fair ever held in Auglaize County." Harry Kahn was seven years old. He later owned a shoe store of his own and continued to promote the county fair for thirty-five years as its secretary.

Born April 22, 1891, to Leon and Hattie (Steinberg) Kahn, he spent some summers at Culver Military Academy and graduated from Wapakoneta Blume High School in 1909. Harry brought the Boy Scout movement into Wapakoneta and organized and coached the first semiprofessional basketball team in the city. His funeral service in 1968 was held at Temple Beth Israel in Lima. He was the only Jewish man I knew as a child.

I smiled when I saw that early ad with the Kahn Brothers' promotion of the fair. When I was growing up, and for many years after, Harry Kahn was known all over Ohio as the number one promoter of the "Big Auglaize County Fair." It was Harry Kahn who got on the fair's loudspeaker and for hours before each grandstand show, announced, begged, wheedled, cajoled and insisted that you had to see the show. Each performance was the biggest and best that had ever been brought to our area. "Hurry, folks! Hurry! You don't want to miss this unforgettable event. Tickets are going fast. Step right up, folks. There are only a few tickets left!" (There were always "only a few tickets left.") Harry Kahn and his showmanship developed the fair into one of the best small fairs in the state of Ohio. His efforts were rewarded with the presentation of the Outstanding Fair Secretary of Ohio award in 1964.

Shortly after I was born, some major changes took place at the fairgrounds. The *Wapakoneta Daily News* of Tuesday, September 16, 1930, announced,

> The first 'night fair' ever held in the county will be held Wednesday evening–and that's something new this year. A pageant entitled 'Depression and Relief of the Ages,' written and directed by C.C. Craig of Hume, will be the evening's feature, though all other departments of the fair will be open. Thursday evening 500 county Farm Bureau people will stage another pageant, 'The Court of Agriculture.' Mammoth flood lights have been put up to light the stage, and hundreds of electric light bulbs have been strung about the grounds and through the exhibit halls." It must have been quite exciting to see the fairgrounds all lit up for the very first time.

One cannot think of the fair without thinking of some of the events that Harry Kahn promoted over that loudspeaker system. The ones that got the most attention were held in the grandstand, and an annual event was horse racing. Across from the huge wooden grandstand stood a small, six- or eight sided open building with a protective roof covering the top. The sides of the two-story structure were about three feet high on both levels with a wooden stairway joining them. As afternoon horse racing began, the judges and announcer entered the lower level and climbed the stairs to the top. The top level's added height provided a good view of the back stretch as the announcer called out his version of the race, at first using a megaphone and in later years with an electric public address system. When no one was around, we loved running up those steps and circling the area high above the ground. Eventually this unique little building was removed. (The infield hasn't looked the same since.)

One of my favorite fair events was the rodeo. I briefly pretended I was a part of ranch life, sitting in awe as I watched cowboys ride bucking broncos, where ropes whirled and spun through the air as they lassoed stray calves, and where angry bulls snorted and bellowed as they twisted and turned in their attempts to unseat cowboys who clung to their heaving backs. It was a dusty sample of the Wild West. I loved every moment of it.

When I was ten or twelve years old, the county's Granges were asked to sell pop in the county fair's grandstand, with a percentage of the profit going to each organization. Kossuth's Salem Grange worked on the fair's last day. That evening, after the grandstand crowd had left and the work was finished, Alma and Helen Hoverman brought out some of their home-grown watermelons. What a feast we had!

Besides all the melon we could eat, we also had one of the most exciting evenings of our young lives. We were the only kids around at that late hour. The carnival folks were ready to tear down their tents and rides, but they allowed us to play their games and sit on their rides, free of charge as they worked. This was my chance! I had always wondered if I could hit hard enough to ring the bell. Grabbing the handle, I whammed that mallet down as hard as I could, but try as I may, the little metal piece just wouldn't go up high enough to ring that elusive bell. Oh, well, on to the merry-go-round.

Sitting astride one of the larger horses, I rode around and around as I watched the kids on the Ferris wheel next door. After riding several times around, the man stopped the giant wheel. He emptied one seat and removed it, then ran the wheel a half turn and after those kids got off, he removed their seat. He continued this routine until every seat had been taken off. I enjoyed the merry-go-round until it, too, had the last horse removed. We could hardly believe we didn't have to pay for all these games and rides! What a night! A child's dream come true!

I continued to hear the voice of Harry Kahn throughout all of my childhood and most of my children's childhood. Along with the years of being at the fair with the church, I was also a 4-H member for eight years and displayed or modeled projects at the fair. I also continued to attend the county fair as an adult. As a 4-H advisor for twenty-five years, I saw all of my young sewers model their outfits at the fair, while competing with my own sewing in the open-class show. I was more successful at sewing than at ringing that little bell. Later, I accompanied my husband as he displayed our new farm machinery for many years. After the end of a 4-H show, we often sat down to rest in late afternoon. About the time we relaxed, the loudspeaker crackled and there was Harry—"Right this way, folks! Get your tickets now! They're going fast!" Sometimes we heard his routine so often, we could have repeated it word for word! There were times when we would gladly have pulled his microphone switch. But Harry was a promoter, and he did the job that he knew best. He brought first-class shows, racing and other events to the county fair and the crowds came!

A great many things have changed at the fair since I was a little girl. When was the last time you saw a family have a picnic on the fairgrounds, eating cold fried chicken out of a wicker basket—men seated on the running boards of their cars and women and children on a blanket in the grass? When you recall riding the Ferris wheel or tilt-a-whirl, do you hear the sound and feel the heat of a gasoline engine, or merely the hum of an electric motor? The blaring rock beat coming from the merry-go-round can't compare to the glorious sounds that emanated from the wheezy old music box! Now, I can only imagine walking past the fair's office in the northwest corner of the old wooden grandstand, seeing Harry Kahn with his microphone in hand, and hearing him remind us one more time of the "Big Auglaize County Fair."

## *The FULLER BRUSH MAN*

Up the sidewalk he came, suitcase in hand. A knock on the door quickly let Grandma know the Fuller Brush man had arrived once again. With a grand flourish, he opened his suitcase in the middle of the living room floor. Inside were brushes for polishing shoes, brushing hair or teeth, cleaning vegetables, brushing lint off clothes, washing insides of baby bottles, scrubbing tired backs—any kind of brush you could imagine. I had no idea there were so many different kinds of brushes in existence! If he was turned away at the door, he gave you nothing, but each housewife who graciously invited him in to show his complete line of brushes was presented a small vegetable brush, absolutely free. Although Grandma seldom bought many of his brushes, we saw enough Fuller Brush demonstrations to keep us in vegetable brushes for several years.

## *The GAS MAN*

A little shed sat just north of our barn when I was a small child. Since this shed (we always called it the "oil house") was within a few feet of the highway, the gas man parked his truck at the edge of the road, then entered the shed and filled the small tank inside with gasoline. We didn't travel much back then so we didn't use a huge amount of gas. The small tank was sufficient.

By parking the gas truck on the road, it was not only easy to reach the tank, but it also saved a lot of wear and tear on Grandpa's driveway. The few car drivers that traveled the road could easily see the truck in time to drive out around it, since they were moving at a rather slow pace of thirty to forty miles per hour. There wasn't a lot of truck traffic on the road, either. Most products were shipped by train back then.

Grandpa always filled his car with gas on our weekly trips to Spencerville. The gas in the shed was basically used for Dad's ditching work. The shed also held an assortment of oil cans and other greasy items that I did not find appealing; thus, I stayed away from it. I had probably been warned by Grandma not to go there because I would get dirty, and grease was difficult to remove from little girls' dresses. There were no pre-wash sprays to take out such stains then. It would be no problem with today's variety of cleaners.

The shed eventually had to be moved to a spot much farther back in the barnyard and away from the road. Although it had been very handy for the gas man to fill, it was also very handy for those thieves who broke in and helped themselves to Daddy's gas and oil. After he put a lock on it and moved it back, the thefts stopped.

As the roads were improved and travel became easier, more fuel was needed for the tractors, trucks, automobiles and Dad's ditching machine. Eventually he had a large 500-gallon gas tank buried on the farm. We then had our own gas pump.

Although the gas man and his big fuel truck made regular stops at our house and were very vital for Dad's business, I barely remember him. But I've never forgotten the sight of his big truck as it came down the road with a metal chain fastened to the underside. The purpose of the chain was to "ground" the truck, eliminating any chance of sparks causing a big explosion due to static electricity. I was always intrigued by that truck as it drove down our road, its chain dangling on the road where it flipped and bounced gaily.

## *The GRAIN BUYER/COMPETITOR*

Ferd Detjen wore many hats. I knew him first as the owner of Detjen Grain Company in Moulton, the buyer of corn, soybeans and other grains that Dad or Grandpa had for sale. When it was harvest time, they occasionally called Ferd to check on the current grain market prices. If they felt the price was too low, they stored the grain until the market was no longer flooded with new grain. Then the price would go back up. If the price suited them, or if there was no more room to store the grain in the barn, they told Ferd they wanted to sell it. He would send out a grain truck.

When I talked to Ferd in the 1980s, he began to laugh heartily as he told me of an incident he had remembered from many years before. My dad talked to him about selling some corn. They agreed upon a price, but by the time Ferd got around to sending his trucks out to load the corn, the price had gone *up* eight cents a bushel. When Dad moped and thought that Ferd was getting the best end of things, Ferd reminded him that "a deal is a deal." The next year Dad decided if the price was right, he would sell the entire crop, 2,100 bushels of corn. When he approached Ferd about selling it, they agreed on a price. And again the price changed by the time Ferd's trucks came for the corn, but this time the price had gone *down* six cents a bushel. With that many bushels, this was quite a loss for Ferd. When he grumbled about it, Dad looked him right in the eye, and, grinning from ear to ear, told him, "Sorry, Ferd, but a deal's a deal!" Ferd laughed out loud as he told me the story.

After Bill and I were married, Ferd was no longer just the grain buyer. Now I found out he was one of Bill's relatives, not just once, but twice. Ferd's grandmother Detjen was a sister to Bill's great-grandfather Wierwille. Not only that, Ferd's mother was a sister to Bill's great-grandma Henschen. When I became interested in genealogy, Ferd shared his family knowledge with me.

We saw Ferd rather frequently. Like Bill and me, he really loved music. Ferd sang in the massed choir that participated in the Auglaize County Centennial in 1948. Bill and I had just met a couple of weeks before and we had each volunteered to join with our church choirs in becoming a part of that large group who would be singing at the centennial celebration at the county fairgrounds. (By the way, fifty years later we again sang in the huge choir celebrating the county's sesquicentennial. What fun!)

Ferd also belonged to the same concert series that Bill and I joined after we were married. Concert tickets were sold for a very reasonable fee, but they provided admission to several concert series throughout this area of Ohio, from Lima to Greenville, from Van Wert to Bellefontaine and most of the cities between. We seldom missed any of these performances. I don't think Ferd did either. We usually saw him in the audiences.

The third hat worn by Ferd was that of our competitor. For many years he was the John Deere dealer located just a mile or so down the road from our Case dealership. We were not just friendly competitors, we were also good friends. Ferd knew my dad and grandpa, and they knew him, although they seldom bought any machinery from him. Bill had started our machinery business before we were married. In all that time we found Ferd to be a fair and honest businessman. We never felt any animosity toward him because of improper salesmanship. I will never forget the strange look on the face of an acquaintance whom we met at the State Implement Dealers' Convention in Columbus. We entered a hotel meeting room and there stood Ferd Detjen. As soon as Ferd saw us, he rushed over and gave me a great big bear hug and clasped Bill's hand warmly. After talking and laughing together for a few minutes, he walked away. The lady looked at me and gasped, "*Who* was *that*?" "Oh," I laughed, "*That* was our nearest *competitor*!" She just stood there with her mouth wide open and a very puzzled look on her face, not knowing quite what to say. Hugging your competitor? Whoever heard of such a thing? Obviously, she didn't know Ferd Detjen!

## *The HIGHWAY MEN*

The unsung heroes of snowy winter nights were the men of the highway department who faithfully manned the big snow plows and cleared the roads to keep traffic moving safely. It was such a comforting feeling to hear the distinctive sound of the plow as it scraped along the road, pushing the snow aside. We could almost predict the weather by how far back those snowplows pushed the snow. If it was way out in the ditch, it usually meant more snow was coming.

During the summer, the state highway men often stopped at our house around noon. They enjoyed eating their sack lunches as they sat under the big maple trees in our side yard. Several had told Grandpa the water from our well was the best drinking water in the whole county. If they were adding stone to our road or spreading oil in front of the houses, they usually stopped for a drink of cool water. After the road was tarred, they continued to enjoy the thirst quenching water and the cool grassy area under our shade tree.

Bill remembers seeing grass growing in the center of the road in front of his house. Adrian Settlage asked at a Platt Deutsch meeting, "Why were the ditches along the country roads so yellow during the summer?" In answering his question, he explained that some of the legumes used for making hay in our modern times were not available back then. Sweet clover was reasonably priced and readily available, making it the ideal form of hay for the horses. Since most of the farmers fed the clover to their animals, the seeds were prevalent in their droppings. As the horses walked on the roads, they left a good supply of these "horsey road apples" adorning the country roads. Although neighborhood birds feasted on the seeds found in the manure, there were more seeds than they could consume. As the rains washed over the droppings, the water drained into the side ditches, taking the seeds with it. In the spring the seeds sprouted and the yellow heads made an attractive path along the roads each summer, thanks to the abundant supply of the horses road "apples."

Bill saw a large number of men, perhaps a hundred, using shovels to dig ditches and widen the road west of his grandpa's house when he was a kid. It was the 1930s and they were working for the WPA. The work was hard and dusty on those hot days, although Grandpa thought some of the men spent a bit too much time leaning on their shovels. (Was that because of weary bones or lazy bones?)

While the country roads were being improved, there was also progress being made on the streets of the area cities. Cousin Norman Davenport remembers his father working in the Public Square in Lima as bricks were being laid for the first time. Norman was less than ten years old as he walked over each day to take his dad's dinner bucket to him.

Times have changed, and super highways are common, but we still owe a vote of thanks to the men who work on the highways and keep them clear and safe. I still take great comfort when I awake in the middle of a cold, snowy night and hear the scraping of the snowplow as it turns down our road.

## *The HIRED MAN*

Dad needed help. He was getting back on his feet financially after the double whammy of Mother's death and the Great Depression. Folks were again getting the money to put in tile for draining their farm fields, so Dad needed someone to help in the business. The farmers always provided someone to lay the tile in the ground after the ditcher had dug the trench, but Dad needed someone to help run the machine while he set up the stakes and figured out the grade. The first hired man I remember was Floyd Leffel, a young man from Kossuth.

Floyd came to work for Dad before I was three years old. My earliest memory of him was of sitting on his lap in the Ferris wheel at the Auglaize County Fair. I was crying my heart out because I was scared of being up so high, and I was sobbing, "Off! I want off!" The operator stopped the wheel and we got off, but it was at least a decade before I rode a Ferris wheel again. (Would you believe the same thing happened again?) When our church ladies provided meals in the dining hall, the kids had plenty of time to see the fair. I was with a girlfriend who wanted to ride the big wheel, but she wasn't allowed to ride alone. After pleading and begging, she finally talked me into riding with her. I remember quite well how unhappy she was when I told the operator to stop the wheel so I could get off. She felt she had been cheated because she hadn't gotten the full ride. I felt sorry for her, but I just couldn't ride that scary thing.

When Dad hired Floyd, he and his bride, Olive Whetstone, set up housekeeping in Dad's house where he and Mother had lived when I was born. One upstairs room had been set aside as storage for the few personal things that Dad and Mother had used. This room was kept locked. Dad used a small building across the driveway from the house as his shop where he did repairs and other work on his ditcher. When the weather was not fit for ditching, or if something needed to be fixed, Dad usually spent most of the day in that shop a mile south of our house.

As a little girl, I occasionally went there with Daddy. As he walked me to the house, Olive greeted us and took us up to that room. Dad unlocked the door and left me there for the rest of the afternoon. I can't describe the feelings I had when I was in that room. I was only eight or nine years old, but somehow I felt my mother's presence when I was there. I suppose that was because it contained her series of Ruth Fielding books, a few pictures of happier days, my baby shoes and dresses, a straight chair and rocker, her college scrapbook, a few pots and pans and other odds and ends. These were the only things that I knew my mother's hands had actually touched. They were very special. Olive was always good about allowing me to be there and when I had finished looking at and handling the things, I locked the door and took the key back to Daddy. Until time to go home for supper, I watched Daddy making his repairs as he pounded the hot metals into the desired shape and used the anvil, the drills and the other shop equipment.

I don't know how many years Floyd worked for Dad. While living in that house, he and Olive had a little girl, Jeanette Sue, and then a baby boy, Kenneth. Eventually Floyd moved his family to Wapakoneta where he drove a truck that delivered gasoline to farmers. I'm sure this was a more reliable job. When he worked for Dad, there were many days when ditching could not be done because of extremely bad weather or equipment breakage. My family had great respect for Floyd, and when my grandmother died, Olive and a neighbor, Claire Place, sang for the funeral. Floyd had been dependable, a good worker and a very kind man whom I remember with great fondness, except for that Ferris wheel ride, of course!

## *The HORSE TRADER*

Some people come into your life, make an impression, and leave. That is the story with Elmer Rasneor. Elmer was a dealer in horses. When Grandpa wanted to buy a horse, it was Elmer whom he visited. Soon after, a truck pulling a horse trailer drove into our barnyard, and Elmer brought out the beautiful branded western bronco, Bobby, who spent the next few years at our house. Then after a couple of years, Elmer returned with his trailer and took Bobby away. Grandpa was getting too old to ride regularly, and I was too young. Don's interest had turned toward something a little more exciting—cars and tractors. They didn't have to be fed and brushed daily and you certainly didn't have to haul out their manure!

## *The HUCKSTER WAGON MAN*

The huckster wagon stopped coming to our house when I was still quite small, so I don't remember much about the man or his wagon. It carried all sorts of things that a farm wife might need. When I asked my fellow genealogy society members what they knew about huckster wagons, a few remembered the wagon coming around to the farming areas. In early years it had been a horse drawn wagon, but though it was still called the huckster wagon, the later model was a truck. It carried bread, canned goods, potatoes, almost anything you could get in a grocery store. It even had candy for those who were lucky enough to have a few pennies to spend. One lady said her mother's huckster wagon had even brought yard goods suitable for aprons and everyday dresses. Another lady said that when her mother needed something they didn't have on the wagon, she ordered it. He brought it the next time. Some wagons came every week, others every other week.

The *Auglaize County Republican,* Thursday, August 4, 1904, had the following item in news from the Sodom area southeast of Kossuth: "Duff Day was unable to take his place on the huckster wagon Monday morning on account of a sprained ankle." Duff was from Kossuth and his route covered the general area where my family lived. Other huckster wagon men were Albert Haller and Dan Sawmiller. Grandpa used to sing me a song called "Old Dan Tucker." Somehow I always associated that name with Dan Sawmiller. Any time I saw Dan, my little girl's mind was saying, "Here comes Old Dan Tucker."

## *The JUNK MAN*

"Well, Mr. Davenport, have you got any junk today?" About twice a year Charlie

Morlock came around to ask if we had junk to sell. Don and I welcomed his appearing, since it meant money in our pockets. Although it didn't amount to much, a few cents from some broken tools or scrap metal—it was ours. When we found a piece of junk, it was piled against the back side of Grandpa's shop where it remained until Charlie came around the next time. He also bought bottles, tin cans, burlap sacks, old coats and rags. Since Grandma crocheted rugs from our rags, he never got any of those.

As a child, I enjoyed Charlie Morlock's visits. He lived just down the road from Dad's farm, and I didn't know anyone who looked, smelled, or sounded quite like Charlie. He spoke with a very heavy German accent, something that intrigued me immensely. His clothes can only be described as *wonderfully* dirty. I didn't know of *anyone* but Charlie who had such a grand assortment of rust, oil, and mud from the junk, the smell of cows and barnyard goop, combined with a day's honest sweat. When Charlie attended area farm sales to buy the junk that no one else really wanted, he usually cleaned up a bit. When he dressed up to attend the funeral of a friend or relative, I scarcely recognized him. Could that really be our friendly junk man?

Charlie had very little formal "book learning," but he knew the junk business. His services were needed on the farms at that time. I don't know when he stopped coming around. Charlie was getting old, and so was his truck. During World War II, most of the schools entered into a contest to see who could bring in the most junk, and we took ours to the school. It was during this time that the Old Hoopie, the car of my earliest memories, finally met its demise. The Hoopie eventually went to the St. Marys Iron and Steel to help us win the war.

One of Don's favorite junk man stories took place in Buckland. Charlie hadn't learned to drive at that time, so he depended on his son, Andrew, to do the driving. Andy was about twenty years old when he and Charlie stopped at Sherm Richardson's restaurant, which at that time was on the east side of Main Street. Charlie's old truck was a Model T Ford that had to be cranked to get it started. While they were inside, a group of older boys decided to have some fun and connected a smoke bomb to the engine, then waited for Charlie and Andy to come out. Soon Charlie walked out and climbed into the cab, while Andrew walked to the front of the truck and started to crank. The first spark set off the bomb, and it began to whistle, then thick smoke started to roll out from under the hood. Getting out as quickly as he could, Charlie took off running and in that thick German accent, yelled back, "Run, Andy, run! She's going to blow up!" The pranksters enjoyed every moment of the show! In the days before accelerator pedals were built into cars, the flow of gas in the Model T was controlled by a handle on the side of the column underneath the steering wheel. As Andy and I reminisced recently, he laughed. "Yep, that's the way it happened. And you know what," he said. "That made me mad and I pulled that handle down and we really took off!"

After Andy got a job at Mersman's, Charlie finally learned to drive his own truck. When he stopped at our house, he usually teased and talked to us for a little while before doing business. When the junk was sold, he counted out those coins into our waiting hands. I always looked forward to his coming, in part because of the money we always got, but also because he was so different from anyone else I knew. Junk was a lot more fun in those days, and there was only one junk man named Charlie Morlock!

## *The LACE MAN*

**B**ill's Aunt Alwina told me of a "peddler" who had come around the New Knoxville area when she was a little girl. He sold lace. I'd never heard of that, but it sounded interesting. As the man held out several pretty pieces, with a heavy German accent, he usually said to her mother, "Cheap, mom! Cheap!" Lace was too extravagant for most thrifty German farm folks, and her mother hadn't bought much of it. The lace was awfully pretty, and Alwina would have liked some on her dresses, but she knew better than to ask for it, even though the man had said it was "Cheap, mom! Cheap!"

## *The LIVESTOCK BUYER*

"**B**ake" is the only name by which I knew him. His proper name was Marion Baker, but I never heard anyone call him that. Many folks probably didn't even know it was his real name.

Bake lived in Buckland in an area that I thought was very special. Buckland is a tiny village built along the former Nickel Plate railroad. Bake lived in a grove of trees east of the main street. The house had some nice porches and shutters, and I always thought it looked like a *romantic* type of home as it nestled back in a wooded area with lots of grass and flowers. When I attended school in Buckland, I often got a glimpse of the house as I passed by.

The railroad ran a short distance from the house, and the Auglaize river was located behind the barns. A wooden railroad trestle crossed that river, and when I stayed overnight with my friend, Mary Jo Bruner, we occasionally walked down the railroad tracks and out onto that trestle. How scary it was to look down through the cracks between the railroad ties and see the water flowing far below! We were always very careful to stay off the trestle if a train was coming. We had heard of people being killed that way, and it sounded like a nasty way to go. When the train whistled for the crossings a couple of miles in either direction, we *immediately made tracks* in getting off that trestle.

Bake's large barn and the small lots around it were quite the opposite of "romantic." They were, at least temporarily, the home of a lot of smelly hogs. The school was over a block away, but on hot spring days with a southeast wind, we could smell those hogs and hear them squealing as they rooted and shoved each other in the outside lots. Bake was a well-known stock buyer and a good friend of Grandpa's. When we had pigs to sell, it was Bake who usually bought them.

Bake sometimes stopped by about the time he thought Grandpa would have a bunch of hogs ready for market. Bake usually took time to talk to us kids. Then Bake and Grandpa would lean on the barnyard fence and look over the animals. They usually discussed the weather, the political situation, the hog diseases going around and other topics of the day. Finally Bake would make a guess as to about how much each hog might average in weight and he was usually not far off. Then they would haggle over prices and finally reach an agreement. Grandpa helped him load up the hogs and then followed Bake to Buckland, where he weighed the hogs. Then he wrote out a check and gave it to Grandpa.

When Don raised his first 4-H pig, she was a fine specimen of hog-ship named Lady

Jean. He took her to the county fair as a market pig, then kept her another year and took her as a sow and litter project. When she delivered only a small litter of pigs, Don decided to sell her. It was Bake who gave him his money. A few years later, I was one of the first girls in the area to take a 4-H animal, a market pig. I was not allowed to stay overnight at the fair as did the boys, but since I was selected to go to a state 4-H camp the same week, I didn't mind. Clarence D. Brown, the county agent, came to our home and judged my pig, awarding it an A.

Eventually, Bake bought that pig and the bottle-fed calf I later raised. The money from these two animals bought my fur coat (which I enjoyed wearing at Wittenberg College) and the Domestic sewing machine I still use. It has sewed my wedding dress and wedding dresses for my daughter and for my granddaughter's Barbie doll. It also sewed nearly all the clothes I've made for myself and for my family. Believe me, that's a bunch! And all because Bake paid a good price for my animals!

## *The MAILMAN*

Who was one of the more important farm visitors in the 1930s? The mailman! He kept folks in touch with the outside world. Radios were not always reliable and tended to fade in and out. Besides that, their occasional sizzling sounds made us wonder if someone was frying a pan of bacon somewhere in the innards of the cabinet! The daily newspaper kept us abreast of the happenings, although the news was already stale by the time it reached the farmer's mailbox the next day. It was the mailman who brought the newsy news, letters from Grandma's relatives in Oklahoma and Missouri, or friends from their road building days in North Carolina. Picture postcards occasionally arrived from someone lucky enough to vacation in distant places such as Niagara Falls, Washington, D.C. and Mexico City.

Colorful seed catalogs made the mailman's load heavy in early January or February as they arrived at the farm homes along his mail route. Many winter evenings were spent looking at the pictures of those luscious vegetables and gorgeous flowers. Could we grow anything that looked that good? Since this was the era of "The Great Depression," money for flowers was scarce. "Vegetables we can eat, flowers we can't," was the motto of many, but Grandma loved flowers, and she was always "giving a start" to someone, then getting a clump of flowers or some bulbs in return. The mailman helped in this exchange of growing things as he occasionally delivered a box of bulbs or a packet of flower seeds from Gene Gerth or Mrs. Burton Callis, Grandma's friends in North Carolina. For years, these ladies enjoyed and shared their flowers.

Of course the mailman brought a few bills, but most things were paid in cash. At our house electricity was made by a Delco, so there was no electric bill. The telephone bill was paid at the Buckland office each month when we happened to be in town. Once a year we received a bill for the local newspaper and *Liberty* magazine. In the 1940s we started taking Grandpa's favorite magazine, the *Saturday Evening Post*. He loved the "Horatio Hornblower" stories! *The Wapakoneta Daily News* showed up each day and the weekly Spencerville *Journal-News* appeared in the mailbox every Thursday. It kept us abreast of things in our neighborhood, although I've never quite forgiven the *Journal* for listing me in their birth announcements as a boy.

The J.C. Penney or Sears Roebuck catalog (nicknamed the Sears and Sawbuck) were favorite items delivered by the mailman. Nicknamed the "wish book," the catalog was leafed through endlessly as we dreamed over pages of things we really "had" to have but seldom got. When the next catalog arrived, the outdated one was moved to the outhouse.

Without a doubt, the most popular item the mailman brought, at least for Don and me, was the Christmas catalog. I dreamed of owning every doll in that catalog. I *loved* dolls and always wanted a Shirley Temple, but never got one. (Sigh!) One of my first dolls was a little one that I played with a lot. When I got a new, bigger doll, I gave the little one to a little girl who had no doll. (I have since found out that dolls like her are quite collectible now and worth money. But my little friend needed it more than I did. She had at least four sisters and two brothers but no doll. Toys were shared by the children, so she was happy to have her own dolly.)

After our Delco wore out and Grandpa signed up for power from Midwest Electric, our mailman faithfully delivered expensive electric bills. But they felt it was worth it to have all the new electrical appliances.

When someone called, "There's the mailman!", we kids usually made a dash for the mailbox. Who knew what exciting things might be in there, especially if it was about time for his most popular delivery, the Christmas catalog. We tried to wait patiently for that wonderful picture book to arrive each year!

## *The NEW CAR SALESMAN*

It was a glorious day when Grandpa decided to buy a new car. He visited the showroom and looked at each model. When the salesman knew Grandpa was interested, he got his name and type of car he wanted. Grandpa took a liking to Nash cars and drove them for several years. I especially remember the Lima Nash salesman, Jake Suever. The Suever family had operated a stone quarry near Delphos. When Grandpa became co-owner of the Davis-Davenport Construction Company, he had somehow gotten acquainted with Mr. Suever and trusted him. If he were going to buy a Nash, it would be from Jake Suever.

A week or so after our visit to the showroom, Mr. Suever drove in with a brand-new car. Emerging from that elegant car, Jake was dressed like a real gentleman—suit, tie, hat, shiny shoes and all. To us country kids, that would be like a man wearing his Sunday clothes during the week. Farmers didn't do that, so we knew when we saw someone *that* dressed up, he was either a preacher, a politician or a "city slicker."

While Mr. Suever explained all the fine points of the automobile to Grandpa and Dad, I sat by the dining room window and looked longingly at the gorgeous car. I knew it was only a matter of time until Grandpa would come in and cheerfully ask, "Anyone want to go for a ride?" We didn't need a second invitation. As we walked to the car, Grandma cautioned us to be very careful not to get anything dirty.

I sat in the back seat, almost quivering from excitement at the thought of driving around in that brand-new car. It had such a wonderful "new car smell" that can't be found anywhere else. The seat was soft and velvety, and I felt like a princess in a new carriage as I stretched to peek out the windows at the familiar neighborhood.

After the ride, Grandpa and Dad looked at the engine and talked business with Mr. Suever, finally dickering for the lowest possible price. When that was reached, Grandpa came into the house and discussed it with Grandma. She helped select the color, since Grandpa was color blind. With that decision made, he went back out and said, "Well, Jake. I'll tell you what! I believe we'll just take one exactly like this if you can get it in light blue." And Mr. Suever grinned and said, "I'll get it!"

Sure enough, several days later Mr. Suever called to tell us the car was ready. We made sure everything was out of the old car, then Grandpa drove us to Lima, and we returned home with *our* brand new 1937 Nash automobile. What an exciting ride that was! I was seven years old and was sure it was the slickest looking, most beautiful car I had ever seen!

Grandpa didn't buy new cars very often, so we seldom saw Mr. Suever. Although it has been decades since that demonstration ride in a new Nash car, I've never forgotten him. Grandpa considered Mr. Suever a real gentleman. A few years ago the *Lima News* mentioned that he and his wife were celebrating seventy years of married life. I thought about contacting Jake Suever and telling him what a fine gentleman my grandpa thought he was. I didn't do it. Wish I had!

## *The NEXT DOOR NEIGHBOR*

Who was the very first man I fell in love with (outside of my family, of course)? Why, it was Joe Frank! Grandpa and Joe, who lived on the first farm west of us, were good friends. They went hunting together each fall and worked side by side on butchering day and at threshing time. When either one needed help, the other was there. As young men, their families had gotten together for an evening of music, fellowship and fun with a group of the neighbors probably once a week. The *Democrat* from September 3, 1914, contained the following. "Mr. and Mrs. Joe Frank entertained a few friends Saturday evening with a cider party and they all claimed Mr. and Mrs. Frank know how to entertain the crowd, and to have them go away wishing the evening longer and wondering when they can come back again for another fine time... At ten thirty a fine lunch was served and at twelve they all departed for their homes, thanking Mr. and Mrs. Frank for their splendid entertaining. They claim Joe still had some cider left, but it is doubtful." Sixteen neighbors enjoyed the events of that evening.

The friendship continued for many years, and our family was there to comfort Joe on that Monday in 1936 when his wife, Rose, died. Later, after he had moved to Texas and found a new wife, he brought her back to introduce her to our family. She was a gracious Southern lady with the sweetest Texas drawl. I was too young to remember much about his first wife, Rose, but I loved this lady, also named Rose. Grandma prepared a special dinner for them. I made the dessert, a cake I had baked from scratch. (There were no boxed cake mixes then!) Rose really bragged about my cake and made me feel very special. See why I loved that lady?

I guess my first memories of Joe Frank are of riding on his old Fordson tractor as he worked in a nearby field. I remember being three or four years old and bravely crossing the road in front of our house. Grandma stood in the yard and watched as I walked into the field and waited for Joe to stop on his next trip around with the plow or disc. Sometimes I carried a pint canning jar full of water for him to drink. He would reach down and swoop me up over the tractor seat and into his lap. We would bounce around the field, laughing and trying to talk above the noise of his old Fordson. Its wheels had metal rims with lugs in them, not rubber tires like today's models. After an hour or so of that bumping and jolting, I would fall asleep in Joe's arms, and he would stop the tractor close to our mailbox, carry me across the road and up to our house. That happened many times. I really missed seeing Joe when I had to go to school. Growing up is tough!

Our family continued to be friends with Joe, even after he had moved to Texas. His new wife and I wrote occasionally, and we sent them an invitation to our wedding, although we knew they couldn't come back to Ohio. I promised them we would visit for a few days on our honeymoon. We stayed several days, and Joe and Bill drove our new car into Breckenridge to receive its 1,000-mile checkup one hot June day. Rose and I drove Joe's car and were to pick them up at the car dealership. As we got into the car, Rose put on a pair of long white gloves that covered her arms. "A lady wants to keep her skin nice and white," she explained to me. The gloves would keep the hot Texas sun from burning her arm through the open window. Remember, there was no air conditioning then.

I don't recall the actual mileage to Breckenridge, but it was a great distance compared to driving in Ohio. We were about halfway there when Rose suddenly gasped, "Oh, I don't remember if I turned the stove off under those black-eyed peas. Well, I guess we just better turn around and go back to check on them." She said it as casually as I might have said it if we were driving the one mile from our house to Kossuth. I couldn't believe we were going to drive all that distance back home, but then again, if they boiled dry it might set the house on fire. Driving longer distances didn't seem to bother in the wide-open spaces of Texas, so back we went. Oh, yes. She had turned the stove off after all.

While visiting Joe and Rose, they took us to Possum Kingdom Dam, the largest dam we had ever seen. The day before our arrival, Joe had thrown his fish line in there and had caught a huge catfish. He kept it alive, brought it home and staked it in his cattle tank. To us, a cattle tank was the oval galvanized metal water tank beside the barn back home, the one we had to pump full of water every day. In Texas, the tank was really a farm pond! We were greatly surprised at the size of that fish as he reeled the line in to shore. Weighing forty pounds, it was the largest catfish we had ever seen, and we were sufficiently impressed! Joe got some bait and poles for us, and we spent a few hours fishing in his cattle tank. While we were fishing, Bill said something about being thirsty. Joe laughed and said, "Well, just kneel down there and get a drink. It's the same water you drink up at the house." I guess Bill gave him a strange look, so he explained that his windmill pumped the water from that cattle tank up to the storage tank above the house. It then drained down into the house, so that the water coming from the spigot was the same water as that in the pond where cows now stood on one side doing their thing in the water, while birds drank on the other side, and fish swam through it all. Sound appetizing? A glass of water sitting overnight left a layer of mud in the bottom, but "when in Rome, do as the Romans." Those people seemed quite healthy, so Bill leaned down and drank. Why didn't they drill wells like we do? Because they always struck that "doggone oil or gas!"

Bill rode with Joe one day as he drove his ancient pickup truck out into the pasture to feed hay to his cows. A rifle rested on the gun rack behind their heads, and as they drove Joe spotted a jackrabbit hiding near a clump of mesquite. These critters can be a real problem for farmers. They multiply as fast as our little rabbits around here, but are much larger and destroy much more of a farmer's crops. Joe suddenly stopped the truck, grabbed his rifle, took quick aim and fired. Bill said they weren't really close but when they walked over and looked at the rabbit, Joe had hit it right through the eyes. He was an excellent shot, and even in his older years, he didn't lose his ability as a sharpshooter.

Joe took us to visit the neighbors, a couple who lived in a very modest house and who seemed like just common, ordinary folks. They were very friendly and really made us feel quite welcome. Their home was built Texas style with their bed in the living room. (Joe and Rose had their bed in a screened-in back porch.) Folks seemed to hunt the coolest spot in the house for sleeping. As hot as it was, I don't blame them.

The neighbors took us to the city to see the fine new home of their daughter and son-in-law. I was very impressed! I hadn't been in many fancy new homes. I thought it was beautiful. I especially noticed that each of the three bedrooms had its own bath, painted or papered in coordinating colors. Quite a new trend for that time—the epitome of elegance for this country girl! Later Joe asked us how we liked the new house. When we told him how impressed we were, Joe agreed that it was really a nice house, but said, "Shoot, they didn't need anything that fancy. After all, her *parents* just live in a plain old house, and *they* are the *millionaires*!" (One time Joe came back to Ohio and jokingly told some of his old neighbors here that he had a millionaire taking care of his cows while he was gone. They just smiled and thought old Joe was pulling their leg, but we had met the man and we knew Joe really *did* have a *millionaire* taking care of his cows.)

One morning we told Joe we would have to leave the next day, but he urged us to stay on for a few more days. He, Rose and some neighbors were hoping we would stay for a party they wanted to give for us that weekend. We had planned our honeymoon to fit in between Bill's farm activities and we had arranged everything according to a timetable so we could get to the Grand Canyon, the Rocky Mountains and other points of interest. We felt we just didn't have time to stay. We have always regretted that, especially after we were marooned for several days in a Kansas flood. A Texas barbecue would have been a much more welcome event! Joe Frank is long gone now and we miss him! Rest in peace, old neighbor!

## *The PIPELINE WALKER/PILOT*

The pipeline walker was a man of mystery. I didn't know his name, nor did I understand his job. Every few weeks he crossed the fields behind our house, and I knew he walked the pipeline to look for leaks. If he met someone working in the field, he spoke a few words and walked on. I knew the pipeline went from Texas to Lima, and in my child's mind I thought that poor man walked every step of that route himself. "How tired he must get," I thought. When we saw him again a few weeks later, I thought, "My goodness, that poor man gets no rest. There he goes, doing it all over again!"

Eventually it was discovered that a low-flying airplane could spot a leak more quickly than a man walking the line, so the job was simplified. From then on, the pipeline plane frequently flew over. This was far more exciting for Don and me, and when we heard the plane approaching, we ran into the yard and waved as long as he was in sight. He had spotted us waving one day and had tipped his wings back and forth to return our greeting. After that, I think he watched for us and continued to tip those wings when we waved. Now that was real excitement for a couple of farm kids

## *The PREACHERS*

With a great-grandpa named *John Wesley* Davenport, you might guess our family had been Methodist. If that doesn't convince you, how about this? His brother was named *Asbury* Nathan and his sister was *Susanna.* (With those names, the Wesley family should be proud!) One of the early family stories pertained to my grandfather's uncle, whom he always referred to as Uncle Bill Bradford. William Bradford married John Wesley Davenport's sister, Elsie Margaret. Uncle Bill was often referred to as a "one-horse preacher" or a "preacher-of-sorts." In other words, he had no formal education and was not ordained, but he felt called to preach at any of the area churches who sought his services. One night Uncle Bill was preaching at the Kossuth Methodist Church. While he was busy preaching inside the church, his young son was quite active outside as he walked from buggy to buggy, *snitching* the buggy whips. His Dad found out about it on the way back to Wapak. Bill Bradford wasn't too happy with his son that night!

Our little country church at Kossuth had quite an assortment of preachers holding that position during my childhood. It was Rev. Robert Herrier who officiated at Mother's funeral. He was followed a few years later by Rev. Rupp and then by Rev. Carey O. Good. It was somewhere during this time that Rev. Seth Painter was invited to have a revival at our church. On March 15, 1942, I tearfully knelt at the altar of the church and accepted Christ as my Lord and Savior.

During Rev. Good's stay, the teenagers' humor of the day was that he was a "good man!" And indeed, he was a good man; but for us kids, he was rather dry and boring. He was elderly and just didn't get too excited about anything. We were on a circuit of four churches at the time and our joint youth fellowship meetings were very exciting to the young people because we got to meet all the kids from the other three churches. While we had a rousing game going or were enjoying a deep discussion, he sat off to the side with his head nodding as he snoozed through the excitement.

Rev. Paul Price was the minister at our wedding, and his wife took pictures during the ceremony. After he left, we had a steady stream of new ministers. The bishop at that time expressed the opinion that any preacher should be able to tell you everything he knew in four years. Then it was time for him to move on. And that was about as fast as he moved them. Bill's church had numerous young men who had gone into the ministry, but I remember making the statement that we never had a preacher long enough for the young people to get well enough acquainted to see them as examples and want to follow them into the ministry. Many of our preachers were students who struggled to keep up with their studies, have enough time to shepherd their little flock and take care of their own families. One young pastor told us that when a group of preachers got together, there was more talk about the size of their homes or the size of their salaries or the size of their golf scores than there was about the number of souls they had led to the Lord. He was not only very surprised, but he was also very disillusioned and disappointed.

Most of the pastors in our little church did not wear formal clerical attire, although one minister insisted on wearing a black robe. He was a tall, long-legged young man and his flock smiled as he rushed down the center aisle each Sunday morning with his long, flowing black robe fluttering in the breeze, giving him the ominous nickname of "The Bat."

Religion was so much a part of the lives of rural people in those days that I really knew very few persons who did not attend church on a fairly regular basis. It was just the thing to do! Small churches have been a very essential part of America, and I am thankful for all the young people in my church when I was growing up. I am also grateful for the large church we now attend because there are so many more resources for spreading the Gospel. But I thank God for all the small churches that continue to dot the countryside across America!

## *The SHOE REPAIR MAN-TELEPHONE BUSINESS AGENT*

Ed McDonald was a man with two jobs. If a pair of shoes had a problem that couldn't be fixed at home, he fixed them at his repair shop in Buckland. He was the only cobbler in the Buckland/Kossuth area, so everyone knew him. He also held the office of Buckland telephone business agent. I don't know exactly what that job's requirements were, but I remember him pulling into our driveway on some kind of telephone business and just sitting there honking his car horn. Now Grandpa and Grandma were not happy when they were hard at work and someone drove in, then sat in the car and honked until they put down whatever they were doing and walked out to see what the person wanted. Often it was a salesman trying to sell something, and our family thought that if the person didn't have enough gumption to come to the door and knock, we wouldn't be interested anyway! But, when they saw Ed McDonald sit and honk, Grandma or Grandpa always went out right away. You see, Ed was physically disabled and could not easily get in and out of a car or walk up to the house. But when it came to shoes, he knew his stuff!

## *The STOREKEEPER*

Ice skating on the canal was one of our favorite teenage activities. If we skated during the day, we often brought a little money to spend at Earl Hoverman's store across the street from the church, just a short walk from the canal. Since it took quite a while to unlace both our high top skates, then put on cold shoes and walk over to the store for a snack, it was easier to just stand up on the toes of our skates (so we wouldn't dull the blades by walking on them.) Looking like awkward ballerinas, we'd prance across the road to Earl's store. Most of the kids had hockey skates that were pointed, not sawtooth on the end like our figure skates, so it required a bit of a balancing act to do this, but hunger won out, and over we went. Although he wanted our business, Earl didn't really appreciate our walking on his wooden floor with those pointy-toed skates. We were just kids and didn't see how it was really going to do that much damage. After all, we had seen him fill customers' oil cans from a drum he kept at the back of the store. Every once in a while the oil overflowed the cans and spilled onto the floor. And besides, we had often seen the old men of the area as they sat by his potbellied stove for hours at a time, telling outlandish stories, chewing tobacco, and spitting on his floor when they missed the coal bucket that doubled as a spittoon. We thought that was far worse than a few tiny dents.

Because he tended to frown upon the kids' actions, he became a target for Halloween pranks. I usually stayed behind trees and watched as the older boys knocked on his door and ran, or put noisemakers against his window. Regardless of what they did, he usually came out with a shotgun, banging away at the air above them and scaring them away. (See why I stayed behind the trees?)

Another of the boys' favorite pranks was to call the store keeper on the telephone and ask, "Do you have Prince Albert in the can?" Prince Albert was a favorite tobacco at that time and it could be purchased in a metal can or in a soft pouch. When Earl replied, "Yes, I have Prince Albert in a can," the boys would reply, "Well, why don't you let the poor guy out?" They would then giggle and hang up.

Earl drove an old Reo truck for many years. He used it to haul supplies to his store, to haul coal to the shed beside it, and for the many other uses he found. I remember it most vividly as he traveled through the countryside each fall, asking for the apples people had not picked in their orchards. He usually got these free for the picking, then took them to the cider press in Glynwood and had them made into the cider that he sold at his store.

Earl's store was a traditional little country store of the 1930s. Originally it had been a hotel. Much was made of the fact that at some time in the past, when the Miami-Erie canal was one of the most common means of travel, a murder had been committed there. Yes, siree! Right there in downtown Kossuth, population less than one hundred. There was a bullet hole in the side of the building to prove it.

Earl had a glass display case where he kept a nice variety of candy, much of it for a penny. He carried a few souvenirs, since State Route 66 was a major north/south road in western Ohio, especially for people traveling to and from Lake St. Marys. He also carried cold meats, a few groceries, motor oil, gloves, fishing rods and tackle, a few spools of thread, fishing licenses, and of course, gasoline. His only gas pump was a model with a glass globe at the top, a real antique nowadays. A handle on the side was pulled down, forcing gas from the tank buried in the ground into the glass globe on top of the pump. Markings on the top specified the amount of gas. If someone wanted five gallons of gas, Earl pumped the handle until the fuel reached the five-gallon mark on the globe. He then stopped pumping and opened the hose, allowing the gas to run out of the globe and into the tank of the car below.

Coal was usually stored in the little shed just north of the store. I remember quite well the large number of circus posters that usually covered its sides. (Don said he wished we had a few of those posters now.)

In his younger years, Earl, like his father, had been a farmer, but when he lost his arm in a corn shredder accident, he no longer farmed, but became the storekeeper, hoping to make enough money to raise his daughters Fern and Nina, and sons, Eugene and Austin. I'm sure life was not easy for him. His wife, Iona, was a very pleasant and likeable lady, but I always felt sorry for her because of one thing. If she wanted the Ladies Aid from the church to meet at her house, she always had the problem of the bathroom. She had none! Even after electricity became widespread in our area and everyone else had indoor plumbing, they did not modernize. Iona didn't let that get her down, though. She prettied up that little outhouse by covering its walls with attractive wallpaper!

Most of the people around Kossuth went to Spencerville for their weekly groceries until World War II started. Like most of our neighbors, we didn't do a lot of shopping in Kossuth, just an occasional loaf of bread or some bologna, and kids often went there for bubble gum or candy after Children's Day practice or a 4-H meeting. With the beginning of World War II, men's heavy cotton work gloves became very hard to find. Each store was given only a small amount to sell. Dad went into the store one day and asked for a pair of gloves. Earl said he had several pair, but he was saving them for his *regular* customers. This made Dad feel bad because we had shopped there about as much as others in the area, but Dad and Grandpa weren't the type to sit by the potbellied stove telling tall tales and drinking pop. They just didn't have the time.

When I was a high school senior, I started taking lessons so I could play the new organ our church had purchased. Although Earl never went to church, he had been its janitor for years. As I practiced every Saturday morning, he usually came in to stoke the furnace or sweep the carpet in winter. When summer came and the church got warm, I opened the windows for fresh air. As I closed them, I began to notice that Earl was always sitting on the bench in front of his store. When I mentioned it to him one time, he told me he enjoyed my music and was sitting there listening to me practice. That was why he had always found a reason to be in the church on cold days and on his front bench on the warm ones. The man I had thought of as a grouch when I was a child was really a lonely man with a soft spot. I didn't see that until I was a young adult, and then it was only because of music, the universal language!

## *The WATKINS MAN*

Vanilla. That was the main item Grandma bought from the Watkins man. She occasionally got a tin can of salve, but I don't remember many other purchases she may have made. I have the lower half of an early Watkins square metal can that Bill's grandpa had sawed off and used to hold nails and screws in his workshop. On the can is a picture of J.R. Watkins with the words "From Ocean to Ocean." Other sides of the can said:

> The Highest Quality, The Neatest Package, The Best Delivery, The Squarest Terms, The Fairest Treatment, The Greatest Uniformity, The Broadest Guaranty, The Oldest Company, The Largest Resources, The Latest Methods, The Most Consumers. All of the above Points of Superiority help to make The Watkins Way, the best merchandising system ever devised. Watkins Spices are but one group of Watkins Products. There are more than 150 in the line. This consists of Household Medicines, Toilet Requisites, Cooking Aids, Soap and Miscellaneous items. They may be purchased only from the Watkins Dealer. Patronize him liberally. Use the complete Watkins Line.

Although the Watkins man carried aspirin and cough syrup, we usually used home remedies or Grandpa purchased something from the drugstore. If stronger medicine were needed, they got it from Doctor Doughty. Friends have told me the Watkins man usually had a stick of licorice or chewing gum for the children.

Another popular item that he handled was fly spray. This came in a five-gallon bucket and was sold by the pint with the farmer providing the container into which it was poured. Watkins men also had sweet smelling soap that was supposed to be much better for the ladies' delicate hands than the cakes of homemade lye soap that most farm wives used at that time. Fancy soap wasn't on Grandma's list. She didn't think of her hard working hands as very delicate or needing to be pampered. In his younger days, Bert DeLong, Grandma's brother-in-law, had been a Watkins man, but if he came to our house, it was long before I was born.

My friends, Dennis and Janet McClintock, Watkins Independent Marketing Directors from Lima, told me of the interesting beginnings of the Watkins Co. J.R.Watkins lived on a farm in Plainview, Minnesota, in 1868. He decided at the age of twenty-eight to sell liniment door to door to the farmers in his area. Every farmer needed a bottle of his liniment to rub on his horses and other animals. Mr. Watkins would make it more available in the desolate Minnesota countryside. Filling a horse-drawn wagon, he started out. Not only did the farmers want his liniment, they were asking for more things. He added other items he thought the wives could use: spices, extracts, cinnamon, home remedies and unique household goods.

His business prospered. By 1885, he moved to a larger building in Winona. The administration building completed in 1911 is still being used. Janet said it is a beautiful building one block long with a lobby adorned with mahogany woodwork, rich Italian marble and mosaics. And it all started with a bottle of liniment!

Spencerville's North Broadway Street looked like this when Dad was a teenager.
When I was a child, Grandpa and I often met many of the "men in my life" on this street.
Kolter's Mill on the left was one of my favorite spots.

## Chapter 35.

# Let's Go Shopping

"I'm running into town. Anybody need anything?" We hear this quite often today. If we run out of eggs, we hop into the nearest car and head for the grocery store to buy a dozen eggs. We glance at the bakery items as we pass by and decide the cinnamon rolls look delicious. Maybe the cinnamon rolls look so good, we completely forget the eggs and have to dash back to the store. Sound familiar?

Buying things in the 1930s was a bit different from today's carefree shopping. First of all, you didn't run to the store every couple of days for one or two items. You planned everything well ahead of time, and your list was complete and ready before you left for that once-a-week trip to the grocery store, the hardware, the drugstore, and so on. Stores often opened at 8:30 or 9:00 and closed at 5:30, five days a week. Most towns had "open night" on Saturday when stores closed at nine. A few observed Friday night shopping hours, and at least one in our area had a Monday night opening. The kids sometimes went to the "movie house" while their parents shopped. Young couples often walked hand in hand down the street, sometimes with parents watching from the family car parked nearby or following at a discreet distance behind them.

Grocery stores of that day were very different. We usually bought our groceries at the Kroger store in Spencerville. Upon entering, Grandpa handed his grocery list to the clerk. She then walked back and forth behind the counter, plucking a can of corn off this shelf, a twenty-five-pound sack of flour off that one. The cereal boxes were usually way up high and she had a special pole with finger-like clamps on the end. The box of cereal would be centered inside those fingers and when they were closed, the box could safely be lifted down to the counter. I always thought that gadget would be fun to play with, but I never got the chance to try it out. My childhood selection of cereal was very limited. There were only a few boxes to choose from—oatmeal and Post Toasties corn flakes were the favorites. When Wheaties came along, they offered simple toys or gifts to entice the children. That worked, and soon other cereals were enclosing a prize for the kids. Other schemes followed for bigger and better toys. Even if you didn't really like the cereal, you ate it to get the box tops that could be accumulated to get a free ring with a hidden compartment, a secret decoder, or some other stupendous gift that would keep children asking for more.

There were no fancy cellophane packages of tomatoes or head lettuce, no plastic bags of potatoes and apples, no frozen foods or boxes of hamburger helper. Produce items such as oranges came in crates or were stacked on tables where you selected the biggest or ripest or prettiest. Eggs were sometimes stacked up in much the same manner as apples.

If you bought a dozen eggs, they were taken off the top of the stack and placed, oh so carefully into your basket or in brown paper sacks. (Ever try handling a sack of eggs?)

Much of the food was sold in bulk. Grandpa always bought twenty-five-pound sacks of flour and sugar. Many stores sold pickles from huge barrels filled with salty brine. There were also barrels of peanuts, still in the shell. Barrels of candy usually appeared a couple of weeks before Christmas, each with a scoop for dipping and a supply of brown paper bags nearby. Since we seldom had candy, Grandpa usually bought several different kinds for Christmas munching. Cheese was plentiful and came in large circles a foot and a half across and at least six inches thick. Using a long butchering knife, the clerk cut off a triangle of the wonderful yellow cheese. What a delicious flavor!

Today, we buy fresh fruits and vegetables year round. Back then there were no refrigerated trucks to bring fresh items from Florida and California to Ohio. We bought baskets of peaches and smaller wooden boxes (Grandma called them lugs) of apricots in the summer. Bushel baskets of apples were sold in the fall. About the only fresh fruit we got in winter were those apples and an occasional orange that usually showed up in the church Christmas treat. We looked forward to these fresh fruits.

Oranges came to the stores in large wooden crates that often made their way to the local farms where they were put to good use. Little girls still play with my small kitchen cupboard Grandpa made from an orange crate. Chicken nests were sometimes made from crates. Others had wheels added and became children's make-believe "cars." Most homes had at least one bookshelf made from an orange crate. Those wonderful orange crates found many uses on the farm.

As Grandma's list of groceries was being filled, the clerk placed all the items on the counter in front of us. Another clerk occasionally set some other customer's groceries on the same counter, next to ours. When we had everything we needed, the clerk added up the cost of each item on a piece of paper and told us the total. Often it was less than $5.00 for a week's groceries. When we had paid our bill, we set our grocery basket on the counter and she loaded the items into it. For those who had brought no basket, she might walk to the storeroom and get a cardboard box that said "Laurel Butter Crackers, 'The taste that tells the tale'." (The crackers came in large metal cans). Perhaps the box said "Ivory soap, ninety-nine and forty-four one hundredths percent pure."

Check books were seldom used. Grandpa paid cash! And there were no credit cards then. (I got my first credit card several years after we were married. I had gone to Lima to the big J.C. Penney department store to buy fabric to make new drapes for the living room windows. The clerk had the material cut and was ready to wrap it when I reached for my billfold to pay in cash. But alas, I had forgotten to put the extra money in. I was very embarrassed and didn't know what to do. Since the material was cut, I was obliged to take it. The clerk, hearing my plight, said, "Oh, that's no problem. Just go to the office and ask for a credit card. That will take care of it." I was opposed to buying anything on credit. My family had raised us to pay cash for everything and if you couldn't pay, then you didn't need to buy the item. But in this case, there was nothing else I could do. I got the card.)

Some families had a running charge account at the grocery store. They often sent one of the kids down to buy an item and just said, "Put it on our account," or "Put it on the books." These accounts were often way overdue and were hard to collect, making it bad for everyone involved. Our family raised as much food as possible on the farm, and never put any groceries on a running charge account. If we couldn't pay cash, we didn't buy it.

Sometimes our shopping included a stop at Forest Croft's Filling Station. In warm weather, a bottle of pop would taste good, and we walked over to the big red metal chest. Laying one half of the lid back over the other half, we searched for our favorite drink. (Grape Nehi for me, thank you!) Ice for the chest was delivered regularly and the glass pop bottles were placed on the ice. As it melted, we had to dig deeper into the icy cold water to find our favorite pop. When we found the one we wanted, we pulled the dripping bottle from the chest, pried the lid off on the opener located at the side, and laid our dime on the counter. Then enjoy!

A trip to Spencerville also meant a visit to the Croft Meat Market across the street. (I don't think our grocery store carried meats in the 1930s.) Croft Meat Market had their own slaughterhouse where the butchering was done, so fresh meat was available daily. The floor of the meat market was covered with sawdust that tickled my bare toes when I wore my summer sandals. Chickens hung from a rack above the counter. Grandpa told the storekeeper just how Grandma wanted a piece of meat cut or sliced and that is the way he cut it. If Grandma wanted a pound of bologna, a tube of the meat was brought from the refrigerated case and placed on the slicer. Turning the handle at the side, he sliced off what he thought would be about a pound. He was usually quite close. When we were ready to leave, he often gave us bones for our dog back home.

Stores didn't have handy little plastic or paper sacks then. It didn't matter if you were buying a pound of hamburger at the meat market, fifty feet of clothesline at the hardware store, or a yard of fabric at the dry goods store, it all got wrapped the same way. Stores had large rolls of strong, light brown wrapping paper that sat on the counter. (A few weeks before Christmas, the brown paper was often replaced by heavy, colored Christmas paper.) When your purchase was complete, the clerk pulled out the appropriate length of paper, lay it on the counter, put your items in the center and wrapped it up. Holding it with one hand, the clerk would reach up to a cone of white cotton string hanging above and, pulling the end down, wrap it around the package. Flipping the package over, the string was then wrapped around the other way. A knot was tied and the string was usually pulled tightly between the hands until it broke. I've even seen clerks break the string by biting it with their teeth.

Buying groceries changed drastically in 1949 with the opening of the new Pangle's Master Market in Lima. The *Lima News* of May 18 announced a new concept in grocery shopping in that new, large store with many wide aisles. Now a shopper pushed a cart through the store and made her *own* selection of food products from huge pyramids of stacked canned goods, from shelves with a wide variety of cereals and crackers, from refrigerated cases of meats, already cut and wrapped in a variety of sizes. Take your pick! Prices were 39 cents for a pound slab of bacon, 59 cents for sirloin steak, chuck roast 45 cents, pork shoulder 29 cents. Two heads of lettuce or a box of crackers were 19 cents each and laundry detergent was 25 cents for a regular size box. Another innovation was the use of uniforms for all employees. But the thing that kept everyone wondering was the newfangled "electric eye" that opened the door automatically as one approached. Real progress! People drove for miles just to shop in this unusual new store.

Shoe stores haven't changed a whole lot since I was a kid, except that you always got your shoes in a box, not a sack. Today you can buy shoes at many different kinds of stores, but in my childhood days, they were usually found only in shoe stores or perhaps the very large department stores. A great new invention appeared in the shoe store one year, an X-ray machine. The idea was to put on a pair of new shoes, then step on the X-ray machine to see how they fit. You could not only see the outline of each shoe, you could see the bones of your feet and where they were in relation to the sides and ends of the shoe. It was easy to see how much "growing room" a child had in his shoes. Kids loved buying new shoes because they could "play" on this machine while the clerk got shoes for Mom or Dad. Thank goodness, we didn't get new shoes very often. Little did we know that X-rays could in any way be harmful!

For everyday items such as gas and groceries, Grandpa usually drove to Spencerville, but for a pair of work pants or new shoes, we shopped in Wapakoneta or at Don's Shop in St. Marys. The men's new suits were usually bought from the Piehl Brothers' menswear store in Wapakoneta or from Bill the Tailor in Spencerville. Grandpa often told of buying a new suit there before going to North Carolina in 1923. At that time, when you bought a suit, they "threw in" the suspenders or belt and perhaps a hat. He was really dressed up when he put on these fancy duds, especially the spats. (They were felt or cloth items that covered the front of men's shoes. Grandpa's were gray. I don't know the original purpose for spats, perhaps to help keep the shoes cleaner. They gave a gentleman a rather dashing appearance.)

One building in which only Grandma and I shopped was the D. Armstrong Co. in St. Marys. We often got fabric there, but, more importantly, this was where Grandma usually bought her "personal items," in other words, the unmentionables that were not displayed in shop windows, in store advertisements, and on television commercials as they are today.

If Grandma and I needed coats or the men needed new overcoats, we usually went to Lima. Sometimes we also shopped in this big city for electrical appliances.

When Grandma and Grandpa finally bought an electric stove and refrigerator, they were careful to buy it closer to home. Grandpa always said you got better service from people you knew and could call by name. When I bought my first washing machine, I got it at a large store in Lima because it was priced a little cheaper. I regretted that more than once. Every time it broke or had a problem, it seemed the machine was filled with wet diapers. When I called them, I was told that the repairman would be out next Thursday. When I lamented, "But it's full of wet diapers that my baby needs now, and this is only Monday," I was told, "Sorry, the repairman comes to your area only on Thursday." Someone finally told us that Whirlpool parts were interchangeable with my machine. From then on, when something broke, I called the Spencerville Whirlpool man, and he came out within hours. When that machine finally had to be replaced, I didn't even hesitate, I called my friendly (and helpful) Whirlpool man.

Hardware stores operated a bit differently back then. It was not self-serve as most are today. Small bins lined one wall and when you needed two 3/8 inch bolts, you told the clerk. He knew just which of those many bins held that kind of bolt and just how much each bolt cost. Unlike today, you didn't have to buy a sealed package with ten bolts in it if you needed only one. Most hardware stores had a ladder that extended to the top of the bins where it hung on a track. Rollers on the bottom of the ladder rested on the floor. If the bolts you needed were near the top of the bins, the clerk grabbed that ladder and rolled it to the area. If your next item was a half-inch wood screw, he rolled the ladder over to that area. If you needed only two of each item, that is what you paid for.

Flashlight batteries often lay in a box on the counter near the cash register and cost about five cents. A shelf lined with kerosene lamps usually had lanterns hanging underneath. As electricity came into the area, more electrical lighting fixtures were displayed. Brooms, mops, shovels and spades were lined up like toy soldiers along the wall. Wicker laundry baskets and wash boards hung nearby. One corner of the store often held a display of bicycles featuring large balloon tires.

Some hardware stores had large coils of rope stored in the basement. The end of the rope was brought up into the store through a hole in the floor where the rope was then measured and cut to the desired length. Log chains came in large barrels or on heavy spools and were also unrolled and cut to the correct length.

There was usually an ample display of guns such as those a farmer might use—shotguns and rifles for hunting and butchering day with a few BB guns for the younger men of the family. The Daisy Air Rifle was the popular one. Bill also had a Crossman Pellet Gun that had to be pumped to build up enough air pressure to propel the pellet. No permits were needed to buy a gun, and farmers wouldn't think of pointing a gun at anyone unless it was an intruder who needed some encouragement to leave the farm. That seldom happened.

Don and I always looked forward to the one or two yearly shopping trips to Lima. We were always happy to see the good-sized display of toys at those large department stores. A trip to Lima also meant getting to eat at a restaurant, something we country kids seldom did. Most restaurants proudly announced their menu on a placard in the front window. We occasionally saw a man walking in front of the restaurant with a menu board across his shoulders. Home cooking was the main selling point and each establishment seemed to have one special item that was its claim to fame. Although it was not too comfortable for Grandpa and Grandma, Don and I thought it was a treat to perch atop a stool at the counter of the F.W. Woolworth five-and-ten-cent store where their plate lunch special sold for a mere pittance compared to today's prices.

Several of the large Lima stores had elevators—The Leader, J.C. Penney, Sears Roebuck, and Montgomery Ward. I always looked forward to Christmas shopping because I knew we would get to ride those elevators. Even riding an elevator was quite different than it is now. There were no automatic doors or buttons to push. Every elevator had an operator, usually a man in a special uniform who pushed down on a little handle that opened the door for you. As he approached each floor, he called out the items found on that floor: "Second floor—ladies' ready-to-wear, lingerie, millinery [hats and bonnets], linens, and bedding. Third floor—Furniture, appliances, yard goods, curtains and drapes." If you didn't know where to find an item, the elevator operator quickly and courteously told you.

The department store clerks didn't have cash registers at each counter. It was fun to watch what happened to your money. A series of belts ran across pulleys and up to the office on the top floor. If a purchase for a $2.99 billfold was made, you might hand the clerk a five-dollar bill. She then put the money, along with the paper listing your purchase, into a container that was placed into a receiving slot on the belt conveyer. She gave it a little push, it would catch the belt, and away it would go to the office upstairs. You could always hear the little clicking sound made by the splicing of the belt as it crossed each pulley. When the office had received it and made the proper change, they put the money and sales receipt into the container, gave it a shove and click, click, click—here came your change. Improvements were later made on this system, and a pneumatic tube was used.

The money was put in a little round cylinder, then inserted into the hollow tube, and "Whoosh!" It started its high speed run. After a few minutes, the little case came tearing back to the clerk's counter with the change. We were fascinated by it all.

Many of the Lima stores where we shopped were on the Public Square. The Sears Roebuck store was in the corner where the Civic Center complex is today. On the corner north of it was the Montgomery Ward store. Across the street was a bank, then a jewelry store, Rowlands furniture store, and one of our favorites for toys, Jones Hardware. Although we didn't get to go there, the Sigma Theater was in the corner. Next to it was a nut shop whose wonderful aroma could be smelled a block away. On those cold winter days, Daddy occasionally bought a small sack of warm, freshly roasted peanuts. Um, um, good!!! We seldom got to the east side of Lima's Public Square, but at least once Grandma had looked for a living room suite at the Good Housekeeping store there. They also had an Isaly's Ice Cream store in that block. (Bill said his family never went to Isaly's because his grandpa was at one time the president of the Equity Union Creamery Company. They visited the Equity Ice Cream store, not Isaly's.)

Another store we often visited was the Stippich Hardware on North Main. If you couldn't find it anywhere else, Stippich usually had it. The Leader Store was just north of the wonderfully fragrant nut shop. Daddy sometimes treated Don and I with fresh nuts. Kresge's 5 and 10 Cent Store was located in the old Faurot Opera House. Newberry's was the first building in Lima to have an escalator—very different and almost scary, but such fun for kids!

I thought shopping in Lima was "big time stuff," but after I was married, I shopped alone in Columbus for the first time and was overwhelmed by the size of the big Lazarus Department Store. We had gone to Bill's implement dealers' convention. While he attended his sessions, I decided to do some Christmas shopping. I had heard about the Lazarus Store just down from the State House, and decided I would get more done if I shopped alone instead of going with a group as some of the other ladies had done. I discovered there were not only a lot more floors of merchandise, but some of the same types of items could be found in several different areas. I finally figured out what "bargain basement" meant and that a similar shirt bought on the seventh floor was not only higher up in the building, it was also much higher up in price!

One of my most confusing things about that big department store was all the different entrances. I had walked from my hotel to the entrance, but when I had finished shopping and went back out on the street, I got a real surprise! Where had they taken my hotel? Nothing was where it should have been. I tried another door, but no luck. By this time I knew I had better ask for help and I finally got pointed in the right direction. I decided there were just too many doors in that store. I was accustomed to the small stores back home. They were much simpler—one room, one floor, and one door! Nothing complicated about that. This country girl had just better stay in the country where she belonged!

People today seem to treat shopping as a hobby or a pleasant way to pass the time, something to do when you want to get away for a day, a change of scenery. When I was a child, there were very few hours or days reserved just for shopping, so you planned ahead to make good use of your time. You didn't wear yourself out shopping . You knew you had to save a little bit of time and energy for feeding animals and doing the milking when you finally got home, sometimes after dark! No "shop till you drop" back then!

## Chapter 36.

# *Bobby, The Western Bronco*

I had been in love with horses for as long as I could remember. Anytime I got a chance to ride one, I did. I rode the *real live ponies* (not to be confused with the merry-go-round ponies) at the county fair until I was so tall my feet nearly dragged the ground. Unlike the ponies of today which are tied to a mechanism that allows them to move only in a circle, we rode these "walking ponies" freely around a circular fenced-in pathway. Dads or moms walked beside the tiny riders. As I got older, I always chose the biggest pony. Imagining myself to be a real cowgirl, I tried to get it to trot or run. Just walking seemed terribly boring! This brought on some stern looks from operators, though.

Grandpa finally bought a horse for Don and me to ride. Named Bobby, he was a real western bronco, complete with brand. I was nearly twelve years old when I first rode him to Rosemary Rothe's house for an afternoon of play. I threw his reins around a post and was showing him off by explaining his brand. As I gently touched it, he was startled and kicked out with his leg. Fortunately there was a gate between us and no one was hurt, but I never surprised him like that again.

Bobby and I had some great adventures. One day I was riding down the road when a neighbor's dog ran out of the ditch in front of us. Bobby was spooked and took off at high speed with me hanging on for dear life. He finally calmed down by the time we got home.

Several times I rode him north to Ramgas' house so I could play with Mary. On the way, we had to pass a field which had farm horses in it. I never knew for sure if I was going to get to play that day or not, because every time we came to that field, he had to look for the other horses. If Mr. Place was using them on the farm or if they were in the barn, we went on to Ramgas, but, if they were in the field, Bobby would not go another step further. He had to stop and chat with those horses. The only direction I could get him to move was toward home. No playing that day!

Once, we were riding in the woods and I was not paying a lot of attention, just gazing at the scenery and looking for squirrels or rabbits. Suddenly I realized a big log and clump of brush were right in front of us. Before I could guide Bobby around it, he took matters into his own hands (hoofs) and up we went, sailing over the whole mess. Needless to say, I was extremely surprised! Believe me, I really hung on for dear life. No one had told Grandpa that Bobby was a jumper.

Did you ever learn something from a dream? I had trouble learning to tie the special knot used to hold down the saddle. I just couldn't seem to get the hang of it. One night while I was sleeping, I saw Grandpa tying that knot over and over in my dream. The next morning I got up, put the saddle on Bobby and fastened it, just as I had seen it in my sleep.

Horses have a way of taking a big breath and filling their tummy full of air while you tighten the belly strap. Then they exhale, giving themselves more breathing room. One time I didn't get the strap quite tight enough and when Bobby exhaled, it was too loose. As I swung up into the stirrup, the weight of my body pushed the saddle down his side and under his belly. He became frightened and put on a bucking show worthy of any Wild West rodeo. I fell off on the first buck and realizing I was in danger of being stomped on, I started rolling away from him as fast as possible. Bobby was well-trained, and as soon as the reins went down he stood perfectly still. The bucking session had really surprised me and perhaps it had surprised him, too. By the time I got up, Bobby was standing quietly as though nothing had happened. Grandpa urged me to get right back on and not be afraid. Good advice!

Hitching posts had disappeared by then, but if we rode somewhere, it was never a problem to find a place to tie him. We dropped the reins, walked away, and Bobby would be in the same spot when we returned.

One of our most exciting times took place on August 13, 1942, when Grandpa rode Bobby to Spencerville to take part in the city's Centennial Parade. We didn't have a horse trailer and Grandpa rode him the five or six miles to town. As they entered South Broadway, Bobby became jittery and did not want to walk on the street because it was brick and made a strange hollow sound under his feet. Grandpa had to really coax him to move on. Bobby wore an authentic set of saddle bags Grandpa had borrowed and we had made a "Pony Express" sign for his sides. Grandpa wore Western work clothes, not fancy "dude" clothes: a cowboy hat, bandana around his neck, and a big grin on his face. What an exciting day! He and Grandpa were the hit of the parade, at least in our eyes! Don rode Bobby home in the dark that night.

Bobby had a habit that we were never able to break. Out West, he had rounded up cattle on a ranch. What a problem he had with our uneducated cows as he often tried to round them up and keep them together in the field. They didn't always want to do that, and I think at times Bobby must have been terribly frustrated with his uncooperative herd.

When the wintry winds blew and the snow came down, Bobby was kept in the barn much of the time. No one wanted to ride when it was bitter cold and nasty. By the time spring came and he was turned loose in the pasture, he was too full of energy for me to handle. Don was getting old enough that he found more excitement in driving four-wheeled vehicles than in riding a horse. Grandpa was just getting too old for such activities and casually mentioned that sometime we ought to sell Bobby. A man drove in one day and Grandpa told me to bring the horse up to the barn. I remember calling Bobby as I walked toward him, but under my breath I was yelling for him to run away so I couldn't catch him. I thought if Bobby wouldn't come to the barn, then maybe Grandpa couldn't sell him.

I was at a 4-H meeting a few weeks later when Mr. Rasneor came to pick up Bobby. They were both gone by the time I got home. As I rode my bicycle past the field, I didn't see the horse. The first thing I asked was, "Where is Bobby?" When Grandpa told me he was gone, I started to cry. I hadn't even gotten to say goodby. I burst into tears as I headed for my little twin bed. I cried through supper and for several hours afterward. Poor Grandpa! He thought it would be easier this way and he didn't know what to do with me. He finally came upstairs and sat on the edge of my bed, "Isn't there something else we can get for you that you would really like to have?" As I lay there trying to think of something, the sobs began to subside and I finally said, “Grandpa, I’d like to have a *real* bed and a *real* room of my very own.”

The little low-ceilinged bedroom above the kitchen had been used by my great-grandpa Schwartz until his death in 1933. Since we had no attic storage room, this became the substitute attic. I remember how much fun it had been to dig around in that room. It contained some fascinating items: our baby bed, Dad’s little cradle and rocking chair, Grandpa Schwartz’s trunk from Germany, boxes of pictures, an old iron bed, old suitcases and the valise which had traveled to North Carolina with Grandpa’s road building company, a huge wicker basket of old clothing which Grandma eventually tore into carpet rags for the many rugs she crocheted, and an assortment of odds and ends which have long since been forgotten. After Grandma had cleaned out this storage room, it became my bedroom. Grandpa built a little closet behind the door and purchased a new “waterfall” style bedroom suite. My memories of Bobby were stored away for happy hours of recollections, and the room that replaced him became my little heaven.

The “Pony Express Rider”
Grandpa Frank rode Bobby in the 1942 Spencerville Centennial parade.

## Chapter 37.

# Cherished Christmas Memories

Christmas wasn't ever mentioned until after Thanksgiving when I was a child. That's the way it was. That's when the stores began to put up their fancy decorations and the mailman delivered our Christmas catalog *Wish Book*. What cherished memories Christmas brings to mind!

The true meaning of Christmas was reflected in our celebration, because ours was a Christian home. We attended church and Sunday school every week, not just at Christmas. No one would think of staying home because he was tired or "stressed out." (That phrase hadn't been invented yet.) There were times, in winter and summer, when all three of our adults were "dead-dog tired" from a week of hard work. Making hay and digging ditches was extremely difficult work, and farmers didn't know the meaning of an eight-hour day. They often made hay or planted corn from sunrise till sunset, then milked and fed the animals long after dark. Even on Sunday mornings, the animals had to be fed and milked before going to church.

A special church program was usually held each Christmas, and someone from our family was most likely included. For several generations, Kossuth Church had continued the tradition of giving a small, brown paper sack of candy, the "Christmas treat," to everyone, young and old, on the Sunday morning before Christmas.

Oranges were a real luxury when my grandparents were young. With no refrigerated rail cars or trucks then, there was no easy method of transporting fresh fruit from Florida or California to Ohio in the winter, so an orange was quite a treat in Grandpa's day. Even when I was small, they were considered almost a luxury. Regardless, at the top of each of those sacks of church candy was a fresh orange or tangerine. Under it were a few nuts, gum drops, chocolate drops (that I didn't like and tried to trade away), coconut bonbons (that I loved and tried to get), peanut clusters, the colorful ribbon candy, a couple of Grandpa's favorite orange "circus peanuts," and the inevitable pieces of cheaper hard candy which had to be sucked on until they melted. If you didn't eat all of your candy in a week or so, the hard candy became so sticky that when you finally got around to eating it, it all stuck together and to the sack. It was hard to enjoy brown-paper-bag-flavored candy. Don used to get upset with me because I ate just a little of my candy each day. He chomped his down right away, then begged me to give him some of mine. I usually didn't, and he'd get unhappy with me because I wouldn't "share." Kids, huh?

It didn't take long to get ready for Christmas. A week before the big day, Grandma brought the little artificial tree down from its storage place behind Grandpa's trunk. She removed the dusty newspaper protecting it and folded down the two dozen or so wire branches which gave it a tree shape. Its short needles were green paper, and the tree stood about thirty-six inches tall. (Check these out at your neighborhood museum. I think they call them feather trees.) We didn't have live Christmas trees when I was a child, and I didn't know of many people who did, since we were recovering from the Great Depression of 1930. It would have been foolish to buy a tree and then dispose of it later. With today's full, realistic looking, long-needled trees, our little tree would appear as a pitiful sight, but those fancy trees weren't around in the 1930s and so we loved our plain little one. I always looked long and wistfully, though, at the Christmas card pictures of families driving home from the woods, horses prancing and a luxurious fir tree sticking out of the back of their sleigh, while smiling, pink-cheeked children covered with colorful quilts waved happily. It was a pleasant picture and I always wished I had been in that sleigh!

We couldn't wait to decorate our tree with its one string of lights. We also had delicate little glass balls that broke into tiny pieces if accidentally dropped or bounced against each other. We had to be extremely careful with them. A fancy glass ball with a pointed tip for the top branch was replaced sometime in the 1940s when Grandma bought a pretty angel with a clear halo that diffused the light from a bulb placed behind it. Now this was real elegance! It's getting a little worn from age now, but that angel still stands on the uppermost branch of our tree each Christmas. (Bill's family had one exactly like ours.) We also had heavy tinfoil icicles that we carefully placed on the tree. They hung down nicely, not like the plastic ones of today that seem to do a better job of clinging to you than to your tree.

Light bulbs were a real aggravation in those days. The bulbs were all wired in series, so if one bulb burned out, out went all the rest. This wasn't a big problem on our little tree, but we had talked Grandpa into buying a real live tree by the 1940s. It was usually much larger and could easily handle two or three strings of lights. That complicated things for Dad or Don, who had the frustrating job of tracing which set of lights was out and then finding which bulb was the culprit. They had to go down the string and unscrew each bulb, then screw in a replacement bulb and hope that the lights would come on. Through this process of elimination, they eventually found the guilty one–often the last bulb on the set! Real frustration came when two bulbs burned out at the same time, and the process was seemingly endless in locating not one, but two bad bulbs. Eventually, new kinds of lights were developed where only the bad bulbs went out. In the 1940s, we purchased our first set of bubble lights. As the various colored bulbs warmed up, the liquid inside formed an endless supply of moving bubbles. How fascinating to relax and watch those never ending bubbles run to the top of each bulb.

"What if Santa Claus doesn't find our tree?" I worried. It was 1936 and a week before Christmas. I was quite ill with bronchial pneumonia. As a six-year-old, I cried because I was going to have to miss my first school Christmas play. But there was something else that worried me. Would Santa Claus find our tree? Because I was sick in my bed upstairs, Grandma had moved the tree to the top of the library table across the room. When Santa came, he wouldn't know the tree had been moved upstairs from its usual place on the dining room table, and I just *knew* he wouldn't leave any gifts. I needn't have worried. The gifts were there on Christmas morning!

That was the year I *didn't* get a dog–not that I really wanted one. Doc Doughty had two very nice daughters, and he brought Ruth along several times when he made his house calls to see how I was doing. Ruth, a teenager at the time, wanted to do something nice for a sick little girl. She had two gifts for me and one of them was a bulldog puppy. I don't know what the adults had to say about it, but it was decided that I didn't need a bulldog at that time. I was far too sick to play with it, and I'm sure Grandma didn't want it under her feet as she made the endless trips from the kitchen to my room upstairs. I really don't remember being greatly disappointed though. After all, a bulldog has a face only a mother could love!

Ruth's second gift was a little package for me to open right away, even though it wasn't yet Christmas. Inside was angel hair! Is angel hair still sold? It was a gossamer thin substance that stretched to cover the entire tree with a sheer, white cobweb effect. When the tree lights were turned on, they shone through it, giving our little tree an ethereal look, as if an angel had touched it. It definitely helped brighten my otherwise cheerless Christmas. Being sick in bed is no fun, especially at a holiday. Praise the Lord that is the only Christmas I've ever spent in bed!

Don and I had our music lessons in Wapakoneta, and we always looked forward to our annual Christmas visit to the basement of Asa Crawford's shoe store after those lessons. Mr. Crawford had the largest display of electric trains we had ever seen, and his basement was open only at Christmas. People drove many miles to see his fascinating display.

He had landscaped the area with tiny trees and houses and buildings—something very unusual at that time. There were bridges and mountains and tunnels. The engines had realistically sounding whistles and even produced smoke. Some cars had sliding doors in the sides and tiny barrels that rolled out onto a platform. Others had miniature milk cans that were placed into nearby trucks. I've seen the huge toy train displays now shown at the Ohio State Fair, and they are wonderful; however, this was sixty years ago. There was nothing like it anywhere around here. I wanted to cry when Daddy said we had watched long enough and it was time to go. I think Don and I could have spent an entire day there and still would not have grown tired of watching those wonderful trains!

Regular shopping was usually done at the small J.C. Penney store in Wapak, but a family Christmas tradition was to go to the big city of Lima to the larger Penney and Montgomery Ward stores. We visited the Leader Store, but since my folks thought most of their prices were too high for the common items we purchased, we just browsed and enjoyed their elegant decorations. The Salvation Army band often played on the downtown street corners or in front of The Leader. I loved listening to their music, although it was usually too cold to stay very long. Like half-frozen saints, they stood with red cheeks and runny noses as they continued to play, even though their fingers had to be freezing. What ever happened to the Salvation Army band? We don't hear it anymore.

We often ate at a restaurant near Lima's public square where home-cooked meals were served. I especially remember the thin slices of roast beef (We had generous chunks of beef at home, not "elegant" thin slices), green beans, mashed potatoes (Real ones! Nothing was instant back then!) with real brown gravy and dressing that was so-o-o delicious! How I looked forward to eating there during our one big shopping day!

We also enjoyed eating at the Kewpee. In 1928 the Kewpee built a drive-in restaurant in downtown Lima near the J.C. Penney store. As we recently shared memories, cousin Norman related that as a youngster in the late 1920 summers, he had gone almost daily to the Deisel Wemmer cigar factory where his mother worked. She gave him ten cents, then he walked over to the Kewpee. He said the Kewpee building was just a tiny place, but it served some mighty delicious hamburgers. With his dime, Norman bought a five-cent sandwich, then walked to the theater in the Public Square where he spent the remaining nickel to watch a picture show. When the show ended, he walked back to the cigar factory and home again with his mother. The Kewpee is still in the same location, with its Kewpee doll trademark and motto "hamburg pickle on top makes your heart go flippity-flop." The food was delicious then and still is, especially my favorites, soup and sandwiches. Really good! How good? So good that when Jeffrey Tennyson wrote his book, *Hamburger Heaven: The Illustrated History of the Hamburger*, he included Kewpee's Hamburgers of Lima, Ohio, in his top ten. Now that's *good*!

The Kewpee parking lot was long and narrow, and cars parked at an angle as they entered. If you wished to eat in the restaurant, you got out and walked inside. If you wanted the food brought to you, you stopped by the door or parked the car and remained inside until a young lady came to take your order. When the food was ready, she brought it out on a tray which she fastened onto the open window on the driver's side. If it was winter, you very quickly brought that tray inside, then hoped you didn't spill anything as you hurriedly rolled up the window.

This was an exciting development—the first fast-food eatery we had seen. But even more excitement came as we were ready to leave and had to head the car out in the opposite direction. But how? The lot was too narrow to turn a car around. A circular turntable was built at the back of the lot sometime in the early 1940s, I was told. As we drove our car onto it, someone started the turntable and it revolved until we were headed out. What fun! People of northwest Ohio drove for many miles to get to Lima, just to eat at the Kewpee and experience that wonderful turntable. Eventually access to the area beyond the lot was purchased by the Kewpee. Today, cars just drive through. Rather ho-hum, wouldn't you say? But if you ask folks over forty if they remember the Kewpee turntable, you will get smiles and nods as it stirs up memories of bygone days. There was no place like it!

We usually had at least one gift to shop for in Jones Hardware in the Public Square, perhaps a pocket knife for Don or a tool for Daddy. One of the features of Jones was that they always had Santa there to talk to the kids. I've thought and thought about it, but I cannot remember ever talking to Santa or sitting on his lap. I guess we knew that the tall, skinny Santa with the saggy pillow tummy who stood on the windy corner beside the Penney store was not the same as the short, chubby Santa in Jones Hardware toy department. We easily figured out those were just Santa's helpers. I never saw the "real" Santa. After all, everybody knows he had no time to waste sitting in toy departments or standing around on street corners. He was far too busy "making his list and checking it twice!"

After a day of shopping and eating at a special restaurant, we had one more exciting tradition. We drove down West Market Street to see the pretty lights. Today, many houses have lights in windows, decorations around doors, and colored lights outlining shrubs and trees. In the 1930s, there were very few decorations anywhere except in the stores and on downtown street lights. Some very rich people living on West Market put up decorations that were really quite nice, at least for those days. (Today, we would consider them run-of-the-mill.) We eagerly looked forward to that pilgrimage to see the fancy houses and lights. That ended our glorious day. A tired little brother and sister were fast asleep by the time we reached home. Years later we enjoyed the vast array of colored lights on the buildings and towers of the Standard Oil Refinery. The hundreds of white bulbs were changed to colored ones for the holiday and everyone enjoyed their beauty.

Christmas was always exciting because of the school program. The younger children rehearsed their musical for weeks as they became toy soldiers, teddy bears, dolls from other countries and other toys that required fancy costumes. Things didn't change much, and a generation later my children were still toy soldiers, snowmen and bells.

Presenting the Biblical account of the Christmas story was left to the older, more mature kids from fourth to sixth grade, complete with angels in floppy white wings, shepherds in dads' bathrobe, and wise men with gifts of moms' pretty perfume bottles and boxes wrapped in gold paper. Teachers had to have nerves of steel as they watched the elegant gold cardboard crowns tip precariously on kings' heads while shepherds' crooks snagged ladies' hats as they herded their flocks of imaginary sheep down the auditorium aisle. All took their parts quite seriously, and I'm sure the Lord must have smiled as He watched the children portray the night of His birth.

Christmas music, much of it sacred, was presented on a different night by the junior and senior high school students involved in band and chorus.

What was the first Christmas ornament you made in school? I proudly took home an English walnut that was cracked in half and painted with silver paint, then glued together with a red ribbon in the center for hanging. We also dipped pine cones in silver paint and tied red yarn at the top. Paper chains were fashioned from strips of construction paper with the ends folded into links and glued together with smears of white library paste. Each link was held tightly between our fingers until the paste dried. When we made paper chains at home, we used homemade flour-and-water paste.

The decoration I remember best was the little foot-high tree made from spools. Several weeks before Christmas, we brought two small wooden spools and three larger ones to school. Most mothers sewed in those days, so empty spools were plentiful. Miss Marsh had someone taper a smaller spool for the top of each tree. Using crayons, we colored one small spool brown and the remainder green, then cut four strips of green crepe paper, each a little wider. Some kind mother volunteered to sew these strips on her sewing machine with heavy thread that we gently pulled to form a circle of green. The paper circles were glued between the spools with the narrow ones at the top and the small brown tree trunk spool glued to the bottom. A tiny silver star was glued to the very top. Now that was a beautiful tree, especially since *we* had made it! I kept mine for a long time, but when it got too bedraggled, it finally went into the furnace. But the happy memory lingers.

When I was old enough to give gifts to the rest of the family, I found the hardest part was not deciding what to give, or even where to find it. The difficult part was trying to wrap the gifts. Scotch tape had not been invented, or if it had, it had not yet reached Auglaize County. We had "holiday stamps," which were about the size of a postage stamp. Grandma showed me how to fold the pretty wrapping paper around a box, then hold it with one hand, pick up a stamp, lick it, press it firmly over the end of the paper and hold it tightly until it dried enough to stay. This worked rather well for boxes with shirts, trousers and longjohns. But Don and I usually gave smaller items such as socks or apron material. Since Grandpa smoked a pipe in those days, we often bought him a pouch or round tin can of tobacco. Now those were a real challenge to wrap! The stamps just didn't cooperate with odd-shaped or soft items. Sometimes I was so anxious that I *over-licked* them. There wasn't enough "goo" left to make them stick and I would have to get another stamp and try again. I just couldn't get a grip on those odd-shaped gifts long enough for the stamps to stick, so it was not unusual to find a package under the tree with one end gaping open, or a series of a half dozen stamps layered over each other, hoping at least one would stay stuck. As I wrap gifts today, I think back to those days and chuckle, then thank the Lord for sticky tape.

One childhood Christmas I never forgot was the year Grandpa told me he was going to do something really special for Grandma. “But you mustn’t tell her,” he admonished me. Grandpa’s usual gift for her would be a slip or blouse, cotton material for a new everyday dress, or a pair of nice silk hose for church (not the heavy cotton she wore for everyday). I was really excited when I heard about this wonderful, unexpected and expensive gift he had planned. How pleased I was that Grandpa shared his secret with me!

A few days later, Grandma whispered to me that she had saved her butter-and-egg money and had planned on buying a really special gift as a big surprise for Grandpa, but I mustn’t tell. Now the excitement was really high! I knew two secrets, and I had to be careful that, like many a child has done, I wouldn’t “spill the beans” and ruin the surprise for everyone. It seemed like a long time until the Big Day, but I kept the secret, and indeed, they were both quite surprised! What were those special gifts? I wish I could remember, but too many years have passed. Neither Don nor I recall them. It may have been Grandma’s gold wedding band or her string of pearls. Grandpa’s gift was either the gold ring with the blue stone or his fancy tie tack and cuff links. Whatever the gifts were, it was unusual for either of them to spend so much of their hard-earned money on each other. We’ve forgotten the gifts, but we’ll never forget the pleasure of that surprise!

One of the German traditions from Grandma’s parents was placing the little Christmas tree in the center of the table, surrounded by a dinner plate for each family member. Santa Claus filled the plate with candy and an orange or tangerine. I didn’t know any other kids who did that, and I thought we were the only ones. A generation later as I met more people from New Knoxville, I found the custom was sometimes used in that area. In fact, after finding that some of my family came from the same German village (Ladbergen) as other New Knoxville folks, I now see many similar customs. That interesting custom may have come from Germany more than a hundred fifty years ago.

As I look back, I realize that not only was our tree much different then, but the number of gifts was small compared to today’s trees with piles of gifts surrounding them. All our gifts fit around the tree with enough room left on the table for the five dinner plates. About the only things that ever sat on the floor or chair were the packages that held Don’s air rifle and the large box containing his typewriter.

It was Sunday, and the announcer’s voice burst into the radio program, “The Japanese have bombed Pearl Harbor.” The day, December 7, 1941, brought disbelief to ordinary citizens all over America. How could such a thing have happened? We had listened just a few days earlier as the friendly voice of the announcer described in detail the large, rubber balloons that made up part of the Macys’ Thanksgiving Day Parade. What fun it was to try to picture each figure in our minds. Rehearsals were in full progress for the coming Christmas programs, and we eagerly anticipated Santa’s visit and the long Christmas vacation with no school. The announcement brought fear to this eleven-year-old, and everyone was uncertain as to what lay ahead. For the next several years, Christmases were rather subdued. Many of the things that were needed in the homes were rationed or were no longer available. Household appliance factories changed over to produce items for the war. As the fighting ceased at the end of the war, America once again returned to a time of peace and prosperity, a time of reflective tranquility.

After the war, Grandma, with encouragement from us kids, always managed to convince Grandpa to buy a real Christmas tree. In those days, they weren't cut until just a couple of weeks before Christmas. When the trees were brought into the house, they were quite green and fresh and, oh, the wonderful pine aroma. The *Evening Leader* of Christmas 1946, advertised fresh Washington fir trees at the Kroger store for 99 cents for a five- to six-foot tree. A nine- to ten-foot tree was $1.99. Too expensive? A three- to four foot-tree cost only 59 cents.

It was almost Christmas when a Wittenberg college friend and I were walking down the hill in the center of the Springfield, Ohio, campus. Somewhere in the distance, church bells were playing familiar carols. I turned to the girl and said, "Aren't those Christmas carols beautiful? Which one is your favorite?" She looked at me in surprise and said, "I'm Jewish! I don't have a favorite carol!" I thought everyone listened to carols. I didn't know anything about her Jewish beliefs. I had heard carols coming from her dorm room radio just as they did from ours. Two weeks before, as we prepared for Christmas, most of us had placed a candle in our window, made paper chains to drape across our rooms, added a crepe paper wreath, or anything simple and inexpensive. We didn't have a lot of spending money, and we knew our families would be decorating properly at home. One evening we took a little tour of the rooms in our hallway, just to see how our friends had decorated. We were quite surprised when we came to this girl's room. No paper chains, no simple candle in the window, not even a homemade wreath! Oh, yes, she had decorations—a *real live tree* about four feet tall with electric lights, tinsel, shiny balls—the whole works!

On the last morning before Christmas vacation, I was the first dorm resident to awaken. (That's what early morning music lessons demanded.) The night before, each girl took her decorations down, packed her suitcase and was ready to leave after her last class of the day. As I walked to the corner near the big wastebasket, I was appalled to see that the little Christmas tree had been dumped upside down into it–lights, tinsel, balls and all. Well now, that seemed almost sacrilegious. I carefully pulled the tree from the wastebasket and stood holding it as I tried to decide what to do. A maid had been hired to sweep the halls and clean our floor's bathroom. I heard her working just around the corner.

Carrying the little tree in my hand, I rounded the corner and approached her. "Do you know someone who will not have a Christmas tree this year?" I asked. Immediately she smiled broadly and said, "Yes, ma'am. I sure do!" "Then please take this tree now and give it to them," I said. She was a very happy lady as she took the little tree from my hands. I suspect it may have ended up in her own living room to be enjoyed by her children. Anyway, some little children enjoyed a live tree that year because a girl who didn't believe in Christmas had the most elaborate decorations in the dorm.

My brother loved candy! My family used to tell the story of trying to fill him up with candy. As a little boy, they set Don in the middle of the floor and gave him a full sack of candy. They figured he would finally get his fill and would not crave it again. But that's not what happened! He ate it all, every bite–then asked for more!

There were some kinds of homemade candies that became traditional in our family. At first Grandma made them, but as we grew older, we joined the fun. A really good recipe for fudge was printed on the side of the tin Hershey's Cocoa can. The fudge had to be taken off the stove at just the right moment or it went to sugar (and even then, the flavor was wonderful). Don got especially good at making that fudge. Today's marshmallowy no-fail fudges are good, but not like his old-fashioned kind! Another favorite was the white divinity that our neighbor, Geraldine Rothe, made. I had tasted some when I was playing with Rosemary, and she gave us the recipe. When Grandma made it, she occasionally dropped in a tiny amount of red food coloring to make the divinity pink. Now it looked pretty *and* tasted good!

We seldom make divinity any more, but a new candy was added. Food samples and recipes were given at Midwest Electric's Christmas open house. I loved the peanut brittle. I hadn't made a lot of candy, so I didn't have the feel of how it should act, but I made my brittle and took it to the family Christmas dinner. It looked and smelled great! But after chewing a while, it became softer and softer and chewier and chewier until it finally stuck to the teeth, definitely not peanut *brittle!* My brother really teased me about that candy, but I wasn't about to give up. I tried it again the next year. That time I cooked it until I thought it was done, then to be sure it was done, I cooked it a little longer. It behaved beautifully, and the tradition started! I think Don usually ate about half of it as he sat close to the candy dish. He looked forward to it every year–the candy lover, remember?

One year my peanut-brittle-loving brother met his match! When Bill and I gained a foster son, Bob Ralston, I soon found we had an even more dedicated peanut brittle lover. After the death of his father, Bob had spent several years in the Xenia Soldiers' and Sailors' Home for Orphans. He never got to help make candy, or wrap gifts, or have a wonderful Christmas. About a week before the big day, I was in the kitchen making the peanut brittle when he saw the peanuts lying on the table, ready to be put in the candy. He gave me a big grin and *sneaked* a handful of those nuts, laughing at his trick as he ran out the door. I yelled, "You're not going to like those!" But he laughed out loud, knowing he had played a real joke on me by snitching some nuts, and he was enjoying it. When he took his first bite of those nuts, his face quickly sobered. He returned to the kitchen, and as he spit them into a wastebasket, he looked at me with a puzzled expression on his face. "What is wrong with those peanuts?" he asked. By then, I was the one who was laughing. "I told you that you wouldn't like them," I grinned. "They are raw. Raw nuts taste awful. They get cooked in the peanut brittle!" When the brittle was finished and had cooled enough to be broken, I called Bob in for a taste. He loved it, and if I hadn't hidden it, I doubt if the peanut brittle would have survived until Christmas. It was Don and Mary's turn to host the event, and we spent Christmas Day with them and their children. After dinner was over, the cookies and candy were set on the coffee table as usual, including the dish brimming full of peanut brittle. Reaching over occasionally, Don would grab a handful and eat it as he and Bill talked. What he didn't notice was that Bob was sitting on the other side of the dish and *he* wasn't doing much *talking*. He was too busy *eating*, making up for all those years of not having homemade candy. Suddenly Don reached for another handful and was shocked to find that the dish was empty. I'll never forget the startled look on his face as he looked at that empty dish and gasped, "It's all gone!" Yep, a candy lover had met his match!

We had just moved to the house near New Knoxville, and everyone looked forward to our first Christmas with a fireplace. The mantel was decorated, and the Christmas cards were beneath it, held in place by tiny clothespins less than an inch long. The scene portrayed the holiday mood of peace and tranquility. Picture postcard perfect!

Since I tried to do the motherly thing of getting up first and going downstairs to turn on the lights and make sure everything was ready, it was Mom who would be starting the fire in the fireplace. Now please understand that Mom knows nothing about fireplaces, but I was told, "Now, Mom, everything is ready for the fire. All you have to do is touch a lighted match to the paper to get it started." When it was burning nicely, I was to call "Merry Christmas" up the stairs, and the family would all rush down to the lighted tree and mantel and a fire blazing in the fireplace. (Just like on the Christmas cards, right?) But that wasn't quite how it went. I turned on the lights, then lit the match and started the fire burning in the fireplace. But, wait a minute! Something was wrong! Those little plastic clothespins had suddenly started spreading apart and the colorful cards were falling in all directions. This was not how it was supposed to go. Forget the picture postcard look! I needed help right now, and I yelled for it, loud and clear!

Down came Bill, Mike, Steve, Nancy and a very excited Bob, all wondering what was wrong. And then I heard someone ask, "Mom, did you open the damper?" Damper? What damper? No one said anything about opening any damper! I didn't even know what a damper was, and I surely didn't know where to find it. Fortunately panic didn't overtake anyone. In just a few seconds the damper was open, and the fire was going nicely. Only a little smoke lingered, and soon the gifts were being opened and life returned to normal. But let me assure you that no one ever forgot that holiday and that Mom no longer lights the fire in the fireplace on Christmas morning. Haven't done it since! Don't intend to!

Another memorable event took place the next year when the whole family was here for Christmas dinner: Grandpa Bernard and Minnie, Don and Mary and their family, Corinne Mitchell (Mary's mother who was like another grandma to our children), Grandma Clara Meckstroth, Bob and his girlfriend, Becky Miller, and all five of us. Mike and Bob were in Bible college and Bob asked if he could present a short devotional. He read from Matthew, the sixth chapter, "But seek ye first the kingdom of God, and his righteousness; and all these things shall be added unto you."[1] Then he told how he had *been nothing* and *had nothing* until he had asked God to save him. As soon as he had turned his life over to Jesus, everything had changed. He now had a real home and a real family who loved him, a wonderful girlfriend, and a church where he could go to worship. Of all God's creatures, Bob felt that he had been most blessed!

After dinner the gifts under the tree were given out. Each family's personal gift exchange was held in the morning at home, but this was when we exchanged gifts with the grandmas and grandpas. Bob walked over and sat on the arm of the couch beside me, then laid a small, thin package in my lap. I quickly unwrapped it. When I saw it, I was so overcome, I couldn't say anything! Huge tears spilled out of my eyes, and I just couldn't blink them back. "What is going on?" everyone wondered. My dad walked over, looked at the gift, then he, too, began to cry. Bill leaned over to look, and his eyes got moist. When I had finally regained my composure and was sufficiently recovered, I read aloud the inscription on the little plaque that was Bob's gift to us. The words were from Matthew 25 verse 35: "I was a stranger and ye took me in!"[2] There were a lot of tears that day, but they were all tears of joy!

---

[1] *The Holy Bible*, King James Translation, Matthew 6:33.

[2] *The Holy Bible*, King James Translation, Matthew 25:35.

## Chapter 38.
# *Grandpa's Park*

"Your grandpa's farm is so pretty, it looks like a park," a lady once told me. Since Grandpa had semi-retired, he delighted in using his time and energy to keep things looking nice. During the 1940s, we hosted the Aufderhaar Reunion two or three times, which was a real incentive to get everything fixed up as much as possible. He and Grandma went all-out to make things pretty.

Grandma loved working in her large flower beds. A half-moon shaped bed extended across much of the side yard. She placed a round rock garden beside a maple. Other maples and a walnut tree grew nearby. She had flowers growing around the house and a vine that climbed the trellis at the end of the porch. Roses trailed across the white fence behind the house.

Pots of flowers sat on the posts at the end of the porch steps, and a brightly colored canvas awning extended over the steps. The porch, with its glider and lawn chairs, provided a perfect spot for relaxing in the evening, that is, until the mosquitoes came.

Grandma wanted a fancy flower bed in the center of the driveway and Grandpa helped her collect stones to be used to outline it, forming a teardrop shape. It *looked* lovely, but what a pain! It became a source of agony for many people. When a car came into the driveway and stopped in front of our door, the driver had to make a big circle out around this bed when he was ready to leave.

After visiting for a while, most people seemed to forget that flower bed, and once they were in the car they could no longer see it. They often cranked the steering wheel to the right and drove directly through the flowers. Although Grandpa raised the bed higher and put larger stones on the curved end, people still forgot it. Only now, instead of driving across the flowers, they got the bottom of their car hung up on those big stones. The more they gunned the engine to get out, the tighter the car stuck. The visitor usually had to come to the house and ask for someone to rescue him. It was especially embarrassing if he happened to be a traveling salesman trying to sell Grandma something she didn't want!

Another of Grandma's special ideas was her "pergola," a wooden ornamental lattice work affair that sat around the pump. She had planted flowers and vines around this also. Grandpa always kept it nicely painted, just as he did the house, barn and outbuildings. All of them were painted white, and for many years the trim on windows and doors was a contrasting golden yellow.

Grandpa saw to it that the grass was kept mowed, either by him or one of us kids (usually Don). Since there were no power mowers at that time, this was no small job. The old reel mower had to be pushed over that large yard at least once a week. There were also no power lawn trimmers then, so the grass around the trees was trimmed by using an old sheep-shearing scissors. I got a lot of blisters from using those sheep shears.

Several times Grandpa made up a batch of whitewash to paint the lower three feet of the trees in our yard. That was frequently done in parks, fairgrounds, and fancy estates of that time. It gave just a little more special park-like look to the farm.

At least once a year Grandpa got his scythe down from its place high up on the wall of the shop (out of the children's reach). Using his whetstone, he went back and forth on that blade until it was sharp as a razor. Swinging the scythe from side to side, he mowed down the grass and weeds out behind the corncrib, henhouse and other buildings where the lawn mower could not go. The orchard was mowed with the big field mower at least once each summer. Grandma always kept the weeds out of her many flower beds, as well as the vegetable garden. All of these special features made the farm very attractive, but it took a lot of time and even more energy to keep it that way. But, yes indeed, it did make Grandpa's farm look a lot like a park!

## Chapter 39.

# *Our Types of Toys*

A little brother and sister stand in a yard, the boy holding the handlebar of a tricycle as the younger sister clasps the handle of a rocking horse. Don was five and I was two when that picture was taken, and we loved those early toys. But for such a happy occasion as picture taking, why did we look so sober? Our friendly dog, Curly, sits obediently beside us, and his expression was nearly as puzzling as ours. We weren't used to Daddy taking our pictures. (It was Depression Days, you know.)

Children of every generation have enjoyed playing with toys of some sort, but the kinds of toys have changed over the years. As little kids, we enjoyed endless hours of playing with Grandma's button box, a metal cigar box with a little latch fastener. She had many kinds of buttons–everything from simple bone buttons to elegant dress buttons with fake diamonds on them, buttons off Grandpa's longjohns and large buttons from heavy winter coats that had worn out. *All* buttons were saved when a garment wore out. You never knew when you might need one of them. They were often reused on other clothing that Grandma made, or they replaced a button that had been lost from a dress or shirt. As a child I sorted those buttons into neat little piles or used a large blunt needle to make long strings of button necklaces and bracelets. There was just no end to their uses. Big ones became cookies for dolls and small ones were pennies or dimes for imaginary shopping in make-believe stores.

Grandpa often entertained us with a piece of string tied at the ends to create a circle. Weaving this through his fingers, he formed a baby cradle and other designs. At one point in his routine, he had us hold out our hands and the string was gradually moved from his hands onto ours. I loved watching him do this over and over again. Unfortunately, I remember very little about how it was done. I recently saw a little girl quietly playing with a circle of string as she sat in a Sunday night church service. As she wove it through her fingers, my mind returned to those days when Grandpa and a circle of string kept me happy for long periods of time. How nice that there are still little girls who enjoy such a simple activity.

Did your Grandpa entertain you with "shadow pictures" on the wall? Ours still had some of the pioneer's creativity in him, and it was fun to use our imaginations trying to guess what animal he was trying to portray just by moving his hands and fingers in different ways.

One day Daddy showed us one of his favorite childhood toys. He called it a magic lantern, and he showed us how to use it. A door in the side of the little square metal lantern opened up, revealing a place to put a lighted candle. Small glass slides could be inserted in a slot in front of the candle. The picture on the slide was then projected on the wall. This lantern had been special to Dad because there were no Auglaize County "picture shows" until long after his birth. With all the modern televisions and computers, I don't think today's children develop their imaginations as previous generations did. It was quite a toy!

Baby chicks and kittens were not exactly toys, but we spent many hours playing with these soft, fluffy little farm animals. Everyone loves to watch two or three small kittens as they play together, rolling and pouncing on each other, running in circles after their tails, chasing each other, and enjoying life to the fullest. Age isn't a factor when it comes to being intrigued by the cute actions of baby farm animals. The wiggly pink piglets, the black and white calves walking unsteadily on spindly legs, cuddly puppies rolling and yipping . . . all of them are cute and irresistible.

I spent my sixth Christmas in bed with pneumonia. One of my gifts was a toy that was ideal for a sick little girl who was too weak to be up and playing. His name was Pluto the Pup. A wooden base, shaped like a bone, held a dog formed by wooden beads linked together with a string running through each bead. The strings came out under the base and had two rings for inserting the fingers. When the fingers pulled the rings tightly, Pluto stood up with head and tail erect. If one ring was left loose, the back part of the dog relaxed and sat down. With the other one loose, his front went down, and when both rings were loosened, he was allowed to lie down. Just a little tug and his head would nod, allowing his long ears to flap. He was a lot of fun, and it didn't take much energy to make him move. Just the right toy for a sick child!

Don enjoyed playing the harmonica he got one year, but when I tried it, I blew a lot of air into it with very little music coming out. There was also a Jew's harp which was fun to play, although each melody came out sounding like the same "twang, twang, twang."

Our Christmas present one year was a new red Radio Flyer coaster wagon. Until the weather was warm enough to go outside, we were occasionally allowed to play with it in the house. One night we had visitors with children about our ages and the four of us spent much of the evening pulling or pushing each other through the house in that new wagon. Suddenly the youngest child got so excited that nature took over and she nearly flooded the inside of our new wagon. I was terribly upset about that and it was quite a while before I stopped talking about the little girl who "wet her pants in my little red wagon."

Our family enjoyed games such as dominoes and checkers. Terry and the Pirates and Monopoly were also good for long winter nights.

A little puzzle that I enjoyed putting together was of cartoon characters, Jake and Lena. Remember them? A Holland windmill's long arm had caught Jake's coat and was beginning to lift him into the air. Lena stood below him, hanging onto his hand to keep him on the ground. All the local people were staring, and as a result one man had upset his cart loaded with apples, another had knocked down a lady as he rode his bicycle, and so on. There was a piece missing, (I think it was Jake's head), so we never got to see the whole puzzle.

Kite flying was one of the first spring and summer activities that took place. Grandpa taught Don and me how to make kites from the colorful Sunday funnies glued together with flour and water paste. Grandpa came up with two narrow strips of wood while Grandma provided the tails torn from old rags. A long piece of fishing line completed the kite. Don could usually get his kite to soar high into the sky, but mine seemed to be afraid of heights. I remember lots of running to get the kite up but not much satisfaction of keeping it there. I guess some people were just meant to be "high flyers," but not me!

Other outdoor activities included riding our little tricycle. As we grew older, that was replaced with bicycles. By the time I was allowed to ride on it, the stone road in front of our house had been tarred, and I often peddled over to Rosemary's house for an afternoon's play. That was hard riding because her road was still gravel. It was even harder for Don to ride up to see his friends, the Rapp twins, Jim and Joe. Not only was their road stone, much of it was uphill.

Don's little electric train was one of our most enjoyable toys. He was usually at the controls as it chugged around the track. It was always exciting when we turned out the lights and watched the train speed through the dark room with its headlights bravely lighting the track a foot or so ahead.

Models were popular items for boys. Don really enjoyed cutting out those little balsa wood airplanes with a sharp razor blade, then gluing them together with that smelly model airplane glue! He had quite an assortment.

One toy that I didn't care for was Don's favorite, his BB gun. Grandpa and Dad taught him the proper use of a gun, and although it was a "toy," it served a very useful purpose—keeping the sparrow and pigeon population under control in the hen house and barn. They were such a nuisance on the farm. They were dirty and left their droppings in the hay and on the machinery. They also ate a lot of the chicken and hog feed. I remember many nights when we went into the darkened barn or the hen house. While I held the flashlight, he shot those dirty birds. Our cats had a feast on those nights! Eventually he got a rifle and we had fresh meat more often–rabbit, pheasant, and squirrel.

I loved playing with doll babies and paper dolls. We took them to school and the girls played together. Coloring books were passed around to one's friends, and each colored a picture and signed her name. I still have nearly all my paper dolls and coloring books. I enjoy looking at them occasionally as I remember the names of my childhood friends. While the boys at school played softball and marbles, the girls played "jacks," jumped rope, and played hopscotch.

When I received a tea set for Christmas one year, Grandpa made a little cupboard to hold it. He added legs and doors to an orange crate, then nailed a smaller, more shallow apricot crate on top. He nailed a shelf in the middle of it, then screwed cup hooks under the open shelf and gave everything a coat of white paint. It was a wonderful play cupboard. Since it was quite sturdy, I later spruced it up for my daughter, Nancy, to play with and then a generation later for her little girl, Heather. A lot of happy hours were spent by three generations of little girls who enjoyed playing with Grandpa's homemade toy.

A weaving set was my gift one year and I proudly displayed a complete set of yarn rugs that I had made for my doll house. Grandma also received a lot of potholders made on that little weaving set.

Reading books has always been one of my favorite activities. One of the first real books I read was one called *Real Live Dolls* or *Dolls That Came to Life* or some such name. It was on the bookshelf in my second grade classroom, and I enjoyed it so much that I read it over and over and over. When I was in junior high school and was allowed to go to the regular school library that was located in one corner of the large study hall, I learned as much as I could about its workings. I went home and set up our *library,* consisting of three little shelves of books. Unfortunately, no one in the family seemed very interested in using my library to *take out* the books. Oh, well! By the time I graduated, I had spent many hours working in that small school library. I was an ambitious reader and enjoyed most of its books.

As a teenager Don acquired a windup Victrola, so we had instant music at our house. The tall cabinet model had doors below the mechanism that opened to reveal a shelf for storing the large round records. I wound that Victrola up and played the gospel song, "Wonderful Words of Life" over and over until I had written down all the words and could sing along with it. I loved hearing the voice of the great tenor soloist, Enrico Caruso. I don't remember what he sang, but I've never forgotten that marvelous tenor voice. Since the Victrola was a hand wound model, we often giggled at the sound of the voices as they reached their peak of performance, only to have the mechanism slowly begin to unwind. The voices got slower and slower and lower and lower until the singing finally stopped. As we cranked the handle on the side of the Victrola, the low gruff voice slowly speeded up until it was once again a high tenor. Today's stereos can't perform that wondrous feat!

It doesn't take fancy toys to keep a child amused. Grandma had rolled a hoop down a hill and Grandpa had bounced a stick off a picket fence. Dad watched a magic lantern that projected pictures on a wall. They were all happy children, as happy as we were with our paper dolls and homemade kites. My children enjoyed more sophisticated toys, but my grandchildren's toys have entered the electronic era. Grandpa would be lost in this world of computers, and imagine, if you will, the look on Grandma's face if she were to compare her simple cornhusk doll with my granddaughter's Barbie.

In 1932, Don and I posed with our dog, Curly, and our tricycle and rocking horse.

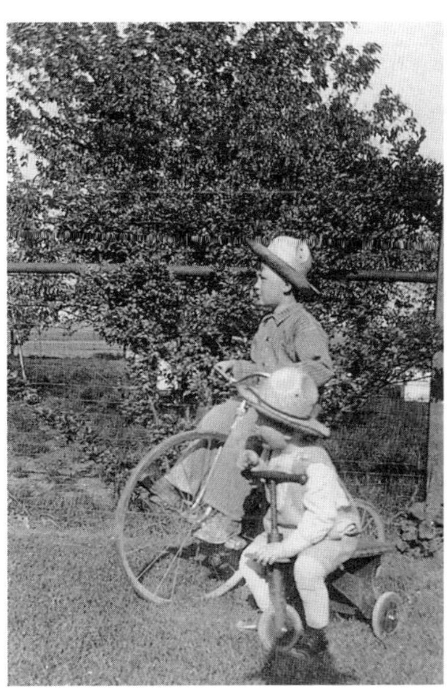

In 1927, Bill posed on his "kiddie car" as big brother, Vernon, sat on the tricycle.

## Chapter 40.

# Uncle Louie and the Horseless Carriage

The first automobile to travel New Knoxville's streets, according to family tradition, was made in 1901 by Bill's Uncle Louie Meckstroth, better known as "Meck." He liked to tinker in his bicycle shop. Neighborhood pals came over one day for a picture-taking session. His brother William (Bill's dad) brought his camera and snapped each man as he posed on one of the motorcycles that Louie also sold. This young man from a farm south of town was interested in new developments, especially vehicles on wheels. Automobiles became the hottest items on the market. Meck eagerly bought a Model T demonstrator and was Johnny-on-the-spot with New Knoxville's first car agency, selling Ford and Reo cars. Among William's glass negatives, we found a picture of Uncle Louie holding the steering wheel of a 1912 Reo with his wife Amanda, sitting proudly beside him. To avoid any form of partiality, there is also a photo of Aunt Mandy at the wheel as Louis sits beside her.

Aunt Mandy looked quite comfortable at the wheel, and her son-in-law, Alfred Henschen, told me that although she had driven a Model T Ford, she didn't do it much after her children were grown. Remember that those early cars had to be cranked to start them, and many women didn't care for that kind of action. They left the driving to the men, although a few sturdy and adventurous younger ladies took the challenge and learned to change tires, fill the tank with gas and add oil.

Uncle Louie must certainly have had some interesting stories to tell in those early automobile days. While browsing through old Auglaize County newspapers (The *Wapakoneta Daily News,* the *Auglaize County Democrat*, and the *Auglaize County Republican*), I found several items about Louie and his cars. This appeared in the January 19, 1911, *Republican*, New Knoxville item: "L.H. Meckstroth intends to put up a two-story garage next summer. Mr. Meckstroth recently returned from Detroit with a 'Ford' machine which he will use as a demonstrating car, he having secured the agency for the Fords—the car for the money."

A few months later, on June 1, 1911, the same paper had this St. Marys R.#3 column: "Ed Katterhenry, Ed Thielk, George C. Thielk and William H. Henschen each purchased a 'Ford' Model T, 1911 automobile from that enterprising business man, L.H. Meckstroth of New Knoxville. This makes seven auto cars that the above named gentleman has sold to local farmers this spring. He does not wait for opportunities but creates them."

Uncle Louie was still quite busy three years later when the April 30, 1914, *Republican* reported: "L.H. Meckstroth, proprictor of a garage and local salesman for the Ford automobile at New Knoxville, has sold nine machines already this season, the purchasers being Dr. William Deerhake, Herman Fledderjohann, Benjamin Henschen, Fred

Schroelucke, Herman Eschmeyer, George Bierbaum, G.R. Wilson, H.W. Hoelscher and Adolph Henschen." (Another headline announced the news that New Knoxville was to get a Sanitary Drinking Fountain.)

This February 22, 1917, *Republican* item was interesting: "Lost–a Ford automobile crank, somewhere in Auglaize County by Charles Bielefeld. Finder will please return to owner and receive reward." Since Mr. Bielefeld was from New Knoxville, this was no doubt one of the Meckstroth Fords. I wonder if he ever found his crank.

And how about this April 5 item from the same year's *Republican*? "Last Saturday was red letter day for the Meck garage. Mr. Meckstroth and his force of workmen delivered 21 Ford cars that day." After reading about Uncle Louie's success that day, I wasn't surprised by an item a few weeks later on May 24: "L.H. Meckstroth, the *'Ford'* man, spent a few days at Columbus last week, trying to scare up some cars. He sells them faster than the company can supply him."

By August 30, this appeared: "Mr. L.H. Meckstroth, the *'Ford Man'*, informed us that he had received a telegram that as early as September he would again be able to secure Ford cars and wishes to announce to the public that he then will be in position to make prompt deliveries. Hence there is no need for hesitating to buy if anyone is in the market for a car."

Uncle Louie's name appeared regularly in newspaper columns for several years. Although he was known for all the new cars he sold, he also did repairs when needed. Most early cars were fashioned with hoods which raised up from the side and folded flat across the top of the engine, making the motor easily accessible. Fenders were quite large then and spare tires were fastened across the back of the trunk or along the side of the engine. Large bumpers protruded from the front and rear. A tool box was vital for any travel, since repair garages and gas stations were few and far between.

This automobile accident was reported on October 4, 1917: "On last Thursday, L.H. Meck, the Ford man, received a call to tug in an automobile. The machine in some unexplainable manner run into Mr. Ervin Stienecker's log wagon in a head on collision. The log wagon is none the worse, but the auto had the wind-shield broken, and the entire front running gear severed from the machine." Animals were afraid of the newfangled vehicles, and folks were often hurt or killed by runaways. It was sometimes necessary for a driver to stop his car when meeting a team of horses. The team was then led past the machine before the engine could be restarted.

Uncle Louis Meckstroth died in 1933, at the age of fifty-five. Aunt Mandy kept the car agency for many years with the help of a manager. The Meckstroth Ford Agency eventually ended, and the garage was sold to Jim Lageman.

Bill's Aunt Alwina said her grandpa, William H. Henschen, was one of the first men around New Knoxville to buy a car. Alwina was three years old and scared to death of that thing. When she was eight or nine years old, the Henschens came for a visit. As the adults spent the afternoon talking inside the house, their sons "showed off" for the benefit of the older girls by driving the car around the barnyard. Alwina was especially frightened by their recklessness and kept her distance on the front porch. Typical kids, I guess.

With the coming of the automobile, New Knoxville's methods of courting changed drastically. Now the young men had to keep their minds on driving. Courting couples had previously held each other's undivided attention, since the horse could be pointed in the right direction and would go home. Bill remembers the story of one gentleman who told his mare to head for the barn, then he reached under the buggy seat and brought out his hymnal. He and his girl sang hymns all the way home.

Bill's grandpa, Fred Wierwille, bought his first automobile the year Alwina was ten years old. While most New Knoxville folks bought Fords and Chevrolets, Fred purchased a larger car, a 1918 Dodge touring car with isinglass windows and an "armstrong" windshield wiper. If you wanted to wipe the rain off the windshield, you grabbed a handle and moved your arm, forcing the wipers to push aside the rain or snow. The car was large with ample space for him, his wife and six children. A neighboring farmer soon outdid him though. Eileen Wessel's Grandpa Haberkamp bought a larger car—a big Buick!

Alwina said there was no antifreeze when her dad bought that first car so he used alcohol to keep it from freezing. In the cold winter weather, he drove the car to church, then drained the alcohol and took it to the nearby home of his half-sister, Mary Cook, where it stayed warm until church was out. Then he put it back in the car and drove home.

Most of the time, Fred didn't use the car in the coldest winter weather. The battery was removed until spring. Since many of the roads were just mud, he used the horse and two-seater surrey to transport his family. They had to stay covered up with lap robes when they rode in the open surrey or the buggy. Eventually he got a single-seat "Cozy Cab" that was closed in with the reins running out from under the front windshield to the horse. Alwina said they thought they really had it good with that cab because it allowed very little cold air to blow inside.

When her dad no longer used that cab, he parked it beside one of the sheds. One day, a neighbor's relative came over and asked if he could buy it. Although it was old, it was better than the one he was driving. Alwina's dad knew the man was rather poor, so he just gave it to him. This man was later killed as he rode to church on his bicycle–run down by a car.

A real treat when Bill was a kid was to have Grandpa drive the car up to Detjen's store in Moulton and bring back a *brick* of ice cream. This box of ice cream was opened and cut into slices so that each member of the family could have one to eat. It was especially good after a day of making hay or other hot, dusty jobs. In the days of horses only, the ice cream would have been melted before they could get it home, so the car served as a necessary tool for that cool treat.

That reminds me of an August 27, 1896, item in the *Republican*: "W.H. Snethkamp of near St. Marys has in his possession the first letter received at the New Knoxville post office nearly half a century ago. He has the distinction also of being the first to introduce ice cream in the village. It was forty years ago last July when ice cream was made for the first time in New Knoxville and Mr. Snethkamp says the people did not know whether it was hot or cold and refused to eat it." Imagine that! Not wanting to eat ice cream!

With the advent of cars, more and better roads were needed. At the beginning of automobile travel, there were no road maps. When seeking directions to someone's farm, my grandpa explained the process. It might have sounded something like this, "Go straight ahead until you reach the fork in the road, veer left until you see a cemetery on the right, turn left there and continue until you come to a large elm tree in the corner of a big field, turn right past the brick house and the farmer you want lives back the lane just beyond the next creek." These directions may have gotten *you* there, but your cousin who lived three states away and recently purchased one of those newfangled horseless carriages might have had a little trouble, especially if someone had just cut down that big elm tree. It was obvious a better system was needed, and the answer came in the form of a road numbering system. This seemed to work well, and eventually road maps made their way into almost every filling station across the country. Of course, they were free and usually contained advertisements of the gasoline products used at that particular station. Our trip out west in 1937 was made easier by those filling station road maps.

For folks living along large rivers such as the Ohio, increased traffic brought the need for large bridges on which to cross the water. Many had slow-moving ferries that couldn't keep up with the increased traffic. A September 10, 1927, *Wapakoneta Daily News* story announced the building of just such a bridge across the Ohio River, the Gallipolis-Point Pleasant vehicular bridge whose cost would be $1,000,000. The steel superstructure was to be done early the next spring, and it was hoped the bridge would be open for traffic by August 1, 1928. The new bridge was to be the very first to be painted with silvery aluminum paint, thus giving it the well-known name of the *Silver Bridge*. A couple of decades or so ago, this *Silver Bridge* suddenly buckled and dropped into the waters of the Ohio River, killing several people who happened to be traveling across it at that time.

In this part of Ohio, we were fortunate to be near two major highways. The Lincoln Highway (U.S.30) north of Lima was a major east-west road across the northern states. Known as the Dixie Highway when I was a child, U.S. Route 25 extended from Michigan down south to the heart of Dixie. The *Wapakoneta Daily News* mentioned in 1930 that the Dixie Highway was to be widened from eighteen feet to thirty feet from Wapak to Cridersville. I am amazed as I think of all that traffic going through the center of downtown Wapakoneta. I remember quite well the big trucks having to make the square corner next to the clock in front of Hartman's Jewelry store. I was almost afraid of that corner because of the traffic and noise as those monstrous vehicles shifted gears, occasionally blowing their air horns to let approaching cars know they needed to make more room for the trucks to turn the square corner.

I wish I had a picture of my grandpa's earliest car. We don't know the model, but it was tiller-steered with a one-cylinder gasoline engine whose sound was "chug, chug, pop, chug, chug, pop." We have snapshots of a few of the family's early vehicles, and it is quite obvious that Dad was a very proud automobile owner as he posed in his Sunday-best beside his shiny new 1923 Model T Ford. A year later, he stands beside the same car, its shine now dust-covered as it pulls a trailer load of corn fodder to the front door of the barn. Grandpa peers down from the top of the load as a skiff of snow on the ground warns that it is time to get the fodder into the barn before real winter weather sets in. Dad labeled the picture "Ford Farming."

There are also pictures of a Four-Ninety Chevrolet and a Chevrolet Baby Grand Touring Sedan with Grandma and Grandpa dressed in their best, suitcase on the running board and the brown leather valise in Grandpa's hand, ready to travel to North Carolina with his road-building company. In another photo, they are seated in a closed-in car with disc wheels and a back seat that's filled with boxes and luggage. The valise rests on top of the pile and Grandma's open door shows her brown fur coat that I remember from my childhood. Was she wiping her nose because of a winter cold or was this a tearful farewell as they returned to North Carolina?

Dad owned a 1928 Pontiac when I was a child. I don't remember what Grandpa drove to church and town, but I vividly recall the 1927 Pontiac Coupe he used on the farm—the Old Hoopie. Dad's "honeymoon car" had also been a coupe (a two-door car with one seat providing space for two or three persons.) I also heard the men of my family speak of a Dodge and an Olds.

One of my early memories was of a car that Grandpa sometimes called a "high-water buggy." Early cars were built much higher up than today's models. We had gone to a Schwartz family reunion in the grove at Uncle Henry's farm north of Spencerville. The car belonged to Dad's cousins, Lois and Carl Seewer. At the age of three I didn't know much about cars, but this car seemed to be *way up high.* The Seewer's son, Junior, was recovering from something contagious, possibly measles, and he wasn't allowed to come out of the car to play with the rest of us. I felt sorry for him and I stood beside the car, looking way up at him, talking to him, but not daring to get too close for fear of getting whatever it was he had! It must have been a miserable day for him.

Although I "drove" the Old Hoopie from Grandpa's lap, the first cars I drove on the road were Dad's 1938 Plymouth and Don's 1940 Studebaker Champion Coupe that had been his graduation gift. My favorite cars were Grandpa's 1937 Nash that we drove to Oklahoma, and the 1948 Nash that took me to college and back many times.

Traveling was often hazardous in the early days of the "horseless carriage," making it obvious that there was a need for new laws for driving. On Friday, September 9, 1927, the *Wapakoneta Daily News* reported that Sam Foos had arrested a lady from Sandusky for not dimming her lights. She was "broke" and didn't have the money to pay the fine. Officials discovered that she, along with her mother and two small children, had spent the night in the women's restroom at the city building. She had only sixty cents and said she had spent her money paying the fine; however, Mr. Foos said he had told her she could mail the money to him when she got home.

It might be of interest to know that this restroom in the city building was still quite new. A July 28 front page story stated: "Comfort Station For Women Now Near Completion." They stressed the need for a donation of a three- to four-foot square mirror of good quality. The main lounge had already been provided a settee by the Chamber of Commerce, and colored curtains had been hung at the windows. Linoleum covered the floors, and the walls were painted blue and pink with electric lights installed inside and out. Ample toilet facilities were located in an adjoining room, and there were "signs erected outside to designate the place to the traveling public and strangers." I don't know if the facilities were there when I was a child. If nature called while we were in town, we usually headed for the ladies' room at the courthouse.

"High Way Deputy Sam Foos" was again mentioned in an August 17, 1927, article when he arrested a man named Geesling, a race horse owner who had not dimmed his lights on the St. Johns highway two miles east of town. "After sounding his whistle over a half-mile stretch of road and shouting to Geesling to halt, Officer Foos put a .38 caliber hole through one of Geesling's rear tires." After repairing the tire, they drove back to town for his punishment. "His failure to stop on the road, his attitude in court and the fact that his automobile smelled of liquor was responsible for the extra assessment by the court." They had "thrown the book at him," so to speak. For the first time ever, they gave Mr. Geesling the maximum fine, $25 and costs. Sounds like a Keystone Cops movie!

Automobiles provided a more rapid means of escape after committing a crime, and now began to play an important part in the life of Auglaize County criminals. A *Wapakoneta Daily News* headline of August 7, 1927, stated: "Post Office At New Knoxville Blown By Yeggs." "Yeggs" was a slang word used to describe a safecracker or burglar. Someone had driven into town in the middle of the night and used nitroglycerin to try to break into the post office safe. They blew off the safe's handle, but were unable to steal its money. Only three or four dollars in change and some stamps were stolen from the office. A neighbor said he had heard some noise, but since those old cars often backfired, he thought it was just the usual night time sounds.

A week later, the paper stated that Mrs. Doris Rice King, a beautiful nineteen-year-old artist and model had gotten her "comeuppance." She was arrested and found to be the wife of a safecracker incarcerated in the Michigan State Prison. She was now being housed in the Auglaize County jail. "Mrs. King is believed to be the driver of the automobile used by a gang of burglars who last week blew the safe in the New Knoxville post office but failed to obtain its contents." She was very curious as to how they had found her, but the sheriff would not divulge that information.

Since a method of keeping track of all the automobiles was needed, a law requiring license plates was passed. When I was young, each little community had its own form of identification. If you saw cars with numbers such as XL121 or XL476 on a license plate, you knew they were from one town. If the letters were XC or DL, they were from another. It was a matter of community pride, since the same letters were used year after year. What fun it was to be a hundred miles or more from home and recognize the numbers on a car. For instance, stories were shared from those who had walked through the parking lot at the Grand Canyon and had seen a car with plates from back home. Right then and there, they stopped to get acquainted and were soon talking like old friends. When the method of issuing plates was changed to randomly scattered letters, a lot of folks were unhappy. That sense of community pride and camaraderie was gone!

When I was a child, folks often left their chickens roam the farm. Occasionally one got on the highway where it was hit by a passing automobile. Pigs sometimes rooted under fences and escaped to freedom, only to be struck by a car. Even the family dog sometimes suffered the same fate. Motorists who hit an animal in our area usually went back to the farmer's house and told someone of the tragedy. I recall a few times when Dad or Grandpa went to the door to inform a family of such an accident and to offer apologies. This gave the farmer a chance to dispose of the animal properly.

When did folks stop waving? If we met another car, the men waved. If a car passed by our house, the driver waved at anyone standing outside. Folks waved when they drove through town. When did this friendly gesture cease?

When thinking of early road hazards, we usually think of mud and rainy seasons, but dry days also brought problems. You have no doubt seen pictures of the well-dressed automobile driver with his close-fitting hat, gloves, goggles and a light-colored duster that covered almost every inch of the man and his clothing. After reading an *Auglaize County Republican* item from July 24, 1890, I can certainly understand the need for such attire. "Logan Township News–The roads are almost impassable owing to the dust which is only three or four inches in depth." That's a lot of dust, don't you think? Cough! Cough!

Bill's Uncle Louis and Aunt Amanda Meckstroth
proudly show off their new 1912 Reo. He owned the dealership.

## Chapter 41.

# The Little Country Church

A child's face peeked through the center of a circle surrounded by petals of crepe paper which formed a human sunflower. My costume was typical of those worn for Children's Day programs in the mid-1930s. I knew my "piece," a short poem about being one of God's little flowers. My friends were roses, zinnias and other assorted flowers in similar headpieces. I loved being a little flower, saying my verse and wearing my prettiest dress. I just couldn't understand why the bigger boys weren't as thrilled as I was with Children's Day programs! (Needless to say, it is now quite obvious!) Several days were spent at church as we practiced for the big day.

The Kossuth Zion Methodist Episcopal Church was located beside the canal in the little village of Kossuth. Since this was a special day, Daddy allowed me to wear my mother's too-big diamond ring which he wrapped with string for a better fit. Grandma also tried to fix my hair up "special." After heating the crimping iron in the coals of the cookstove, she wet her finger in her mouth and quickly touched the metal to see if it was hot enough. If it was too hot, it could burn my head if she accidentally touched it. When it was just right, she picked up a few strands of my straight hair and held the crimper there until the heat had secured the wave. Although I dreaded the procedure, I was thrilled with the results which greatly improved my appearance, (or so I thought). Instead of my usually straight hair, I now had beautiful wavy ridges. Since roses were usually in bloom, I looked forward to having one pinned in my waves. It was indeed a most wonderful night for little girls!

My first Sunday school teacher was Katherine Zuber. Grandpa's old trunk still holds a valentine that I received from her in 1933 when I was three years old. It's not in the best of shape since I had absentmindedly chewed one corner. I don't remember much about those days, but I still know the first song she taught us. No, not "Jesus Loves Me!" It was "I'll Be a Sunbeam." "Jesus wants me for a sunbeam. I'll be a sunbeam for Him!"

Since candy was rather scarce, we eagerly awaited the Christmas Sunday school treat each year. I would guess this tradition came with the merger of the German Zion Church and the Kossuth Methodist Episcopal Church. Regardless of age, everyone received a brown paper sack of candy at the close of the service. I don't know who looked forward to that Christmas treat the most, my sweet-toothed Grandpa or me!

One man stands out in my earliest memories of church—J.W. Hoverman. (His name was Justice, but in German the J sounds like a long U, so he was usually called Ust Hoverman.) He was the church treasurer. As the money was collected from each class, it was counted into a little wicker basket. The classes came together at the close of the service and the secretary's report was read: how many had attended and how much had been in the offering that day. The secretary then took that little basket down the side aisle to Mr. Hoverman. He always sat in the same pew, and as she approached, he stood up and pulled open the side pocket on his suit coat as she dumped in the money. He took it home and as the preacher's salary needed to be paid, or more coal bought, or whatever the need, he paid the bill. Most men at that time had only one suit and since he held the office for so many years, I often wondered if the lining of his pocket wasn't getting a little thin and might tear someday, allowing all that money to pour out on the floor. It never did!

A lot of activities took place in that small church. One year we learned all the books of the Bible. Stored somewhere in the bottom of Grandpa's trunk was a ribbon with many colors and shapes of construction paper and on each was printed a Bible verse I had memorized. Other (less spiritual) activities included potty breaks for the children. These were a lot more frequent during summer sermons than winter ones. The reason? Because the bathroom was a two-seater outhouse located on the canal bank near the church. It was just too cold in the winter, but summer excursions broke the monotony of long-winded sermons that little ones didn't understand anyway.

The church windows were opened on the hot summer Sunday mornings, but we were too short to look out the window while sitting down. We had other methods of entertainment, though. We used the funeral home promotional fans to keep ourselves cool and occupied. We especially liked the kind with three cardboard "blades," joined together at the bottom. There were other kinds, but these were the most fun because they could be folded into one narrow piece, then flipped open to again form a full fan. If the sermon became too boring for us children, we could playfully fan each other or spend the time opening and closing the fans. But shhhh! Don't tell the preacher!

Other activities included skipping stones across the canal after church, buying penny candy at Earl Hoverman's store across the street, church ice cream socials, harvest suppers, class parties and homecomings when former members and preachers came back to visit. I especially remember the year when Rev. Herrier and his family returned. He was my first minister, and I had a good time that day playing with his daughter who was about my age. A man named Versteeg was the first District Superintendent I remember. His German accent was so thick that most of the congregation couldn't understand him. This wouldn't have been a problem for those who formed the original church!

In the 1830s a circuit riding preacher from Sidney came through the Kossuth area where early settlers were of German and English descent. He made stops in seven communities: Kossuth, New Knoxville, Spencerville, Sidney, Piqua, Greenville, and St. Johns. In 1870 the Kossuth Methodist Episcopal Church building was dedicated, and for seven years it was used jointly by both the English and the German congregations. In 1877, the German congregation decided to build their own church. The German Zion Church was built a mile east of Kossuth, where it continued for fifty years. When both buildings began to need major repairs, leaders met in 1927 with the hopes of uniting the two congregations and building a new church. By this time the German Zion members could speak English, so this seemed to be the time to merge. Incorporation papers for the Kossuth-Zion Methodist Episcopal Church were drawn up and signed by leaders of both churches. A dedication day bulletin included familiar names from the Kossuth area: Rothe, Eisley, Hoverman, Bowers, Graessle, Reed, Carnes, DeLong, and Whetstone.

The last service in the German church was held on June 5, 1927, when Rev. F.W.

Mueller, D.D., of Philadelphia, delivered a very inspiring message. His father had dedicated the church fifty years earlier. Shortly after this, the Zion building was dismantled and moved to the new location where parts were used in the construction of the new church. The curved ceiling of the new sanctuary was taken directly from the German Zion church. On Armistice Day, November 11, 1928, the new church was dedicated.[1]

Clarence Zimmerman remembered the day quite well, although he was just a little boy. With Ben Eisley in the lead, followed by the little children, then the adults, the members marched from the old church to the new one. (The original church building sat across from Sandkuhl Tile and was later used as the Salem Grange Hall until the organization disbanded. Sadly for the old-timers, this building was recently torn down.)

A year or so after its dedication, the area around the new church was landscaped. The new plantings were dedicated to the memory of my mother who had just died.

One of the most memorable activities of the church ladies involved operating the dining hall at the Auglaize County Fair. When the new church was built, the ladies chose the basement as their project. They would pay for its entire cost by serving church suppers and dinners for area farm sales. When the possibility of serving meals at the county fair dining hall was made known, they decided to try it.

A group from Cridersville had operated the hall for a few years. A 1927 *Wapakoneta Daily News* states that meal tickets cost fifty cents and they hoped to serve 1,500 persons. It said they had been quite successful at their first attempt the year before. Kossuth must have secured permission to operate it a few years later. Serving meals at the dining hall throughout fair week provided the main source of money for those ambitious ladies to not only pay off the cost of the basement, but also to eventually finish paying off the entire mortgage on the new church.

Ladies arrived early in the morning to fry the bacon, sausage and eggs for breakfast. The hall would be filled with farmers who had come to tend their display animals, with carnival and ride people who were delighted to get a home-cooked meal, and with fair board members who needed a good breakfast before the start of the day's activities. When breakfast was over and the dishes were washed, more ladies arrived with homemade pies, cakes and huge pans of homegrown vegetables and meat. Many of the breakfast crowd returned at noon, along with others wanting a good dinner.

The church-cooked dinners were usually excellent with huge bowls of vegetable or noodle soup, chicken sandwiches, or a plate lunch of delicious fried chicken or meat loaf with mashed potatoes and gravy, green beans, slaw, and those wonderful homemade pies or cakes. The evening meal was similar, and equally delicious.

As small children, we stayed in a little room in the corner of the hall where a table and daybed had been set up. I remember more than one nap on that daybed. When we were a little older, Rosemary Rothe and I went out to see the fair. Occasionally we had saved some money or begged some from our folks so we could enjoy a ride or ring a cane. How we loved showing off the little glass vases or colored dishes we had won. I took mine home and packed them away in Grandpa's trunk for my future home.

Serving these meals at the dining hall each year was a gigantic task with everyone from the church helping when they could. Those who couldn't be on their feet for long hours remained at home and baked several pies a day, or they peeled potatoes for hours on end. There were no mixes or instant anything at that time, so everything was made from scratch. That is why it was so good! Retired men like Grandpa often helped during the day, while others came for supper and the dishwashing that followed. I don't know when the ladies stopped operating the dining hall, possibly in the 1940s. If you ask me, though, there haven't been such delicious home-cooked meals on the fairgrounds since then!

The Ladies Aid from the church was quite an active group. Besides all the work they did to help maintain the building and support the mission work of the church, they also had a wonderful time of fellowship as they worked together. The December 17, 1925, issue of the Spencerville *Journal-News* had the following: "The Ladies Aid of the Kossuth M.E. Church closed the contest at the December meeting on the 'Friendship Quilt'." I wondered if the winners were the ladies who finished their part of the quilt first, sewed the most squares, or sewed the neatest stitches? I have no idea, but the defeated side was "to banquet" the winning side. The losers were Mrs. Ross Bowers, Mrs. J.W. Rothe, Mrs. Harmon Wright, Mrs. P. [Peter] Leffel, Mrs. Clarence Whetstone, Mrs. Sam Graessle, Mrs. Dan Sawmiller, and Mrs. L.A. Reed. Winners included Mrs. Jacob Leffel, Mrs. Clarence Leffel, Mrs. Herman Rothe, Mrs. A.T. Haller, Mrs. A. [Al] Carnes, Mrs. D.B. Graessle, Mrs. Floyd Jacobs, Mrs. F.H. Davenport and Mrs. B.H. DeLong. (Mrs. Davenport was my grandmother and the initials should have been H.F. Since Grandpa went by the name Frank, people assumed his name was Franklin Henry instead of Henry Franklin.)

The banquet, held at the country home of Mrs. J.W. Rothe, featured a four-course meal. The first course consisted of "chopped cabbage and one cracker upon which a small lighted candle was placed." After many jokes and much laughter, the ladies went to the dining room where the real banquet was served. It sounded like a day of fun, didn't it? This event took place before my time, but all of these ladies were still active when I was a little girl. Most of them still have grandchildren living in the area. Although these ladies have all been gone for a good many years, somehow I can still picture them gathered around a table, laughing and enjoying their work together. I wonder, does the Lord have quilts for His faithful saints who can gather together as they stitch and chat about their heavenly lives?

When I was a child, nearly every lady in the church belonged to the Ladies Aid. One of their projects was making clothing for the Indian Mission in New Mexico. It was operated by the Metzgers, sister and brother-in-law of Iona Hoverman, the local storekeeper's wife. A few years after I was married, I made a little blue dotted Swiss dress to be sent to the Mission. My pattern said to use the child's arm measurement to cut the elastic for the sleeve. The dress was a size two and I had no little girl to measure—but I had a little boy. I finished the dress and then decided to try it on him to make sure everything would fit properly. Now this little boy had lots of blonde curls. Since I already had two boys, I thought I might never have a little girl, so I grabbed the camera and took a picture of my son in that little dress. I've never embarrassed him by showing it around, but it was a cute picture. (Just for the record, a few months later, I had my girl.)

Eventually the Methodist Church merged with the United Brethren church and the Ladies Aid was changed to the Women's Society of Christian Service. We were no longer a local group, but were governed by rules sent down from district offices. Several former Ladies Aid members chose not to join the *newfangled* WSCS. Where we had sewn clothing and purchased gifts and wrapped them for the Worthington Children's Home, we were now told to send money and they would buy what was needed for the children. Somehow, that just didn't give the same feeling of satisfaction that we had when using our time and talents to pour our love into something created especially for an orphan. (I think that is why I enjoy going to our church one day a month to sew hospital gowns, aprons, baby layettes, and other items for use by our missionaries, much as the old Ladies Aid had done).

Were we ever stepping up in the world! Our church actually voted to buy an organ. At fifteen I was chosen as assistant pianist, but now in my senior year, I became the organist. I've been an organist for more than fifty years–either there or at Lima Baptist Temple.

The Gleaners Sunday School Class was the real "action" group in the Kossuth church. It no doubt started with the merger of the two churches. The class members were young couples about the age of my dad and mother, which made for an abundance of children about my age. Grandpa Frank was their teacher for *many* years, and later Dad taught the class. The Gleaners class continued for fifty years with basically the same people the entire time.

Each month the class held a party at the home of one of the couples. They loved the fellowship at those monthly meetings. I think the ladies tried to outdo each other by bringing their tastiest dishes. It was wonderful eating! After supper, the adults gathered in the host's living room for devotions and discussion of church problems and blessings.

We children headed outside. If there was an outside light, we played until long after dark. Some of our favorite games were hide and seek, red rover, cowboys and Indians, and tag. With all the kids joining in, everyone had a good time, although we usually came home with an abundance of chigger and mosquito bites. Maxine Erhart was hurt rather badly one night as she ran through a barnyard. A barbed wire fence had been placed around a cow lot, but none of us saw it in the darkness. As she ran, she caught her leg on one of the sharp barbs and it ripped the skin wide open, causing a quick trip to the doctor. After that experience, we were a bit more careful as we played after dark.

"Leave it to Nellie," they laughed. A wiener roast was held at the home of Harmon and Nellie Wright. Nellie was a lot of fun, and when someone dared her to roast a wiener on a manure fork sitting by the barn, she pulled the fork out of the manure and quietly walked to the house. A few minutes later she returned with the fork, put two wieners on it and roasted them. When they were finished, she took them off, put them in buns, and offered one to the person making the dare, while she ate the other one. Everyone laughed, and it was a night no one ever forgot. (Yes, she had washed and sterilized the fork!)

I was nine years old, too young to be a member of the Youth Fellowship, so it was a big occasion when I was invited to play my accordion for them. Teenagers Clarence Zimmerman and Dean Reed drove me to the meeting. Playing for the "big kids" was really special for a little girl. As I got older, I was eager to join the group. There were four churches on our circuit at that time: Walnut Grove, Olive Chapel, Christie Chapel, and Kossuth Zion. The monthly youth meetings alternated among the churches, so we became acquainted with kids representing at least five or six school districts. We had some interesting programs, as well as some really fun times!

With four churches on the circuit, a system was devised to share the preacher's time equally. While Kossuth held their church service first, Walnut Grove was having Sunday school. Then the pastor drove the few miles to Walnut Grove where their Sunday school service had just ended and they were now ready for "preaching," as some folks called it. Both churches had only Sunday school the next Sunday while the preacher split that day between Olive Chapel and Christie Chapel churches. Again, to be absolutely fair, Kossuth had preaching first during the first half of the year, then the routine reversed and Walnut Grove had it first during the remainder of the year. Eventually the circuit was changed. "Preaching" came every Sunday. Some folks wondered if it wasn't a bit too often, though.

I remember hearing of some difficulties of trying to get four churches in agreement on circuit matters. Each one had to pay its share of the preacher's salary and of the money sent to the district for missionary costs, district superintendent and his staff, children's home, and all the other things that the denomination supported. Kossuth was still paying for their new building, and everyone was trying to recover from the Great Depression. One of the churches had two or three fairly wealthy families and had no problem meeting their financial needs. One day one of their members made the statement at an official board meeting that "if you prayed more, maybe you could pay more." Believe me, that didn't go over well with the people, especially since some of his neighbors knew his lifestyle away from church.

Our church was always active in the Tri-township Sunday School Conventions. They covered an area of three townships and were well attended. Each church presented special music, readings, and such. Our family frequently helped to represent the Kossuth church. Dad sometimes played a violin solo, or the Davenettes played. There were still a lot of times when I ended up doing an accordion solo. One year another accordion player did "Whispering Hope," the same number I had chosen. I was very embarrassed. She played it first and I didn't have anything else prepared. I never again played that number at the Convention.

Two of the most important events of my life took place at the altar of that little country church in Kossuth. At the age of eleven, I attended a week-long revival there, and when Rev. Seth Painter, the evangelist, had the altar call on March 14, 1942, I went forward and asked Jesus into my heart. Although I was just a child and had never done anything very bad, I knew I needed Jesus to guide my life, and I accepted Him as my personal Savior. I've never regretted that decision. I'm very grateful that my children and grandchildren have all made the same choice and that they also love the Lord.

The other vital decision in my life was the joyous event of June 24, 1951—my wedding day! On that day Bill and I made an important promise to each other and to God, and for forty-seven years we have kept it, through thick and thin!

---

[1] *Program of Dedicatory Services,* "History," Kossuth Zion Methodist Church, November 11 to 18, 1928.

This picture of the Royal Oaks Sunday School Class from the Kossuth Zion Methodist Church was taken April 13, 1924. Dad wrote the names on the back. Standing left to right: Walter Leffel, Harley Leffel, Bernard Davenport (dad), Eva DeLong (teacher), Edgar DeLong, Homer Grassley, Clarence Whetstone. Seated: Orlo Reed, Vilas Whetstone, Theodore Zimmerman, Alton Reed, Fred Whetstone, George Point, and Arthur Zimmerman.

It was a busy year in the small Kossuth Church.

Babies dedicated on November 28, 1954, included: Robert & Betty McDonald with John Joel, Ray & Margaret Wagner with Robin Elizabeth, Donald & Ruth Rothe with Christine Kay, Bill & Glenna Meckstroth with Michael Allen, Donald & Mary Davenport with Marilyn Lee, Robert & Sue Leffel with Rex Edwin, Robert & Miriam McCune with Mark Eugene, Harold & Rea Bowersock with Janet Elaine, and Rev. Gerald & Shirley Erter with Hope Ann.

## Chapter 42.

# ♫ Make a Joyful Noise ♫

The Scriptures frequently mention music: harps, trumpets, singing. Music has played a very important part in my life. As small children, Don and I heard Dad practicing some very high-class music on his violin and I remember with joy the happy times when Grandpa got out his "fiddle" and Grandma chorded on the piano as they played the old songs—"Turkey in The Straw," "Oh, Susanna," "Red River Valley" and others they had played years before for barn dances, "play parties" and family get-togethers.

The September 3, 1914, *Auglaize County Democrat,* "Out West" column states: "Mr. and Mrs. Frank Davenport purchased a new piano Wednesday at the fairgrounds." They had signed up for a free piano at an Auglaize County Fair drawing. When they were chosen the winner, they went to the music store to claim their prize. The piano was a cheap model, so they asked if they could pay the difference for a more expensive one. The store agreed. That new piano got more publicity than many people ever get. Read on:

> There certainly was a fine time at Mr. and Mrs. Frank Davenports last Saturday evening, when quite a few friends gathered to try their new piano, and they certainly tried it good and proper, with Frank Davenport, Fredus Daniels, and Alga Montague on violins. The men said they are trying to keep their arms in good practice to cut corn this week. At ten o'clock Mrs. Davenport called them to the dining room, where there was a fine display of musk and water melons and lots of fruit prepared for them. They helped themselves and they certainly did justice to the layout. The friends departed at the midnight hour, thanking Mr. and Mrs. Davenport for their good entertaining and looking forward to next Saturday night. Those present were: Mr. and Mrs. Bert Montague, Mr. and Mrs. Frank Ward, Mr. and Mrs. Fredus Daniels, Miss Esta Ward, Alga Montague, and Mr. and Mrs. Frank Davenport and son, Bernard.[1]

Another night of music was recorded much earlier in the August 4, 1904, *Democrat.* It states in part: "Music from the phonograph was listened to and afterwards the party was entertained by the sweet notes of a violin in the able hands of Frank, Fredus and Lewis Daniels and Frank Davenport and the organ played by Mrs. Grant Daniels." Since Grandpa's uncles (Frank, Lewis and James Richard Daniels), all played fiddles, their dad (Abner Daniels), may also have been a fiddle player. There is really quite a story about James Richard. When his daughter-in-law wrote to me several years ago, she explained that when he left Minnesota in the 1870s, he had "tucked his fiddle under his arm and walked to Idaho" where he homesteaded land, married and raised his family. So, my family's interest in music dated back to at least my great-grandparents' generation. My mother also loved music. She played the piano. With such a musical family, how could I *not* like music?

My public musical *debut* took place at the Kossuth M.E. Church when I sang with the other little kids, then recited my Bible verse for a Children's Day program. It was scary, but tremendously exciting and I loved it.

As little children, Don and I could both sing a melody without wavering. I'm sure the school teachers must have been pleased because many youngsters "can't carry a tune in a bucket."

"What's your favorite class in school?" Daddy had asked. That was easy. "Music," I replied. Our teacher sometimes brought a windup Victrola with her to class. After turning the handle to wind it up, she'd place a large round record on it and then start it. She asked us to put our heads down on our desks so we would not be distracted while she told about the music as we listened to it. My childhood teacher explained the music in such a way that I learned to understand and love it. Most vivid were the pictures she described as we listened to "In the Hall of the Mountain King" and "Till Eulenspeigels Lustige Streiche." I loved the big booming sounds of the mountain king and was intrigued by the antics of poor Till who seemed constantly to be a problem. When we heard a certain little melody, we always knew Till was in trouble again.

A knock on the door when I was eight years old really opened my world to music. A door-to-door salesman, Mr. Fitzsimmons, representing the Wurlitzer Company was selling parents on the idea of accordion lessons for their children. Dad purchased a 24 bass accordion for my first lesson at the Wurlitzer Studio in St. Marys. When I returned after two weeks of practice, the teacher asked me to play a certain note. I wasn't sure where it was and I turned to Daddy with a pleading look. The teacher saw that and smiled as she said, "It won't help to look at Daddy. He doesn't know!"

After just a couple of lessons, the teacher told Dad I was catching on quickly and suggested I transfer to the advanced teacher, Freda Hooper (now Mrs. Oliver Hoge.) She told Dad I would quickly outgrow the small accordion and she suggested trading it for a full size 120 bass model. Dad agreed and my next lesson was on a beautiful new accordion with my name, "Glenna Mae," set in rhinestones on the front. I still play it.

Along with about thirty area kids, I became a part of the accordion band directed by Miss Hooper. One year we were invited to join other groups for a massed accordion band concert at a large park. The girls wore identical gypsy dresses of colorful yellow striped fabric. Although Don took violin lessons in Wapak, he was invited to join us for that concert. The previous day he had gone fishing on Lake St. Marys with relatives and acquired a horrible sunburn. With blisters on his back and shoulders, he could barely stand the touch of his white shirt. The director placed him in the back row where, hopefully, no one would accidentally touch him.

We were allowed to go swimming in the park's pool after the program. Grandma had helped me pick out my first swimsuit, a pretty one with a cute ruffle around the bottom. Most of the other girls wore the old style tank suits, but my suit was the latest fashion. Two girls kept telling me that this was not a swimsuit, it was a playsuit. And I very indignantly informed them it was not a playsuit, it was a *swimsuit*! Oh, the memories of childhood.

How do you get kids to practice? I was motivated by the big gold stars placed on my music, by a family that greatly encouraged me, and by the fact that my mother was up in heaven watching me. I certainly didn't want to disappoint her. That often kept me on the straight-and-narrow. Grandma also used good psychology by giving me a choice. After we had finished "redding up" the supper table, I could either practice for an hour or I could wash dishes. Well, what would you do? I didn't like washing dishes, so I practiced!

Playing the accordion led to lots of performances before church, school and community groups. Nearly everyone I knew who played accordion learned one rousing melody–"The Beer Barrel Polka." I knew it quite well from memory and was usually asked to play it at community meetings. (It must have been quite a sight–this skinny little girl with the great big accordion squeezing out that peppy polka!) One Sunday morning I played a solo for our church service. When I finished, someone asked me to play "The Beer Barrel Polka." I couldn't believe they would ask for that particular polka–and in church, yet. When I hesitated, the request was repeated. I looked at Daddy and he nodded, so I played it! (I doubt that there are many folks today who can say they have played "The Beer Barrel Polka" in the sanctuary of a church during a Sunday morning worship service!)

Dad and Don played violins, and I played my accordion in a trio. With a name like ours, Daddy called us the Davenettes, little davenports. He thought the name quite appropriate for a daddy and his two little Davenports, ages nine and twelve. The Davenettes eventually played for most community organizations. One year we were to be featured at the Midwest Electric annual meeting held at the St. Marys armory. Daddy thought we would look more professional if I wore a long formal dress for the occasion. He, Grandma and I went shopping for a suitable one. That became one of the most trying days of my childhood. There *were no formals* for children. I was tall and thin and could wear smaller ladies' sizes, but those dresses allowed more than ample room for a couple of body parts that I hadn't quite developed yet, so I looked like a little girl playing dress-up in adult clothes. I think the day ended in tears for me and frustration for Grandma and Daddy. I don't know what I finally wore for that program, but it was *not* a long formal!

Eventually my teacher told Dad I had developed well musically, and she suggested he find a more advanced teacher. Lucille Seibert from Wapakoneta was eager to have me as a student. She had graduated in 1919 from Blume High School with my dad, and she knew of his love of music. She was sure I would practice. Many students didn't. Don and I both became members of her band, which included Vivian Arnold's stringed instrument students and Lucille's accordion and marimba students.

One Christmas, I was asked to play my accordion at a special children's program at the Wapakoneta theater. I knew some of the kids from school and Santa came with gifts for all of the other kids, but there was none for me! I didn't understand at the time, but this was a party for the county's underprivileged children. My folks explained it to me later.

"She shouldn't lift anything heavy for a long time," the doctor said. After appendicitis surgery on my eleventh birthday, the lessons on that heavy accordion ended. Although I was no longer able to play it, I still enjoyed music enough to pick out hymns on Grandpa and Grandma's piano. Dad finally decided I should take piano lessons. We visited an old friend, Maya Helmstetter, in St. Marys, but she told Dad she didn't take beginners. After listening to me play, she knew I had learned the basics with my accordion lessons and took me at once. She continued my lessons every other week until my high school graduation.

When Maya's mother became ill, her bed was placed in the dining room adjacent to the music room. She always asked Maya to open the door just a crack so she could hear me play. She said I put so much feeling into the music, and she loved hearing it. Maya agreed. The more they bragged about it, the harder I tried to make music come to life with emotion and meaning. Maya and her sister's shared a long-time friendship with my dad. She also influenced my life and helped me prepare for my musical interview for college.

A humorous event took place years later. After Maya, her mother and sisters had all passed away, a public auction of their belongings was held at their home. Due to the large crowd and lack of space in the small yard, the city closed the street in front of their house. Furniture and other belongings were placed there. As I arrived at the sale, I noticed the music had been packed in boxes on the closed-in front porch. A lady was taking books from one box and putting them in another. As I watched her at work, I wondered what she was doing. I finally figured out that she was placing all the things *she* wanted in two boxes. There were numerous boxes of beginner music, of violin solos and trio music the Helmstetter sisters had used to entertain World War I troops overseas. I didn't need any of this music.

Maya had been a church organist for many years. I knew she had a lot of organ music, as well as several books of duets for piano and organ. That's what *I* wanted. Well, so did the other lady. She had packed her boxes with exactly what I wanted. When those boxes were taken out to be sold, I waited patiently beside them. As the bidding started, I was amazed to find no one seriously bidding against me. Where was the lady who had stacked the boxes for herself? After I had safely purchased both of them, I saw her talking up a storm with some friends. As I picked up my boxes, she saw me and realized she had goofed. Rushing over, she gave me a nasty look and spluttered, "But *I* wanted those boxes!" I knew that. I just said, "I'm sorry, but so did I! You should have bid against me!" She complained and insisted I sell them to her, but I just smiled, picked up my boxes and headed for my car. On the way, a lady whom I did not know, stopped me and said, "I saw that whole thing. That woman is a local musician. She's arrogant and didn't deserve the boxes after what she did. I'm glad you got the music. You handled the *old biddy* quite well." What could I say? I smiled and walked on.

But back to those childhood piano lessons. As soon as I could play well enough, I became the assistant pianist at the Kossuth church. I accompanied the singing at youth meetings and other church functions. I certainly was embarrassed one night when our youth group visited another group at Spencerville. Their pianist hadn't come. I was drafted, against my will, to accompany the singing. I'd never heard their choruses, and while they sang lustily in *a mile-a-minute* style, I could in no way sight read the unfamiliar music and keep up with their fast pace. I felt humiliated, but afterward I thought, "Hey! No one else could even *play* the piano. At least I tried." Hindsight is wonderful, isn't it?

Mary Jo Bruner, Bonnie Elsass and I had sung in the junior high school chorus. In our high school days, we formed a vocal trio, singing for graduations and other special programs. I especially remember singing "The World is Waiting for the Sunrise" at our Junior Prom. We also participated in the high school chorus, girls' ensemble and mixed chorus. I eventually became one of the pianists for those groups.

The only band instrument offered to me in junior high was a tuba. Dad said it would be too heavy for a little girl to carry when marching. We turned it down. I always wanted to play in the band, but how could I march carrying a piano or even an accordion? The glockenspiel was what I wanted to play, but someone else was already playing it.

"If you are going to study music in college, you need to get some experience in the band," cautioned Lester Smith, our new band director when I was a senior. He had directed the well-known Lima Westinghouse Band that was popular during World War II. He encouraged me to come to band practice. "We'll let you play the cymbals." There wasn't much to learn with cymbals, but even so, he managed to really embarrass me one day. We were playing a lively march in which I was to play a really big cymbal crash. Somehow my hands didn't bring them together evenly and the sound resembled a dull "clunk," rather than a nice ringing cymbal. Mr. Smith stopped the band, looked right at me, a dignified senior heading for college, smiled broadly and asked, "What happened? Did you get your nose caught in it?" Talk about embarrassing! My face was red as I felt complete humiliation.

About that time, the Kossuth church decided to buy their first organ. I again became a student of Lucille Seibert, this time for organ lessons. The committee ordered an organ exactly like the one at the Buckland Church. Dad made arrangements for me to practice there after school. By the time our new instrument arrived, I knew how to play it, and was selected as the organist. This became a little difficult when I went to college. A college rule allowed students to return home only once a month unless that month contained a holiday. I came back as often as possible and enjoyed playing the new organ. The congregation was also interested in hearing my progress from month to month.

When Grandma needed major surgery after my second year in college, I left school to stay home and help take care of her. I never went back, and contrary to the opinion expressed by my piano professor, I never regretted my decision. I have enjoyed my music and praise the Lord for giving me the talent to "hear" music, just by looking at it!

Several neighborhood children took piano or organ lessons from me. At least two are now church organists. Most of the parents made arrangements for their children to ride the school bus to our house for lessons, and then pick them up later. A rather humorous event occurred one day. Elaine had finished her lesson but Mrs. Cook, who was my most reliable parent, was not there. Thinking she had probably been detained somewhere, we sat and talked. After a half hour, Elaine and I were getting concerned. Other mothers were occasionally late, but not Elaine's mom. I finally went to the phone and called. When her mother answered, I told her Elaine was finished with her lesson. There was a long pause and then a gasp, "Oh, my goodness! I forgot all about her! I was busy and thought she had gotten off the bus and gone up to her room to play. I'll be right over!" She apologized several times and just couldn't believe she had forgotten her own daughter. (When we met many years later, she reminded me that her husband had taken the car and she had to come for Elaine on a tractor. We still laugh about the events of that day.)

The love of music carried down through the next generation, when we formed a family group, The Harmony Cousins. Our children became members of the high school band, chorus, and other musical groups. One or more have also been active in church choirs and orchestras, the OSU Men's Glee Club and the Lima Area Concert Band. Now the musical bug has bitten the grandchildren, and they are learning to play instruments. Our entire family is grateful to God for the talents which He has given us. We have tried to use them for His work whenever possible. Thank you, Lord, for the gift of music!

---

[1] *Auglaize Democrat*, "Out West," September 24, 1914.

*FROM THIS:*

"The Davenettes,"
Dad, Don and I in 1939

*TO THIS:*

The Harmony Cousins
Back row: Don Davenport, Steven Meckstroth, Michael Meckstroth, Bill Meckstroth
Middle row: Roger Davenport, Linda Davenport, Nancy Meckstroth, Richard Davenport
Seated front: Mary Davenport, Marilyn Davenport, Glenna Meckstroth

## Chapter 43.

# *Old Time Pill Peddlers*

"Grandma, the walls are moving!" I wailed. From my place on the couch, I could see the walls moving back and forth in little waves above my head. They had never done that before and when I told Grandma, I'm sure she must have been puzzled. When she walked over and felt my forehead, she found out I was burning up with fever. She immediately hurried to the telephone and cranked it one long turn. When the operator asked, "Number please," Grandma asked for long distance to Doc Doughty in Spencerville. Within a half hour he arrived and took my temperature with the thermometer from his little black bag. The reading was not good–one hundred three-and-a-half degrees. Doc didn't take long to make his diagnosis. "It's pneumonia," he sighed. I was only six years old, in the first grade, and there was no cure for pneumonia! Penicillin had not yet been discovered; therefore, most people died. Doctor's medicine helped control coughing, but the only cure for pneumonia seemed to be to just "sweat it out" by keeping many warm blankets on the patient until the sweating flushed the poisons out of the body. This is what Grandma did with me. Doctor Doughty faithfully drove the six miles out to check on me many times, and although I missed the whole Christmas vacation plus nineteen days of school, I finally recovered from the dreaded ailment.

(A neighbor's daughter, a young school teacher who still lived at home, had pneumonia a year or so later. The doctor had told them to keep her covered, but when she got so terribly hot, she begged her mother to take off some of the heavy blankets. Her mother finally did and she eventually died! The poor mother was heartsick and for many years blamed herself for the death.)

"My tummy hurts!" I can't count the number of times I used to say that, but I remember that it often meant several doses of Doc Doughty's bitter tasting stomach medicine. I almost envy the sweet-tasting medicine and tiny pills the kids of today receive from their doctors. After taking that nasty stuff for several years, my stomach aches came to an abrupt end on the first hours of my eleventh birthday. My pains had come because my appendix had slowly grown around the intestines, and when everything shut down one Saturday night, I ended up with emergency surgery. Since that was such a traumatic experience for the whole family, I really should explain the events of that night.

At one time, Don and I had our music lessons on Saturday night in Wapakoneta. Dad left Don off at the home of his violin teacher, Vivian Arnold, and then took me to the home of my accordion teacher, Lucille Seibert. When the music lessons were over that night, Daddy took us to Abbott's Shoe Store for a new pair of shoes for me to wear on Easter. I had looked forward to getting those much needed new shoes for church. Saturday night was the big night in town, a time to "see and be seen." The shoe store was busy that night.

As we waited, I began to feel sick. I was anxious for those new shoes, but I finally told Daddy that I just didn't feel well. I wanted to go home. I'm sure that surprised him, and he took us home at once. I headed for the couch, but the longer I lay there, the worse I felt. They finally called Dr. Doughty at Spencerville and asked him to come out. Other than the pneumonia five years earlier, I had not had any serious health problems. Doc hurried to our home and after examining me, he came to the conclusion it was appendicitis and told the family I would need surgery at once.

My mother's death in a hospital was still fresh in my family's minds, and upon hearing that immediate surgery was necessary, poor Grandpa was so overcome that Dr. Doughty had to dig into his little black bag and locate some pills for Grandpa so he would feel able to accompany us to the hospital.

My family explained to me on the way that St. Rita's was a Catholic hospital where I would see a lot of nuns. They didn't want me to be afraid of the long black, flowing habits with big wing-like sleeves and large head coverings that were worn at that time. I had never seen a nun, so they were right! I would have been very frightened if they had not told me what to expect.

I don't remember a whole lot about the surgery. Usually ether was used to put a patient to sleep, but because of my pneumonia a few years before, they used some other gas. When they put the mask over my face and told me to breathe deeply, I decided I wasn't going to breathe at all. *No one* was going to start *cutting* up *my* tummy! But I finally had to take a breath and when I did, I heard someone say, "Happy Birthday!" It was now past midnight, and I was suddenly waking up on the 22nd of April 1941, my eleventh birthday. Imagine that! The surgery was over!

The hospital priest came to my room in the morning and wished me a happy birthday. Then he eagerly explained how he would make plans for a birthday party for me–complete with cake and ice cream. Although I was really in pain, that sounded good to me. I had never had a birthday party. But a nurse said, "I'm afraid there will be no party for this little girl. She won't be eating for several days." I was really disappointed! There went my birthday party!

They placed me in the children's ward with five other little girls. The name Margaret was shared by three of them, so the nurses called them Margaret A, B, and C. One of the Margarets loved to pick on everyone, and when Grandma came in to see me, she said, "Boy, your mom is really old!" I said, "She's not my mom. She's my grandma! I don't have a mom!" Then she really made fun. "She is not your grandma! She's your mom! Everyone has a mom!" "No, they don't," I replied. "My mom died when I was a baby, and now she's an angel, and I don't have a mom!" And I burst into tears. A nurse came in then and scolded Margaret, and she finally stopped teasing.

At every meal, a tray was brought in for the other five girls, but all I ever got was a tiny bowl of broth with no salt and a cup of tea with no sugar. Yuck! (And you wonder why I don't drink tea?) By now I was getting weak from hunger. Either intravenous feedings had not yet been developed or they just didn't try it on me. After five days of watching all the other girls eating nice things and getting ice cream snacks, I made a decision. I started crying and made up my mind I wasn't going to stop until they brought some food. It worked! When my tray arrived on Thursday, it held a plate full of food. Yes, real food!

What a change has been made in surgical procedures. I lay in that hospital bed for ten days, *bed pans* and all! (When I had surgery in 1995, I was up and walking within hours. Oh, the pain of it all.)

Doc Doughty had been faithful in checking on me while I was in the hospital. On the eleventh day, I was finally allowed to go home, but only in an ambulance where I could lie down. Spring had come, and the ride, although bumpy, was exciting. I was finally out of the hospital and thrilled to look out of the ambulance window and recognize the area as we approached home. For the next two weeks I had to stay quiet and rest a lot. By the end of May, I finally made it back for the *last* day of school. Our class had a picnic in the woods across from the school building. I looked forward to swinging on the wild grape vines that grew on the trees. But while the rest of the kids ran and played, I had to sit by the teacher and watch. Some picnic, huh?

Doctoring was much different in those days. If you were really sick, the doctor made house calls. He entered your house carrying his little black bag filled with the tools of his trade: the stethoscope to hear your heart beat, the wooden stick to press on your tongue as you obediently said "Ahhh," and the thermometer flavored with the nasty tasting alcohol in which it was stored. There were a few pills and bottles of dark liquid, a bottle of iodine, tweezers and a scalpel for minor surgery, everything a country doctor might need.

Doctors seemed to be rather plentiful in this area of Ohio, even in my grandparents' early days. The November 12, 1891 *Auglaize County Republican* offered this Kossuth item: "Our new doctor, H.N. Wood has his office rooms in the basement of the America House," the local Hotel in that tiny little country village. I wonder if this might have been the doctor who came to deliver my Dad when he was born eight years later?

Even illness did not escape the notice of newspaper reporters of those earlier days. In the September 22, 1910, *Auglaize County Republican*, the Sodom area reporter wrote: "Mrs. C.W. Brincefield called on Mrs. F. Davenport Tuesday afternoon." Just a week later, the same paper reported that "Mrs. Frank Davenport who has been quite ill for some time is improving nicely." Two weeks after that, on October 13, it said "Mrs. Frank Davenport is slowly improving at this writing." By the time another two weeks had passed, the paper reported, "Frank Davenport, wife and son Bernard, spent Sunday as guests of 'Bill' Montague and family at Elm Tree Hall." Hooray for Grandma! She was well again!

Dr. Fledderjohann is a legend around New Knoxville. He was Bill's distant relative and many stories have been told about his life. In an interview published in the St. Marys *Evening Leader* in 1949, I read his personal account of his doctoring days in the 1880s. Concerning the birth of babies, the reporter asked, "'How long before confinement would they engage you?' [His answer was] 'Sometimes a bashful young man would meet me on the street and say that they might be needing me in a month or two, but without telling me what for. At other times they would rush into the office when I had the office full and say: 'My wife's having a baby and you have just got to come at once,' and that would be the first I knew of it. Only about half my patients would see me before hand.'" He mentioned delivering three babies within an hour at nearby Kettlersville, a tiny rural village.

The interview continues, "During the flu epidemic following World War I, there were occasions when he saw as many as 100 patients in a day and went 48 hours without sleep and that he became so tired that he was unable to reach up to the upper shelves of his office for medicines."

The Spencerville *Journal-News* in 1942 published a two-part series of "Echoes of Days

Past and Gone" as told by Dr. J.R. Welch. He had been a physician in Spencerville for 60 years and died at the age of 83 just before the final two chapters of the series were completed. He spoke of getting off the train (about 1882) in a drenching rain. As he ate in the hotel dining room, a boy came in hunting a doctor to go see his sick father. The doctor he was looking for was in the bar room, too drunk to go. The new doctor agreed to go as soon as he could put on dry clothing.

After changing clothes, he headed across the street to A.C. Harter's general store for some rain gear. (My great-grandfather, Charles Marion Briggs, worked at that store for his brother-in-law, A.C. Harter. Who knows, he may have made the sale.) "I purchased a pair of hip gum [rubber] boots and a belt to which the top of the boots were fastened. Then a gum coat and hat which made up my new wardrobe." He then walked to the livery stable where they loaned him a buckskin colored pony. The mud was nearly knee deep, and after mounting, he found they were playing a trick on him. This pony had not been broken to ride. The doctor had spent some time on a farm in Indiana and had broken several horses and he stated that "after some little time and persuasion with the whip, we understood each other better, and reached our destination seven miles out in about an hour."

Dr. Welch later told of buying a good horse named Jim. "I have slept many miles in the saddle at night, after making a call. I could turn him toward home, and take a nap. I always woke up when he stopped at the barn door. He felt disgraced when [the] harness was put on him, and would not budge until it was taken off." The doctor finally bought a horse to pull a cart or buggy that he used in the daytime. He rode Jim only at night.

The condition of roads made travel nearly hopeless. Dr. Welch continued, "The roads were all mud and due to shaded conditions of roads, many of them mere trails through the woods, they never dried up only when they froze, and then they were so rough that one could not drive faster than a horse could walk."

The doctor mentioned one rainy Sunday night when a team of horses was pulling his buggy on a muddy road near Fort Amanda. "I had a lantern on the dash and I was watching the wheels fill up, and was wondering how much farther I could go before something would happen. The doubletree broke and I was two miles from my destination at two o'clock in the morning and it was pitch dark and raining hard. I tied one horse to the fence and rode the other one to my destination. After taking care of my patient, I explained the situation to the man of the house and he found another doubletree and went back with me. At breakfast time I was back home and ready for the next experience.

Dr. Welch added, "Another experience that still lingers in my mind is another night trip. I was riding Jim up the east side of the canal on a road that was [a] trail through brush and over-hanging trees . . . . This strip of brush was alive with screech-owls, and every little way from one to half a dozen of them would dart down and hit me and the horse and deliver a blood curdling scream. Jim did not like it any better than I did and immediately went into 'high.' I never traveled that road after night again."

One of his most dangerous calls took him in 1885 or 86 to the Hartford area east of Spencerville. "Arriving at the bridge, I discovered that the east half of it was gone and that the river was up and full of floating ice. I noticed fresh wagon tracks going down to the river on the south side of the bridge, and I made up my mind someone had been there and had forded the river. I was not familiar with the depth of the water at this place, because there had been a bridge to cross on during all the time that I had been here.

"I rode into the water fully expecting to swim the horse, but almost as soon as he left the bank he went clear under the water. I found out later that a large hole had been made there when gravel had been hauled out by farmers."

The doctor continued, "The current was very swift and full of ice. I turned Jim's head down stream, and we went under the bridge and came out on the same side of the river that we went in on. I started back to my office three miles away, and by the time I arrived there my clothing was frozen stiff. While I was thawing out and getting dry clothing on, a man came in and told me that a Mr. Ham Miller had driven in the river soon after I left and drowned his wife, child, and team." Life was not easy in the country.

The first doctor I visited was Dr. Doughty. My grandparents had always gone to him. His office was much different from the sterile offices of today. First of all, it was located on the second floor above the Spencerville bank. To get there, we had to climb up that *long* flight of *steep* stairs. If we were too sick to make the climb, he occasionally came down to the car to see us or he came to our house. He made several house calls, especially at night, to see Grandpa or me.

Doc Doughty's massive grandfather clock occupied a prominent place in his waiting room and once I was inside, I always looked at the clock. The gold pendulum slowly swung back and forth as the clock ticked away the minutes while we waited patiently for him to finish. The office doors and woodwork were warm brown oak, and the oak chairs had leather cushions. There were no small chairs, toys or coloring books for the children; but then, we never had to wait very long. There were no appointments. Seldom did more than two or three people get sick at the same time. When it was my turn, Doc opened the door and smiled at Grandpa and me as we went in—no registering at the desk or filling out endless forms, no nurse or bookkeeper. Doc was the only one there, and he did it all! He sat down at his roll top desk and after hearing my symptoms, he looked into my eyes and ears and nose. With his stethoscope, he listened to my heart and usually thumped me gently on the back. When he had the problem diagnosed, he didn't give me a drug store prescription. No, Doc *peddled his own pills*.

One wall of his office was covered with large bottles of pills and flasks of liquid medicines. Taking a large bottle of pills from his shelf, he counted out the amount he wanted and slipped them into a little white envelope. If medicine was needed, he took a bottle off the shelf and poured some into a smaller bottle, popped a cork in the top and handed it to me. After chatting a few minutes, he said, "Well, I guess that's about two dollars worth." Grandpa paid my bill and we went home.

Most people didn't go to the doctor every time they had a little pain. People were more active and stayed in reasonably good health. The men often took Hinkle's Pills and the ladies depended on Lydia Pinkham's medicine. For colds and coughs, our family bought Luden's Cough Drops and rubbed Mentholatum on our chests and noses. For a sore throat we coated our neck with Mentholatum and pinned a sock around it. A clean sock out of the drawer wouldn't work as well as one we had just pulled off our foot. For several winters after I had pneumonia, Grandma made me wear what she called a pneumonia jacket. It consisted of a square of *wool* flannel that she placed over my chest and pinned to my underwear shirts. My goodness but that thing did itch! I could hardly study for scratching in those warm school classrooms!

When I was quite small, I used to have a lot of earaches, especially at night. Doc told Grandpa what to do. He got out of bed and carried me downstairs, then lit his pipe and ever so gently puffed a little of that warm smoke into my ears. Soon I was asleep, and he carried me back up to bed. As I think back to those days, I really laugh as I think of the picture Grandpa and I must have made in the middle of the night—me in my flannel jammies sitting on Grandpa's lap as he puffed away on his pipe, dressed only in his longjohns. The only robe he ever owned was the one we bought him when he was in his 70's and had surgery .

My earaches continued after I got into school. I spent many a day sitting beside the hot water register with my ear resting on my wool mittens which lay against that warm metal. Of course, the teachers knew that I had nearly died of pneumonia in the first grade and that I was a poor little girl with no mommy, and so I probably received a *whole* lot more than my fair share of sympathy. Soon, the other little girls and boys began to have earaches and placed their ears near mine. I guess they thought it was fun, sitting by that heater all day. They soon got tired of it and returned to their seats.

Believe me, it was no fun sitting so close to all the heat with that wool pneumonia jacket itching like crazy and an ear throbbing badly. If that wasn't enough pain, those hot water pipes would occasionally emit a cracking and banging sound that didn't help. It nearly sent my ear into spasms. Fortunately I outgrew the problem and haven't had an earache since. I haven't worn an itchy pneumonia jacket either, but I must confess, I still use the dirty sock treatment when I have a sore throat. Hey, it works!

Another cure-all that was used a lot at our house was liniment. It was good for bruises, bumps and sprains, aches in the back, side, or legs. And the smell opened up the sinuses. We also kept Vaseline on hand and smeared it liberally on cuts, burns, windburn and dried out hands.

One of the most dreaded diseases of any time was typhoid fever. Grandma had mentioned that her sister had once had it. Sure enough, the October 24, 1895, *Auglaize County Republican* stated in the Salem Township news that "Miss Matilda Schwartz is quite sick with typhoid fever. She has been staying in Kossuth, where she was attending school. She was removed to her home last Friday." A week later the paper revealed that "Miss Matilda Schwartz, whom we made mention of before is very low at this writing with typhoid fever." I am happy to report the rest of the story. She survived and became one of my favorite relatives.

## *The EYE DOCTOR*

I had trouble seeing the fine print on the blackboard when I was about eight years old. This prompted my first trip to the eye doctor. Daddy took me to Wapak to see Dr. Clem Hartman. He did his eye doctoring in a little room behind the showroom of his jewelry store. His first act was to put some drops in my eyes that left me half-blinded for a while. I remember a feeling of near panic as he put the machine so close to the front of my face and stared into my eyes. To this day, I am bothered by this. I often get the feeling I want to burst out laughing when the eye doctor gets extremely close. That would give the doctor a shock, huh? (Do I have a psychological problem? Maybe I should ask someone.)

Test results showed I needed glasses. But what color tint should they be, what shape and size frames? Today there is a wall of frames from which to choose, as well as a choice of colors. Back then you had only one choice . . . plain gold metal circles with clear glass.

Period! Certainly nothing glamorous, and I certainly didn't like them, but that was it!

I wore those glasses for two or three years. Then one day I got hit in the side of the head with a softball that bent the frame. I knew I was in trouble. When my brother was playing ball several weeks earlier, he had taken off his glasses and put them in his back pocket. He forgot about them and later sat down, breaking them. I knew Dad was not too happy about having to buy him new ones. I wasn't looking forward to a similar scolding, so I just didn't say anything. I never wore the glasses again. Fortunately my eyes seemed to have corrected themselves. It was not until I was in college and used my eyes for long hours of studying and reading music that I finally had to return to wearing glasses.

## *The DENTIST*

My first visit to a dentist didn't come until my permanent teeth had come in. Like my dad, I had a couple of teeth that were out of line. He thought I should have them checked. When he was young, Dad had worn bands on his teeth. It was the only way they knew to straighten crooked teeth and it had apparently *hurt like everything*. He didn't want me to have to go through that. When the dentist said I was a little young yet to worry about it, we forgot it. Several years later when I was well into my teen years, I really wanted my teeth to be straighter. I went to a different dentist who told me my teeth were now set and that it was too late to change them. Oh, great! My mouth was stuck with those teeth! (Since that time, they have found out that even older people can have good results with the use of braces. Too late smart, huh?)

Going to the dentist was no fun in those days. They did not have the modern technology and high speed drills of today, just big drills that made a lot of noise and hurt like crazy! Things got a bit nasty if you had cavities or had to have teeth pulled. Just cleaning them was bad enough.

A dentist (I believe in North Carolina) had put in a gold tooth for Grandpa Frank. That shiny tooth fascinated me as a child. I remember sitting on Grandpa's lap, trying to touch it with my finger. He made snapping motions at me and tried to catch my finger in his mouth. We had a lot of fun with that tooth! Years later, when he finally had his teeth replaced with a set of false teeth, I wanted him to have that tooth put in the new set, but he didn't agree to that. Later, as the price of gold climbed sharply, I wondered what he had done with that gold tooth.

I was about ten years old when Grandma was advised to have her teeth all pulled. She chose a new dentist, Alvin Noble, from St. Marys. He had just gotten out of the navy and was using the latest equipment. At that time it took months to get all your teeth pulled—just a few teeth each week until they were all out, then a long waiting period while the gums healed before getting the new plate. I usually went with Grandma and Grandpa when they went to the dentist.

Near the dentist was the office of Dr. Harry Briggs, a chiropractor who just happened to be my great-uncle, Grandpa Briggs' brother. My folks had told me that he was a relative of mine. I asked if I could see him, since I didn't know many of my mother's family. One day they took me over to his office so I could meet him. He had said to sit down until he finished with his patient, and since my appendix had been taken out several weeks before, he said he would give me a free treatment. As we sat in that waiting room,

I began to get nervous. His patient seemed to be in extreme pain. She loudly groaned and moaned and made quite a fuss. The longer we sat, the more nervous I became as I listened to her agonizing sounds. Finally I could take it no more. I didn't want him working on me if it was going to hurt that much! I convinced Grandpa and Grandma that I had to get out of there. It was several years before I finally met Uncle Harry. But Uncle Harry was not the only chiropractor in the family. Mother's brother, Marion, and his son, John, were also chiropractors. I never did get my free treatment from Great-uncle Harry!

## *The HEALTH PROBLEMS*

The county health doctor and nurse came to school each year to examine the children. This included head inspections for lice. (I never had any, although I used to wonder when Grandpa tucked me in bed at night and said, "Good night, sleep tight, don't let the bed bugs bite!") We also had patch tests for tuberculosis and shots for other diseases. X-rays were routinely used for finding tuberculosis. I was really frightened after my first such test at school. If there was a problem, the student was called into the office. I was the only one in my class to get called in. There were suspicious shadows on my x-ray. I was about convinced that I had tuberculosis, for which there was no definite cure, and I was sure that I was probably going to die before I could graduate in a half-dozen years. Suddenly one of them asked me if I had ever had pneumonia. When I told them I'd had it when I was six years old, they suddenly smiled and said, "Then those are scars from the pneumonia." Hallelujah! I wasn't going to die after all!

Chest x-rays were stressed as something we should have regularly. The big portable x-ray bus was parked at every festival and county fair, at local parks and at Lima's Public Square during heavy shopping times. Public announcements were made on radio and in the papers as to where that bus would be. Everyone was encouraged to get those free chest x-rays. No one ever thought too many might be harmful.

A quarantine sign on the door of a house was a common sight when I was a child. If someone got the measles or mumps or scarlet fever, or any of the other infectious illnesses, the county health doctor came around and fastened a large sheet of paper on the door with big letters saying, "QUARANTINE!" For a serious epidemic affecting everyone, this meant no one was to enter or leave the home. For most of the less serious childhood diseases, the father was allowed to go to work as usual.

What happens when we have problems with our mind? We now have psychologists and psychiatrists, but back in the days of my grandparents, parents, and even my own childhood, we had never heard of such a thing! If you had a problem, you talked to your family or friends, to the preacher or Sunday school teacher, or to the family doctor who always had a sympathetic ear. People visited their relatives every week or two, and they talked over their problems. There was always someone around with whom you could share your thoughts and discuss answers to any concerns you might have. And there were always the neighbors. After all, they usually listened in on your phone calls so they already knew your business! And if everything else failed, you could share your problems with the family dog. The cows and pigs were also quite good at listening. (The pigs probably wouldn't give you more than just a grunt but you could depend on Bossie's sympathetic eyes. Many folks today don't even have that!)

How many times had I as a child sat under the quilting frame and listened to grownups talking? More than I can remember. While Grandma sat with relatives and sewed for hours on the quilts she often helped make, I huddled under the frame and tried not to step on their toes. I was engrossed in my own childish pastimes and paid little attention as they discussed what to do about a husband who wouldn't pick up his clothes, about children who had moved a thousand miles away, about various health problems, new recipes, and other topics that were equally boring for me. But the point was, when you listened to your relatives' problems, you found out that they had the same problems you did. Even more important, some of their problems and worries made yours look small and insignificant! Anyway, who needed a psychologist when you had sympathetic listeners like Aunt Tillie?

## *"WHAT DID HE DIE OF?"*

"What did he die of?" That seemed to be the first question people asked when there was a death in the family years ago. So what did people die of? What caused deaths back in the late 1800s to mid-1900s?

Many of the children suffered or died because of whooping cough, typhoid fever, scarlet fever, and pneumonia. Some suffered from "quincy." After a trip to the dictionary, I found that quincy was acute tonsillitis, often accompanied by fever and the formation of an abscess. Measles were quite common and were best treated by keeping the child in a darkened room, since too much light might harm his eyes. How well I remember my comment when told that I was getting a good case of chicken pox. With childish practicality, I blurted out, "But I haven't been out with the chickens!"

Adults often died of the grippe (influenza or flu), consumption (tuberculosis), contagious blood poison, catarrh (nose and throat inflammation), biliousness (I remember Grandma talking about a bilious stomach and a sour stomach), lung fever, fits (sudden or violent attack of a disorder such as epilepsy or apoplexy), and inflammation of bowels. Other deaths were caused by the flux and by dysentery. One of the worst plagues this area has ever seen was the cholera epidemic of 1848, 49 and 50. It was then that so many of Bill's Fledderjohann relatives (nine) died within eleven days.

The flu epidemic of 1918 claimed a lot of America's World War I soldiers, as well as many back home. One victim was Bill's Aunt Ella Wierwille who died at the age of fifteen. Grandpa Frank Davenport's Uncle Nate died in 1919 of tuberculosis. The obituary headline read: "White Plague Takes Its Toll." The disease was quite prevalent. Zella Eversman's mother, wife of Dr. Fledderjohann, died of TB after doing the only thing they knew, going "out west" to a drier climate. New mothers often died of "child bed fever," and many older folks died of cancer or, like Grandpa Frank's grandma, of dropsy (abnormal accumulation of thin, watery fluid in the body, edema or swelling). Many just died of "old age."

Some died as a result of crude surgeries, sometimes performed on kitchen tables by the light of a kerosene lamp. My grandparents' generation often referred to surgery as "going under the knife," a ghastly description, I think. A headline in the August 1, 1927, *Wapakoneta Daily News* said, "Dr. R.C. Hunter Goes Under Knife" The sub-line read "Health Commissioner Is Appendicitis Victim Upon Reaching National Guard Camp." Dr. Hunter was a captain in the St. Marys Guard unit and was not feeling well when they headed for summer training at Camp Perry near Toledo. Upon arrival he was taken to a hospital for surgery. As a child, I often saw Dr. Hunter and his health nurse as they visited our school.

Accidents were very prevalent from falling trees. Two of the first young New Knoxville settlers, including a Meckstroth, died when a tree fell on them as they cleared their land of virgin timber.

Home remedies were used in every household. In those days of muddy roads and horse drawn conveyances, a serious burn or cut needed emergency measures. Many older folks, including my great-grandma, read scripture verses to stop the bleeding, to draw the fire out of a burn, or to stop hiccups. Grandpa and Grandma Davenport told of a neighbor who couldn't get his hiccups to stop. They lasted for days and his stomach became so sore he could no longer eat. His wife telephoned a neighbor who quoted Bible verses over the phone, and the hiccups stopped instantly.

Each family seemed to have a favorite folk remedy. When a wart developed on one of my fingers, Grandpa had the cure. "Break off a piece of milkweed stem and put the 'milk' on it," he had said. It would dissolve the offending wart if done consistently. Would you believe it actually did? But when Bill recently noticed a wart, I looked in the fence rows and along the creek and couldn't find even one milkweed plant. Shucks, our modern methods of weed control have eliminated the cure for warts.

Many folks were hurt or killed by runaway horses, by falls from bridges, barns or trees, and by injuries from threshing machines and corn shredders. Some died in house fires and others drowned. There were many horse and buggy accidents involving interurbans or trains. New hazards arrived with the advent of the automobile.

The old newspapers had a lot of advertisements for medicines to cure your every ailment. One extolled the benefits of using "Raus Mit 'Em" corn plaster. My grandparents often said "Raus Mit 'Em" when they were urging us to go outside to play or to do our chores. It is German and means "out with them." The name alone should have helped eliminate those corns. A 1926 newspaper had this ad: "Skinny Men, Rundown Men, Nervous Men–take McCoy's Cod Liver Oil Compound Tablets." I smiled as I read of another old time medicine, a special concoction advertised in the 1898 *Auglaize County Democrat:* "Dr. Williams Pink Pills for Pale People." Feeling pale? Those pink pills ought to cure it, don't you think?

## *EXCERPTS FROM A DOCTOR'S JOURNAL*

The following information was compiled from a book, *Day to Day Journals of Andrew J. Foreman, M.D.*. I found it to be of great interest. It was transcribed by his niece, Eunice (Snider) Miller. Eunice graciously allowed me to use excerpts from the journal.

Dr. Foreman was an active family doctor in eastern Auglaize County during the 1880-1900 era. As the name suggests, it was a day-to-day journal. To aid in the book's readability, I have arranged some items by categories. Of special interest are those that list the various methods used by Dr. Foreman's patients to pay their bills. The first item deals with the question, "What type of service was rendered and what was the cost?"

## DOCTORS SERVICES AND COSTS–1880-1900

Patient visit and medicine - $1
Extracting bone from throat - $1
Liniment & bandages for hand - $.50
Lancing abscess for little boy - $.50
Dressing foot - hired boy - $.50
Dressing hand, gunshot wound - $.50
Reducing dislocated elbow joint - $10
Wife in labor - varied from $3 up.
Extracted grain from little boy's nose - $.50
Extracted bean from little boy's nose -$2.00

Paregoric for babe - $.50
Camphor for wife - $.25
Miscarriage - $3.00
Extracting tooth - $.25
Exam for insurance - $5.00
Quinine - $.25
Salve - $.15
If forceps were used, $10.

The doctor visited and changed the dressing of a burned "babe" every day from May 25th through June 1st, then twice a day from June 2nd to 5th. Each of these visits cost $1. The visits stopped abruptly after the two visits on June 5th, leaving the impression that the poor baby died. He visited one patient every day for 46 continuous days. Twelve days after his last visit, the entire bill was paid—a total of $40.50.

This leads to the second question, "How did people pay their bills?" Money was quite scarce in those years and the doctor seemed to have taken his patient's financial situation into account when settling the bill. I have divided the various methods of payment into five categories.

HAULING:

Stove $1; Gravel $4; Load of lumber $.50; Load of shingles $1.50

WORK:

Killing hog $1; Plowing & scraping $3; Road work $3; Cording wood $.25; Sawing wood two days $2.50; Shop work $2; Sawing lumber $18.20; Washing $.50; One day's work $1.25; Cutting wheat $7; One day picking apples $1; Splitting wood $1; Day and half shingling hen house by father-in-law.

FARM SUPPLIES:

Colt $19.75; Horse pasture $.75; Breeding sow $.50; 3 loads straw $4.50; 2 hogs 320 pounds @ 5¢ pound $16; 2 cords wood $1; 30 bushels corn @ 28¢ bushel $8.40; 2 bushels wheat $1.70; Load of wood $1.50; Load of hay $1.80; Oats 30 bushels @ 20¢ bushel $6; 440 feet lumber $4.40.

PRODUCE:

15 pounds beef $.85; 2 bushels potatoes $.80; Maple syrup $1; Sorghum 3 gallons $1.20; ½ bushel hickory nuts $5; 8 bushels 3 pecks potatoes @ 50¢ bushel $4.40; 15 pound turkey $1.50; Fish $.25; 2 hams $10.50; 115 ½ pounds beef @ 6¢ $6.93; 5 gallons maple syrup $5; 2 gallons gooseberries $1; Coffee & sugar $.52; Eggs & sugar $.28; Coffee and *nice* soap $.84; 1 pound butter $.15; 1 dozen eggs, (prices ranged from 7¢ to 16¢ dozen, possibly depending on color and size of eggs or on the needs of patient); Sugar and apples

$.75; Eggs, sugar and soap $.55; Pickles $.50; 2 hogs $12; Dried apples $.28; 3 pounds hominy $.15; Peaches, eggs and butter $.48; Bread $.75; ½ bushel apples $.35; 6 heads cabbage at $.45 and ½ bushel turnips and 1720 pounds hay @45¢ hundred $8.19. As you can see, they offered anything they might be able to produce on their farm or in their garden.

MISCELLANEOUS:

Tinware $.50; Shoes $3.25 for one pair and $4 for a later pair; Credit for four and a half days at court $4.50; 2 pair rubbers $1.25; Groceries $.81; Coffee mill $.50; Muslin & calico $3.04; Broom $.50; Stove polish $.15.

The good doctor seemed willing to accept most any method of payment which his patients were capable of developing, whether it be for money, for goods or for services rendered. I was a little surprised that I did not see any chickens used as a form of payment, since they were very common around nearly every home at that time. Dr. Foreman also seemed to have a lot of "patience" as well as "patients." He accepted what they had and put the rest on his books until they could find something else to pay on the account. I found these facts to be a very interesting study in making-do in an era when there was little money for even the barest of necessities. This was indeed a "kinder and gentler world," a time when folks were willing to "work things out" with sympathy and compassion.

---

[1] *Day to Day Journals of Andrew J. Foreman, M.D.*, Personal journal, used with permission from Eunice Snider Miller, 1997.

## Chapter 44.
## "To Make the Best Better"

How do you get an entire 4-H club into a two-door Model A Ford? Easy! You put four girls in the front seat, two deep, beside the advisor. Then you squeeze the other four into the rumble seat behind. That is how our entire 4-H club went to our picnic at Ft. Amanda in about 1943. It was great fun, but thank goodness, it didn't rain!

"Dean Reed's 4-H pig just died. It got too hot," someone called excitedly as he ran into the Auglaize County Fair dining hall where our church ladies served meals. I was a little girl and was fast asleep on the daybed in the tiny room in the corner of the building. This was my very first memory of anything pertaining to 4-H. With no electric fans in any of the buildings or barns, the hot and humid day had been difficult for everyone, especially the animals. This pig had overheated and died. Farm boys usually took animal projects, but Dean lived in the village of Kossuth where raising a pig had been quite an accomplishment. The ladies felt especially sad for the young boy who had worked so hard to prepare his animal for the fair, only to have it die before it could be judged. Everyone hurt for him.

When Don was old enough, he joined the Kossuth Gleaners 4-H Club. Three years later I followed his example by joining the Maids of Kossuth. In *The ABC's of Sewing,* I made a pincushion and pot holder, but it was the tea towel I remember best. We girls sat on the porch railing of a member's home, stitching the hems on our tea towels for our first projects. The stitches had to be tiny and evenly sewn—something quite difficult for our clumsy little fingers. We did a *little* stitching and a *lot* of ripping and groaning that day!

County Health Nurse, Pauline Menges, always gave health exams on judging day. This was as stressful as the project judging. Were we too tall or too thin or would she find something terribly wrong with us? She was in charge of the Auglaize County Fair's first aid building. We eventually became good friends as we sat on a bench in front of the building and talked. More than fifty years later, as I visited Pauline in a rest home, we recalled those early 4-H memories.

For several years, my friend Rosemary and I rode our bicycles around the area south of Kossuth as we collected money for the TB drive sponsored by the County 4-H. Tuberculosis was a very bad disease at that time. A man from our church was confined for many months at the Lima TB hospital, and we felt we were being a big help by collecting funds. We also met some really nice people on those bike rides.

Since her family was all grown, Mrs. Dave Rohrbach, who spoke with a strong German accent, loved having little girls stop and chat with her. Another kind lady, Mrs. Ross Bowers, always had fresh cookies for us to eat. We usually received a snack from Orlo

Whetstone's wife, Bernice. They were newlyweds. As I look back, I wonder how, at the age of only eleven or twelve years, we had the nerve to go knocking on the doors of all those people we did not know to ask for money for TB. It was a little scary when someone answered our knock for the first time. Would she be nice or was she a grouch? Although Rosie and I didn't know all these people, our families knew everyone living in the area and knew we were safe. In those days people looked after each other.

4-H camp sounded exciting, and in my third year in 4-H, Daddy allowed me to attend Camp Harbor View located on Grand Lake St. Marys east of Celina. A large dining hall sat at one end of the campgrounds with rustic wooden cabins on each side–boys on the west side and girls on the east. I especially enjoyed getting to swim every day in the lake. I also enjoyed craft time, and still have the cork-covered autograph album and decorative felt sunflower pin I made. They weren't very elegant, but I found I really enjoyed crafts. (And still do!)

Camp was such fun that I attended the next year. It was during that time that my most embarrassing moment took place because of a pair of "unmentionables." World War II was in full swing. Elastic was needed for the war effort, so we could no longer buy panties with elastic at the top. (Oops! We didn't say that word! It was too personal! Grandma referred to such items as bloomers.) Bloomers covered a whole lot more of the subject.) Anyway, ladies' underpants now came equipped with waistbands at the top and a button to keep them closed. (A real nuisance, especially for little girls!) After lunch one day, I was walking through the center of the campgrounds when the worst possible thing happened! My button popped. Down dropped my britches. I grabbed them, hoisted them to my knees and ran like the dickens to my cabin. We were supposed to rest for an hour after lunch before going swimming. I think it took that whole time for my face to change from its fire engine red back to a normal pink. Believe me, I was really happy when the war ended. Once again we could buy undies with elastic!

I looked forward to attending camp the next year, but a lot changed during that time. World War II was at its peak, and German soldiers were being taken prisoners. Almost overnight, our fun-filled 4-H camp suddenly turned into a prisoner of war camp.

Because Grandma's old treadle machine would not sew evenly, especially over several layers of material, I had some problems with sewing projects. Grandma always said my dad had ruined her machine when he tried to sew the isinglass curtains for his car back in the 1920s. To solve the problem, Grandma took me over to Aunt Tillie's house to use her machine. This worked fairly well for the small items, but when it came to making dresses, complications arose. Grandpa had to drive us over and then come back and get us later in the day. It not only took time, it also used up precious gas. There was a war on, you know! Although Grandma and Aunt Tillie had done a lot of sewing, they just didn't know the "fancy sewing" rules of 4-H. Sewing lost its appeal, and I never took another sewing project. However, I listened carefully to the judges as they inspected the other girls' projects. I decided I *was* going to learn the rules so I *could* do it right. (Some ladies called it "sewing the 4-H way" and they considered it much too picky!) Today, I will challenge any of those former 4-H sewing winners. On my own, I learned "the 4-H way" and have the proof—a drawer full of ribbons, rosettes and "Best of Show" honors from several area fairs and the Ohio State Fair!

Victory gardens were popular, and in 1944 I helped the war effort by taking two projects, Vegetable Gardening and Canning. I preserved the foods I had grown. The two projects worked well together and I won a special pin from the Sears Roebuck Company for my efforts. Grandma didn't own a pressure canner, so she canned tomatoes using the open kettle method. The hot water bath was used for everything else. She didn't own a can lifter, either, but just grabbed the hot cans with a potholder or dish rag and lifted them in and out of the huge kettle of boiling water. As a young teenager, I was almost afraid to lift those heavy, hot cans. One of my first purchases as a bride was a pair of the scissors-like lifters. (No more burned hand from boiling pots for me.)

Eager to help win the war, 4-H and school kids collected milkweed pods each fall. The fuzz inside was used as a replacement for the kapok that was no longer available. The world's main source of kapok was from plantations in the Dutch East Indies which had been occupied by the Japanese. Kids scoured the fence rows and field corners, under bridges and along streams for the milkweed pods. We were told it was used mainly for life jackets for the navy and for flight jackets worn by pilots, navigators, and airmen. It was a warm and very lightweight replacement for kapok. An article in the September 9, 1944, issue of *Science News Letter* says, "The buoyant, waterproof floss in two bushels of pods is just enough to stuff one of the 1.2 million life jackets the Navy needs to protect the lives of fathers, brothers and friends at sea." A survivor of a torpedoed ship could be kept afloat for 140 hours in a storm-tossed ocean. We worked hard, hoping the pods we had picked would, indeed, save someone's life. We were proud to have done our part.

Have you been to a mock wedding? Our yearly program for the local Grange was meant to inform, but was also a lot of fun. Along with a summary of our year's activities and showing off our 4-H projects, we always presented something entertaining. One of our favorites was a mock wedding. The girls dressed up as the men and ladies of a wedding party. Some wore their dads' suits as the groom, preacher, best man, and ushers. Others were bridesmaids, flower girls and mother-of-the-bride, each dressed in one of her mother's dresses which would be long on the little girls. The father-of-the-bride was usually in bib overalls and carried a shotgun. The bride was, of course, dressed in white, anything white, meaning her gown might be a white flannel nightgown or a fancy slip with a long veil extending into a train made from a lace curtain directly from some poor mother's living room window. As the advisor played *Here Comes the Bride* on the piano, the solemn–but comical–procession entered the room. The more ridiculous the attire, the funnier. The audience loved it, and so did we!

What other kinds of projects did I take in 4-H? I sewed a guest towel, apron, handkerchief and two dresses. I also raised the garden, took two canning projects, had two foods projects, and, although girls in our county didn't take animal projects, I raised a pig and 150 cockerels (young roosters.)

Junior Leadership was a new project when I was sixteen. A one-week summer camp was held at Camp Ohio southeast of Columbus to explain the project and urge people to develop their leadership skills. My cousin, Carl Seewer Jr., and I were chosen to attend this first camp. Since most of the campers were seventeen or eighteen, I was one of the youngest there. The war was just over, and several foreign exchange students were brought to the camp as speakers. This was Ohio's very first Junior Leadership Camp, and we placed several important 4-H items in a time capsule which was buried on Vesper Hill, to be opened in twenty-five years. (Did someone do that?) Although he was up in years, we felt quite honored to have the founder of 4-H, A.B. Graham, visit our camp.

What should be our life's work? One camp activity was a series of aptitude tests to help us make that determination. Questions included such things as, "Would you rather read a book or play ball?" That one wasn't hard for me because I loved to read. "Would you rather be a housewife or a cleric?" Housewife I understood, but what was a cleric? There were other questions involving clerics. I had heard of clerical collars and assumed a cleric was a preacher. I certainly hadn't planned on doing any preaching, so I marked "no" on all of those questions. It wasn't until later that I found out they were referring to a cleric as a bookkeeper or clerk. Oh, well! I didn't want to do that either.

The young man in charge of that first JL Camp was Jack Mount. He was a real gentleman, and everyone respected him. I was quite surprised to meet him again fifty years later as Dr. John Mount, a retiree who had worked himself up through the state 4-H office, to become a Dean and Vice President at The Ohio State University. He continues as a most enthusiastic supporter of Ohio State and the OSU Men's Glee Club. Our Michael had gotten acquainted with him there. After all those years, we again met at one of the Glee Club concerts. What fun!

In my seventh year in 4-H, I took a market pig project and Jr. Leadership. My job was to help and encourage five younger members. I have a picture of those eager little girls, seated on folding chairs in the stone parking lot by the Grange Hall. They are all grown, and several have grandchildren who are 4-H members.

Since Grandpa had built a picnic stove in our yard, I took outdoor cookery for my third project. In a county demonstration contest, I showed how to lay a campfire. Well, imagine that. I won! Three other girls from my club were also winners, and we would all go to the Ohio State Fair for the first time. Rosemary Rothe won the top clothing award with her wool suit, and Phyllis Seibert and Imogene Ramga made refrigerator cookies for their team demonstration.

What a time we had at state fair! Herman and Geraldine Rothe drove us to Columbus the day before our contests. There were no motels then and the hotels were mostly downtown, so all of us stayed in one of the many homes on Eleventh Avenue that had a "Rooms for Rent" sign tacked on the front porch. In the morning we had to hunt a grocery store. The girls had forgotten something, (was it butter?) that they needed for their demonstration.

How did my demonstration go? Don't ask! My bonfire logs had stacked nicely and stayed in place at the county contest, but when I gave the same demonstration at State Fair, the logs rolled wildly with a mind of their own. I was really flustered, but the 4-H motto says: *"To make the best better!"* I had done my best!

I no longer joined 4-H after I turned eighteen. All the books, pins and ribbons were placed in Grandpa's old trunk in the corner of my room, and I went off to college. The towels, bean bag and pot holders of my early 4-H projects were packed away with the books and awaited the time when they would be brought out and used in my own home. My 4-H days were finished, or so I thought!

Well, not quite! I eventually spent seventeen years as an adviser with my old 4-H club, the Maids of Kossuth, and another eight years with the Cheery Sunbeams after we moved to New Knoxville.

I have made a sizeable investment of my life in 4-H—eight years as a member and twenty-five as an advisor. My three children grew up with 4-H as a way of life. Each was a ten-year member, attended numerous county camps, was awarded trips to nearly every state camp, and filled out numerous report forms to apply for many award pins. As a result, the State 4-H Council selected each of them as winners of a trip to National 4-H Club Congress in Chicago. Michael won in the Electricity project, Steven in Horticulture, and Nancy in Home Management. Interest in 4-H continued for several years as Michael volunteered as a counselor at State 4-H Club Congress at The Ohio State University. Nancy and her husband, David, have been advisors for several years in Allen County.

Now comes the next generation of 4-H kids as our grandchildren, Heather and Brian, are well on their way to repeating the cycle. Let's hear it for 4-H!

Carl "Junior" Seewer and I at Ohio's first 4-H Junior Leadership Camp, Camp Ohio, 1946

My 1948 4-H Junior Leadership project was helping younger members.
At left: Roberta Mack, Alice Daniels, Janice Zimmerman, Roxanna Long, and Betty Lou Daniels

## Chapter 45.

# Monday Was Wash Day

Did your Grandma wash and rinse her clothes or did she "warsh and rench" them? I've heard both laundry day expressions, but Grandma's important Monday morning question was, "What's the weather like today?" Was the sun shining so she could hang the clothes outside? Wash day was rather tedious before the invention of automatic washing machines and clothes dryers. It was the sun that dried the clothes as they hung on the clothesline, dancing and flapping in the breeze. When days were damp or bitter cold, drying clothes became a real chore.

If there were just a few small items to wash, Grandma usually filled her granite pan from the hot water storage tank on the side of the cookstove. She set it in the kitchen sink and washed out the small items. The big items waited for the difficult job of weekly wash day. In earlier days, wash water had to be heated in a large boiler which sat on top of the kitchen range. By the time I came along, water was circulated through a heating coil that was placed in the furnace, providing hot water for Grandma's wringer washer in the basement. Although it was a great improvement over her "tub and scrub board" method, it was still a very tiring day for Grandma. She always wore cotton dresses with fairly long sleeves, and on wash day those sleeves were rolled up to stay dry as she immersed her arms up to her elbows in water that was much too hot for my delicate little hands. It didn't seem to bother her as she pulled the clothes out of the washer and up to the wringer at the back of the machine.

Occasionally the clothes bunched up and were too thick to go between the hard rubber rollers or a button would not lie flat as it went through. Then Grandma had to hit the release, allowing the rolls to separate wide enough to rearrange the pieces. Wringers were dangerous and ladies who were careless often lost strands of long hair as they were literally pulled out by the moving rollers. Grandma kept her long hair braided or wrapped tightly and pinned securely to the top of her head. I was still quite small when she showed me how to hit the release bar across the top of the wringer if anything ever got caught in it. (Bill's mother always had a problem with her arm because she had gotten it caught in a wringer when she was young.)

Grandma still had a few cakes of homemade lye soap, although I remember best the cakes of P&G (Proctor and Gamble) or Fels Naphtha soap. There were no boxes of powdered soap or bottles of liquid. The cakes of soap had to be shaved with a sharp knife before being put into the wash water to dissolve. In small pans used for hand washing, she swished the cake of soap back and forth until the water was sufficiently soapy.

Since the same water would have to be used for everything, the laundry was sorted according to color. The white things were always washed first, then the others according to color and degree of dirt. The dirty overalls and dark things made up the last load.

Perhaps this would be the spot to insert a piece of advice that was given to both Bill and me when we were children. If we were going away, we were usually reminded to put on good, clean underwear. After all, what if we had an accident and ended up in the hospital? Those people would see our dirty or torn old underwear. Heaven forbid!

When washing white clothing, Grandma usually added a little bluing to the rinse water. This helped the whites to dry whiter. She usually used a light coating of starch on my little dresses and the men's dress shirts. Like nearly every other housewife of that time, my grandma used *Argo* starch. It was mixed with water and then cooked on top of the stove. If Grandma wasn't really careful when stirring the starch, she might get a lump or two that usually formed a stiff little blob in the middle of a dress or white shirt when she ironed. Clothing which had been immersed in the starch was usually wrung out by hand so that the starch didn't mess up the wringer rolls.

Drying the laundry could be a difficult task. On nice summer days everything was hung on the clothesline in the back yard. Grandpa had tied one end of the line to a big limb of the maple tree beside the house and the other end to a wooden post near the outhouse. Two-pronged wooden clothespins were used to pin the laundry to the clothesline. Once everything was hung, there could still be a problem. If the farm fields were being disked or manure was being spread, dust occasionally blew toward the clothesline, allowing a light film of dirt to coat everything. Grandma usually checked to see the wind direction and what was going on in the fields before starting the wash. In winter, when coal was burning in the furnace, she occasionally saw a few tiny black specks of soot on Grandpa's white Sunday shirt. Sometimes there were other problems. A few times the clothesline broke, and down came the whole line of clean clothes. I also remember a time when the overloaded line broke the old post and everything landed on the ground. It was not a pleasing sight to a hectic housewife who had spent a six-hour morning doing the laundry. Since our clothesline was rather long, Grandma used a long pole to prop up the middle of the line where it sagged from the weight of the wet clothing. This pole also had a nasty habit of breaking, allowing shirts hanging in the center of the line to get "Ring around the collar"...and cuffs...from flapping against the ground below. If the day was especially windy, we could expect to find clothes lying all over the back yard. They flapped until the pins finally worked loose, and I laughingly said that on a windy day, we might find our clothes in the next county.

A lot of folks left their chickens run around in the yard, but Grandpa always kept ours in a fenced-in lot. If the week's wash landed on the ground accidentally, it was on relatively clean grass, not chicken droppings. Every so often a low flying bird might decide to drop some doo-doo just as it flew over the clothesline. Oh, dear, its aim seemed to be uncannily accurate!

On clear winter days, Grandma usually hung the laundry out to freeze dry. Many times as I went out to take it down in the evening, everything was frozen stiff, including my hands by the time I finished. I was almost afraid I might *break* things when I tried to fold those frozen pieces to fit into the clothes basket. The towels and Grandpa's long johns were the slowest in drying and they often had to be brought in and hung across chairs to finish drying near the hot air registers. I remember twirling merrily around the cold back yard with Grandpa's frozen-stiff longjohns as my unlikely dance partner. Kid stuff, huh?

Another problem we sometimes encountered in summer was bees and bugs relaxing in the warm sunshine on the clean clothes. Occasionally one got wrapped up in the sheets and was unknowingly escorted into the house, only to be discovered walking across the bed in the middle of the night. Even worse were the times they hid inside the clothing. One day after I was married and had a family, I had hung the wash on the line to dry. My teenaged son needed a clean pair of jeans for band practice. He hurried out to the clothesline, grabbed a pair off the line, and stepped into them. Before he could zip the zipper, he realized he had a problem. A bee already occupied his pants. I was looking out the kitchen window at that moment, and what a dance that boy performed!

When heavy rain or snow storms were raging outside, the laundry had to be hung on lines crisscrossing the basement. This left everything limp, yet stiff with wrinkles that defied even the best and hottest of flat irons. Grandma's only solution seemed to be to sprinkle the clothes with water until they were quite damp and then to iron them.

Most people took great pride in their work, and doing the laundry was no different. There seemed to be some sort of unlisted rules to this business of laundry. For instance, in many areas it was a real challenge to be the very first to get the damp clothes hung on the line to dry. My friend, Eileen Wessel, remembered hearing her mother tell of someone who actually hung dry sheets out as soon as she got up, so it would look like she was the first in the neighborhood with laundry on the line. Another challenge was to have the whitest whites in the neighborhood. Of course, there was a common practice of modesty among the housewives. Underwear, especially the female variety, was hung on the line farthest away from the street, behind the sheets and towels where they were discreetly concealed from prying eyes. My great-aunts lived in the city where these unspoken rules were more noticeable.

Ironing day was almost as difficult as wash day. The cookstove had to be kept hot all day, since the irons sat directly on its surface. A roaring fire was great in the winter and helped to keep the kitchen warm and cook the meals, as well as to heat the irons, but that meant a lot of extra work and heat in the house in summer. Although we didn't have one, many of the homes had "summer kitchens" in which to do those chores, allowing the rest of the house to stay relatively cool.

My grandma had two kinds of irons when I was a child. The first was a one-piece iron with a metal handle attached. As it heated on top of the stove, the handle also became quite hot and a pot holder was wrapped around the handle before picking it up to start ironing. To see if it was hot enough, Grandma turned it on end and touched her finger to her moist tongue, then quickly tapped the bottom of the iron. If it made a satisfactory sizzling sound, it was ready. The trick was to be extremely fast and then the finger was not burned. (This iron now serves as my kitchen door stop.) The other was a two-piece model. The bottom metal section sat on the hot stove, but the handle was detachable and stayed cooler. With two bottom sections, one could be heating while using the other. Either model was very heavy and very hot. When I got old enough to help, I always seemed to touch that hot iron somehow and had the scars to prove it.

Grandma heated those irons on her stove until the power lines came through our area. Then I could scarcely believe how light and cool her newly purchased electric iron was. The early electric irons didn't produce steam, so I bought a special little sprinkler head with a cork plug which was inserted into a water-filled pop bottle. This made it easy to shake water over the clothing, dampening it before ironing; however, Grandma continued to use her hand to sprinkle the water on her clothes. It was hard to break an old habit.

After Grandma died, I did the laundry for Grandpa and Dad, as well as for Bill, myself and our three children. There were no wash-and-wear clothes then, so everything had to be ironed. Although some ladies ironed sheets, pillow slips, and undies, I never felt that was necessary. With five men and boys wearing shirts for school, everyday, and church, and the dresses, blouses, and skirts for Nancy and me, there was a huge amount of ironing, One long, tiring day I ironed forty shirts! Yes, I was proud of those clean, pressed shirts, but by the time I had finished, I was worn to a frazzle.

After I was married, Bill bought an automatic washer—no more up-to-my-elbows in hot water or worrying about getting something wrapped around a wringer. Just push a button, the water entered, washed the clothes, spun the water out, and shut off. What luxury!

Our basement was lower than the Prairie Creek a mile down the road. After a big rain the water often overflowed the creek banks and flooded Route 197. When that happened, I knew there would be water in our basement. It sometimes got up rather high. We knew it would ruin the washer, so Bill built a platform about a foot high, and the washer sat on it. With two little ones in diapers, the laundry had to be done, high water or not.

There was a little problem one wash day. Our basement walls had been built with sand and gravel from the gravel pit near the local Prairie Creek. These materials were not quite pure and as a result, the basement walls under several area houses, including ours, had deteriorated due to the impurities. Grandpa had put a new wall up against the old basement wall, hoping to salvage it. This left a ledge at about eye level.

I was busy doing the laundry one day and after several loads, my eye suddenly noticed something. Oh, no! My heart nearly stopped! There, on that ledge, not more than three feet from my face lay a four-foot long snake. Talk about heart failure! I knew Bill was gone but I ran outside and yelled for Grandpa. He was working nearby and quickly brought a spade with which to give it a whack. It tumbled to the floor and slithered under the washer platform. There are a lot of dark corners in a basement, and Grandpa's eyesight was not the best, so Mr. Snake got away. That night when Bill got home he found and killed it. Needless to say, I did not do another ounce of laundry until Bill and one of our employees had covered every hole in the basement that was big enough for even a little mouse to get through. That was the last snake we saw, but believe me, *one* was *enough.*

When Michael was just a baby, my grandpa Briggs died, and I inherited a small amount of money. After thinking it over, I decided the best thing I could buy was a clothes dryer. From then on I hung the laundry outside in good weather, but plopped it in the dryer on bad days. Bill had also built a platform for it. Now my wash days really became a joy!

When we moved to New Knoxville, the closed-in back porch became a laundry room. As a school project, Nancy painted it with cheerful, bright colors, making it a colorful and sunny room, even on less than cheerful days! We were quite surprised to come home from church on our twenty-fifth wedding anniversary, and after being led to the laundry room, found a new washer sitting there, a gift from our precious children. My grandma with her tubs of hot water and heavy heated irons would not believe the luxury I now have. What more could the heart desire on wash day?

## Chapter 46.
# Cisterns, Wells and Farm Fires

Is that a swimming pool in the basement? No, not quite! Nearly every farm in our area had a cistern just outside the kitchen, but in Bill's childhood home, it was in the basement. Most cisterns were large concrete tanks which held rain water. When it rained, the water ran into the spouting at the edge of the roof, then into the cistern where it was stored for use in the kitchen, laundry and bathroom. We called this "soft" water. People didn't have water softeners then, so we were usually cautioned not to use too much water for baths, for fear the cistern would run dry.

When this happened, as it occasionally did during dry summer weather, we sometimes tried to pump enough well water into the cistern to help us get along until it rained. But even when it was mixed with the soft water, the well water was much too hard and full of minerals such as iron. It left the clothing stiff and dingy.

About the time we got married, we heard of a milk hauler who used his truck to deliver water to those folks whose cisterns had gone dry. The water was purchased from the city of Celina, then sold to area farmers. Although the water was soft, it also smelled very fishy. Why? Because it had originally come from Grand Lake.

Cistern water often became "riled up" after a storm, especially in the fall when decaying tree leaves plugged the spouting, causing the water to be dirty. At one time, Grandma kept a large barrel under a section of spouting where leaves did not accumulate. That clean water was saved just for washing hair. Cleaning the cistern water when it was dirty was a rather simple task. The concrete lid of the cistern was lifted off and a box of "Old Dutch Settler" was sprinkled into the water. That did the trick and the residue soon settled to the bottom.

A friend who grew up in Minnesota explained how vital cisterns were to survival in their bitter cold winters. Even as a child, she had to take her turn going outside to stir the cistern water to keep it from freezing. It was the only water they had—for use in the house, for dishes, baths, everything—even fighting fires if needed.

Nearly all farms had their own well which produced *hard water.* This referred to the drinking water obtained by using the outdoor pump to draw it up from out of the ground. Don and I spent many hours pumping that handle up and down to fill buckets of water for the house. A bucket of drinking water sat on the back porch table with a tin cup beside it. When I was just a little girl, I liked to watch the cows drink out of the stock tank by the barn as they noisily took in great gulps of water. I remember a few times when I leaned over that bucket of water on the porch, then put my head down and slurped and gulped just like the cows. I thought the water tasted better that way, much better than drinking it out of the tin cup which we all shared. No one ever caught me at it, so I was never punished. ("Shhhh, don't tell anyone!")

Grandpa eventually buried a pipe from the pump to the barn. By turning a knob, the water was closed off at the well, forcing it into the pipe leading to the oval-shaped galvanized cattle-tank beside the barn. The cows drank several times each day, so we had to pump it full every evening. I pumped that handle up and down with one arm until it got tired, then I pumped with the other arm until it wore out, then I'd stand directly behind the pump and use both. Oh, my aching arms! Keeping that tank full was a real pain for Don and me!

Some folks in Kossuth didn't have wells. They used the town pump located at the intersection of State Routes 66 and 197 in the center of the village. There was a concrete or stone trough beneath the pump when I was just "a little shaver." A man traveling those routes could stop and give his thirsty horses a drink of fresh water. A tin cup hung on a wire hook and the man could also enjoy a drink for himself. Everyone used that cup.

When horses were no longer seen in town, the trough was disposed of, but I don't think many Children's Day practices or summer youth meetings were ever held without some kids gathering around the pump for a cool drink. The little church across the street got awfully warm on summer Sunday mornings and it was common for us to *just have to have a drink* after church. "Be careful crossing the road!" adults usually cautioned. Route 66 through Kossuth was on the direct route used by Lima sportsmen when traveling to Lake St. Marys for a Sunday afternoon outing.

A new pump was eventually installed, one with a hole in the top. Now we could hold our hand over the bottom of the spout and pump, causing the water to spurt out the little hole and form a stream just like a water fountain. Now that fresh cold water tasted even better. As health laws improved, a sign posted nearby proclaimed the water safe for drinking.

Although wells weren't of much use in fighting fires, the water from cisterns was often used during farm fires. Fires were rather common when I was a child. Everyone used wood or coal for the heating stove in the living room and a cookstove in the kitchen. That was all the heat some houses had. Bedrooms were often extremely cold. A heating stove usually sat in the living room with a register in the ceiling above, allowing some heat to reach the bedrooms upstairs. I have seen several homes with scorched wallpaper where the stove pipe entered the chimney. Occasionally homes burned because of fires that started there. I don't remember our house having anything but a furnace in the basement; however, the patched hole under the dining room wallpaper remained as hidden evidence that a heating stove had once stood there.

In rural areas such as ours, fire departments were small, volunteer organizations. If the alarm rang, men came from all directions—the storekeeper leaving his customers, the barber stopping in the middle of someone's haircut, and the mechanic dropping his wrench and hurrying off with grease still on his hands. When the cistern water had been used up, the firemen filled the truck's tanks at nearby gravel pits, creeks or the Miami-Erie canal a mile west of us. Fire safety was one of the main points for keeping the canal open in this area, even though it was being filled in elsewhere.

As a little girl, I sometimes went to play with the LeMarr children down the road. My grandparents' best friends had lived in the house and when they moved, they left an old buggy in the shed. We loved that contraption and bounced up and down and side to side—that's how it would feel in a stagecoach traveling across the prairie with the enemy in hot pursuit. We always outsmarted them and made it to safety just as the cavalry arrived.

After the LeMarrs moved, Leonard and Jennie Spacht and their children moved into the house. One early morning in 1945, we awoke with shadows from a fire dancing on our bedroom walls. When we ran to the window and looked to the east, we could see Leonard's house was burning. I had never seen a house fire and I nearly got sick to my stomach at the sight of that familiar place burning. Had the children made it out safely so early in the morning when everyone would still be sleeping?

Grandpa and Dad dressed quickly and went downstairs. When a sudden knock was heard on our door, Grandpa rushed to open it. There stood a man, obviously shaken up and seeking help. He had been driving to work on Route 66 west of the canal. As he entered the area, he saw the fire and turned east, driving toward it. The flames were directly ahead as he traveled down the road. Not being familiar with the area, he didn't realize the road ended in a deep ditch a half mile from the fire. Keeping his eyes on the fire, he had driven toward it, then stopped abruptly as his car dropped into that deep ditch. He needed help in getting out and since the fire trucks had arrived, my family knew there was little they could do at the fire. Driving a tractor over to his car, they pulled it out of the ditch. Thankfully, neither he nor the Spacht family were hurt. Our farm was usually a very quiet place. Either a fire or a wreck would have been enough excitement for one day, but with both events at the same time . . . oh, my!

Fire isn't funny, but we had a scare that seemed humorous–after it was over. When our children were young, we were watching a TV movie about the giant German airship, the Hindenburg, that had crashed and burned in New Jersey in 1937 with a loss of more than thirty lives. As the movie progressed, we watched in awe as flames licked at the sides of the giant craft. Suddenly someone smelled smoke. Sure, we watched the airship burn, then smelled smoke. Very realistic! Wait a minute! Then we realized we *were* smelling smoke. Someone shouted, "Look, there's smoke curling up behind the TV." Sure enough, there was smoke! In seconds, the plug was pulled and the TV set was carried out to the front porch. Upon examination, its insides were found to have shorted out. Indeed, we had smelled smoke. We were grateful we didn't have to use our cistern water to fight a fire that day, but we did have to buy a new television. Needless to say, if they rerun the burning of the Hindenburg, *I'm not sure we will watch*!

## Chapter 47.

# *Parks Are For Play*

Cedar Point sounded like a wonderful park, but because of the depression and then World War II, we had never visited it. Our children were teens when we chaperoned their church youth group as they spent a day at this amusement park. We had a wonderful time and later, as I was telling Grandpa about it, he smiled and said he had been there when he was a young man. I must confess, I thought Grandpa was a bit confused. It couldn't have been the same place. This was way up on Lake Erie. He must have been thinking of Russells Point at nearby Indian Lake.

That sounded more reasonable in his horse-and-buggy youth, but as I researched travel back then, I realized folks from across Ohio could drive a horse and buggy to the nearest interurban or train station. Week end excursions were quite popular at one time and a 1914 *Auglaize County Democrat* featured this large advertisement:

> Weekend Excursion to Sandusky via The Western Ohio Railroad. [Our area called it The Interurban.] Tickets good going every Saturday and Sunday, on Cleveland Limited only, returning until Monday Evening. Spend this week end at Cedar Point, Put-In-Bay, Lakeside, Marble Head or Kelley's Island. Reached by boat from Sandusky. See agents or address C.O. Sullivan, Traffic Mgr. or C.F. Cramer, Tran. Pass. Agent.[1]

When the train pulled alongside the pier in Sandusky, a ferry waited to transport the hundreds of eager young passengers to the Point each day. At that time Cedar Point was on an island that could only be reached by boat or by ferry. Later, those coming in by car took the ferry over and parked beside the big roller coaster. I once saw a picture of the "Leap the Dips" roller coaster that was built in 1892 and dismantled in 1935. Grandpa may have enjoyed that coaster. Cedar Point's 125th anniversary was recently celebrated, so it had indeed been there in the 1890s and Grandpa certainly knew what he was talking about!

In its early days, Cedar Point was best known for its extensive beaches. At one time a circular swing stood in the water and the riders whirled and dipped in and out of the waves. In Cedar Point's anniversary TV special, one lady revealed that an occasional swimmer lost a swim suit on that whirling, plunging ride.

Gordon Park at Villa Nova on nearby Lake St. Marys was our closest amusement park. The St. Marys *Evening Leader's* "1992 Back To The Future Progress" special edition featured pictures and stories of the park during its hey-day in the 1920s and 30s. Its roller coaster was the tallest and biggest one in Ohio at a cost of $50,000. There was also the

Old Mill, a boat ride that ran through a 1500 foot tunnel and slid into the lake. Bill's Aunt Alwina remembered riding in a little boat that followed a water filled "trough" around curves as it slid down. Other rides were a merry-go-round, Ferris wheel, miniature train ride, chairplane swings, pony rides, and the usual funhouse and penny arcade games. A 200-passenger boat provided rides on the lake with a Calliope playing on the rear deck. Shucks! I was born too late for all of that!

My "drinking" days began and ended (all in the same day) at Gordon Park. I remember our family spending the day there when I was three years old. As I saw the vast expanse of the lake for the first time, I gasped in surprise—so much water in one spot and so big compared to the canal back home. My memories of the park are sketchy, but I didn't forget one thing. It was a hot day and I was thirsty. As we walked past one stand, I saw something pretty and foamy being poured into a glass. I wanted some. Daddy tried to tell me I really didn't want any of that, but like most three-year-olds, I insisted that I did. He finally bought some, (perhaps to teach me a lesson), and although it had looked pretty as it bubbled into the cup, it tasted horrible and smelled even worse. I had just taken my first (and last) taste of beer. Thus ended my drinking days! I guess that was really a very important day in my life, though. When I became a teenager, it was *easy* to say, "No, thanks!" to any drinks that were offered. A man came to our church when I was about ten years old and spoke about the evils of strong drink. He concluded by giving each of us a card that said we promised never to drink alcoholic beverages. I gladly signed mine and kept the promise. After that first taste, I *certainly* didn't want to go through that *again*!

Although the park was gone by the time I was a child, Villa Nova maintained a picnic and swimming area. When I took accordion lessons from Freda Hooper, her studio enjoyed a picnic there. Her guest for the day was a good-looking young man named Oliver Hoge. He had brought a camera and spent much of the day trying to take pictures of Miss Hooper. She giggled and ran behind trees as she tried to hide from him. I was about nine years old and I thought it was all rather silly. If she would *just stand still* and *let* him take the pictures and get it over with, he would *stop* pestering her and she could come play games with us kids instead of hiding from him all day. (P.S. They were married a short time later!)

We looked forward to our summer visit to see two big black bears that lived in Lima's Faurot Park. Located underneath the bear pit was a special area where the bears hibernated for the winter. Sometime during or shortly after World War II the bears and pit disappeared. I recently saw a picture of that pit. Hanging on the fence was a sign saying "Do not feed the bears. $10 fine." Guess what? A man was standing beside the sign . . . feeding the bears!

I was a little girl and was eager to join the other kids who splashed and frolicked nearby in the shallow pool surrounding a fountain of cascading water that tumbled and churned as it fell. This was even more fun than watching lazy old bears.

"Mairzy Doats and Doesy Doats and Liddle Lambsy Divy." Over and over, the Celina Lake Festival loudspeaker played that new tune, a favorite of the 1940s. The lively number is now so far outdated that I couldn't find anyone who was willing to even guess at the spelling, but we all knew that when the song was slowed down, it really said, "Mares Eat Oats and Does Eat Oats and Little Lambs Eat Ivy." I know it's silly, but everyone loved the catchy tune. The highlight of the Festival was a parade of elegantly decorated boats and floating barges that seemed to drift along the West Bank of the lake in front of the crowd watching from the shore. I thought they were so beautiful! But I couldn't get that silly tune out of my head.

One of the tiniest parks in our area was located between Kossuth and Spencerville at historic Deep Cut. It had only a pump with a little roof over it, a picnic table, and a tiny winding path that led down into the deep area beside the water. Grandpa and I often stopped at the pump for a drink of water as we returned from shopping in Spencerville. On the hillside just down the road sat an old house. Those folks were poor and we often saw the lady of the house pushing a baby buggy along the side of the road with one or two little kids in it. Occasionally it also held a sack or two of groceries and sometimes the buggy was filled with twigs and branches that she'd picked up along the road or at the park. She always had the buggy, but we were never sure of its contents!

When Don was a freshman, he joined the Future Farmers of America, an organization designed to teach young men how to farm and to take care of animals. Their teacher planned a week of summer fun as he rented a cabin at O'Connor's Landing on the east side of Indian Lake. Families were invited to spend one day with them and it was there I enjoyed my first canoe ride. Rowing a boat was a lot of fun but why did my canoe keep going in circles?

Fort Amanda is a small, but historic park in Auglaize County. According to Lima's David Johnson, the fort was built by Lt. Colonel Robert Pogue, a quartermaster with Gen. "Mad" Anthony Wayne, and named for his eleven-year-old daughter, Amanda. The active fort was occupied during the War of 1812 and had been vital to the development of northwest Ohio when Indians still roamed the area. As a child, I ran up and down the many winding trails through the park and down the steep slopes to the Auglaize River below. One needed very little imagination to hear the soft hush of dozens of moccasin clad feet as they walked the trails decades before, searching for the many deer that roamed the area or catching fish in the Auglaize River. As children, we soaked in the history of the area as we enjoyed the safety and freedom to run and play in the park. At one time, a man was said to have hidden from the enemy by crawling into a large hollow tree. Such a tree stood beside the path leading to the monument which had been patterned after the old fort. In true pioneer spirit, we crawled into the tree and hid too!

As a teenager, my Dad had delivered the Gettysburg Address when the large monument was dedicated on July 4, 1915. What was that day like, I wondered? Hundreds of people had parked their buggies and Model T's in neighboring fields and had walked through the woods to the monument in the center of an open field. I'm sure many browsed through the old cemetery located in the park, possibly looking for the graves of their ancestors who may have died during early Indian battles or in the War of 1812. It must have been quite a day!

The park was a favorite picnic area for local groups. We visited at least two or three times a year with the 4-H club, church youth group, Dad's Sunday School class or the Ladies Aid Society. Several times we stood at a respectful distance and watched in silence as baptismal services were held in the shallow waters of the Auglaize River. My high school senior class took a "skip day" and some of us spent several hours at the park. We rejoiced in the fact we were now adults and would soon leave high school, yet we were apprehensive about the future. The day gave us a chance to recapture our lost childhood while trying to bolster each other's spirits as we stepped into the world of adulthood.

Russells Point was "the" place to go when I was a teenager. Located on nearby Indian

Lake, the amusement park's main attraction was the large wooden roller coaster that wound its way through the park. A replica of a huge fat lady stood in front of the funhouse and laughed endlessly. When I first saw her, I smiled, then laughed out loud and thought it was funny, but her raucous cackle soon became overbearing and after a few minutes, ear plugs would have been appropriate. We walked on down the midway.

One of Bill's favorite hangouts was the roller skating rink near the park where kids from many miles away met for a night of fun. Bill and a carload of his friends from New Knoxville spent many hours there, usually on Saturday night. Those guys loved to skate.

One evening Don, Mary, Bill and I went to "The Point," as it was often called. After listening to the spiel of a man who displayed a unique slicer, we watched as he easily made perfect slices of fruits and vegetables. What a marvelous gadget! Mary and I quickly convinced our guys we each needed one. Amazingly, those slicers worked quite well. I used mine for many years, but alas, it was made of plastic and finally broke.

Russells Point was also known for the large curved bridge spanning a channel leading in from Indian Lake. It extended from the main part of the midway to a large, boat-shaped restaurant on the other side of the water. The lighted bridge made an exciting place to enjoy a view of the park and the small boats that cruised through the channel beneath. It was even more special when accompanied by that certain young man.

Russells Point was best known for its large outdoor dance floor. Most of the Big Bands of the 1940s and 50s played there, bands led by Glenn Miller, Guy Lombardo, Wayne King and others. One night a group of kids from my school watched the event under the moonlight. The area was so crowded we couldn't get in, but it was a fantastic experience just to stand outside the fence and hear the wonderful *big band* playing popular songs of the day: "Stormy Weather," "Sentimental Journey," "Moonlight in Vermont," and my favorite . . . "In the Mood."

How sad my generation felt as we watched that wonderful playground literally fall apart. Trash littered the area, buildings began to crumble, and the decision was finally made to sell the land and clean up the area. After everything of value was removed from the park, the public was invited to come in and take the remaining things as souvenirs. Soon the little cars and trucks from the kiddie rides, the signs advertising the funhouse, and the fat lady were all gone. (I don't know who was lucky [or unlucky] enough to get that laughing fat lady!) The land was sold and although the bridge remains, condominiums now sit where years before were heard the screams of happy teenagers riding the roller coaster and the sounds of a fat lady who laughed endlessly.

We occasionally visited other parks at family reunions or near the homes of distant relatives, but parks are parks. The main attraction then was the same as today, a place to enjoy and have fun, from the swings, teeter-totters, and sliding boards of childhood play to the more mature toys of the Ferris wheel and the roller coaster!

Although State Fair isn't really a park, it has many of the same attractions–lots of rides, beautiful flowers, and plenty of things to see and do. Don, Mary, Bill and I decided to go to State Fair soon after our marriages. It was the first visit for the others and we were eager to see everything. Our early start provided a close parking place. That was nice since we had taken our dinner. Mary made one of her scrumptious chocolate cakes with real fudge icing! How wonderful that tasted! We had also taken a thermos jug of lemonade made from real lemons. Each time we got tired of walking, we went back to the car for another slice of cake and cup of lemonade. As the thermos jug began to empty, we added a little more water, but the lemonade still tasted quite good. Later we added more water and it still tasted good. Visiting that huge fair was an educational experience but we have often laughed about that jug of lemonade which lasted the whole day!

World's Fairs were really big happenings around the turn of the century and although none of my family attended, the *Auglaize County Democrat* of Thursday, September 14, 1893, told of several New Knoxville couples who had attended the World's Columbian Exposition in Chicago. Bill's distant relatives, H.H. Meckstroth and wife and Dr. H.F. Fledderjohann did attend at that time. "How interesting! I wonder what they saw."

The feature theme of the Exposition was structural steel and electricity. The biggest attraction was a new ride made by George Washington Gale Ferris, the giant Ferris Wheel. The World Book Encyclopedia states this wheel had a diameter of 250 feet and weighed a total of 150 tons. Thirty-six cars carried sixty persons for a total of 2,160 people riding the wheel at one time. Wow! The cars were like small barns with roofs over the top and three foot high sides. Picture the size of that monstrous wheel compared with today's smaller rides that stand about 45 feet high, carrying 12 to 15 seats. After the event was over, the Ferris Wheel was taken apart and moved from Chicago to St. Louis for the St. Louis World's Fair in 1904. Since Bill's Grandpa Wierwille attended that fair, he may have ridden the Giant Wheel. Its dimensions were overwhelming. But alas and alack, after the 1904 fair, the world's largest Ferris Wheel was taken apart for one last move—to the junk yard. Yes, it was sold for scrap! Imagine that!

---

[1] *Auglaize County Democrat,* Advertisement, July 23, 1914.

## Chapter 48.

# The ABC's and Me

I was Grandpa's girl and went everywhere with him. Why did I have to change my life by going to school? Were the ABC's that important? After boarding the big yellow bus and spending my first day in school, I decided school was fun. Each evening I ran to show Grandpa what I had learned that day. After my coloring papers had been properly looked at and praised by family members, they were carefully stashed away in Grandpa's trunk to be treasured and protected. The ABC's took on new meaning for me.

With papers to show and the praises that followed, I not only enjoyed school, I especially loved Llewena Marsh, my teacher. She had ridden with my dad to Wapakoneta Blume High School seventeen years earlier, and had also taught Don. I enjoyed the little songs she taught us, especially those that were a part of circle games such as London Bridge, Ring Around the Rosey and Farmer in the Dell. After school was out that spring, she did the unthinkable. She stopped teaching and married Sam Chrismer. Llewena never forgot us, though. Because we had been her last class, she made us feel really special by hosting a party in our honor when we graduated twelve years later.

Yes, I liked almost everything about school except writing class. Why? Because we had to use scratchy, metal quill-type pens for those early writing classes. Each child had a wooden holder into which a metal writing tip was placed. If that tip became bent, a new one could be inserted. The writing process seemed endless as we dipped the tip into an ink bottle, wrote a few words, then dipped again.

The writing tablet's pretty example showed nice overlapping O's resembling stovepipes. My O's looked more like a fractured balloon with an obvious puncture wound made by my pen's sharp point as it pushed through the paper. Even worse were the continuous up-and-down slashes which often tore the paper as we pressed too hard. How we detested those scratchy pens.

The fountain pens that we used later had rubber bladders that had to be filled regularly and often left unsightly ink blobs (vaguely resembling creatures from outer space) on the papers. Fortunately, ball point pens were developed before I graduated.

Buckland School was small, and although it had to compromise in some areas, it gave us a superior education. Due to small classes, the second grade was usually split between the first and third grade teachers, so I had Ilo Winget for second and third grades. Vivian Myers taught our fourth grade and the routine was repeated with a split fifth grade. Frances Bierhup taught fifth grade, but after she also got married, Elizabeth McClure became my sixth grade teacher. (Several years later, when Bill and I first met, we discovered Miss McClure had also been his teacher at the New Knoxville school.)

Grade school meant special adventures, such as an occasional overnight visit with a girlfriend. I spent my very first night away from home at Mary Jo Bruner's house. She was a "city" girl. Well, Buckland was actually a little rural village, but it seemed like a city to me. I carried my little cardboard suitcase on the bus with me that morning. When the school bell rang at the end of the day, it seemed strange not to get on the school bus. Instead, we hurried down the street to Mary Jo's house. Her mother had a piece of cake with caramel icing for each of us. I'd never had caramel icing and I thought that was about the best cake I had ever eaten. We played until bedtime. I was a bit homesick that night, so Mrs. Bruner placed a little lamp beside the bed. It had a celluloid shade with a picture of Niagara Falls that moved, making the water appear to be tumbling down the falls. From then on, my visits to Mary Jo's house included watching Niagara Falls until we fell asleep.

One afternoon Mary Jo and I hurried to her house. She had a brand new set of twin baby sisters, Joan Sue and Janet Lou. Now we moved to the guest room, and the twins stayed near their mother and daddy. I loved watching those babies and tried to tell Grandma that although Mary Jo had a little sister, Margie, and now the twins, *I* would be satisfied to have just *one* little sister. My words were in vain! I just didn't understand, and I was even more confused when one of the twins later became ill and died. That was such a shock. I thought only old people died.

Alice Hager, another "city" girl, lived near the railroad track. The train's whistle seemed awfully loud. I wondered if I would be able to rest that night, but after several hours of play, I quickly fell asleep. I didn't hear a train whistle all night.

Grade school brought some really special days. Everyone made a fancy box to hold the Valentines which we brought for classmates. These were shoe boxes covered with construction paper, frilly little paper lace doilies, and a strip or two of crepe paper that we ruffled by pulling the edges. I saved those precious valentines for several years, storing them at the bottom of Grandpa's trunk. They lay beside the crumbling leaf collection from Biology, the tiny paper party umbrella, and the "lucky" four leaf clovers. I found them one pleasant summer day as I sat in the front yard, listening to the Bob White's mating call as I casually watched the fluffy clouds gliding silently overhead.

School birthday parties were also special. Spring, with its warm weather, had come by the time my birthday arrived on April 22. My eleventh birthday came on Sunday, and when a friend teased me about giving me my birthday spanking on Monday, I told her I was going to "play hooky" from school. As fate would have it, I didn't get to play hooky. I was in the hospital with an emergency appendectomy!

Good Friday was observed in a special way at school. The entire student body, with the exception of the two or three Catholic families, walked to the local church and participated in an afternoon service. Rev. C.C. Ryan, affectionately known to the kids as "Pappy Ryan," was the local pastor at that time. After a hymn and scripture, Rev. Ryan preached. He usually gave a vivid description of his visit to the Holy Lands, something of which we knew very little. I listened intently as he described the Sea of Galilee, the walls of Jerusalem, and especially the Mount of Olives, Garden of Gethsemane, and the empty tomb.

As Don and I waited beside the road for our school bus, Mel Fryer from Spencerville occasionally stopped and asked if we wanted to ride with him. Mr. Fryer was one of my junior high teachers and how important I felt climbing out of a teacher's car. This was during the heyday of the Big Band Era, and Mr. Fryer played in a well-known local band that occasionally played for proms and area programs. To us students, he was a celebrity.

"A passion for poetry." That describes Homer Tennant, our junior high English teacher. Our assignment each week was to memorize a poem and to write an original poem or story. Writing poetry was sheer panic for most of the class, especially the boys. I enjoyed it and still have every poem and story I wrote–well, almost every one. Someone usually rushed in at the last moment and said, "Say something that rhymes. I need a poem."

Although I never really learned to crochet or tat, I did learn a few knitting basics for a grade school Thanksgiving program. Several of us Pilgrim ladies were to sit in our log house, talking and knitting. The teacher showed us a few basic stitches to give us the authentic Pilgrim-lady look. Her efforts were successful and we looked quite impressive! But since Grandma hadn't learned to knit, my newly-found talent was forgotten about as quickly as it had been learned.

Because of another school program, I also learned to dance the *Highland Fling*. We portrayed girls from Scotland and, wearing plaid skirts, we hippity-hopped around the stage in good style. It may not have impressed a Scotsman, but when I saw the dance performed professionally in Scotland years later, I remembered many of the steps.

Programs were special for me. Daddy allowed me the privilege of wearing my mother's diamond engagement ring for many school programs. He always wrapped it with string so it wouldn't slip off my finger, and for those big events, I always felt so close to the mother I had never known.

Rural communities enjoyed "Community Farmer's Institutes" each year. I was fortunate. Not only did I get to attend the weekend institute at the Kossuth Grange Hall, I also enjoyed another one held during the week at Buckland School. Several weeks before the Institute, a poster contest was held, and the posters were then put on display. I enjoyed art, but never won a prize. There were a few kids who were not great at "book learning," but they were quite artistic. They usually won the poster contest.

Besides the speakers on various topics of interest to farmers, there was always a play put on by the local folks to end the two-day event. The plays were usually comedies that attracted everyone in the neighborhood. They were even more humorous because the people we saw every week at meetings, church, or the local feed mill became one-night actors with makeup and new personalities. Hours of practice were needed, but it raised everyone's spirits when the community joined together in guffaws and belly-laughs that rang through the building. One lady had a most uncomfortable habit of forgetting her lines, then just ad-libbing the first thing that came into her mind. She did it with such a straight face that everyone else looked lost, while she appeared to be the only one who knew her part. Just after we were married, Bill and I participated in a play at Kossuth. This gal caught me off guard when she ad-libbed after forgetting her lines. Now what? I did some ad-libbing of my own and we were soon back on track. The play was a huge success.

We had no cafeteria when I started school. I took my lunch in a little green dinner pail on which Daddy painted my initials, GMD. The school finally developed a cafeteria when I was in junior high. Warm meals were provided for a small fee, (possibly 25¢.) I didn't take my lunch again unless the cafeteria was closed for some reason. Don's high school basketball practice came right after lunch. The guys always stopped in the kitchen to eat any left over food from lunch. His favorites–macaroni and cheese and Spanish rice.

I smile as I think back to that first school cafeteria. The kitchen was in a corner of a room that was sometimes used as the shop classroom. As the guys sawed and sanded in the work area in the adjoining room, a sifting of fine sawdust often covered the cafeteria tables and benches. Although the cooks did their best to keep everything clean and sanitary, very little in that old cafeteria would pass today's inspections. But we thought the food was great. These local ladies did their best to provide us with tasty "home cooked" meals.

When the tables in the cafeteria were filled, we ate in the vocational agriculture room. The FFA (Future Farmers of America) met in this room. Its symbol, a stuffed owl, peered down at us from a top shelf, giving me a creepy feeling that something was watching me as I ate. Another occasional overflow lunchroom was the science lab, which was even more challenging with its cabinets of specimens preserved in formaldehyde, its shelves of vile smelling chemicals, and ugly sinks which had soaked up too many acids.

I planned to attend college and took college-prep classes in high school. Most of the girls went into home economics classes, but you see, I didn't like to cook. The reason was simple. Grandma cooked with a pinch of this, a handful of that and three-fourths of a coffee cup of something else. My pinches and handfuls and cups weren't the same size as hers. How frustrating! I was also shy when it came to working in a kitchen. At least two girls in my class had from six to eleven brothers and sisters and they helped cook all the time at home. They *knew* what they were doing. I didn't. I felt much more at home working in the library rather than volunteering in the cafeteria, even if it meant a free meal that day. For some reason, I couldn't get out of helping one time, and then I found that I had worried needlessly. All I was asked to do was butter slices of bread and put fruit cocktail into little bowls. What a relief! I thought I would have to help stir big pots of soup or make endless pans of macaroni and cheese.

Thinking of high school brings back other memories. One is of Miss West, a rather buxom older lady on whom the boys loved to play tricks. One time they put a thumb tack on her chair. When she sat down, it stuck into her girdle, and she walked around the rest of the day with a tack in the crease of her backside, something which the boys thought was hilarious. Then there was Miss Beulah Jones, our high school English teacher. As we read the *House of Seven Gables,* she made the story so real that we chose New York and Boston for our class trip instead of New York and Washington, D.C., as other classes had done. We saw the house with the seven gables and the spreading chestnut tree that inspired the poem "The Village Blacksmith." In Boston Harbor our group visited the historic ship, *Constitution*, better known as *Old Ironsides.*

Of course, I can't forget Miss Kilmer, the feisty little math teacher who was always pointing her finger at us as she looked for gum chewers. One day she made me come to the front to spit my gum into the wastebasket. But I didn't have any gum. She even looked in my mouth trying to find it. (Was I absentmindedly moving my mouth or did I deliberately try to confuse her?) Miss Kilmer was a good math teacher. She made sure we learned our lessons well.

Kenneth Crim, a fine Christian man, was superintendent of Buckland School when I graduated. While participating in a computer class several years ago, Bill became acquainted with Mr. Crim, who mentioned he had taught at Buckland. "My wife, Glenna Davenport, graduated from Buckland," Bill told him. Mr. Crim smiled. Believe it or not, after all those years, he still remembered me. I was surprised and really quite pleased!

"Homework assignments are much too long," we had said. "She acts as if her's is the only class we have," we had argued. Something had to be done about this new young teacher. Kids in one of Lima's *big city* schools had written a petition against one of their teachers. We decided that was the thing to do. Mary Jo agreed to sign it first if I would write the petition. The other kids encouraged me, and I began to write. The finished petition was signed and delivered to the teacher one morning. By noon word had circulated through the school, directly to the superintendent's office. With a very somber face, he walked into our room, excused the only girl who had refused to sign our petition, and while she blissfully walked home for dinner, we sat and listened as he verbally chewed us into fine pieces throughout our noon hour. His final words were that we would receive no dinner and we were to each go to that teacher and personally apologize for our actions. By the time he left, most of us were feeling a bit sorry for our rather exciting adventure, and we did as we were told. We apologized! I must confess that we had made our point, though. Our homework assignments became shorter.

Nine boys and three girls made up my chemistry and physics classes. Not a bad ratio if you like those subjects. I didn't, but they were required for college entrance. The boys were very ingenious, especially in chemistry. They usually managed to make some kind of strong smell that permeated from the basement laboratory to the whole school above. One favorite concoction wreaked of a strong banana smell that was sickening, but the worst were those that smelled like rotten eggs and dead mice. Then the boys discovered chloroform. A mouse had been brought to class, and with one whiff of chloroform, the boys put him to sleep in seconds. Then they held him out the window for a breath of fresh air, and suddenly he was wide awake. This was repeated until the teacher returned from an errand and realized what was going on. And so ends the tale of the sleepy mouse!

One class met after lunch in a room with a bad lock on the door. The kids hurried upstairs after lunch and rushed into the room, then shut the door. When the teacher came, she couldn't get the door to open. The kids on the inside called out encouragement, "Try wiggling the door knob." "Hit it hard with your shoulder." "Twist the knob back and forth." She usually gave up and got the janitor who had to take the door off the hinges. That old lock had been really tricky! No matter how hard the teacher pulled and twisted, the door wouldn't open. It was really quite simple, though! If you were lucky enough to be on the inside, you had only to turn the knob and it opened. The janitor finally caught on and put a new lock on the door.

My speech class participated in the local "Prince of Peace" contest. We had to memorize one of several prepared speeches, then in our most dramatic voices, present it in a contest. At the last minute, the judge was not able to come. An unqualified local man substituted. My speech teacher was shocked when he selected a young man as the winner. She told me I had done the best job, so I was disappointed. The young winner was killed in the Korean War shortly after that, and I knew that award was the only thing he had ever won in his short life. Somehow, losing the contest no longer seemed so important.

Since the junior class was in charge of the senior prom, we were allowed to miss a couple of afternoons of classes in order to decorate the gymnasium and turn it into a fancy ballroom. A group of us rode in a pickup truck to Grandma's north farm to pick up stones which would be whitewashed to form into a garden path. The stones were heavy, and it was hard work picking them up, but shucks, any excuse for skipping school was worth it.

The teaching staff had selected me as editor of the school paper in my junior year.

That created a problem. The editor was usually chosen from the top students in the *typing* class, but I hadn't been able to work typing into my schedule. One of the advantages of a small school was that the teachers tried to solve problems such as this. The typing teacher put me into a class that had one pupil–me! I took first-year typing sitting in one corner of the second year typing class where I worked at my own speed. By the end of the year, I had caught up with the others and was prepared for college and the job of school paper editor.

My senior year was the most exciting, and Great-grandpa's old trunk was eventually crammed with program folders, prom favors, trip souvenirs and a wide assortment of other items deemed worthy of preservation. It was a year with lots of music: the school musical whose setting resembled Switzerland, the girls' vocal trio, playing the piano for the high school choir and finally becoming a member of the band. Marching in the Auglaize County Centennial parade that summer was my most memorable band experience.

There were a lot of fun activities and orneriness that senior year. After lunch each day, our very young, very pretty homeroom teacher had a fixed routine. As she entered the room, she always went to her desk and got her pencil, then walked over to the pencil sharpener. Grasping the tip end of the sharpener handle daintily between her thumb and finger, she quickly turned the handle in such a way that her fanny put on quite a show. The boys loved it! One day they decided to have some fun. They wrapped a tiny snake around the pencil sharpener handle. As usual, the pretty teacher entered the room, got her pencil from her desk and walked to the sharpener. Just as she reached for the handle, one of the boys asked her something. As she moved her head to talk, she turned the handle as usual. That little snake was right on schedule and quickly unwound, flying right into her face. I'm sure the men at McName's feed mill at the other end of town could have heard her scream. Shame on those ornery boys!

My entire graduation class was made up of just nineteen members:

Janice Sprague    Donald Mack    Alice Hager
Kenneth McName    Mary Jo Bruner    Mary Ramga
Paul Holtzapple    Carmen Bodey    Dale Place
Glenna Davenport    Bonnie Elsass    Dick Place
Harmon Holtzapple    Betty Lambert    Mary Hall
Morris Dingledine    Dale Wilges    Bill Place
Kenneth Ziegenbusch

A few days before graduation, the class decided to take a "senior skip day." At least one carload of boys drove to the Forty Acre Pond for a swim, while most of us spent the day at Ft. Amanda Park. (Today's schools would strongly disapprove.)

When the final grades were compiled, Mary Jo and I were announced as valedictorian and salutatorian and were asked to present speeches on graduation day. Our senior class trip started a day or so later. For some of my class members, this was their first time away from home. One mother said she didn't know if she could get along without her son. One impertinent boy piped up, "Put her on ice. She'll keep!"

Our bus stopped in Philadelphia for a tour of Independence Hall and the Betsy Ross home where the first American flag was made. Then we drove to New York City for a few days of sightseeing: Radio City Music Hall with its gorgeous chandeliers and Rockette dance troupe, a boat cruise around Manhattan with the Statue of Liberty in the distance, a very foggy evening at Coney Island, a visit to Chinatown and to the Bowery. We also visited the newly organized United Nations at Flushing Meadows and heard a speech by Eleanor Roosevelt, widow of the former President.

Lost in the Big Apple? Now that was an experience that Mary Ramga and I shared as we walked through the heart of New York City with the rest of our group, gawking at tall buildings and staring into fancy store windows. We had never seen a store window filled with wigs. After staring at those elegant hair pieces for a few minutes, we walked on, then suddenly realized the other kids were out of sight. Thinking we could catch up, we walked faster. But we still saw no one we knew. Finally we accepted the fact that we were alone and lost in the middle of Manhattan. "Stay calm!" we reassured each other, "we'll ask someone." Although we asked several people, including a policeman, how to get to our hotel, it was never where they said it should be. As our last resort, we hailed a taxi that finally returned us to the hotel. We were over a mile from it and although it cost us a few dollars, we gladly thrust some money into the driver's hands and ran to the safety of the hotel's front door where the class was waiting for us. Needless to say, our chaperones were enormously relieved to see us!

After the excitement of New York, Boston seemed rather mild and quiet. While there, we naive country kids had the unique experience of eating with chop sticks. Oriental foods were quite scarce, and in downtown Buckland, they were completely nonexistent at Sherm's Restaurant. We soon realized chopsticks were not our ideal eating utensils. The experiment turned out to be a very humorous event!

On our return trip, we stopped in Toledo at the home of our young teacher of the "snake episode." Fortunately, she didn't hold a grudge against us, and we thoroughly enjoyed the delicious breakfast she prepared for us. As we returned to our waiting families back at Buckland, it was a bitter sweet time for those of us who enjoyed school and our classroom friendships. We knew this would be the end of those close-knit relationships. Some of us would be leaving soon for college, the military, waiting jobs and marriage. For others, it was an escape from the ABC's and the freedom to do as they pleased. For all of us it was, "Look out world, here we come!"

Buckland High School's operetta, "In Grand Old Switzerland," was held in the fall of 1947. Soloists in the center are Glenna Davenport, Delbert Cook, Mary Jo Bruner, and Juanita Wells. Kneeling in front are Glen Place and Rex Place.

"Freshman Initiation" at Buckland High School 1944
The senior class was in charge (and my brother was one!) The girls wore boys' clothes to school and the boys dressed like girls. That night the new freshmen were guests at their first high school party. It was a fun day for everyone.

Sitting: Carol Hughes, Bonnie Elsass, Mary Jo Bruner, Mary Ramga, Betty Lambert
Kneeling: Mary Hall, Glenna Davenport (that's me!), Carmen Bodey, Carol Minkner, Alvaretta Lee, Alice Hager
Standing: Dale Place, Donald Mack, Paul Holtzapple, Kenneth McName, Harmon Holtzapple, Kenneth Ziegenbusch, Bill Place, Dale Wilges

## Chapter 49.

# The Swing's the Thing

Where's the best place to sit when shelling peas or snapping green beans? There was no doubt about it. When I was growing up, there was only one *best* place and that was the old wooden porch swing. I sat at one end of the swing and Grandma placed the big dish pan full of freshly picked peas, still nestled tightly in their green pods, between us. A small pan sat on each lap as we took a handful of pods from the large pan and shelled out the little round peas, popping them into our small pans.

My legs didn't reach the floor yet, and as we sat side-by-side on the swing, the only movement was the gentle swaying motion we made as we shelled the peas and tossed the empty pods into the five-gallon bucket sitting on the floor between us. Whether it was shelling peas or snapping beans or just relaxing after a hot day, the old porch swing was always a welcome spot.

Grandpa found the swing to be the ideal place for reading the day's mail. The mailman usually came just before dinner, and while Grandma busied herself in the kitchen, Grandpa relaxed for a few minutes in the swing. Taking out his blue everyday handkerchief, he wiped the perspiration from his forehead, then sorted through the mail. Hopefully there would be no bills. By the time Grandpa had covered the high spots from the *Wapakoneta Daily News*, Grandma had dinner ready.

Porch swings are great places for children to play and Don and I got our chance to enjoy it after dinner when the adults had gone back to work. We had to be careful that we didn't swing too high, though. If the back of the swing happened to bang into the wall behind it, the sound would echo through the house, and we could be in trouble. We tried swinging longways back and forth a few times, but that was never very rewarding. Too much effort for such a small ride!

Our swing hung on the back porch which was enclosed with windows and doors that opened up to let the fresh air and sunshine inside. We could listen to the sounds of the night as we sat in the swing after a full day's work. Since the windows had screens, the neighborhood mosquitoes sang their evening song on the outside while the swing sang its squeaky song on the inside. No one bothered trying to *fix* the sound with a squirt from Grandpa's oil can. After all, the song of the swing was as much a part of the enjoyment as was the sound of the crickets chirping in the shrubbery just outside.

Dolls! Dolls! How I loved dolls! Many summer afternoons were spent sitting in the swing where I dressed my favorite doll, the rubber Betsy Wetsy, in the many outfits Grandma and I had made for her. I also rocked my big baby doll and dressed her in some of the real baby clothes I found in Grandpa's trunk in the corner of my room. They are a little worse off for the wear, but I thought it was really special that my doll baby could wear the same dresses I had worn as a baby. I also liked to swing as I gently cradled the old doll with the cracked face. Had she belonged to my mother? I never knew! I wish I had asked Grandma. I also had two little sets of Dionne Quintuplets–certainly more than enough dolls to keep a little girl busy for hours.

Occasionally I brought one or two of the barn kittens into the porch and sat quietly petting them as they snoozed in my lap. We weren't supposed to play with kittens in the house, so I had to make sure they didn't run through the open door into the kitchen.

With pillows tucked in the corner, the porch swing was an ideal spot for reading books. The gentle swaying motion was an added charm, and I read every book in the house and many of those from the school library. We never went to a "city" library.

The old porch swing also heard Grandma and me as we discussed the day's events while peeling the supper potatoes, made plans for the coming day while husking the yellow ears of sweet corn from the garden, discussed the birds and bees while cleaning the hulls from the homegrown strawberries, and contemplated the neighborhood news while snapping the freshly picked green beans. Work went faster as we talked and swung gently to and fro. Sometimes Grandma softly sang one of the old hymns. It was while we were working and swinging that I bombarded Grandma with questions a little girl needed to know. "What was I like when I was a baby?" "Why don't we give names to all the piggies and calves like we do the kittens?" "Why do other girls have mothers and I don't?" "My girlfriends have baby sisters, so Grandma, why can't *you* get me a baby sister?" I really put her on the spot with that question, didn't I?

Swings are notorious as "spooning spots" for young lovers, but unfortunately Bill and I never got the chance to try it out. The old swing finally fell apart before our courting days. Sigh!

There's something very relaxing about a porch swing, something very non-threatening. A swing is a warm and homey spot. It seems to encourage and thrive on daydreams and friendly conversation. Every home needs one!

## Chapter 50.
# "Back Home Again in Indiana"

Grandpa had always been a Democrat, but when President Franklin Roosevelt ran for a third term in 1940, Grandpa decided it was time for a change. As he put it, "Two terms are enough for anyone!" Grandpa became a Republican.

When he heard that Republican candidate, Wendell Willkie, was going to speak in his hometown of Elwood, Indiana, on August 17, Grandpa and Dad decided we should go hear what he had to say. Elwood is located near Indianapolis, about 100 miles from our home. On a very hot, sticky summer morning, Grandpa, Grandma, Dad, Don and I piled into Grandpa's Nash Rambler and headed west.

Getting there was no problem. It was that bumper to bumper traffic at the outskirts of town that caused trouble for a lot of people. Traffic moved at a snail's pace and cars began to heat up. So did some of their owners. Most of those drivers had pulled off and parked by the side of the road until the cloud of steam subsided. Then, hopefully, someone would be kind enough to let them back in line. "My goodness, Daddy, won't we ever get there?" I wondered. It seemed like an eternity before we eventually found a parking spot. The crops had been harvested from many of the fields, so area farmers turned them into parking areas for all those visitors to their town.

After considerable walking, we finally arrived at main street just before the parade was to pass by. The Hoosiers wanted to "cheer on" their hometown boy. Grandpa and Grandma were reaching their more mature years by this time, and Grandma just wasn't able to handle all those hours of standing, first for the parade and then for the "long-winded speeches" at the wooded Callaway Park. Most of the listeners sat on the ground or stood for the entire afternoon. Dad decided to go shopping and when he came back he carried a little footstool for Grandma to use. Today that stool sits in Don's living room where I fondly remember it as *The Wendell Willkie Stool.*

Callaway Park was large, and we could barely see Mr. Willkie. I have no idea what he said or what my family thought of his speech. At that time politics didn't interest me, and I didn't really understand what the fuss was all about. I was ten years old and my day was just a great adventure.

By Roosevelt's fourth term, the adults in my family were all staunch Republicans. I broke with Grandpa's new political image, though, and accepted the patriotic little token offered by the Democrats at their Auglaize County Fair booth. It was a practical little square pencil sharpener, one in which you inserted a pencil and turned it around until the sharp edges cut away the wood, leaving a nice point on the lead. Every kid wanted one. With the war on, the patriotic message painted in red, white, and blue was appropriate.

Franklin Delano Roosevelt used the following symbol quite often in his campaign.

can
We will Win
must
FDR

The president died before completing his fourth term and the pencil sharpener became dull. It eventually found its way into Grandpa's trunk.

Years later, shortly after our marriage, we glimpsed a little different view of politics. We attended several Auglaize County young Republican meetings and when our county president decided to run for State President of the Young Republicans, he asked all the members to attend and support him. We decided to go and see what politics were really all about. What an eye-opener! We had made signs and were prepared to "talk up" our candidate on election day. We went to our hotel bed that night with eager anticipation of a rousing display of banners and cheering support. Imagine our surprise when we awoke the next morning and found out that while we slept, the campaign managers had met in a "smoke-filled room" and worked out an agreement. After certain concessions were made, our candidate was to be the new president and his opponent would be the vice president. Our anticipation and eagerness to wave banners and support our candidate were suddenly down the drain, and our efforts were no longer needed. We've always voted but have never gotten personally involved in politics. That event burst our political bubble!

A Cleveland, Ohio, band marches in the
"Wendell Willkie Hometown Parade," Elwood, Indiana, 1940.

## Chapter 51.
# Antics and Escapades

Art Linkletter's *House Party,* a popular 1950s afternoon TV program, featured a daily segment with Mr. Linkletter talking to children. The antics of the kids brought many smiles and prompted a book, *Kids Say the Darndest Things*! The kids were very open and candid, often telling things like, "Mom said I shouldn't make faces," or "Daddy told me not to pick my nose," or even more graphic comments. Needless to say, the program became very popular and my three preschoolers loved to watch. The program was so popular that it returned to the TV screen with Bill Cosby and Art Linkletter as hosts. Since most people enjoy the antics of children, I include these true family stories, not to pick on anyone, but to share the innocence of childhood with those who may have grown cynical. Perhaps the stories will bring a tear or smile.

Born in 1840, Great-grandfather Heinrich Schwartz was a little boy in a militant, peasant-oriented Prussia. There was no time for foolish play. Grandma told me about one of her dad's tasks as a small boy. At that time, the forests belonged to the government or to wealthy landowners. It was against the law to break off branches or cut down trees, even small ones. Only twigs or sticks lying on the ground could be picked up. As a small boy, it was his job to find any fallen twigs and limbs and take them home to use in the stove. A grandson told me that when Henry was a child, he was very hungry one day when he came into the house. He walked over to a pot boiling on the cookstove, lifted the lid and peered into it. His mother slapped his hand and reprimanded him severely for his actions. She assured this little son that he was to be a worker, not a pot watcher. It sounds quite innocent today, but it was taken quite seriously in the 1840s in Germany!

In later life, this immigrant proved to have a sense of humor with a "streak of orneriness." After a mill accident, only a stub of Henry's index finger remained on his right hand. Sometimes he used that stub when teasing children. His grandson, Chester Schwartz, remembered being teased by a playful poke with that finger. It was not something that he reserved for family members, either. Harold Daniels told of going to Albert Haller's store as a child. As Henry and his dad stood and talked, Henry playfully poked the little boy in the ribs with his finger. There wasn't much padding on those little ribs and Henry didn't realize the strength he had in that finger.

Henry's daughter, my grandma Davenport, created her own form of fun when she brought the cows home each evening. Henry had five daughters before having two sons and another daughter, so the girls had to work like men to maintain the farm. Grandma was the real tomboy of those girls. As the sun began to sink into the western sky each day, Grandma walked to the woods to bring the cows home for milking. She usually climbed on the back of one of the cows and rode it home, sometimes even standing up as it plodded slowly toward the log barn. Her sister, Tillie, said that her Dad was not too happy about it, but he never said a whole lot as long as the cows came to the barn and gave their usual amount of milk.

Grandpa Frank also had his share of childhood stories. His family had driven a team of horses pulling a covered wagon to settle in Wisconsin in 1879 when he was two years old. A wooden board fence surrounded the Davenport yard, and one day the little boy ran up and down, banging the fence with a stick in his hand–thump, thump, thumping against each board. It was great fun for the little tyke as he attracted the attention of the big dog just on the other side of the fence. The dog was getting a bit agitated by the time someone took note of the situation and rescued the little boy before things got nasty. Grandpa's innocent fun could have become a huge disaster because the "dog" which was becoming very irritated by all the noise was, in reality, a Wisconsin bear!

When Grandpa was a teenager, he and his friends went Halloweening one night. An elderly gentleman living on a farm south of Kossuth had a cow which was his most prized possession. The boys decided to hide that cow as a prank. While the man slept, they led it through the underbrush to a hiding place beside the canal. Every morning the boys walked through the brush and weeds as they carried food and water to the cow. Then they milked it and returned home, only to repeat the event again that evening. The old man fussed when he couldn't find his cow, but animals occasionally wandered away and were later found by neighbors. After a week or more, the boys realized their *trick* was causing *them* more problems than it was the old man. That night they walked the cow back home and tied her in the old man's barn. I'm sure he was delighted to see her, but no doubt wondered where in the world his cow had been all that time. No one ever told, not even the cow!

Other Halloween devilment included placing a spring wagon on top of a windmill and a buggy atop the peaked roof of a barn. Both were difficult tasks and no doubt required more energy than they were worth. A nighttime climb to the top of a windmill or school flagpole for the purpose of hanging a "slop jar" (also called a "night owl"), was simpler and produced satisfaction with much less effort.

When Grandpa was a young man, life around Kossuth was not always peaceful and serene. In fact, an 1890 *Auglaize County Republican* article described Kossuth as an unincorporated village "where law and order are unknown." Like many canal towns, the saloon was one of the busiest places in town. Grandpa hadn't yet married when a man came out of the saloon one day and called him a very bad name. Grandpa was usually rather quiet, but he slugged the guy! Before the fellow could figure out what had hit him, Grandpa went to the constable, told him he had just hit a man, and he paid the one dollar fine. Grandpa told us that no one was going to call him *that* and get away with it. As he explained it, "By paying the fine, the man couldn't take me to court because I had already paid for my actions." Very good thinking for a country boy, although I couldn't imagine my peace-loving, Sunday-School-teaching grandpa doing such a thing! I guess his patience just ran out.

Grandpa maintained a spirited outlook on life, even as he grew older. I was a teenager when my school bus stopped in front of our house one memorable day. I could scarcely believe my eyes as I looked at my grandpa standing in the front yard. "What is so unusual about that?" you may ask, but you see he was standing–on his head. I didn't know he could do that and wasn't sure why he was doing it then when he was more than seventy years old. He explained that he'd been having pains in his side, and the doctor thought it might be appendicitis. Someone told Grandpa that if he stood on his head, he wouldn't need surgery because the appendix would drain. When he was young, he had learned to stand on his head as a clown with the *Uncle Tom's Cabin* stage show, so there stood Grandpa, upside down, trying to cure his pains. What happened? By the next week, he was in the hospital where the appendix was surgically removed. Standing on his head didn't cure Grandpa's appendicitis!

Grandpa was also involved in another event when I was a little girl. Aunt Tillie and Uncle Ed lived in the country near Kossuth. We had gone to visit and, as usual, Aunt Tillie was pointing out all her new flowers to us. One particular flower was quite attractive and she called out to Grandpa, "Look here, Frank!" Grandpa turned to look and just as he did so, Tillie slipped and tumbled to the ground with feet high in the air, petticoat and dress flying up to her neck. Grandpa stared in shocked silence for a moment, then burst out laughing as he helped her get back on her feet. Needless to say, she was occasionally teased about that display.

The next generation of stories started when my dad was a tired little boy who enjoyed sleeping more than parties. His parents were young and active in the community. Grandpa joined his cousin, Freedus, and uncles, Lew and Frank Daniels, as they played their fiddles for various parties, barn dances, and activities in the area. Grandma occasionally chorded on the piano if one was available. Dad was a little boy, but he went along to the parties. When he got sleepy, he pulled the adults' coats into a little nest and went to sleep. Parties were fun for grownups, but a good nap was much more enjoyable for a sleepy little boy.

One of the most oft-told stories about the escapades of my dad was that of his ingenious method of feeding the chickens. Using a sharp nail, he drilled a hole in a grain of corn, then tied a string through the hole and threw it on the ground with a few other grains of corn. When an unsuspecting old hen gobbled up the grain, he pulled the string and the grain of corn came back out. Then he fed it to some other unsuspecting chicken. He thought it was great fun until his parents caught him in the act.

Dad had several skirmishes when he was in high school. Actually, Dad was quite active on the Spencerville football team during his first three years of high school. When he transferred to Blume High School in Wapak, he missed the fun and excitement of playing on that team. Since Blume didn't have a team, Dad decided to correct that situation at once. He talked to several boys about starting a football team. His enthusiasm was not only dampened quite soon, but his school career nearly ended when he was called into the superintendent's office. Mr. Drummond very sternly informed him that Blume did not *have* football, did not *want* football, and that if he continued with his efforts to start a team, he would be *expelled* from school. Dad got the message and went on to graduate. But apparently he planted a seed. Three years later the 1922 yearbook boasted that the school now had its first football team.

I guess schools have always had more than their share of pranks. A 1925 *Wapakoneta Daily News* headline read: "SMELLED AWFUL! Limburger cheese placed on a steam radiator in a Buckland Schoolroom by one of the boys during the absence of the teacher Wednesday brought about an investigation by authorities." This incident did not involve any of our family, but a fourteen-year-old youth from the village confessed his crime, and school was out for a short time while doors and windows were opened to air out the building. Since it was January 23, it probably didn't take long for things to air out and cool off in the building.

And now comes the antics from my generation. I guess I was a fussy baby, but my family knew I had a good reason. My mother died when I was seven months old. After that Grandpa and Grandma had quite a time finding a milk that *agreed* with me. Apparently they found something that did the trick, though. As you may have already noticed, I lived!

Unfortunately, (and to my shame), I was allowed to drink my milk from a bottle until I was five years old. Since they had a problem finding something that worked, they allowed me to keep drinking from those bottles to be sure I would get enough calcium. Was I going to have to drag those dumb baby bottles to school with me? No, one day, I realized I was just too old to hang onto them any longer and I told Grandma I wanted to break all of them. Grandpa helped me carry them out to the old shop where I threw them, one at a time, against the side of the building so the pieces would fall into the trash pile below. That action gave me some kind of deep satisfaction, knowing I had made the decision to dispose of them myself. After sucking on rubber nipples all those years, the milk didn't taste right out of a glass. The result? I don't like milk.

Tucked away in the bottom of Grandpa's trunk, just below my baby shoes, was a little infant feeding dish. That baby dish holds a touch of my past. I guess it is a good thing it can't talk. Did my brother make the small chip on the side, or did I? Was I banging my little spoon too hard? Did someone try to feed me some of Grandma's homemade cottage cheese which I detested and with a grand sweep of my little hand, I sent that poor dish crashing to the floor with a clunk? Can't you just picture me sitting in a high chair with that dish in front of me, trying to balance a spoon somewhere between my fingers and my elbows, mashed potatoes and gravy smooshed across the big grin on my face? That grin was quite obvious in my one-year-old baby picture. Now if you can picture that, add this to the view. When sorting through some of Bill's family things, I found his baby dish, exactly like mine with the same little pictures on the outer rim. Where mine had a "puss 'n boots" painted in the bottom, his had three little children. But his isn't chipped!

In our rural area, we didn't have a designated *Trick-or-treat Night* when kids dressed up and spent several hours running door to door, collecting enormous amounts of candy as they often do today. Dressing up in masks was usually a school activity. Grade school children *dressed up* for Halloween and walked to other classrooms where the other students tried to guess each person's identity. No one bought fancy costumes then. Masks were simple and were used for several years by someone else in the family. Half-masks resembling the Lone Ranger's were cheaper. I was one of the tallest in the class, so there was usually no problem in identifying me.

One Halloween, Don and I decided to dress up and visit the neighbors, Bob and Helen Mack and their two children, Joe and Roberta. Grandma helped us find some things for costumes. We knew full well that if we walked down the road to Mack's, they would immediately know it was us, but Don had a bright idea. We would go through our woods, climb the fence and walk across the field to their home. It sounded good to me, but the deeper we got into that dark woods, the less I thought of the idea. The woods had always been friendly during the day, but now it was dark and desolate. Each step in the silence of the night seemed to explode with the crackle of broken twigs beneath our feet, and I shivered under my costume as I struggled to keep up with Don. Tree branches waved about us, occasionally moaning and groaning in the evening breeze. I was rather scared until we finally left the woods and climbed the fence where we walked with ease through the empty field.

Helen welcomed us at the door, and the children were wide-eyed as they stared at the two strangers. After a few words of welcome and a handful of candy for each of us, Don and I retraced our steps back across the field. Joe recently told me that he had watched us until we had climbed the fence and disappeared back into the darkened woods. We had kept our identities secret, but as we stumbled through the woods toward home, I wasn't sure it was worth it. I guess Don agreed. We never did it again.

Like most brothers, Don liked to tease. We usually got a drink of water before going to bed. As I walked through the darkened dining room toward the kitchen, he often hid behind the chimney, then jumped out and yelled as I passed, scaring the daylights out of me. Don didn't behave one day and Grandma said she was going to punish him. He sassed back, "You'll have to catch me first!" then took off running around the kitchen table with Grandma chasing him. We were not allowed to talk back to adults and that day he had to pay the price for his sinful actions.

My second grade classroom was just across the hall from the stage entrance at the Buckland School. Don's fifth grade was practicing for a program on the stage. His teacher didn't think he was behaving properly and brought him over to our room where he had to stand in the corner. I was so embarrassed! I wanted to pretend I didn't know him. Years later, Don told me that this particular teacher was always picking on him. He finally figured out the reason. After he had misbehaved a sufficient number of times, she felt it was then her duty to have a conference with our dad. She was an "old maid school marm," and Don said, "I think she picked on me so she and Dad could get together for those conferences." Dad was a widower and was thought to be a "prize catch." But this teacher's tactics didn't work!

How did I learn to swim? I learned while floating around Stoner's gravel pit on an inner tube. A group of Kossuth kids went swimming there one afternoon and as I floated by, my ornery brother got the bright idea of pushing me off the inner tube. I did a lot of spitting and sputtering, but for the first time in my life, I swam! The water in that area of the gravel pit was over my head so what other choice did I have? Drown? That didn't sound too appealing!

How did I learn to ice skate? A pair of ice skates was under the Christmas tree when I was about thirteen. Since Don was old enough to drive, he took me along to the pond near the canal and I changed into my new shoe skates. Leaning against a tree for support, I gingerly stood up on the ice. From out of nowhere came my brother who had been a good skater for several years, and as he whizzed by, he gave me a gentle shove out onto the ice. No, I didn't skate off into the sunset. Ice skating didn't work quite like swimming. With no tree to support me, I flopped onto the ice in a less-than-graceful heap and slid to the middle of the pond.

But the story ends happily. It took me a while, but I did eventually skate well and Don usually took me with him when he drove to Kossuth for an afternoon or evening of skating fun. In retrospect, my brother's brash actions actually were a blessing in disguise. I'm not an athletic person, and I might not have had the nerve to get involved in seriously learning to skate and swim. As it was, I learned to skate well enough to really enjoy it. After seeing my first Sonja Henie movie, I nearly killed myself, though. I tried to do some of the fancy things this world famous figure skating champion did. I knew she had smooth ice on a sheltered pond, while my ice was roughed up by the windblown waves freezing on the flowing canal and fallen twigs strewn across it. What I didn't know was that her skates were figure skates designed for such fancy skating. Mine were hockey skates designed for fast skating, definitely not for figure eights and spins. I didn't stand a chance! How we loved it when occasionally there was no wind, and the water would be smooth as it froze into ice! The big boys had a fast game of hockey on those days. I know I am much too old for such things now, but when I see a frozen creek or pond on a cold, crisp morning, I have an urge to put on skates and again enjoy the wonderful feeling of gliding over smooth ice with the wind blowing past me. Ah, those were the good old days!

As Rosie and I were riding bikes to Spencerville one afternoon, we rounded the big curve north of Kossuth and met a car. In trying to get safely to the side of the road, we collided. Her pedal caught in the spokes of my front wheel, bending them badly. Not knowing what to do, we bent them back far enough for the bicycle to be ridden and pedaled on into town. We stopped at Forest Croft's filling station and he straightened the spokes so well that you could scarcely tell it had been wrecked. I was afraid I would be grounded since mine was a brand new bicycle!

Maple syrup time was always exciting when I was a child. The sap was collected from the maple trees in the woods and yard and this "sugar water" was boiled down in the oven of the old wood cookstove until it became a thick syrup. It took a lot of water to make a pint of syrup. One year Grandma had finished boiling some syrup and had put it in a pint can and left it to cool on the kitchen table. She had spilled some water on the floor and as she reached for a towel to mop it up, my brother Don chased me into the kitchen. As I flew past the table, my foot slipped in the water and down I went. Throwing out my arms to catch myself, my hand accidentally caught the jar of maple syrup sitting on the table. To make a long, sticky story very short, the can of syrup landed on top of my head and the sweet goo literally ran down my hair, across my face, and oozed down my arms. Not only was I a sticky mess, all of Grandma's efforts in making the syrup were wasted. Hours of work and nothing to show for it! But one good thing came from the whole sad episode. Several years later, it became the subject of my first speech for my Wittenberg College speech class. It was recorded for posterity.

One of my most sorrowful escapades happened the day I hurried to get something from Grandma's dining room buffet and yanked open a side door. Several of the dishes that had been stacked inside suddenly fell to the floor and broke. Every soup bowl in the set became a part of the mess left on the floor. I couldn't believe they had toppled out so easily, and I was heartbroken. These were no ordinary dishes! They were the special ones Grandma had longed for over the years. Every piece was very thin, delicate and gorgeous. Oh, I was so very sorry! Grandma had always said I was to have them someday, and now I had ruined the set for her and for myself as well.

Years later, after Grandma was gone, Grandpa asked me to take the dishes home. He said he would never use them, and he was afraid they might get broken before I had a chance to inherit them. As I packed them carefully for the move, I was amazed to find that all eight soup bowls were there. Although I didn't know it, Grandpa and Grandma had written to the company and found out that replacements were still available. In spite of my childhood carelessness, many years later I inherited a complete set of pretty dishes.

One day while playing in the barn, I did something that really upset Daddy. I quickly ran to the house. As I slammed the door, I realized he was just a short distance behind me. I skipped up the stairs and into the bathroom. (I thought I was safe there.) As Dad climbed the stairs he called out, "Where are you?" In my most innocent voice I answered, "I'm using the bathroom, Daddy!" I guess I thought that excuse would be good enough for him to leave, but he didn't. He sat down on the top step and waited. I hoped to "out-wait" him, but as I sat and thought about it for a while, I finally decided the longer he had to wait, the more trouble I would be in. I finally turned the handle (so he would know my business had really been necessary, you know!) and I went out. I don't remember my punishment, so it couldn't have been too bad. The worst thing was just sitting there worrying about what it *might* be.

I had heard Grandpa tell his story about the man who called him a bad name, and it made a deep impression on me. One day when Don had teased me more than any little girl could stand, I called him the worst thing I could think of–that same name. I had no idea what those three letters stood for or what it really meant. I just thought it sounded about right for a pesky, teasing brother. The problem was that someone else heard me say it. I was immediately paraded inside and told to sit on a kitchen chair where I soon learned what S.O.B. meant. When I called my brother that name, I had, in essence, just called my mother a bad name. That nearly broke my heart. Everyone had told me how wonderful my mother was and how they hoped I would grow up to be as sweet as she was. I cried and cried for being such a wicked little girl and promised I would never, ever say that again. I was cured that day and never took up swearing as a hobby!

When I asked Bill about some of his childhood antics, he couldn't think of any. Now do you suppose he never got into trouble? Maybe it pays to have a bad memory.

When they were in their late teens, Bill and his brother, Vernon, had some experiences with snakes. Snakes had always been a part of farm life. The two young brothers were fishing in the creek behind the barn. The fish were to go into a bucket of water about three feet behind the fishermen. After a period of time, they looked back and were startled to see a snake coiled in a circle around it. They scared it away, but he certainly hasn't forgotten the shock of seeing it so close to where they had been contentedly fishing.

When he was about ten or twelve years old, Bill was fishing from a concrete abutment beside the bridge. His dog, a blend of collie and shepherd, was down by the creek where he found a three or four feet long snake. Bill watched as the dog began to tease and irritate the reptile. After a certain amount of this, the snake decided it had enough and, as Bill watched, it began to wrap around the dog. Bill said he didn't know what to do, and, as he watched, it squeezed the breath out of his dog. When the dog finally fell down and lay still, the snake uncoiled itself and slithered away. About that time, the dog got up and shook itself, then looked over and saw the fleeing snake. That dog was now angry and he took out after the snake. When the dog was finally finished with him, Mr. Snake looked like shredded meat.

Many times, as Bill plowed ground in a swampy area, he saw blue racers which had come out of the nearby woods. Some were up to eight feet long and often ran down the furrow in front of his tractor. Sometimes they could be seen running across the ground with their heads sticking up above the top of the grass. If he was close enough, Bill would unhitch his pull-type plow and take off after them with the tractor. Although he was driving about fifteen miles an hour, it sometimes took a little while to catch up with the snake. They wanted to eliminate them from the farm, so he tried to run over the snake with the tractor. When the back tire was on top of him, he slammed on the brakes and the skidding tread would chew up the critter. But enough about snakes.

"It was a dark and stormy night!" That's how Snoopy always starts his story in the funny papers, isn't it? Bill was a young man when he had an interesting experience one dark and stormy night. He had been working plowed ground on his grandpa's farm. The summer day had been very hot, and as he worked, a severe thunderstorm suddenly came up around midnight. He drove the tractor back to the pickup truck, turned off the key and dashed to the truck just as the rain started pelting down. Opening the door, he dove into the driver's seat and slammed the door behind him. Grabbing the handle, he started winding up the open truck window. Suddenly . . . Wham! Into his lap jumped Spike, his dog. Being all black, Spike visually melted into the darkness. Since this dog was part greyhound, it was easy for him to jump through that window. But the sudden unexpected jolt nearly scared the daylights out of Bill!

Much as a magnet draws metal to it, mud seems to attract farm kids and we have certainly had our share of mud-versus-kid episodes. Children are as adventurous as a nest of half-grown kittens, eager to explore every nook and cranny around them. One day when he was about three years old, our first-born, Michael, went exploring. This was not unusual. As I looked out the kitchen window, I usually followed his progress from the swings to the tree to the garage and on to the corncrib. When I could no longer see him, I usually called and within seconds, I would hear his answer or see him. One day, he disappeared from sight and when I couldn't locate him from any house windows, I ran outside and called his name. After a couple of calls, I finally heard a faint, faraway cry.

I eventually located my little boy standing in the middle of a sea of mud just behind the hen house. Although his boots were stuck, he was not about to wade out and leave them there. I finally put on Daddy's big buckle-up boots and headed for the mud hole. When I lifted him straight up, he popped right out of those little rubber boots. Balancing him on my hip, I reached down to rescue the boots. As I pulled them out of the mud, they sounded much like the sucking sound made by a cow's hoof when she pulls it out of a manure pile. After a firm conversation about the disasters of mud holes, he promised he would never set foot in one again. He tearfully explained that when the mud started closing in on his little boots, he was afraid he was going to just disappear into that hole.

Two or three years later, when Steven was five and Nancy three, they had a similar encounter with mud. (Apparently Michael had learned his lesson earlier! He was not involved!) When I didn't see them for a while, I ran outside and started calling their names. I didn't hear a thing as I frantically ran from the house to the barn to the garage to the hen house. They were in none of these places. I called their names over and over. Finally I heard a very faint cry. "Where are you?" I called. Then I heard Steven's plaintive cry, "Here! In the field!" My eyes searched the large field behind the hen house and there, at the farthermost end of the farm, stood my little runaways. When I yelled for them to come to the house, they just stood and looked at me. Again I yelled, this time with the emphasis loud and clear, "You come to the house *right now!*" Convinced I meant it, they obediently started for the house. It wasn't until they were quite near that I realized they were both walking in stocking feet. Now, mind you, this was winter. It was cold. I was quite alarmed when I realized they had walked on that cold, rough ground all the way from the back of the farm with only thin little socks on their feet. They had to have been about frozen. I shook my head in dismay as I instructed them to "Go to the house and get those muddy clothes off while I get the boots. Then I'll give you a bath and you are going right to bed!"

Following their muddy foot prints, I traced them to an even more muddy dead furrow at the back of the field. But where were their boots? I saw nothing but a smooth sea of mud. Finally I spotted a half inch of something sticking up. When I pulled, it was a little rubber boot. "Now where are the other three?" I wondered. I finally realized the only way to find them was to use my hand as a shovel and start digging. When I found the other boots, they were completely buried in the soft slime. I was not a happy mommy, but by the time I carried those muddy boots all the way to the house in the cold winter air, I had cooled off enough to see the humor of it all. After a quick bath and a long nap, my forlorn little wanderers were properly repentant, and we were all grateful that they had not been hurt or caught pneumonia.

Our family's last great episode of kids-versus-mud took place recently when Kevin and Elizabeth Davenport were playing outside, got too close to mud that just "sucked them in," and what do you know? They were stuck. When their parents, Diane and Roger Davenport, (my nephew) told me, I just smiled and said, "Well, I guess it just runs in the family!" Now that little Matthew has joined the family, I wonder, "Will he be next?"

Well, those are some family escapades. There isn't room to print them all, but I assure you we had an abundance of humorous kids antics in raising three active youngsters.

Dad's Spencerville High School 1917-18 football team posed beside the school.
Front row, left to right: Bernard Davenport (my dad)-center, Emerson Tone-guard, Carl Wolfe-end, Professor Charles Rish-manager, Fred Rupert-end, Ralph Greer-guard, Ira Beeryman
Back row: Roy Slygh, Harvey Spyker-halfback, Gerald Sisler-half back, Carl Helwig-quarterback, Arthur Miller-halfback, Walter Leffel-tailback

## Chapter 52.

# Working Together to Win a War

Where were you when Pearl Harbor was bombed? You could ask anyone old enough to remember that day and they could tell you the exact circumstances under which they heard the terrible news. It began an era that no one could forget. America was plunged into the most widespread and worst years of fighting anyone had ever seen, and it had started with an air raid and bombing of the naval base and airfield at Pearl Harbor in Hawaii. The attack left the entire area in a shambles. Americans were stunned! Who would believe that such a thing could have happened? Although Hawaii was not yet a state, we were closely aligned with it and our fleet of ships filled the harbor near Honolulu.

So, where was my family? We went to Sunday school and church as usual that winter Sunday morning. When we arrived home, Grandma took dinner out of the oven, and we sat down to eat. Someone flipped the radio on. We listened in shocked silence as the horrible details were announced. We had followed the stories of Hitler marching his army through some of the smaller European countries, then occupying them, but we certainly didn't expect to be involved. Now Japan was putting us into the thick of it.

Within hours, President Franklin D. Roosevelt had declared war on the aggressors and was broadcasting a radio plea for volunteers to help in the war effort. American boys stood in line to volunteer for military service while others were drafted. Overnight, our lives had changed drastically. Dad belonged to the Gideons, a group of Christian businessmen who came into our classrooms and gave a New Testament to each fifth-grader. Now he joined with other Gideons as they stood in bus depots and train stations, giving the precious little books to the young men as they left for distant military camps.

Almost immediately, certain items needed for the war effort became scarce. Gasoline was rationed and a national speed limit of 35 miles per hour was put in place. Fast driving wasted too much precious gasoline. Huge signs were placed in strategic spots showing Uncle Sam pointing his finger and asking, "Is This Trip Really Necessary?" Grandpa's gas allowance got us to church each Sunday and to Spencerville for groceries. By saving a little each week, we could occasionally visit relatives in nearby towns.

With the beginning of rationing, Dad was asked to serve on the county tire Rationing Board, and was allowed a little extra gas to attend board meetings and to keep his ditching machine running. Productive land helped the farmers to supply food for the troops.

What items were rationed? I remember gasoline, tires, meat, shoes, and sugar. There may have been others, but those were the most obvious to our family. Rationing cards were distributed in each community, usually at the school, and each family adapted to the rules as best they could. Many country families worked out a system much like the one used by Grandma and Aunt Tillie. Grandma needed more sugar to preserve the fruit grown on our farm. Aunt Tillie lived in Lima then, didn't can fruits, and never used her full sugar allotment. Since she had to buy her meat, those were the stamps she needed. We raised our own meat, so the two sisters traded–sugar stamps for meat stamps. Most farm families had the same problem and solved it the same way.

Because food was rationed, many special recipe booklets in colors of red, white, and blue were made available to housewives. The recipes used honey or saccharin in place of sugar and they stretched meats as far as possible. Grandma's wartime copy of *Variety Meats*, published by National Livestock and Meat Board, lists recipes for some of the less popular cuts of meat: tongue with rice and spinach, breaded brains, kidney loaf, sweetbread salad, liver pancakes, braised heart with apples, and tripe a la Creole. How do these goodies sound? Page 4 of *Recipes for Today,* published in 1943 by General Foods Corporation, lists "My wartime food rules:"

1. "Get down to good plain food." (They suggested using soups, stews, and meat loaves which used meat sparingly, also lots of fresh-grown vegetables.)
2. "Work harder planning, buying, and cooking." (We were to use healthy foods and then make them look and taste good so the family would like them.)
3. "Buy the most for the money. . . ." (They stressed using good tasting and nourishing foods that would also save time and fuel. They mentioned reading the labels for nutritional information, and so on. Few people ever read a label.)
4. "Learn all about the food rations. . . ." (We were asked to read what the government had to say and when changes took place, we were to take them in "good heart." They urged us to "show that famous American ingenuity, like Grandmother did.")
5. "Never waste a bit of food. . . ." (We were urged to find ways to use all of it by learning from "olden times, or from neighbors and experts.")

Ration books became a source of many problems, but also of much humor. I don't know of a family who didn't have their ration books go through the washing machine at least once or twice. Occasionally folks went to town for groceries and discovered they had left those pesky rationing books at home. No meat or sugar for today and no gas to come back tomorrow.

For those who may wonder about the rationing rules, the following appeared in area newspapers in 1942. "Gasoline Rationing Questions Answered–Washington, Oct. 1–Answers to some of the questions most frequently asked about gasoline rationing, now effective in the east and soon to be extended nationwide to curb driving and conserve tires, follow:"

1. Q. When does gasoline rationing become effective nationally?
   A. Sometime around Nov. 22.
2. Q. How will motorists obtain ration books?
   A. By registration at public schools on dates yet to be announced.
3. Q. How much gasoline will the average motorist receive?
   A. A little under four gallons weekly.
4. Q. What are the different kinds of ration books?
   A. There are "A" books, "B" books, "C" books, "D" books, "S" books, "E" books, and "R" books.

5. Q. What is the "A" book?
   A. It is the basic ration book for passenger cars, providing little less than four gallons of gasoline weekly for an estimated 2,880 miles of driving a year.
6. Q. If the "A" book does not provide enough gasoline for his proven occupational needs, can a car owner get a supplemental ration?
   A. Yes, he may obtain a "B" book by proving a need of more than 150 miles of occupational driving monthly: forming a car-sharing club with some other persons, or show that he is unable to do so and that alternative means of transportation are inadequate.
7. Q. Who is entitled to receive "C" books?
   A. Special categories of drivers, including physicians, police, firemen, war workers, etc.
8. Q. Who receives the other classes of ration books?
   A. "D" books are issued to motorcycles; "S" books to trucks, buses, and taxis; "E" and "R" books to non-highway users such as boats, tractors, etc.
9. Q. May the owner of two cars get two basic rations?
   A. Yes, he may obtain an "A" book for each car.[1]

School buses received sufficient gasoline and tires to run their daily routes, but all other school trips were canceled. As school children we did our part as we peeled the tinfoil from chewing gum wrappers, tried not to make mistakes on school papers which then required using rubber erasers (many of the new pencils did not have erasers on the top), and saved milkweed pods to replace the kapok that was no longer available. Stale lard and used grease were saved for making munitions, and glass and tin cans were collected. Paper was scarce, so we used the back side of our school papers for homework. Used envelopes were cut apart and grocery lists or other notes were scribbled on them. Everyone did everything possible to assist in the war effort. It wasn't called that, but recycling was a common thing in those days.

Big scrap drives were held in many communities. In New Knoxville the school classes competed in bringing in the most junk. (Bill helped his class become the winners.) Kids saved pennies to buy Savings Stamps and when we had enough, we traded them for War Bonds. Signs saying "Buy Bonds and Stamps Today" appeared on big billboards, in store windows, on post cards and envelopes—wherever they could be used to remind folks to support the war effort. Movie stars and politicians took part in huge bond rallies to promote the sale of bonds and stamps. Magazine advertisements were full of red, white and blue patriotic symbols and we often saw signs that said, "Keep America Free" and "A Slip of the Lip Could Sink a Ship."

Manufacturers switched from making refrigerators, stoves, and automobiles to military trucks and engines for tanks or airplanes. Old appliances had to last a bit longer, or we did without.

A few new phrases were "price controls," "ceiling price" and "wage freeze." Congress gave the President power to freeze wages and prices. A ceiling price was put on items, allowing a store owner to sell under, but not over that amount. Signs read "Ceiling Price $1.40, our price $1.29." Labor unions also promoted a "no-strike" policy to insure supplies would reach the military when needed.

Until this time in history, most women had remained in the home, but as men were drafted into the military, women began to replace them in the offices and factories. The phrase, “Rosie the Riveter” became quite well-known as women became riveters in building the ships and planes used in the war. I don’t remember that any of my friends’ mothers went to work in factories, but we heard of others who had put on slacks, tied their hair in a pony-tail or put it up in a snood to keep it out of the machinery, and worked alongside the men still working in factories. And heaven forbid, there was even talk that many were soon able to out-cuss the men.

Cities and towns all over the United States, even little ones like Buckland, built towers on top of their tallest buildings to be used as observation towers for the search of enemy aircraft. Buckland’s tower was atop the fire station. Volunteers learned to identify airplanes by sight and sound. Although it may sound useless now, at that time those volunteers felt they were really doing something important to help the war effort. We didn’t know if an attack would come to America, so everyone tried to do his part.

Victory gardens became the popular means of providing food for one’s family. Gardens showed up in unusual places: along roadsides and railroad tracks, in vacant lots and back yards, and even on the lawns of town squares. Whole communities divided plots of land at the edge of town into individual gardens. After working at jobs all day, people walked to their gardens each evening to plant and weed and harvest. There was very little theft then and people respected items belonging to others. The evenings of working together as they discussed the day’s events were a real time of togetherness and patriotism. I tried to do my share with my victory garden and canning 4-H projects.

Cloth for making clothes and household items was almost impossible to buy. Fabrics were being used for military uniforms and underwear, for towels and tents, for mattresses and bedding needed to supply all the new military camps that sprang up almost overnight across America. With a shortage of yard goods, the housewives used what they had on hand, much as they had during the depression. Now that we were at war, the twenty-five pound white sugar and flour sacks became dish towels and nice homemade undies.

The feed sacks which were plentiful on most farms were again being put to use. The sacks in which Grandpa bought his chicken feed and hog supplement were used for hand towels. An occasional little dress sometimes appeared on clotheslines with the words, Baby Pig Starter, showing faintly. Ingenuity finally took over, and the feed sacks began to show up in bright stripes, floral and other prints that were more suitable for clothing. When Grandpa had his feed ground at the Kossuth Mill, he carried the corn and other ingredients there in burlap sacks. The mash or supplement that was added came in these fancy bags. He didn’t have a large bunch of hogs or chickens, so Grandpa needed only one or two sacks of supplement at a time. Grandma suggested he try to get two sacks alike so she could make something a little larger than the aprons so easily made from just one sack. I loved going along in the summer to pick out my favorite prints. If I was lucky, I might find enough for a dress. When Don and I were in school, poor Grandpa had a problem, though. Even after Grandma started sending a sack along to match designs, Grandpa occasionally brought home one with the exact same pattern–but in a different color. You see, Grandpa was color blind.

Feed sacks were used for everything: new window curtains, slip covers for old chairs, shirts for the men and boys, pajamas, dresses, blouses and robes for the ladies and girls. Some communities had style shows and the only requirement was that everything had to be made from feed sacks. And those ladies were really clever!

The *Hoard’s Dairyman* ran an interesting feature on feed bags. In an earlier column,

Lois J. Hurley had asked her readers to send comments about their use of feed bags. I especially enjoyed one from New York: "In 1948, my family moved from the Bronx to Staten Island to become instant farmers on five acres, horses, a Guernsey cow, two pigs, chickens. We got conned into buying White Leghorn cockerel chicks for one cent each; how they could eat. That's how we wound up with many beautiful feed sacks."

He continued, "I had bought a 1929 Model A four-door sedan for $15. The inside upholstery was pretty bad, so I did the whole inside over with feed bags, using the same pattern but in different colors."

"When I married the girl up the street, off we went on our honeymoon–John Deere green with yellow wheels–lined with mash bags–New Jersey, Pennsylvania, New York State, Thousand Island, King's Highway in Canada, and back to Staten Island. 'Them were the good old days.'"[2] Today one sack is worth several dollars.

While sitting in my classroom at school, word came that Homer Kuck had been shot down and was missing. We were saddened by this first casualty in the area because his wife, Annabelle Herron, had attended Buckland school a few years earlier and many in the area knew Homer. Later, word from the government revealed that Homer was a prisoner of war. He was released at the end of the war and returned to his home in New Knoxville. As he later reminisced about his days as a war prisoner, Homer told Bill that it was the most demoralizing experience of his life. Although he revealed only his name, rank and serial number, the Germans knew all about his life back home–the name of his town, the members of his family, and even the name of his Sunday school teacher.

Who were the men who spent part of the day at school asking questions of teachers and school officials? Everyone was curious. The rumor eventually spread through the building that these strangers were U.S. Army officials, the Secret Service, or members of FBI. Why were they in our little town? The whispers mentioned a local young man who was now serving under Uncle Sam. The visit by these dignitaries prompted a whole lot of stories and speculation.

Several months later we were told the young man had been thoroughly investigated and was now working in a classified area where he was not allowed to reveal anything about his job. I see him quite often, and although fifty years have passed, he still does not talk about his activities during the war.

Everyone was encouraged to "write to our boys." Even my grandparents wrote to several men, including Robert Schrolucke, a young man from Kossuth. In return, Bob wrote from Camp Claiborne, Louisiana, in 1943, "Got your letter OK. Glad to get it. I know someone is thinking of me at least. I wish I was home to plow your garden." Bob had plowed our garden for several years before going into the armed forces and he later wrote, "Received your card and letter yesterday. It makes a fellow feel like he's got something to come home for." Mail written by service men was postage free. Although I was only eleven when the war started, I did my part and wrote several letters to my cousin, Charles Briggs, whose birthday was on the same date as mine. I couldn't understand the censor reading those letters first, though. Some letters came to us with sections clipped out by the censor.

Grandpa occasionally wrote to his younger half-brother, Homer Davenport, who served in the Military Police. When he occasionally made it home, I thought he was so handsome in his uniform! Homer's job was one which few people want—hunting down the men who went AWOL (absent without official leave.) Sometimes men who were ready to get on a ship for overseas would suddenly break rank and run. They just couldn't face that possibility of death. Most servicemen's mothers had a flag in the front window with a blue star for each son or daughter in military service. These men didn't want to turn that blue star into the gold one which honored those who had died. Homer's job was to track down these men and bring them back to face prison terms, using force if necessary. Although he was not a big man, Homer was very physically fit and as tough as nails. He told Grandpa it just tore at his heart, though, to hear those men pleading with him and to see the tears streaming down their faces as they begged. But he knew his job was to return them as prisoners to accept punishment.

The hardest thing for parents was the waiting and wondering if they would receive one of the dreaded letters from the government saying their son was missing, or worse yet, killed in action. There were two young men from the Kossuth area killed in that war, Lester "Red" Daniels and Norman Skinner. We attended the funeral of Norman, whom I had known as the ornery, full-of-fun young man who lived on the next farm. That military funeral made a deep impression—the flag-draped coffin as it was lowered into the grave, the guns' loud salute, and the bugler playing "Taps" in the quiet country cemetery. War had suddenly come very close to home.

Another sign of the war came to our community when the former 4-H camp, located on the north shore of Grand Lake St. Marys near Celina, found a different type of occupant. Where we happy 4-H kids had once played and slept, German prisoners of war now occupied tents around the flag pole, while guards lived in the little cabins. I don't know how many men were interred there or how long they stayed, but in talking to friends, I learned that a group of prisoners was taken each day from the camp to the tile mill in New Knoxville. Folks weren't supposed to talk to them, but when they found some of those prisoners understood the local Platt Deutsch, conversations took place. Some prisoners knew people back home who were relatives of these local people.

I occasionally saw a truckload of prisoners go through Kossuth. During tomato harvest, they made the daily trip to Delphos to work in the canning factory. The closed-in truck had its back door up and an armed guard stood at the rear of the truck, gun in his hands, ready to be used if needed. We could see the prisoners behind him, some standing and others seated, perhaps on bales of straw.

Most of the German prisoners were happy to be here, away from the war and fighting. Speaking Platt Deutsch, they told the people in New Knoxville that in America they received good meals each day and had clean, warm clothes to wear and a dry bed in which to sleep. Back in Germany, food had been scarce. Many days they ate only dry brown bread and thin soup, yet they were expected to fight. Their uniforms had begun to wear thin, and they had very few heavy winter clothes. When the war ended, many prisoners didn't want to return to Germany. They had to go back, although some returned later and became American citizens.

Music played a large role in the war effort. The big band era was in full swing and some of the well-known war songs of the day were: "The White Cliffs of Dover," "When the Lights Go On Again All Over the World," "Comin' in on a Wing and a Prayer," and "Praise the Lord and Pass the Ammunition." "Chattanooga Choo-Choo" and "String of Pearls" were favorites. "In the Mood"was rather unique. Just when you thought the music was over, it started again. The favorite band director, far above all others, was Glenn Miller. It was a shock to everyone when he was killed on his way overseas to entertain the troops. Bob Hope became a legend with his faithful visits to hundreds of World War II military camps, ships and airfields around the world.

Lima had one of the few "free canteens" for military personnel in the United States. From November 1, 1942, until October 16, 1945, the people of the Lima area met every train coming into town. All service personnel were given milk, sandwiches, cookies, candy and coffee. Lima's canteen was known all across the country. Every serviceman riding through hoped his train would stop for snacks. In fact, one young man heard about the Lima Canteen when he was fighting in Africa. He was delighted to finally see it. *The Allen County Pictorial History* states that "On July 30, 1943 the Putnam County *Vidette* reported that the canteen could use any excess red ration stamps for ten days after the expiration date for the purchase of meats and cheese for sandwiches. Each day 500 or 600 sandwiches were served to our men and women in the military." The *Lima News* of January 2, 1944, lists the following amount of food served for Christmas: "200 lbs. Coffee, 245 lbs. ground meat, 12 turkeys, 12 chickens, 3 large hens, 1 goose, 4 gallons meat spread, 1 gallon chicken spread, 300 lbs. cheese, 4,200 eggs, 200 popcorn balls, 1,200 pieces fruitcake, 60 bushels apples, 700 quarts milk, 1,300 loaves bread, 70 gallons mayonnaise, 62 gallons relish, 12 lbs. fudge, 300 individual pies, 12,000 cookies."[3] Groups from as far away as Kossuth helped provide those snacks. I remember baking cookies to send to the canteen. I was a young teenager and would have been happy to have helped distribute them to all those good-looking soldiers; but, alas, I was never given the chance. I think those in charge preferred older, more motherly ladies. I am amazed as I think of the unselfishness of all those families. Grandma didn't receive extra sugar stamps for baking those cookies. She sacrificed our own sugar to make the treats for the soldiers.

Ernie Pyle's name was quite familiar. A war correspondent who lived with the boys in the thick of the European and African battles, Ernie wrote his observations to newspapers back in America, telling the humorous and the sensitive aspects of war. He kept the home folks in touch with the events over there. The nation was saddened when they heard he had been killed by a Japanese sniper. Several years ago we visited his grave site in the National Military Cemetery at the top of the Punchbowl in Hawaii.

Wartime hosiery brought some unexpected problems. Ladies' hose had come in two types. Grandma's everyday stockings were made of heavy cotton and were held up by elastic garters. For Sunday, she wore shear silk hose that were quite delicate. The tops of these were fastened to girdles or garter belts. Both styles always had a seam down the back where they were sewed together. Some brands used a very dark seam which supposedly made the legs appear slimmer. (There were no pantyhose then.) Because silk was used during the war for making parachutes, only the heavy cotton hose were readily available. Ladies who were fortunate enough to have a pair or two of silk hose were very careful when handling them. They snagged quite easily. The younger ladies hated the ugly cotton hose, but it was either wear them or go barefoot. A humorous consequence of the war resulted when these young gals decided to make their own *fake* hose, using a liquid "make-up" to cover their legs. When it was painted on, the colored legs looked like hose. There was even a special pencil used to draw the dark seam down the back. These new "hose" looked quite good on nice, sunny days, but look out when it rained. Your fancy hose, seam and all, tended to run down your legs and disappear into your shoes!

After the war, nylon hose began to appear on the market. How we marveled at the new technology in these manmade fibers. When holding up a pair of silk hose, the shape of a leg was defined. Sold in little flat boxes, each was delicately folded into a protective tissue paper to avoid possible snags. Now, as we held up the new nylons, we wondered how anything so small would ever stretch far enough to fit over our legs. Since I was still a skinny little kid, the silk hose bagged and drooped, but amazingly, the new little nylons stretched without breaking a thread and still fit perfectly after several hours. What a wonderful new invention!

A small air show was held one day at the old Baty Road Airport on the west edge of Lima. The loudspeaker announced that packages of nylon hose would be dropped out of an airplane. Most of us teenage girls wore bobby sox with saddle shoes or "penny" loafers. (The loafers had a little area in the front in which a penny fit perfectly. If you wished to be in style, you had to be sure your penny was in place.) Since having nylon hose was not that important to me, I didn't run across the airfield as the older girls did, screaming and grabbing and fighting to get those falling packages of nylons. In fact, I thought the whole thing was a little bit foolish!

When I first started wearing those long nylons, it was such a struggle to keep the seam straight on my leg that I'm afraid some of my first ones looked like I had a struggling fish worm crawling down the back of my leg. The manufacturers eventually noticed the problem and eliminated the troublesome back seam. No one ever really missed it. It may have made the leg look slimmer, but only if the seam was straight!

When Franklin Roosevelt died near the end of the war, it was the new President, Harry Truman, who was finally able to proclaim "PEACE!" So, where were you when that announcement of peace was declared? The war's end was another time that most people did not forget. We were at home. I ran to the chicken house yelling the good news to Grandpa. In nearby towns, the church bells were rung, but I don't remember attending any big celebrations. There were many prayers of heartfelt thanks expressed at the next Sunday church service. My, but we were all so relieved to have the war over. Now life could return to normal! Like our neighbors, we felt as though a ton of bricks had been lifted from over us. A real period of peace, prosperity and goodwill followed. Items were no longer needed for the war effort, and appliances began to return to the market. Names were put on waiting lists for new cars, although rumors were that some money placed into the hands of unscrupulous dealers might persuade them to move your name to the top of the list.

Now that the war was over, the very air smelled of freedom and peace as the nation's sons and daughters returned to the arms of waiting families and friends in hometowns across America. It was a great time to be alive.

---

[1] Newspaper article clipped by a 12-year-old (me) in the fall of 1942, unable to locate original source.

[2] Lois J. Hurley, "From Day to Day," *Hoard's Dairyman*, March 25, 1983, used with permission.

[3] *Lima News,* Lima, Ohio, January 2,1944, used with permission.

## Chapter 53.
# "Kilroy Was Here"

Kilroy was here!" Those words showed up in every spot imaginable during and shortly after World War II, often in the most unlikely places all over the world. As American soldiers captured a town in Germany, they might walk through its streets, only to find "Kilroy Was Here" scribbled on the wall of a bombed out house or the back of a street sign. In our school, it was scribbled on chalk boards when no one was looking. It appeared on the inside cover of textbooks (very much discouraged) and in chalk on the wall behind the stage curtains (also discouraged). We saw it scrawled on the sides of hundreds of boxcars and tankers as trains rolled through the countryside, or scribbled in the dust on the trunks of parked cars or the sides of trucks moving along the highways. It was written in chalk on the fences surrounding vacant lots and on the walls of downtown buildings. Lamp posts and traffic signs were decorated with it. As soldiers returned from France and Italy, as sailors returned from the South Pacific, as Marines landed on distant shores and returned in victory, all had seen the sign where they had been fighting in the far corners of the world.

Never before or since has such a simple thing attracted so much attention. Often it was accompanied by the simple little drawing of a long-nosed man, hands holding him up as he peeked over a wall. As my dad, brother and I toured Columbus during that time, we stepped out of the elevator at the top of the giant AIU Tower, and found ourselves face to face with those famous words, "Kilroy Was Here." American ingenuity sent that little phrase into nearly every nook and cranny around the world!

Everyone knew about it and talked about it, but no one seemed to really know how, by whom, or where it had all started. Oh, there were many rumors and stories were abundant as to how it had come about, but very few people knew the origins of the phrase. A Reminisce Magazine article revealed the true story.

James J. Kilroy counted rivets at the Fore River Shipyard in Quincy, Massachusetts during World War II. Workers were paid by the number of rivets installed and it was his job to count the rivets, then make a chalk mark so they wouldn't be counted again. Some men, however, returned after Kilroy went off duty, erased his mark and got paid double. When the boss realized there was a problem, he told Kilroy to find out what was going on. As a result, Kilroy made his check mark, then in king-sized letters, wrote "Kilroy Was Here." Ordinarily the marks would have been covered with paint, but due to the wartime urgency, there wasn't time to paint the ships and Kilroy's inspection mark traveled around the world. It was a catchy phrase that became very popular with servicemen everywhere and those three simple words became a sort of morale booster. It was often used as a code.

If two friends were to meet, the first to arrive might scrawl "Kilroy Was Here" on a nearby wall or building, especially if he had to return to duty before the other serviceman arrived.

So many Kilroys claimed to be the original that in 1948 the Transit Company of America offered a prize to the person who could prove he had been the real war-time "Kilroy." James Kilroy needed money for Christmas presents for his nine children but was reluctant to enter because he thought the prize–a trolley car–was foolish. His wife convinced him he should enter and the children could use the prize streetcar as a playhouse. Over forty Kilroys showed up, but with the backing of the Fore River Shipyard officials and some of the riveters, James Kilroy was declared the "real" Kilroy.[1]

---

[1] Richard O'Donnell, *Reminisce Magazine*, July/August 1994, used with permission.

Kilroy Was Here!

## Chapter 54.
# Travels After the War

Once World War II was over and tires became available and gas was plentiful, the travel bug bit our family. Don had just graduated from high school, and he and Dad planned a trip "Out West" to visit our old neighbor, Joe Frank, in Texas and to see Dad's cousin, Otho Crawford, in Oklahoma. It was a three-week adventure for the two Davenports–father and son.

Always an outdoors man, Joe took them to his favorite fishing grounds at nearby Possum Kingdom Dam where they caught some nice fish. Joe and Grandpa had done a lot of hunting each winter. Though he was now older, Joe was still a good shot and brought down a deer while they were there. When Dad made plans to leave after a week, Joe and Rose protested, "No, you're not. We've got too much deer meat and fish to eat. You've got to stay and help eat this up." So, they stayed for another week.

Since Don had learned to ride our horse, Bobby, he was eager to participate when invited to join the exciting adventure of a real roundup. A Spencerville *Journal-News* article dated March 13, 1947, included this account: "During that time they enjoyed some real Texas ranch atmosphere, as Don says 'not from behind the horn of a car going 60 but from behind the horn of a real western saddle cinched to a real western cowpony and plenty of real mesquite and cactus country to ride thru.'" Instead of *playing* cowboy as we had as children, Don now had the chance to *be* a real cowboy, at least for a few hours. He loved it!

The local country club sponsored a party one evening at the elegant yacht club. One of Joe's young neighbors got Don a blind date for the event. Don said it had been a very interesting evening.

Joe took Dad and Don into town shopping one day. New clothes were still rather difficult to get after the war, but Don saw some work clothes that weren't sold in our part of the country. They were called Levi's. He told Joe, "I ought to have some of these clothes, a pair of Levi's and a Levi jacket. We've never seen them back home." In Texas they were just ordinary work clothes that could be bought at the local clothing store. Joe knew the owner, and gesturing toward Don, he said, "My friend here wants to get some clothes today. He wants a pair of boots. And have you got any Levi's?" The store owner said, "Well, I'm kind of short on Levi's." "Well," Joe persisted, "He wants a pair of Levi's and a hat and a Levi jacket." In his mind, the store owner reviewed his inventory.

After Don got his boots and a good hat, Joe said, "You better look back there and see if you can't find a pair of Levi's and a Levi jacket." The storekeeper went to his back room and returned with some clothes he had just "found" there. Don got really duded up in *real* cowboy clothes. Although cowboy boots and Levi's are common here now, they were a rare sight at that time. Don's new duds brought some admiring glances back in Ohio.

After leaving Joe and Rose Frank's home, Dad and Don drove north to Oklahoma to visit Dad's cousin, Otho and Dorothy Crawford. Otho ran a welding shop where he had done a lot of business in the oil field boom days. When that slowed down, he utilized his equipment in a small factory making propane tanks similar to those now used on gas grills and in motor homes. He also made steam turbine-driven electric generators for the oil fields in South America. The wells were booming at that time, and although they didn't have electricity because they were out in the boon docks, they had steam that they were using to power their rigs. Otho made electric generators to run off the steam boilers, thus enabling them to provide ample light for night time operations.

Otho became friends with a man who was wounded in World War II. As the man lay on his bed recuperating, he put his mind to work developing a carburetor. He drew the blueprint, and Otho was going to produce the carburetor in a hangar at an ex-army airfield he had leased. Otho was to be paid one dollar plus the cost of the carburetor for each one he built.

Dad and Don got to see one of the carburetors in action. It had been put on a standard Chevrolet car and was proving to be very economical, getting twice the mileage. The same carburetor was hooked up on a little Briggs and Stratton engine and on a big oil field engine. It handled the big engine as easily as the little one.

As Don explained it, the carburetor had a ring in it, a venturi. The ring was connected to a tapered needle valve. The air coming through the carburetor lifted the ring, which opened the needle valve. The more air that went through, the more fuel it put in, so it was always balanced. It was an updraft carburetor because of the way it was designed. However, he had put a big curve in a pipe in order to install it on his Chevrolet (which took a down draft carburetor). It worked quite well,

The developer's health improved enough that he could get around and one day he drove up to Otho's place. Otho said to him, "How about taking these cousins for a ride in your car?" He quickly agreed, then showed them its benefits. "You can't flood the engine when you try to start it," he pointed out. Pulling out the choke on the car, he said, "Well, you know women have trouble with the chokers." This was back in the days before automatic chokes and he said, "I'm going to show you what this carburetor will do." He pushed the starter button, but with the key turned off. (Back then, the key didn't activate the starter; there was a separate "starter button" that usually worked even when the key was turned off.) He cranked the engine and cranked it and cranked it some more. At last he said, "It ought to be flooded, hadn't it?" Dad said, "I'd think so!" He said, "Well, let's crank it a little more to make sure." So he cranked it some more. Finally he said, "Now, probably you would imagine it would be flooded and when you start it you would expect to see a lot of black smoke coming out. Now look back at the exhaust and see what happens." He turned the key, hit the starter and it just took right off with no smoke—nothing!

The car had been run for several thousand miles, and when they tore the engine down, Don saw the valves. They looked like they were brand-new. The oil didn't get dirty, but had stayed green. The engine didn't know the top speed. It just ran! It had been patented under the name of Russell Carburetor.

Before they could get into full production, word somehow got out about this unusual piece of equipment. Other people began to come to the man and ask, "Will you sell us the carburetor?" At first he had said, "No," but they kept after him and finally got the price up high enough that he sold his patent rights. When the owner sold the patent rights, Otho wasn't allowed to build any more carburetors. Unfortunately, that was the last anyone saw of the carburetor. It totally disappeared. Had it worked too well?

With the war over and the trip behind him, Don was ready to look ahead to the future. The time spent with Otho had been exciting. As Dad and Don traveled the highways toward home, they discussed the future. The direction in which Don would go became evident. A short time after his return, he registered at welding school in Troy. Don and Dad were two of a kind–mechanically minded men. Like father, like son!

**Chapter 55.**

# Aboard the Dudley H. Thomas

He was barely out of his teens, and now he was heading for Greece! For those desiring to see the world, World War II had provided plenty of opportunities.

After graduating from high school in 1944, Bill had been exempted from military service because the local draft board felt that he was needed by his grandfather to help on the farm. He later tried to enlist and took the Air Force scholarship test, scoring the second highest in the group. When taking the physical exam, however, he found out that with the end of the war in sight, the age requirements had changed, and his military career crashed before it ever got off the ground.

Meanwhile, Bill's brother had married and started a family. After the birth of their second child, his wife experienced some problems and was hospitalized. Bill's mother agreed to help out by bringing the baby home with her. With Bill, both of his grandparents, his mother, and a newborn baby living in the same house, things were sometimes quite hectic.

A young man from New Knoxville, Reuben Deerhake, had become involved in an activity that interested Bill. With the war over, various relief organizations were sending ships loaded with items to help the war-torn countries get back on their feet. Reuben had worked on a ship taking animals overseas. Bill considered the possibilities for a similar trip leaving November of 1946. By then the crops would be harvested and Grandpa could handle the other chores.

Bill signed up for a trip sponsored by the Church of the Brethren's Service Center, working with the United Nations Rehabilitation and Relief Administration (UNRRA). The organization was sending horses to Greece to replenish their farms with the animals needed for planting and harvesting crops. Men accustomed to working with farm animals were recruited to accompany the horses and care for them. Although the voyage lasted just two months, some of the friendships have continued a lifetime.

One of these friendships was with Lowell Hoover, a young farmer from Abilene, Kansas, who was married and the father of two little girls. He was very active in his Brethren Church and felt this would be an opportunity for service. Bill and I were married five years after the trip and since our honeymoon would take us near their area, Bill thought we should visit the Hoovers. We spent a couple of days on their farm and felt quite at home with their family. From that time on, we exchanged Christmas letters each year, but we saw Lowell only twice in all those years. As he was passing through Ohio on his way to a Messiah College Board of Directors meeting in about 1960, he flew into Dayton where we picked him up for an overnight visit.

We were so glad to see Lowell, but I felt I needed to apologize for the condition of his bedroom. I was redecorating our only guest bedroom when he called. It was to be our little boys room and their smaller room would be given to Nancy. I had removed the wallpaper, there were no window curtains, and the only extra bed we owned was a tiny little single bed that sat forlornly in the middle of that bleak, bare room. Bless his heart, Lowell didn't say one word of complaint.

Years later, after spending a few days with Steve at LeTourneau College in Longview, Texas, we drove up to Abilene for a brief stop at the Hoover farm. We had a nice visit with his wife, Dorcas, but Lowell was on a mission trip in Africa. Our second visit with Lowell came in October, 1996. After the death of his beloved Dorcas, he eventually remarried. He and his new wife, Doris, drove through Ohio and spent a weekend with us.

We knew the Hoovers loved music and since we had tickets to the Lima Area Concert Band in which Nancy played, they got to meet her, David and our grandchildren. "I've heard about you all of my life," Nancy told Lowell. As we talked later, Nancy made this very revealing comment, "Mom, did you know that when I was a little girl and we got the Hoovers' Christmas card and letter every year, I thought, 'Wow! My Mom and Dad really know some important people!' The only Hoover I had ever heard of was those who made the Hoover vacuum cleaners."

Lowell occasionally saw another member of the group that made the trip to Greece, Henry Reist of Mount Joy, Pennsylvania. After visiting us, Lowell gave Henry our address and phone number. As I answered the phone six months later, it was Henry. He was coming through our area and would like to see us. I didn't tell Bill he was coming. Would you believe that when Henry walked into our house, Bill looked at him a few minutes and called him by name, although the last time they had talked was when they were both teenagers more than fifty years ago?

Although the wives had some knowledge of the trip, the visits from these men to our home and the reminiscing that followed, led each man to recall long forgotten details.

When Lowell volunteered for the trip, he stipulated that it should take place after the wheat had been planted, but that he wanted to be back by Christmas so he could spend that special holiday with his family. When Lowell received a call to come to Maine for a shipment, he turned it down. His wheat planting was not yet completed. "Was I ever thankful I had," he told us. "They had a longshoreman's strike up there, and I would have been stranded in Maine for a month."

Henry's trip started when he and three friends piled into an old Ford pickup truck and drove to Norfolk. His brother had already made two trips taking animals overseas. Now it was Henry's turn.

Since he didn't own a car, Bill hitchhiked much of the way, getting a ride from Wapakoneta to Vandalia, Ohio, and another to Charleston, West Virginia. There he bought a bus ticket to Newport News where he was to meet the rest of the group. Upon arrival, Bill met a sailor who took him under his wing and walked him right into his first "chow line." The man explained that when asked what he wanted to eat, he was to answer "full house." He would then get a plate filled with everything they had for that meal. But as he followed his new friend down the chow line, no one questioned him or asked for identification. When Bill said the magic words, his plate was piled high with a variety of food. He was well fed on that first shipboard meal, but as Bill later told me, "I probably shouldn't have been on that ship. It was not the vessel on which I was scheduled to sail."

The ship he was supposed to be on was the HMS *Dudley H. Thomas,* which sailed under the British flag. According to Lowell, it was a *Liberty* ship which had been commissioned in Pensacola, Florida. It had been used during World War II for shipping military supplies overseas. It still had a gun mount on the fan tail (back end) that had helped defend it during the war. An emergency helm was also located there with a heavy iron enclosure about four feet tall to protect the area from flying bullets if attacked. *Liberty* ships were mass-produced as quickly as possible and were made from cement covered with steel plating. Since many of them were likely to be hit by torpedoes, they needed to be as cheap and expendable as possible–definitely not the "Cadillac" of the ship industry.

As the men assembled aboard the *Dudley H.*, they were an excited group. For most of them, this was the first trip out of the country. As they sailed out of the harbor that first evening, the water was calm, and everything was peaceful and serene. Small rooms with three sets of double bunk beds were to become their home for the next two months. After the initial excitement was over, Bill climbed into a top bunk and was soon asleep.

On his first morning at sea, as Bill walked out on deck, he noticed quite a few of the men standing at the rail looking down at the water below. "I wonder what they are looking at?" he thought, and he stepped to the rail to see what was so interesting down there. It was then he realized this was not a sightseeing event. These men were quite busy "feeding the fish" as a result of severe seasickness. Since this pastime didn't appeal to him, he went on to the galley and ate a hearty breakfast. Bill was one of the very few who were not afflicted with the symptoms. Lowell said he didn't feel well for three days. Just the thought of food brought renewed trips to the rail for some men, and one poor soul suffered from seasickness throughout the entire voyage. For him, it was a very long trip!

Bill was one of the youngest of the thirty-five or so volunteers. Each man had to have a physical exam and the necessary immunizations for the trip; however, no passports were needed. The first task had been to register at the Brethren Service Committee office. They then received $2.50 for each day they were in port while waiting to ship out and this would be added to the $150 for making the trip. A full page of instructions had included directions to the Kresge 5¢ & 10¢ store in Norfolk where the three photos necessary for the Seaman's card could be taken for 50¢. Although the cards listed them as "cattlemen," Bill's ship carried horses. The crew nicknamed them the "cowboys."

The longshoremen were responsible for loading and unloading the animals and their food and water, but once they were on the ship, the volunteers (mostly farmers) were to feed, water and care for the horses. Each man was to feed and take care of a certain number of animals, making sure the horses stayed on their feet at all times. Horses can sleep standing up, but if one were to lie down, they were to try to get it up. If it would not respond, they were to call one of the two veterinarians aboard the ship. Horses who lay down usually never got up, but died of pneumonia. Of the 400 or so horses on board, Lowell thought 55 had died on the trip to Greece. These were hoisted up out of the hold of the ship and dropped overboard for burial at sea. Bill said it became an increasingly sickening sight to see these wheezing, sickly horses dying and being dumped overboard.

When feeding the horses, one had to be very careful. Bill once referred to them as "western nags." They had come from the western states and were not "broken." Some were rather wild and mean. Bill and Lowell remembered one man receiving a rather severe bite in his shoulder. They smiled as they remembered seeing two horses whinnying and really creating a fuss as they stood back to back, "kicking the slats out of each other."

For many years Bill had worked with horses on the farm back home. He knew that most horses would nuzzle you first and lightly nibble at your shirt, then suddenly clamp down for a mouthful. He said he had felt these Greece-bound horses nibbling several times, but he had jerked quickly out of their reach before they could take a full-sized bite out of him.

As they made their way across the ocean, the travelers seldom saw another ship. If they did, it was usually quite a distance away. As Bill watched one day, a ship approached on what appeared to be a collision course. "I didn't know if they were playing 'chicken' or what," Bill commented, "but they just kept coming, cutting directly across our bow." Realizing the ultimate outcome, the captain of the *Dudley H.* ordered his engines reversed. "They were so close that if our captain hadn't reversed the engines, the ships would have collided," Bill added. Lowell and Henry were both a bit surprised to hear this story. They had been below deck and had never heard about the near miss.

The cattlemen were told to stay away from the ship's regular crew, since many of them were rather tough characters who had traveled the world. Most of the cattlemen were naive farmers who were very inexperienced in the ways of seagoing men. Bill was wandering around the deck one day when he noticed one of the regular crew having trouble with a grease gun. The man was producing a long line of profanity that was in no way improving the workings of the tool. Bill had greased farm machinery back home with an identical style gun, so he asked, "Can I take a look at the grease gun? Maybe I can fix it for you." This prompted another outburst of profanity, directed, not at the grease gun, but at Bill. Since nothing else was helping, the man threw the gun directly at Bill. He said, "I'm not sure if he was throwing it *to* me or *at* me, but I caught it." Since he had experienced the same problem himself, Bill thought he knew the solution. After removing an air pocket from the grease tube, he handed it back to the crewman, saying, "Here, try it. See if it works now." It worked well, and the man thought Bill was the hero of the day. By the time the crew had eaten their next meal, word had spread that Bill had done something good for one of the sailors. Bill laughed as he told us, "It changed my image." Hearing this, Lowell said, "I wondered about that. I thought Bill had gotten a little special treatment." He laughed heartily as he said it.

Bill was six-foot-three-inches tall and quite thin. Someone in the crew gave him the nickname "Slim." As Bill was talking to the ship's captain one day, the man said, "Slim, would you like to steer the ship?" Bill seized this unique opportunity. For several minutes he took the wheel of the *Dudley H.* Upon hearing this, Lowell grinned broadly and just shook his head.

There wasn't much to do on the ship after the horses were fed and cared for. Some men wrote letters home, although they couldn't be mailed until they reached shore. Bill didn't try the scheme, but some cattlemen developed a system to wash their dirty clothes. Using a very long rope, they tied one end around a burlap sack in which they had placed their clothing and the other end was tied to the ship. The sack was thrown overboard where it trailed in the ship's wake. After the clothes were thought to be clean, they were hauled back on board and rinsed in clear water to eliminate the salt residue. Although some of the men thought it was a great idea, Bill didn't share their enthusiasm. "It looked to me like a good way to lose your clothing in the middle of the ocean," he laughed.

Watching porpoises is an enjoyable way to kill some time. Bill said the "landlubber" farmers often stood on deck and watched the happy sea creatures at play. They splashed and flipped and swam along the bow and the sides of the ship as it moved through the water. Some were real clowns and seemed to enjoy showing off, accompanying the ship for miles.

Like Bill, many of the men left their beards grow during the voyage over. It just seemed like a good thing to do. Bill was surprised to find he was producing a nice crop of *red* hair on his face. Although they may have looked a bit scraggly, most of the cattlemen kept themselves clean. One man, however, failed to pay much attention to his personal hygiene, even though they had encouraged him to clean up. When his body odor had become quite objectionable, some of the others decided it was time to take matters into their own hands. They took him out on deck and set him down on an upturned bucket. While one man held his feet solidly against the deck, another forced him over backwards with his hands held down on the deck behind him. Taking a bucket of cold water and a scrub brush, they scrubbed his body until he finally agreed to finish cleaning himself and then let him loose. Those bristles not only made his skin a healthy pink, they produced a shade more like "scrub brush red," but he had learned a lesson.

And then there were those cooks! Were they serious, or was this a show to furnish some fun and humor for the crew and farm boys? Bill wasn't sure, but he said the two black cooks on the ship occasionally had a merry chase around the butcher block with the chaser wielding a huge butcher knife in a menacing manner. It certainly gave those farm folks a touch of excitement and a strong determination to stay out of the cooks' path.

One of the cooks was a man of massive proportions who was quite adept at using that long butcher knife. Several times Bill had seen him emerge from the ship's cooler below deck with a huge quarter of beef slung over his shoulder, then mount the steps to the kitchen on the main deck above. Plopping the entire quarter of meat on the butcher block, the cook grabbed that razor sharp butcher knife. With one very quick and very powerful stroke, he sliced out a huge slab of steak for the next meal. It was amazing and humbling to watch this huge man at work.

As the *Dudley H.* approached Gibraltar, the supply of hay for the horses began to run low. The decision was made to stop there for more hay. It was the middle of the night when they pulled into the harbor, only to find out there was no hay available. After other arrangements were made, the ship left the harbor and entered the Mediterranean Sea, proceeding toward Algiers where they would try again. As they arrived in that city, the men were given shore leave and were allowed to spend some time as tourists while the hay was located and loaded onto the *Dudley H.*

Having been confined to the ship for two weeks, the men were anxious to put their feet on solid ground. So, before leaving the ship, the cattlemen were warned that for safety's sake, they needed to travel together in groups of at least two or three men. Bill and a man named Frank Kobielski stayed together. Kobielski had been in Algiers during the recent war and was going to take Bill to a place with which he was familiar. As they walked further and further from the ship, Kobielski began to realize they were not in the right area. He cautioned Bill that as they walked to the next street corner, they were to casually look down the street, then slowly turn around and head back in the direction from which they had come. The main thing was to show no fear and stay calm. As they walked down the narrow streets, Arab men squatted in the open doorways, eyeing the strangers suspiciously. Dressed in burlap type cloaks with the traditional head covering of that area, the men slowly sharpened their glistening knives in the hot Algerian sun as their eyes followed every movement of the intruders. While trying nonchalantly to make a quick return to their ship, Bill heard Kobielski quietly say, "If we panic and start to run, we'll never live long enough to tell about it." Now that was not a very pleasant thought, and Bill forced himself to remain calm. The *Dudley H.* looked extremely good to the two men as they returned to the safety of its deck a short time later. They heaved a sigh of enormous relief.

While walking down the streets of Algiers, Bill had noticed water running along the gutters at the sides of the streets. "That wasn't rain water," he laughed as he and Lowell explained. This was the waste from the street restrooms. These consisted of a three-foot high fence along the side of the street, behind which you stood in public view from the waist up while doing your duty. Rather embarrassing, I should think! I wondered about the ladies, but after thinking it over, I realized there were no female tourists at that time. The few local ladies who ventured out to buy food were still clad in the long gowns with face veils. I assume they would have stayed in the privacy of their homes for such necessities.

Lowell remembered that while in Algiers, the ship's Third Mate had imbibed too much strong drink. When he returned to the ship, he was so drunk that the regular crew had locked him up in the former ammunition room until he was once again sober.

Bill spent many hours on deck, just watching the sea and sky above. One evening as they moved through the Mediterranean, the sea was so calm that it looked like a giant piece of glass. The sun was setting slowly in the west, its reflection forming a mirror image in the water. Only the ripples of the ship's wake disturbed the tranquil picture. It was so breathtaking it gave the viewer a strange feeling of being too perfect.

According to Lowell's memory, it had taken two weeks to cross the ocean and another week for the stops at Gibraltar and Algiers and for the trip through the Mediterranean Sea. As their ship sailed through the Aegean Sea, someone saw an uncleared mine left over from the war floating near the ship, and they discovered they were off course. They passed safely beyond it.

One of the most beautiful sights of the trip was also seen on the Aegean. A large sailing ship with full sails unfurled glided silently through the water with unbelievable grace and beauty. It was picture postcard perfect.

As the *Dudley H.* entered the Piraeus (pronounced Pie-ree-us) Harbor near Athens, Greece, the men saw a highlight of the trip, the first glimpse of the Acropolis, the ancient fortified hill which rose high above the city of Athens. At its topmost point stood the magnificent Parthenon with its white marble Doric columns glistening in the sun like a gigantic crown. Dating back to more than four hundred years before the birth of Christ, the Parthenon presented a sight that created an unforgettable welcome to Athens as the *Dudley H. Thomas* approached its moorings, its cattlemen standing at the railing, gazing in awe at the unforgettable panorama before them.

In contrast to this beautiful sight above the harbor, the harbor itself displayed the reality of war—wrecked ships that had been sunk and were now partially visible as they lay in their watery resting places. Several U.S. Navy ships were also docked in the harbor. As Bill and a couple of friends walked by a destroyer, he asked the sailor standing watch at the gangplank if they might tour the ship. The man phoned the officer in charge who not only gave his permission, but sent someone to guide them. They were made to feel quite welcome and were given a tour of the ship where, as Bill put it, "Everything was spit and polish." After seeing that ship's cleanliness and shine, the *Dudley H.*, with its motley crew and *horsey* smelling cattlemen whose scent permeated the air around it, now looked and smelled more like an old farmer's tub.

Another vessel anchored in the harbor was the USS *Roosevelt*, an American aircraft carrier that had been completed at the close of the war. A beautiful yacht was let down from the deck of the *Roosevelt* and its officers were taken to shore in style. Nothing quite that fine for the men of the *Dudley H.,* though!

Many were the unusual sights that greeted these country boys as they stared at this strange land so far from home. Most had never been in a country touched by war. The area had been occupied by the Axis forces, and some of the local people later showed the men pieces of the German money that they had been forced to use during the occupation. The bombed-out buildings were a sad sign of the stark reality of the recent fighting. The war was still quite fresh in their minds. They were happy to be liberated.

Bill remembers seeing open trucks with little boys sitting on top of loads of small hard rolls or loaves of bread that were tossed down to the customers and store owners. It didn't appear to be a very sanitary arrangement, but years later we saw many such conveyances as we toured Egypt and the Holy Lands.

Lowell remembered the distinctive smell of the fish markets with the dead fish lying in the sun to dry. After seeing them, he said he wasn't too anxious to order fish for dinner. Bill remembered seeing turkeys and chickens being led down the street on their way to market, a twine string tied about each neck as the owner encouraged his unsuspecting flock to their slaughter.

Most of the men took walking tours of the city or rented a taxi. Henry went to see Corinth, while Bill went to Mars Hill. Henry commented about the beauty and the workmanship of the Parthenon. He was amazed at the snug fit of the huge marble pieces forming each massive column. They were squared off for a perfect fit without the use of any mortar. Quite amazing for that day! [Bill mentioned that the taxi in which he had ridden was a Roosevelt car. He had seen lots of Ford cars, but never a Roosevelt.]

While the "cowboys" were enjoying their shore leave, the surviving horses were unloaded. With this finished, the empty ship was moved out into the harbor; possibly to make room for other ships to enter and unload, but more likely for the "other" unloading job. While it was in the open harbor, local men were hired to clean out the horse stalls. The accumulation of manure was then dumped into the water, as well as several barrels of garbage sitting on the deck which Bill had seen (and smelled). (Similar barrels had attracted his attention as he had initially boarded the ship. They had also been dumped into the ocean after leaving Newport News.)

Many of the cattlemen boarded the *Dudley H.* before it was moved into the Greek harbor, but Bill and the two others didn't get back in time to get aboard. They hired a small motor launch to transport them to the ship that was now anchored far from shore. A strong wind came up, and as the tiny launch braved the rough waters while transporting them to the ship, it had bounced about, much like a cork bobbing on a cascading creek.

As the motor launch drew alongside the ship, the pilot of the little boat motioned toward a Jacob's ladder, a rope affair hanging down the side of the *Dudley H.* Nodding toward Bill, he yelled something, but the wind was so strong it had blown his words away. Bill said, "Although I couldn't understand his language, I knew exactly what he wanted me to do." With one quick leap, Bill grasped the ladder and hung on. As he looked back at his friends in the boat, the giant wave that had enabled him to catch the ladder had suddenly dropped twenty feet or so directly below him. Resisting the urge to look again at the frightened faces of his friends staring up at him, he hung onto the ladder, gripping each rung as he climbed up the side and into the safety of the *Dudley H.* One by one, the others waited for the wave to crest, grabbed the ladder and climbed aboard as the little motor launch bobbed on the churning sea below. It was one of those unforgettable moments that would be best to remember, but not repeat.

As Bill and Lowell talked about those long-ago days, Lowell mentioned one fellow who'd been a woman chaser and had done a lot of running around. He did not make the return trip, and they never heard what happened to him. Maybe his sins finally caught up with him!

With the return voyage under way, the cattlemen were left with nothing to do and a lot of time in which to do it. Henry was ambitious and found himself a job. During the remainder of the trip, he donned a white jacket and assisted the cooks in serving the meals. As he visited us, he proudly took that very jacket out of a box and modeled it for us, proving he was still able to fit into it. He also surprised us by showing us a nearly complete set of daily menus from the *Dudley H.*

As Lowell and Bill remembered various aspects of the trip, a most vivid event of the return trip came to mind. One officer, either the purser or the steward, was a short, stocky man who had gone into the galley and was arguing with the cooks about wasting too much food. Bill watched in awe as that large cook who had toughened his muscles by carrying quarters of beef on his back, now tried a new tactic. Reaching out with one arm, he grabbed the officer by his collar and shirt front, then literally picked him straight up into the air and plopped him down outside the galley door, telling him his place was out there and not in the cooks' kitchen. The cook took care of the food in the way he thought best. The officer's face turned white with fear and rage, but he didn't stick around long enough to argue the point.

Although it was December, the weather over the ocean was mild. The men spent hours relaxing and enjoying the luxury of idleness. Henry mentioned that each Sunday a very brief worship service was conducted by a young man who planned to someday be a preacher.

As Bill walked on deck one night, he heard beautiful Christmas music floating through the air. Following the sound, he located the source. It came from a tiny radio in the cabin of the head cook. Leaning against the railing outside the small porthole, Bill enjoyed the beautiful sounds. Suddenly the cook looked through the porthole and saw him. "What are you doing out there?" he demanded. "Just listening to your beautiful Christmas carols," Bill replied. Was this huge man going to become upset and pick Bill up by his shirt collar and set him overboard? No, he opened the door and stuck his hand out, wiggling his finger at Bill as he said, "Come on in, Slim. You can hear it better inside." Bill stepped into his small cabin, and for the next hour or so the two men, one a giant black cook who sailed the seas and the other a skinny white farm boy from Ohio, sat and listened and talked as they had a good time together, enjoying the common bond–*music*.

It became increasingly evident that the *Dudley H.* was not going to make it home for Christmas. Christmas far from home is often a little difficult, and this was Bill's first time to be away. His family had stressed the sacredness of the holiday and had always attended church, then had a nice dinner. Although a rumor was heard that food was getting a little scarce, the cooks had saved some special items for Christmas Day. One favorite was mincemeat pie. The only holiday celebrations on the *Dudley H.* were those meals. Henry's Christmas Day menu read:

> "*S/S DUDLEY H. THOMAS,* At Sea. December 25, 1946. Breakfast: Chilled fruit juice, Hot oatmeal, Assorted dry cereals, Cheese omelette, Eggs to order (fried, boiled, scrambled), Grilled bacon, Bread and butter, Fried potatoes, Coffee, Tea, Milk. Dinner: Green olives, Mixed pickles, Chicken gumbo soup with crackers, Roast turkey, Cranberry sauce, Gravy, Stuffing, Creamed ham on toast, Asparagus, Mashed potatoes, Carrots, Bread and butter, Ice cream, Coffee, Tea, and Milk. Supper: Button onions, Relish, Roast prime ribs of beef au juice, Ham rice yamboley, Sweet potatoes, String beans, Roast potatoes, Pickled beets salad, Bread and butter, Preserved pineapples, Mince pie, Coffee, Tea and milk. Night lunch." [1]

That sounds like a really good day around the *Dudley H.* mess table, don't you think? (Bill grinned when he remembered that "mince pie.")

As Bill walked past the galley after that Christmas supper, the cook stuck his head out and motioned for him to come closer. "Hey, Slim," he called out, "Could you use another piece of pie?" Bill didn't need a second invitation. He was Johnny-on-the-spot, ready to enjoy that second piece of mincemeat pie.

The seas were calm on December 25 and 26, but as Bill put it, "That night all hell broke loose." He awoke to find himself rolling and banging against the sides of the bunk. The ship was rolling so violently that in order to keep himself in the bunk, he had to wrap his arm around an upright bar in the railing surrounding his top bunk, then lay across his arm and hand. The ship was listing to either side at an angle of thirty-five degrees or more in waves of forty to fifty feet. Bill said he could see the degrees as they registered on the emergency helm on the rear gun mount. They had come dangerously close to the red mark representing the "point of no return."

The *Dudley H. Thomas* was 429 feet long, as Bill remembered it, and too short to ride the crest of two waves. Instead it bobbed up and down in the trough of each wave, making a very rough ride. The sound of the howling winds was quite evident, but even more sobering was the feel of the ship. As it crested each wave, the bow dipped and was submerged in the next wave while the propeller emerged from the water with its blade tip violently shaking the ship.

As it plunged back into the churning water, the ship was again shaken by the motion. The *Dudley H.* was taking a real beating. At one point, the captain made an inspection of the ship. He noticed several cracks in the structure, and Bill overheard him say, "The ship is beginning to weaken and break up in spots. This will be her last trip over." How comforting!

The men were forbidden on deck and had to go down into the hold of the ship, walk through the boiler room and up the other end to get to the mess hall for their meals. Bill said, "After all that, we got only cheese and crackers to eat." It was so rough the cook wouldn't even try to fire up the stoves to prepare a full meal. That didn't bother some of the men, though. With the rough seas, they were back to feeding the fishes!

At another time, Bill asked the captain, "How fast do you think we are going?" The captain's reply was, "Just look out there! You can see how fast we are going! We're going *backwards*!" Then he looked at Bill with a twinkle in his eye and said, "*Officially,* we're going two knots!"

Since the storm had slowed them down considerably, the supply of food began to run low. Bill said there were still raisin cookies to eat, but they had worms in them. Since there wasn't a whole lot of other food to eat, Bill ate the cookies, worms and all. Making a face, he said, "But oh, did those things ever give you gas! Whoee!"

The *Dudley H.* finally made its way back to America, this time to New York City. It cruised into the New York harbor on December 30, giving its cattlemen-now-turned-passengers a clear view of Ellis Island and Liberty Island with its Statue of Liberty. There is no more impressive sight than that statue which welcomes each ship to New York Harbor. (Although many American families entered through Ellis Island, all of our ancestors came before the arrival of the Statue and the use of Ellis Island as a port of entry.)

Once the *Dudley H. Thomas* had anchored in the harbor, the cattlemen boarded a small boat for the ride to shore. Although the temperatures had been mild during most of the return trip, Henry remembered receiving a cold and nasty welcome to the city. Heavy coats were dug out of duffel bags as the men prepared for the winter weather. Henry said he had trouble sleeping that first night, though. He had become so accustomed to his shipboard bed rocking in a regular rhythm that his landlubber bed was too still for good sleeping.

Most of the cattlemen were eager to return to their families. Henry and his friends returned to the Ford pickup which they had parked two months earlier and headed for home, but Bill and Lowell decided to stay in the *Big Apple* long enough to see the New Year's Eve celebration in Times Square. As they left the ship, part of the regular crew asked Bill to go with them to the Flying Dutchman, a bar that was a favorite with them. To have received such an invitation from these seasoned sailors of the sea was indeed an honor, but it was not the type of Christian lifestyle Bill enjoyed. He thanked them kindly, explaining that he had made other plans.

What were those plans? Wanting to see some of the high spots of New York, they hailed a taxi which drove them to Madison Square Garden. "What a wild ride!" Bill commented. After traveling for several weeks at a slow steady pace, this hectic taxi ride, weaving at breakneck speed through New York traffic with horns blaring, was a real challenge to the nerves. They arrived safely at Madison Square Garden and Bill enjoyed seeing his first ice hockey game between the New York Rangers and a Canadian team. A visit to Radio City Music Hall was a special treat as they saw a movie and a stage extravaganza that included a precision dance team, the Rockettes, who still make regular appearances there.

As evening approached, native New Yorker, Frank Kobielski, escorted Bill and Lowell into Times Square where they blended into the crowd of thousands who thronged the area, waiting patiently for the giant ball to drop at midnight signaling the birth of the New Year. The crowd shuffled slowly around the streets of the Square. The three men walked side by side with their arms joined tightly to stay together. Mounted police officers kept everyone moving in an orderly fashion as other officers on foot mingled with the crowd. When someone had imbibed too much and slumped to the ground, he was immediately spotted, and, with an officer on each side of him, he was dragged to the sidewalks.

The *luckiest* drunks were those who had passed out early in the evening. They were dragged into the doorways of the closed stores where they could sleep it off in relative comfort. Those who passed out later in the evening lay farther out near the streets and occasionally got walked on, stumbled over, or kicked aside by the mass of humanity assembled there. What a way to celebrate, huh?

Bill and Lowell agreed that it was indeed an experience they would never forget, but it was also one that they had no desire to ever repeat. Lowell was anxious to return to his family in Kansas, but Bill decided to spend a little more time in the area. Boarding a night train for Washington, D.C., he spent the next day on a bus tour of the city. Upon his return to the train station, he boarded an Ohio bound train for Cincinnati where he spent some time with his Aunt Emma. Returning home as he had started, he again put his thumb into action and hitched a ride to Moulton, riding in style on a wooden box in an open school bus chassis. The driver sat beside him, also on a box with only a windshield to protect them. One more wave of the thumb and Bill caught his final ride on a Hoge Lumber truck which brought him to the corner of the farm. From there, he walked the quarter of a mile to the house. Praise the Lord, the farm boy had finally returned! Welcome home! It's 1947!

---

[1] Menu from *Dudley H. Thomas*, December 25, 1946

The *Dudley H. Thomas* was the temporary home of these "seagoing cowboys" during part of 1946. Bill is standing to the right of the big cook in the back row.

## Chapter 56.
# *College Capers*

When was the decision made that I should go to college? I think it was shortly after I was born! Let me explain. When my mother graduated from Ft. Wayne Business College in Indiana, she had two prized possessions, a wardrobe and a steamer trunk. My family always told us that Don was to receive her wardrobe, and I was to get the trunk for college use. After Mother died, her mother (my grandma) was very bitter and took back practically all of Mother's possessions. We never got the trunk or wardrobe. My family always felt sad because of her actions. She saw me only four times in my life, and never knew my mother died because of a doctor's error.

Because I had heard the word "college" used so often, I always assumed that several years down the road, I would go to college–future time and place unknown.

I knew very little about college men. My first experience came when my friend, Mary Jo, entered summer school immediately after graduation. One day she asked me to double date with her and two college friends. I'd never had a blind date before, but I agreed, and our foursome headed for Lima for an afternoon of bowling. Now I had never bowled, but I had heard stories of people getting fingers caught in bowling ball holes. Since I was taking organ lessons at the time, I knew I needed every finger to be healthy. I had also heard embarrassing stories of gutter balls, and with my luck, I would no doubt be quite good at making them. (I was not known to be excessively athletic.) I had also heard of people who had actually been dragged down the alley with a ball. Ha! I was a skinny kid and could almost picture that happening! "Woe is me," I thought as we approached the bowling alley. Imagine my relief when it proved to be closed for the day! Oh, joy, joy, joy! Then what did we do? I have no idea. We probably ate something and eventually went home. I wasn't greatly impressed with the college boys, and I'm sure they weren't impressed with me!

Which college would be best for me? The music department at Wittenberg College in Springfield, Ohio, seemed to be the best choice. On a nice summer day after high school graduation, Dad, my grandparents and I drove to the campus. We met the Dean of Women who assured Dad they would take good care of me. That fall I registered as a freshman in the School of Music.

There is much that could be told about the daily routine of college life, the classes, the friends made, the endless hours of music practice . . . but why bore you with those details? Instead, I'll give you the highlights and humorous glimpses of my college years.

"Well, isn't that strange," I thought. I learned to drive in my early teens and all my friends had also driven for several years. I couldn't imagine any young person, especially a man, not knowing how to drive. Yet, at the get-acquainted party, I met a young man from New York City who had never driven a car. Noticing my surprise, he explained. Where would he learn to drive in the heart of a big city? There were large parks, but you wouldn't want a first-time driver weaving through a park with children playing, joggers running, horse drawn carriages clip-clopping and so on. Schools didn't have drivers' education, so he would have had to pay for lessons at a driving school. That cost big money! With easy access to city buses and subways, he didn't need to drive. When I considered his point of view, I could easily understand. I wouldn't have driven, either. I learned a lot about city living that day.

Since all the college dorms were filled, I was one of more than thirty girls assigned to Mercycrest, an off-campus institution that housed college students on the third floor, working girls on the second, and a public dining hall, Catholic chapel, and private rooms for the Sisters of Mercy nuns and priest on the first floor. The building resembled a castle. My roommate and I had the tower room. Our square bedroom held twin beds, dressers and clothes wardrobes, with a smaller round tower room for the study area. Since the "castle" was set on a hill, our tower view was beautiful, especially at night as the city lights twinkled below us.

I loved weekends and Sunday mornings when the vibrant sound of church bells drifted up from the city below. Because of our unique situation, we were often "shown off" to visitors from both the Lutheran college and the Catholic church. They seemed to know that our room was kept spotless (well, almost!), and our study time was often interrupted by our housemothers or the Mother Superior as visitors toured the facilities. How fortunate I was. Ours was the only room housing just two girls. Other rooms had as many as eight. College was a new playground for some of them, and studying was not their greatest priority. Perpetual turmoil prevailed in some rooms from too many roommates, an overabundance of girl talk (mostly about boys), sloppy living habits, leftover snacks and so on. A few of the more serious students occasionally knocked on our door for some peace and quiet study in our tower room.

Our meal arrangement was absolutely fantastic! The girls' dorms had their own dining halls, but they were several blocks away. We were given instructions to eat our breakfast and evening meals in the public dining room on our first floor. While the dorm girls ate macaroni and cheese with peaches for dessert, we ate anything we wanted from the restaurant menu: steak, fried chicken, fresh fish on Fridays, a wide selection of vegetables and salads, and best of all–the fresh baked pies and ice cream for dessert. Everything was delicious! And if that weren't enough, our noon meal was eaten on campus in the *boys'* dining hall. If I remember correctly, we were not to sit at the same table with the boys, but that didn't mean we couldn't talk to those at the next table. A few hundred boys and thirty-one Mercycrest girls wasn't a bad ratio, was it? I think every girl on campus was jealous of our wonderful food arrangement.

The mile-long walks from Mercycrest to the music school helped wear off the effects of those breakfast sweet rolls before our eight o'clock class. After a day or two of classes, we found a shortcut behind the football stadium. As I walked home alone after a late class that first afternoon, I received a real shock! Our little high school didn't have a football team, so I had never been near a player in uniform. As I walked along enjoying the late summer sunshine, a door at the back of the stadium burst open and out ran the whole team dressed in full uniform—padding, helmets, and all. They seemed to be giants, ten feet tall and five feet across. (Maybe I should explain that several Wittenberg players were big, husky guys from Pittsburgh who wore Steeler sweatshirts and were tough, tough, tough!) Just the size of those guys was overwhelming, and I stopped in my tracks, sucking in my breath while trying to disappear into the concrete walls of the stadium until those giants had passed. That was my welcome to football. But, hey, those big guys won our games!

It's strange, but even with that mile-long walk in sunshine, rain or snow, I was always early for music school classes, while girls living in the dorm next door were either late or they slid into their seats just seconds before the tardy bell rang.

"If you want to attend church, meet in front of Ferncliff Hall," we were told. My friend, Betty Wade, and I walked from Mercycrest to the dorm. Small groups of girls stood on the sidewalk, this one for Lutherans, that group for Catholics, the Methodists over here, and so on. Someone walked us to the bus stop where we rode to the downtown Methodist Church. We got better acquainted as we walked to the church. (Although we were welcomed at the door and attended that church for the next two years, no one ever invited us home for a Sunday dinner, nor did we ever attend any of the young people's activities, church suppers or other social events.)

By the next year, we knew the routine. Betty and I stood in front of Ferncliff, waiting for girls who might want to go to the Methodist Church with us. Only one chose to go. (Well, after all, Wittenberg *is* a Lutheran school!) The next Sunday, even that girl decided to go to a Lutheran Church with a friend. When we heard what had happened, we were thankful for her decision. She had never been away from home, and after two weeks of school, she was in a mental turmoil that led to a breakdown during the service. She had cried out quite loudly, creating quite a scene. Her new friends were extremely embarrassed and didn't know how to handle her or the situation. She had to be removed, was sent home to her family and never came back. Although we really felt sorry for the girl, Betty and I were quite thankful she had decided to be a Lutheran that day.

I was rather surprised when I saw the music school. It consisted of three older houses joined together by walkways. A few classes were even held in a basement room. Since there was no air conditioning in those days, this room was more comfortable in warm weather. Professor John Bennett Ham was a favorite. He was always considerate of his students. That's why we didn't believe it when he announced a test for the day before Christmas vacation. Would our beloved professor really do such a thing? Sure enough, he passed out the test papers and said he would be right back. We struggled with the test, very disappointed that Professor Ham would really let us down like this. In a few minutes he returned, carrying a large box in his hands. Now what? Would you believe that sweet man had a box filled with goodies and our struggle suddenly turned into a full-fledged party? What a surprise! We loved John Bennett Ham! Before we left the classroom, however, he made us all promise we would never tell next year's students about his little "test." He admitted doing this for several years. No one had ever told. He loved pulling this Christmas surprise on his unsuspecting students!

A phonograph disc was to record our first attempts in speech class. The topic was: "A true experience from your life." After contemplating my choices, I told of the day I slid through a puddle of spilled water and knocked a can of precious homemade maple syrup over on my head. My class found it quite amusing and I was grateful that the speech received better results than the gooey experience. The professor was impressed.

I made some good friends at the Wittenberg music school. A couple of the older girls, vocal music majors, asked me to accompany them as they sang at various meetings in area churches. I always felt shy because I was younger, and I never knew what kind of "clunker" piano was going to be in those church basements and meeting halls. Most of all, I was scared to death *I might make a mistake.* That would be embarrassing! But these girls were sweet Christian gals, and they knew that *I* would not get upset at them if *they* made a mistake!

My teacher and I were the only ones in the music school for my first semester early Saturday morning lessons. Everyone was still snuggled in warm beds, sound asleep. Saturday lessons stopped the next semester and I decided that would be a good time to practice, since no one else was awake. I was still bashful about having others, especially professors, listening as I practiced. Those old wooden music school floors often creaked when someone walked by, and my piano professor had a nasty habit of standing outside practice room doors while listening to his student's struggle. That really made me nervous and I developed a sixth sense that told me he was there. I would stop playing until he left, so those early Saturday practices were great–the professor was still in bed asleep.

"You are expected to practice one hour every day for each music lesson you have each week," our professor had told us. With one organ and two piano lessons, I was expected to practice three hours a day. One semester I added a vocal lesson and had to practice *four* hours a day. I also had the usual amount of classes (geography, English, speech, sociology, etc.), each requiring homework. With four hours daily practice, a music lesson nearly every day, the other classes with all their homework–well, it really kept me hopping. Upperclassmen had often asked during my first few weeks of school what I was studying. When I replied, "Music," they usually turned with a look of pity and said, "Oh, you poor girl!" It didn't take long to understand exactly what they meant.

Sigma Alpha Iota, the ladies' music honorary, had high standards. Dad hoped I would qualify for membership. Grades were essential, but the student's personality, musical ability and actions were also scrutinized. Mine were found appropriate, and I was thrilled to be asked to pledge SAI. Pledges presented a concert for members and alumni. I chose a Bach organ number which, like most Bach music, required an abundance of footwork. I remember one lady saying, "That young lady will never be a one-foot organist."

After our acceptance into the sorority, we were asked to bring our Bibles to the ceremony. Each pledge was sent to a separate room to read and meditate on I Corinthians 13, often referred to as the "love chapter." Even today, as I read that chapter, I still think of that night and its quiet reflection. The Lord has so abundantly used music in my life.

As an official member of SAI, I attended meetings, teas and a special formal Christmas banquet. We also presented regular recitals. I recall one day when we did some painting at the music school. We were not a social organization or a group of snobs. (Snobbish girls were not invited to join.) We were a group of girls who dearly loved music and had worked hard to get where we were

I was a country kid who didn't know better, and I mentioned that only punch was served at their "teas." After my comment, the decision was made to actually serve tea at the next fancy event. Everything looked quite elegant as we honored our alumni members by using an exquisite silver tea service. Prim and proper. What did I drink? Punch! I don't like tea!

The "Spring Sing" was one of the most popular Wittenberg campus events. A singing contest among the social organizations was held in the evening outside one of the stately old campus buildings. The fraternity men presented their music one week and the sorority gals performed the next. *Every* member was *required* to sing with his or her group, and the director had to be a student member of that society, usually a music major. If I remember correctly, one number was required, then each society presented a number of their choice. Judges selected the group with the best musical sound. I know for a fact that one girl "stood" with her sorority sisters, but although her mouth moved, she did *NOT* sing. No, not even one note! As the old saying goes, "she couldn't carry a tune in a bucket." That poor young lady! Her sorority sisters jokingly threatened her with bodily harm if she so much as let out a peep!

A required student fee covered the cost of musical concerts, ball games, plays and other college events. Music majors were expected to attend all musical programs. I enjoyed them, but my favorite was the Springfield Symphony Orchestra with the full, rich sounds of its strings. I enjoyed the other concerts featuring opera stars, great instrumentalists, dance troupes and so on. And then there were those student recitals which we were expected to attend. I must confess that voice majors with their long operatic arias sometimes lulled us to the point of sleep. Like many of my friends, I guess you might say we just tolerated them!

Although many of us "Mercycrest girls" asked to live there our second year, it was no longer available to students. We were sent to Ferncliff, a regular college dorm. Instead of the early morning mile walk to the music school, I now lived next door. So was I still early? Well, sometimes, but most of the time, I ran down the sidewalk at breakneck speed, sliding into my seat as the bell rang. Sound like the previous year's girls? Yep! I was one of *them* now!

Because we were in Ferncliff, we had to eat all our meals in the dorm's dining hall. Hello, macaroni and cheese–goodby, coconut pie! How we missed our steak and fancy foods, especially those wonderful homemade pies from the Mercycrest public dining room.

I didn't know my new roommate, Marian Danekind, but we soon found that each of us had an ornery streak. More than once when I was studying in bed, she folded the thing up into the wall with me yelling bloody murder as I lay spreadeagle upside down and flattened between the mattress and the wall. Cleaning under those fold-up beds was a cinch. They were also nice for a get-together among neighbors, but my goodness, they were such a temptation for horseplay among roommates. We certainly had our moments!

Since the dorms did not serve supper on Sunday nights, many of the students walked to the Lutheran church near the campus where a light supper was served to anyone attending the Sunday night youth meetings. I went with friends a time or two, and although the food was good, I just didn't feel comfortable with the liturgy. The day of fast-foods had not yet arrived, so like many others, I stayed in the dorm and either didn't eat, or made a meal of popcorn or snacks.

A friend decided one evening to make rice for her supper. She was not a "born and bred" Susy Homemaker. In fact, I don't think she had ever done much cooking. She dumped a box of rice into a pan, added water, and started cooking it over the gas hot plate in our floor's tiny "kitchen." That so-called kitchen consisted of a chair and a hot plate sitting on a cupboard. I heard her fussing over her pan, and, sticking my head in the door, I asked if she was having problems. Judging from the looks of things, my question was a bit foolish. The expanding rice had now filled her pan and was bubbling and boiling down onto the hot plate and across the counter, down its side and onto the floor. Rice seemed to be everywhere! I think she had started with enough rice to feed about half the dorm. What a mess! Those Sunday nights without suppers were quite a test of ingenuity for some of us.

A young lady across the hall knew how to take care of those meals and snacks. Her bottom dresser drawer was filled with food. Her family owned a delicatessen which kept her drawer filled with cheese, crackers, salami and much more. One night she invited us over for a snack. We had seen a mouse jump out of the dresser drawer earlier in the day, and for some reason, we weren't very hungry. This plump young lady claimed she had a gland problem, but we thought it was more of a bottom-dresser-drawer-problem.

Eventually food machines were installed in our dorm. Then we could buy pop, candy bars or sandwiches. One night Marian and I walked down to the machines to look for something for supper. She put her money in the sandwich machine, and out dropped two. I put money in the pop machine, and down came two. There was no one to whom we could report the error, so we enjoyed our cheap supper that night.

A new addition came to Ferncliff Hall that year. The laundry room with its sink-lined wall acquired a new piece of equipment, one of those newfangled "automatic" washing machines. This was the first one we had seen, and suddenly the popular entertainment was to gather up our laundry and spend the evening there. In a March 6, 1950, letter to my family, I wrote, "They installed a Bendix Washamat here Saturday. You have to put a quarter in the slot, and it washes, rinses, and damp dries. I'm going to save up my clothes and pay the quarter next week." For a quarter, we could not only get our laundry washed, we could also have an hour or so of fun sitting in front of that glass-doored Bendix washer, watching our colorful clothing twirl around and around. "There goes my red blouse!" and "Look quick, there's my new green sweater!" "Look at all the bubbles!" became familiar phrases. Until that time, I had usually saved up my laundry until I went home. Many students sent their dirty clothes home in laundry boxes, and the rest did their laundry in the deep tubs on the third floor. They had to suffer the indignities of brushing aside wet laundry hanging on ropes strung around dorm rooms. My roommate was from Michigan and seldom got home, so her only choice was to do her laundry upstairs and hang it in our room to dry. Occasionally Bill called me on the only first floor phone down the hall, so I had to jump up from my study desk and run, sometimes getting slapped in the face with a wet slip as I rushed by. My roommate plowed through the wet clothes quite often as she rushed to the phone. Her boyfriend lived on campus and called almost every night.

That newfangled washer created a full-fledged problem one night. Its load of clothes became lopsided and as it whirled and spun, it began to take a "walk," traveling across the room. It lunged into one of the sinks and knocked it completely off the wall. Word traveled fast and almost everyone showed up at some time that night to see the damage. Unfortunately, we were not there to actually witness the "*walking* Bendix" in action. Alas, that was about as exciting as our college life got in those days.

It was a warm spring night, and Marian and I had a touch of spring fever. Although we were in our pajamas, we suddenly had a deep urge to eat ice cream. We were not supposed to go out during week nights except to the library, but after talking the situation over, we finally came up with a plan. Rolling up the legs of our pajamas, we put on our most innocent looks, grabbed our spring coats and a book, and proceeded to the lobby of our dorm where we signed out for the library. Feeling slightly guilty, but enjoying the beautiful evening, we walked straight to the library. "Yes," we could honestly say, "we went to the library." Then we walked around the side of the building and proceeded across the back of the campus to the nearby drugstore. The forbidden treat was thoroughly enjoyed, and we giggled and laughed as we walked past the library door, then back to our dorm where we signed in and hurried to our room. Not trusting anyone to keep our little secret, we never told the other girls of our spring fever excursion that evening.

I had another late night adventure one year. My roomie became angry at me for some reason, something so insignificant that we didn't remember afterward what the problem had been. In a sudden burst of temper, she had grabbed her little water-filled paperweight and threw it. It was a heavy round glass ball which contained a winter scene whose snow fell when shaken. It hit the mirror on the dresser behind me. The mirror shattered with pieces flying all over the dresser scarf and out across the floor. Later that night she apologized with a contrite heart, admitting that she had not really aimed it at me. Then she originated one of the world's craziest ideas and convinced me it would solve the problem.

Nearby was an empty room. It had a dresser just like ours and our key fit that room. After everyone was asleep, we would exchange dressers. At about two o'clock in the morning, we crept out of bed and quietly started the process of moving the dressers. Rollers on the bottom would make this job a cinch. Well, not quite! As we started to roll one, it squeaked and squawked in a most horrendous noise that shattered the silence of the sleeping dorm. We quickly realized this wasn't going to be an easy task. It would be necessary for us to actually pick the dresser up and carry it into the hall, around the corner, past the girls' bathroom and down about three doors. "Please, Lord, don't let anyone have to use that bathroom in the middle of the night," we prayed. After some huffing and puffing, we finally got our dresser to the other room; then, drawing on all the strength we had left, we started the process of bringing the unbroken dresser back to our room. We struggled down the hall, glancing around to see if we would be detected. Around the corner we shuffled with our heavy load, down three doors, and inside to the safety of our room. Had we actually made it? We quietly closed the door on the completed job and silently congratulated ourselves on our success.

We were worn out from carrying those heavy metal dressers and were weak from exhaustion and fear of being caught, yet the whole picture seemed so ridiculous we collapsed in giggles on our beds. We didn't get much sleep that night, but we didn't get caught either. I've always felt a little guilty about that broken mirror, even though I was not the one who caused it. The room was a spare that was seldom used, and we never heard anything more about it. How did I get roped into such a shenanigan? As one of the Nuns proclaimed in *The Sound of Music*, "Father, forgive me for I have sinned!"

Not every evening brought fun and excitement for us. After homework was finished, we had many very quiet evenings when we sat with pillows behind our backs, leaning against the wall with our feet stretched across the bed in front of us. Then we did our little homemaker routine. Marian was quite adept at knitting, and while her needles clicked a steady tune as she knit her boyfriend a sweater, I carefully embroidered several pairs of pillow slips and guest towels. These went home with me and were packed away in Grandpa's trunk which I now proudly called my "hope chest."

I was going "steady" with a young man named Bill and was beginning to wonder if college life was really for me. My grades were excellent. I had gotten along quite well with the people and classes. So what did I dislike most about college?

John Thomas Williams had two grand pianos in his studio. As I entered for my lessons twice each week, I was expected to put my books on his piano, then sit at the other piano and play everything without music during those seemingly endless lessons. Oh, how I hated that! I had never been good at memorizing music (and still can't!). He was trying to make a concert pianist of me, and I was really just a country girl who enjoyed music. After all those hours of lessons and practice, I was getting tired of the whole routine. I had never lived in town and didn't enjoy city life. I wanted to see the sun come up and go down. I wanted to see the corn and animals grow. No, I had finally had enough of the life in a college dormitory, enough of living in town, and more than enough of memorizing piano lessons! If I didn't quit, I was afraid I would hate music for the rest of my life, and I certainly didn't want that to happen! Besides, a diamond ring assured me that a young man waited patiently back in Auglaize County.

The last event of the school year was the Alma Mater pageant held in The Hollow behind the library. Guests sat on the grassy slopes as the pageant unfolded in front of them. For several weeks, the girls' physical education classes had learned folk dances and special numbers for this grand day. Bill sat in the audience as I portrayed a slave girl dressed in rags, hair disheveled, face dirty, quite a pathetic sight. I had to walk among the *rich* people, calling out "Baksheesh! Baksheesh!" as I pleaded for their help, their money and their sympathy. My acting job was so realistic that Bill wanted desperately to help me out of my pathetic situation, yet there was nothing he could do! I did such a convincing performance that spring afternoon that my big, six-foot-three-inch-tall hero almost cried real tears. Hey, that's impressive! I wonder, is it too late for an acting career?

These girls from Mercycrest dorm at Wittenberg College in 1948 were told to say "cheese."
First row, left to right: Carol Stevens, Joan Hodges, Betty Wade, Jan Baker, Bambi Faun
Second Row: Jane Noel, Vivian Hehl, Audrey Korn, Mary Lou Morgan, Verna Hoyt, Imogene Fox, Jo Parker, Mickey Hanlin
Third Row: Patsy Anthony, Sonja Hillgreen, Katherine Mansfield, Jo Young, Margaret Richards, Gail Kollie, Millie Stokes, Sally Bell, Mary Liz Willer
Fourth Row: Miss Frances Smith (dorm mom), Virginia Gross, Glenna Davenport, Mary Pearson, Sister Betty Amstutz (dorm mom), Mimi Loetz, Gerry Jewel, Martina Jacobsen, Carrol Taepke

## Chapter 57.

# Meeting the In-laws

Meeting one's future in-laws for the first time is usually a *shaking-in-the-shoes* event. What will we have in common? How will we differ? Knowing that Great-Grandpa Heinrich Schwartz and Grandma Charlotta Briggs had both been born in Germany may have given me a false sense of security about the extent of the differences. In hindsight, I was totally unprepared for what I discovered, not only about my future in-laws, but also about my own lack of knowledge about what it meant to be German.

My first impression of Bill's family was that they were certainly quiet folks, especially at meal times. After the food was placed on the table, Bill's grandpa asked the blessing in German, which of course I did not understand. As we ate, conversation was scarce and almost strained, with few sounds other than that of chewing, swallowing and an occasional burp. (In some countries this is a sign that the meal is satisfactory, so the tradition may have been brought from Germany.) When everyone had finished eating, Grandma closed the meal with a prayer—in German of course. I soon learned that the routine never varied.

Meals in Bill's family home were very different from those in my home where food was usually accompanied by good conversation. That was when my family talked out problems, discussed the activities of the day and made plans for the week ahead. Many dinners, especially on Sunday, were filled with comments about the Sunday school lesson or the morning sermon. I especially remember Grandpa and Dad's vivid discussion of the Biblical account of Belshazar and the "handwriting on the wall" from the fifth chapter of Daniel. Occasionally, "roast preacher" seemed to be the topic after a particularly boring sermon. Although Bill remembers similar meals like that, my first meal at his house was certainly different from those talkative meals at my house.

Much of the quiet atmosphere was probably due in part to shyness and to the fact that Bill's grandparents felt more comfortable speaking Platt Deutsch, the German dialect used in their homes. Great-grandpa Schwartz had spoken German, but his children knew only a few phrases. It was not until I met Bill's family that I learned to more fully appreciate the German dialects. Just as the Bostonian English differs from that spoken in the heart of Dixie, so were there differences in the forms of the German language used throughout Germany in the 1800s. *Platt* (low) *Deutsch* (German) was used primarily in the low or marshland areas of north and northwestern Germany. Most of those from New Knoxville learned Platt Deutsch at home as their mother tongue (until World War II) and it was the language used in everyday life. *Hoch* (high) *Deutsch* (German), was used in the southern, more mountainous regions of Germany. Martin Luther's translation of the Bible resulted in high German becoming the language of the church, and today's "German." Bill's parents studied High German in school in order to read German Bibles, hymn books and newspapers. English, which was learned at school, was used when dealing with those from "outside" the community. It was also used for legal forms and record keeping, since low German was usually not used in a written form.

Many of those who left Germany and came to America were tired of being involved in wars between fighting counts and barons, and naturally settled among relatives and friends who shared the same dialect and faith, and were "German-like-us." It is of interest that New Knoxville residents (from Ladbergen) and Minster residents (from Oldenburg) spoke the same dialect but had differing faiths, while New Bremen folks spoke a slightly different dialect but had the same faith. Jake Meckstroth once mentioned how difficult it had been to talk with his cousins from New Bremen because they talked "funny."

Platt Deutsch was also used outside the community, but with different motives! Some of the young people of southwestern Auglaize County would speak in Low German, knowing that the kids from other areas of the county could not understand them. They could talk about the English-only speakers to their faces, then smile and look quite innocent as they walked away. Only another German speaker would know the difference.

Bill's grandmother had never needed to learn much English. She was seldom far from home where her family and friends all spoke the Low German. Since I spoke only English, she sometimes had difficulty communicating with me. Many times she would start to tell me something, then pause and say, "Ach, how you say that?" when she couldn't think of the English words. Bill or his mother would come to her rescue. Grandpa had gotten around more, so his English was much better.

Most mealtime visits were on Sunday evenings, especially when I had come home from college for the weekend. Bill would pick me up late in the afternoon and we would stop at his house before he took me back to Wittenberg College in Springfield. After supper was over, Bill would head to the barn and do the milking and other chores, and his grandpa would head to the rocking chair and radio. If the weather outside was cold, I usually helped Bill's mom and grandma clean up in the kitchen, while Grandpa listened as Drew Pearson, (whom he called Drew Pierce) reported the evening news. As soon as the news was off, Grandpa started twisting the dial. Sometimes he would find some pretty music, and I would think, "Oh, leave it there. That's so beautiful." But after only a minute or two, the dial was turned to some other station. As I began to get interested in that program, another twist, and it changed again. That really bothered me! But if the weather was warm, I sometimes kept Bill company in the barn, although we were careful not to get emotional. As with many Germans, any sign of affection was seldom shown among his family members, although I still felt accepted by them. Several years later, I embarrassed the daylights out of Bill's grandpa. He was quite ill in the hospital and as we prepared to leave, I gave him a big hug and a kiss. He loved it, but his face was certainly red!

After getting better acquainted with the family, attending each other's churches was the next big step for Bill and me. Just as I was unprepared for the silence of his family, I was equally unprepared for what awaited me in his church. Chores had run long, so we arrived a few minutes late. It was also a special holiday service and empty seats were hard to find. I felt as if everyone was staring and whispering as we sat down. After all, I was an outsider whom the older people had never seen. I was quite relieved to be sitting at last, but within minutes, a little old lady walked directly to me, stopped, then frowning down at me, said something in a voice loud enough to be heard in the front row of the sanctuary.

I just stared at her. I had no idea what she had said. As every head turned to look at me, I wanted very much to disappear through the floor. I gave Bill a dumbfounded look as he said we had to move. "Why?" I wondered. "We got here first." Taking my hand, Bill gently urged me up, and we finally found another place to sit. Never before had I been so publicly embarrassed, and I decided it would definitely be a cold day in July before I would ever return to *that* church. (I did eventually return.) When the service was over, I finally found out what the commotion was all about. The chair I was sitting on *belonged* to the lady because a special hearing device was available beside it, enabling her to hear the service. She was not only German, she was also quite deaf! That was why the whole church knew that *I* was sitting in *her* seat. They understood her German. I didn't!

Meeting Bill's family also meant a crash course in German names. I had no trouble with my family's German names of Schwartz and Frech, but Wierwille, Grotholtman, Feldwisch, Fledderjohann and Katterheinrich (pronounced as "Fledderjohn" and "Katterhenry" in New Knoxville) were a bit more challenging. Indeed, some who had moved out of the community changed the spelling to match the way they were pronounced in New Knoxville. Other relatives actually dropped the "heinrich/henry" and are just called Katter. Although Kuckherman was an early local name, there are none in the current phone book. The descendants use only "Kuck." Auglaize County's German names can be a real challenge! We have a lot of fun with our road name—Weifenbach. The sign at the west end says "Wief . . ." but it is "Weif . . ." at the east end. When I mentioned this to a county road official, he just shrugged his shoulders. The road is only one mile long, so who cares? Hmmm! [At the time of this new printing, the sign on the east end has been run down by a car, and now the signs are spelled wrong on both ends.]

Given names were sometimes more confusing than family names! Many of the newly married immigrants from Germany continued the German tradition of repeating names. If a child named Hermann Heinrich Adolph died as a baby, the next boy born might be given the exact same name. In some cases, the same names were used for two children but the order reversed for the second child. Others gave all the children the same first name–Hermann for instance. The first son might be Hermann Heinrich, the second Hermann Wilhelm, and the third Hermann Adolph. Bill's ancestors, Herman Heinrich Fledderjohann and wife, Christine Elisabeth (Holtkamp), used this method when naming their sons in the 1820s.

Many of the immigrants had three given names and a family surname. Bill's great-grandfather was Herman Heinrich Wilhelm Wierwille. Sometimes it is difficult to locate all three names. By combining the marriage, christening and birth records, I was finally able to locate all of my grandmother's names–Charlotta Adelheid Dorothea Frech of Petershagen, Prussia.

Although the Methodist church in which I was raised was the result of a merger of German and English-speaking congregations, not all ethnic communities were so quick to break down the barriers that separated them from the rest of the world. I learned, as did others like me, that just because one marries into an ethnic community, it does not mean that one will be accepted as a part of "them." Many of the very old folks around New Knoxville were suspicious of strangers. Outsiders were rarely welcomed with open arms. Many years ago, I went into one of the local grocery stores to buy some smoked sausage. While the clerk weighed a ring of the sausage for me, she asked, "You going to have sauerkraut and potatoes with this?" "Yes," I replied, "that's what I'm having." She wrapped the sausage in a sheet of paper, and as she tied the string around it, she said, "I suppose you'll serve it with mashed potatoes. That's the way most people fix it." My reply was, "No, I cook chunks of potato and then put them in with the kraut and sausage." She looked a bit surprised and said, "Oh, that's the way the Germans fix it." "Yes, I know!" I answered. "I had Ladbergen ancestors who came here in 1845. I'm German, too!" Her answer—an abrupt, "Oh!"

Bill was related to both Ferd and Zella Eversman. One day Zella asked about my family. She had known me for more than thirty years, but not my ancestry. "Well, Zella," I said, "my great-great-grandparents came from Ladbergen to New Knoxville in 1845." With a twinkle in her eye, she burst out laughing. "Ach," she said, "you *are* one of us!"

Bill and I have smiled many times as we remember a special anniversary planning meeting in New Knoxville many years ago. Someone suggested the history of the town be written by a local retired school teacher whom they named. She was very capable and would have done a marvelous job, but an older person spoke up and said the job really should be given to a native, someone who was *from* New Knoxville. I later found that, although this teacher had lived and taught school in New Knoxville for forty years, she had been *born* in some other area and had only married a local man. Even with her talent and years of teaching experience, she was not considered a wise choice for the job, simply because she had not been *born* there. We just shook our heads in wonderment!

I also learned that barriers, such as language and customs, not only kept the outside out, but they sometimes kept things in. Bill said the young people of New Knoxville had been encouraged to stay in town to eat after ball games. Local businesses then benefited from the money. Eating out was seldom done by Bill's family. When we occasionally took his mother to eat in a restaurant, she was very ill at ease when ordering from a menu. She usually waited for us to order, then said, "I'll take what they ordered."

Wars, especially those involving Germany, created some tense situations for a few Auglaize County residents of German ancestry. While some outsiders wondered about the patriotism of these communities, it was quite apparent as to whom they gave their allegiance. Many of those who had immigrated to the United States had been peasants who had worked the fields of wealthy landlords. Zella told me of an incident involving Ferd and an older relative, possibly his grandfather. Ferd wasn't sure how his grandpa was going to accept his involvement in World War I as an American soldier, since Grandpa had been born in the same Germany that was now considered "the enemy." As the two men talked, Ferd's grandpa explained that as a young man back in Germany, he had been compelled to work very hard. An overseer on a horse had ridden through the fields where he was working and the man's favorite tool was a whip that he used liberally on the young peasant workers' backs. His grandpa's advice to Ferd roughly translates to: "Kill all those bastards you can!"

World War II was also a trying time. Although many local residents had corresponded with family members back in Germany, they remained sensitive to what non-Germans in the area might be thinking. The New Knoxville school sponsored a scrap drive with a huge stack of junk piled out behind the school. That small community also gave more than their share of young men to fight in that war. Homer Kuck from New Knoxville was the first prisoner of war I had heard of. Zelotes Eschmeyer was also a prisoner. Many local men just a few years older than Bill had flown numerous bombing missions, fought in the Battle of the Bulge, crossed the Pacific in the belly of a submarine, landed on Iwo Jima and spent years in a prisoner-of-war camp. These patriotic young men had served their country with pride.

After the war, people in Germany faced shortages of food and clothing of all kinds. They had no money with which to buy needed items. Relatives in New Knoxville, as well as Americans across the country, responded to their plight with generous hearts, and a stream of packages crossed the ocean to war-torn Europe. Bill's neighbors, Lawrence and Lydia Schroeder, had sent used clothing and shoes to relatives there. Their daughter, Dorothy Egan, told of receiving pictures showing her German cousins wearing the dresses and other clothing that she and her siblings had outgrown. She remembered hearing her folks talk about sending letters and boxes, then wondering if the clothing would still fit their children after it finally arrived. They wrote letters of thanks and were extremely grateful for anything they received.

These German relatives were farmers whose main interest was in staying alive. They were not responsible for the war. Germany had experienced a time of depression much like our own here in America. When they voted Hitler into office, they were voting for a man who promised jobs, food for their tables and a stable economy. American families voted for the same things when Roosevelt took office here. Little did any of us know what lay ahead. When folks from this area get together with distant relatives and friends from Germany, the conversation seldom turns to the topic of war. Many of the people traveling here were children in the 1940s and have traumatic memories of seeing loved ones killed and of hiding in the woods while American bombs destroyed their homes. Unexploded bombs are still found occasionally. It is very difficult for them to speak about the war.

Several years ago I bought a box of articles at an estate auction. In it were a couple of letters from people in Germany. These were translated into English, and I feel parts of them should be included here. One was written on August 10, 1952, several years after the war's end. It started, "My dear friends in America, We received your dear letter on August 8th. and we were very happy, and especially about the package we received three weeks ago and which surprised us very much." She mentioned that they were finished with their harvesting and threshing, but that it had not been a good year. It had not rained since planting time and the heat had set new records. Because the crops were dead, many of their animals had to be sold. "Just the war has left much behind, twice our money has depreciated in value. These are all things that kept us back. In America that hasn't happened yet." She then mentioned that a couple of young men had left for Australia. She rather wistfully wrote, "If I were young again I would emigrate too. Now I want to talk about the dresses. Hedwig was especially pleased about the coat. She said she'd always wanted one like it, and most of the things fit. The shoes fit me too. Hedwig has a bigger foot. The stockings and shirt fit Eugene. I want to thank you again for your kindness."

Another letter was dated October 3, 1952. "We received your dear package with much pleasure and we can use just everything. I was especially pleased with the jacket, because I had none and so now my wish to have one is fulfilled. The girls are sending you their kindest regards and thank you for everything as it happens you have the same figure as they." During this time, there was some conflict between some of the nations, and the news spoke of possibly going to war over the problem. She wrote:

> What news do you get in America about the war? We hope and wish that the statesmen can manage to agree without arms. All of us recently had to sacrifice our husbands and

> children. Isn't life hard enough to bear already? Then comes unemployment, the refugees and the high cost of living. No one seems to get along the way we should in these times. If only we could finally be at peace all over the world. Is your son still at home in your country or is he far away from you? I lived through such conditions for seven years and I know what it means to be a soldier's wife. I hope we shall be spared from having to go thru it a second time. Does your husband still have work? What will happen to us here, I don't know, there is so little. And layoffs because of high prices. All this time potatoes cost 15 marks per 50 kilos, who can pay all this and yet we all want to live. It must be better where you live and so we are doubly glad when you can occasionally send us something.

Although I obviously noted many differences between my husband's family and community and my own, there were also numerous ways in which I found myself identifying with many of their ways and stereotypes. One of the first things one associates with being German is ethnic foods, and especially cabbage prepared as sauerkraut. Germans supposedly all love sauerkraut. It was quite common for Bill's family and mine to make large crocks of kraut each fall. It was so much a part of the German identity that Bill remembers that his first school bus, with its wooden body and spoke wheels, was often referred to by local people as the "cabbage crate."

Bill and I attended a few basketball games while dating. New Knoxville's team was envied by area schools because its tall, husky, basketball players made it the powerhouse of the county athletic league. Because of their German ancestry, they were sometimes referred to as "kraut heads." This prompted someone to roll a head of cabbage across the basketball court during a tournament game in St. Marys! It didn't seem to bother the players, though. New Knoxville eventually went on to play in the state tournament in Columbus. Of course, none of the old-timers ever forgot the game in which New Knoxville beat Buckland by a *final* score of 2-0. I think that game made the *Guinness Book of World Records*!

There are a few foods that seem to shout "German." Summer sausage, blood puddin' and liverwurst were also frequent dishes on most old German dinner tables. They were homegrown, cheap and filling. I smiled as I read a paragraph from a 1949 *Evening Leader* interview with New Knoxville's Doc Fledderjohann. When asked about epidemics, he told of a certain typhoid epidemic.

> The [epidemic] almost wrecked me. Four adults died from it, and many others recovered but were left in a weakened condition. One after another these contracted pneumonia and began to die, and I was almost frantic because I had those lives on my hands and some were beyond help. And sometimes people wouldn't obey orders and insist on feeding my Typhoid patients 'wurst' and cheese and other solids. I sometimes barked and growled and snarled at them like a dog and some of them said I was a grouchy old cuss.

Another traditional German food was *zwieback*, a kind of dried bread. How do you make it? Lola Lammers says she makes hers from a sweeter dough than that used for baking regular bread. Although some people make it into loaves which they slice, she makes hers into buns that she bakes, then pulls apart with two forks and places on a cookie sheet to dry in a warm oven. (That is the way her mother did it!) The bread is left in the oven overnight or for an entire day. She said most people then dunk it in coffee as they eat it. Bill said when he was a child, he dipped his into hot cocoa. Whether you dipped it, lay it in a coffee-soaked saucer, covered it with fruit and sugar or just ate it plain, it was considered a necessary item in homes of most German descendants around New Knoxville.

I also felt quite at home with the thriftiness of Bill's family. My grandpa, like Bill's, had saved every box, can and board for future use. My grandma washed bread wrappers and used them again, just as Bill's mother and grandma did. I heard of one father who took things a bit too far, though. His children felt deprived because they had not been allowed to attend a movie as their friends had done. But Father solved the problem. He attended the movie by himself, then came home and told the rest of the family about it, describing the plot in detail. It saved some money that way!

Bill's grandpa, as did mine, took great pride in his farm and house. Years later, I smiled as a distant relative assured me she would not be too anxious to move to New Knoxville as we had just done. She had heard that if you lived in town, you had to mow your lawn the same day as the neighbors or you would be in trouble. Everybody's lawn had to be the same length at the same time. Well, I don't think it's quite that bad, but if you drive through southwestern Auglaize County, you will notice that the houses and yards are usually well kept in this area of German ancestry.

My family also seemed to share much of the same philosophy of child rearing and respect for authority as Bill's family. During both of our childhoods, the rule in most homes seemed to be, "Children are to be seen and not heard!" This was especially true when there were visitors in the home. We were reminded of our manners in church and in school, as well as at home. I will never forget the humiliation I felt the day our school superintendent passed me in the hall outside my first grade room. I was so accustomed to saying, "Yes, ma'am," and "No, ma'am" to my female teacher that I had automatically answered his simple question with a "Yes, ma'am" instead of "Yes, sir." The words flew out of my mouth, and I knew at once I had made a mistake. My face surely must have turned quite red, and I felt the great inner flush of embarrassment at my poor use of manners.

This desire for children to have good manners had also been developed in Bill's family. He remembers as a little tyke, sitting on the lap of his Grandpa Ernst, better known as "Squire" Meckstroth, during the church service. Ernst gave him a nickel which he carefully placed in the church collection plate as it passed, then he had to sit quietly during the remainder of the church service. Bill's cousin, Ralph Hoelscher, remembered his family teaching him to say hello to Grandpa Ernst. If he said, "How do sir, Grandpa!" Ernst would respond with a penny which he was allowed to keep. Bad manners were not tolerated, but for him, it paid to be proper.

Sometimes those old Germans had some "funny" ideas about respect and saving face. I have heard numerous stories of family members who got angry with each other over some simple little thing, but never resolved the problem. Now, perhaps several decades later, those who were originally involved are dead and their children (or grandchildren in some cases) are still not speaking, although they don't always know why. The reason was probably buried with a deceased family member. Relatives continue to silently pass each other at weddings and funerals and keep right on going with not even a "How Do!"

An older lady told me of a situation that took place many years ago. Her family drove many miles over rough roads to visit a sick relative in this area. When they arrived, the man's wife wasn't even going to let them in to see him. After a brief discussion, she finally consented. They had a final visit with him before he died a few weeks later.

My grandma used to talk about her dad being so stubborn (or was it that he just demanded so much respect?). I thought of that as I listened to a story from a local farmer's son. After studying a particular problem on the farm, he made a suggestion to his father as to how the problem could be remedied. His dad didn't like the idea. Then one day, after sufficient time had passed, the father came up with a "new" idea. In reality it was the son's idea with just enough modifications that Dad could now claim it as his own. Then it was all right to make the changes. Since most German mothers tried to keep their distance from any confrontation, she assured Father his idea was a good one. After he had returned to the barn, she quietly praised the son for his intelligence. Although both parents and son knew the truth, it helped Father "save face." Remember the threshing story? Jell-O was frivolous until Father got a taste, then he suggested buying it.

I continue to learn what it means to be German, as do those reared in New Knoxville. The old Platt Deutsch is no longer the common language heard in the area, although occasional get-togethers bring conversation and the sharing of youthful tales. Local historical societies in southwestern Auglaize County also attempt to preserve the German heritage as a means of educating current and future generations about their ancestors' endeavors. These forums also provide opportunities to learn about one's family from the stories and other folklore that are discussed.

Meta (Meckstroth) Hoge enjoyed telling a family story she had heard about a visit from Napoleon. Napoleon had allegedly ridden through the German countryside, pillaging and stealing. He had stopped at the relatives' home and stolen their horse which they desperately needed. In its place, he left his old, worn-out nag that was of no use on the farm.

According to another story handed down in this area, a love affair between a count and a nun was responsible for Ladbergen being Protestant instead of Catholic. I once heard an older lady say that her ancestors had been in church the day the change from Catholic to Protestant was made. Supposedly, Count Philipp of Hessia, had become a follower of Martin Luther. His cousin, Mechthilde, a nun had also listened carefully to Luther's comments. She eventually left the convent and became a Protestant. Count Konrad of Tecklenberg (which included the area around Ladbergen) fell in love with Mechthilde and they were married, but only after he, too, became a Protestant.

This story was verified in the book *Ladbergen* by Friedrich Saatkamp. The marriage in May of 1527 made Mecklenburg the first county in Westphalia to become Protestant. Although nearly every church member accepted the change, three or four farmers in the Ladbergen area chose to stay with their Catholic upbringing. They either moved or attended church in neighboring towns. The book *Ladbergen* says, "According to another old word-of-mouth tradition, the Reformation came to Ladbergen when the preacher simply changed from wearing the white robe of the Catholic Church one Sunday to the black robe of a Protestant preacher on the next." [1]

When cheap farm land became scarce around New Knoxville, many left the area in the 1870s and 1880s, taking some of their "unique" ways with them as they settled in Holland, Indiana; Le Sueur, Minnesota; and Garner, Iowa. Familiar names still appear in the phone books of these four areas.

One of Zella Eversman's favorite stories was about a determined German relative of both Bill and her husband who had moved on to Garner, Iowa. At the outbreak of World

War I, many people decided it would be best to use English instead of the language of the "enemy." Thus the pastor of the Garner church announced that church services, as well as catechism classes, would no longer be taught in German. One lady was very much offended by this and made her feelings known. Her children would not be allowed to attend the class. She would teach them at home because, as Zella quoted her, "Everyone *knows* that *God is German* and that the Bible does not translate right into English!"

Many times we have smiled about that story. As I later related it to another New Knoxville relative, Bud Zuege, he started laughing, then said, "Let me tell you the rest of the story. When I was a boy, my family went to Garner to visit relatives. As we participated in the church service, we stood up to sing. While everyone else sang in English, this same family still sang in German." Of course, the words didn't match and the boy was terribly embarrassed to find himself in the midst of the confusion. This incident took place in the late 1940s, so these folks were really *determined Germans*. But, after all, why not? "God *is* German!" Right?

---

[1] Friedrich Saatkamp, *Ladbergen*, English translation by Dean Hoge 1985, Kleins Druck-und Verlagstat, Lengerich, Westfalia, Germany, pp. 38-39, used with permission.

Bill's grandparents celebrated 60 years of marriage in 1954.

Seated on ground: Ronald Cottrell, Jim Meckstroth, Vernon Frederick Meckstroth Jr., Laura Lee Wierwille, Rebecca Meckstroth, Joanne Wierwille, and Marylou Meckstroth

Seated: Alwina (Wierwille) Niemeyer, Emma Wierwille, honorees Fred and Anna Wierwille, Clara (Wierwille) Meckstroth, Caroline (Wierwille) Cottrell, Harry Wierwille

Standing: Oliver Niemeyer, Glenna (Davenport) Meckstroth, Bill Meckstroth, Vernon Meckstroth, Betty (Roby) Meckstroth, Ashley Cottrell, Wilhelmina (Strasburg) Wierwille

## Chapter 58.

# "I Love You Truly"

How did we meet? Well, we were both going in circles at the time! On this particular night, a group of guys from New Knoxville had driven to Lima and walked up the ramp to the second floor skating rink on West Market Street. (Recently I was quite surprised to find that cousin Norman Davenport had helped lay the wood and sand that original skating rink floor.) Roller skating had been a regular part of Bill's life, and for his New Knoxville crowd, this was just another night of the usual routine with the guys.

It definitely had *not* been a regular routine for me. In fact, I had skated a grand total of only two or three times when a girlfriend invited some of us girls to go skating that summer evening. We had just graduated from high school and drove to Lima expecting a night of fun and clean activity. During the evening, my friend Grace pointed out a young man whom she knew and said, "He's a really nice guy. Why don't you ask him to skate when they have *ladies' choice*?" The rink was crowded, and most of the young men were skating rather rapidly, but she pointed to the one. At the appropriate time, I went over and asked the young man to skate. We had a good time talking, but when I went back to my friends, Grace informed me I had asked the wrong person. Oh, well, it didn't really matter. Homer and I enjoyed talking, and when the skating ended for the night, we went home.

A week later she again called to ask if I would go skating. I had no other plans, so I went. The same New Knoxville guys were there, and Homer, the young man with whom I had skated the week before, came over and sat down. As we talked, another young man skated over and sat on the other side of me. After saying hello, this newcomer asked me to skate with him and I accepted. As we skated, he said, "You like music, don't you?" I smiled and said, "Yes, I do, but how did you know?" He quickly replied, "Because you skate in time with the music. Most girls don't." Bill and I skated together several times that night, and he asked to take me home. I had come with the girls, and I always thought a girl should go home with the person who had brought her, so I turned him down. On the way home, Grace asked me what I had thought of Bill. That seemed odd, but then she told me he was the one she had pointed out the week before. Well, what do you know? I had mistakenly asked Homer Henschen, but now I had met the right one. But guess what! When I finally walked down the aisle to become Bill's bride, there stood Bill's cousin Homer–our best man!

A few days after meeting Bill for the first time, a strange car drove in one evening, and someone knocked on our door. I wasn't expecting anyone and was upstairs. Grandma invited him to sit down in the living room and called up the stairway to tell me I had company. When I came down those steps, Bill said he thought I must have been the little sister to the girl he had met. I was wearing my favorite summer outfit which I had definitely outgrown, a pretty, flowered cotton dress with puffed sleeves, a ruffle circling the yoke and a hemline that was high above my knees. With my hair in pigtails, I looked about twelve years old. When I recognized him and started talking, Bill finally realized I was actually the same girl.

That was the summer of Auglaize County's 100th anniversary. We were both taking part in a special choral program to be presented by singers from the entire county. We talked briefly at the practices held at St. Paul's Church in Wapakoneta and realized we were both participating in a centennial talent show that was to be presented at the fairgrounds. On our first official date, we competed *against* each other at the talent show. Although neither of us won, we had a good time. Bill sang "The Big Bass Viol" and I *squeezed out* a march, "Under the Double Eagle," on my accordion. After the contest, we walked around the fairgrounds together, enjoying the many township displays of antiques and historical items pertaining to the county's beginning. We tasted some of the foods, talked to friends, and were thrilled with the special fireworks. It was a great night of celebration for the county, and by the end of the evening we realized we enjoyed each other's company.

A few weeks later, I headed for my first year at Wittenberg College in Springfield, Ohio. Since their rules allowed students to go home only once a month, we usually saw each other then. It wasn't long before Bill not only came to see me at home, he soon began coming to Springfield for an occasional visit or to bring me home and back again.

During the next summer we saw each other more frequently. What did we do on our once-a-week dates? Since Bill couldn't come over until his milking was finished, we occasionally just sat and talked, drove into New Knoxville for a soda at the Dairy Bar or drove to Lima where we munched on a hamburger from the Kewpee. Since we both loved music, we spent many evenings at the local drive-in movie theaters enjoying the fabulous musicals such as *Brigadoon, State Fair, South Pacific*, *Oklahoma*, the "road" films with Bing Crosby, Bob Hope, and Dorothy Lamour. We also enjoyed the wonderful Nelson Eddy-Jeannette McDonald musicals. These evenings were always filled with appreciation for those great musicals.

One night we attended a movie at the Gloria Drive-In Theater north of Lima. At one point in the musical, Bill leaned over and kissed me. This may sound like something out of a movie, but believe it or not, at the very same moment we both clearly heard bells ringing. Now wasn't that romantic? You know of course there were really no audible bells, but we knew at that moment that we definitely were in *LOVE!*

Bill planned a day in Columbus to help celebrate my twentieth birthday. While there, he purchased a diamond engagement ring. As we returned home that evening, he stopped at a small roadside park in Bellefontaine and slipped the ring on my finger. When I went back to college Sunday night, I didn't mention the engagement ring, but as I was in the girls' restroom washing my hair, a friend came in. I didn't think she would notice the diamond among all those soap bubbles, but I was wrong. In a few minutes, a gang of friends descended on me and literally picked me up and placed me under a cold shower, clothes and all. Most of the newly engaged girls were either dunked under the shower or into the fountain at the center of the campus. Since it was "after hours" and girls were not allowed out, I was lucky. I got the shower! Dunkings in the fountain drew very large, noisy crowds of well wishers and involved either a quick trip to the dorm or wearing some very soggy clothes to classes, as well as ruining a perfectly good hairdo in the middle of the day. I was thankful my dunking came while my hair was already wet. My long hair was very hard to dry, and I knew of only one hair dryer in the whole dorm!

When word got out that I was engaged, a group of guys from the Dorm League came to serenade me. This was usually done by the fraternity men when a girl was "pinned" (received her boyfriend's fraternity pin) or when she received her diamond engagement ring. Usually girls who did not live in sorority houses or date fraternity men were seldom serenaded, so I felt quite privileged to receive the honor from my friends there.

My roommate, Marian Danekind, and her Dorm League boyfriend, Don Hanson, invited Bill and me to attend their elegant spring banquet. The girls wore long formal dresses, and the guys were in nice suits. The custom of tuxedos for parties and weddings was unheard of then. Out on the farm, the only tuxedos I had seen were in the movies.

From my first day in college, I had wanted to learn more about being an organist, but when I played for John Thomas Williams, a red-haired Welshman who was the head of the School of Music at Wittenberg, he asked me to play the piano, not the organ. When I mentioned playing the accordion, he snorted and said he didn't even consider it a proper musical instrument. He apparently decided I had enough talent to make it as a concert pianist and immediately scheduled one organ lesson and two piano lessons a week. He was my piano teacher and taught the theory classes that I most certainly did not enjoy. I wanted to make music, not write it.

"I see you are wearing a diamond," he said as I sat down for my next piano lesson. He was not happy with my engagement and immediately started preaching to me during lessons. He said that girls who got engaged usually had big dreams, then quit school. He certainly hoped I was not contemplating doing that. He felt I would regret it the rest of my life since I was really too young to know what was best for me. (I had planned on quitting, but hadn't told him and so the more he ranted, the more I was convinced that I was doing the right thing.) Even his wife, who was in charge of our music sorority, joined his crusade to keep me in school. She told me she thought it was a shame that I would be living out in the country where none of the *finer things of life* were available. She didn't know that Dad and I belonged to a concert series and that Bill and I had tickets for the concerts as well as for the Lima Symphony. We had attended performances by some of the greatest opera singers, symphony orchestras and instrumentalists in the world. (Contrary to Professor Williams' dire prediction, I have never, ever regretted leaving college. No, never! Not even for one moment!)

I did not return to college for my junior year. Are you surprised? Grandma had surgery and I was kept busy for several months taking care of her and doing the housework. Bill came to see me once or twice a week, and life went on without Professor Williams and his side-by-side pianos.

That was a busy summer for Bill. He worked with his Grandpa on a fifty/fifty basis. He paid half of the bills and received half of the profits (and because he was a strong young man and Grandpa was old, I think he did about ninety percent of the work.) Since he couldn't come see me until the work was all done, many nights he didn't arrive until 8:30 or 9:00. By then, most people were going home, and Route 33 in Moulton was quite busy. He often waited several minutes while the traffic cleared enough for him to safely cross. Imagine that, a traffic jam in tiny downtown Moulton!

That fall was exciting. Don and Mary got married and asked me to be her bridesmaid.

Daddy wanted me to be twenty-one years old before I got married, so we set our wedding date for the following June 24, 1951. One day Grandma and I went to Lima and purchased material for my wedding dress. I spent most of the next spring designing and sewing it.

As the wedding day approached, Mary, who was to be my matron of honor, planned a surprise shower for me. Rosemary Elsass, my bridesmaid, was to bring me to the party. She and I had sat together on the school bus for most of my school years, and we had visited in each other's homes. Her parents had both been born with hearing and speech loss, so our visits were always interesting.

I almost missed my own bridal shower. Since my bridesmaid was rather shy, we sat and talked for over an hour before I finally suspected something was happening and went with her. A lot of my friends from the Kossuth area were at Mary's, and as they waited for me, they cut pictures, words, and cartoons from magazines to describe our first date, the kiss, what our wedding would be like, what our children would look like, and so on. That funny book still brings smiles and memories of that night.

While we were decorating the church for the wedding and reception, Grandma's chicken cooked gently on the stove at home. Chicken sandwiches were to be served at the rehearsal dinner at our house that night. As we returned home, we smelled something. Oh, no! The chicken was burning. Grandma was quite concerned, but somehow she saved it, and everything went well at the rehearsal and dinner afterward. Tables were set in the living room and the dining room for the guests: the bride and groom (that's Bill and I); Grandpa and Grandma; Dad (bride's father); Bill's mother; my brother, Don, (usher) and his wife Mary (matron of honor); Rosemary Elsass (bridesmaid); Bill's cousins Homer Henschen (best man) and Ralph Hoelscher (usher); Charlene Sandkuhl (flower girl) and her parents, Charles and Evalyn; Rev. and Mrs. Paul Price (the preacher and amateur photographer); and Mr. and Mrs. Ferd Eversman (Zella was the organist for the wedding.) Fred Katterheinrich (vocalist), was unable to attend the party.

There is an interesting little story about three generations of flower girls. Do you want to hear it? When my parents were married in 1926, one of their flower girls had been Evalyn Leffel. It was Evalyn and Charles Sandkuhl's daughter, Charlene, who was my flower girl in 1951. When Charlene married Charles Dille in 1964, my daughter, Nancy, was their flower girl.

Our wedding day was hectic. Since I was the church organist, I played for that Sunday's morning services as usual. Everyone knew I was to be married that afternoon, and as the minister preached on and on, a few members of his congregation became rather nervous. Was he going to stop preaching in time to allow the bride to get ready? He did, and I made it in time.

Our wedding was rather simple with one floral arrangement between the candles on the altar and each of the girls carrying a bouquet. The attendants wore taffeta dresses made from the same pattern as mine—Mary in yellow and Rosemary in light green. My dress, like theirs, was floor length in white satin and lace featuring a circular train.

The music was lovely. Zella showed off the organ to good advantage. Fred's voice was as beautiful as I had remembered it. We enjoyed listening to the half-hour of music before the ceremony, Bill from a Sunday school room near the altar, and Dad, the girls and I from the basement. At the appointed time, Zella began to play the "Bridal Chorus" (you know–"Here Comes the Bride.") Rosemary and Mary started down the aisle, then Dad and I followed as he gently held my arm, smiling proudly with tears in his eyes.

It seemed like only moments until we had exchanged rings, kissed, and hurried back down the aisle to our new green Ford waiting just outside. As Bill and I were driven away, we attracted a lot of attention with our decorated car, the big "JUST MARRIED" signs, and a trail of assorted tin cans clanging behind. We drove to a St. Marys photographer for our official wedding pictures, although the preacher's wife had taken snapshots of the service. All pictures were black and white then, and wedding portraits were very expensive, especially when colored by someone using paints made for that purpose.

We quickly returned to the church and cut our beautiful cake with the small lighted church on top. While our guests enjoyed cake and punch, we opened our gifts—a common practice in those days. Not only did everyone want to see what we had received, I think some also wanted everyone to see what *they* had given the newlyweds. The day had been extremely hot, and as we opened the gifts, someone noticed a huge storm coming. Immediately most of the people from New Knoxville arose, congratulated us and hurried home. Others stayed and sat and talked to each other and to us until the heavy thunderstorm had passed. During that time we had a chance to sample the cake and punch. We also found that Helen Mack and Geraldine Rothe, whom we had asked to serve refreshments, had faced a problem. We had forgotten to bring a fancy, ribbon decorated knife to cut the cake. (No, Grandpa didn't whip out his pocket knife, wipe it on his pants, and offer it to them.) The problem was quickly solved when Helen, who lived next door to the church, hurried home, tied a bow on her fancy knife, and we cut our cake in style.

After most of the guests had left, I changed into the pink organdy dress I had made and put a white picture hat on my head. As the sun shone brightly after the shower, we started for Greenfield, Indiana, where we had reserved a motel room.

It was late when we reached the motel and we both agreed we were starved. All we had eaten since lunch was cake and punch, so we walked across the road to a nice restaurant where we ordered big steak dinners.

It seemed really strange to wake up to the unfamiliar sounds of a stone quarry located just behind the motel and to realize Bill did not *have* to get up to start the milking or drive the tractor. It was a relaxing time for both of us. We didn't have to be anywhere by a certain time. That day we drove through Indiana, Illinois and into Missouri where we visited the Meramec Caverns near Stanton. These were the largest caverns we had ever toured, and we stared at gorgeous stalactites and stalagmites, one of which was a colorful arrangement resembling organ pipes. Our guide shared historical facts: the cave had been used during the Civil War, it had also been an underground railroad station for helping escaped slaves, one area had been a hideout for outlaw Jesse James and his gang, and newlyweds from a radio show were honored with a room for the night. I'm glad it wasn't us. Although the cave was beautiful, it was cold and dark and damp.

That night we stayed at a nearby motel, the Hill Top, named because–oh, you guessed it! It was at the top of a hill. Bill wanted to take a picture of our room, so I placed my slippers by the side of the bed. We agreed it gave the picture a "homey" touch.

Quite a few years ago, a popular song about "getting your kicks on Route 66" described the main road, one lane in each direction, leading from Chicago into the southwest part of the United States. While driving down this winding and well-known route, we never really knew what was going to be around the next bend. Many Ozark mountain housewives spent their days sewing. Clotheslines full of brightly colored homemade quilts and comforters often greeted us as we rounded a bend in the road. Each lady seemed to try to outdo her neighbor who lived around the next curve.

One hot afternoon, we saw a barn built against the side of a mountain, nestled between the rocks and trees at the edge of the road. A large window opened out toward the road and a homemade sign announced, "Dairy Queen." We had never seen a Dairy Queen, but the drawing of an ice cream cone told us this would be a good place to visit on a hot day. We enjoyed that unexpected cool treat. It was several years before DQ arrived in our area.

We visited Dad's cousin Otho and Dorothy Crawford in Shawnee, Oklahoma. They had been to Ohio several years earlier and their daughter, Judy, and I had written occasionally. When we arrived, we met their youngest daughter, Barbara, and her little girlfriend. After they had run into the next room to play, Bill mentioned that this was his first trip West and that he had never seen an Indian. Dorothy laughed and said, "There's one in the next room!" Their little girl's friend was a full-blooded Shawnee.

We spent two days with them. Otho drove us around the area where we saw the State Capitol in Oklahoma City with its many oil wells on the front lawn. Bill enjoyed seeing Otho's machine shop and the things on which he was working.

The Will Rogers Museum in Claremore, Oklahoma, was interesting. I was a cowboy lover from way back, and Will had been a well-known cowboy/humorist. He, along with pilot Wiley Post, had died in a plane crash several years earlier. This museum contained many of his personal belongings such as his saddles and the Indian items he had collected.

As the temperature climbed higher, we were surprised to see our first air conditioner at a restaurant in Miami, Oklahoma. Water dripped from a tank onto a porous material. As air blew through that, the evaporation cooled the air entering the building. Since the atmosphere was so dry in Oklahoma, it did a great job. We were impressed.

We enjoyed the many Burma Shave signs that were prevalent along Route 66. Then we began to see another set of interesting signs. The first one said, "Jackrabbit 100 miles." Further down the road another said, "Jackrabbit 75 miles." These signs continued until we were down to three miles, then two, and finally one. By this time, we were more than a little curious as to what the Jackrabbit was. These signs had definitely aroused our interest! When we actually got to the Jackrabbit, it was—just another of the many trading posts scattered every few miles along Route 66. With their advance publicity, you better believe that nearly every car had to stop and see what The Jackrabbit was all about. Like all the other folks, we just had to buy a few souvenirs there. Looking to the future, we purchased a little set of turtle clips at each end of a ribbon—bib holders. (We put them to good use three years later.)

Texas is mighty big, but we managed to locate my old neighbor, Joe Frank, and spent several days with him and his wife, Rose. We enjoyed fishing, visiting neighbors and just having a good time talking. We even drove to Breckenridge to have our new car serviced.

After leaving Joe's, we pointed the car toward Carlsbad Caverns in New Mexico. Now we are talking *big caves* with Carlsbad. We sat at long tables and ate box lunches in the large lunchroom located at the bottom of the cave. Another room was so large that it would have held several houses. We decided they could have put half of our nearby village of Kossuth inside it. Our guide explained that the lights in this huge room would be turned off briefly and asked if anyone would panic in the dark. Everyone in our group did well, but I can understand why it would bother some folks. With absolutely no source of light in that deep underground cave, we began to understand the real meaning of the word "black." That evening we returned to the cavern entrance and took pictures at sunset as millions of bats living inside flew from the mouth of the cave into the night sky. It was quite a sight!

Somewhere in the desert area of New Mexico, a sandstorm descended on us. The temperature was 119 in the shade—and believe me, there was no shade! Joe and Rose Frank had given us a very thoughtful wedding gift—a thermos jug. We kept it filled with cold water. Occasionally I wet a washcloth and sponged Bill's face to keep him cool enough to drive. The windows had to be kept closed to keep the sand out. Even so, some fine grit filtered through. By evening, a thin layer of dust covered everything in the car, including us.

An Indian powwow was in full swing when we pulled into Flagstaff, Arizona. We were fortunate to get a room at a motel, since tourists flocked to the area from several states just to enjoy the activities. The owners suggested we drive through the local fairgrounds to see the tepees and families cooking over open fires, just as their ancestors had done. We learned a little about their lives as we saw slabs of beef jerky hanging from nearby trees and enjoyed the dances and songs they provided for tourists. Most families had traveled by pickup truck, and each one seemed to have the truck bed loaded with children who were loving all the excitement and attention! We'd never seen anything like it in Ohio.

As we drove back to our motel, we smiled as we watched one native American trying to sell a souvenir bow and arrow to another. They were really having fun! Another man was selling some very nice watermelons from the back of his truck. We bought one and took it to our motel room where we broke it open and feasted. Although we had no silverware, it was definitely an "all you can eat" dessert. After eating our fill, we climbed into bed for a much needed night of sleep after all the difficult driving and the excitement of the powwow. Just as we were drifting off to sleep, a hair-raising howl brought us upright in our bed. "What was that?" I cried as I nearly jumped out of my skin. Just behind our motel stood a large mountain whose rocky area rose almost straight up. Somewhere a coyote was calling out to his lady friend on the next mountain. We had never heard such a wild outpouring of sound. My goose bumps will never forget it, although Bill offered these comforting words, "Just go to sleep. It's only a dog howling." Dog, my foot.

While driving to the Grand Canyon the next morning, I was not feeling my best. I don't know if it was *all* that watermelon, the scare of that wild coyote's howl, drinking the alkali water from that area, the extreme heat, or maybe it was a combination of all of the above. When we arrived at the park, we decided *not* to take the donkey ride to the bottom. (I could picture myself falling off my donkey on that steep descent into the Canyon.) After seeing their promotional movie of the trip, I was glad I hadn't gone. Some of the paths were just wide enough for one donkey, then the ground dropped sharply for several hundred feet below. A fall from that height would not have been a pretty sight.

By the next day I felt much better, and we stopped briefly for some sight-seeing at the Petrified Forest and Bryce Canyon. We later saw volcanic rock and copper mines. As we headed north toward Utah, Bill let me drive for a while as he napped with his head on my lap. I decided to open up that new car and see how fast it would go. The road stretched straight ahead as far as the eye could see and there was not a car in sight. And there was no speed limit. As my foot went down, the speed went up and up and up. It finally leveled off at 105 miles per hour. I'd never driven that fast before and I haven't done it since.

Furthermore, I don't ever intend to. But it is too bad that Bill slept through it all!

As we arrived at a motel in Salt Lake City, we asked the clerk what there was to do in town that evening. She said there really wasn't much to do unless we liked music and wanted to attend the Mormon Tabernacle choir's weekly practice. It couldn't have worked better! We had heard them many times on their radio worship services and loved their music. It was a wonderful evening! The next day we attended the organ concert in the Tabernacle and enjoyed every minute of its beautiful sounds. We marveled at the tremendous acoustics of that large auditorium and were amazed that such a building could have been built nearly one hundred years earlier without the aid of modern technology.

That afternoon, we drove out into the countryside for a look at the Great Salt Lake. Because it was so hot and dry, the lake was smaller than normal, making the desert around it much larger. Everything was extremely dry, and the ground was covered with deep cracks. It was one of the most forlorn areas we had ever seen with absolutely nothing growing there.

As we drove near Pike's Peak on Sunday morning, we tuned our car radio to the service from the Mormon Tabernacle. That was really special! The choir was singing the wonderful music we had enjoyed at their practice a few days earlier.

From the dust storms in Arizona to the snow in the Rocky mountains, it was quite a change. We hadn't brought coats (Hey, it was July!), and as we drove higher into the mountains, we began to shiver. I was surprised to see hardy little wild flowers growing in the dirt between the clumps of snow. Bill turned on the car heater to warm us up a bit. At one point, he stopped, we jumped out and threw a few snowballs, then dived back into the warm car.

Driving in the Rocky Mountains was a bit scary in 1951. The roads were quite narrow with barely enough room in some places to meet another car. The scariest thing was that many of those winding curves had no guardrails. To slide off the road there meant a plunge of thousands of feet to the valley below. In many places we were high above the clouds. We watched their shadows moving through the valley below us. As we drove to the city of Denver, we were invigorated by the clean, crisp pure air.

After the mountain driving, the flatlands of Kansas were indeed a welcome sight. We drove through Salina (pronounced like our Celina, Ohio), then on to Abilene where Lowell Hoover lived. He and Bill had met on the liberty ship, *Dudley H. Thomas* as they took care of horses being shipped to Greece after World War II. After all those years, Bill wanted to see his friend again. Since they had invited us to stay with them for a day or two, we drove into Abilene, asked for directions at the grain elevator and drove out to Lowell's farm. We were warmly welcomed, and enjoyed our time with them and their family. Their little son, Steve, became our special friend. (He now runs the farm since Lowell is older and semi-retired.)

Our first day at Lowell's was beautiful as we toured his farm and neighborhood, but in the middle of the night, a tremendous thunderstorm roared through the area. The rain poured all night long, drenching everything. It continued to rain for the rest of our stay. The Acres brothers, who had also been on the trip to Greece, lived nearby. Lowell encouraged us to visit them.

After leaving Abilene, we had a brief visit with the brothers. They also asked us to stay for a day or so. Since they had just butchered, they insisted there was plenty of fresh meat and fresh garden produce. Wouldn't we please stay? Bill didn't know them very well, and since the time we had allowed for our honeymoon was getting shorter, we decided to drive on, even though the rain continued to pour, making driving difficult.

We arrived in Florence, Kansas, that afternoon and visited Bill's great-uncle and his family. We enjoyed a rainy afternoon with them. They also wanted us to stay all night. Some of their children were visiting, and the house really wasn't large enough for more company, so we drove on. (We would have had to sleep on a couch or the floor. We found out weeks later that had we stayed, we would have been caught in their flooded house. They awoke to find water had filled their basement and was rising rapidly until it reached a depth of three feet in the house. They lost everything. How thankful we were that we hadn't stayed!)

That night was unforgettable! We didn't know the area, and as we drove through the downpour, we repeatedly saw flares and high water signs blocking roads. Each time, we turned and drove down another road until it ended in water, then changed directions and continued to drive. My built-in radar kept us going north and east, always in the direction of Kansas City.

By now, we could see that the land was flooded in all directions. Boats were taking people out of their homes' upstairs windows. Many farm buildings were nearly covered by water. Miraculously, we did not drive through any water, but we could see that in this flat country, water was lapping both sides of the road on which we were driving. I was thankful it was dark out there.

We finally reached the town of Emporia, Kansas, late that night and knew we had to stop. After crossing a little bridge, Bill turned the car in at the new motel just beyond. I stayed in the car while he went in to ask for a room. Again, we were fortunate. There was still an empty room, but they were very puzzled as to where we had come from, since the road was under water. Bill assured them we had just driven in on that road. The motel clerk looked at him in disbelief and, turning quite pale, said, "You couldn't have! That road has been closed all day!" Bill emphasized that we had indeed come in on that road and that we had not driven through a drop of water. The clerk was still not convinced and shook his head in wonderment.

After the stress of the day's difficult driving, we knew we needed some rest and recuperation. By morning the rain stopped. When we walked to the motel dining room for breakfast, the waitress apologized for having to serve day-old rolls and bread. Because of the flood, trucks with fresh supplies could not get into town. They informed us that there was *ten feet* of water over the bridge we had crossed the night before. As we walked over and looked at the fast-moving water, we thanked the Lord for bringing us safely to this brand new motel located on a hill high above that raging torrent.

Behind the motel were railroad tracks where a train had been halted, well above the river. Those people had to be rescued. What do you do when you are marooned and can't go anywhere? We called to tell our family we were all right and would be a few days later than we had planned. (I guess we didn't describe many details. They told us later they had pictured us sitting on the top floor of a hotel in the middle of town with water swirling around us.)

We spent some time looking around this town of Emporia. I bought enough fabric and thread from the local J.C. Penney store to make a skirt. While listening to the flood news on the radio, I hand-stitched my new skirt together. Since I was now a married lady, I thought I should try to look more mature. Bill and I talked it over and devised a plan to accomplish that. Adult ladies didn't wear long hair at that time, so with my sewing scissors in his hand, Bill started whacking off my long hair. (Needless to say, by the time we finally arrived home my family was quite surprised at the change in my appearance.)

Emporia was aware of the need for some form of entertainment and relaxation for its many stranded visitors, so they arranged a special program at a local auditorium. Students from Emporia College provided entertainment. I especially remember young ladies from Hawaii who demonstrated a hula dance, our first view of this exotic entertainment. The evening closed with square dancing.

After a couple of days, we heard that one lane of the highway leading to Kansas City was now open. We packed quickly and left. That beautiful new road had been so battered by the water that it washed out underneath, allowing the pavement to collapse within hours after we had driven over it. Again, the Lord had taken care of us! Several giant oil storage tanks were burning fiercely as we entered the southwest edge of Kansas City. A few days after our return, we saw newsreel pictures of the flood at the nearby Wapa Theater. I gasped as we watched the familiar scene and saw those same burning tanks.

As we drove out of Kansas City and the flood area, we heard that a levee had broken and that a road we had traveled just minutes before was now covered with water. Thank you, Lord, for another day of protection.

Thankful to be away from the devastation, we crossed Missouri into Illinois. Since we were in the vicinity, we visited Abraham Lincoln's tomb and other historical areas.

That night we were anxious to get home and drove a bit later than we should have. Vacant rooms seemed to be very scarce. We finally found one at an older motel somewhere in Illinois. Although it was clean, the nearest thing to luxury was a tiny fan placed in the open window. The July day had been extremely hot and very sticky. That fan buzzed away all night long, causing a problem for us! On this, the last night of our honeymoon, I awoke to find my big, gentle husband swatting me with both hands. I finally realized he was still asleep. As I woke him, he explained that bees had been swarming around him and he was swatting at them. Now where would he get that idea? Couldn't have been that fan buzzing away!

I kept a notebook of that 1951 honeymoon with a record of every penny we spent, as well as some other facts. For instance, the speedometer registered 600 miles when our new Ford left home and 6,121.9 on our return. We traveled 5,521 miles and averaged 15 ½ miles per gallon. As we look back on those prices now, we are truly amazed. It cost us $330.26 or an average of $16.51 daily. (We stayed with friends or relatives occasionally, and that cut the total cost.) Several motels charged only $4 nightly while the most expensive at Carlsbad Caverns had cost us $6.12. Meals were priced from $.75 to $1.50 each. Pop came only in tall glass bottles and cost ten to fifteen cents. Gas prices ranged from 23 to 31 cents a gallon. (Don't we wish we could go back to that?) An oil change was $1.63, and a bottle of hair tonic cost 36 cents. We crossed the Mississippi River on Monday, June 25, at 4:18 p.m.; at 9:00 in the morning of Wednesday, June 27 we saw five combines in one field in Oklahoma; we crossed the Continental Divide at 3:45 on Monday, July 2 in New Mexico; on Tuesday, July 3, at 2:40 we visited Meteor City, Arizona, population 2. Of course we had to stop for ice cream in Truth or Consequences, New Mexico. Everything was new and exciting to us.

July 2, 1951–Crossed the Continental Divide at 3:45, drove through lots of desert, very hot 119 degrees. [And that was in the shade.]

After checking my little notebook, I smiled at the amount of money we spent for an average day of our honeymoon. It looked something like this:

| | |
|---|---|
| $2.76 | Gas, 10.6 gallons, El Paso, Texas |
| .10 | Ice, El Paso, Texas |
| 2.50 | Breakfast Las Cruses, New Mexico |
| .62 | Ice Cream, Truth or Consequences, New Mexico |
| 2.32 | Gas, 8 gallons, Truth or Consequences, New Mexico |
| 3.00 | Gas, 9.7 gallons, Pie Town, New Mexico |
| 2.73 | Supper, Springerville, Arizona |
| 1.00 | Tips for the day |
| 4.00 | Motel, Springerville, Arizona (lady played organ for us). |

That little notebook listed every article of clothing and personal items that I took on the honeymoon, plus all the items in my "hope chest" that I had made, bought, or been given for our future home. I recorded the names of the states whose licence plates we saw as we traveled: Mexico, Canada, Japan, and all 48 states. [Hawaii and Alaska became states later.] Interesting names we saw: the city of Pie Town in New Mexico, and in Utah the Motel 4 U, (the word Motel was quite new. It was not even listed in my 1948 *Webster's Collegiate Dictionary.*) Most places were called "tourist cabins," "tourist courts" or "tourist camps" such as Done Roamin Camp. I wondered if a Davenport family owned the Daven-Haven Tourist Court. Texas boasted names such as the Pick-A-Rib Barbecue, Sour Mug Ranch, and inns named: Du-Kum-Inn, Do-Drop-Inn, and Sho-Me-Inn. We also saw a huge stack of deer, elk and moose antlers with a sign saying: "Largest pile of antlers in the West." That was impressive until we saw that same sign and stack of antlers in at least three or four other places. One of the cutest names was on a dance hall near Salt Lake, Utah. It was appropriately called the Salt Shaker.

We seemed to have made every moment special on that trip. Bill and I recently spent a happy evening looking through the pages of my little notebook as we remembered our wonderful honeymoon. We were newlyweds once again!

This is the little country church at Kossuth as it looked at our wedding in 1951.

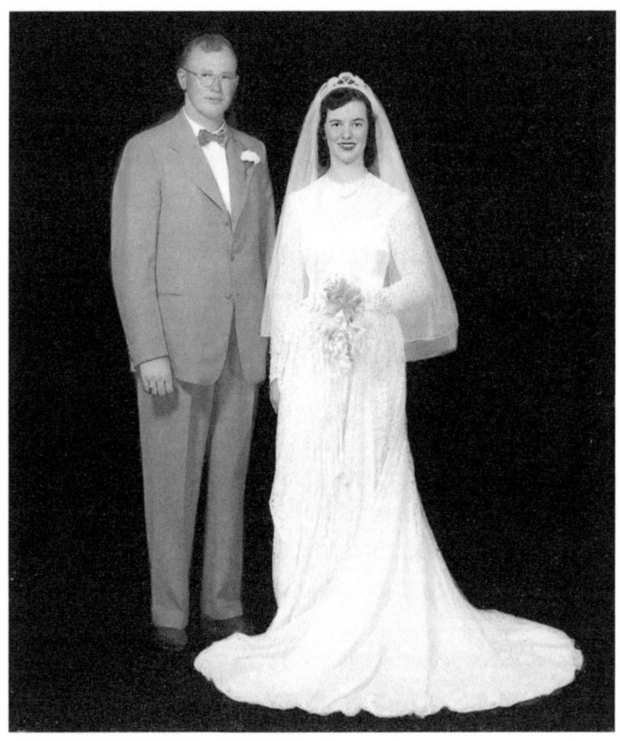

Bill and I on our wedding day, June 24, 1951

Our wedding party

Left to right: flower girl Charlene Sandkuhl, bridesmaid Rosemary Elsass, matron of honor Mary Davenport, the bride Glenna Davenport, the groom Bill Meckstroth, best man Homer Henschen, ushers Donald Davenport and Ralph Hoelscher

## Chapter 59.
# *Help! We're Being Attacked!*

"Whomp! Whomp!" The sound of shotguns blasted outside the windows. It was obvious that this was the night! In our neighborhood, the young people had a "belling" for newlyweds and tonight it was our turn. Some areas called it a "chivaree," but by either name it was still the same thing, an evening with lots and lots of noise and fun! Since the belling was rather like a welcoming ritual for the newly-marrieds, it usually took place a few weeks after the wedding.

I never heard if my parents or grandparents had a belling. An October belling party was held in 1914 for some of their neighbors, and judging from the size of the crowd, I would guess that the Davenports were among the guests:

> Mr. and Mrs. Lewis Fritz have gone to housekeeping on what was the Leb Williams farm, where they were given an old-time "belling" Friday evening by about sixty people and there were about as many ladies as there were men in the crowd. We can't tell from here whether the ladies have eaten all their candy yet or not, but we are sure of one thing, and that is, the bellers certainly gave them plenty of noise, and they all departed at a late hour, wishing Mr. and Mrs. Fritz a long and prosperous life.[1]

But now it was our turn to be belled. Since Grandpa and Grandma had not yet finished their new house next door, Bill and I spent our first few weeks of married life with them. As we sat together in the living room one evening, we suddenly heard the blast of shotguns just outside the window. We had been a part of other bellings and we knew the routine. Grandpa and Grandma grinned from ear to ear as they listened to the cacophony of sound. Some young men shot their guns, others held an old dinner bell that they rang vigorously, still others banged a large round saw blade with a hammer. The girls joined the fun by beating on old pans or clashing pie tins or lids together. What a racket!

The noise stopped as we went to the door for a closer look. Then our friends escorted us to a waiting pickup truck. Bill and I seated ourselves on bales of straw in the back of the truck as several friends sat across from us or stood near us, shooting those old double-barreled shotguns occasionally, ringing the bells and banging the saw blade. The sharp reverberations and piercing sound made our heads ring! We knew from experience that we might as well go along with their fun, so we held our hands over our ears and grinned.

After a drive through the countryside with several carloads of friends tooting horns as they followed behind, our hosts drove us the five miles to downtown Spencerville. The noisy procession drove slowly down North Broadway with horns blaring, bells ringing, and guns exploding. The idea was to attract attention. Well, it certainly did! Everything came to a halt as shopkeepers and customers looked out, curious as to the cause of all the commotion. Bellings were fairly common and everyone smiled as they waited for the excitement to start. Friends helped us down from the truck and I was urged into our next mode of transportation, the same wicker baby buggy in which I had been pushed about town twenty-one years earlier. Many a young lady had to perch in a wheelbarrow as her new husband tried to balance her and traverse that route. Although our baby buggy was quite stable, it was also a bit more embarrassing.

As traffic eased to the sides of the busiest street in town, Bill had the privilege of pushing me in my baby buggy down the center of the street amid the cheers of the huge Saturday night crowd of shoppers. For two blocks in the heart of town, Bill good-naturedly pushed me as the truck and cars followed behind, horns tooting, bells ringing, friends cheering and guns ker-powing.

When the fun was over, the shopkeepers returned to their usual Saturday night business and we climbed back into the rear of the truck. We soon found out we were not headed for home though. Would you believe that, after a half-hour drive through the countryside, we were doing a repeat performance for the benefit of Bill's friends? He had to push me down the main street of New Knoxville in my baby buggy. My neighbor's son, Joe Mack, who was a teenager at the time, recently told me he almost got into trouble that night. He and a friend decided to place some Limburger cheese on the engine of a nearby car, but were caught in the act by the local law officer and the deed was never done. I laughed as Joe reminisced about the night and his near-brush with the law.

The next stop was home. There we enjoyed the good wishes of our friends as we were served ice cream and cake. It wasn't until we went to bed later that we found the rest of the fun. A few of the girls had remained to get the refreshments ready after we had departed for our ride. They had tied our underwear into knots, short-sheeted the bed and filled it with crackers, turned pictures to the wall, and tied our clothes together. Had we lived alone in our own home, we would have had more of a mess to clean up. They would have "done" the whole house. By living those few weeks with my grandparents, they had only our bedroom in which to play their silly tricks. As I said, I knew the routine. I had done my share of belling! All in all, it was quite an evening and a very exciting and proper beginning for our new life together!

---

[1] *Auglaize County Democrat,* October 29, 1914.

Here is the baby who rode in the buggy. "Grandpa's little girl" is one year old.

This is the little boy who grew up and married Grandpa's little girl. He's five months old here.

## Chapter 60.

# *French Fries—Not Corn Fritters*

First anniversaries are especially happy occasions ranking right up there near the top of the importance ladder, just one step behind weddings and new babies, but between graduations and paying off the mortgage. What a bag of mixed emotions are brought on by the memories of our first wedding anniversary. It was a hot, dry day that June 24th, 1952,—ideal for making hay. Bill spent the day wiping sweat and breathing dust, but the cows would be well fed next winter. My day passed quickly as I tried to keep one step ahead of the weeds in the garden, then picked the large crop of raspberries.

Although it was rather late by the time we were cleaned up and ready to go, we started driving with eager anticipation of this first anniversary celebration. Bill's church choir had enjoyed a party at the West Milton Inn, located about sixty miles south of us. He had bragged about the good food and unique setting of the old Inn and had promised a feast there on our first anniversary. I really looked forward to the evening and to the wonderful food he had mentioned. The Inn's specialty, corn fritters with syrup, sounded very tasty.

After traveling through several little towns along the way, the car, purchased for our honeymoon, suddenly decided to die. We have since heard the definition of FORD–Found on Road Dead. It was a Ford and believe me, the description fit it to a T that night. In order to be prepared for the long honeymoon trip the year before, we had joined the American Automobile Association (AAA). Our membership had expired just before our anniversary, but after some deep discussion, we decided to renew it. Now our decision would pay off. Bill raised the hood, looked over the balky engine's innards, and determined the problem was a broken rotor arm in the distributor. He walked to the nearest house, called the AAA, and asked them to bring a new part. A short while later, their mechanics arrived with the needed part which they quickly installed. After an hour or so of delay, we were again heading south to West Milton.

Several cars were standing in the parking lot as we pulled in beside them, then walked to the door of the Inn. But what was this? The door was locked. We knocked and someone finally came to the door. "I'm sorry," she said, "The Inn closes at nine o'clock." Glancing at our watches, we saw that it was just a few minutes after nine. Hindsight is always better, and we are not as shy now as we were then. Had we told them it was our first anniversary, that we had experienced car trouble, and that we had looked forward to this night for a whole year, they might have welcomed us, even though it was a little after closing time. But, as I said, we were too shy to say anything and so we dejectedly walked to the car and drove away, not knowing where to go.

There were no Interstate Highways to travel to larger towns. Fast foods had not yet come into the picture. Our only hope was to find another restaurant still open in one of the smaller towns between there and home. Each of these towns usually had only one restaurant. As we drove through town after town, we began to realize that this was not going to be a storybook anniversary. Everything was closed by now. Bill heaved a sigh of relief as we drove through downtown Sidney and noticed the lights were still on in the well-known Spot Restaurant. There seemed to be no other choice. It certainly wasn't the wonderful meal we had anticipated, but by then we were so hungry, we weren't too particular. Just get us some food! And so our very unromantic first anniversary was spent sitting in a booth at the Spot eating the only food they had left, hamburgers and fries. It was indeed a memorable night–but not for the reasons we had anticipated! We dined on hamburgers and French fries instead of steak and corn fritters.

Now, here we are fifty years later.

# *Great-Grandpa's Trunk*

As our memories are made, so our memories are lost
And life rushes by just the same,
With brief moments of sadness and moments of joy
And sometimes a moment of fame.
As we traverse life's road with a twinkle and smile,
We try to meet friends with a grin
But with families scattered both here and abroad,
The ties that should bind have worn thin.
All the lessons we learned at our forefathers' knees
Are wisdom and words from the past
But they teach and instruct us of steps we should take
To slow down a life that's too fast.

How I long for the days of simplicity and peace
When folks showed their care and their love,
When each Sunday meant church and a day to give thanks
And recognize God up above.
There was time for our families to share hours together,
To talk about problems and woes
And our elders gave wisdom for solving each task
And soon we had conquered our foes.
We relaxed and made time for the friends who stopped by,
Made time at a beck-and-a-call.
We enjoyed life together and lived it with zest
And work was a task shared by all.

Now I've told you the tales from Great-grandfather's trunk
And all of the stories are true,
So I hope you've learned something of life in the past.
These memories are my gift to you!

# INDEX

# *Have You Read?*

You may also wish to read the author's second book, *Surviving World War II: Tales of Ordinary People in Extraordinary Times.* It is a fascinating collection of oral histories of the war's survivors: prisoners of war, both Americans in Germany and Germans in Russia and America; the GIs who guarded them on land and sea; foreign war brides now living in Ohio; military ladies who served at home and near European battle fronts; children who grew up under Hitler's strict rules; a Jewish lady whose family escaped Germany just in time; a U.S. airman who was rescued by the Dutch Underground and the lady from The Netherlands who helped get him to safety. Two of the former prisoners, one of whom actually worked within two or three miles of the author's residence, were interviewed in their homes in Germany.

Also included is information about Camp Perry, Ohio's main POW camp, and its branch camps throughout Ohio and N.E. Indiana. There are personal memories of ex-GIs who saw the Germans in various U.S. military camps, and of civilians who worked beside the prisoners in factories and on farms. There are numerous stories of the daily life of the prisoners of war—their work, play, religion, illnesses and deaths, strikes, and escapes. Their experiences in America gave them a preview of what democracy was all about and it helped them prepare for the improvement of their circumstances, once they were returned to their German homeland. You will also want this one-of-a-kind book in your home library. It is highly recommended by military personnel and others.

"I had a hard time putting this book down because of the genuine people aspect that is presented. I am pleased that someone has taken the time to save the memories of part of the 'Greatest Generation' and present our former enemies and now allies as human beings."

–Lt. Colonel Ralph W. Green Jr., U.S. Army, retired, State Adm. Camp Perry, Ohio.

"While reading Glenna's thoroughly researched book, I constantly questioned the unbelievable reactions of the Americans, especially the women who befriended the German POWs. The stories are overwhelming and Surviving World War II gives much food for thought."

–Lt. Colonel Jean Neidhardt, U.S. Air Force, retired, Virginia Beach, Virginia.

"Now, before it is too late, it is important that the lives and the words of those civilians in and out of uniform on both sides be preserved and remembered. She has done a marvelous job of saving and organizing those memories for us and for the future."

–Dr. Violet I. Meek, Dean and Director, Emeritus, The Ohio State University at Lima.

". . . I have been deeply impressed by the contents of this most remarkable book. In my 51 years as a Marine and veteran's advocate, I have heard many similar stories but have seen few in print."

–Adj. Gen. David Goliver, Retired Veterans Advocate, Elida, Ohio.

# About the Author

## "What Do You Mean I'm a Boy?" she asked.

"Don't believe everything you read in the paper. Imagine my surprise to find that, according to one account of my birth, I was a boy! Since Dad and Mother already had one, I am sure they would have noticed the difference. Therefore, I must assure you that the statement was (and still is) very much incorrect."

"Since April 22 was a popular birth date in Mother's family, I chose that day to be born. My uncle Marion Briggs had selected that date many years earlier. Cousin Charles Briggs also liked the date and was born a few years before my arrival."

"The thirty-first President of the United States, Herbert Hoover, was in office at the time of my birth in 1930, and the Great Depression was in full swing, but my interests lay elsewhere at the time, so I ignored politics (and almost everything else.)"

The above paragraphs are Glenna's account of her birth. Born to Bernard and Lena (Briggs) Davenport on a farm near the village of Kossuth in western Auglaize County, Glenna lost her mother at the age of seven months. Her dad took his children, Glenna and her brother, Don, home to live with his parents, Frank and Nora Davenport. With three generations in the home, family stories were many and varied—a hay wagon encounter with a rattlesnake, meeting a celebrity on the canal tow path, threshing and butchering on the farm, lots of fiddle music, a belling and a baby buggy, living through "The Great Depression" and World War II, the men in her life before marriage, and many more.

Glenna enjoys playing the church organ, genealogy and sewing. She is retired, lives near New Knoxville, Ohio, and is Mom to Michael, Steven, Nancy, and son-in-law, David. She's grandma to Brian and Heather. Although she has written newsletters, various papers, poems, and stories over the years, this is her first published book.

As you read through its pages, perhaps you will feel you are a part of this loving farm family and will enjoy the humor that flows freely throughout the book. Hours of research have gone into preparing the stories for accuracy and authenticity. May each story bring a smile as you remember similar tales from your own childhood or learn for the first time what life was like in earlier days.